TRIBAL CRIMINAL
AND PROCEDURE

Tribal Legal Studies Series

SERIES EDITORS: Jerry Gardner (Cherokee), Executive Director,
Tribal Law and Policy Institute
Heather Valdez Singleton, Program Director,
Tribal Law and Policy Institute

This series began as a collaborative initiative between the UCLA Native Nations Law and Policy Center and four tribal colleges. It is designed to promote education and community empowerment through the development of resources for and about tribal justice systems.

American Indian tribal court systems deal with a wide range of difficult criminal and civil justice problems on a daily basis. Culturally based legal training is one of Indian country's most pressing needs, as tribes assume responsibility for a growing number of government functions, such as child welfare and environmental control, and tribal courts continue to expand as the primary sources of law enforcement and dispute resolution for tribal communities. This book series is designed to develop legal and technical resources for tribal justice course offerings and materials, so that they reflect community thought, philosophy, traditions, and norms, and serve to strengthen tribal government and leadership.

BOOKS IN THE SERIES
Introduction to Tribal Legal Studies (2004), by Justin B. Richland and Sarah Deer. Alta Mira Press.
Tribal Criminal Law and Procedure (2004), by Carrie E. Garrow and Sarah Deer. Alta Mira Press.
Sharing Our Stories of Survival: Native Women Surviving Violence (2007), edited by Sarah Deer, Bonnie Clairmont, Carrie A. Martell, and Maureen White Eagle. Alta Mira Press.
Introduction to Tribal Legal Studies, second edition (2010), by Justin. B. Richland and Sarah Deer. Alta Mira Press.
Tribal Criminal Law and Procedure, second edition (2014), by Carrie E. Garrow and Sarah Deer. Alta Mira Press.
Structuring Sovereignty: Constitutions of Native Nations (2014), by Melissa Tatum, Miriam Jorgenson, Mary Guss, and Sarah Deer. UCLA American Indian Studies Center.

For more information on the series see: www.TribalLegalStudies.org

This project was supported in part by Grant No 2012-IC-BX-K001 awarded by the Bureau of Justice Assistance. The Bureau of Justice Assistance is a component of the Office of Justice Programs, which also includes the Bureau of Justice Statistics, the National Institute of Justice, the Office of Juvenile and Delinquency Prevention, the Office for Victims of Crime, and the SMART Office. Points of view or opinions in this document are those of the authors and do not necessarily represent the official position or policies of the U.S. Department of Justice.

TRIBAL CRIMINAL LAW AND PROCEDURE

Second Edition

CARRIE E. GARROW AND SARAH DEER

ROWMAN & LITTLEFIELD
Lanham • Boulder • New York • London

Published by Rowman & Littlefield
A wholly owned subsidiary of The Rowman & Littlefield Publishing Group, Inc.
4501 Forbes Boulevard, Suite 200, Lanham, Maryland 20706
www.rowman.com

Unit A, Whitacre Mews, 26-34 Stannary Street, London SE11 4AB

Copyright © 2015 by Rowman & Littlefield

All rights reserved. No part of this book may be reproduced in any form or by any electronic or mechanical means, including information storage and retrieval systems, without written permission from the publisher, except by a reviewer who may quote passages in a review.

British Library Cataloguing in Publication Information Available

Library of Congress Cataloging-in-Publication Data
Garrow, Carrie E., 1969– author.
　Tribal criminal law and procedure / Carrie E. Garrow and Sarah Deer. — Second edition.
　　pages cm — (Tribal legal studies series)
　Includes bibliographical references and index.
　ISBN 978-1-4422-3228-0 (cloth : alk. paper) — ISBN 978-1-4422-3229-7 (pbk. : alk. paper) — ISBN 978-1-4422-3230-3 (ebook : alk. paper) 1. Indians of North America—Legal status, laws, etc. 2. Criminal law—United States. I. Deer, Sarah, 1972– author. II. Title.
　KIE3305.G37 2015
　345.730089'97—dc22
　　　　　　　　　　　　　　　　　　　　　　　　　　　　　　　　　　　　2014044289

∞™ The paper used in this publication meets the minimum requirements of American National Standard for Information Sciences—Permanence of Paper for Printed Library Materials, ANSI/NISO Z39.48-1992.

Printed in the United States of America

CONTENTS

Foreword to the Second Edition by Duane Champagne   ix

Preface to the Second Edition   xi

Notes on Law   xv

CHAPTER 1
Introduction to American Criminal Law Concepts   1

CHAPTER 2
Comparing Tribal Criminal Law and American Criminal Law   13

CHAPTER 3
Using American Criminal Law to Control American Indian Nations   37

CHAPTER 4
Traditional Law Today   55

CHAPTER 5
Introduction: What Is Criminal Jurisdiction?   87

CHAPTER 6
Traditional Criminal Jurisdiction   93

CHAPTER 7
Limitations on Tribal Criminal Jurisdiction Imposed by the United States   101

CHAPTER 8

Exercising Jurisdiction over Crimes Committed by Non-Indians   115

CHAPTER 9

Criminal Jurisdiction as Defined by Tribal Courts   149

CHAPTER 10

Tribal Criminal Jurisdiction Reform: The Tribal Law and Order Act and the Violence Against Women Act   165

CHAPTER 11

State and Tribal Court Collaboration   191

CHAPTER 12

Overview of Criminal Laws: Statutes and Procedures   209

CHAPTER 13

The Mental State   219

CHAPTER 14

A Closer Look at Criminal Elements   241

CHAPTER 15

Is Helping a Criminal Act? Preliminary Crimes and Accomplice Liability   249

CHAPTER 16

Criminal Defenses   261

CHAPTER 17

The Burden of Proof   287

CHAPTER 18

Rights of Criminal Defendants   299

CHAPTER 19

The Law of Arrest   313

CHAPTER 20

Interrogations and Confessions: The Right to Remain Silent   335

CHAPTER 21

Search and Seizure   367

CHAPTER 22

The Exclusionary Rule: Remedies for Civil Rights Violations   405

CHAPTER 23

The Right to an Attorney/Advocate   425

CHAPTER 24

Defendant Rights at Trial   455

CHAPTER 25

Victims' Rights   485

CHAPTER 26

Sentencing: Fines and Incarceration   507

CHAPTER 27

Tribal Restorative Justice   555

Glossary of Terms   591

Index   599

About the Authors   631

Foreword to the Second Edition

BY DUANE CHAMPAGNE

The inspiration for this series of textbooks on Tribal Legal Studies comes from many places but the multiple paths have led to a common outcome. Jerry Gardner, series co-editor, has long worked in the Native tribal court and law-training field. Over the years, he and colleagues have provided numerous weekend, weeklong and one to four day trainings to tribal legal personnel from all over the United States. The goal was to offer information and training so that tribal governments could build and improve their courts and legal departments. Many tribal communities and leaders realized that exercising sovereignty required the capability to manage disputes and exercise law and order on Native reservations.

Many tribes want to include traditional methods of legal resolution, emphasizing restorative justice rather than the punitive methods that predominate within U.S. law and court systems. If tribal communities are going to exercise sovereignty, they must do so in ways that emphasize their cultural values and maintain order and commitment among tribal members. Tribal communities have too long lived under legal and court regimes that did not express their sovereignty or their ways of managing and sustaining social and cultural relations. The task of educating Native leaders and court personnel about federal, state and tribal law is of paramount importance, as Native governments and communities work toward more effective governments that will express Native values and protect native rights.

Jerry Gardner and his colleagues found that weekend and short seminar courses were useful for many, but did not provide enough depth and breadth for the needs of a well-trained legal and court staff. Consequently, in an effort to provide more sustained information and training, a curriculum for Native legal studies was created at the New College in northern California in the 1980s. The experiment lasted only briefly, as few tribal people wanted to travel to California and stay away from their home reservations for the sustained periods necessary to complete a couple years of coursework.

Joining with faculty at UCLA such as Carole Goldberg and Duane Champagne, a new Tribal Legal Studies strategy was formed. This project was initially funded through the U.S. Department of Education by way of a FIPSE (Fund for the Improvement of Post-secondary Education) grant. A course curriculum was created for four Native-controlled community colleges: Salish Kootenai College, Dine College, Northwest Indian College and Turtle Mountain Community College. For five years, from 1998 to 2003, courses were delivered and curricula revised. Our plan was to deliver the courses in the heart of Indian country, where the people lived and the Native legal issues and institutions were day to day events.

A major difficulty in delivering Tribal Legal Studies courses for tribally controlled community colleges was the scarcity of funds for appropriately trained legal personnel, as well as a dearth of curriculum material. The Tribal Legal Studies Series directly addresses the latter problem. The textbook series includes federal, state, and tribal legal information in lesson formats that heretofore were not available. Students are encouraged to research the legal cultural and norms of their own traditions and include them in solving the legal issues of their contemporary communities. We hope to provide information that will make students more aware of legal and cultural issues necessary for them to understand and serve the interests of their Native communities and governments.

Students are encouraged to follow multiple paths through this Tribal Legal Studies Series. Some may wish to continue their dedication by enrolling in law school—but now armed with training in Native legal principles and knowledge that few law schools offer. We think such law students approach the law in a more sophisticated manner and will be better prepared to interpret and understand American law in ways that will serve Native communities. Other students may wish to use the courses in preparation for assuming the responsibilities of political office, for gaining skills necessary to fulfill tribal or Bureau of Indian Affairs jobs, or for training to serve in tribal courts or as community legal advocates. Community members who have greater understanding of federal, state, and tribal law will be better tribal citizens and will be in a much better position to evaluate and strengthen Native courts, law, constitutions, government organizations and policies.

It is our sincere hope and belief that the Tribal Legal Studies Series will lead to better educated tribal citizens, leaders, and policy makers and will support and help strengthen Native Tribal governments and legal institutions that express Native values and understandings that will produce greater capabilities for exercising and protecting Native sovereignty.

Duane Champagne
(Turtle Mountain Band of Chippewa)
January 2015

Preface to the Second Edition

The publication of this Tribal Legal Studies Series is the culmination of a dream of many people throughout Indian country to formalize and institutionalize tribal legal education through collaboration between tribal justice systems, tribal colleges and to open access to institutions of higher learning to tribal community members who might otherwise have geographic challenges.

We are pleased to offer this new revised edition of *Tribal Criminal Law and Procedure*, which incorporates new excerpts and the most up to date information on recently passed federal laws impacting tribal justice systems in Indian country, including the Tribal Law and Order Act (signed into law in 2010), which among its other provisions, authorizes tribes to exercise "enhanced" sentencing authority beyond limitations put in place through the Indian Civil Rights Act of 1978. This new edition also incorporates the 2013 Violence Against Women Act Reauthorization, which includes for the first time authorization for participating tribes to exercise "special domestic violence criminal jurisdiction" over non-Indians. Detailed information on these laws and their potentially significant impact on tribal criminal jurisdiction is woven throughout this second edition with a new chapter 10 devoted to the topics. This volume also includes a new chapter 11 on tribal-state court collaboration, a practice which has shown great promise in finding solutions to jurisdictional challenges.

Since the publication of the first edition in 2004, the Tribal Law and Policy Institute (TLPI) has continued to collaborate with a variety of organizations to deliver the Tribal Legal Studies curriculum, including the University of California, Los Angeles (UCLA) Native Nations Law and Policy Center, particularly through their Tribal Learning and Community Educational Exchange (TLCEE) program.

The Tribal Legal Studies Series was initiated in 1998 as a collaborative effort between the University of California, Los Angeles (UCLA) Native Nations Law and Policy Center, the Tribal Law and Policy Institute, and four tribal colleges (Turtle Mountain Community College, Salish Kootenai College, Dine College and Northwest Indian College) to develop, pilot and implement Tribal Legal Studies curricula at tribal community colleges. This initial kick off effort would not have been possible without the dedication and commitment of both Duane Champagne, UCLA Professor of Sociology and former Director of the American Indian Studies Center, and Carole Goldberg, UCLA Professor of Law. The current phase of the Tribal Legal Studies project has been funded through a grant from the U.S. Department of Justice's Bureau of Justice Assistance (BJA) to TLPI.

The Tribal Legal Studies Series has been designed to provide a Legal Studies certificate program, a two-year Associate of Arts (A.A.) degree and/or Associated of Applied Science (A.A.S.) degree in Legal Studies, a possible four-year Bachelor of Arts (B.A.) degree in Legal Studies and to increase tribal college course offerings.

The Tribal Legal Studies Series is designed to prepare students for employment with tribal governments and tribal court systems as judge, advocate (prosecutor, defender, or civil advocate), paralegal, victim advocate, court appointed special advocate (CASA), court administrator, court clerk, probation officer, social service personnel, law enforcement personnel, and other positions related to the administration of justice in Indian country. The target audience for the Series includes students who plan a career working for tribal courts or governments, students with a specific interest in specific careers such as students planning further careers in law. The books can also be used as in-service training for current tribal employees and the community at large. Moreover, the series serves as a gateway to those students who become interested in law school or other higher education opportunities.

A central component of the Tribal Legal Studies Series is the belief that community based collaborative development of tribal law and policy is crucial. To that end, these volumes ask students to reflect on their own communities and how law and policy is realized at the local level. This unique approach puts tribal culture and tradition in a central role in law making.

The Tribal Legal Studies Series is designed to enhance American Indian and Alaska Native communities and tribal justice systems on at least three different dimensions. First, it empowers tribal court staff (current and future) to provide leadership and shape their own futures and their communities by providing them with the legal knowledge, cultural knowledge, and advocacy skills needed to successfully complete this program and to go on to law school and other higher education opportunities. Second, it promotes tribal self-determination and enhances tribal sovereignty by strengthening, improving, and empowering tribal justice systems, and thereby, building tribal capacity to create positive change and promote social and economic community development. Third, it strengthens the links between tribal courts and tribal community colleges by enriching the tribal college legal curriculum, enhancing their capacity to meet the needs of their communities and serving as gateways to higher education, and building partnerships between tribal college and mainstream institutions.

We anticipate that the publication of these textbooks and the accompanying instructor guides will greatly facilitate the dissemination of a Tribal Legal Studies curriculum to other tribal colleges and colleges with programs throughout Indian country. We hope that the publication of these textbooks and instructor guides will thereby benefit all of Indian country.

Heather Valdez Singleton
Tribal Legal Studies Series Co-Editor

Jerry Gardner (Cherokee)
Tribal Legal Studies Series Co-Editor

Notes on Law, Non-Indian Anthropologists, Terminology, Juvenile Justice and First Nations

Tribal Case Law

This book includes tribal case law that has been published in reports or on the Internet. This textbook should not be used as a replacement for legal research for pending cases. Some of the cases may have been overturned by subsequent decisions and therefore should not be used as legal authority. Only a few tribes are represented in this text. We encourage readers, students, and instructors to consult local tribal case law (if available) to supplement the materials. We have done major editing on some of the cases to facilitate the educational value. For example, we have edited most footnotes and citations out of the tribal case law. In addition, portions of case law that are irrelevant for this textbook are omitted so that students can focus on particular issues.

Practitioners should always consult the original cases and read them in their original context before using or citing as law. Many of the cases include references to other tribal, federal or state law. It is important that this textbook not be relied upon as binding precedent.

We do not include long portions of text from federal or state case law because this is a textbook concentrating on tribal law. References to federal and/or state case law are kept to a minimum, except where the law has impact for tribal judicial systems (for example, Oliphant v. Suquamish, which limits tribal criminal jurisdiction over non-Indians).

Tribal Statutes

This book also includes many tribal statutes that have been published on the Internet. We have indicated the date of enactment of these tribal statutes whenever that information was available. These tribal statutes, however, may have been revised, supplemented, and/or overturned by subsequent tribal legislative actions. Consequently, tribal statutes included here should not be used as legal authority without additional research. Only a select few tribes are represented in this text. We encourage readers, students, and instructors to consult local tribal statutes (if available) to supplement the materials.

Practitioners should always consult the full tribal statutes and read them in their original context before using or citing as law. References to federal law are kept to a minimum, except where the law has impact for tribal judicial systems (for example, the Indian Child Welfare Act).

Non-Indian Anthropologists and Historians

We have used a few reports or accounts from non-Indian anthropologists or historians. We realize that these accounts may not always be consistent with the beliefs and/or legal procedures of Native peoples. We include them as a starting point for discussing traditional methods of dispute resolution and crime control among indigenous peoples. We encourage readers, students, and instructors to read critically and form independent analysis of the passages.

Terminology

There are a number of difficult issues with regard to the use of particular terminology while discussing tribal legal systems. David E. Wilkins and Heidi Kiiwetinepinesiik Stark provide an excellent analysis of these terminology issues at the beginning of their book American Indian Politics and the American Political System (2011):

> Throughout the book several terms are used interchangeably in referring to indigenous peoples in a collective sense—tribal nations, tribes, Alaskan Natives, indigenous nations, and indigenous peoples. But when we refer to individual indigenous persons, we generally use only Indian or American Indian. Of all the terms most used, Indian is easily the most problematic (though some argue that the term tribe is pejorative and hints strongly of colonialism), and we use it with some hesitation for two reasons: first, because of its obvious geographical inaccuracy, and second, because it erroneously generalizes and completely ignores the cultural diversity evident in the hundreds of distinctive indigenous nations of North America, each with its own name for itself. One could thus argue that continued usage of the term attests to surviving vestiges of colonialism.
>
> Nevertheless, the terms Indian and American Indian remain the most common appellations used by indigenous and non-indigenous persons and institutions, and so it is frequently used in the text when no tribal name is specified. We have, moreover, intentionally avoided using the phrase Native American, despite that term's

popularity among mainstream academics in recent decades, since it causes more confusion than the one it purports to replace, as it can be applied literally to any person born in the Americas. The expressions Native peoples and Native nations may be less confusing, but these terms and the intriguing phrase First Nations, which are all popular in Canada and among some Alaskan indigenous groups, have never quite caught on in the United States among indigenous nations or policymakers.

What complicates matters, of course, is that there is no single term that is acceptable by all indigenous people all the time, and even people within specific native communities sometimes disagree on which name they prefer (e.g., Navajo or Diné; Chippewa, Ojibwe, or Anishinaabe; Iroquois or Haudenosaunee), and on whether they would rather be identified as tribal communities (which emphasizes their kinship affiliation) or as national entities (which, while not discounting kinship ties, tends to place greater emphasis on an independent political character and a right to engage in diplomatic relations with other nations or states, like the United States or other polities).

Of course, federal law and policy have vacillated on these terms as well. But we shall see that despite assimilative efforts, federal lawmakers continue to recognize the sovereign character of indigenous communities regardless of whether they are called tribes, nations, or peoples.

In this book, we will use a variety of interchangeable terms. The terms include Indian/ Native/Native American/indigenous as well as Tribes/Nations/governments and traditions/customs/values/beliefs. It is expected that these terms will assist in the learning and comprehension of this textbook.

Juvenile Justice

This textbook focuses on tribal criminal law as it may apply to adult defendants. For most children and youth under 18, the American system and the tribal systems are considered separate and distinct from the criminal justice system. Juvenile cases usually are framed as delinquency or child protection cases instead of criminal cases. However, many of the principles found in this book (for example, arrest and interrogation) might be applicable in the juvenile justice setting.

Note about First Nations

In Canada, the Native population is often referred to as "First Nation" or "Aboriginal." We rely on some Canadian sources because of parallel socio-legal history and First Nations' legal traditions and practices provide insight into tribal criminal law and procedure that are also applicable to American Indian nations.

Visit www.triballegalstudies.org for more information.

Introduction to American Criminal Law Concepts

Chapter 1

Beginning a tribal law book with an overview of American legal principles may seem odd. As most Native people know, tribal **criminal law** and justice has been harmed by various acts associated with colonization. American criminal law has been used as a weapon of colonization, to criminalize indigenous cultural practices. Federal and state governments have enacted numerous laws and policies in attempts to change tribal justice systems from those based on traditional indigenous laws to systems using American criminal justice principles. Today, tribal police, prosecutors, and courts work tribal justice systems that sometimes clash with and sometimes cooperate with state and federal governments. We believe it is important to understand the principles of American criminal law and its impact on tribal criminal justice systems, in order to understand the context within which tribal justice systems operate today. It is also this context that helps tribal leaders understand the work that is continually needed to strengthen and rebuild tribal criminal justice systems based on tribal laws and policies. It is with this belief and hope in mind that we begin our journey into tribal criminal law and procedure with a basic overview of American criminal law and its impact on tribal justice systems.

The American legal system divides conflicts into two categories—civil and criminal. Criminal law concerns those norms or rules that, when violated, are considered to be an offense against the entire community. Acts such as murder, theft, assault, and rape are considered acts that harm all of society. Since these acts are considered an offense against society as a whole, a criminal legal action is usually (1) prosecuted by a government attorney and (2) titled as "The People," "The State," "The Tribe," or "The Nation" versus the accused defendant. Furthermore, the available remedies or sanctions in a criminal action include imprisonment, whereas imprisonment is not usually available as a remedy in a civil action (except through the court's contempt power to enforce court orders). Consequently, criminal law is sometimes called **penal law** because it imposes punishments on the accused if the accused is found guilty of violating the law. Criminal law defines the various offenses prohibited by a community. Criminal procedure, which is covered in the later chapters, refers to the process in place to protect the rights of individuals during the government's investigation and prosecution of a crime.

Civil law refers to norms and rules that are supposed to be followed in the legal relationships between individual citizens or corporations or with the government. These legal relationships include business contracts, family legal relationships created by marriage or adoption, property relationships such as ownership and leases, and the duties and obligations that arise between parties entering these relationships. When these kinds of relationships are violated, they are considered to cause harm to the individual offended.

The distinction between criminal and civil law is not always obvious. For example, in the civil example in table 1.1, could a government decide that not repaying a loan actually harms all of society instead of just a single person? If so, could neglecting to repay a loan be considered a criminal act? Often a wrongful act can be considered a violation of criminal law and civil law. For example, a person can be prosecuted criminally for homicide and also be subject to a civil suit by the victim's family for wrongfully causing the victim's death.

Traditional tribal law often does not draw a distinction between actions that harm all of society and actions that harm an individual. Regulating problem behavior often has involved a variety of responses, from individual responses to clan responses to tribal responses. The following case addresses the difference between traditional Navajo law and the modern Navajo Nation Criminal Code and how the traditional concept of restitution is now handled in the modern Navajo criminal justice system.

Table 1.1. Distinction between Anglo-American Criminal and Civil Law

Example of a Criminal Case	Example of a Civil Case
Martin hits Robert. All of society is harmed by this action. Therefore, Martin can be prosecuted by the government in the criminal justice system. The case is named "Government v. Martin." Martin can be punished for his behavior.	Robert loans money to Martin. Later, Martin refuses to repay the loan. Robert is harmed by Martin's refusal. Therefore, Robert can sue Martin in civil court. The case is named "Robert v. Martin." Martin can be ordered by the court to repay the loan.

Supreme Court of the Navajo Nation
Navajo Nation v. Blake (1996)
24 Ind. L. Rep 6017 (1996)
Before Yazzie, Chief Justice, Austin and Sloan (sitting by designation), Associate Justices.
The opinion of the Court was delivered by: Austin, Associate Justice.

Blake was charged with committing seven criminal offenses after he was apprehended for starting a fire that destroyed two businesses in Tuba City, Navajo Nation (Arizona): The Pizza Edge Restaurant and Dahl Chiropractic. Blake pleaded guilty to the offenses of criminal damage and criminal entry, 17 N.N.C. §§ 351, 380 (1995), in exchange for dismissal of the other charges. The criminal complaints for the two remaining offenses listed $2,000 and $72,000 as the amounts of restitution requested by the business owners for damages. Discovery revealed that the owner of the Pizza Edge Restaurant had insurance to cover his losses. Whether Dahl Chiropractic had insurance to cover its losses is not known.

During negotiations on a **plea agreement**, the prosecutor informed Blake that restitution would not be sought; therefore, it was not a point of contention, nor included in the final agreement. The parties dispute whether the court accepted the plea agreement and the record is of little help in this regard. . . .

The court did not hear any evidence concerning the businesses nor the alleged damages incurred by the owners, perhaps, because the case did not proceed to trial. Also, restitution was not a recommended sentence either by the plea agreement or the Navajo Nation during sentencing. Nonetheless, the court, on its own, awarded $2,000 and $74,000 as restitution to the two business owners. Blake uses these facts to argue that the district court erred when it awarded restitution without a hearing and considering evidence.

Our modern criminal law, as it is found in the Navajo Nation Criminal Code, is foreign to traditional Navajo society. Navajos, traditionally, did not charge offenders with crimes in the name of the state or on behalf of the people. What are charged as offenses today were treated as personal injury or property damage matters, and of practical concern only to the parties, their relatives, and, if necessary, the clan matriarchs and patriarchs. These "offenses" were resolved using the traditional Navajo civil process of "talking things out." Nalyeeh (restitution) was often the preferred method to foster healing and conciliation among the parties and their relatives. The ultimate goal being to restore the parties and their families to hozho (harmony).

These concepts supported a request for restitution in a juvenile proceeding in a prior district court case. In the Matter of D. P., 3 Nav. R. 255, 257 (Crownpt. Dist. Ct. 1982), the court discussed the Navajo traditions of putting the victim in the position he or she enjoyed prior to the offense, punishing in a visible way to show a wrong was punished, and giving an offender a means to return to the community by making good for a wrong. Id. The court concluded that "not only is restitution permitted under Navajo custom law, but indeed it was so central to Navajo tradition in offenses that it should be presumed to be required in any juvenile disposition." Id. While we agree that restitution is central to Navajo tradition, we do not, at this point, address whether restitution should have presumptive value in criminal cases.

Restitution, a time-honored American Indian practice, entered the tribal criminal codes through the early Bureau of Indian Affairs (BIA) Code of Federal Regulations (CFR) (often referred to as "Law and Order Regulations"). For example, a provision in the 1938 BIA regulations states as follows:

In addition to any other sentence the Court [CFR Court] may require an offender who has inflicted injury upon the person or property of any individual to make restitution or to compensate the party injured, through the surrender of property, the payment of money damages, or the performance of any other act for the benefit of the injured party. Federal Register, at page 956 (May 18, 1938).

In 1958, the Navajo Nation Council adopted, wholesale, the BIA Law and Order Regulations and made it the Navajo Nation Criminal Code. See Navajo Tribal Council Res. No. CJ-45-58 (passed July 18, 1958). Upon adoption, the restitution provision found in the BIA regulations became a part of Navajo statutory criminal law. Restitution, therefore, is firmly embedded in Navajo common law and in modern Navajo criminal law. With this background, we now turn to the issue raised by Blake.

Blake agrees with the Navajo Nation that the district court has the power to award restitution to the business owners upon his guilty plea to criminal damage. Blake, however, takes issue with the court's award of restitution without notice to him and an evidentiary hearing on the issue. Blake believes that the applicable subsection in the criminal statute, 17 N.N.C. § 380(C) (1985), requires a hearing and the court must be satisfied of certain factors before awarding restitution.

Subsection 380(C) states as follows: "*Restitution.* The court, in addition to or in lieu of the sentence, may require the offender to pay actual damages for the benefit of the injured party" (italics in original). Blake believes that the words "actual damages" and "injured party" in the subsection mandates an evidentiary hearing, because, without a hearing, it would be impossible to identify the injured party. Blake also argues that on any claim for damages, there must be evidence presented in support of that claim, because our law is damages cannot be speculative. *Wilson v. Begay*, No. A-CV-05-86, slip op. at 10 (decided March 8, 1988).

We agree with Blake. Before restitution can be awarded under the criminal code, and specifically subsection 380(C), the court must be satisfied with these minimal factors: 1) Is restitution appropriate in the case; 2) Who is the injured party; 3) What is the extent of the loss or injury; 4) What kind of restitution is appropriate and 5) If money is to be paid, what amount would satisfy the actual damages requirement? We believe these factors satisfy the rudiments of traditional Navajo due process apparent in this criminal statute. We trust the district courts will fashion approaches to ensure that the mandates of the statute are fulfilled.

Finally, Blake's guilty plea came before the district court on a plea bargain. Under our law, the district court need not accept the exact terms of a plea bargain. The court should warn the defendant that it may disregard the agreement and impose the full sentence allowed by law before accepting the plea. If the defendant still wishes to enter a guilty plea, the court should proceed to sentence. See *Stanley v. Navajo Nation*, No. A-CR-06-90 (decided November 5, 1990).

The decision of the Tuba City District Court on restitution is reversed and the issue remanded to that court for a new hearing.

Social Harm and Norms

What makes a crime different from other wrongful acts? It may be "wrong" to be impolite, but is it a crime? When does bad behavior become a crime? "Crime" refers to an act that society has deemed harmful—sometimes called a "social harm." The injury suffered involves a violation of rights and duties owed to the community as a whole. The community has deemed the act a violation of the community's well-being and an act that should be punished.

Who decides which acts are socially harmful? Crimes typically are based on social norms. Norms are standards accepted by the community or society against which the society judges someone or something. In the American system, the government defines crimes, based on the society's notion of what is a crime, through criminal laws and establishes a criminal justice system to enforce these laws. The legislatures adopt written laws and enforce them through the use of police and prosecutors. Figure 1.1 diagrams the process of delineating how American society identifies and handles crimes. Table 1.2 lists some examples of behavior that the American system defines as criminal acts and their public purpose. As the table illustrates, the criminal justice system is designed for the protection, not of individual victims, but rather of society as a whole.

As society changes, most communities periodically redefine their criminal laws. What was a crime in a tribal community two hundred years ago may not be considered a crime today. Changes have occurred in tribal criminal justice systems as interaction with American ideas and assimilation tactics have forced nations to adopt some American components into their justice systems. For example, prior to adopting a written constitution, the Choctaw punished witchcraft by execution. However, the new court system adopted by the written constitution prohibited the killing of a witch. American and European societies have gone through similar evolutions.

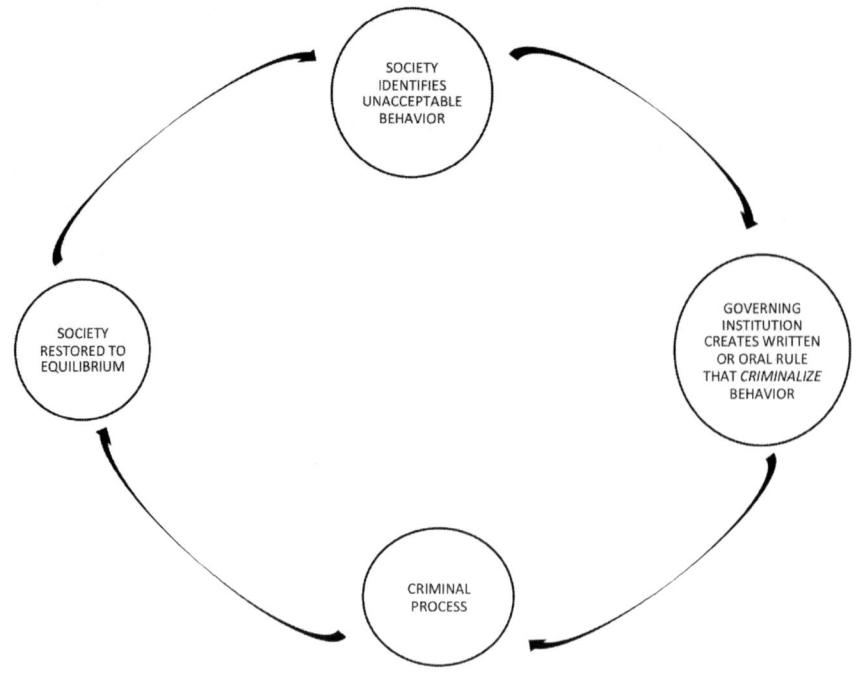

Figure 1.1. Regulating Offensive Behavior

Table 1.2. Types of Crimes in Anglo-American Law

Type of Crime	Examples	Purpose
Crimes against the government	Treason, spying	Protection of national security
Crimes against persons	Murder, rape, kidnapping, assault, battery	Protection of persons against violence
Crimes against homes	Burglary, arson	Protection of safety and security in one's home
Crimes against property	Theft, robbery, vandalism, fraud	Protection of private property
Crimes against public order	Disorderly conduct, alcohol and drugs	Protection of public peace, order, and safety
Crimes against public morals	Prostitution, gambling, use of alcohol and drugs	Maintaining traditional morality
Crimes against the environment	Pollution, smoking, toxic waste dumping	Preserving public health and the natural environment

Consider this statement from Lawrence Friedman:

> Heretics were burned at the stake in medieval Europe; there is no such crime today. Colonial Massachusetts put witches to death. In antebellum Virginia and Mississippi, two slave states, black runaways, and any whites who helped them, committed crimes. Selling liquor was a crime in the 1920s, during Prohibition. It was a crime during the Second World War to sell meat above the fixed, official price; or to rent an apartment at excessive rent. These are now extinct or obsolete crimes.[1]

Enforcement

In the American system, criminal law is enforced by the government, as part of the police powers of the government. The initial response to crime is usually provided by law enforcement officers, such as city, county, or state police or the Federal Bureau of Investigation. Law enforcement officers investigate the crime and then provide the evidence to a prosecutor. The prosecutor is responsible for proving the facts of the crime to a judge or jury.

The Response to Wrongdoing

In American judicial systems, people who are convicted of crimes are punished or disciplined for their criminal acts. There are four main theories of the purposes of punishment in American law. One is **retribution** or the belief that a person who violates society's law deserves to be punished. Another theory, which is called **deterrence**, holds that punishment will discourage others from doing wrong. For example, if Martin punches Robert and has to go to jail, other people will be less likely to hurt one another because they do not want to go to jail. **Incapacitation** is the theory that punishment will prevent a person from continuing the criminal behavior. For example, if a drunk driver has to serve time in prison, the driver will be unable to engage in drunk driving for the time spent behind bars. A fourth theory of punishment is that it should focus on **rehabilitation**, or helping offenders reform their lives. These theories are summarized in table 1.3.

A criminal justice system can combine one or more of these goals. For example, Martin may go to jail as punishment for punching Robert. He is unable

Table 1.3. Four Different Theories of Criminal Punishment

Retribution	Take legal revenge for harm done to society
Incapacitation	Make it impossible for a criminal to reoffend for a period of time
Deterrence	Discourage other people from committing crime
Rehabilitation	Convert criminals into noncriminals

to commit violent acts while he is in jail (incapacitation), but the system may also offer counseling and education to help Martin become a better person (rehabilitation) and address the problems that caused him to commit a crime.

Not everyone agrees on what the main purpose of the criminal justice system should be. For example, some view the current federal laws on possession of drugs as too harsh because the laws impose lengthy prison sentences. Some argue that defendants who are charged with mere possession of drugs should be ordered into drug treatment programs to undergo rehabilitation instead of being subject to long periods of incarceration. Others argue that the lengthy prison sentences provide retribution and deterrence. Many traditional indigenous legal systems are based on rehabilitation or restoring communities and individuals to peace. It is up to each community to decide the basis or purpose of its justice system.

Overview of Criminal Law Structures

There are two primary categories of laws in the American criminal justice system. The first category is criminal laws (examples include assault, robbery, theft). Each crime contains elements, which include an act and a mental state. The second category concerns the process (procedure) for arresting and prosecuting a suspect.

The American criminal justice system requires certain procedures to be followed before a court can convict an individual for a crime. Many of these requirements apply in contemporary tribal courts as well. The procedures are necessary to protect the rights of the defendant and increase the likelihood that only guilty people will be convicted and punished. Tribal criminal procedure law can be found in tribal constitutions, tribal statutes, tribal case law, and the Indian Civil Rights Act.

The path of a criminal case begins when law enforcement becomes aware of a potential crime. The police may witness the crime, but usually it is reported by someone. Once evidence is gathered and the defendant is arrested, the police file a report with the prosecutor. The prosecutor reviews the report. In some jurisdictions, prosecutors call together a grand jury, which is a group of citizens that examines the evidence and then determines whether to charge the individual with a crime. In most states and tribes, the prosecutor determines whether to file criminal charges against the individual. If the individual is in custody, he or she is then arraigned on the charges. Arraigned means informed of the charges, brought before a judge, and allowed to enter a plea of guilty or not guilty.

If the individual is not in custody, an arrest **warrant** may be issued, and the individual, now called the defendant, is arrested on the warrant and brought to court. Or the defendant may be given a ticket or summons, which is an order to appear in court. Once the defendant is in court, then he or she is arraigned.

Defendants are presumed innocent until proven guilty. Unless there is a risk of flight or harm to the community, the defendant should have an opportunity to post **bail** and stay out of jail pending trial. The case then proceeds to trial. Generally, pretrial conferences are held to determine whether a plea will be negotiated or the defendant wants to proceed to trial. The judge often hears motions to determine what evidence will be allowed at trial.

At the trial, the prosecutor must prove each element of the crime and must prove that the defendant committed the crime (this is called the burden of proof).

The defendant has the option of presenting a defense. The defense may introduce evidence to demonstrate that he or she did not commit the crime or to justify the act. Many tribal governments have adopted this basic structure in their own contemporary criminal courts.

Figure 1.2 provides a general overview of the chronology of an American criminal trial. The items in italics are not used in every trial. The shaded area contains the actual trial process.

Conclusion

The distinction between criminal and civil law is sometimes difficult to define. And Indian nations did not often make this distinction in their traditional laws. A wrongdoer simply faced whatever consequence that was proscribed by the act. In American law, criminal law prohibits certain harms or actions against the community and the wrongdoer faces the possibility of imprisonment. Civil law regulates relationships between individuals, businesses, and the government, and civil wrongdoings generally do not result in incarceration. Crimes are acts that have been deemed social harms by the community. Social harms will vary from community to community and will also change as the community changes. In the American criminal justice system punishment is based on four theories or purposes: retribution, incapacitation, deterrence, and rehabilitation. Among many Indian nations, traditional and modern tribal laws focus on rehabilitation. As you work through the chapters and read the various cases, determine what theories of punishment the courts are using.

Questions

1. How does a crime differ from a civil wrong?
2. Did the practice of restitution change in the Navajo Nation? If yes, how so?
3. Which one of the four theories of punishment do you think should be the main goal of a criminal justice system? Explain your answer.

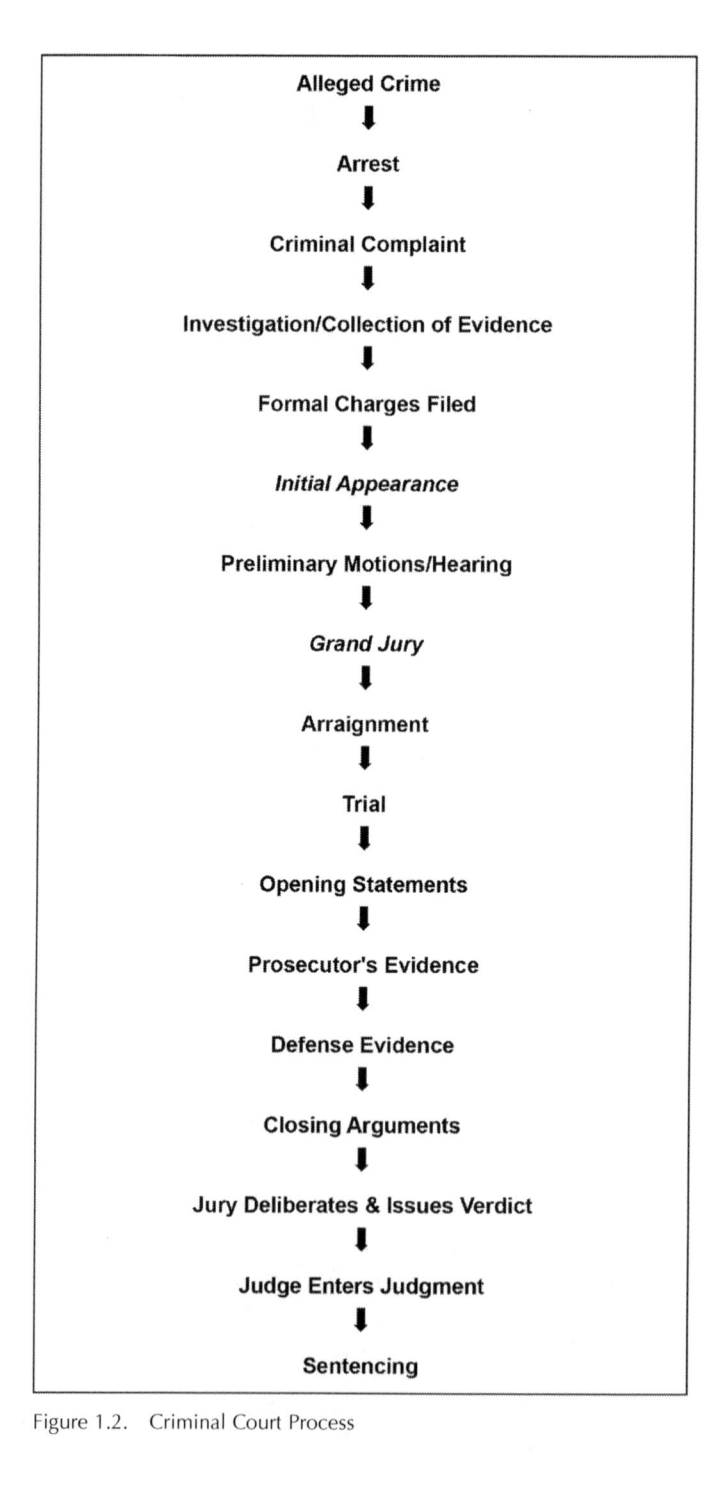

Alleged Crime
↓
Arrest
↓
Criminal Complaint
↓
Investigation/Collection of Evidence
↓
Formal Charges Filed
↓
Initial Appearance
↓
Preliminary Motions/Hearing
↓
Grand Jury
↓
Arraignment
↓
Trial
↓
Opening Statements
↓
Prosecutor's Evidence
↓
Defense Evidence
↓
Closing Arguments
↓
Jury Deliberates & Issues Verdict
↓
Judge Enters Judgment
↓
Sentencing

Figure 1.2. Criminal Court Process

In Your Community
1. What have been your experiences with the criminal justice system as it is applied by state or federal governments within your community?
2. Do you think the local nontribal criminal justice system is a good system? Why or why not?

Terms Used in Chapter 1
Bail: The temporary release of a prisoner in exchange for security given for the due appearance of the prisoner.
Civil law: The norms and rules that are supposed to be followed in the legal relationships that individual citizens or corporations have with each other or the government.
Criminal law: The norms or rules that, when violated, are considered to be an offense against the community as a whole rather than against an individual party.
Deterrence: The theory that punishment of an individual will discourage others from doing wrong.
Incapacitation: The theory that punishment will prevent a particular criminal from continuing the criminal behavior, at least during the period of the punishment.
Penal: Concerning a penalty for breaking a law.
Plea Agreement: An agreement between the prosecutor and defendant whereby the defendant agrees to plead guilty to a particular charge in return for some concession from the prosecutor.
Rehabilitation: The restoration of someone to a useful place in society.
Retribution: Punishment or revenge for a previous act.
Warrant: A document issued by a court that gives the police the power to do something.

Note
1. Lawrence Friedman, *Crime and Punishment in American History* 7 (1994).

Suggested Further Reading
Joshua Dressler, *Understanding Criminal Law*, 6th ed. (2012).
Lawrence M. Friedman, *Crime and Punishment in American History* (1994).

Comparing Tribal Criminal Law and American Criminal Law

Chapter 2

Indigenous traditional laws sometimes look very different than contemporary American laws. As a result, those unfamiliar with tribal laws often make misjudgments about tribal justice systems. Early settlers from Europe sometimes concluded that Indigenous people did not have law because they did not see Native people doing anything that resembled legal systems in Europe. In fact, all governments have systems that structure and regulate their communities in accordance with custom and tradition. Tribal nations have always had legal systems, and many continue today with a foundation in unique custom and traditional principles.

As noted in chapter 1, the American legal system draws an important distinction between the criminal legal system and civil legal system. This distinction has not always existed in many Native communities. For example, many tribal governments have treated any harmful acts as potentially harmful to all of society. (In other words, there was no private "civil" action in these tribes.) Other tribes allowed individual clans to respond to wrongs they suffered at the hands of others. (This would mean that there was no overarching "criminal" system that punished wrongdoers on behalf of the entire community.)

Defining which acts constitute "crimes" in Native cultures is often a very complicated task. Historically, many non-Native researchers did not understand traditional law and used European or American standards when observing tribal law at work. Thus, a researcher may have assumed that a tribe had no law, but if she understood the Native language belief-system, she would be able to see the legal system at work. Part of the confusion comes from language differences. Many Native languages, for example, do not have a word for crime. A trader who lived among the Chickasaw in the 1700s noted that the nearest expression for the word crime is *haksi*, which is used to convey the idea of a person's being criminal, and that although the original meaning was deaf, it came to signify drunken, roguish, wicked, or sinful. Many tribal laws did not focus on the bad behavior of a person, but rather on the positive, expected behavior of all people. As you read the following sections, think about how your traditional law is different from American law.

Most tribal laws and customs were transmitted orally from generation to generation through stories, songs, and speeches. Unlike European or American laws, laws were not written down. However, tribal nations did have ways of recording these laws. Among the Iroquois Confederacy, the laws included the Great Law, which was recorded on wampum belts, and other oral customs or rules of conduct "looking toward the security of person and property and the general stability of the clan."[1] Native people often use stories to teach their customs, beliefs, and laws. Law comes from values and beliefs, but it can also be derived from stories or symbols that are tied to the beliefs of the people. A story provides a method for integrating and communicating a complex backdrop of experiences, thoughts, and fundamental beliefs.

Stories are a crucial component of traditional law and teach important concepts. Often Native stories taught beneficial behavior and actions, making Native laws very positive, as opposed to a book that listed punishable actions, such as criminal statutes in the United States. The stories frequently described good and bad consequences to teach people, adults as well as children, to make right choices.

The Foundation of Traditional Law

Contemporary American lawyers focus on law which has been written by humans (legislatures and councils). When practicing law, these lawyers do research to identify which laws apply (statutes) and how the court system interprets those laws (cases). American law is also generally considered to be secular (nonreligious). In many Native belief systems, however, laws are given by a Creator and therefore have a spiritual foundation.

Understanding the spiritual foundation for tribal law is a critical component of practicing tribal law. Traditional law in many Native societies is often based on values, duties, and responsibilities that are closely linked to spiritual beliefs. These spiritual values created the framework for responding to problem behavior. Many of these systems focused on responsibilities of people (e.g., to be respectful, to honor the ancestors) rather than a list of prohibited activities. For example, a Native person in Canada asked the following questions at an aboriginal policing conference, "Why does your law, from the Ten Commandments to the criminal code, speak only of what people should not do? Why don't your laws speak to people about what they should be?"[2]

The Haudenosaunee Great Law is based on beliefs about the Creator. Strong spiritual beliefs in the Creator regulate behavior more than written rules about right and wrong. Because the Creator was the source of the law, there was very little crime among the Haudenosaunee people prior to intermingling with settlers and the introduction of alcohol. The Haudenosaunee people believe in the Great Spirit as their creator, who is the source of earthly blessings and blessings after death. The Great Spirit is given thanks for all things, including the changes in the seasons; the fruits of the earth; and the preservation of their lives, social privileges, and prosperity, and is continually asked for further protection. The Haudenosaunee also believe in the Evil-minded, who created monsters, poisonous reptiles, and poisonous plants. Humans stand between them and, with their free agency, control their own destiny. A life of trusting and following the Great Spirit gives one shelter against the Evil-minded.

Social Harm

In many ways, tribal conceptions of social harm can be much broader than those in the American legal system. One important reason is that the basis of much traditional law is spiritual. As a result, social harm can include mistreating animals and trees or acts of witchcraft, which is "the use of powers in selfish, hurtful, or destructive ways."[3]

Another important aspect of social harm within tribes is that some tribes rest more on community-based rights or duties and others more on individualized rights or duties. This difference can affect what is considered a social harm and can also determine whether a community organization or an individual should rectify a harm.

The following story, from the Iroquois or Haudenosaunee, includes a discussion of social harm in society.

The Two Brothers

Joseph Bruchac, *Iroquois Stories: Heroes, Heroines, Monsters and Magic*, The Crossing Press, 18–22 (1985).

It was not long after she had fallen from the Sky-World and the earth had been made as a place for her to stand, that the Sky-Woman gave birth to a beautiful daughter. Together they lived in peace upon this world, which rested upon the turtle's back, until the daughter became a woman.

One day she came to her mother and said, "Mother, while I slept in the meadow, I felt a wind sweep over me and I heard someone whisper sweet words into my ear."

Then it was that the Sky-Woman knew the West Wind had taken her daughter as his wife.

Soon the daughter of the Sky-Woman grew heavy with child and from her stomach the voices of two children could be heard.

One of the voices was angry and quarrelsome. "My brother," it said, "let us tear our way out. I think I see light through our mother's side."

The other voice was loving and gentle. "No, my brother," said the other voice. "We must not do that, for it would cause her death."

Before long the time came for the brothers to be born. The good-minded brother was the first and entered this life in the normal way. But the brother of evil mind tore his way through their mother's side and she died when he was born.

The Sky-Woman was saddened at her daughter's death. She looked at the children who stood before her. "My grandsons," she said, "your mother has gone before us to that good place where all who live good lives shall dwell some day. Let us bury her now and something good may happen."

Then the brother who was good of mind helped to bury his mother's body, while the other brother, the Evil Mind, paid no attention and either slept or cried for food.

Soon green shoots rose from their mother's grave. From her fingers came the bean plants, from her feet came the potatoes. From her stomach came the squashes and from her breasts, the corn. Last of all, from her forehead, grew the medicine plant, tobacco.

Then the Good Mind listened to his grandmother's words teaching him, telling him how to shape the earth and bring good things to be used by the humans who were to come. When she finished, she departed, back into the Sky-World, where she still looks down on us through the nights as the moon, our grandmother.

Then the Good Mind touched the earth and from it grew the tall elm tree, which gives its bark for the lodges of the people.

But the Evil Mind struck the earth and the briars and bushes with thorns sprang up. Then the Good Mind touched the earth and from it flowed the springs of pure water. But the Evil Mind struck the earth, kicking in dirt to muddy the springs. Then the Good Mind touched the earth, making the rivers and running streams to carry people from place to place, with currents flowing in each direction. But the Evil Mind made rapids and falls and twisted the streams, throwing in great rocks so that travel would not be an easy thing. Then the Good Mind made animals and birds and creatures friendly to human beings, to be his companions and provide him with food. But the Evil Mind made evil creatures: The Flying Heads and the monster bears, great horned serpents, Stone Giants and beings who would trouble the lives and dreams of the people.

So it was that in the two brothers all that was good and all that was evil came to this world and the long contest between the Good and the Evil Minds began. And even today, this world we walk in is made of both good and evil things. But if we choose the Good Mind's path, remembering right is greater than wrong, we will find our reward at journey's end.

The Individual and the Community

Many tribal traditional legal systems typically focus more on social harm done to the community rather the harm done to a single individual. One reason traditional laws were designed to protect the community is that the spiritual beliefs of many tribes instructed individuals about their duties and responsibilities to families, clans, and the tribe. In addition, a family or clan was the basis for survival, so the beliefs and laws were designed to protect the family or clan, not simply the individual.

Hopi elder Albert Yava explained: "In our Indian way of looking at the world the individual isn't important, only the group. We forget the names of our heroes and villains, while remembering what the group did, for good or evil, and how it met challenges and dangers, and how it lived in balance with nature."[4] Self-interest was intertwined with tribal interest, and thus the general good and the individual good were often virtually identical.

For the Haudenosaunee, a person's duties and responsibilities were more important than personal rights and privileges. William Newell, a Mohawk author who lived in American society, noted the difference:

> Above all I should call your attention to one of the most outstanding principles of the League of the Iroquois, and that was the idea that man's rights and privileges never exceeded his duties and responsibilities. The principle which we find in the Old Indian league differed from our own ideas on the subject in that in modern times the majority of us think only of our rights and privileges. We fight for them, we cheat to get them, and we shirk our duties to avoid our responsibilities and obligations. The old Iroquois was just as determined that he would do his duty and assume his responsibilities.[5]

The following passage illustrates the importance of responsibility to family members in the traditional justice system of the Pomo Indians:

> ## A Man without Family
> Told by Tom Jimerson (Pomo)
> Burt and Ethel Aginsky, *Deep Valley*, Stein and Day, 18–19 (1967).
>
> What is man? A man is nothing. Without family he is of less importance than that bug crossing the trail, of less importance than spit or dung. At least they can be used to help poison a man.
>
> A man must be with his family to amount to anything with us. If he had nobody else to help him, the first trouble he got into he would be killed by his enemies because there would be no relatives to help him fight the poison of the other group. No woman would marry him because her family would not let her marry a man with no family. He would be poorer than a newborn child; he would be poorer than a worm, and the family would not consider him worth anything. He would not bring renown or glory with him. He would not bring support of other relatives either. The family is important. If a man has a large family and a profession and upbringing by a family that is known to produce good children, then he is somebody, and every family is willing to have him marry a woman of their group. It is the family that is important. . . .
>
> The family was everything, and no man ever forgot that. Each person was nothing; but as a group, joined by blood, the individual knew that he would get the support of all his relatives if anything happened. He also knew that if he was a bad person the head man of his family would pay another tribe to kill him so that there would be no trouble afterward and so that he would not get the family into trouble all of the time. That is why we were good people.

Tribal traditions vary widely—while many tribal traditions focused on community rights, many also emphasized individual rights. As Bruce Miller, a professor of anthropology, notes, "[I]t would be a serious mistake to underestimate the strength of the individuals' moral conceptions in Native groups."[6] Tribal cultures that focused on individual rights include the Yurok people. Traditionally, The Yurok believed that every wrongdoing or violation of personal rights could be exactly compensated and every individual measured in terms of property. Under traditional Yurok law, all wrongdoings are committed against the individual, not against the community. Because rights and injuries are personal to the individual, there was traditionally no overarching social mechanism or institution that dispensed justice. A punishment would have been considered a new offense against an individual. As a result, settlement for any wrongdoing was done through negotiation or compensation, and each side was responsible for pursuing the matter or defending himself or herself. Traditionally, the Yurok believed that every wrongdoing or violation of personal rights could be exactly compensated and every individual privilege could be measured in terms of property.[7]

The Comanche also traditionally based their law around the individual, and responsibility for any legal action rested with the injured or aggrieved party. However, if the aggrieved held back or was afraid to pursue a claim, the community would view that person as a coward. Thus, the aggrieved was righting a personal wrong while upholding the community standards.[8]

The Iroquois traditionally considered some crimes as crimes against the whole nation, and other crimes were a matter of concern to only the family of the offender and the family of the victim. Witchcraft, according to Iroquois beliefs, is a crime against the whole nation, and it is the nation that dispenses justice. However, theft, adultery, and murder are considered to be family or individual concerns.[9]

Enforcement

Bad behavior was dealt with according to custom and tradition. Most Native communities did not use the words "prosecutor" or "police"; those are English words and concepts. The varying beliefs of each Nation dictated which entity performs the enforcement function.

The Iroquois Confederacy used social or political entities to resolve wrongdoings and impose punishment. Crime was rare because life revolved around the clans, wrongdoing was contrary to the interest of the clan, and thus wrongdoing was contrary to the interest of the individual. If wrongdoing did occur, clan leaders took responsibility for it.[10] If the accused and the victim belonged to different clans but a council of clans could not resolve the issues, the matter was referred to the nation's council, which determined guilt or innocence and amount of compensation. Further, the councils were not the only entity that enforced the law. Parents were also responsible for enforcing laws and disciplining their children; the Iroquois believed that failure to discipline caused weak children. Keepers of the Faith were also enforcers as they acted as the censors of the people and possessed the authority to report evil deeds to the council.

The chiefs among the Osage assumed a similar role; they were responsible for maintaining peace among their people. If individuals were threatening to kill one another, the chiefs stepped in to try to restore peace. When a tribal member was murdered, peace gifts were given to the victim's family. If the family was not satisfied with the gifts and still wanted to take the murderer's life for compensation, the chiefs would step in and restore peace. If the family was still not appeased, the chiefs would expel the murderer from the community, which was the harshest punishment. If the murderer's family refused to offer peace gifts, the community would step in and offer the gifts, and the leader of the murderer's relatives would be expelled from the community.

Among the Comanche, the enforcers, or those who addressed social harms, acted as individuals:

> Comanche law-ways functioned without benefits of courts. As might well be expected, in view of the ambiguity of powers of political chieftains, there were no public officials endowed with law-speaking or law-enforcing authority. Comanche law was neither legislated nor judge made. It was hammered out on the hard anvil of individual cases by claimant and defendant pressing the issues in terms of Comanche notions of individual rights and tribal standards of conduct.[11]

The Blackfeet used a combination of mechanisms for enforcing laws. Among the Blackfeet, the Men's Societies served partly to preserve order among the camps, on marches, and on hunting parties. When an individual was killed, the victim's relatives possessed the authority to avenge the murder by killing the murderer or the first member of the murderer's family whom the victim's family met. Vengeance could be avoided, however, with a payment of great value.[12]

Traditional Administration of Justice

In many tribal cultures, there were specific people or societies who were in charge of intervening in a criminal act. Kirke Kickingbird (Kiowa) explains some of these systems:

> In many tribes, "soldiers" shared responsibility with the kin group for the administration of justice. Such police societies, which were subordinate to the chiefs and the tribal council, existed in the majority of the 32 Plains tribes. "Soldiers" performed all the duties that white society distributed among police, prosecutors, judges, and penal authorities. They prevented and detected violations of the tribal order and meted out punishment. In certain tribes, the Menominees for example, they functioned as prosecutors as well. In some tribes they were called upon only during special times such as the buffalo hunt, or when the chiefs of the council requested them to act. In others, their activities were full time. The extent of their jurisdiction varied from tribe to tribe.[13]

Traditional Criminal Procedure

The Menominees and other central Algonikan peoples developed formal, three-party judicial proceedings for the prosecution of crimes. A member of the police society, or *mike-suk*, served as an investigator and prosecutor, while the pipe-holder, or *sukanahowao*, who was also a warrior chief, acted as defense attorney. The trial was complicated by the presence of a distinguished "police go-between," who acted as a mediator in negotiating a settlement between the accused and offended parties.[14]

The Response to Wrongdoing

Philosophically, most tribal legal systems had a different approach to the concept of consequences. Native culture often focused on rehabilitation or restoring peace and harmony to the individual and the community. A typical tribal worldview considers events in a cyclical pattern (see figure 2.1), which applies to criminal behavior. In order to avoid permanent disruption in a system, the goal is to maintain peace and functioning of the community—not the punishment of behavior or the prevention of future crimes. The method of restoration may have been banishment to protect the community from future harm or gifts from the wrongdoer's family to restore peace. The emphasis is on restoring individuals to harmony rather than on establishing guilt or innocence.

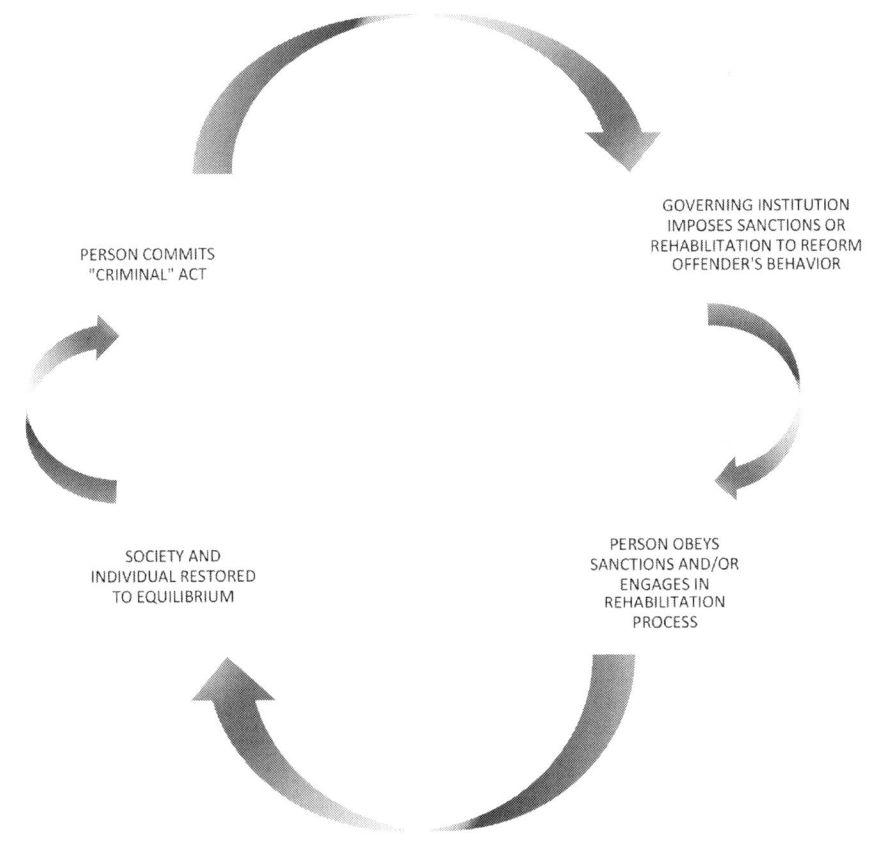

Figure 2.1. Restorative Justice

For example, the Osage system was based on restoring peace, and the Osage people would not risk their peace and harmony for the loss of one life. The community's well-being was most important, and their laws protected the community. The chiefs worked to restore peace and, if restoring peace proved impossible, expelled the individual who was preventing peace.

Some Native nations' customs required compensating individuals exactly for the harm that occurred, while others paid more attention to restoring the individual or the family harmed. The Yuroks' punishment was based more on compensation and the injured individual's worth. The killing of a man in good standing required fifteen strings of dentalium, red obsidian (used for blades; the red was rarer than the black), a woodpecker scalp headband, other property, and a daughter.[15]

The Comanche system was based more upon restoration. Using a system of negotiation and settlement, the Comanche restored the individual harmed through payment of horses, guns, blankets, or clothing. If the victim was a warrior, he would often request a favorite horse of the offender's as settlement. This request was a settlement or restoration. The family of the victim was entitled to the life of the murderer, and the case was closed once his life was taken.[16]

The Iroquois also focused upon restoring peace, either by removal of the offending individual or by **condonation**. Condonation is the forgiving, pardoning, or overlooking of an offense by treating the offender as if he had done nothing wrong. However, some crimes could not be pardoned. Among the Iroquois, treason resulted in immediate execution. Treason, according to the Iroquois, consisted of revealing the secrets of preparing medicine for good fortune or giving other information or assistance to the enemies of the tribes. When a murder occurred, the family was allowed to take the life of the murderer, but the possibility of condonation was allowed. A gift of white wampum sent on behalf of the offender was an attempt at condonation. If it was accepted, it wiped out the memory of the event. If the victim's family did not accept the wampum, family members could take the life of the offender whenever they wanted.

This practice extended to foreigners who may have been harmed in Iroquois territory. However, the judicial authority was aimed not at punishing the murderer but at preventing discord or war that might arise through vicarious **atonement**. Among the Huron and the Iroquois, the gifts were offered in solemn ceremony with sayings such as, "By this we wash out the blood of the slain; By this we cleanse his wound; By this we clothe his corpse with a new shirt; By this we place food on his grave." The victim's family could refuse the gifts, and in this case the murderer was given to the family as a slave.[17] The Iroquois also believe in supplying bad consequences for misbehavior. Any man who beat his wife was led to a red-hot statue of a female and told to beat it as he beat his wife. As he beat it, sparks would fly off and burn him.[18]

Other tribes focused on healing the wrongdoer and restoring him to the community. Rupert Ross, a non-Native legal scholar, has concluded that Anishinaabe (Ojibway) people find it easier to forgive wrongdoers because their notions of blame are different from those of Western societies. The Ojibway believe that most offenders could not have avoided the wrong acts, so there is less blame, and forgiveness takes on a different form. For example, when one domestic-violence offender was sentenced to jail time and was about to be led off to jail, a circle of fifteen elderly women formed a circle around him and proceeded to hug and kiss him and whisper in his ear. Elders from Sandy Lake Band articulated this philosophical difference between beliefs about restoration and beliefs about punishment in an application to the Canadian government for justice funding. The application read in part:

> Probably one of the most serious gaps in the system is the different perception of wrongdoing and how to treat it. In the non-Native society, committing a crime seems to mean that the individual is a bad person and must be punished. . . . The Indian communities view wrong doing as a misbehavior which requires teaching, or an illness which requires healing.[19]

As illustrated by the following story, the Cheyenne also focus on restoration and rehabilitation. Although a person may be removed from the community as punishment, the offender can be restored to the community following rehabilitation.

High Backed Wolf, Pawnee Punished by the Bowstring Soldiers and Rehabilitated

Karl N. Llewellyn & E. Adamson Hoebel, *The Cheyenne Way*, W.S. Hein, 6–9 (1941).

Pawnee was a Southern Cheyenne when he was a very young man, but in his later years he lived up here with us. He was all the time looking out after the people's morals and counseling the boys on good behavior. I have heard him tell his story many times when I was a youth, because he was always telling it to us as a lesson. He had been an awful rascal down there in Oklahoma, stealing meat from people's racks, taking their horses for joy-rides without asking them for them, and then when he got to where he was going he would just turn the horse loose and let it wander back to its owner—if it did. He was disrespectful to people and sassed them back. Everyone thought he was a mean boy, and whatever happened in the camp, he got blamed for it. This story I am going to tell happened just after that trouble Wolf Lies Down had over the borrowed horse when the soldiers made the rule that no one in the camp could take another person's horse without permission. This is what Pawnee used to tell us:

Down there [in Oklahoma] were two spotted horses well liked in their family. One day I took them and headed west. Three days passed and I found myself still safe. Now I was out of trouble's way, so I began to feel pretty good. On the fourth day, as I looked back I saw some people coming up. "It is nothing," I thought, "just some people traveling." When they overtook me, I saw they were Bowstring soldiers [one of four Cheyenne soldier troops] after me.

"You have stolen those horses," they cried as they pulled me from my horse. "Now we have trailed you down." They threw me on the ground and beat me until I could not stand; they broke up my weapons and ruined my saddle; they cut my blankets, moccasins, and kit to shreds. When they had finished they took all my food and went off with the horses, leaving me alone on the prairie, sore and destitute, too weak and hurt to move.

The next day I started back, traveling as best I could all day long. I knew there was a small camp of buffalo hunters out and for them I was looking. I traveled all day. The next day I thought I would die. I had no food, only water. Late in the afternoon I camped on a creek. My feet were bleeding and I could not walk farther. I crawled slowly on my hands and knees to the brow of a high hill to find a place to die. I waited in mourning. Far to the south of me I could see the rolling country; to the west my view was blocked. My pipe and tobacco were gone. Without smoke I sat there thinking of a great many things as I watched the blood drip from my swollen feet.

As I gazed steadfastly into the south, a hunter came up the hill from behind me. When he saw me he stopped and watched me for a long time. After three days and two nights in my condition I must have been nearly deaf, for I did not hear him until he spoke from his horse right behind me. I was naked. I fell over in fright when I heard his voice start out in the silence.

This man dismounted and hugged me. He wept, he felt so bad at seeing my plight. It was High Backed Wolf, a young man, but a chief. He put his blanket about me and took me home. The camp was on the creek below, hidden just around a bend where I had not seen it. His wife gave me food and nourished me. Then High Backed Wolf sent for the chiefs who were in the camp. Four or five came, one of whom was a soldier chief.

High Backed Wolf spoke to the soldier chief first. "This is the first time since I have become a big [tribal] chief that I have happened upon such a poor man; now I am going to outfit him. Until he is fixed up, I shall ask no questions. Then we shall learn how he came to be naked. I am not going to ask you to give anything unless you wish to do so. I know this man," he said. "He is a great smoker. But I shall give him no smoke until he has first eaten." (In my own mind I said, "I'd rather smoke first.")

First they gave me a little soup; then some meat.

High Backed Wolf then filled the pipe. As he held it to the five directions he prayed, "This is my first good act as a chief. Help this man to tell the truth." Then he held the pipe for me to smoke; then he gave it to the next man and to the others. Now he faced me again. "Now you tell the truth. Have you been caught by enemies and stripped? Or was it something else? You saw me smoke this pipe; you have touched it with your own lips. That is to help you tell the truth. If you tell us straightly, Maiyun [the supernatural] will help you."

I told them the whole story. I told them whose horses they were, and I told them it was the Bowstrings who had punished me. High Backed Wolf knew I was a rascal, so he lectured to me. "You are old enough now to know what is right," he preached. "You have been to war. Now leave off this foolishness. If it had been that I had not ridden out into the hills today you would have died. No one would have known the end of you. You know how we Cheyennes try to live. You know how we hunt, how we go to war. When we take horses, we take them from enemies, not from Cheyennes. You had better join a military society. You can learn good behavior from the soldiers. Yet I ask only one thing of you. Be decent from now on! Stop stealing! Stop making fun of people! Use no more bad language in the camp! Lead a good life!"

"Now I am going to help you out. That is what I am here for, because I am a chief of the people. Here are your clothes. Outside are three horses. You may take your choice!" He gave me a six-shooter. "Here is a mountain-lion skin. I used to wear this in the parades. Now I give it to you." He offered me all these things and I took them.

The others gave me beaver skins to braid in my hair, beads, and extra moccasins, and two more horses.

Then High Backed Wolf ended it. "Now I am not going to tell you to leave this camp. You may stay here as long as you wish. I shall not tell you which direction to go, west or south." I had a sweetheart in the south, but when these people did this for me, I felt ashamed. I had all those things with which to look beautiful, but I did not dare to go back, for I knew she would have heard what the Bowstrings had done to me. I thought it wisest to go north until the thing was dead.

When the Arrows were next renewed, the Foxes put up their lodge to get more men. I went in [joined]. Still, I never got it out of my head that it had been those Bowstrings. Whenever my Fox troop was on

> duty I was out looking for those men or their families to do something wrong. I always looked for a Bowstring to slip, so I could beat him well. I stayed with the Northern Cheyennes a long, long time, until the Horse Creek Treaty. Though I came to be a chief of the Fox Soldiers among the Northern people, I never amounted to much with the Southern bands. Those people always remembered me as a no-good.
>
> You boys remember that. You may run away, but your people always remember. You just obey the rules of the camp, and you'll do all right.

Stigma

In many traditional Native communities, society's ridicule served as a strong element of social control. The embarrassment and shame associated with committing a social harm served as a strong deterrent.

> For mild persistent misconduct [among the Blackfoot], a method of formal ridicule is sometimes practiced. When the offender has failed to take hints and suggestions, the head men may take formal notice and decide to resort to discipline. Some evening when all are in their tipis, a head man will call out to a neighbor asking if he has observed the conduct of Mr. A. This starts a general conversation between the many tipis, in which all the grotesque and hideous features of Mr. A's acts are held up to general ridicule amid shrieks of laughter, the grilling continuing until far into the night. The mortification of the victim is extreme and usually drives him into temporary exile or, as formerly, upon the war path to do desperate deeds.[20]

The following story illustrates the Iroquois response to bad behavior and the stigma that wrongdoing can bring upon a person.

> ### Battle with the Snakes
> Joseph Bruchac, *Iroquois Stories: Heroes, Heroines, Monsters and Magic*, The Crossing Press, 18–22 (1985).
>
> There was a man who was not kind to animals. One day when he was hunting, he found a rattlesnake and decided to torture it. He held its head to the ground and pierced it with a piece of bark. Then, as it was caught there, he tormented it.
>
> "We shall fight," he said and then burned the snake until it was dead. He thought this was a great jest and so, whenever he found a snake, he would do the same thing.

One day another man from his village was walking through the forest when he heard a strange sound. It was louder than the wind hissing through the tops of tall pine trees. He crept closer to see. There, in a great clearing, were many snakes. They were gathered for a war council and as he listened in fright he heard them say:

"We shall now fight with them. Djisdaah has challenged us and we shall go to war. In four days we shall go to their village and fight them."

The man crept away and then ran as fast as he could to his village to tell what he had heard and seen. The chief sent other men to see if the report was true. They returned in great fright. "Ahhhh," they said, "It is so. The snakes are all gathering to have a war."

The chief of the village could see that he had no choice. "We must fight," he said and ordered the people of the village to make preparations for the battle. They cut mountains of wood and stacked it in long piles all around the village. They built rows of stakes close together to keep the snakes out. When the fourth day came, the chief ordered that the piles of wood be set on fire. Just as he did so they heard a great noise, like a great wind in the trees. It was the noise of the snakes, hissing as they came to the village to do battle.

Usually a snake will not go near a fire, but these snakes were determined to have their revenge. They went straight into the flames. Many of them died, but the living snakes crawled over the bodies of the dead ones and continued to move forward until they reached the second row of stakes.

Once again, the chief ordered that the piles of wood in the second row of defense be set on fire. But the snakes crawled straight into the flames, hissing their war songs, and the living crawled over the bodies of the dead. It was a terrible sight. They reached the second row of stakes and, even though the people fought bravely, it was no use.

The snakes were more numerous than fallen leaves and they could not be stopped. Soon they forced their way past the last row of stakes and the people of the village were fighting for their lives. The first man to be killed was Djisdaah, the one who had challenged the snakes to battle.

It was now clear they could never win this battle. The chief of the village shouted to the snakes who had reached the edge of the village: "Hear me, my brothers. We surrender to you. We have done you a great wrong. Have mercy on us."

The snakes stopped where they were and there was a great silence. The exhausted warriors looked at the great army of snakes and the snakes stared back at them. Then the earth trembled and cracked in front of the human beings. A great snake, a snake taller than the big-

> gest pine tree, whose head was larger than a great longhouse, lifted himself out of the hole in the earth.
> "Hear me," he said. "I am the chief of all the snakes. We shall go and leave you in peace if you will agree to two things."
> The chief looked at the great snake and nodded his head. "We will agree, Great Chief," he said. "It is well," said the Chief of the Snakes. "These are the two things. First, you must always treat my people with respect. Secondly, as long as the world stands, you will never name another man Djisdaah."
> And so it was agreed and so it is, even today.

Traditional Criminal Law and the Spirit World

Cherokee laws were traditionally closely intertwined with spiritual beliefs and ceremonies. These laws represented strong spiritual beliefs that guided the Cherokee people throughout their lives. The following excerpt describes the foundations of traditional Cherokee law. As you read the passage, identify some of the American elements of criminal law (social harm, enforcement, and stigma) as they exist in the traditional Cherokee system.

Traditional Law Ways and the Spirit World

Rennard Strickland, *The Fire and the Spirits: Law from Clan to Court*, University of Oklahoma Press, 10-12 (1982).

Four kinds of **deviation**s were recognized by traditional Cherokee law: deviations which constituted an offense against the supernatural or Spirit Beings, against the entire community, against the clan, and against an individual Cherokee. Four distinct authorities were empowered to determine deviation from these norms. Supernatural norms involving, as they did, the relationship between man and Spirits were, in the Cherokee view, automatically detected. In fact, according to reports . . . there was "no hiding place where the Spirits did not see." Most public offenses were brought before a tribal group much like a court, composed of the seven clans. Deviations which were offenses against individual members of the clan were resolved in accordance with a pre-established duty based upon particular relationships between the clan member and the offense or offender. Offenses against an individual involved little more than personal response. Divine judgment might be sought for deviations on any of the levels.

Again, the agent assigned the task of applying sanctions for any deviation was clearly delineated along one of the four lines. Divine retribution for violation of Spirit norms might be immediate or prolonged, against either the individual or the entire village. Public punishment of an established nature followed conviction for a public offense. Clan violations were avenged by individual members of the offended clan, for individual retribution was achieved by the person offended. Divine assistance might be sought for punishment of non-spiritual norm deviations.

Each Cherokee village had two distinct governmental structures, a white, or peace, government and a red, or war, government. The white government was supreme in all respects except the making of war. During times of peace the white government controlled all tribal affairs. In times of war the red government was in control of all tribal affairs. The two governmental structures were never in operation at the same time. The white government was essentially a stable theocracy composed of the older and wiser men of the tribe, who constituted a tribal **gerontocracy**. The red organization was, on the other hand, flexible, responsive to changing conditions and controlled by the younger warriors.

The Seven Counselors Court was a peace organization composed of selected officials from the white government. The officers operating the peace society were (1) the chief of the tribe or the high priest, (2) the chief's right-hand man, (3) seven prime counselors representing the seven clans, (4) the council of elders, (5) the chief speaker, (6) messengers, and (7) a number of officers for specialized ceremonial functions. Evidence indicates that all the officers above the level of messenger sat at the white court. The organizational structure was repeated in each of the tribal villages of any size large enough to be represented by each of the clans.

Deviations from established norms which offended community expectations were tried in the courts of the villages. A Cherokee trial was essentially a matter of oath saying. The accused was brought before the assembled officers. The offenses against him were presented by a court prosecutor, who was generally the chief's right-hand man. The court was free to question in any manner desired. No "attorney" was allowed to represent the individual on trial. There were no juries, and the counselors and court did not act in that capacity but rather placed the accused upon a sacred oath which required him to state his own innocence or guilt. Violation of the oath would prevent the ghost from passing to the Nightland, and, therefore, the punishment for the offense with which the accused was charged would, in the view of the traditional Cherokee, be less grave than having one's ghost remain forever wandering as a result of violation of the oath. ....

Clan investigation was never formalized into an actual court procedure but represented an investigation by clan members most immediately concerned with deviations. It was a corporate reaction, but it was never institutionalized into a court procedure as in community sanction enforcement. The offended members of the clan reacted, often immediately, as in the case of the individual who might seek revenge or retaliation for the offenses against his person.

Women constituted a special class within the operation of Cherokee laws. They might serve as a court designed to punish offenses which were affronts to them and the tribe growing from the regulations of women. The lawgiver recited a "female lecture," when tribal laws were given, and was reported to be "sharp and prolix" as "he urges them with much earnest to an honest observance of the marriage-law." To violate the rules of female cleanliness was "at the [risk] of their lives." Women were themselves granted the right to enforce these regulations, especially those relating to the obligations of widowhood and adultery. . . .

The most thoroughly documented study of Cherokee norm deviations center around the clan blood regulation of **homicide**. The clan was, without doubt, the major institution exercising legal powers. The survival of important sources of information on murder regulation was assured for two reasons. Control of murder was no doubt an ancient and major public-order question among the Cherokees and had become fully institutionalized. A second factor which accounts for our detailed knowledge of the regulation of murder is the fascination which this crime held for white travelers who noted the cases with considerable detail. The following statements represent the general Cherokee attitudes towards control of murder:

1. Homicide was an offense against the blood of the clan.
2. The ghost of the murdered clansman could not pass from the earth until the blood had been revenged.
3. Revenge for the murder rested with members of the clan of the victim and was a sacred duty.
4. Blood revenge required the death of a member of the clan of the murderer.
5. Clans were corporate units for revenge purposes, all being brothers.
6. It was desirable to kill the murderer himself, but if he was not available, then a member of his clan, especially a close relative of the murderer, might be avenged.

7. Revenge was a duty and fell to the oldest male relative of the victim's generation, generally his oldest brother. To fail to avenge was to be held up to public ridicule.
8. There were no degrees of murder. The necessity of revenge to free the ghost was the same whether the death was accidental or deliberate.
9. There was no need for a public trial, witnesses, or hearings. The clan member with the duty of revenge would determine guilt. If assistance was needed, he could call upon other members of his clan.
10. The members of the clan of the murderer might serve a self-policing or protecting purpose by executing the member of their own clan and thus eliminate the risk that innocent clansmen might be made to suffer the blood revenge.
11. An individual who had innocently or by accident taken the life of another might flee to one of four "free cities," or "sacred cities of refuge," where the murderer would be safe. A priest might offer the same protection on sacred ground in any town.
12. Compensation was occasionally possible, but only with the replacement of a member of the clan through capture of a prisoner or delivery of the scalp of an enemy in blood revenge. No fixed monetary compensation appears to have existed in the primitive system.
13. Execution in blood revenge could be carried out by any means selected by the clansmen designated to make the revenge.
14. The clans served as public executioner but this often increased the chances of public disorder with the danger of blood feud. However, generally the sanction was so strongly supported that the clan which suffered the blood revenge considered the execution justified.

One of the most serious blood-regulation threats to the Cherokee community stemmed from the presence of a witch who could cause sickness and death. . . . Witchcraft was considered a **capital crime**—more dangerous than homicide. Some witch cases might be tried by the Seven Counselors Court, but generally there were no trials, no witnesses; the dangers were too great. All that was required to ensure execution was "to accuse him and refer to some instance of painful disease of death."

One of the most difficult tasks of law under a clan-revenge system is to prevent escalation of revenge into open clan warfare and blood feud. The buildup is easy to understand because the revenge killing is a private act with no public determination of fairness. In most instances the consensus of support for the system was so great that the retaliation produced no additional revenge, and, in fact, the revenge killing was occasionally executed by the clan of the murderer. However, there is a record of "one instance [in which] a man was killed as a witch who had several brothers. These avenged his death by killing the witchkiller. His relatives avenged his death, and so it went on till seven individuals were killed. . . ."

The clan-blood relationship explains why there was so little social emphasis attached to male sex practice in the matrilineal structure of the society. Clan membership, inheritance, and social status depended upon the mother and her family. Sexual activity constituted little threat to society unless there was a violation of clan-intermarriage restrictions. As Chief Blanket, an informant for Cephas Washburn, explained, "Every mother knows who are her children, but fathers have not such knowledge. My wife was a singing bird [and] had four [children] while she lived with me, and she said I was their father."

Public punishment was rare and was inflicted by officers chosen for the purpose. Tribal humiliation was common and was administered by the entire tribe. An effort was made to select individuals related to the offense in cases of assaults, arson, or witchcraft. If the punishment involved death, a member of each clan constituted the execution group to prevent the danger of revenge. Apparently there was no institutionalized post of public executioner. In the instance when an acknowledged witch was put to death, "These executions were accomplished by a company designated by the headmen of some village, within whose jurisdiction the witch resided." Priests might provide the more common punishments, such as scratching the legs of young warriors who violated prescribed codes of military conduct. Scratching of the young was often the duty of the mother's brother.

The temptation to abuse individual or clan punishments was great. There are recorded instances of abuses in the punishment of witches. Any enemy found it simple to suggest crop failures or unexplained deaths were the result of witchcraft by an old enemy or a bitter rival. . . .

Spirit or supernatural punishments might be invoked in response to violations of the norms of society. The Spirit World was often called upon to atone for deviations affecting the community, the clan, and the individual. These divine punishments were not, however, automatic and must be requested by the offended Cherokee. Most often such assistance would be sought when supernatural forces were needed to determine guilt for the offense. Divining crystals were regularly used to determine the location of stolen property and the name of the thief. . . .

A great pride was involved in acceptance of justified punishment. The Cherokee was resentful of one who did not accept his punishment. The practice of scratching the young was more often a ritual related to powers rather than punishment. War leaders are said to have scratched harder and deeper when warriors flinched when being scratched as punishment for violation of a battle-order. . . .

Violation of established order might result in punishment of the entire tribe. It was believed by the Cherokees that the severe smallpox epidemic of 1738, which is said to have reduced [the] population by one-half, was "brought on by their unlawful copulation in the night dews." The violation of the Divine Spirit order was considered the cause. The dangers of women violating "their lunar retreats" illustrate individual violations being vested upon an entire tribe. Adair (an Irish trader who lived among Indians of the Southeast in the eighteenth century) notes that "Should they be known to violate that ancient law, they must answer for every misfortune that befalls any of the people, as a certain effect of the divine fire."

Within this universe of divinely ordered laws the Cherokees faced the question introduced by the arrival of the white man—the question of adapting their laws to new or changing circumstances. Adaptation was begun with a form of supernatural fiction found among many primitive people and probably used by the ancient Cherokees.

Conclusion

All criminal justice systems have the same basic goal: protect citizens from harmful behavior. The mechanisms by which this goal is achieved may differ. Even the philosophies for how harmful behavior should be addressed can differ widely. However, the end result is the same. People are held accountable for their behavior and the safety of the community is preserved.

Questions

1. Did tribal cultures traditionally distinguish between criminal and civil law? Explain your answer.
2. The story of Pawnee ends with Pawnee encouraging the young boys to behave well because of the importance of reputation. Do you think Pawnee's bad reputation among the Cheyenne was a type of stigma for his criminal acts?

3. Is ridicule, as described in the passage about the Blackfoot, an effective way to address criminal behavior? Why or why not?
4. According to Strickland, what beliefs formed the basis of Cherokee law?
5. How were victims of crime treated under traditional Cherokee law?

In Your Community

1. Describe some beliefs in your culture that form the basis of your tribal law.
2. Are stories or symbols used in your nation to teach values and laws? What are some of the stories you have heard, and what do they teach?
3. Traditionally, who enforced the law among your people? How did they enforce the law?
4. How did your nation traditionally punish people? Was the punishment based upon compensation or restoration?
5. Did your nation traditionally focus on restoring the community or the individual?

Terms Used in Chapter 2

Atonement: Amends or reparation made for an injury or wrong.
Capital Crime: A crime punishable by death.
Condonation: The implied forgiveness of an offense by ignoring it.
Deviation: Departure from established procedure or philosophy.
Gerontocracy: Government based on rule by elders.
Homicide: The killing of a person.

Notes

1. Sara Henry Sites, *Economics of the Iroquois* 107 (1904).
2. Rupert Ross, *Dancing with a Ghost: Exploring Indian Reality* 170 (1992).
3. Michael Cousins, "Aboriginal Justice: A Haudenosaunee Approach," in *Justice as Healing, Indigenous Ways* 148 (Wanda D. McCaslin ed., 2005).
4. Albert Yava, *Big Falling Snow* (1978).
5. William B. Newell, *Crime and Justice among the Iroquois Nations* 47 (1965).
6. Bruce G. Miller, "The Individual, the Collective, and Tribal Code," 21 *American Indian Culture and Research Journal* 107-129 (1997).
7. A. L. Kroeber, *Yurok Law and Custom: The California Indians: A Source Book* 391 (1971).
8. Ernest Wallace and E. Adamson Hoebel, *The Comanches: Lords of the South Plains* 224, 226 (1952).
9. Newell, *supra* note 5, at 47, 51.
10. Lewis Henry Morgan, *The League of the Iroquois* 321 (1851).

11. Ernest Wallace and E. Adamson Hoebel, *The Comanches, Lords of the South Plains* 224 (1952).

12. *See* Esther S. Goldfrank, "Changing Configurations of the Social Organization of a Blackfoot Tribe during the Reserve Period," *Monographs of the American Ethnological Society* (1961).

13. Kirke Kickingbird, "In our Image . . . After Our Likeness: The Drive for the Assimilation of Indian Court Systems" 13 *American Criminal Law Review* 675, 678 (1976).

14. *Id.*

15. Kroeber, *supra* note 7, at 399.

16. Wallace and Hoebel, *supra* note 11, at 226, 232.

17. Francis Parkman, *The Jesuits in North America in the Seventeenth Century* XLI-LXII (1899).

18. Sally Roesch Wagner, *Sisters in Spirit: Haudenosaunee Influence on Early American Feminists* 66 (2001).

19. Ross, *Dancing with a Ghost*, 59, 61-62.

20. Clark Wissler, *The Social Life of the Blackfoot Indians* 24 (1911).

Suggested Further Reading

Pat Lauderdale, "Indigenous North American Jurisprudence," 38 *International Journal of Comparative Sociology* 131 (1997).

John Howard Payne, *Indian Justice: A Cherokee Murder Trial at Talequah in 1840*, University of Oklahoma Press (2002).

Using American Criminal Law to Control American Indian Nations

Chapter 3

As conflict over land and resources grew, the American legal system and its predecessors (Spanish, British, and French) used criminal law as a tool of destruction. Criminal justice systems were used to outlaw cultural practices and traditions and punish those who participated. Through the justice system, federal officials attempted to control Native people who were attempting to fight for their nations' sovereignty, culture, and land. Criminal law and the justice system were also used to impose Western values of punishment and to outlaw tribal mechanisms for addressing "criminal" behavior. In addition, the American system was imposed on Native nations as a method of indirect rule enlisting Natives to impose American law on their own people.

American Indian nations' history with the American legal system resulted in immense distrust and skepticism toward the modern criminal justice system. Today, some tribal members even distrust their own tribal justice programs, especially those that are funded by the federal government. The following excerpts provide an analysis of how the American criminal justice system was used to control tribal communities and restrict their sovereignty.

The Failure of Criminal Law

Criminal law was used by the federal government to confine indigenous people to reservations, but failed to protect them from harm by colonists. Although used to punish Indigenous people for practicing their culture, it was rarely used to protect Indigenous people from the criminal conduct of colonial settlers.

> Luana Ross, *Inventing the Savage—The Social Construction of Native American Criminality*, University of Texas, 15-16 (1998).
>
> Genocide against Native people was never seen as murder. Indeed, in the Old West the murder of Natives was not even a crime. Native men and women, their humanity cast aside, were commonly referred to as "bucks" and "squaws." Those not exterminated faced dire circumstances. For instance, the state of California enacted "The Act for the Government and Protection of Indians" in 1850, amended in 1860. Despite the title of the act, it allowed white people to simply take Native children, those orphaned or supposedly with parental consent, as indentured slaves. The law also "virtually compelled Indians to work because any Indian found 'loitering or strolling about' was subject to arrest on the complaint of any white citizen, where upon the court was required within twenty-four hours to hire out arrestees to the highest bidder for up to four months."

Controlling Indian Nations with Courts and Police

The Office of Indian Affairs (OIA), which would become the Bureau of Indian Affairs (BIA), believed that the legal systems of Native people were insufficient for controlling behavior. Moreover, these federal agencies also viewed many traditional practices as crimes. As a result the OIA created Courts of Indian Offenses (also called CFR Courts—referring to the Code of Federal Regulations) that outlawed many cultural practices. Today, there are still more than twenty CFR courts in operation but nations now exercise more control over these courts.

The Law and Order Apparatus

> Thomas Biolsi, *Organizing the Lakota: The Political Economy of the New Deal on the Pine Ridge and Rosebud Reservations*, University of Arizona, 7-8 (1998).
>
> One technology deployed by the OIA for controlling Indian behavior was the agency courts and police forces. In 1883 the Interior Department **promulgate**d a code providing for a court of Indian offenses for each agency, to be presided over by three Indian judges appointed by the commissioner on the recommendation of the agent. The court had jurisdiction over **misdemeanors** and civil matters as these were defined under the laws of the state or territory in which the reservation was located. The court also had jurisdiction over what were termed Indian offenses. These included the Sun Dance, new plural marriages, the practices of medicine men, destruc-

tion of property, payment for cohabiting with a woman, intoxication, and trafficking in liquor. In actual practice, the agent often enforced the code without a court of Indian judges; he also had veto power over the decisions of judges. Punishments included detention in the agency guardhouse, fines in cash and/or hard labor, and withholding rations.

The agent enforced the code with Indian policemen appointed and paid by the OIA, over which he served as commander. The Pine Ridge agent swore in fifty Oglala men in 1879 "to serve the Great Father [the president] and him only." The first action was to prevent departure of an armed Cheyenne party—some Cheyenne resided on Pine Ridge—which intended to join Sitting Bull's band of hostiles in Canada. The leader of the Cheyenne party was shot and killed, and the agent reportedly told the Oglala, "Remember that you have seen the power of the police; they represent the Father."

The criminal cases actually handled through the law and order apparatus concerned, principally, not infractions by medicine men and Sun dancers, but the kinds of misdemeanors—particularly liquor violations—which one would find in any non-Indian community. There was a heavy incidence, however, of cases involving illicit sexual relations and prohibited domestic arrangements. The OIA wanted to insure documentable paternity through legalized marriage/divorce in order to facilitate the determination of heirs in probating trust property . . . , and in order to prevent claims for rations for children unsupported by a father. Toward this end, the agencies systematically issued marriage licenses free of charge after 1900. Neither the agencies nor the courts of Indian offenses were authorized by law, however, to grant divorces. The agencies punished couples cohabiting without a license as well as legally married individuals who divorced by "Indian custom" and moved in with new spouses while still legally married to the original spouse. These practices account for the numerous cases listed as adultery, bastardy, bigamy, fornication, and illicit relationship. Sentences for such offenses on Rosebud Reservation in 1930 ranged from thirty to sixty days' detention.

Courts of Indian Offenses

The Courts of Indian Offenses imposed federal regulations to prohibit misdemeanor offenses. And they also used the federal regulations to prohibit cultural practices and behavior the OIA deemed immoral. The following passage comes from a Congressional Report. Read through the offenses listed below and discuss what might be the impact on Indigenous people and nations.

Rules for Indian Courts (1892)
H. R. Rep. No. 51-1, pt. 5, at 28-31 (1892)

For the purpose of these regulations the following shall be deemed to constitute offenses, and the judges of the Indian court shall severally have jurisdiction to try and punish for the same when committed within their respective districts.

a. *Dances, etc.*—Any Indian who shall engage in the sun dance, scalp dance, or war dance, or any other similar feast, so called, shall be deemed guilty of an offense, and upon conviction thereof shall be punished for the first offense by the withholding of its rations for not exceeding ten days or by imprisonment for not exceeding ten days; and for any subsequent offense under this clause he shall be punished by withholding his rations for not less than ten nor more than thirty days, or by imprisonment for not less than ten nor more than thirty days.

b. *Plural or polygamous marriages.*—Any Indian under the supervision of a United States Indian agent who shall hereafter contract or enter into any plural or polygamous marriage shall be deemed guilty of an offense, and upon conviction thereof shall pay a fine of not less than twenty nor more than fifty dollars, or work at hard labor for not less than twenty nor more than sixty days, or both, at the discretion of the court; and so long as the person shall continue in such unlawful relation he shall forfeit all right to receive rations from the Government.

c. *Practices of medicine men.*—Any Indian who shall engage in the practices of so-called medicine men, or who shall resort to any artifice or device to keep the Indians of the reservation from adopting and following civilized habits and pursuits, or shall adopt any means to prevent the attendance of children at school, or shall use any arts of a conjurer to prevent Indians from abandoning their barbarous rites and customs, shall be deemed to be guilty of an offense, and upon conviction thereof, for the first offense shall be imprisoned for not less than ten nor more than thirty days: Provided, That for any subsequent conviction for such offense the maximum term or imprisonment shall not exceed six months.

d. *Destroying property of other Indians.*—Any Indian who shall willfully or wantonly destroy or injure, or, with intent to destroy or injure or appropriate, shall take and carry away any property of any other Indian or Indians, shall, without reference to its value, be deemed guilty of an offense, and upon conviction shall be compelled to return the property to the owner or owners, or, in case the property shall have been lost, injured, or destroyed, the estimated full value of the same; and in addition he shall be imprisoned for not exceeding thirty days; and the plea that the person convicted or the owner of the property in question was at time a "mourner," and that thereby the taking, destroying, or injuring of the property was justified by the customs or rites of the tribe, shall not be accepted as a sufficient defense.

e. *Immorality.*—Any Indian who shall pay, or offer to pay, money or other thing of value to any female Indian, or to her friends or relatives, or to any other persons, for the purpose of living or cohabiting with any such female Indian not his wife, shall be deemed guilty of an offense, and upon conviction thereof shall forfeit all right to Government rations for not exceeding ninety days, or be imprisoned for not exceeding ninety days, or both, in the discretion of the court. And any Indian who shall receive, or offer to receive money or other valuable things in consideration for allowing, consenting to, or practicing such immorality, shall be punished in the same manner as provided for the punishment of the party paying, or offering to pay, said consideration.

Federal Criminal Jurisdiction as a Method of Control

Federal agents were not content with the creation of courts of Indian offenses. The BIA wanted federal courts to have criminal jurisdiction over Native people so that American laws could be used to govern Native people directly. The BIA repeatedly asked Congress to grant federal courts criminal jurisdiction on Indian territories. In 1883, the U.S. Supreme Court issued a decision called *Ex parte Crow Dog*, which ruled that the tribe had exclusive criminal jurisdiction over the murder, a murder committed by a Brule Sioux man (Crow Dog) against another Brule Sioux man (Spotted Tail). Because the decision was so controversial, the BIA was finally successful in its efforts to convince Congress to enact the Major Crimes Act in 1885. The Major Crimes Act imposed federal criminal jurisdiction on tribal nations without their consent. The following excerpt explains the importance of this law.

Crow Dog and the Western Justice System

Sidney L. Harring, *Crow Dog's Case: American Indian Sovereignty, Tribal Law, and United States Law in the Nineteenth Century*, Cambridge University Press, 129-141 (1994).

The Supreme Court's Decision

What is remarkable about the Crow Dog decision's recognition of tribal law as an inherent attribute of sovereignty is not that the Supreme Court had any respect for Brule law or even knew anything substantive about it. Characterizing the case as one of "red man's revenge," the Court hardly bothered to conceal its contempt for tribal institutions. Yet at the same time, Crow Dog upheld Marshall's recognition of tribal sovereignty in Worcester, a significant statement given the heightened Indian–white conflict fifty years later. Although the holding was based conservatively on narrow grounds—that congressional ratification of an 1877 Sioux treaty that contained general language securing "orderly government" and making the Sioux "subject to the laws of the United States" did not reverse a long-standing government policy toward Indians, "as declared in many statutes and treaties"—the Court went beyond the scope of the decision and offered important statements of late-nineteenth-century Indian policy. While accepting the justice and logic of recognizing the right of the tribes to maintain their own legal institutions, the Court also made it plain that it did not respect tribal institutions and that ultimately they must give way to "civilization." The case is memorable for both its strength and its weakness, as well as for the Court's fundamental inability to come to terms with the complexity of Indian–white relations or with a legal strategy to give effect to tribal sovereignty.

The unanimous opinion, written by Justice Stanley Matthews and delivered on December 17, 1883, fourteen months after the original appeal to the territorial supreme court, was rooted in well-developed doctrines of Indian law. It strongly supports the traditional conception that treaties are made between nations of people, and it interprets the Sioux treaties of 1869 and 1877 in ways that give greatest effect to tribal sovereignty. The Crow Dog opinion was a **watershed**, the legal divide where a traditional Indian policy that recognized the equality of tribal peoples and respected their national sovereignty last stood against the rise of the BIA policy of **assimilation**, which would dominate federal Indian policy for the next fifty years.

The Court's decision has two distinct parts. The first is a detailed analysis of the language of the treaties that formed the basis of the prosecution's case. The second is a statement of national policy regarding tribal sovereignty and the law of tribal people that was a central part of that sovereignty. The first of the treaty provisions orders that "if bad men among the Indians shall commit a wrong or **depredation** upon the person or property of any one, white, black, or Indian . . . the Indians herein named solemnly agree that they will . . . deliver up the wrongdoers to the United States to be tried and punished according to its laws." This clause, according to Justice Matthews, was taken out of context by the courts and needed to be read in conjunction with its preceding clause, which provides for punishment by the United States of any bad men among the whites who committed any wrongs upon the Indians. This was a common provision for the prosecution of crimes between Indians and persons of other races and was found in most of the treaties with Indian tribes. It did not refer to crimes committed between Indians of the same tribe.

The second provision, from the treaty of 1877, involved the language "and Congress shall . . . secure to them an orderly government; they shall be subject to the laws of the United States, and each individual shall be protected in his rights of property, person and life." The Court took this statement to mean nearly the opposite of the interpretation given it by Judge Moody of the territorial court and the BIA:

> The pledge to secure to these people, with whom the United States was contracting as a distinct political body, an orderly government, by appro-

priate legislation thereafter to be framed and enacted, necessarily implies, having regard to all the circumstances attending the transaction, that among the arts of civilized life, which it was the very purpose of all these arrangements to introduce and naturalize among them, was the highest and best of all, that of self-government, the regulation by themselves of their own domestic affairs, the maintenance of order and peace among their own members by the administration of their own laws and customs.

The Court went on to describe this relationship in **paternalistic** terms: "as a dependent community who were in a state of pupilage, advancing from the condition of a savage tribe to that of a people who, through the discipline of labor and by education, it was hoped might become a self-supporting and self-governing society." There is no denying the clear recognition of a contract between two political entities with equal sovereignty and of Indian tribes' natural right to maintain their own order and peace and to administer their own laws and customs.

Finally, the Court strongly stated the traditional reason for recognition of tribal law for Indian people:

It is a case where . . . that law . . . is thought to be extended over aliens and strangers; over the members of a community, separated by race, by tradition, by the instincts of a free though savage life, from the authority and power which seeks to impose upon them the restraints of an external and unknown code, and to subject them to the responsibilities of civil conduct, according to rules and penalties of which they could have no previous warning; which judges them by a standard made by others and not for them, which takes no account of the conditions which should except them from its exactions, and makes no allowance for their inability to understand it. It tries them not by their peers, nor by the custom of their people, nor the law of their land, but by superiors of a different race, according to the law of a social state of which they have an imperfect conception, and which is opposed to the traditions of their history, to the habits of their lives, to the strongest prejudices of their savage nature; one which measures the red man's revenge by the maxim of the white man's morality.

A strong statement of the integrity of Sioux law emerges, one that could undermine the assimilationist policy of the BIA.

Yet the language had changed since the Cherokee cases of the Marshall court. There was a strong tone of racism, combined with a clear message that tribal law was somehow **transitory**, a mechanism to assist in the inevitable transition from savagery to civilization. While adopting Marshall's legal theories, with their respect for tribal sovereignty, the Court also implicitly adopted the assimilationist ideology of the day. The result was an unsatisfactory fit.

Although Crow Dog is always understood as a significant decision in Indian law, it may be ironic that the most important set of considerations in the case had nothing at all to do with the status of the Indian tribes. Crow Dog was also a capital criminal case. The U.S. Supreme Court, at the time, heard few criminal appeals. At the federal court level, there was no right of appeal at all of an ordinary federal criminal case until 1879 when a right of appeal to the circuit courts was created. It was 1889 before a criminal appeal could be taken to the U.S. Supreme Court. (Crow Dog's case, of course, could be appealed because it raised a constitutional question, that of treaty rights.) When the Supreme Court first came to hear criminal appeals, it reversed a great many of them, evidently appalled by the quality of criminal justice in many remote courts. To the Supreme Court, death penalty convictions had to show a level of integrity difficult for frontier justice. Crow Dog's offense, committed with an uncertain mental element under an uncertain legal status, may simply not have warranted the death penalty in the eyes of the justices. Still, it seems the federal Indian law questions disposed of in the opinion are too elaborate to have been simply intended to save Crow Dog's life.

Crow Dog returned to the Rosebud Reservation to continue as a leader of the traditional faction, derisively labeled the "kickers" by the Indian agent. He left the reservation, leading Ghost Dancers into the Badlands in 1890. Later he was a leading opponent of allotment, refusing to accept his allotment until 1910, when he was seventy-eight years old. His agent repeatedly asked BIA authorities in Washington to remove Crow Dog from the reservation because he was a "troublemaker." According to the agent, the reversal of his conviction was responsible for his arrogant attitude. This, of course, was not true. Crow Dog was deeply grounded in tradition, all his days a leader of traditional Brule.

There is no record of the number of cases of Indian killings that were directly affected by the Crow Dog decision. Ironically, the only other Indian who was released from prison because of the Supreme Court's decision was Spotted Tail's son. On May 29, 1884, five months after the decision, Spotted Tail, Jr., Thunder Hawk, and Song Pumpkin had become involved in a dispute with White Thunder, an extension of the same factional struggle that gave rise to Crow Dog's case. Young Spotted Tail, unable to inherit his father's power within the tribe, went to the camp of White Thunder, a respected older chief, and took one of White Thunder's wives. White Thunder immediately responded by raiding Spotted Tail's camp and taking some prize ponies. As a further insult to Spotted Tail, White Thunder killed the ponies, a sign of great contempt. Spotted Tail gave chase and became enraged when he found several of his ponies shot by the side of the road. Upon arriving at White Thunder's camp, Spotted Tail and his friends opened fire. In the exchange, White Thunder and Song Pumpkin were killed and White Thunder's father fatally injured.

Showing how little the doctrine of **stare decisis** penetrated the BIA, the Indian agent ordered Spotted Tail and Thunder Hawk to proceed to Fort Niobara and put themselves in the custody of the military. Both were locked in the guardhouse. There then followed an extended exchange of letters and telegrams between the agency and Washington over their disposition.

While the BIA proceeded in a confused manner, the Sioux once more resolved the matter: the council met and decided to allow Spotted Tail and Thunder Hawk back on the reservation and agreed to take responsibility for their conduct. The council sent this information to the agent, who forwarded it to Washington along with a letter from Spotted Tail and Thunder Hawk requesting to be "paroled" from the guardhouse. On September 2, the commissioner of Indian affairs, citing Crow Dog, requested that the secretary of the interior order the release of the prisoners. This was done on October 4. Spotted Tail and Thunder Hawk had been illegally imprisoned in a military guardhouse for four months while the BIA reluctantly gave effect to the Supreme Court's holding.

Law for the Indians: The Major Crimes Act

Since 1874, the BIA had been attempting to persuade Congress to extend federal jurisdiction over certain serious crimes committed among Indians but had been singularly unsuccessful. After 1880, this annual effort was joined by eastern Indian reformers, especially the Indian Rights Association (IRA), which advocated broad legislation that would make Indians subject to the same law as whites and, abandoning federal jurisdiction, make tribal Indians subject to full state or territorial criminal and civil law. The IRA was founded in Philadelphia in December 1882 by Henry Pancoast and Herbert Welsh. Where other Indian reform groups focused primarily on humanitarian aims, the IRA believed that Indians were capable of assuming full citizenship but had been held back by protective and paternalistic practices. The full extension of law and legal rights to the Indians became a central theme in IRA work, and the organization had considerable success lobbying in Congress. Many members' voices were added to the "popular outcry" over the Crow Dog decision. Among the proposals before Congress in 1884 was an IRA draft "Act to Provide for the Establishment of Courts of Criminal Jurisdiction upon Indian Reservations."

The IRA proposal was much broader than the Major Crimes Act that Congress ultimately adopted. It would have created an "agency court" for each Indian agency, with the Indian agent serving as judge. This court was to apply the complete criminal law of the state or territory in which the reservation was located, except for capital offenses, which would be tried in U.S. circuit courts. Convicted felons would serve their sentences in guardhouses on the reservations or be turned over to U.S. marshals and treated as other federal prisoners. These courts would operate without juries; appeals could go only to the commissioner of Indian affairs, not to any federal court. Civil actions against Indians would be **cognizable** in "any court in the United States," including state courts. This court structure would have put Indians under the complete legal force of U.S. law with few due process protections.

The logic behind this position was paternalistic: Indians needed to be protected by U.S. law but also to be held responsible under this law in order to prepare them as citizens. This reasoning was outlined in detail in a major IRA pamphlet, "The Indian Before the Law," by Henry Pancoast, published the year before the Major Crimes Act. After reviewing the legal status of the Indian, Pancoast went on to discuss different proposals for projecting U.S. law on Indian tribes. He opposed the BIA plan to extend a few criminal laws to the Indian tribes and try those crimes in local courts. Part of his reasoning was based on the practical difficulty in doing this, given the distances involved. Pancoast also wanted a far more **repressive** criminal justice apparatus to deal with misdemeanors and offenses against white standards of morality:

> In disturbances on an Indian reservation in particular there is the greatest necessity for a prompt, decided and inexpensive settlement of dispute . . . some firm and consistent power on a reservation that shall systematically and impartially enforce such simple rules of morality and justice as do not conflict too hardly with the primitive character of Indian customs or ideas.

... Side by side with the power of religion and the power of education to redeem the remnant of this people, there should stand the power of law.

Such a system would have increased the power of the BIA over the tribes through its protectionist and paternalistic policies. However, the BIA neither needed nor desired such an expansive act to get the same measure of power. Already, it was experimenting with extralegal forces of Indian police under the control of Indian agents and informal "courts of Indian offenses" that were in no way restricted by the need for a formal statute. Moreover, the imposition of such a formal legal role on the Indian agents raised potential bureaucratic problems for the BIA that could be avoided by keeping the existing informal system for the agents and removing the "major crimes" to federal courts. Put bluntly, extending the full force of U.S. law to Indian reservations was likely to control the BIA as well as the Indians, and the BIA was unwilling to give up the extralegal power it held over the tribes.

The Senate had rejected the BIA's original 1874 proposal for a major crimes act because such legislation was inconsistent with existing notions of tribal sovereignty. Since the late 1870s, virtually every annual report of the secretary of the interior and of the commissioner of Indian affairs had advocated the passage of a major crimes act. Interior Secretary Carl Schurz wrote in his 1879 report:

> If the Indians are to be advanced in civilized habits, it is essential that they be accustomed to the government of law, with the restraints it imposes and the protection it affords. [A] bill was introduced at the last session of Congress providing ... that the laws of the respective States and Territories relative to certain crimes, shall be ... taken to be the law in force within such reservations, and the district courts of the United States ... shall have original jurisdiction over all such offenses committed within such reservations.

The 1881 report of Schurz's successor, Samuel Kirkwood, written before the killing of Spotted Tail, repeated this argument and justified it with reference to "Apache outrages":

> Further legislation is, in my judgement [sic], necessary for the definition and punishment of crime committed on reservations whether by Indians in their dealings with each other, by Indians on white men, or by white men on Indians. A good deal of uncertainty exists on these points, which should be removed. It is also important that the liability of Indians who

engage in hostile acts against the government and our people should be declared more clearly and fully. During the present year the Apaches have committed many outrages in New Mexico and Arizona. . . . Are they prisoners or war criminals? Should not the liability of Indians thus engaged be clearly defined? Should not all crimes committed on reservations be clearly defined, the punishment thereof fixed, and the trial therefore provided in the United States Courts?

Henry M. Teller, who succeeded Kirkwood, repeated this request in his 1882 and 1883 annual reports. In the 1884 annual report, his successor, L. Q. C. Lamar, specifically used the Crow Dog case to justify the same measure and to misrepresent Sioux tribal law:

> I again desire to call attention to the necessity for legislation for the punishment of crimes on the Indian reservations. Since my last report, the Supreme Court of the United States decided in the case of Ex parte Crow Dog, indicted for murder, that the district court of South Dakota was without jurisdiction, when the crime was committed on the reservation by one Indian against another. If offenses of this character cannot be tried in the courts of the United States, there is no tribunal in which the crime of murder can be punished. . . . It will hardly do to leave the punishment of the crime of murder to a tribunal that exists only by the consent of the Indians of the reservation. If the murder is left to be punished according to the old Indian custom, it becomes the duty of the next of kin to avenge the death of his relative or some one of his kinsmen.

Examples of Indians going unpunished for murder also produced a different interpretation of the savage character of tribal society and the inadequacy of tribal law. Bishop H. Hare, an Episcopal missionary among the Sioux, recognized the force of tribal law by reverse argument: because tribal law was being destroyed, the tribes were becoming disorderly:

> Civilization has loosened . . . the bonds which regulate and hold together Indian society in its wild state, and has failed to give the people law and officers of justice in their place. Women are brutally beaten and outraged; men are murdered in cold blood; the Indians who are friendly to schools and churches are intimidated and preyed upon by the evil-disposed; children are molested on their way to school, and schools are dispersed by bands of vagabonds; but there is no redress. It is a disgrace to our land. . . . And . . . the efforts of civil agents, teachers, and missionaries are like the

struggles of drowning men weighted with lead, as long as by the absence of law Indian society is left without a base.

This language, quoted as part of the BIA commissioner's 1883 plea for such legislation, illustrates the relationship between the extension of criminal law to the Indians and the broad assimilationist goals of the Indian service: the work of teachers and missionaries needed to be protected by the criminal law.

Although the Major Crimes Act of 1885 was a clear departure from existing law, it was consistent with the move away from a policy based on treaty rights recognizing Indian sovereignty and toward one of dependency and forced assimilation. This policy shift, many years in the making, reflected broad national social and economic changes following from rapid westward expansion but was also bound within the contradictions of John Marshall's Worcester opinion. Even Marshall had assumed that given some protection of U.S. law, the tribes would ultimately assimilate into the mainstream of U.S. life. By the 1880s, it was obvious that the tribes would not cooperate, that, on the contrary, traditional culture remained strong everywhere in tribal America. Crow Dog's case embodied the failure of federal Indian policy. Spotted Tail, a government-imposed chief, had not been willing to educate his children in a government school and had blocked the extension of railroad lines across his lands. Yet he was dead as a result of a factional conflict with traditional Brules who would yield nothing to the American nation, and his killer freely walked the Rosebud Reservation, challenging the authority of the government.

The Major Crimes Act was an easy solution to one piece of this problem: federal criminal law could be imposed on those who violated U.S. law. Congress had resisted such a policy since 1874, but the facts of Crow Dog gave the BIA a sharp tool with which to prod congressional action. Presented with a portrayal of Spotted Tail as a loyal and courageous chief leading his people into productive roles as U.S. citizens—and one of Crow Dog as a "savage" who would lead his people into a continuation of the Indian wars, a murderer freed by a U.S. Supreme Court applying an **anachronistic** Indian policy—Congress appeared to have no other choice.

The whole matter occupies fewer than five pages of the Congressional Record, and those pages are largely filled with confusion over language. The simultaneous consideration of a stronger federal law to prohibit the sale of liquor to Indians received far more detailed discussion. This lack of attention itself testifies that although the Major Crimes Act may have been a sharp departure from existing Indian law, it was consistent with existing Indian policy.

The discussion in Congress cannot be called a debate. As presented by Congressman Cutcheon of Michigan for the Indian Affairs Committee, the bill's reasoning directly paralleled BIA policy and even borrowed language from the BIA commissioner's 1884 annual report:

> I believe it is not necessary for me to say that this amendment is in the direction of the thought of all who desire the advancement and civilization of the Indian tribes. It is recommended very strongly by the Secretary of the Interior in his annual report. I believe we all feel that an Indian, when he commits a crime, should be recognized as a criminal, and so treated under the laws of the land. I do not believe we shall ever succeed in civilizing the Indian race until we teach them regard to the law, but amenable to its penalties.
>
> We all remember the case of Crow Dog, who committed the murder of the celebrated chief Spotted Tail. He was arrested, tried by a Federal tribunal, and convicted of the murder, but the case being taken to the Supreme Court of the United States upon **habeas corpus**, it was there decided that the United States courts had no jurisdiction in any case where one reservation Indian committed a crime upon another. Thus, Crow Dog went free. He returned to his reservation, feeling, as the Commissioner says, a great deal more important than any of the chiefs of his tribe. The result was that another murder grew out of that—a murder committed by Spotted Tail, Jr., upon White Thunder. And so these things must go on unless we adopt proper legislation on the subject.
>
> It is an infamy upon our civilization, a disgrace to this nation, that there should be anywhere within its boundaries a body of people who can, with absolute impunity, commit the crime of murder, there being no tribunal before which they can be brought for punishment. Under our present law, there is no penalty that can be inflicted except according to the custom of the tribe, which is simply that the "blood avenger"—that is, the next of kin of the person murdered—shall pursue the one who has been guilty of the crime and commit a new murder upon him.

Congressman James Budd of California objected to including assault among the **enumerated** offenses, and it was agreed that courts of Indian offenses were adequate for such crimes. Some congressmen supported the IRA's desire to extend federal and state law to include all crimes among

Indians, even misdemeanors. Others were concerned whether the law should be extended to include the tribes within the Indian Territory. The closest the matter came to policy debate is in an exchange that shows that Congress was aware of the threat the bill posed to traditional Indian policy, if not tribal sovereignty:

> Mr. Hiscock: I would like to inquire of the gentleman from Michigan if he believes that all of these Indian tribes are in such a condition of civilization as that they should be put under the criminal law?
>
> Mr. Cutcheon: I think if they are not in that condition they will be civilized a great deal sooner by being put under such laws and taught to regard life and the personal property of others.
>
> Mr. Budd: This provision is as much for the benefit of the Indians as it is for the whites; because now, as there is no law to punish for Indian depredations, the bordermen take the law into their own hands, which would not be the case if such provision as this was enacted into law.
>
> Mr. Hiscock: That may all be true; but when we bring in a bill here, year after year, appropriating many millions of dollars to support and care for these Indians, and treat them as irresponsible persons, it seems to me that policy is not in the line of the policy indicated by this amendment, which proposes to extend to them the harsh provisions of the criminal law.
>
> Mr. Budd: We would like to change the policy of the Government in that respect.
>
> Mr. Hiscock: Then you had better defeat the present bill.
>
> Mr. Budd: We can do it in the way we propose here without defeating the bill.
>
> Mr. Cutcheon: We want to change the law a little in the direction of law and order.
>
> Mr. Ryan: And civilization.
>
> Mr. Cutcheon: Yes, and civilization.

Budd was mistaken about the current state of Indian law in his remarks about the need for a major crimes act. "Indian depredations" came under the scope of the "bad Indian" extradition clauses that had been a feature of virtually all treaties. Nor, apparently, was he aware that the Major Crimes

Act applied only to crimes committed between Indians while on a reservation. He was not the only congressman mistaken about the law.

Congressman Warner of Ohio asked whether the proposed amendment "conflicts with any treaty **stipulations**." Congressman Cutcheon incredibly answered, "Not that I am aware of." Warner responded, perhaps sarcastically: "I think that ought to be known positively." The discussion then went into financial matters. The whole appropriations bill passed on a vote of 240 to 7, with 77 members, including Hiscock, not voting. The Senate, after even less discussion, passed a narrower version. The two versions were reconciled in conference, and the bill became law on June 30, 1885. The Indian nations in Oklahoma, recognizing their special status, were excluded from the law, leaving them complete criminal jurisdiction over Indians within their territory.

Though pleased that the final act followed closely their original proposal, BIA officials were concerned that without a substantial appropriation of funds, the legislation would have no impact. Local federal, state, and territorial authorities were often not interested in crimes on Indian reservations and might be deterred from pursuing felons under the act by the high cost of such prosecutions. This was the reason that Kagama, whose case was the first under the Major Crimes Act to reach the U.S. Supreme Court, went free.

Conclusion

The tragic facts of the killing of Spotted Tail give rise to a wide range of reactions. But these cannot obscure the central issue: Brule law was functioning and able to settle the dispute. The U.S. Supreme Court recognized tribal sovereignty and deferred to Brule law. That was the law in the United States of 1883. This law was based on a long tradition of recognizing tribal sovereignty. It also made sound policy sense: the tribes were best able to adjudicate intertribal disputes. This result does not depend on any taking of sides in the dispute between Spotted Tail and Crow Dog: whatever the underlying reasons for the killing, the Brule Sioux were in a better position to know and judge them. They had a right to do so. That is the essence of tribal sovereignty.

The desire of the BIA and U.S. Indian policy makers generally to destroy tribal sovereignty is well documented. Tribal law was an essential element of that sovereignty. The killing of Spotted Tail, a great chief, provided these people with an opportunity to defame Brule law—"red man's revenge"—so they could substitute U.S. law. The framework for this attack on Brule law was already in place, deriving from nearly a dozen attempts to try Indians for intertribal killings in the years immediately before and after 1881. But the killing of Spotted Tail was the perfect test case. Ironically, it was also an isolated case: in all the factional struggles sweeping two hundred reservations in the late nineteenth and early twentieth centuries no other chief was killed. This must testify to the capacity of tribal law to mediate and contain disputes. Clearly, the army and the BIA police lacked the capacity to serve as bodyguards to all the chiefs, no matter how much power the U.S. government was able to muster in Indian country.

Conclusion

Criminal justice in tribal nations today must be understood in a historical context. Criminal law was a tool of colonization. Rather than providing protection from harm it was used to punish Indian people for leaving their reservations and practicing their culture. It's within this context tribal courts and tribal governments work to strengthen and rebuild their own justice systems.

Questions

1. The history of criminalizing Indian customs and practices has led to a general distrust of American criminal justice systems. Do you agree or disagree? Why?
2. Why was it so important for the OIA to control the Lakota people?
3. Why do you think the OIA created the Court of Indian Offenses and punished these behaviors?
4. What was the U.S. Supreme Court's ruling in *Ex parte Crow Dog*?
5. What was Congress's reaction to the Court's decision in *Crow Dog*?
6. Bishop Hare reported that the destruction of tribal law was leading to more crimes among the Indian people. Do you agree with his assessment?

In Your Community

1. Are there examples of the federal or state government trying to control your nation through the criminal justice system? Describe them.
2. Do you think your tribal nation has a resistance to establishing a contemporary criminal justice system? Why or why not?

Terms Used in Chapter 3
Anachronistic: Chronologically misplaced.
Assimilation: Made similar; caused to resemble. A tribal government is "assimilated" if it looks and operates exactly like the Anglo-American government.
Cognizable: Capable of being known.
Depredation: A destructive action.
Enumerated: Mentioned specifically; listed one by one.
Habeas corpus: A judicial order normally given to a jail or detention facility to bring a person to court so a decision regarding whether the imprisonment is legal can be made.
Misdemeanor: A criminal offense less serious than a felony that is usually punishable by a fine or less than a year in jail.
Paternalistic: Like a father; benevolent but intrusive.
Promulgate: Formally put a law into effect.
Repressive: Restrictive of action; exerting strict control on the freedom of others.
Stare decisis: (Latin term meaning "Let it stand.") The rule that when a court has decided a case by applying a legal principle to a set of facts, the court should stick by the principle and apply it to all later cases with clearly similar facts.
Stipulation: A condition or requirement in a contract or agreement.
Transitory: Continuing for only a short time.
Watershed: A place where two things separate.

Suggested Further Reading
Kathleen Joan Bragdon, "Crime and Punishment among the Indians of Massachusetts, 1675–1750" 28 *Ethnohistory* 23 (1981).

Vanessa Ann Gunther, *Ambiguous Justice: Native Americans and the Legal System in Southern California, 1848–1890* (Michigan State University Press 2001).

Carol Chiago Lujan and Gordon Adams, "U.S. Colonization of Indian Justice Systems: A Brief History," 19 *Wicazo Sa Review* 9 (2004).

Dian Million, "Policing the Rez: Keeping No Peace in Indian Country," 27 *Social Justice* 101 (2000).

Frank Pommersheim, *Broken Landscape: Indians, Indian Tribes, and the Constitution* (Cambridge University Press 2009).

James Riding In, "The United States v. Yellow Sun et al. (The Pawnee People)," 17 *Wicazo Sa Review* 13 (2002).

Luana Ross, *Inventing the Savage: The Social Construction of Native American Criminality* (University of Texas Press, 1998).

Traditional Law Today   Chapter 4

Just as tribal governments have evolved and changed over many years, so have criminal laws and procedures. This chapter introduces the inclusion of traditional tribal values and beliefs in contemporary criminal law.

The introduction of coercive American law enforcement was disruptive to many tribal governments. Given this disruption, there are many challenges for contemporary tribal governments in developing a strong criminal justice system. One of the biggest challenges facing contemporary tribal courts is the incorporation of traditional indigenous legal principles. Because many tribal cultures have experienced the imposition of American criminal law principles, it can be especially challenging to restore the traditional practices of Native people in a modern context.

The Navajo Nation government is an example of a tribe that bases much of its law on traditional values. The Navajo courts often use Navajo words to describe certain legal principles. The following article describes how even the structure of the court system is based on Navajo common law.

The Philosophy of Criminal Justice

Indians, Ant Hills and Stereotypes
Chief Justice Robert Yazzie in Wanda D. McCaslin, ed., *Justice as Healing: Indigenous Ways*, Living Justice Press, 121-133 (2005).

A few years ago, I did a presentation on traditional Navajo justice to judges from five western states. After the talk, two state judges went outside. One said to the other, "What did you think of Chief Justice Yazzie's description of Navajo common law?" The other judge laughed and replied, "He didn't mention staking people to ant hills!" Obviously the judges saw too many Western movies. Unfortunately, there is a popular stereotype that Indian justice is rough justice; that Indians used punishments such as staking people to ant hills, running them through a **gauntlet** of people armed with clubs, or stringing an offender (usually shown in the movies as a White offender) up in the sun to bake. That is an unfortunate stereotype. One of the reasons I want to speak at this important conference is that people such as myself, as Indian leaders, need to do more to educate the general American public about Indian ways.

The main issue posed for this conference is, "What is the judicial role in sentencing?" This session is designed to address restorative and reparative principles. "Restorative" is defined to mean "the process for renewing damaged personal and community relationships." "Reparative" is defined to mean "the process of making things right for those affected by an offender's behavior." In other words, how can we help victims? We use only one word for both ideas: peacemaking. The Navajo term is Hozhooji Naat'aanii, and while it is difficult to completely translate its concepts into English, I will simply translate it as "talking things out in a good way."

We know that it is unique because it incorporates traditional Navajo concepts on how to respond to crime. I will describe the policy's concepts of "talking things out," the "traditional probation officer," and how we use Navajo peacemaking before charges are filed, at the time of plea, prior to sentencing, and after sentencing.

Talking Things Out

The traditional Navajo response to crime is not staking the offender to an ant hill. It is to talk the problem out with respect. In traditional Navajo society, everyone was equal. There was no strong "chief" who heard a dispute and made a decision for others. In fact, the idea of someone with power and authority making decisions for others is entirely contrary to Navajo morals. We believe in a high degree of freedom, but we call it "freedom with responsibility" (in the words of our Associate Justice Raymond D. Austin).

What is an offender? It is someone who shows little regard for right relationships. That person has little respect for others. Navajos say of such a person, "He acts as if he has no relatives." So, what do you do when someone acts as if they have no relatives? You bring in the relatives! Victim rights is an important issue. What do you do about them? There too, you bring in the relatives!

Vincent Craig, our chief probation officer, once told me a story. He said that an oral history came down to him that in the old days, many young women became pregnant while herding sheep. The woman's family would then approach the man's family to talk out a settlement. That is what I mean by bringing in the relatives.

Didn't Navajos have any kind of civil leadership? Certainly. Our traditional leader is a naat'aanii. That refers to someone who speaks well, plans well, and bears himself or herself well. Another stereotype is that Indian men are strong, dominant leaders. Navajo women were naat'aanii too. They still are. A naat'aanii is not a "chief." A naat'aanii isn't just an advisor. A naat'aanii is someone who is considered so wise in his or her community that people listen. Today, we call a naat'aanii a peacemaker. We have over 250 of them in 110 local communities called "chapters."

When someone has [a] problem, we can appoint a peacemaker to handle it. The peacemaker uses the "talking out" process to address it. Who is invited to attend the discussions? The victim and his or her family. The offender and his or her family. Friends, neighbors and anyone else who is involved in the matter or affected by it will be invited to attend or can attend.

The procedure is fairly simple. First, there is a traditional prayer to put people in the right frame of mind for the talking out. Often, a peacemaker will choose an elder to say it. Then, everyone has their say about what happened. They also have their say about how they feel about what happened. We like to say that the most important piece of paper in the procedure is the tissue, and emotions are on the table. Opinion evidence is freely allowed, within the bounds of saying things in a respectful way. After all that is done, there is "the lecture." That means that it is time for the peacemaker to do some teaching. The peacemaker will relate parts of the Hajine Bahane, our creation lore, and apply it to the problem. The old "stories" are actually a form of precedent which everyone respects. That, by the way, is why peacemaking is not "mediation." Most mediators are also called "neutrals," which means they don't express an opinion about the problem they are handling. Peacemakers have very definite opinions about what they hear while talking things out.

Finally, based upon the prayer, venting, discussion, and knowledge of the traditional way of doing things, the people themselves usually reach a consensus decision about what to do. Planning is actually a central Navajo justice concept, and the people plan a very practical resolution to the problem. Today, we put it in writing and the parties sign it.

In one recent case out of our Crownpoint court, a woman was charged with threatening and the illegal discharge of a firearm because she went to her nephew's house, threatened to shoot his dogs, and shot off a gun near the dogs. She was found guilty after a trial. She then asked Judge Loretta Morris if she could go into peacemaking. When the judge said "yes," fifteen family members got together and reached a resolution. All fifteen signed the agreement and asked the judge to dismiss the charge after a cooling off and reconciliation period. The judge agreed and ordered dismissal of the charges if it appeared that the peacemaking decision was still working after thirty days. That shows how creative the process can be.

The Traditional Probation Officer

Our sentencing policy uses the concept of "traditional probation officer." Let me explain it this way: In the Navajo way of thinking, when someone "acts as if they had no relatives," relatives have certain responsibilities. It is shameful to have a relative who acts out against others. That hurts your relationships with others. So, you assume responsibility for your relative's actions. The same holds true of victims. If my relative is hurt, I have a responsibility to step in and help.

There is an action verb in our policy which is important to understand. It is nalyeeh. You can translate it in a couple of different ways. It can be translated as **"restitution"** or "reparation." Articles on indigenous traditional law often use that translation. However, those are nouns, aren't they? I said an action verb. The other translation is that it is a demand to be made whole. It is also a demand to enter into a respectful discussion of the hurt. The aim of nalyeeh is not punishment or the correction of a person. That would violate the Navajo maxim, "It's up to him." Instead, the aim is correction of the action. It is to cure the harm caused by bad "conduct."

The offender's relatives play a very important part in nalyeeh. It is they who actually pay the money, horses, or goods. Once they have done that, they will keep an eye on the offender to make certain he or she will not offend again. Our policy provides for a peace bond, signed by relatives, for the same purpose.

That told Navajos they were not competent to solve their own problems. The other aspect of the traditional probation officer concept is that we want communities to reassume their proper role in resolving community problems.

Peacemaking in the Criminal Justice System
Our sentencing policy provides for peacemaking before a charge is filed, after one is filed, before sentencing, and after sentencing. This is how it works:

Many courts have diversion programs in the prosecutor's office where someone will be sent into some form of community justice in place of filing charges. Most often, **deferred** prosecution is used as the incentive. We had a demonstration program in our Chinle court where we diverted DWI [driving while impaired] cases into peacemaking, and it was very successful. We found that the talking out process works to change attitudes about drinking and driving. Our judges can also divert into peacemaking at the time of plea.

I think we have a good way to address [victims'] rights by using peacemaking to recommend a sentence. The victim can participate or not (but often they do). The parties can then reach a consensus about a sentence and recommend it to the judge. I want to stress that when I say "consensus," everyone has to agree. What, you might say, if the victim is coerced? That is why we have the victim's relatives attend. Does that give the defendant a slim chance of a favorable outcome? His or her relatives get to speak too. Also, our peacemaker with an opinion will have some influence on the decision. While peacemakers do not make a decision or impose one, they have an important say about how things should be concluded.

In sum, we want the families of offenders to take responsibility for their relative and the families of victims to speak with the victim. In a situation where a victim is afraid to face the perpetrator, it is the victim's relatives who can do the talking.

There is something else important about the traditional probation officer concept. In 1892, Western courts were imposed on Navajos. Why would you use peacemaking after a sentence has been imposed? Most courts use the suspended imposition of sentence, suspended execution of sentence, or probation to try to get defendants into treatment programs, pay restitution, or do community service. Sometimes that works, and sometimes it doesn't. However, we all know about the defendant who attends the alcohol or counseling program only because there is a possible jail sentence hanging out there. You know how they look: Arms folded; angry stare; the barriers are up. In peacemaking, you can make a defendant want to go into alcohol treatment or counseling.

In one peacemaking involving domestic violence, the defendant was full of denial; he made light of his actions; and he blamed his wife for the whole thing. It was the man's sister who straightened him out, showed him his alcohol problem, and told him to stop making excuses for his own actions. See how relatives get the job done?

There is a fifth use of peacemaking I haven't mentioned. The Navajo Nation is 25,000 square miles big. It is bigger than nine states of the U.S. It's something like the Texan who said that it took him three days to drive across his ranch. A Navajo replied, "Yeah, I once had a truck like that too." We don't have enough police to patrol that large an area. In fact, most Indian nations have a police force only half the size of a normal rural police force.

Most of our peacemaking cases are walk-ins where the people themselves bring the case. Rather than call the police, many people call a peacemaker. People are using peacemaking for family squabbles, alcohol-related behavior, family violence, and even such controversial things as sex offenses. It works.

Conclusion

This is how Navajos respond to crime. We found that we can use traditional methods in a modern court system. We are ahead of the curve when it comes to restorative or reparative justice. We call it peacemaking. The final point I want to make is this: Peacemaking is also good horse sense. (I like that Anglo expression, because we Navajos love horses.) We see that our ancestors were pretty smart. They had human dynamics figured out and knew psychology long before Freud. Peacemaking simply taps the wisdom of our communities, involves them in the process, and responds to their needs. It makes offenders look at themselves and at the consequences of their actions. Many victim assistance programs forget that victims have families, and they are one of the best resources to help. That's the Navajo response to crime in a nutshell.

Using Traditional Criminal Law in Tribal Courts

Today, many tribal governments incorporate tribal traditional law into their written law. There are different methods for using traditional law in tribal court, but a common goal is to ensure that all tribal law reflects the nation's customs and traditions. The case excerpts that follow illustrate how several different tribal judges consider traditional law in criminal cases. As you read the cases, notice the potential clash between American concepts of criminal law and traditional beliefs. Consider how the judges have tried to balance sometimes competing philosophies.

District Court of the Cheyenne-Arapaho Tribes

In Matter of Sacred Arrows (1990)
3 Okla. Trib. 332
TAH-BONE, Chief Judge.

On June 29, 1990, Mr. Jasper H. Washa Sr., Edgar Heap-of-Birds, Samuel C. Hart, Cheevers Heap-of-Birds, and George Sutton, Headsmen, Chiefs, and Tribal Members of the Southern Cheyenne Tribe, petitioned the Cheyenne-Arapaho District Court for return of the (4) Sacred Arrows used in rituals of the Cheyenne Ceremonies; a Cedar Chest, among the contents, a Buffalo Hide; and a Ti Pi cover with pegs.

The Court was requested to issue a prejudgment order directing the respondents to return possession of the sacred items to Alfrich Heap-of-Birds. Affiants believed that these sacred items would be removed out of the jurisdiction of the Cheyenne Tribe if they were not recovered immediately.

A prejudgment Order was issued, and a show-cause hearing was scheduled for July 11, 1990 should the respondents take issue with the prejudgment Order.

The Order was served on the respondents by tribal police, and an attempt was made to recover the sacred items. The tribal police were accompanied by Arrow Priest, Chiefs, and Headsmen in order to transfer possession in the proper traditional manner. The respondents refused to comply with the Order, electing to show cause. Floyd Blackbear and Bill Red Hat, Jr. advised the Court that a ceremonial meeting had been called by the respondents on June 6, 1990, to discuss a permanent site of the Sacred Arrows.

Furthermore, an objection was raised concerning the tribal court's jurisdiction over a purely Cheyenne tribal traditional matter. The respondents advised the Court that this matter could only be handled in a traditional manner. The tribal police were advised to withdraw, but were to remain within the area to prevent any confrontation by the opposing parties and to safeguard the Sacred Arrows.

On July 5, 1990, George Sutton, Cheyenne Chief, Jasper Washa, and Leo Penn advised the Court, via affidavit, that the meeting of July 6, 1990, could not be called by the respondents, but required the consent of the Chiefs and Headsmen of the Cheyenne Tribe, according to the traditional ceremonial way. Another request was made to secure the possession of the Sacred Arrows.

A second attempt was made on July 6, 1990, by Alfrich Heap-of-Birds and Cheevers Heap-of-Birds, who were accompanied by the tribal police to take possession of the Sacred Arrows. During the attempt to restore possession to Alfrich Heap-of-Birds, fighting erupted at the Ti Pi site. There was grave concern that the Sacred Arrows would be damaged and people injured. The tribal police elected to withdraw, having been previously advised to accompany the plaintiffs to peacefully recover the Sacred Arrows, but to avoid any manner of conflict.

In light of the escalating situation, a Stay Order was issued on July 6, 1990 in order to prevent any further confrontations and to allow additional time for the appropriate traditional Societies, Chiefs, and Headsmen to gather and resolve this issue by the proper ceremonial procedures.

On July 11, 1990, a show-cause hearing was held at the District Court of the Cheyenne-Arapaho Tribes of Oklahoma, attended by the respondents; the petitioners did not appear. The respondents provided the Court with written materials concerning the meeting of July 6, 1990; notice that a meeting had been called for July 6, 1990; Sweet Medicine's Old Time Rules; Statement of Edward Red Hat I, dated November 3, 1981; an article by Zachary Gussow. Also present during this meeting were Jeanette Ita and anthropologist Carl Schlesenger, both from the University of Oklahoma, Norman, Oklahoma.

The Respondents urged the Court to consider this matter as a traditional matter which must be resolved with the Cheyenne Tribe, and that great care is taken procedurally to protect the integrity of the Sacred Arrows and the persons involved with the handling of those sacred items.

The Court has been contacted by many concerned Tribal Elders and members, as well as members of the Northern Cheyenne Tribe in regards to this matter. The most responsible advice that has been given is that both parties to this dispute should meet at a neutral site in a peaceful and responsible manner according to the traditional procedure and resolve this long-standing dispute.

The Tribal Court will not and cannot decide who the Arrow Keeper is. The Tribal Court's involvement in this matter has been limited to honoring the requests of various tribal citizens for assistance, which all tribal citizens have a right to do so. However, tribal courts cannot merely simulate the state and federal courts in interpreting and applying tribal laws. The Tribal Court has the duty of incorporating centuries of customs and traditions within the framework of the new Constitution. As in this case, it is not an easy task. Applying the Tribal Code of Laws to a traditional and religious conflict results in tension and conflict between the Tribal Code of Laws and traditional customs and traditions. Because of these dilemmas, Anglo-American concepts of fairness and civil rights are sometimes inappropriate, in their raw form, to Indian communities. These concepts can be applied only in conjunction with the unique cultural, social, and political attributes of the Indian heritage.

IT IS THEREFORE ORDERED that the Tribal Court of the Cheyenne-Arapaho Tribes of Oklahoma has decided that the question of who is in rightful possession of the Sacred Arrows should be left to the Headsmen, Chiefs, and the Cheyenne tribal members themselves, which is in accordance with tribal traditional practice and procedure.

SO ORDERED.

Colville Confederated Tribes Court of Appeals
Laurie Watt, v. Colville Confederated Tribes (1998)
25 ILR 6027, 2 CTCR 43, 4 CCAR 48
Before Chief Justice Dupris, Justice Bonga and Justice Stewart. The opinion of the court was delivered by: Dupris, C.J.

Summary of Proceedings
Background Information: At the trial court level, Laurie Watt entered a guilty plea to the charge of Driving Without a Valid License. The Court entered a sentence of jail and fine, with some of the sentence suspended on conditions. Ms. Watt appealed, claiming that the Court should have suspended the jail time and fine based on tribal custom.]

Facts
[Ms. Watt] entered a guilty plea to the charge of Driving Without A Valid License. The prosecutor's office made a recommendation of a fine of $500.00 with $200.00 suspended and sixty (60) days in jail with fifty-five (55) days suspended. The appellant's attorney recommended [Ms. Watt] be allowed to work community service hours in lieu of the jail time because of extenuating circumstances regarding the care of the appellant's young child. The Trial Court did not accept these recommendations. The Trial Court did not enter specific findings on the record regarding the basis of its rulings. However, the record on appeal includes information taken at the sentencing. . . .

[Ms. Watt] argues that the Trial Court abused its discretion by not allowing her to serve her jail term through community service contrary to Tribal custom and tradition.

Discussion
Did the Trial Court abuse its discretion by not substituting community service in lieu of jail time, contrary to Tribal custom and tradition?

The Court of Appeals must review two things in this appeal: (1) whether there is a custom or tradition regarding the use of community service in lieu of jail time; and (2) whether the Trial Court abused its discretion in failing to allow the appellant community service in lieu of jail time.

As to the first question, there is nothing on record to support the appellant's argument regarding custom and tradition. Appellant cites no authorities regarding the nature of punishment prior to the statutory law of the Tribes. (Citation omitted.) At best the appellant has supported her arguments with [guesswork] of what she believes custom and tradition [are] regarding punishment. She has failed to meet even a minimum burden of showing what [are] custom and tradition. We so hold.

Next we decide whether the Trial Court abused its discretion by failing to allow community service [instead] of jail time in this case. . . . The record must show a clear abuse of discretion between the facts of the case and the sentence entered by the trial judge. We must be shown that the record does not support the trial judge's findings. We cannot find that in this case. As the [Tribe] has pointed out, the record before the trial judge at the time of the sentencing shows numerous similar offenses by [Ms. Watt].

The record also shows that the sentence is well within the statutory limits for the offense charged. We hold that this appeal shall be dismissed and this matter remanded to the Trial Court for disposition consistent with this ruling.

It is so Ordered.

Stewart, J concurring.

In 1971 I was working for Highway Safety on a grant from the Department of Transportation out of Washington D.C. This Reservation in the mid-1970s had the highest fatality rate of any place in Washington State between Omak and Coulee Dam. I was keeping record at the time, and decided we should have some kind of driver's license for the five hundred (500) Tribal employees who drove Tribal vehicles. Fifty percent of our drivers did not have any kind of a state driver's license. There were five program directors who did not have a license. I started a program to teach people to drive, and made every employee who drove have a Tribal license. The first year the Tribes saved $1,000.00 on insurance.

The public defender we have at this time is a compassionate person, well able to make sure the people he represents are protected under the law. I wouldn't have it any other way. Now it is not unusual to have twenty-five cases in one day. The whole Court staff, and the Police Department, Prosecutor's Office, Probation Office, as well as the Public Defender's Office (and maybe a few departments I have forgotten to give credit to) are all over-worked.

Quite often the public defender will get stuck in a pattern, take the easy way out, and file any number of cases saying "arbitrary and capricious," yet when the Court of Appeals says "enough!" he can write really in-depth on an issue. He can write something to be proud of.

This case is one of his new ideas, well worth thinking over. From what I remember, the Tribes did not have jails to hold people in who violated the law. He is right. It reminded me of when I first worked in Law and Order as a new Game Warden and officer. The Fish and Game Committee sat me down and said: "You are new to the job, but we have had Tribal police for hundreds of years before the white man came. We didn't have much law breakers, but we did have some. The worst thing that would happen in the old days was, a young buck would ride his horse through the camp too fast. Some of the Elders would call him out and say, 'Don't do that again.' It usually worked, but sometimes he would do it again. The same Elders would call some of the other young men and say, 'Take him out back of the camps and beat him up.' If he did it again, the Elders would tell the young people to take him out and kill him."

Our old laws like those I was told about do not work because the world is changing. We still must protect our people from the ones who do not obey the law, or accept it as the Tribes write it up. The Colville Tribes has one of the leading Courts. We have to set the standards, not only for our own people, but because we have laid the foundation for the smaller tribes to use as guidelines for their courts.

We, as the Court of Appeals' Justices for this Tribe, cannot control what the federal courts, or the state courts, or the county courts do. We are responsible to this Tribe to set standards for the cases to build on from where we are now. If the standard for a cement foundation is one bucket of water, three shovels of sand, and a shovel of cement is working and has worked for years, we cannot be led down the path of change by putting too much water or sand, and a half a shovel of cement to keep our foundation from crumbling.

A law without a penalty is only advice. The penalty of the law is the cement of the foundation. Contempt of court comes in many forms, e.g., not wearing a dress coat, or a tie, or not speaking loud enough to be heard. Other examples include not following a court order to pay a fine, even if it is community service, or not obtaining a driver's license, or driving without a license. This all falls within contempt for the Court.

The Probation Department reported that defendant Watt did not comply with past court orders; the officers arrested her several years ago for no valid license. The Trial Court gave her a fair and just sentence, and yet a case that should not have been filed in the Court of Appeals has cost the Tribes thousands of dollars at this time.

The briefs from the Prosecutor's Office listed most of the reasons. No insurance for an unlicensed driver is high on the priority list. I feel if we let a chosen few get away with disregarding Court orders, we are not putting our finger in the leak that could wash out the dam of violations and erodes away the hard-earned foundations that have been laid for years. I did not mean this to be this long. Please forgive my rambling and simple way of putting things on paper. I feel we can only uphold the Trial Court's decision. Let the majority rule in this case.

Nisqually Tribal Court of Appeals
Michael Stepetin, III, v. Nisqually Indian Community
1 Northwest Indian Court System 224, 20 Indian L. Rep. 6049 (1993)
Before: Chief Justice Rosemary Irvin, Associate Justice Elizabeth Fry, and Associate Justice Charles R. Hostnik.
Hostnik, Associate Justice.

Michael Stepetin, III, an enrolled member of the Nisqually Indian Community, was charged with the offense of **reckless** driving, alleging that on September 3, 1990, at or about 8:00 P.M., he drove a truck at a high rate of speed on a gravel road on the Nisqually Reservation. The complaint further alleged that tribal community members were in the vicinity, though no one was struck or injured. Unfortunately, a dog was struck and killed. Mr. Stepetin exercised his right to a jury trial. The trial was conducted on May 14, 1991. The jury did not find Mr. Stepetin guilty of reckless driving, but did find him guilty of the lesser included offense of **negligent** driving. From this conviction, Mr. Stepetin appeals to this Court.

Mr. Stepetin's reckless driving charge was based upon Washington State statutes. Resort to the Washington State statute was made pursuant to a provision of the Nisqually Indian Community's Law and Order Code, which states as follows:

Where state law . . . does not conflict with the Tribal Code, the Tribal Court may resort to and enforce any state statute within tribal jurisdiction.

Nisqually Law and Order Code, Ch. I, Sec. 1(c); recodified 1991 as Nisqually Tribal Code, Sec. 1.02.03(c).

Issues Presented
Mr. Stepetin raises three issues in his appeal:
[issues #1 and #3 omitted]
2. Whether the Nisqually Law and Order Code provision incorporating Washington State statutes is impermissibly vague.

Vagueness of Nisqually Incorporation Provision
The Nisqually Indian Community has enacted a provision which states as follows:

> Where state law . . . does not conflict with the Tribal Code, the Tribal Court may resort to and enforce any state statute within tribal jurisdiction. Nisqually Law and Order Code, Ch. I, Sec. 1(c); recodified 1991 as Nisqually Tribal Code, Sec. 1.02.03(c).

The defendant contends this language is impermissibly vague because it does not provide notice to the members of the Nisqually Indian Community regarding what state statutes are to be enforced. The defendant further contends this language is an impermissible delegation of legislative power to the Tribal Court. . . .

We begin our analysis by noting that, in general, a strong presumption exists in favor of a statute's validity, and this court is obligated to find the statute constitutional, if at all possible. . . .

The principle underlying the vagueness doctrine is that no one is to be held criminally responsible for conduct which he or she could not reasonably understand to be **proscribed**. In making that determination, we are to determine whether the statute gives a person of ordinary intelligence fair notice that certain conduct is forbidden. This is a component of **due process**. The Indian Civil Rights Act provides that no tribe, in exercising powers of self-government, shall deprive any person of liberty or property without due process of law. 25 U.S.C. Sec. 1302(8).

The statute in this case, on its face, does not prohibit any conduct. It does not require the Tribal Court to resort to and enforce any state statutes, but clearly leaves discretion to the court to do so.

Therefore, the ultimate issue addressed by the vagueness argument is whether this provision of Nisqually law was adequate to give fair notice to Mr. Stepetin that his conduct was prohibited by the Nisqually Tribal Code. Mr. Stepetin was alleged to have driven a truck at a high rate of speed along a gravel road on the Nisqually Reservation. Tribal members were in the vicinity and though no one was injured, a dog was struck and killed.

Any reasonable person should know that this type of conduct is prohibited in any community. However, we agree with defendant's counsel when he stated the issue as not whether Mr. Stepetin knew this conduct was wrong, but whether he knew it was a crime. The Nisqually incorporation statute does not advise Mr. Stepetin, or any other Nisqually Tribal member, that driving a motor vehicle in this manner was a crime. Therefore, we find that the statute is impermissibly vague.

We are aware that on the Nisqually Reservation word may travel quickly throughout the Reservation. However, we do not believe that this is, or should be, a substitute for proper enactment, enforcement, and notice of ordinances by the Community. . . .

Where prosecutors or law enforcement officials may impose their personal **predilections** in determining what should be permissible behavior under a statute, such a provision is unconstitutional. . . .

Chief Justice IRVIN, concurring in part and dissenting in part:

> I am most surprised at the majority opinion and in strong disagreement with its conclusion that Mr. Stepetin had inadequate notice that his conduct could be criminally sanctioned under the laws of the Nisqually Indian Community. As a tribal trial and appellate judge for fourteen years, having served over twenty different tribes, having presided as the trial judge at the Nisqually Reservation for one-and-one-half years, and having been a part of the lives of those tribal people, I have to conclude that Nisqually custom and tradition combined with the tribal history of enforcement of the state statute at issue provided adequate warning to the appellant that his conduct could be sanctioned in the manner it was.

The doctrine of vagueness of a statute originated in the non-Indian community. Federal cases, state cases, and even those from other Indian reservations have little, if any, applicability to the facts of the present case. One must interpret the disputed statute in the context of the Nisqually Indian Community, a physically small and close-knit community of tribal people whose lineage and customs have intertwined for hundreds of years. C. Carpenter, Fort Nisqually: A Documented History of Indian and British Interaction 1–19 (1986); H. Haeberlin & E. Gunther, The Indians of Puget Sound 7–8 (1930); R. Ruby & J. Brown, A Guide to the Indian Tribes of the Pacific Northwest 150–52 (1992).

I. THE CENTRAL ROLE OF TRADITIONAL MORES IN THE TRIBAL COMMUNITY

Tribal jurisprudence does not spring from European roots, but stems from tribal traditions, practices and teachings that predate the introduction of Anglo-American law in this country. These traditions and customs constitute the original body of tribal law, the role of which is in many ways analogous to that of common law crimes in the Anglo-American tradition.

The Tribe's original laws and conflict-resolution mechanisms have altered over time in response to policies imposed by the United States and sometimes carried out by the state and local governments. The shift imposed on the Tribe from being the dominant culture possessing unrestricted territorial rights to being a minority culture whose territories have been severely reduced to reservations and federal trust lands has also caused them to change. These changes, however, have not altered the fact that the roots of tribal justice are deeply grounded in tribal custom and tradition, not in the non-Indian culture.

A. *The Nisqually Indian Community Has Not Adopted the Provisions of the U.S. Constitution*

In his brief Mr. Stepetin argued that the Nisqually Tribe, by language in the Nisqually Tribal Constitution, has guaranteed to its members the protections of the U.S. Constitution. The language cited for this proposition is as follows:

Section 1. Enumerated Powers

The Community Council of the Nisqually Indian Community shall exercise the following powers, subject to any limitations imposed by the statutes or the Constitution of the United States. Nisqually Const. Art. V, Sec. I

It is clear from the above provision that the Nisqually Indian Community has not adopted the provisions of the United States Constitution and statutes of the United States as its own. In this section of its Constitution, the Tribe has merely expressed its intent that whatever limitations are imposed on the tribal community by federal law are to be followed. Therefore, the Nisqually Tribe is not subject to the constitutional limitations that apply to the states or the federal government, and the appellant's due process rights are not defined by these laws. As discussed below, Mr. Stepetin's due process rights derive from Nisqually tribal customs and traditions and from Title I of the Indian Civil Rights Act (ICRA), codified at 25 U.S.C.A. Sections 1301–1303. The Indian Civil Rights Act has been "imposed by the Statutes . . . of the United States" and is thus applicable to the Nisqually Indian Community.

B. The Hybridization of Traditional Law and Anglo-American Jurisprudence
1. Tribal Sovereignty and the Role of the Tribal Court

Indian tribes are **quasi**-sovereigns, not states of the Union. They do not exercise their tribal authority as an arm of the federal government. Each tribe is also a sovereign separate and apart from any other tribe. . . .

During the period of the federal policy of assimilation tribal practices were suppressed by both federal and state governments, leading to the loss of many of the traditional practices of Puget Sound tribes. Tribes have varied in how they have filled the void this created.

The Nisqually Tribal Court has come to take on aspects of U.S. jurisprudence because of the Tribe's quasi-sovereign status. The law of Anglo-American society is preserved and transmitted in writings, rather than in the oral manner customary to tribal people. Due to the superimposition of Anglo-American written law over tribal oral custom and tradition, the Nisqually Tribe has adopted many of the procedural forms of federal and state tribunals, as well as some substantive provisions. As with other Western Washington tribes, the further sophistication of the Nisqually Tribe's courts was necessitated by the need for the Tribe to be self-regulating under the ruling of *U.S. v. Washington* in order to secure its fishing rights. . . . This meant, in part, having tribal court decrees which can be understood and given credence in the federal and state courts. I would hold, however, that none of these evolutionary changes have overturned or supplanted traditional law where it is practiced and has not been clearly or specifically changed by the Tribe.

Tribal statutes which have been adopted in **derogation** to tribal tradition should be regarded with caution. Just because tribal communities have sometimes given paper recognition to non-Indian practices and Anglo-American law principles in their laws does not necessarily mean that such apparent adoption of non-Indian legal concepts and practices should be taken at face value. Tribal practices and traditions have always been oral, and it is very rare that any tribe intends to supplant these with a formal writing.

Tribal courts as they presently exist are not a traditional forum for tribal people. For the Western Washington tribes, the need to assert treaty hunting and fishing rights, territorial jurisdiction over the reservations, and the tribal interest in their children given legal protection in the Indian Child Welfare Act, has caused tribal courts to become more complex and to take on aspects of non-Indian jurisprudence to gain respect in the non-Indian community. The courts have also taken over some of the functions originally performed by tribal elders in providing a forum to resolve disputes in the community and in sanctioning members for conduct the community will not tolerate. In performing any of these functions the court must be fundamentally fair and evenly address the needs of the tribal community in order to maintain legitimacy and respect.

The relational aspect of tribal courts, in which the tribal court serves as a dispute resolution forum for a tribal community which consists of related families, is an important way in which the function of tribal courts differs from that of non-Indian jurisprudence. Rigid rules, fashioned as precedent for adjudications but ignoring the internal dynamics of the tribal community, may not serve justice at all. In contrast, equitable considerations and procedures allowing flexibility in dispute resolutions may often be more responsive to the relational needs of the tribal community.

2. The Due Process Clause of the Indian Civil Rights Act

The requirements of the Indian Civil Rights Act (ICRA), 25 U.S.C.A. 1301–1303, imposed on the Tribe by the United States government, must be viewed within the context of the cultural expectations and the dynamics of the tribal community. Section 1302(8) of the ICRA states that "No Indian tribe in exercising powers of self-government shall deny to any person within its jurisdiction the equal protection of its laws or deprive any person of liberty or property without due process of law...."

In the interpretation and determination of due process rights under ICRA, each tribe must be treated with regard to its own individual composition and territory. In many cases, large tribes with large reservations have adopted the Federal Rules of Procedure and/or have incorporated state substantive laws into their codes. Case law from these tribal courts does not necessarily fit smaller reservations with strongly integrated communities, tribes with a different economic base and practices, or tribes with more relaxed procedures or simplified law and order codes.

C. The Defendant Had Notice Under the Customs, Mores and Traditions of the Nisqually Indian Community That He Would Incur Sanctions for Behaving in a Manner Which Endangered Lives

The majority, paraphrasing the defendant's attorney, states the issue of adequate notice as "not whether Mr. Stepetin knew this conduct was wrong, but whether he knew it was a crime." But traditionally, for a member of what is now the Nisqually Indian Community, there was no difference between wrongful conduct and that which was societally sanctioned. Interview with Barbara Lane, Ph.D., anthropologist specializing in Northwest Native American customs and traditions (Jan. 7, 1993). To say that the defendant knew that he had violated a community standard but that he did not know there was a written statute making this violation illegal is to make a distinction without a difference.

Mr. Stepetin drove recklessly on the Nisqually Reservation in a manner that not only endangered property but also human life, and ended up killing one family's pet dog. Traditionally, when conduct such as this occurred within the tribal community, it was customary for someone who represented the victim to go to the family of the person who caused the loss and demand satisfaction or payment. If the person refused to make some offering of regret or payment, the event would upset relationships between families and risk starting a feud. If no offering was made, the leader of the community or some respected elder or a person of standing in the community would frequently step in and try to settle the dispute.

The Nisqually Indian Community is a close-knit society located on a small, rural reservation, where many families are closely or distantly related to one another. Mr. Stepetin has lived in this community all of his life. He knew that the type of behavior he engaged in could result in tribally-imposed sanctions. The Nisqually Trial Court imposed a fine and restitution. Both of these penalties are closely in line with traditional penalties, which could also have included making an offer of regret to the injured family, shaming, or in the extreme case, banishment. Although the trial court was enforcing a state statute, its actions were closely in line with tribal tradition.

In conclusion, Mr. Stepetin's knowledge of those common social duties imposed by traditional tribal mores constitutes adequate notice that his conduct could trigger tribal sanctions.

Little River Band of Ottawa Indians Tribal Court of Appeals
Champagne v the People of the Little River Band of Ottawa Indians
WL 6900484 (2007).
Rosemary Edmondson, Justice.

I. Introduction
There are many trickster tales told by the Anishinaabek involving the godlike character Nanabozho. One story relevant to the present matter is a story that is sometimes referred to as "The Duck Dinner." *See, e.g.,* JOHN BORROWS, RECOVERING CANADA: THE RESURGENCE OF INDIGENOUS LAW

47–49 (2002); Charles Kawbawgam, *Nanabozho in a Time of Famine*, in OJIBWA NARRATIVES OF CHARLES AND CHARLOTTE KAWBAWGAM AND JACQUES LEPIQUE, 1893–1895, at 33 (Arthur P. Bourgeios, ed. 1994); Beatrice Blackwood, *Tales of the Chippewa Indians*, 40 FOLKLORE 315, 337–38 (1929). There are many, many versions of this story, but in most versions, Nanabozho is hungry, as usual. After a series of failures in convincing (tricking) the woodpecker and muskrat spirits into being meals, Nanabozho convinces (tricks) several ducks and kills them by decapitating them. He eats his fill, saves the rest for later, and takes a nap. He orders his buttocks to wake him if anyone comes along threatening to steal the rest of his duck dinner. During the night, men approach. Nanabozho's buttocks warn him twice: "Wake up, Nanabozho. Men are coming." KAWBAWGAM, *supra*, at 35. Nanabozho ignores his buttocks and continues to sleep. When he awakens to find the remainder of his food stolen, he is angry. But he does not blame himself. Instead, he builds up his fire and burns his buttocks as punishment for their failure to warn him. To some extent, the trick has come back to haunt Nanabozho—and in the end, with his short-sightedness, he burns his own body.

The relevance of this timeless story to the present matter is apparent. The trial court, per Judge Brenda Jones Quick, tried and convicted the defendant and appellant, Hon. Ryan L. Champagne, a tribal member, an appellate justice, and a member of this Court, of the crime of attempted fraud. Justice Champagne's primary job during the relevant period in this case was with the Little River Band of Ottawa Indians. Part of his job responsibilities included leaving the tribal place of business in his personal vehicle to visit clients. While on one of these trips, Justice Champagne took a personal detour and was involved in an accident. The Band and later the trial judge concluded that his claim for reimbursement from the Band was fraudulent. Judge Quick found that Justice Champagne "attempted to obtain money by seeking reimbursement from the Tribe for the loss of his vehicle by intentionally making a false assertion that he was on his way to a client's home at the time of the accident." Justice Champagne was neither heading toward the tribal offices nor toward a client's home.

Like Nanabozho, Justice Champagne perpetrated a trick upon the Little River Ottawa community—a trick that has come back to haunt him. It would seem to be a small thing involving a relatively small sum of money, but because the Little River Ottawa people have designated this particular "trick" a criminal act, Justice Champagne has burned himself.

Among the many legal arguments made before this Court at oral argument that will be addressed later in this Opinion and Order, Justice Champagne argues that the tribal customs and traditions of the Ottawa people do not recognize the crime of "attempt." Justice Champagne further appears to argue more generally that the Little River Band statute adopting relevant Michigan state criminal is inconsistent with Anishinaabek traditional tribal law and therefore this Court should not apply it to him.

These are laudable and compelling arguments relating to the seeming contradiction between tribal goals to develop a modern and sophisticated legal system based on Anglo-American legal models while attempting to preserve the cultural distinctiveness of Ottawa culture through the development of tribal law and the preservation of tribal customs and traditions. *See generally* Michael D. Petoskey, *Tribal Courts*, 67 MICHIGAN BAR JOURNAL, May 1988, at 366, 366–69; FRANK POMMERSHEIM, BRAID OF FEATHERS: AMERICAN INDIAN LAW AND CONTEMPORARY TRIBAL LIFE 66–67 (1995). As such, we take these arguments seriously. In other factual and legal circumstances, we *might* be compelled to consider such an argument as dispositive, but this matter does not oblige us to question current tribal law. As Justice Champagne all but admitted at trial and at oral argument, he attempted to procure money that was not owed him by the Little River Band for his own purposes. It is not obvious to this Court that Justice Champagne's failure in his attempt should excuse him from liability. More importantly, Justice Champagne does not and cannot identify an Ottawa custom or tradition that would excuse him for his actions. In fact, it would be a sad day for this community to acknowledge that an action reflecting an intention of an individual to fraudulently procure money from the Band is excused because the word "attempt" does not exist in Anishinaabemowin, as Justice Champagne alleged at oral argument.

As the remainder of this Opinion and Order shows, we have no choice but to AFFIRM the judgment below.

III. Discussion

Justice Champagne offered several legal challenges to the complaint filed against him by the Little River Band. Justice Champagne's challenges derive from his pretrial motions that, respectively, asserted that the complaint should be dismissed for (1) lack of a criminal statute; (2) lack of probable cause; and (3) lack of jurisdiction. On August 21, 2006, the trial court denied the motions to dismiss and filed an Opinion and Order. Justice Champagne sought review of these motions to dismiss from this Court. We declined to address the merits of the motions at that time. Justice Champagne raised additional legal arguments in his notice of appeal and at oral argument on May 4, 2007.

We address each of these legal arguments in turn.

A. Jurisdiction

As always, we must begin our analysis with jurisdiction, for this Court has no authority without jurisdiction. *See generally* CONST. art. VI, § 8. Justice Champagne asserts that the Little River Band does not have territorial jurisdiction over this matter. We disagree.

The Constitution of the Little River Band of Ottawa Indians provides that "[t]he territory of the Little River Band of Ottawa Indians shall encompass all lands which are now or hereinafter owned or reserved for the Tribe . . . and all lands which are now or at a later date owned by the Tribe or held in trust for the Tribe or any member of the Tribe by the United States of America." CONST. art. I, § 1. The Tribal Council has defined the criminal jurisdiction of this Court to include the territory of the Band and all American Indians. *See* Law and Order—Criminal Offenses—Ordinance §§ 4.02–4.03, Ordinance # 03–400–03 (last amended July 19, 2006); Criminal Procedures Ordinance § 8.08, Ordinance # 03–300–03 (effective Oct. 10, 2003). In other words, this Court has jurisdiction over all crimes committed on both reservation lands and trust lands of the Little River Band. Such lands include the lands upon which the Little River Band's governmental and commercial entities rest.

The Constitution provides that the Band must exercise jurisdiction over the Band's territory, subject to three limitations. Specifically, the Constitution provides that "[t]he Tribe's jurisdiction over its members and territory shall be exercised to the fullest extent consistent with this Constitution, the sovereign powers of the Tribe, and federal law." CONST. art. I, § 2. As to the *first* limitation, the Constitution mandates that this Court take jurisdiction over criminal matters arising within the territory of the Band that involve tribal members. The Constitution provides that this Court must "adjudicate all . . . criminal matters arising within the jurisdiction of the Tribe or to which the Tribe or an enrolled member of the Tribe is a party." CONST. art. VI, § 8(a)(1). *See also* Tribal Court Ordinance § 4.01, Ordinance # 97–300–01 (Aug. 4, 1997). As the trial court correctly concluded, the locus of the crime was the territory of the Little River Band, not the accident location or Justice Champagne's residence. The act of attempted fraud against the tribal government committed by a tribal member such as Justice Champagne is within this definition of the Band's jurisdiction.

As to the *second* limitation, the Constitution authorizes the Tribal Council "to govern the conduct of members of the Little River Band and other persons within its jurisdiction" through the enactment of ordinances and resolutions. CONST. art. IV, § 7(a)(1). The Little River Band is a sovereign nation capable of exercising the inherent governmental powers that every sovereign retains in accordance with its governing, organic documents. In this instance, the Constitution authorizes the government to exercise criminal jurisdiction over its members. The Tribal Council has adopted a criminal code and authorized a prosecutor to exercise the sovereign powers of the Band to prosecute the criminal code. *See* Tribal Court Ordinance § 8.02, Ordinance # 97–300–01 (Aug. 4, 1997). *See also* Law and Order—Criminal Offenses—Ordinance §§ 4.02–4.03, Ordinance # 03–400.03 (last amended July 19, 2006). As such, the sovereign powers of the Band as defined by the Constitution and the ordinances of the Tribal Council authorize the prosecution of this matter.

As to the *third* limitation, federal law, nothing in federal law prohibits the prosecution of Justice Champagne for this crime. Congress reaffirmed the federal recognition of the Little River Band in 1994. *See* Pub.L. 103–324; 25 U.S.C. § 1300k–2(a). In that statute, Congress expressly reaffirmed "[a]ll rights and privileges" of the Band. 25 U.S.C. § 1300k–3(a). Federal law has long recognized the rights and authority of federally recognized Indian tribes to exercise criminal jurisdiction over American Indians for crimes committed within Indian Country. *See, e.g.*, 25 U.S.C. § 1301(2) (recognizing tribal authority "to exercise criminal jurisdiction over all Indians"); *United States v. Lara*, 541 U.S. 193, 124 S.Ct. 1628, 158 L.Ed.2d 420 (2004); *United States v. Wheeler*, 435 U.S. 313, 98 S.Ct. 1079, 55 L.Ed.2d 303 (1978); COHEN'S HANDBOOK OF FEDERAL INDIAN LAW § 9.04 (Nell Jessup Newton et al. eds. 2005). In short, the Band possesses ample authority recognized under federal law to prosecute Justice Champagne.

In his pre-trial motion, Justice Champagne argued that the State of Michigan should have exclusive jurisdiction in this matter. At oral argument, Justice Champagne asserted that the federal government should have exclusive jurisdiction. Justice Champagne is incorrect on both counts. As Judge Quick pointed out:

> Defendant is a member of the Tribe. The allegation against Defendant is that he engaged in criminal conduct against the Tribe. To assume a sovereign other than the Little River Band of Ottawa Indians has jurisdiction over this matter would be tantamount to determining that the Tribe has no power to govern its own affairs. Certainly, the Tribe's right of governance is unquestionable. The Little River Band of Ottawa Indians, through its inherent power to rule itself, does have jurisdiction over this matter. *Champagne I, supra*, at 6.

Regardless of whether either the State of Michigan or the United States has jurisdiction over this matter, this Court is obligated by the Constitution of the Little River Band and by the ordinances of the Tribal Council to assert jurisdiction.

B. *Right to Jury Trial*

Justice Champagne was tried by the trial court below without a jury on the basis that the tribal prosecutor declined to seek jail time in this matter. Justice Champagne now asserts that he had the right to be tried by a jury of his peers under the Indian Civil Rights Act (ICRA). Justice Champagne is mistaken.

Persons subject to the criminal jurisdiction of the Band and charged with "an offense punishable by imprisonment" have the right to a six-person jury trial in accordance with tribal law. CONST. art. III, § 1(j) ("The Little River Band in exercising the powers of self-government shall not ... [d]eny to any person accused of an offense *punishable by imprisonment* the right, upon request, to a trial by jury of not less than six (6) persons.") (emphasis added). Assuming without deciding that ICRA applies to the Little River Band, the Constitutional provision here mirrors the provision contained in the Act. *See* 25 U.S.C. § 1302(10) ("No Indian tribe in exercising powers of self-government shall . . . deny to any person accused of an offense *punishable by imprisonment* the right, upon request, to a trial by jury of not less than six persons.") (emphasis added). The Tribal Council has determined that where the tribal prosecutor informs the Court and criminal defendants before trial that the People will not seek jail time, no right to a jury trial attaches. *See* Criminal Procedures Ordinance § 8.02, Ordinance # 03–300–03 (effective Oct. 10, 2003). We concur in this assessment about the right to a jury trial. *See* CONST. art. VI, § 8(a)(2). As such, no right to a jury trial ever attached in this matter.

C. Lack of a Criminal Statute

The Little River Band's Tribal Council has both adopted an indigenous criminal code and incorporated provisions of the Michigan state criminal law statutes as a means of exercising its constitutional authority "to govern the conduct of members of the Little River Band. . ." CONST. art. IV, § 7(a)(1). The Band charged Justice Champagne with attempted fraud in accordance with the Law and Order—Criminal Offenses—Ordinance § 11.02, Ordinance # 03–400–03 (last amended July 19, 2006) (criminalizing and defining "fraud") and the Tribal Court Ordinance § 8.02, Ordinance # 97–300–01 (Aug. 4, 1997) ("Any matters not covered by the laws or regulations of the Little River Band of Ottawa . . . may be decided by the Courts according to the laws of the State of Michigan."). Through the state law incorporation statute, Section 8.02, the Band asserted that Michigan Compiled Laws Section 750.92 also applies to Justice Champagne. Section 750.92 is the State's "attempt" statute and provides, "Any person who shall attempt to commit an offense prohibited by law, and in such attempt shall do any act towards the commission of such offense, but shall fail in the perpetration, or shall be intercepted or prevented in the execution of the same, when no express provision is made by law for the punishment of such attempt, shall be punished. . . ." The Little River Band's criminal law statute has no parallel provision criminalizing "attempt." Justice Champagne, who attempted to defraud the Band but failed, was charged under this collection of statutes.

Justice Champagne forcefully argues that the lack of an indigenous "attempt" statute excuses his actions. His argument rests on the basis that the Little River Band's choice to incorporate elements of Michigan's criminal code is an abrogation of tribal sovereignty and a violation of tribal customs and traditions. This appears to be a facial attack on the validity of Section 8.02. As Judge Quick noted, however, "It does not diminish a sovereign's power to enact, by incorporation, laws as set forth by another jurisdiction, particularly when it is a matter of convenience. . . . Certainly, when the Tribal Council enacted specific laws, it could have done away with Ordinance # 97–300–01, Section 8.02. This, it did not do. There, the Ordinance is binding on Defendant." *Champagne I, supra,* at 2. Regardless, whether or not the Tribal Council's decision to adopt state law was wise is irrelevant—the statutes apply to Justice Champagne as a member of the Band. We are bound to apply the law of the Little River Band. *See* Tribal Court Ordinance § 8.01, Ordinance # 97–300–01 (Aug. 4, 1997).

At oral argument, Justice Champagne referred this Court to his separate opinion in our 2006 decision in *LaPorte v. Fletcher*—Am. Tribal Law—2006 WL 6351711 (Little River Band Tribal Court of Appeals 2006) (Champagne, J.). Justice Champagne represented the opinion to mean that the tribal courts should refrain from applying state law, especially where it is inconsistent with tribal customs and traditions. That opinion, the reasoning of which both of the other justices deciding that matter explicitly rejected, has no precedential value to this Court. Moreover, the subject of the separate opinion—whether the losing party to a closely contested civil suit should receive an award of attorney fees—is all but irrelevant to this matter. Finally, the separate opinion—arguing on a general level that tribal law should be used to bring the parties together to make the parties whole—tends to support a view that does not favor Justice Champagne's position in this matter. As noted in the introduction to this opinion, it does no justice to the tribal community to excuse the actions of a presiding appellate justice in attempting (and failing) to defraud the Little River Band.

D. Demand for Traditional Judges

Justice Champagne argues that the trial court incorrectly denied him a trial before "traditional judges." At oral argument, Justice Champagne suggested that his case should have been heard before the Peacemaker's Court or perhaps through a sentencing circle. However, Justice Champagne offers nothing in either the Constitution nor tribal statute or regulation that creates an *entitlement* to be tried before "traditional judges." Without an entitlement guaranteed by tribal law, there is no right. Justice Champagne's claim to a right to a trial before "traditional judges" must fail.

Conclusion

This Court is aware of the gravity of a criminal case involving a sitting appellate justice as a defendant. It is a sad day for the Little River Band Ottawa community and to this Court to be forced to sit in judgment of one of its own, but we are obligated to do so. At oral argument, Justice Champagne raised the possibility that his prosecution was "political." We have no doubt that Justice Champagne's assertion is true, but not in the way he means it. As one of the leaders of the community—*ogemuk*—Justice Champagne was held—and should be held—to a higher standard of conduct. *See generally* CONST. art. VI, § 2(a); art. VI, §§ 6(b)(1)-(2). As to Justice Champagne's claim that he was singled out by other leaders of this community, we have no competence or authority to make judgments as to the sound discretion of the tribal prosecutor to initiate a criminal proceeding.

> For the above reasons, we AFFIRM the judgment of the trial court.
> IT IS SO ORDERED.
>
> ## Order
> The Opinion and Judgment per Judge Brenda Jones Quick and dated December 1, 2006 convicting Hon. Ryan L. Champagne of the crime of attempted fraud is AFFIRMED in its entirety.

The next case, *Nelson v. Yurok* is not a strictly criminal case. The Appellant was charged with a civil infraction. However, the discussion of traditional law could be applied in the criminal setting as well.

> # Yurok Tribal Court of Appeals
> *Nelson v. Yurok* (1999)
> WL 35015757-1999
> DOUGLAS W. LUNA, Justice.
>
> ## Introduction
> This matter came before the Yurok Tribal Court of Appeals pursuant to Appellant's Notice of Appeal filed on October 13, 1997. Appellant appeals the Opinion and Order of the Yurok Tribal Court. The Tribal Court, after a trial de novo, found the Appellant had violated the Yurok Tribal Fishing Rights Ordinance (YTFRO) and imposed the maximum fine of $200, which was suspended on condition that Appellant comply with Tribal law for the following year. The Special Judge, appointed for purposes of holding a de novo trial, restored Appellant's previously suspended fishing rights on the condition that he comply with YTFRO for one year.
>
> ## I. Jurisdiction
> This Court has personal jurisdiction over the Appellant because he is an enrolled member of the federally recognized Yurok Indian Tribe. The act which is the subject of this appeal occurred within the exterior boundaries of the Yurok Indian Reservation, giving rise to territorial as well as personal jurisdiction. This Court has subject matter jurisdiction on this case pursuant to Yurok Tribal Court Interim Ordinance and YTFRO § 8(a) concerning permissible and prohibited fishing. The Yurok Reservation is open to the taking of anadromous fish by eligible fishers for subsistence and ceremonial purposes unless specifically closed by YTFRO or a properly adopted pre-season or in-season adjustment.

II. Factual Background

On Wednesday, September 25, 1996, at approximately 4:30 p.m., California Fish and Game Warden, Richard Banko, observed Appellant in the process of dip-net fishing at the mouth of the Klamath River and notified the Bureau of Indian Affairs (BIA). At approximately 5:30 p.m., BIA officer, Tami Fletcher, arrived at the scene. Officer Fletcher found Appellant in possession of several salmon and cited Appellant pursuant to YFTRO § 8(a) for fishing during closure hours pursuant to the Yurok Tribe's 1996 Harvest Management Plan (Plan). The BIA seized Appellant's dip-net and salmon, as provided for in the YTFRO.
[deleted procedural background]

IV. Issues on Appeal

In his Notice of Appeal, Appellant lists several grounds for his appeal from the de novo trial decision. Since the Appellant failed to submit a written brief and failed to appear for the scheduled oral arguments, the grounds for his appeal are based upon his Notice of Appeal and consolidated into two issues:

1. Was the Appellant denied procedural or substantive due process in the de novo trial?
2. Did the Appellant's conviction violate Article IX of the Yurok Constitution which protects "traditional practices" from infringement by acts of the Yurok Tribal Council?

V. Discussion

Even though the Appellant failed to do more than file a Notice of Appeal, he raises an issue worth addressing. That is, in the exercise of its authority, may a tribe regulate tribal members' exercise of traditional practices regarding their right to fish? Throughout this case the Appellant represented himself. It is because of this pro se status that we will discuss first in general terms the applicable tribal law, the legal concepts of due process and equal protection, and apply them to the Appellant's specific arguments raised in his Notice of Appeal. We will then discuss the second constitutional issue and the underlying feature of his case regarding the rights of individual tribal members in relationship to their tribal government.

The applicable to Appellant's appeal are the Yurok Constitution, the YTFRO, the Yurok Tribe's 1996 Harvest Management Plan, and the Tribe's September 11, 1996 "Advance Notice of In–Season Adjustment."

The Yurok are a fishing people and the Tribe's Constitution and fishing laws are expressly designed to conserve and restore the severely depleted Klamath River anadromous fishery for current members and future generations. The first paragraph of the Preamble to the Yurok Constitution states:

> *Our people have always lived on this sacred and wondrous land along the Pacific Coast and inland on the Klamath River, since the Spirit People, Wo-ge, made things ready for us and the Creator, Ko-won-no-ekc-on Ne-kanup-ceo, placed us here. From the beginning, we have followed all the laws of the Creator, which became the whole fabric of our tribal sovereignty. In times past and now Yurok people bless the deep river, the tall redwood trees, the rocks, the mounds, and the trails. We pray for the health of all the animals, and prudently harvest and manage the great salmon runs and herds of deer and elk. We never waste and use every bit of the salmon, deer, elk, sturgeon, eels, seaweed, mussels, candlefish, otters, sea lions, seals, whales, and other ocean and river animals. We also have practiced our stewardship of the land in the prairies and forests through controlled burns that improve wildlife habitat and enhance the health and growth of the tan oak acorns, hazelnuts, pepperwood nuts, berries, grasses and bushes, all of which are used and provide materials for baskets, fabrics and utensils.*

The last paragraph of the Preamble expressly provides:

> Therefore, in order to exercise the inherent sovereignty of the Yurok Tribe, we adopt this Constitution in order to:
>
> 1) Preserve forever the survival of our tribe and protect it from forces which may threaten its existence;
> 2) Uphold and protect our tribal sovereignty which has existed from time immemorial and which remains undiminished;
> 3) Reclaim the tribal land base within the Yurok Reservation and enlarge the Reservation boundaries to the maximum extent possible within the ancestral lands of our tribe and/or within any compensatory land area;
> 4) Preserve and promote our culture, language, and religious beliefs and practices, and pass them on to our children, our grandchildren, and to their children and grandchildren, on and on, forever;
> 5) Provide for the health, education, economy, and social well-being of our members and future members;
> 6) Restore, enhance, and manage the tribal fishery, tribal water rights, tribal forests, and all other natural resources; and
> 7) Insure peace, harmony, and protection of individual human rights among our members and among others who may come within the jurisdiction of our tribal government.

Article IV, § 5 of the Yurok Constitution vests the Yurok Tribal Council with "the legislative power of the Yurok Tribe," including: [T]he authority to enact legislation, rules and regulations not inconsistent with this Constitution; to further the objectives of the Yurok Tribe as reflected in the Preamble to this Constitution; administer and regulate affairs, persons and transactions within Tribal Territory; enact civil and criminal laws . . . *manage Tribal lands and assets.*

The judicial power of the Yurok Tribe is vested in the Tribal Court. Yurok Const. Art. VIII.

The YTFRO, as amended June 6, 1996, "was issued by the authority of the Yurok Tribal Council as provided by the Constitution of the Yurok Tribe." YTFRO § 1(a) provides:

The purpose of this ordinance is to protect the fishery resources and, therefore, tribal fishing rights by establishing procedures for the conservation of fish stock and exercise of federally reserved fishing rights. This YTFRO is intended to allow fishing opportunity to Yurok Tribal members, while at the same time assuring adequate spawning escapement and the attainment of conservation objectives. Section 8(p) of the YTFRO provides: "Dip net and hook-and-line fishing: eligible Indians may engage in dip net fishing or angling at all times on the Reservation except when expressly prohibited." The YTFRO § 10(a) provides that "the Yurok Tribal Council shall adopt pre-season and in-season changes to this YTFRO for resource conservation and management purposes." Notification of such adjustments "shall be posted at Tribal offices and other places as determined by the Tribal Council." YTFRO § 10(c).

The YTFRO § 1(d) and § 2(b) provides for prosecution in tribal court, or other courts of competent jurisdiction as well as penalties for any violations. The first violation of §8 by illegal fishing is punishable by "forfeiture of all fish seized and by a fine of not less than fifty dollars ($50) nor more than two hundred dollars ($200)." YTFRO § 13(a)(1).

Enforcement is accomplished by law enforcement officers pursuant to YTFRO § 12(b).

The Yurok Tribe's 1996 Harvest Management Plan ("Plan") sets forth the fisheries resource management requirements of the Tribe for 1996. The Plan specifies that in Area 1, which is the mouth of the Klamath River where Appellant was fishing, subsistence fishing after August 1 is allowed "during the same time period as commercial fishing," unless the commercial fishery is closed, in which case subsistence fishing is allowed at all times (except 9 a.m. to 5 p.m. Monday). Plan § III(B). In turn, commercial fishing in Area 1 was allowed only before 6 a.m. and after 6 p.m. on the day Appellant was fishing at 4 p.m. Plan § IV. As set forth in the September 11, 1996 "Advance Notice of In-Season Adjustment" ("Notice"), the commercial season was extended through September 30, 1996, and "regulations for subsistence fishing remain unchanged."

In short, on the day in question, Wednesday, September 25, 1996, Appellant was entitled to fish at the mouth of the Klamath with his dip net before 6:00 a.m. and after 6:00 p.m. Instead the Appellant chose to fish for an unknown number of hours before the 6:00 p.m. opening. Appellant was first observed fishing at 4:30 p.m. and was cited at 5:30 p.m.

Appellant has repeatedly and freely admitted that he was fishing at the time and place he was cited. He has further admitted that he had prior notice and warning that he was fishing in violation of Tribal law. On appeal he implies for the first time, but does not directly state, that he may not have had adequate notice of the fishing restrictions due to insufficient publication by the Tribe. To accept Appellant's notice argument is to ignore his repeated admissions that he had prior notice and had been warned that he was illegally fishing. It is also to ignore his testimony that he knew at least two locations where the notices are posted. At the de novo trial, Appellant complained that where the notices are posted in Klamath, the glass cover sometimes fogs over, or the notice may be torn down. The Tribe correctly argues that the Appellant certainly knows how to contact the Tribal officer or fisheries department in order to confirm current restrictions. Instead, Appellant admits that he takes no interest in, or responsibility for, Tribal law: "When I go fishing, I just go fishing." It is this contention that is at the heart of this case.

C. Constitutional Issue

The second major issue in this case is the Appellant's claim that the fishing restrictions of the YTFRO and Plan violate the Yurok Constitution's Article IX protection of "traditional practices," specifically his supposed right to dip-net at any time and place he wants. He bases this argument on the ground that the Tribal resource conservation laws are irrational and Tribal members have an absolute right to those resources. At the de novo trial, Appellant offered his opinion, but no factual or scientific evidence, that the Tribe's resource conservation laws are irrational.

The Tribe responded with several arguments. First, it is common knowledge that the salmon fishery of the Klamath River is in severe decline and requires careful management to restore and maintain the fishery for present and future generations. The Tribe's fishing YTFRO and Plan, on their face, demonstrate the Tribe's careful efforts to do so. Second, the Tribe's efforts are mandated by the Yurok Constitution itself, which dictates that the Tribe "restore, enhance, and manage the tribal fishery." Appellant ignores this mandate, relying instead on Article IX and its protection of traditional practices.

Third, the Tribe's Fishing YTFRO and Plan do not deny Appellant his traditional practices. Appellant is free to dip-net on the days and times prescribed, which are ample to provide him and all Tribal fishers food and livelihood. Had he simply waited a couple of hours on the day he was cited, Appellant could have fished lawfully and unhindered for twelve straight hours.

Fourth, it is frivolous to suggest that the constitutional protection of traditional practices strips the Tribe of any authority to regulate such practices to preserve a critical resource for generations to come, particularly when such conservation is expressly mandated by the same Constitution. In effect, the conservation regulations assure that Tribal fishers will be able to continue their traditional practices for years to come.

Fifth, it is a commonplace of statutory construction that the more specific provision of law controls the less specific. Here, the constitutional fisheries conservation mandate is more specific than the broad protection of traditional practices. Even if some conflict were implied between these two constitutional provisions, they can be harmonized by acknowledging that the specific conservation mandate is regulatory, not prohibitory of traditional practices, and is in fact necessary to assure the health of the fishery so that Tribal fishers will have traditional practices to carry on.

Sixth, it is for the Tribe, not Appellant as an individual, to determine what is a rational and appropriate fisheries policy. If Tribal members disagree with the policies of their elected Tribal Council and the Tribe's technical fisheries staff, they are but one election away from changing those policies.

Based upon the entire record including the Tribe's Preamble provisions cited earlier, we find the Tribe's argument compelling. The Tribe's exercise of its governmental powers was based upon a legitimate, rational constitutionally provided mechanism to protect its tribal resources. There was no constitutional violation when the Yurok Tribe exercised its governmental authority to protect its resources by limiting a tribal member's right to fish in accordance with its ordinance and Harvest Management Plan.

D. *Indian Rights*

We note the Appellant's basic argument centers on the concept that his definition of a "traditional practice" for exercising his fishing rights is flawed for a number of reasons. First as noted above, the Yurok tribal government has exercised its rights in accordance with federal and tribal law to define the areas and times for fishing, as correctly noted by the Special Judge. YTFRO § 8(p), concerning dip-net fishing, provides that "eligible Indians may engage in dip net fishing or angling at all times on the Reservation except when expressly prohibited."

We also note that the Appellant's claim of a right to exercise of "traditional practice" to fish any time he wishes violates the notion of rights and obligations between any government and its governed. That is, government relies upon the fundamental foundation that there is no such thing as individual sovereignty. Tribal governments are sovereign domestic dependent nations within the United States; individual tribal members are not. More importantly, tribal governments, in the exercise of power, also rely upon two fundamental rules of traditional Indian law.

With regard to "tradition," tribal governments and individual Native Americans still maintain a fundamental relationship that pre-dates other societies. We call these concepts the first two rules of Indian Law.

> The First Rule is: Bring honor and respect to the family, clan and tribe.
> The Second Rule is: Live in harmony with nature.

> If this case is analyzed in accordance with the First Rule, this means that the Appellant must take positive action to restore honor. If the Appellant abided by the de novo court's decision and complied with tribal law for one year, he would restore his honor and bring respect back to his family, clan and tribe, and he would be living in harmony with nature.
>
> In this case, we note that the Yurok Tribe has placed greater emphasis in its Constitution regarding the Second Rule to live in harmony with nature, over that of traditionally exercising a fishing right.
>
> Finally, we note even if the Appellant's claim of a "traditional practice" is wrongly analyzed as a property right, he would still be subject to the tribal government's restrictions. The great scholar, Felix S. Cohen, noted that when looking at the dependency of individual rights upon the extent of tribal property:
>
>> The individual Indian, claiming a share in tribal assets, is subject to the general rule that he can obtain no greater interest than that possessed by the tribe in whose assets he participates. [Handbook of Federal Indian Law, p. 185 (1942)].
>
> In the case at hand, the Appellant has no greater rights than the Tribe. The Tribe has placed upon itself and its members a traditional obligation of living in harmony with nature. The judgment of the de nova trial court is hereby affirmed.

Conclusion

Tribal nations have strong foundations on which to build a contemporary criminal justice system. Although the introduction of American legal systems has been disruptive, many tribal nations today have found ways in which to incorporate traditional values and cultural norms in their court systems. Traditional values and spiritual principles are often a core aspect of today's tribal criminal justice systems.

Questions

1. According to Justice Yazzie in "The Navajo Response to Crime," how does the Navajo Nation use its traditional law today?
2. According to Justice Yazzie in "The Navajo Response to Crime," how are a victim's rights protected in the Navajo legal system?
3. Is *In Re the Case of the Sacred Arrows* a criminal case or a civil case? How do you know? Is it important that the tribal judge label this conflict criminal versus civil?
4. In *Watt v. Colville*, why do you think Judge Stewart filed a concurring opinion? What kind of information is available in the concurring opinion that is not available in the majority opinion?

5. In the *Stepetin v. Nisqually* case, describe the different approaches to criminal law found in the majority opinion (written by Justice Hostnik) and the dissent (written by Chief Justice Irvin).
6. In the Stepetin case, what does the term *quasi-sovereign* refer to? Is this a valid term for a tribal court to use?
7. In the Nisqually case, do you think the law against reckless/negligent driving was too vague?
8. How does the court incorporate a traditional tribal story into its decision in the Champagne case?
9. Does the defendant in *Yurok v. Nelson* successfully raise cultural defenses? Why not?

In Your Community
1. What are the basic beliefs of your nation's traditional law?
2. How is traditional law used in your tribal court? Give an example.
3. Is restitution part of your traditional law today? How was restitution dealt with traditionally?
4. How has your law changed over the years?

Terms Used in Chapter 4
Deferred: Postponed or delayed.
Derogation: A partial repeal or abolishment of law by a later law.
Due Process: Refers to the legal right to have notice, a chance to present his/her side in a legal dispute, and to have a fair hearing.
Gauntlet: A form of punishment in which people armed with sticks or other weapons arrange themselves in two lines facing each other and beat a person forced to run between them.
Hybridization: A combination of two dissimilar systems to form a new system that is a mixture of the originals.
Negligent: Failing to exercise a reasonable amount of care in a situation.
Predilections: Strong likings; predispositions in favor of something.
Proscribed: Prohibited or forbidden.
Quasi: Latin term meaning "sort of."
Reckless: Can mean "careless and inattentive" or "a willful disregard for the life of others"—usually involving more than negligence.
Restitution: Act of restoring a wronged or injured person to the person's condition before the wrong, loss, or injury.

Suggested Further Reading

William C. Bradford, "Reclaiming Indigenous Legal Autonomy on the Path to Peaceful Coexistence," 76 *North Dakota Law Review* 551 (2000).

Robert D. Cooter and Wolfgang Fikentscher, "Indian Common Law: The Role of Custom in American Indian Tribal Courts," 46 *American Journal of Comparative Law* 287 (1998).

Chapter 5

Introduction: What Is Criminal Jurisdiction?

Jurisdiction is the power of a government to exercise authority over people, property, and land. Indian nations had power over their people and land long before Europeans ever set foot in what is now called North America. A court's jurisdiction is the power of a court over a geographic area, an area of law (like divorce law or criminal law), or a given person or property.

As seen in table 5.1, there are several categories of jurisdiction. Personal jurisdiction is the power of a tribal court over a particular person to bring them into court, often called *in personam jurisdiction*. *In rem jurisdiction* is jurisdiction over property. Subject-matter jurisdiction is the power of a court to hear the type of case and relief requested. Criminal law, traffic law, and fish and game law are all types of cases that a criminal court might hear as part of its criminal subject-matter jurisdiction. Territorial jurisdiction is the power to hear a case that occurs within a specified area of land.

In addition, the terms *exclusive* and *concurrent jurisdiction* may sometimes be used. Jurisdiction is exclusive when only one government can exercise a power. **Concurrent jurisdiction** exists when more than one government can exercise authority at the same time. If the federal government and a tribal government both have the right to hear a case, then they are said to have concurrent jurisdiction.

Table 5.1. Different Types of Jurisdiction

Jurisdiction	Power
Personal Jurisdiction	Power of a court over a specific person
Subject matter jurisdiction	Power of a court to hear a specific kind of case
Territorial jurisdiction	Power of a court to hear a case that occurs within a specified area of land

Tribal courts address the following jurisdictional questions in determining whether the tribe has authority over a particular case.

1. Did a criminally wrong act (as defined by the tribe) occur (criminal as opposed to civil subject-matter jurisdiction)?
2. Did the act or any significant part of the act occur in Indian country (territorial jurisdiction)?
3. Who committed the crime? Is the person a tribal member of the prosecuting tribe or some other tribe? Some tribes will address this question at the beginning of the case, while other tribal courts require the defendant to raise this question (personal jurisdiction).
4. Does any other government have jurisdiction over the crime (concurrent or **exclusive jurisdiction**)?

The following provisions from the Poarch Band of Creek Indians' Code demonstrate the Band's assertion of jurisdiction in criminal matters:

Poarch Band of Creek Indians' Code

4-1-2 Personal Jurisdiction—Criminal
The Tribal Court shall have criminal jurisdiction over the person as follows:

a. *All enrolled Tribal members, or other federally recognized Indians for any violation of a criminal offense contained in the Tribal Criminal Code . . . when the criminal offense is alleged to have occurred on or within the reservation or within the territorial jurisdiction of the tribe; or*
b. *All enrolled Tribal members, or other federally recognized Indians who commit a criminal offense as set out in the Tribal Criminal Code . . . by their own conduct or the conduct of another for which they are legally accountable.*
   1. *The conduct occurs either wholly or partially on or within the reservation or territorial jurisdiction of the tribe; or,*
   2. *The conduct which occurs outside the reservation or territorial jurisdiction of the tribe constitutes an attempt, solicitation or conspiracy to commit an offense within the reservation or territorial jurisdiction of the tribe and an act in furtherance of the attempt or conspiracy occurs within the reservation or territorial jurisdiction of the tribe; or,*
   3. *The conduct which occurs within the reservation or territorial jurisdiction of the tribe constitutes an attempt, solicitation, or conspiracy to commit in another jurisdiction an offense prohibited by the Tribal Criminal Code . . . and is also prohibited by the other jurisdiction.*

4-1-3 Jurisdiction Over Property
The Tribal Court shall have civil and criminal jurisdiction over property, real and personal, as follows:

a. All property located on or within the reservation and/or territorial jurisdiction of the tribe;
b. Any property which has been unlawfully removed from the reservation or territorial jurisdiction of the tribe;
c. All property of the Poarch Band of Creek Indians wheresoever located.

4-1-4 Subject Matter Jurisdiction
a. The Tribal Court shall have subject matter jurisdiction over all civil actions in which the Tribal Court has jurisdiction over the person or property;
b. The Tribal Court shall have jurisdiction over all criminal matters alleged to be committed by tribal members, members of other federally recognized tribes within the reservation and jurisdiction of the Tribal Court.

4-1-5 Original and Exclusive Jurisdiction
a. The Tribal Court shall have original and exclusive jurisdiction over all civil matters within the jurisdiction of the Tribal Court.
b. The Tribal Court shall have original and exclusive jurisdiction over all criminal offenses committed within the territorial jurisdiction, of the tribe by enrolled members of the tribe, or other federally recognized Indians, except to the extent that the Major Crimes Act or other Federal Laws provide for criminal jurisdiction on Indian Reservations, or within the territorial jurisdiction of Indian Tribes, and in that event, the jurisdiction shall be concurrent with the United States Government. The State of Alabama shall have no jurisdiction, criminal or civil, within the reservation or territorial jurisdiction of the tribe and there shall be no concurrent jurisdiction with the State of Alabama with respect to the jurisdiction of the tribe for civil or criminal matters, unless and only to the extent that approval has been given for the same by the Tribal Council.

Tribal jurisdiction is a logical extension of inherent sovereignty and the right to self-government. In other words, criminal jurisdiction is the power of Indian nations to regulate criminal conduct or behavior. Although the U.S. government has imposed numerous limitations on the powers of tribal courts, tribal jurisdiction remains an important part of the power of self-government.

Criminal jurisdiction is a critical element of the right to self-governance. In addition to protecting people from crime, it gives tribes the power to protect their people, culture, and nation. If an Indian nation has jurisdiction over a criminal case, then the nation's law, based upon the nation's values and beliefs, will be applied to the actions of a wrongdoer. This power is especially important given the differences between tribal criminal justice and American criminal justice discussed in Chapter 4. Many tribes will focus on rehabilitation rather than on only punishing the offender.

Criminal jurisdiction in Indian country is a confusing maze of rules and restrictions. Historically, tribes exercised criminal jurisdiction over their members and over individuals who came into their territory. Over the past several hundred years, however, the U.S. government has sought to diminish the criminal powers of tribes. The purpose of this section of the book is to give an overview of traditional criminal jurisdiction exercised by tribes and then discuss contemporary tribal criminal jurisdiction. We will also address mechanisms or methods for preserving tribes' criminal jurisdiction and examine how tribal courts have addressed questions regarding jurisdiction.

Conclusion

The power of a government to exercise authority over people, property, and land is jurisdiction. Before a court can hear a criminal case, the court must determine if they have jurisdiction over the crime, offender, and the place where the crime took place. Jurisdiction, or the power to exercise authority over people, places, and property, is an inherent and critical component of sovereignty and the right to self-government. Chapters 6-10 will illustrate the federal government's laws that have impacted this inherent right to protect tribal people and lands.

Questions

1. Why is jurisdiction important to sovereignty?
2. What is the difference between exclusive and concurrent jurisdiction?
3. Why does the Poarch Band of Creek Indians tribal code mention the state of Alabama in its criminal jurisdiction statute?

In Your Community

1. Does your tribal code contain a statement of criminal jurisdiction? If so, does it address personal, subject-matter, or territorial jurisdiction?
2. Do you think your tribal code criminal jurisdiction statute is adequate? If not, how could it be improved?

Terms Used in Chapter 5

Concurrent jurisdiction: Two or more governments can exercise power or jurisdiction over an issue.

Exclusive jurisdiction: Only one government can exercise power or jurisdiction over an issue.

Suggested Further Reading

Frank Pommersheim, "The Crucible of Sovereignty: Analyzing Issues of Tribal Jurisdiction," 31 *Arizona Law Review* 329 (1989).

Kevin K. Washburn, "American Indians, Crime, and the Law," 104 *Michigan Law Review* 709 (2006).

Kevin K. Washburn, "Federal Criminal Law and Tribal Self-Determination," 84 *N.C. L. Rev.* 779 (2006).

Traditional Criminal Jurisdiction

Chapter 6

"Jurisdiction" refers to legal power. Prior to the imposition of American law, each tribal nation had the legal power or authority to deal with harmful behavior on its own terms. While the tribes did not necessarily refer to this power as "jurisdiction," tribal customs determined the extent of tribal power. The Haudenosaunee Great Law addressed the Confederacy's jurisdiction:

> Roots have spread out from the Tree of the Great Peace, one to the north, one to the east, one to the south and one to the west. The name of these roots is The Great White Roots and their nature is Peace and Strength. If any man or any nation outside the Five Nations shall obey the laws of the Great Peace and make known their disposition to the Lords of the Confederacy, they may trace the Roots to the Tree and if their minds are clean and they are obedient and promise to obey the wishes of the Confederate Council, they shall be welcomed to take shelter beneath the Tree of the Long Leaves.[1]

Thus, the Confederacy had jurisdiction over anyone who followed the Roots to the Tree and promised to obey the Council. Anyone who came freely into Iroquois territory and lived among the Iroquois was subject to their laws. If a member of the Confederacy chose to submit to the laws of foreign nations, the member forfeited any birthrights or claims on the Confederacy and the territory of the Confederacy.[2]

The Osage also exercised criminal jurisdiction prior to contact with the Europeans. The leaders known as the Little Old Men developed laws that gave them jurisdiction over wrongdoings. The laws came about during a time when people were eager for war, and when they went to war, the effort was disorganized, and the captives who were brought back were tortured and killed. Also, leaders often brought trouble upon the whole tribe by committing crimes such as rape or murder. As a result, the Little Old Men retired to the Lodge of Mystery and decided upon a "new road," which included laws or commandments against murder and killing captives. The chiefs now had jurisdiction over killings and disputes and made every attempt to restore peace through gifts when wrongdoings occurred. When restoring peace was impossible, the offender was expelled in order to maintain peace. The Osage laws included jurisdiction over captives of war. The chiefs had the authority to save the lives of the captives and make the captives members of the tribe.[3]

When the Choctaw Nation adopted a written constitution in 1860, its government was divided into three branches, and the courts were granted jurisdiction over criminal and civil cases. The Choctaw also had laws addressing how to deal with non-Choctaw wrongdoers. Under the Treaty of 1866, all Choctaws, whether born, intermarried, or adopted, fell under the jurisdiction of Choctaw law. In addition, the Treaty of Separation and the compact signed at North Fork Village in 1859 gave the Choctaw jurisdiction over the Chickasaws, Cherokees, Creeks, and Seminoles who lived among them. The compact and treaty also allowed for **extradition** of Chickasaws, Cherokees, Creeks, and Seminoles. Under the treaties of 1855 and 1866, the Choctaws agreed to deliver criminals demanded by the state and federal authorities. There was no **reciprocal** obligation, but the Choctaws offered rewards for wanted criminals, so neighboring states would often return the offenders.[4]

Governments have different time frames for bringing a criminal complaint. These laws are called *statutes of limitation*. In the Creek Nation, the traditional statute of limitation was a year—all crimes were washed clean during the annual harvest busk.

> Every year, in August, each family comes together to celebrate the Harvest Festival, at which time they renew everything that has served them during the past year. The women break and smash to pieces all their household appliances and replace them with new. This is the day that they eat, for the first time, the new corn and that the priest or medicine man of the district kindles the new fire and administers the new war medicine to all the assisting men. The Indians observe this ceremony so religiously that those among them who have no old maize to subsist them till this time would eat roots rather than touch the new maize. This is also the time that they forget and forgive all their past enmities. Any Indian who, after the festival, should renew a former quarrel would forfeit the good opinion of all the others.[5]

These examples illustrate that tribes, prior to adopting American court systems, exercised criminal jurisdiction over members and nonmembers. Before the rules of criminal jurisdiction were written, the tribes' customs and traditions established jurisdiction.

Many tribal nations had strict rules about geographical boundaries. There were consequences for disrespecting the territorial rights of neighboring tribes. In 1987, the Witsuwit'en people authorized a report about their traditional jurisdiction in a case seeking land rights for its people in British Columbia. The following passages explore this principle of respect:

> Antonia Mills, *Eagle Down Is Our Law: Witsuwit'en Law, Feasts, and Land Claims*, University of British Columbia Press (1994).
> Chief Tsanaloo (Robert Abraham) of Burns Lake said:
>
>> All the clans own the territory. . . . Before our time each clan they know, they use their territory and they never have any problem. When they go out on their hunting ground they trap. . . . When they take up the name of the clan in the feast hall, they witness it. When they take up the name, the territory goes with it. (p. 52)
>
> Chief Gwis Gyen (Stanley Williams), a Gitsak chief from Gitwanga spoke:
>
>> It is one of the duties of the chief who is seated at a very important place at the table to oversee the use of the huge territory. Should the nephew of the chief want to use the land he is obligated to come to the chief to ask if he can use that land. For this reason he is carefully picked by his colleagues to hold the land and to look over the use of the land. It is the chief's duty at all times to control the hunting grounds, the fishing grounds, the berrying grounds. And it is his decision that is vital at all times. For this reason the chief knows his own territories and guards his own territories and he must know the boundaries of all the other clans. It is his duty and he is trained to know the boundaries of the clans. (p. 53)
>
>> One of the firmest laws in the Witsuwit'en system holds that you do not go on someone's territory where you do not belong without asking permission. "Whoever has been on the trapline before will say, 'That hill or that lake, you can't pass that.'" They use trees as landmarks or creeks. Maybe one side of a creek belongs to one tribe and the opposite side would belong to someone else. Chief Gisdaywa told the story of someone who was following a bear he had wounded when it crossed over the boundary into someone else's territory. He could hear people down on the other side of

> the boundary, so he shouted, "Bear coming down. If you kill it you can get the meat but I get the hide!" (p. 144–145)
>
> To go onto territory where permission has neither been sought nor granted constitutes a serious offense of trespassing. A person caught trespassing might be a warning the first time (often in the form of being given a symbolic feather); however, a persistent offender could face severe consequences, including death. (p. 145)

The following story, as told by an Athabascan elder, describes the exercise of criminal jurisdiction over Russians who came to Alaska:

> ## Taa'ii'tì (English Translation)
> Johnny Frank Taa'ii'tì, in *Neerihiinjik* (Craig Mishlered, ed.), Alaska Native Language Center (1995).
>
> There were some hard times at Old Crow during the time Òol Tì' was living there.
>
> The Russians came to Valdez about that same time. They landed their ship for the first time.
>
> Lots of things were available from them for a long time after that.
>
> The first boat did not go back, and the Alaska Natives used up all the steel on it (laughs).
>
> They brought knives, ice chisels, canes, spear heads, axes, and lots of useful little stuff, saws, and milled lumber.
>
> Then they went over again to pick up more things. And this time they brought back lots of beads.
>
> We didn't know anything about money.
>
> The only thing the Indian bought were different kinds of colored beads. They traded many furs for beads and stoves.
>
> The chief there was a man named Taa'ii' Tì'.
>
> He was really wise.
>
> When the Russians landed there, they fooled around with the Indian women during the night. There were lots of men in the big ship.
>
> The chief named Taa'ii' Tì' told them not to bother the women, but they still did it, so he told them,
>
> "Don't ever do that again!" He spoke very loudly.
>
> The Russian men he was talking to at that time were feeling his body muscles like this (gesturing) and said to him:
>
> "You have a weak body, why are you talking?"
>
> He was like a President himself so he was really mad when they told him that.
>
> He didn't say another word until everyone went to bed.

The next morning, he reminded them not to do it again, but they still fooled around with the women, even the married women.

The people in the village told him about it. The Russian men were sleeping at that time.

They were all sleeping in tents, and Taa'ii' Tì' got his cane and hit all of them.

They all cried out in pain.

While doing that, he reminded them that they underestimated him and that his body was not weak.

He only spared four men who would take the boat back over (to Russia).

They didn't like it, but what would they do about it?

He ordered the rest of the men away to continue what they were being punished for.

So the four men invited him to return with them since they knew that he knew their own leader too.

The captain of that ship asked him to return with them. "Okay, yes," he said.

So he went over with them (laughs).

When they arrived (in Russia) they took him to the President there.

Taa'ii' Tì' told him about the shipload of men that went over to Alaska and how he killed them all that one morning.

The President asked the four men why Taa'ii' Tì' did what he did, but they kept quiet, for it was their fault after what they did over here.

Then the President told Taa'ii' Tì' to come to him, and right there, Taa'ii' Tì' told him what the men did over in Alaska.

"I'm chief over in Alaska just like you are the leader here."

Taa'ii' Tì' told the Russian President that his men sexually molested the married women every night while their husbands slept.

Someone told him about them so he warned them not to do it again. But they still did it.

He warned them twice about it.

They had made fun of him, saying how weak he was, and it was no use speaking loudly to them, and that's why he killed them (laughs).

He also told the Russian leader that he left only four men alive so they could tell the President about it.

That President was glad to hear about it.

"If that ever happens again, you have my permission to kill them all," he said.

"You are a good man. That is why you even had these men tell me about it," he told him.

Then he gave Taa'ii' Tì' half a shipload of things.

He told him, "I'll give you everything every year from now on."

Conclusion

Traditional tribal authority was limited in a variety of ways. Some Native cultures had strict geographical boundaries that limited territorial jurisdiction. Others exercised authority over all citizens, regardless of where they might physically be. Many tribes exercised jurisdiction over anyone who came into the community. Understanding these jurisdictional rules is helpful when interpreting the extent of tribal authority today.

Questions

1. How did tribal nations assert jurisdiction prior to colonization?
2. What was the role of victims (and victims' families) in determining jurisdiction in some cultures?
3. How did the Creek people prepare for their annual harvest ceremonies? How does this relate to criminal jurisdiction?
4. How was territorial jurisdiction governed by the Witsuwit'en people?
5. Did Taa'ii' Ti' exercise criminal jurisdiction over Russians?
6. Why did Taa'ii' Ti' leave four men alive? What was the response of the Russian president?

In Your Community

1. Did your nation traditionally have criminal jurisdiction over members and nonmembers?
2. Who exercised jurisdiction traditionally?
3. Are there elements of your traditional jurisdiction in your law today?

Terms Used in Chapter 6

Extradition: To give up (an alleged fugitive or criminal) to another state or nation at its request.

Reciprocal: Interchanged, given or owed to each other.

Notes

1. Iroquois Constitution Sec. 2.
2. Iroquois Constitution Sec. 58.
3. John Joseph Matthews, *The Osages: Children of the Middle Waters* (University of Oklahoma Press, 1961).
4. Angie Debo, *The Rise and Fall of the Choctaw Republic* (University of Oklahoma Press, 1961).

5. Ouis Leclerk Demilford, *Memoir, or a Cursory Glance At My Different Travels and My Sojourn in the Creek Nation* 153 (Geraldine DeCourcy, trans., John Francis McDermott, ed., R. R. Donnelly & Sons, 1956).

Suggested Further Reading

John Philip Reid, *Patterns of Vengeance: Crosscultural Homicide in the North American Fur Trade* (Ninth Judicial Circuit Historical Society, 1999).

Chapter 7

Limitations on Tribal Criminal Jurisdiction Imposed by the United States

Understanding contemporary tribal criminal jurisdiction requires an exploration of intrusions by the federal government upon tribal jurisdiction. Tribal jurisdiction is an **inherent** governmental power. It remains unchanged unless Congress provides specific language removing federal recognition of that power or the Supreme Court refuses to recognize a specific exercise of tribal jurisdiction. Through acts of Congress and Supreme Court decisions, the federal government has restricted its recognition of tribal criminal jurisdiction. A brief overview of the legislation and Supreme Court cases is given in the following text.

"Indian Country" as Defined by Federal Law for the Purposes of Criminal Jurisdiction (18 U.S.C. § 1151)

In order to make laws that affect tribes, the U.S. government has defined the land areas over which these laws will have territorial jurisdiction. The U.S. government defines this area as "Indian country." The definition of *Indian country* is in 18 U.S.C. § 1151:

a. all land within the limits of any Indian reservation under the jurisdiction of the United States Government, notwithstanding the issuance of any **patent**, and, including rights-of-way running through the reservation, (b) all dependent Indian communities within the borders of the United States whether within the original or subsequently acquired territory thereof, and whether

b. within or without the limits of a State, and (c) all Indian **allotments**, the Indian titles to which have not been extinguished, including rights-of-way running through the same.

Whether or not a particular act happened on land defined as Indian country will influence which government (tribal, state, or federal) has jurisdiction to prosecute the offense. Some federal criminal laws affecting tribes apply outside Indian country (e.g., some gambling offenses).

The term *dependent Indian communities* was interpreted by the U.S. Supreme Court in *Alaska v. Native Village of Venetie Tribal Government*, 522 U.S. 520 (1998). The Court ruled that dependent Indian communities refers to a limited category of Indian lands that are neither reservations nor allotments and that satisfy two requirements: (1) the lands must have been set aside by the United States for the use of the Indians as Indian lands; and (2) the lands must be under federal superintendence. The Court also held that Tribe's land granted under the Alaska Native Claims Settlement Act did not meet the definition of *Indian country*. Thus, most lands owned by Alaska Native villages, tribes, or corporations do not qualify as Indian country. As a result, it has been very difficult for Alaska tribal governments to exercise criminal jurisdiction as they are not recognized as having lands they can exercise jurisdiction over.[1] As of 2014, the Bureau of Indian Affairs is developing regulations that may allow Alaska tribal governments to place land into trust, thereby restoring territorial jurisdiction.

The General Crimes Act (18 U.S.C. § 1152)

The Indian Country Crimes Act—more commonly known as the General Crimes Act, 18 U.S.C. § 1152—gave federal courts criminal jurisdiction over crimes between Indians and non-Indians committed in Indian country. This law, initially enacted in 1817, provides as follows:

> Except as otherwise expressly provided by law, the general laws of the United States as to the punishment of offenses committed in any place within the sole and exclusive jurisdiction of the United States, except the District of Columbia, shall extend to the Indian country.
>
> This section shall not extend to offenses committed by one Indian against the person or property of another Indian, nor to any Indian committing any offense in the Indian country who has been punished by the local law of the tribe, or to any case where, by treaty stipulations, the exclusive jurisdiction over such offenses is or may be secured to the Indian tribes respectively.

Under this law, non-Indians committing crimes against Indians in Indian country were subject to federal prosecution.[2] Cases in which Indians committed crimes against non-Indians in Indian country were, by this law, still under the subject-matter jurisdiction of the tribe if tribal law handled them first. Tribes continued to have exclusive jurisdiction over all crimes committed by Indians in their territory, regardless of the victim. This was true because tribal criminal jurisdiction was seen as part of a tribe's inherent sovereign power (powers that were fundamental to a tribe's authority as an independent nation prior to U.S. domination) to maintain social order among its members within its territorial boundaries.

The Major Crimes Act (18 U.S.C. § 1153)

The Major Crimes Act was enacted in 1885 as a response to *Ex parte Crow Dog*, 109 U. S. 556 (1883). As discussed previously, in *Ex parte Crow Dog* the U.S. Supreme Court held that, in the absence of federal statutes limiting tribal criminal jurisdiction, tribes possessed complete, inherent, and exclusive criminal jurisdiction in Indian country. *Ex parte Crow Dog* interpreted the General Crimes Act as excluding crimes between two Indians and, thereby, upholds exclusive tribal criminal jurisdiction over crimes between Indian defendants and Indian victims.

The Supreme Court's decision in *Ex parte Crow Dog*, along with a misrepresentation of tribal society as "lawless," led to the passage of the Major Crimes Act of 1885. This act was the first assertion of federal criminal jurisdiction over crimes committed by Indians against Indians in Indian country and constitutes a major inroad into the exclusive criminal jurisdiction that tribes previously held.[3]

The Major Crimes Act grants federal courts, concurrent with tribal courts, criminal jurisdiction over Indians who commit any of its designated offenses. The act grants federal courts concurrent criminal jurisdiction when the listed offenses are committed by an Indian against the person or property of another in Indian country. The Major Crimes Act does not strip tribal courts of their jurisdiction to handle the same offenses. Many tribes do not pursue the major crimes offenses, often due to the misconception that they do not have the authority, the belief that the federal courts will handle the offenses, or a lack of resources. In addition, tribes must follow certain sentencing limitations imposed by the Indian Civil Rights Act (ICRA) that sometimes make prosecuting a major crime impractical. As tribes revise their tribal codes, however, more are incorporating and prosecuting the major crimes.

When it was enacted in 1885, the Major Crimes Act provided federal jurisdiction over seven enumerated crimes committed by Indian defendants. The Major Crimes Act has been amended numerous times, most recently in 2013, and now covers more than a dozen major crimes. As amended, 18 U.S.C. sec. 1153 now reads:

> (a) Any Indian who commits against the person or property of another Indian or other person any of the following offenses, namely, murder, manslaughter, kidnapping, maiming, a felony under chapter 109A, incest, a felony assault under section 113, an assault against an individual who has not attained the age of 16 years, felony child abuse or neglect, arson, burglary, robbery, and

a felony under section 661 of this title within the Indian country, shall be subject to the same law and penalties as all other persons committing any of the above offenses, within the exclusive jurisdiction of the United States.

(b) Any offense referred to in subsection (a) of this section that is not defined and punished by Federal law in force within the exclusive jurisdiction of the United States shall be defined and punished in accordance with the laws of the State in which such offense was committed as are in force at the time of such offense.

In a challenge to the Major Crimes Act, the Supreme Court in *United States v. Kagama*, 118 U.S. 375 (1886), sustained the power of Congress to extend federal criminal jurisdiction over Indian country as a function of its "guardianship" of Indians.

Intrusion of State Jurisdiction in Indian Country: Public Law 280 (18 U.S.C. 1162)

In 1953 Congress passed Public Law (PL) 280, transferring federal jurisdiction over crimes occurring in Indian country to certain named states (California, Minnesota, Nebraska, Oregon, and Wisconsin; and then Alaska upon statehood). States that were required to accept this transfer of jurisdiction are called "mandatory" states. Other states were given the option of asserting jurisdiction and are called "optional" states. PL 280 did not take eliminate tribal criminal jurisdiction; state jurisdiction pursuant to PL 280 is concurrent with tribal jurisdiction.[4] The legislation added yet another layer of complexity to the picture of criminal jurisdiction: whether a tribe, a state, or the federal government has the power to prosecute a crime depends on who committed the crime (Indian or non-Indian) and where it was committed (Indian country or not, and in what state). The impact of this statute varies from state to state and from tribe to tribe.[5]

PL 280 has been the source of much tension and frustration about the criminal justice system since it was originally passed in 1953. The law was passed without tribal consent or consultation. From a state perspective, the law provided no additional funding or taxing opportunities, making law enforcement on Indian lands a very costly endeavor. Developing collaborative and coordinated legal systems with local counties has been difficult in some communities.

In 2010, the Tribal Law and Order Act offered tribes a new alternative to deal with concerns about PL 280. Chapter 10 provides more information.

Intrusion of State Jurisdiction in Indian Country: Other Grants of Criminal Jurisdiction to States

PL 280 is not the first or last federal law granting states concurrent criminal jurisdiction. Kansas was the first state granted concurrent criminal jurisdiction on

Indian reservations in 1940. The act did not remove federal jurisdiction. In 1948 New York State was granted concurrent criminal jurisdiction over Indian lands within the state. And in 1950, New York was granted concurrent adjudicatory civil jurisdiction, which became effective in 1952. Both states argued for the grant of jurisdiction citing the lack of tribal courts, ignoring completely the nations' current court systems and traditional dispute-resolution processes.

Subsequent to PL 280, several states were able to obtain concurrent criminal jurisdiction through land claims settlement acts. The Massachusetts Settlement Act states the Wampanoag Tribe of Gay Head (Aquinnah) shall not have any jurisdiction over nontribal members and cannot exercise any jurisdiction in contravention with the civil regulatory and criminal laws of Massachusetts and the Town of Gay Head. And tribal lands are subject to Massachusetts and the Town of Gay Head's civil and criminal jurisdiction. Several other Indian nations are subject to state criminal and civil jurisdiction due to settlement acts, for example, the Narragansett Indian Tribe, the Miccosukee Tribe of Indians of Florida, and the Mashantucket (Western) Pequot Tribal Nation. The Mohegan Tribe is subject to concurrent criminal jurisdiction of Connecticut. The Maine Indian Land Claims Act includes the Penobscot Indian Nation, Passamaquoddy, and later the Houlton Band of Maliseet Indians, and grants state criminal and civil jurisdiction, removes federal jurisdiction under the Major Crimes Act, and requires that any subsequent federal legislation dealing with Indian nations specifically mention Maine or the Indian nations within Maine. And the Aroostook Band of Micmacs is subject to concurrent state criminal and civil jurisdiction as well. The Catawba Indian Nation is also subject to state criminal and civil regulatory jurisdiction, as well as the limitation that any federal laws subsequent to their settlement act must specifically be made applicable in South Carolina. The Alabama and Coushatta Tribes of Texas and the Ysleta del Sur Pueblo are subject to state civil and criminal jurisdiction. The Paiute Indian Tribe of Utah is subject to state criminal and civil jurisdiction.[6]

Upholding Tribal Sovereignty: *United States v. Wheeler,* 435 U.S. 313 (1978)

The U.S. Constitution protects individuals against double jeopardy (being prosecuted for the same crime twice by the same government). In *United States v. Wheeler* the defendant was prosecuted and convicted in the Navajo Nation's tribal courts and then in federal court for the same crime. The defendant claimed the later federal prosecution violated his right against **double jeopardy**. The U.S. Supreme Court ruled that the source of the power to punish offenders is an inherent part of tribal sovereignty and not a grant of federal power. Thus, because the two prosecutions were by separate sovereigns, the Navajo Nation and the United States, the subsequent federal prosecution did not violate the defendant's right against double jeopardy.

No Criminal Jurisdiction over Non-Indians: *Oliphant v. Suquamish Indian Tribe et al.*, 435 U.S. 191 (1978)

Until 1978, tribal governments had full power to exercise criminal jurisdiction over non-Indians. In *Oliphant v. Suquamish*, 435 U.S. 191 (1978), the Supreme Court ruled tribes no longer possessed criminal jurisdiction over non-Indians. Oliphant was a non-Indian charged with a criminal offense in the Suquamish Tribal Court. He challenged the tribe's criminal jurisdiction over him, arguing the tribe did not have criminal jurisdiction over non-Indians because this power had been given up to the federal government. Holding the tribe had lost that authority, the Court mistakenly held that attempts to exercise criminal jurisdiction over non-Indians were a relatively new phenomenon and that few tribes had anything resembling a court at that time, and thus criminal jurisdiction over non-Indians was not a power practiced historically. The Court stated although Congress never expressly removed criminal jurisdiction over non-Indians, that removal was **implicit** in its legislative actions. According to the Supreme Court, any criminal jurisdiction over non-Indians that tribes exercised in the past was lost by submitting to the overriding sovereignty of the United States.

The following passage from Oliphant describes the court's reasoning:

> But an examination of our earlier precedents satisfies us that, even ignoring treaty provisions and congressional policy, Indians do not have criminal jurisdiction over non-Indians absent affirmative delegation of such power by Congress. Indian tribes do retain elements of "quasi-sovereign" authority after ceding their lands to the United States and announcing their dependence on the Federal Government. See *Cherokee Nation v. Georgia*, 5 Pet. 1, 15 (1831). But the tribes' retained powers are not such that they are limited only by specific restrictions in treaties or congressional enactments. *Oliphant v. Suquamish Indian Tribe*, 435 U.S. 191 (1978).

Tribal Criminal Jurisdiction over Nonmember Indians: *Duro v. Reina*, 495 U.S. 676 (1990) and the Congressional *Duro*-Fix

Only six years after *Oliphant*, the ability of tribal courts to exercise criminal jurisdiction over **nonmember Indian**s was challenged. Duro was an Indian, but not an enrolled member of Salt River Pima-Maricopa Indian Community. At a hearing in 1984 before the Salt River Tribal Court, Duro challenged the tribal court's jurisdiction over his misdemeanor prosecution. The tribal court ruled that *Oliphant* concerned criminal jurisdiction over non-Indians, not nonmember Indians, and thus the court had jurisdiction over the defendant. Duro appealed this decision through the federal courts. Six years later, the U.S. Supreme Court, in *Duro v. Reina*, 495 U.S. 676 (1990), extended the logic of *Oliphant* and held that because of their domination by the United States, tribes also no longer possess criminal jurisdiction over offenses committed by nonmember Indians when such crimes are committed in Indian country. The Court ruled that the power to prosecute nonmember Indians was a power surrendered by tribes in their submission to the overriding sovereignty of the United States. Thus, the tribes had no criminal jurisdiction over nonmember Indians. Or, put another way, tribes had criminal jurisdiction only over their own enrolled members.

After the *Duro* decision, tribes worked with Congress to restore recognition of tribal criminal jurisdiction over nonmember Indians by amending the language defining the "powers of self government" in the ICRA of 1968 (25 U.S.C. 1301) to "the inherent power of Indian tribes, hereby recognized and affirmed, to exercise criminal jurisdiction over all Indians." These ICRA amendments are commonly referred to as the congressional *Duro*-fix. This *Duro*-fix was initially enacted by Congress on a temporary basis in 1990 (PL 101-511) but then made permanent in 1991 (PL 102-137). The amendments recognized that tribes have inherent jurisdiction over nonmember Indians.

Nonmember Indians, however, challenged this congressional *Duro*-fix. They contended it was a delegation of federal authority rather than recognition of inherent tribal sovereign authority. If the federal courts held that Congress's *Duro*-fix was a delegation of federal authority, charging a nonmember Indian in both federal and tribal court would be double jeopardy because the tribal government would be exercising federal authority not its tribal authority.

In an affirmation of tribal sovereignty, the U. S. Supreme Court ruled 7 to 2 in *U. S. v. Lara*, 541 U.S. (2004), that double jeopardy does not apply since the tribe acted in its capacity as a sovereign authority when it prosecuted the nonmember Indian under the *Duro*-fix. In effect, the Court held that the congressional *Duro*-fix was recognition of inherent tribal sovereign authority rather than a delegation of federal authority. It should be noted, however, that the decision did not address all possible challenges to the tribal criminal prosecution of nonmember Indians. It is likely, therefore, that nonmember Indians will continue to challenge tribal criminal jurisdiction over them.

Tribal criminal jurisdiction is changing rapidly due to congressional recognition of other aspects of inherent sovereignty. Chapter 10 focuses specifically on the Tribal Law and Order Act and the Violence Against Women Act.

The Criminal Jurisdiction Maze

The jurisdictional maze set forth by the above legislation and U.S. Supreme Court cases is summarized in tables 7.1 and 7.2 from the Indian Law and Order Commission Report.[7] Table 7.1 addresses criminal jurisdiction in PL 280 states and non–PL 280 states. It is important again to note that as long as the defendant is a tribal member, tribal courts possess jurisdiction, regardless of the offense. Table 7.2 gives an overview of the federal court cases and legislation that have affected tribal criminal jurisdiction.

Table 7.1. General Summary of Criminal Jurisdiction on Indian Lands (Details vary by Tribe and State)

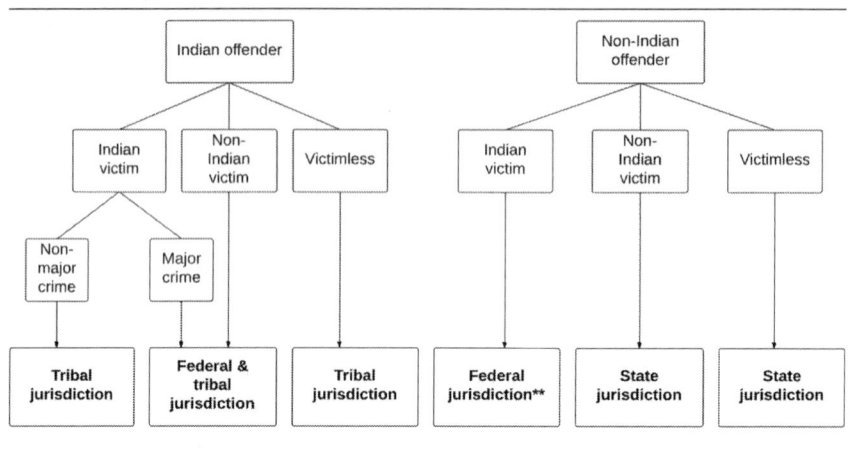

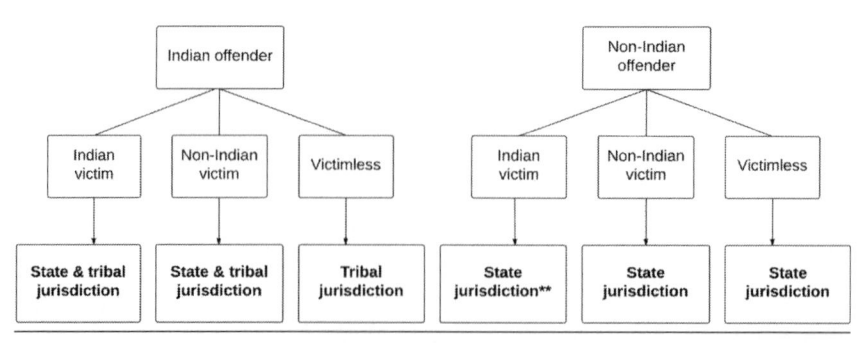

*Under the *Tribal Law and Order Act of 2010*, tribes can opt for added concurrent Federal jurisdiction, with Federal consent. Neither this tribe-by-tribe issue nor the various configurations of "Optional 280" status are shown in this chart.

** Under the *Violence Against Women Act Reauthorization of 2013* (VAWA), after 2015, tribes may exercise Special Domestic Violence Jurisdiction with the Federal govenment and with States for VAWA-defined domestic violence crimes.

Source: From The Indian Law and Order Commission, "A Roadmap for Making Native America Safer, Report to The President and Congress of The United States."

Table 7.2. Major Statutes and Cases Affecting Indian Country Criminal Jurisdiction

Act or Case	Reference	Year	Description
Trade and Intercourse Act	1 Stat. 137 §137	1790	Asserts that a state can punish crimes committed by non-Indians against Indians under the laws of the state.
General Crimes Act	18 U.S.C. § 1817	1817	General federal laws for the punishment of non-Indian crimes are upheld in tribal lands; Indian offenses remain under tribal jurisdiction.
Assimilative Crimes Act	18 U.S.C. § 13	1825	Extends coverage through federal enforcement of certain state criminal laws in certain federal enclaves.
Worcester v. Georgia	31 U.S. (6 Pet.) 515	1832	State laws have no rule of force in Indian country.
U.S. v. McBratney	104 U.S. 621	1881	Provides for exclusive state criminal jurisdiction over crimes between non-Indians for offenses committed in Indian country; rule later extended for "victimless" crimes.
Ex parte Crow Dog	109 U.S. 556	1883	Reaffirms tribal self-governance and the absence of state jurisdictional authority in Indian country, as well as federal jurisdiction in cases of intra-tribal crimes
Major Crimes Act	18 U.S.C. § 1153	1885	Extends federal jurisdiction to include authority over Indians who commit 7 (later amended to 16) felonies
United States v Kagama	118 U.S. 375	1886	Upholds the Major Crimes Act based on Congress's plenary power over Indian affairs.
General Allotment Act (Dawes Act)	25 U.S.C. § 331	1887	Created individual Indian land parcels, held in trust by the federal government for individual Indians and Indian households, out of reservation lands, eventually leading to so-called "checker-boarded" jurisdiction as some parcels moved from trust to fee status.
Indian Country Act	18 U.S.C. § 1151	1948	Defines the scope of federal criminal jurisdiction over Indian lands.
Public Law 83-280	18 U.S.C. § 1162; 25 U.S.C. § 1360	1953	Transfers federal jurisdiction over Indian lands to 5 mandatory states (Alaska added upon statehood), excepting 3 tribes, without tribes' consent: optional for other states, also without tribes' consent.
Public Law 83-280, amended	18 U.S.C. § 1162; 25 U.S.C. § 1360	1968	Allows states to request retrocession of Indian country jurisdiction (a return of jurisdiction to the federal government).
Indian Civil Rights Act (ICRA)	25 U.S.C. § 1301	1968	Details rights tribes must provide defendants in their courts while restricting tribal courts to misdemeanor sentencing only.

(continued)

Table 7.2. (continued)

Act or Case	Reference	Year	Description
Indian Self-Determination and Education Assistance Act	25 U.S.C. § 450	1975	Allows for the reassertion of control over tribal services through self-governance contracts and other mechanisms.
Oliphant v. Suquamish Indian Tribe	435 U.S. 191	1978	Holds that tribal courts lack any criminal jurisdiction over non-Indians for offenses committed on Indian lands.
United States v. Wheeler	495 U.S. 313	1978	Double jeopardy does not apply in cases subject to concurrent federal and tribal criminal jurisdiction.
Duro v. Reina	495 U.S. 676	1991	Prevents Tribal courts from exercising criminal jurisdiction over non-Indians for offenses committed on Indian lands.
ICRA, amended	25 U.S.C. § 1301	1991	So-called "*Duro*-fix" reaffirms tribal jurisdiction over *all* Indians, not just member Indians.
Tribal governments' consent for federal capital punishment	18 U.S.C. § 3598	1994	Requires that no Indian may be subject to a capital sentence unless the governing body of the tribe has first consented to the imposition of the death penalty for crimes committed on the tribe's lands.
United States v. Lara	541 U.S. 193	2004	Affirms that separate federal and tribal prosecutions do not violate double jeopardy when a tribe prosecutes a nonmember Indian.
Tribal Law and Order Act	25 U.S.C. § 2801	2010	Enhances federal collaboration with tribal law enforcement agencies, expands tribal courts' sentencing authority to felony jurisdiction by amending ICRA to permit incarceration for up to three years per offense, while allowing multiple offenses to be "stacked."
Violence Against Women Reauthorization Act	127 Stat. 54	2013	Restores tribal criminal jurisdiction over non-Indians in Indian country for certain crimes involving domestic and dating violence and related protection orders.

Source: The Indian Law and Order Commission, *A Roadmap for Making Native America Safer, Report to the President and Congress of the United States.*

Conclusion

Through legislation and court cases, the federal government has narrowed its recognition of tribal criminal jurisdiction. These federal laws have negatively affected tribal sovereignty. Because of the intrusion of federal and/or state legal systems without tribal consent, it has been difficult for tribal nations to operate their legal systems without interference. As discussed in later chapters, Indian nations continue to overcome these barriers in order to provide justice and safety for not only tribal citizens, but to all people who live and visit their lands.

Questions

1. Which federal law or Supreme Court case do you think was most damaging to tribes' criminal jurisdiction? Explain your opinion.
2. Which federal law or Supreme Court case do you think did the least damage to tribes' criminal jurisdiction? Explain your opinion.
3. Why do you think so much of criminal jurisdiction in Indian country depends on the tribal membership of the defendant and the victim? Do you think this is a good way to determine jurisdiction? Why or why not?

In Your Community

1. This chapter lists some major federal actions that affected almost all tribes. There are some federal laws and U.S. Supreme Court cases, however, that affected individual tribes or tribes within a particular state. If any such laws have affected your tribal nation, explain how the laws have impacted your tribal government's jurisdiction.
2. Are there any issues regarding the nature of your tribal territory that may affect criminal jurisdiction? For example, some reservations include non-Indian **fee land**. How does this affect your tribal government's ability to address crimes in your community?

Terms Used in Chapter 7

Allotments: Shares or portions; distribution of land.
Double jeopardy: Putting a person on trial more than once for the same crime.
Fee land: Land that is owned free and clear without any trust or restrictions.
Implicit: Implied or understood although not directly expressed.
Inherent: A natural part of; a permanent feature of.
Nonmember Indians: Indians who are citizens of a different tribe.
Patent: A grant of land by the government to an individual.

Notes

1. For a more in-depth discussion of the challenges faced by Alaska Natives see *The Indian Law & Order Commission's Report, A Road Map for Making Native America Safer*, Chapter 2: "Reforming Justice for Alaska Natives: The Time Is Now," http://www.aisc.ucla.edu/iloc/report/index.html.

2. Under the Assimilative Crime Act (18 U.S.C. § 13), if the crime is not defined by federal law, the federal government may incorporate an applicable state statute.

3. We will explore in chapter 8 how it is possible that tribes may still exercise concurrent jurisdiction (i.e., have parallel, noncompeting authority) to hear and try these crimes even though the federal government now has the authority to prosecute these crimes as well.

4. *Southern Ute Tribe v. Frost*, 19 Indian L. Rep. 6132 (S. Ute. Tr. Ct., 1992).

5. For an in-depth discussion on the impact of PL 280 see the following: Carole Goldberg and Duane Champagne, *Law Enforcement and Criminal Justice under Public Law 280*, http://www.tribal-institute.org/download/pl280_study.pdf; Sarah Deer, Carole Goldberg, Heather Valdez Singleton, and Maureen White Eagle, *Final Report: Focus Group on Public Law 280 and the Sexual Assault of Native Women*, http://www.tribal-institute.org/download/Final%20280%20FG%20Report.pdf.

6. For an overview of various state jurisdictions in Indian country see http://www.tribal-institute.org/lists/tjsa.htm.

7. Indian Law and Order Commission, *A Roadmap for Making Native America Safer*, Report to the President and Congress of the United States, November 2013, 2, 7, http://www.aisc.ucla.edu/iloc/report/index.html.

Suggested Further Reading

Robert T. Anderson, "Negotiating Jurisdiction: Retroceding State Authority over Indian Country Granted by Public Law 280," 87 *Wash. L. Rev.* 915 (2012).

Christopher B. Chaney, "The Effect of the United States Supreme Court's Decisions during the Last Quarter of the Nineteenth Century on Tribal Criminal Jurisdiction," 14 *BYU Journal of Public Law* 173 (2000).

Michael C. Duma, "Kansas' Criminal Jurisdiction in Indian Country: Why the Kansas Act Is Unnecessary, Outdated, and Unfair," 50 *Washburn L. J.* 685 (2011).

Jerry Gardner and Ada Pecos Melton, "Public Law 280: Issues and Concerns for Victims of Crimes in Indian Country," Tribal Court Clearinghouse (1999), http://www.tribal-institute.org/articles/gardner1.htm.

Carole Goldberg, *Planting Tail Feathers: Tribal Survival and Public Law 280* (UCLA American Indian Studies Center, 1997).

Vanessa J. Jimenez and Soo C. Song, "Concurrent Tribal and State Jurisdiction under Public Law 280," 47 *American University Law Review* 1627 (1998).

Ken Peak, "Criminal Justice, Law and Policy in Indian Country: A Historical Perspective," 17 *Journal of Criminal Justice* 485 (1989).

Kevin Washburn, "American Indians, Crime, and the Law," 104 *Mich. L. Rev* 709 (2006).
Kevin Washburn, "American Indians Crime, and the Law: Five Years of Scholarship on Criminal Justice in Indian Country," 40 *Ariz. St. L.J.* 1003 (2008).
The Indian Law and Order Commission, "A Roadmap for Making Native America Safer, Report to The President and Congress of The United States," http://www.aisc.ucla.edu/iloc/report/index.html.

Chapter 8

Exercising Jurisdiction over Crimes Committed by Non-Indians

Although tribal nations retain criminal jurisdiction over Indians, tribes have struggled to respond to crimes committed by non-Indians since the 1978 Supreme Court decision *Oliphant v. Suquamish*.

The Violence Against Women Act 2013 reauthorization recognizes tribal criminal authority over certain acts of domestic violence committed by non-Indians (see details in Chapter 10). However, as of 2014, tribal criminal jurisdiction over other crimes committed by non-Indians is still not recognized by the federal government. Even though the state or federal government technically may have criminal authority over non-Indians, prosecution of crimes committed on the reservation by non-Natives has often been a low priority of state and federal law enforcement and prosecutors. This leaves a significant gap in the prosecution of non-Native offenders.

Tribal nations have been using creative mechanisms to hold offenders accountable for their behavior regardless of their citizenship. This section provides a few examples of what tribes are doing to address the criminal jurisdiction gap.

- Treaties
- Civil Authority
- Arrest and Remove/Cross-Deputization
- Consent/**Stipulation**
- Civil **Contempt**
- Exclusion
- Forfeiture

Treaties as a Basis for Criminal Authority

Some tribes retain criminal jurisdiction through their treaties with the United States. This is an important aspect of criminal jurisdiction, and tribes with treaties should carefully examine their treaties to determine whether they address jurisdiction. The case on p. 123 illustrates the way treaties may affect tribal jurisdiction and also shows how custom and tradition, as discussed earlier, provide criminal jurisdiction.

Jurisdiction over Non–U.S. Citizens

The Eastern Band of Cherokee Indians Court recently ruled on the issue of exercising jurisdiction over a non-Indian who is not a U.S. citizen. In this case, the Cherokee Court concludes that the *Oliphant* case is inapplicable to non–U.S. citizens. Read the following case and consider if you agree.

Eastern Band of Indians, Cherokee Supreme Court
Eastern Band of Cherokee Indians v. Torres (2005)
2005.NACE.0000007 (VersusLaw)

These cases were consolidated for trial in the Cherokee Court on December 10, 2003. The defendant moved to dismiss the charges for lack of jurisdiction of the defendant on the grounds that he is not an Indian. The Court entered an order denying the motion to dismiss on January 27, 2004, and notice of appeal to this Court was filed on February 10, 2004. The appeal was argued in this Court on July 23, 2004.

All parties stipulated that defendant Torres is a citizen of the republic of Mexico (United Mexican States).

Defendant Torres was charged with driving while impaired and failure to stop for a stop sign on September 10, 2003. While released on bond for these charges, defendant on September 21, 2003 was charged with driving while impaired and driving while license revoked. Again, on pre-trial release, defendant was charged with second-degree child abuse of an enrolled member on November 13, 2003. During this time period, defendant was living at 4031 Wrights Creek Road (the residence of an enrolled member), which this Court takes judicial notice is located in Indian Country within the Qualla Boundary (the reservation of the Eastern Band of Cherokee Indians in North Carolina). The record discloses that defendant was associating with at least two female enrolled members of the Eastern Band of Cherokee Indians, and that the alleged child abuse occurred at 4031 Wrights Creek Road.

The traffic violations occurred on public highways in Indian Country within the Qualla Boundary. Defendant's breathalyzer test on September 21, 2003 gave a result of .17 Alcohol Content. The defendant's alcohol content at the September 10, 2003 arrest was .11. Both arrests were at intersections of tribal roads with US 19 and in populated areas. Defendant is 37 years of age and had been issued a North Carolina driver's license.

The population of the Qualla Boundary, both permanent and temporary, is becoming larger and more diverse. Approximately 8,500 enrolled members live on the Qualla Boundary. More people visit Cherokee than any place in North Carolina, some three (3) million visitors a year. This case is not a unique, stand-alone case. It is not unusual for foreigners to appear in the Cherokee Court, in civil, criminal and infraction cases.

We now turn to the issue of jurisdiction.

This is a case of first impression. The issue for decision is: Does the Cherokee Court, an independent tribal court of the Eastern Band of Cherokee Indians, a federally recognized Indian tribe, have jurisdiction to try and to punish the defendant Torres, a citizen of Mexico who is not an Indian, for violating the criminal laws of the Eastern Band of Cherokee Indians? We answer the issue, yes.

Our research does not disclose any authority directly addressing this issue. We consider that the better reasoned analysis requires and supports the conclusion that the Cherokee Court does have criminal jurisdiction over non-Indians who are not citizens of the United States, i.e., aliens.

In reviewing issues of jurisdiction the Court is guided by Chapter 7, Section 2 (2000) of the Cherokee Code. Section 2 (c) states: "The Judicial Branch shall not have jurisdiction over matters in which the exercise of jurisdiction has been specifically prohibited by a binding decision of the United States Supreme Court, the United States Court of Appeals for the Fourth Circuit or by an Act of Congress."

Our research does not disclose any Act of Congress specifically prohibiting the exercise of criminal jurisdiction by Indian tribal Courts over non-Indians who are not citizens of the United States. Nor do we find any such decision of the United States Court of Appeals for the Fourth Circuit.

The Supreme Court of the United States has addressed the criminal jurisdiction of Indian Courts in four opinions during the last twenty-five years. The Court has reviewed jurisdiction over non-Indian citizens of the United States, *Oliphant v. Suquamish Tribe* (1978); jurisdiction over member Indians, *United States v. Wheeler* (1978); and jurisdiction over non-member Indians, *Duro v. Reina* (1990); *United States v. Lara* (2004). Each of these cases specifically involved the rights of citizens of the United States. Throughout its extensive history of jurisprudence regarding Indian tribal sovereignty, the Supreme Court has never considered the powers and status of the Tribes with regard to non-citizens of the United States. The Cherokee Court, drawing upon history and references from precedent concluded that the Eastern Band of Cherokee Indians maintained the "inherent authority" to prosecute non-citizens of the United States.

The appellant relies entirely on *Oliphant*. He only cites two additional authorities, *Duro* and Chapter 14, Section 1.5 of the Cherokee Code. Appellant argues that *Oliphant* holds that Indian tribal courts do not have jurisdiction to try any non-Indians on criminal charges. Stated again, that Indian tribal courts only have criminal jurisdiction over Indians. Appellant fails to perceive the issue before the Court.

It is true that since the Marshall trilogy, *McIntosh*, *Cherokee* and *Worcester*, the United States Supreme Court has referred to Indian tribes as "dependent sovereign nations." This Court agrees that Indian tribes are prohibited from exercising those powers of autonomous states that have been expressly terminated by the United States Congress and those powers inconsistent with their status, as dependent sovereign nations. *Oliphant*. Congress has not expressly limited the jurisdiction of Indian tribal courts over non-Indians in criminal cases.

This Court holds that neither Congress nor the United States Supreme Court nor the Fourth Circuit Court of Appeals has specifically prohibited the jurisdiction of Indian Tribal courts over non-Indian aliens of the United States on criminal charges.

A careful reading of *Oliphant* supports this conclusion. The Court in *Oliphant* does not address this issue directly. Oliphant and Belgarde were not aliens, but were citizens of the United States. Historically, the United States in its treaties and agreements with Indian tribes from the earliest days had two basic goals: to gain land from the Indians, and to protect citizens of the U.S. The first treaty, the 1778 treaty with the Delaware nation, stated that neither party to the treaty could "proceed to the infliction of punishments on the citizens of the other. . . ." Treaty with the Delaware's, Article IV, 7 Stat. 14. In the Treaty with the Shawnees, Article III, 7 Stat. 26 (1786) we find the reference to "any citizen of the United States. . ."; like provision in the Treaty with the Choctaws, Article IV, 79 Statue 22 (1780) "any citizen of the United States." Surely, the United States did not intend to protect English, Spanish, Dutch and other aliens, from the Indians.

The Court's restriction of its holding in *Oliphant* to "non-Indian citizens of the United States" has a significant historical basis, and is consistent with the Court's concerns of liberty, justice and fairness justifying the Court's ruling prohibiting the exercise of criminal jurisdiction over non-Indian citizens of the United States. The Court has traditionally recognized this distinction between citizens and non-citizens. Over a century ago, the Court indicated that the general "object" of Congressional statutes regarding Indian country was "to reserve to the courts of the United States [criminal] jurisdiction of all actions to which its own citizens are parties on either side." *In re Mayfield* (1891) (quoted in *Oliphant*).

In nine separate places in the majority opinion in *Oliphant*, Justice (now Chief Justice) Rehnquist refers to "non-Indian citizens of the United States." The defendants in Oliphant were "non-Indian citizens of the United States." As stated above, and in *Oliphant*, history supports the conclusion that in its relations with Indians, the United States was protecting the citizens of the United States and not all non-Indian people. It is noted that the Congressional Review Commission in 1977 concluded that "there is an established legal basis for tribes to exercise jurisdiction over non-Indians." Final Report of the American Indian Policy Review Commission 114, 117, 152-154 (1977). The committee did not refer to the question of jurisdiction over non-Indian aliens.

A brief review of the history of the Cherokees reveals that in negotiating with the Cherokees the primary intent of the United States was the protection of the liberties of citizens of the United States. Six of the first nine treaties executed by the Cherokees and the United States contained special provisions applicable only to United States citizens. The first article of the Hopewell Treaty includes: ". . . the Cherokees shall restore all . . . citizens of the United States . . . to their entire liberty." 7 Stat. 18 Article 8. Article X holds that "all travelers, citizens of the United States, shall have liberty to go to any of the tribes or towns of the Cherokee to trade with them." No right of trade was granted for non-citizens. In the Treaty of the Holston River, 7 Stat. 39 (1791) the activity of citizens of the United States is restricted without reference to those not citizens, thus leaving non-citizens who venture into Indian Country to their own devices for protection. See also, Second Treaty of the Holston River (1798), Article VII, 7 Stat. 62 (freedom of travel); Fourth Treaty of Tellico (1805), Article II, 7 Stat. 95, (travel); Second Treaty of Washington (1816), Article II, 7 Stat. 139, (freedom of navigation of rivers and waters within the Cherokee Nation); (use of ferries and public houses.) Id.

When considering the inherent powers of tribes, the United States Supreme Court has held that tribes retain all powers of autonomous states except those which have been expressly terminated by Treaty or Act of Congress, or which are inconsistent with their status as domestic dependent nations. *Oliphant*, at 208. With the exception of limitations on the power to transfer of land and to exercise external political sovereignty, considerable sovereign power remains within the Tribes. "Indian Tribes are unique aggregations possessing attributes of sovereignty over both their members and their territory." *Lara*, at 204, (quoting *United States v. Mazurie*, 419 U.S. 544 (1975)). This sovereignty exists in large part to protect the political integrity, the economic security, or the health or welfare of the Tribe. *United States v. Montana*, 450 U.S. 544 (1981). The Court has held the exercise of tribal power legitimate where it concerns "a tribe's authority to control events that occur upon the tribe's own land." *Lara* at 204. Over a century ago, the courts of the United States recognized that the Cherokees "have and exhibit the same interest in the enforcement of the law and in the protection of personal and property rights as the United States citizen resident therein. In some sense they have the higher interest, because they are owners of the soil, and constitute the more fixed and permanent population." *Carter v. United States*, 1 Indian Terr. 342, 37 S.W. 204 (Ct App. Ind. Terr., 1896).

The Court in *Oliphant* holds "But from the formation of the Union and the adoption of the Bill of Rights, the United States has manifested an equally great solicitude that its citizens be protected by the United States from unwarranted intrusions on their personal liberty. . . . By submitting to the overriding sovereignty of the United States, Indian tribes therefore necessarily give up their power to try non-Indian citizens of the United States except in a manner acceptable to Congress." *Oliphant* at 210.

The law of *Oliphant* can be summarized in the following: "Such an exercise of jurisdiction over non-Indian citizens of the United States would belie the tribes' forfeiture of full sovereignty in return for the protection of the United States." *Oliphant* supra. By accepting the protection of the United States, Indian tribes did not relinquish their inherent sovereign powers of criminal jurisdiction over non-Indians who were not citizens of the United States, such as Torres.

In *Oliphant*, all the authority relied upon (treaties, opinions and statutes) sought to protect the liberty of United States citizens from Indians. The Court was not concerned with the protection of aliens in dealing with Indians. Nor has the United States Supreme Court specifically expressed the protection of aliens as a reason to limit the sovereignty of Indian tribes.

The Court in *United States v. Lara*, supra, re-affirms many of the principles supporting our decision in Torres, e.g. "The common law conception of crime as an offense against the sovereignty of the government"; "Indian tribes are unique aggregations possessing attributions of sovereignty over both their members and their territory." In several places the Court in Lara again refers to the interest of the United States in protecting citizens of the United States: ". . . whether the . . . Due Process or Equal Protection Clauses prohibit tribes from prosecuting a non-member citizen of the United States."; "non-member Indian citizens of the United States . . .", "We hesitate to adopt a view of tribal sovereignty that would single out another group of citizens, non-member Indians, for trial by political bodies that do not include them." Kennedy, J. concurring, states: "Lara, after all, is a citizen of the United States. To hold that Congress can subject him, within our domestic boundaries, to sovereignty outside the basic structure of the Constitution is a serious step. . . .The National Government seeks to subject a citizen to the criminal jurisdiction of a third entity . . . subject American citizens to the authority of an extra-constitutional sovereign. . . ." *Lara*, at 212. Justice Souter, in dissent, cites *Oliphant* for its holding that "Indian tribes therefore necessarily give up this power to try non-Indian citizens of the United States. . . ."

Therefore, we hold that *Oliphant* does not control the Torres appeal. Oliphant concerns Indian tribal court jurisdiction of criminal cases against non-Indian citizens of the United States. Torres concerns Indian tribal court jurisdiction of criminal cases against non-Indian aliens of the United States.

We hold that the sovereign power of inherent jurisdiction of the Eastern Band of Cherokee Indians to try and punish non-Indian aliens of the United States has not been expressly terminated by Treaty, Act of Congress, or specifically prohibited by a binding decision of the Supreme Court of the United States or the United States Court of Appeals for the Fourth Circuit.

Counsel did not brief or argue the issue of whether jurisdiction by the Eastern Band of Cherokee Indians of criminal cases against non-Indians who are not citizens of the United States, i.e. aliens, is inconsistent with the status of the Eastern Band of Cherokee Indians as a "dependent sovereign nation." However, we find this issue to be essential to the resolution of this appeal. We have reviewed this issue, and hold that the court's jurisdiction over non-Indian aliens on criminal charges is not inconsistent with the status of the Eastern Band of Cherokee Indians as a "dependent sovereign nation."

After the arrival of non-Indians to what is now the United States of America and before the existence of the United States of America, the Cherokee Indians exercised inherent jurisdiction over all non-Indians found within Cherokee Country. Following the formation of the United States of America, the Cherokee Nation entered into treaties with the United States over the years recognizing its relation with the United States as a "dependent sovereign nation," and the federal government assumed its fiduciary obligations for the Cherokees. As demonstrated previously in this opinion, this relationship resulted in the Cherokees giving up criminal jurisdiction over non-Indian citizens of the United States as being inconsistent with the status of the Cherokees as a dependent sovereign nation.

Not so, as to non-Indian aliens of the United States. In order to govern itself, manage its own affairs and safeguard its people as well as visitors (including citizens of the United States and aliens) to Cherokee Country, criminal jurisdiction over non-Indians aliens is an exercise of the inherent power of the Cherokee Nation, and is essential.

Torres, and all aliens who violate criminal laws within the United States will be subjected to a strange court, under strange laws, in a strange land, whether the court is federal, state or tribal. The Cherokee Court provided Torres with all the protection and assistance that he would have received in federal or state court, including appointment of counsel, due process, speedy trial, bond and right of appeal. In addition, after defendant exhausts all of his remedies in the Cherokee Court, he may petition the United States District Court for a writ of habeas corpus and federal appellate review. So, Torres, or any alien, is not prejudiced by receiving a trial in tribal court. See 25 U.S.C. 1301 et seq. (1968).

The decision in Oliphant holds that the inherent sovereign power of criminal jurisdiction of tribal courts over non-Indians has not been specifically curtailed by treaty or act of Congress, but that such jurisdiction is inconsistent with the status of tribes as dependent sovereign nations. As set forth above, we conclude that Oliphant is not a specific ruling as to tribal jurisdiction over non-Indian aliens. We do not find any authority (by treaty, statute or judicial opinion of the United States Supreme Court or Court of Appeals for the Fourth Circuit) holding that tribal criminal jurisdiction over non-Indian aliens is inconsistent with the status of Indian tribes as dependent sovereign nations. The Cherokee Nation had such jurisdiction in 1492; it has it today.

The facts of this case demonstrate the necessity of preserving the criminal jurisdiction of the Eastern Band of Cherokee Indians over non-Indian aliens of the United States in order to protect the safety, health, economic development, liberty and the general welfare of the Eastern Band of Cherokee Indians and all other people who live, work or visit on Tribal lands. The records of the Cherokee Court disclose that aliens of the United States are seeking and receiving the protection of the Cherokee Court in criminal cases arising on the Qualla Boundary against enrolled members of the Eastern Band of Cherokee Indians. To allow criminal jurisdiction when an alien is the victim and deny jurisdiction when an alien is the perpetrator, would indeed be inconsistent with the status of the Eastern Band of Cherokee Indians as a dependent sovereign nation.

This Court's ruling today is in accord with the federal government's current policy of self determination with the Indian tribes by seeking greater tribal autonomy within the framework of a "government to government relationship" with federal agencies. The present policy has a goal of decreasing tribal dependence on the federal government and the development of strong and stable tribal governments. See 25 U.S.C. Sec. 450 a (b). A contrary ruling would indeed serve to frustrate this national policy.

Further, the Court's holding, and the federal policy of self-determination of Indian tribes, is consistent with and supported by established norms of customary international law. See The Paquete Habana, 175 U.S. 677, 700 (1900); International Convention on the Elimination of All Forms of Racial Discrimination (ICERD); *Lawrence v Texas*, 539 U.S. 558, (2003) (citing *Dudgeon v United Kingdom*, European Court of Human Rights); *Grutter v Bolinger*, 539 U.S. 306 (2003) (Ginsberg, J. concurring); International Capital Law as an Interpretive Force in Federal Indian Law, 116 *Harvard Law Rev.* 1751, 1762 (2003); International Law and Domestic Courts: Enhancing Self-Determination for Indigenous People, 5 *Harvard Human Rights J.* 65, 68 (1992).

This ruling is also supported by the traditions, customs and culture of the Eastern Band of Cherokee Indians.

The order of the Cherokee Court denying defendant/appellant's motion to dismiss is affirmed, and this case is remanded to the Cherokee Court. (footnote omitted)

The following case involves an Indian defendant. However, it also gives some examples of how treaty rights could be interpreted to support jurisdiction over non-Indians.

Supreme Court of the Navajo Nation
Russell Means v. District Court of the Chinle Judicial District (1999)
1999.NANN.0000013 (VersusLaw)

This is an original action for a writ of prohibition under 7 N.N.C. Sec. 303 (1995) to prevent or remedy an act of the Chinle District Court which is allegedly beyond that court's jurisdiction, namely denying Russell Means' ("petitioner") motion to dismiss criminal charges against him. Judge Ray Gilmore denied the petitioner's motion in an opinion and order on July 20, 1998. The petitioner then sought a writ of prohibition from this Court.

The petition alleges that the Navajo Nation lacks criminal jurisdiction over the petitioner, who is a member of the Oglala Sioux Nation. Alternatively, the petitioner requests this Court to prohibit the Chinle District Court from exercising criminal jurisdiction, because a prosecution would violate the equal protection provisions of the 1968 Indian Civil Rights Act, the Navajo Nation Bill of Rights at 1 N.N.C. Sec. 3 (equal protection), and the fifth amendment of the United States Constitution. The petitioner also broadly asserts that the Navajo Nation has no criminal jurisdiction over non-Navajo Indians under the Treaty of June 1, 1868 between the United States of America and the Navajo Nation; that the petitioner has not consented to criminal jurisdiction by virtue of his marriage to a Navajo and residence within the Navajo Nation; and that 25 U.S.C. Sec. 1302(2), as amended to recognize Indian nation criminal jurisdiction over nonmember Indians ("Duro Fix" legislation), is not permissible "preference legislation" but instead legislation which violates equal protection of the law. The nub of the equal protection challenge is that while the Navajo Nation "cannot" prosecute non-Indians, the Nation is trying to prosecute the petitioner as a nonmember Indian.

Given the allegations of the petition and the petitioner's formulation of the issues, we will decide the following questions:

1. Does the June 1, 1868 Treaty between the United States of America and the Navajo Nation recognize Navajo Nation criminal jurisdiction over individuals who are not members of the Navajo Nation or Tribe of Indians?
2. Has the petitioner consented to the criminal jurisdiction of the Navajo Nation by virtue of his assumption of tribal relations with Navajos . . . ?

I

On December 28, 1997, the Navajo Nation charged the petitioner with three offenses: threatening Leon Grant in violation of 17 N.N.C. § 310 (1995); committing a battery upon Mr. Grant in violation of 17 N.N.C. § 316; and committing a battery upon Jeremiah Bitsui, also in violation of 17 N.N.C. § 316. Threatening has a maximum potential penalty of imprisonment for a term up to 90 days, a $250 fine, or both, and battery has a maximum potential penalty of incarceration up to 180 days, a $500 fine, or both. The Navajo Nation Criminal Code of 1977 provides, at 17 N.N.C. § 225, that a defendant found guilty of an offense may receive a multiple sentence, with the sentence to run concurrently or consecutively. The petitioner faces a maximum exposure of 450 days incarceration, a fine of $1,250, or both, along with the payment of restitution to the victims of the alleged offenses. 17 N.N.C. § 220(C).

The petitioner filed a motion to dismiss the three charges on January 23, 1998, and the district court held an evidentiary hearing on the motion on April 14, 1998. The petitioner voluntarily testified at the hearing to relate his connections with Navajos and the Navajo Nation. The court denied the motion on July 20, 1998.

Before summarizing the testimony elicited during the April 14, 1998 hearing, this Court will use judicial notice to describe the demography of the Navajo Nation and its criminal justice problems.

A

The Navajo Nation is the largest Indian nation in the United States in terms of geographic size. It has 17,213,941.90 acres of land (approximately 25,000 square miles) as of 1988, including Navajo tribal trust land, land owned in fee, individual Navajo allotments, and various leases. The Navajo Nation membership is the second largest of all Indian nations within the United States, with a total estimated membership of 225,298 persons as of 1990. The 1990 population of the Navajo Nation was 145,853 persons of "all races," with 140,749 American Indians, Eskimos and Aleuts, and 5,104 individuals of "other races." Of that population, 96.62% was Indian and 3.38% was "non-American Indian." Of the American Indian population, 131,422 individuals were Navajos and 9,327 were "other Indians." Therefore, the percentage of nonmember Indians in the Navajo Nation population was 6.39%. There were 126 Sioux Indians residing within the Navajo Nation as of 1990. . . .

[T]he Navajo Nation courts are addressing the serious criminal and social problems of drunk driving, assaults and batteries (including aggravated assault and battery with deadly weapons), sex offenses against children, disorderly conduct, and public intoxication. Many of the crimes against persons are acts of in-family violence, and the civil domestic abuse restraining order numbers show that family violence may be the most serious social problem in the Navajo Nation.

Given the United States Indian education policy of sending Indian children to boarding schools, Indians in the armed services, modern population mobility, and other factors, there are high rates of intertribal intermarriage among American Indians. As noted, at least 9,327 "other" or nonmember Indians resided within the Navajo Nation in 1990. They are involved in some of the 27,000 plus criminal charges in our system and in the 3,435 plus domestic violence cases. The questions are whether nonmember Indians should have de facto immunity from criminal prosecution, given the failure of federal officials to effectively address crime in the Navajo Nation, and whether this Court should rule that thousands of innocent victims, Navajo and non-Navajo, should be permitted to suffer. We must sadly take judicial notice of the fact that, with a few exceptions, non-Indians and nonmember Indians who commit crimes within the Navajo Nation escape punishment for the crimes they commit. The social health of the Navajo Nation is at risk in addressing the petitioner's personal issues, as is the actual health and well-being of thousands of people.

Recent United States Justice Department statistics confirm the severity of the situation. . . . [The following statistics apply to reservation and off-reservation crimes.]

> American Indians experience per capita rates of violence which are more than twice those of the U.S. resident population.
>
> Rates of violence in every age group are higher among American Indians than that of all races.
>
> Nearly a third of all American Indian victims of violence are between ages 18 and 24. This group of American Indians experienced the highest per capita rate of violence of any racial group considered by age—about 1 violent crime for every 4 persons of this age.
>
> Rates of violent victimization for both males and females are higher among American Indians than for all races. The rate of violent crime experienced by American Indian women is nearly 50% higher than that reported by black males.
>
> At least 70% of the violent victimizations experienced by American Indians are committed by persons not of the same race—a substantially higher rate of interracial violence than experienced by white or black victims.
>
> American Indian victims of violence were the most likely of all races of victims to indicate that the offender committed the offense while drinking.
>
> The 1997 arrest rate among American Indians for alcohol-related offenses (driving under the influence, liquor law violations, and public drunkenness) was more than double that found among all races. Drug arrest rates for American Indians were lower than average. . . .

These are unpleasant facts. However, they point to the need to exercise criminal jurisdiction over all who enter the Navajo Nation. Indian nation courts are at the front line of attempts to control crime and social disruption. They share a common responsibility with police, prosecutors, defenders, and social service programs to address crime and violence for the welfare of not only the Navajo People, but all those who live within the Navajo Nation or reside in areas adjacent to the Navajo Nation.

Indian nations cannot rely upon others to address the problems identified by the Bureau of Justice Statistics. The Navajo Nation courts have primary jurisdiction to deal with criminal offenses and they must be free to exercise that jurisdiction.

B

The petitioner is a member of the Oglala Sioux Nation. He was 58 years of age as of the date of the hearing, and he resided for ten years within the Navajo Nation from 1987 through 1997. He was married to Gloria Grant, an enrolled Navajo woman. Leon Grant, whom the petitioner is charged with threatening and battering, is a member of the Omaha Tribe, and Jeremiah Bitsui, whom the petitioner is charged with battering, is Navajo. . . .

The petitioner complained of a lack of hospitality toward him when he resided within the Navajo Nation. He said he could not vote, run for Navajo Nation office (including judicial office), become a Navajo Nation Council delegate, the president, vice-president, or be a member of a farm board. In sum, he could not attain any Navajo Nation political position. He said he could not sit on a jury and received no notice to appear for jury duty. That may be because the petitioner was not on any Navajo Nation registration or voter list and he was not on the voter registration list for Apache County, Arizona. He complained at length about his inability to get a job or start a business because of Navajo Nation employment and contracting preference laws.

The petitioner's national reputation as an activist is well-known. On cross-examination, the prosecution attempted to develop the petitioner's active participation in the public and political life of the Navajo Nation. The prosecution highlighted the petitioner's attendance at chapter meetings and elicited the fact that subsequent to a 1989 incident when Navajos were shot by Navajos, he led a march to the court house for a demonstration to make a "broad statement" about political activities of the Navajo Nation.

The "facts" the petitioner related during his testimony are only partially correct. While it is true that there are preference laws for employment and contracting in the Navajo Nation, they are not an absolute barrier to either employment or the ability to do business. There are many non-Navajo employees of the Navajo Nation (some of whom hold high positions in Navajo Nation government), and non-Navajo businesses operate within the Navajo Nation. The ability to work or do business within the Navajo Nation has a great deal more to do with individual initiative and talent than preference laws. The petitioner was most likely not called for jury duty because he did not register to vote in Arizona. Non-Navajos have been called for jury duty since at least 1979. The 126 Sioux Indians listed in the 1990 Census can be called for jury duty if they are on a voter list and are called. If the petitioner was an indigent at the time of his arraignment, he would have been eligible for the appointment of an attorney.

II

The first issue is whether the June 1, 1868 Treaty between the United States of America and the Navajo Nation gives the Navajo Nation courts criminal jurisdiction over individuals who are not members of the Navajo Nation or Tribe of Indians. We will first discuss the 1868 Treaty as a source of criminal jurisdiction and then apply it.

A

There is a general and false assumption that Indian nations have no criminal jurisdiction over non-Indians and nonmember Indians. While the United States Supreme Court ruled that Indian nations have no inherent criminal jurisdiction over non-Indians in *Oliphant v. Suquamish Indian Tribe*, and that there is no inherent criminal jurisdiction over nonmember Indians in *Duro v. Reina*, criminal jurisdiction over nonmembers can rest upon a treaty or federal statute. The Supreme Court reserved the issues of affirmative congressional authorization or treaty provisions in both cases. Therefore, we will examine whether the Navajo Nation Treaty of 1868 is a source of Navajo Nation criminal jurisdiction over nonmember Indians.

The basic canons of treaty construction are:

1. A treaty must be construed as the Indians understood it.
2. Doubtful or ambiguous expressions in a treaty must be resolved in favor of the given Indian nation.
3. Treaty provisions which are not clear on their face may be interpreted from the surrounding circumstances and history.
4. A treaty is not a grant of rights to Indian nations but a grant of rights from them, with reservations of all rights which are not granted.
5. Treaties with Indian nations are the law of the land under the treaty clause of the Constitution.

B

The Treaty between the Navajo Nation or Tribe of Indians and the United States was negotiated at Fort Sumner, New Mexico Territory, on May 28, 29, and 30, 1868, and it was executed there on June 1, 1868. The United States Senate advised ratification of the Treaty on July 25, 1868, and President Andrew Johnson proclaimed it on August 12, 1868, 15 Stats. 667. We are primarily interested in language found in Article II of the Treaty, which we will call the "set apart for the use and occupation" clause, and that in Article I, which we will call the "bad men" clause.

Article II of the Treaty, 15 Stats. at 668, begins with a boundary description and then says that "this reservation" is "set apart for the use and occupation of the Navajo tribe of Indians, and for such other friendly tribes or individual Indians as from time to time they may be willing, with the consent of the United States, to admit among them. . . ." Federal courts use this language as the basis for Navajo Nation civil jurisdiction. The Supreme Court held that the Navajo Nation retained its inherent criminal jurisdiction over members in *United States v. Wheeler.*

The plain language of Article II indicates that the Navajo Reservation exists for the exclusive use of not only Navajos, but other Indians, either as tribes or as individuals, where both the Navajo Nation and the United States agree to their admission. Given that the jurisdiction of our courts is recognized in the Article II language, Indians such as the petitioner who are permitted to reside within the Navajo Nation fall within the same grouping as Navajo Indians in terms of the Treaty's coverage.

We see this provision applied in the historical record. On September 27, 1881, Agent Galen Eastman wrote to the Commissioner of Indian Affairs to inform him that about forty Pah-Utes (Paiutes) had arrived in a starving condition and were begging for food. They said "they were going to cease their predatory life and use the hoe thereafter." The Navajo reply was that "if the Great Father is willing, we will try you again and be responsible for your good behavior for we used to be friends and have intermarried with your people and yours with ours . . . but if you return to your bad life, thieving and murdering we (the Navajos) will hang you." Obviously, thinking of the language in Article II of the Treaty, Eastman asked for instructions.

The "bad men" among either "the Indians" or "Whites" language has been litigated in various contexts, but the closest interpretation on the issue of criminal jurisdiction was in the case of *State ex rel. Merrill v. Turtle*, 413 F.2d 683 (9th Cir. 1969). There, the State of Arizona arrested a Cheyenne Indian within the Navajo Nation using the "bad men among the Indians" Treaty language as its justification, and the court ruled that the arrest of an Indian had to follow the extradition provision in the "bad men" clause. 413 F.2d at 686. The "bad men" clause has been used as the basis for concurrent civil jurisdiction in the Navajo Nation courts. *Babbitt Ford, Inc. v. Navajo Indian Tribe*, 710 F.2d 587, 595 (9th Cir. 1983). . . .

General William T. Sherman said [to the Navajos about problems with non-member Indians]: "The Army will do the fighting, you must live at peace, if you go to your own country the Utes will be the nearest Indians to you, you must not trouble the Utes and the Utes must not trouble you. If, however, the Utes or Apaches come into your country with bows and arrows and guns you of course can drive them out but must not follow beyond the boundary line."

There are two foundations for criminal jurisdiction in the Treaty of 1868, the history of its negotiation, and its application: those who assume relations with Navajos with the consent of the Navajo Nation and the United States are permitted to enter and reside within the Navajo Nation, subject to its laws, and non-Navajo Indians who enter and commit offenses are subject to punishment. That is what

General Sherman told the Navajos who were assembled behind the fort hospital on June 28, 1868. It is quite obvious from Galen Eastman's September 17, 1881 letter to the Commissioner of Indian Affairs that the Navajo leadership was thinking of admitting Paiutes to the Navajo Nation, and if they were admitted, they would be subject to punishment for theft and murder by Navajos.

Therefore, we conclude that the Chinle District Court has criminal jurisdiction over the petitioner by virtue of the 1868 Treaty. The petitioner entered the Navajo Nation, married a Navajo woman, conducted business activities, engaged in political activities by expressing his right to free speech, and otherwise satisfied the Article II conditions for entry and residence and Article I and II court jurisdiction.

III

We previously held, in *Navajo Nation v. Hunter*, 6 Nav. R., No. SC-CR-07-95 (decided March 8, 1996), that the Navajo Nation has criminal jurisdiction over individuals who "assume tribal relations." How does that comply with the indications in the *Duro* decision that intermarriage alone does not constitute sufficient consent for criminal jurisdiction?

We have previously ruled that our 1997 Navajo Nation Criminal Code will be construed in light of Navajo common law, and the Supreme Court approved Navajo common law in the Wheeler decision. While there is a formal process to obtain membership as a Navajo, that is not the only kind of "membership" under Navajo Nation law. An individual who marries or has an intimate relationship with a Navajo is a hadane (in-law). The Navajo People have adoone'e or clans, and many of them are based upon the intermarriage of original Navajo clan members with people of other nations. The primary clan relation is traced through the mother, and some of the "foreign nation" clans include the "Flat Foot-Pima clan," the "Ute people clan," the "Zuni clan," the "Mexican clan," and the "Mescalero Apache clan." The list of clans based upon other peoples is not exhaustive. A hadane or in-law assumes a clan relation to a Navajo when an intimate relationship forms, and when that relationship is conducted within the Navajo Nation, there are reciprocal obligations to and from family and clan members under Navajo common law. Among those obligations is the duty to avoid threatening or assaulting a relative by marriage (or any other person).

We find that the petitioner, by reason of his marriage to a Navajo, longtime residence within the Navajo Nation, his activities here, and his status as a hadane, consented to Navajo Nation criminal jurisdiction. This is not done by "adoption" in any formal or customary sense, but by assuming Tribal relations and establishing familial and community relationships under Navajo common law.

There is another aspect to consent by conduct. In *Tsosie v. United States*, 825 F.2d 393 (Fed. Cir. 1987), the Federal Circuit Court of Appeals discussed the "bad men among the Indians" language, saying that "[i]t is evident from the

> negotiations that the Navajos were not to be permanently disarmed, and could defend their reservation. They feared attacks by other Indian tribes, which they could repel, but pursuit and retaliation it was hoped they would refrain from, leaving that to the United States Army. The 'bad men' clause is not confined to United States Government employees, but extends 'to people subject to the authority of the United States.' This vague phrase, to effectuate the purpose of the treaty, could possibly include Indians hostile to the Navajos whose wrongs to the Navajos the United States will punish and pay for: thus the need for Indian retaliation would be eliminated." Id., at 396.
>
> Avoidance of retaliation and revenge is clear in the Treaty of 1868. General Sherman urged Navajos to leave the neighboring Mexicans to the Army, but he told Navajos they could pursue Utes and Apaches who entered the Navajo homeland. The Treaty speaks to the admission of Indians from other Indian nations. The thrust of the "bad men" clause was to avoid conflict. We use a rule of necessity to interpret consent under our Treaty. It would be absurd to conclude that our hadane relatives can enter the Navajo Nation, offend, and remain among us, and we can do nothing to protect Navajos and others from them. To so conclude would be to open the door for revenge and retaliation. While there are those who may think that the remedies offered by the United States Government are adequate, it is plain and clear to us that federal enforcement of criminal law is deficient. Potential state remedies are impractical, because law enforcement personnel in nearby areas have their own law enforcement problems. We must have the rule of peaceful law rather than the law of the talon, so we conclude that the petitioner has assumed Tribal relations with Navajos and he is thus subject to the jurisdiction of our courts.
>
> [The Court found that the Chinle District Court had jurisdiction over Means under the Treaty of 1868 and because Means consented to criminal jurisdiction, and that he was not denied equal protection of the law. The case was remanded back to the Chinle District Court for trial.]

Civil Authority

Tribes sometimes use civil laws to regulate the behavior of non-Indians. One example of this strategy includes using civil traffic infractions rather than criminal misdemeanors. Civil laws are also used often in child protection cases to ensure jurisdiction over non-Native parents. Another area in which civil laws are often used in place of criminal laws is natural resources, such as fish and game, to ensure that the natural resources of the tribe are protected.

The following tribal statutes address behavior of non-Indians.

Red Cliff Band Civil Traffic Code § 14.1.1
The Tribal Council of the Red Cliff Band of Lake Superior Chippewa Indians finds that the operation of motor vehicles on reservation threatens and has a direct effect on the political integrity, economic security and health and welfare of the tribe and its members. Pursuant to the inherent powers of the Red Cliff Band to exercise civil authority over the conduct of members and non-members operating motor vehicles on reservation, the Tribal Council of the Red Cliff Band has enacted this Red Cliff Traffic Code regulating traffic within the boundaries of the Red Cliff Reservation.

White Mountain Apache Fish and Game Code § 6.3
Except as otherwise provided in this Code, all matters arising under this Code shall be adjudicated in the White Mountain Apache Tribal Court following the filing of a Civil Complaint naming the White Mountain Apache Tribe as plaintiff, by the Authorized Officer alleging the violation, or by legal counsel for the Tribe.

Police Power to Arrest and Remove
Generally, tribal police retain the power to stop and detain any person suspected of criminal activity and to hold that person until state or federal law enforcement authorities arrive and take control of the individual. The police may also escort individuals off reservation property. Chapter 11 focuses on tribal-state collaboration and cross-deputization.

The following tribal laws demonstrate this power:

Oglala Sioux Tribe Law and Order Code § 112 (1996)
All persons hunting, fishing, cutting wood, driving livestock, peddling, or doing any commercial business on Trust Indian Allotments without the permission of the owner; or Tribal land on this Reservation without the permission of the Oglala Sioux Tribal Council, may be forcibly ejected from the Pine Ridge Reservation by a police officer, officer of the United States Indian Service, or Tribal police, and may be turned over to the custody of the United States Marshal or Sheriff or other officer of the State of South Dakota or Nebraska, for prosecution under Federal or State law.

Consent or Stipulation of Non-Indians
Some tribes exercise criminal jurisdiction through the consent of non-Natives. For example, in order to obtain a fishing permit, the tribe may require individuals to consent to criminal jurisdiction. Thus, if any crimes occur, the tribe may retain jurisdiction because the non-Native has consented.

The following statutes address consent to jurisdiction:

White Mountain Apache's Permits Require Consent to the Tribe's Jurisdiction

A. *Any persons to whom a Hunting or Recreation Permit is issued by the Department shall be required to sign a Permit Agreement before any such permit shall be valid. The Agreement shall be in substantially the same form as provided in Section B below. The form shall be signed by the applicant in the presence of the permit dealer who issued the permit, or his agent.*

B. *Permit Agreement Form: I hereby agree that the following terms and conditions govern my use of the permit, my presence on the White Mountain Apache Reservation, and my use of Tribal resources and services:*

1. *I agree to obey all Tribal laws and regulations.*
2. *I consent to the jurisdiction of the White Mountain Apache Tribal Court as the forum for the resolution of any civil disputes which arise from my presence on the Reservation and/or use of Tribal resources and/or services.*
3. *I understand that permission for me to enter the White Mountain Apache Reservation is conditioned on my obeyance of Tribal laws and regulations and that violation of such laws and regulations makes me a trespasser and may subject me to arrest, tribal and federal court action, expulsion from the Reservation, and seizure of property as security for payment of potential financial obligations to the Tribe.*
4. *I understand that permits are required for all Recreational Activities and for taking wildlife on the Reservation.*
5. *Swimming is prohibited on the Reservation.*
6. *I understand that the willful use of Tribal resources or services contrary to the terms of Tribal law or regulation constitutes theft of Tribal assets and is a violation of Tribal and federal law.*
7. *I agree to be bound by the penalties and liquidated damages provisions of Tribal law in the event that I am found liable to the White Mountain Apache Tribe for violations of Tribal law.*

White Mountain Apache Fish and Game Code § 3.2 (2000).

The following case considers whether a non-Native can consent to criminal jurisdiction in the Port Gamble tribal court.

Port Gamble S'Klallam Tribal Court of Appeals
Port Gamble S'Klallam Tribe v. Michael Hjert (2011)
10 NICS App. 60

I. Facts
Between September 2009 and September 2010, Michael Hjert, a non-Indian, was charged in the Port Gamble S'Klallam Tribal Community Court under separate

cause numbers with multiple alcohol related offenses. Hjert pled guilty to those offenses. His sentences included detention, probation and fines.

On November 29, 2010, Hjert was charged with another alcohol related offense. In the complaint the Tribe alleged Hjert was a "Non Native American defendant who has consented to Tribal jurisdiction." The consent form signed by Hjert states:

> With this form, you are being requested to consent to the criminal jurisdiction of the Port Gamble S'Klallam Tribal Community. **YOU DO NOT HAVE TO CONSENT TO JURISDICTION.** If you do not consent, this Tribe will not prosecute you. The matter may be referred to the county, state, or federal authorities for prosecution, however.
>
> If you do consent, this written consent is limited to this one incident only. However, more than one charge may arise out of this one incident.
>
> Also, if you consent, you are not necessarily saying you are guilty of any offenses. You may still maintain your innocence even if you do consent to be prosecuted by the Port Gamble S'Klallam Tribal Community.
>
> Further, this consent will continue throughout the case. For example, if the Court finds you guilty of an offense and orders you to pay a fine or participate in counseling, you cannot later withdraw your consent to avoid obligations imposed by Court orders.

At a hearing held on January 19, 2011, the judge *sua sponte* dismissed the charge and related probation violation allegations on the grounds the Tribe lacked subject matter jurisdiction under *Oliphant v. Suquamish Indian Tribe*. An order dismissing the offense and all the prior offenses was entered on January 25, 2011.

The Tribe appeals from the dismissal order. The Tribe contends the Community Court had jurisdiction to try and punish Hjert based on Hjert's consent to the Tribe's criminal jurisdiction.

II. Decision

This issue in this case is whether the Port Gamble S'Klallam Tribal Community Court had jurisdiction to try and punish Hjert, a non-Indian for a crime committed on the Reservation based on his consent. The trial judge ruled it did not under the United States Supreme Court's holding in *Oliphant*.

. . .

Under Article I of the Constitution of the Port Gamble S'Klallam Tribe:

> The jurisdiction of the Port Gamble S'Klallam Tribe shall extend over the following, to the fullest extent, except where prohibited by codes, statutes, ordinances or resolutions of the Port Gamble S'Klallam Tribe ("Tribal Law") or *applicable federal law*:
>
> 1. All persons, property and activities within: (1) the confines of the Port Gamble S'Klallam Reservation as established by Proclamation dated June 16, 1938, and

(2) such other lands as may hereafter be added thereto, and (3) other lands held or acquired by the Port Gamble S'Klallam Tribe or for the benefit of the Port Gamble S'Klallam Tribe

Title I of the Port Gamble S'Klallam Tribe Community Court General Rules provides. "[t]he Port Gamble S'Klallam Community Court is vested with the fullest personal, subject matter and territorial jurisdiction permissible under applicable law." PGSTC 1.02.01 (emphasis added). When PGSTC 1.02.01 is read in conjunction with Article I, the Tribe's intent is to assert its jurisdiction unless prohibited by its own codes or applicable federal law and to authorize its court to exercise personal, subject matter or territorial jurisdiction where permitted by applicable law.

We find no Tribal law that specifically prohibits the court from asserting criminal jurisdiction over a consenting non-Indian. But, that does not end the inquiry. First, we must determine whether the Tribe's asserted jurisdictions prohibited under applicable federal law. If we find it is not, we must then determine whether the Port Gamble S'Klallam Tribe has vested its Community Court with the authority to assert the Tribe's criminal jurisdiction over a consenting non-Indian.

Tribes have criminal jurisdiction over their members. That authority derives from a tribe's retained sovereignty. *United States v. Wheeler*. Tribes have criminal jurisdiction over nonmember Indians because Congress has recognized that inherent power. *United States v. Lara*. Tribes also possess the inherent sovereign powers to exclude non-members from tribal lands. *New Mexico v Mescalero Apache*. The authority to exclude necessarily includes the lesser authority to set conditions on their entry and continued presence through regulations. See *Merrion v. Jicarilla Apache Tribe* (the power to exclude "necessarily includes the lesser power to place conditions on entry, on continued presence, or on reservation conduct.").

The seminal case on the issue of a tribe's criminal jurisdiction where the defendant is a non-Indian is *Oliphant*. In *Oliphant* the United States Supreme Court held that tribes do not possess inherent criminal jurisdiction over non-Indians. In that case the Suquamish Tribe, which like the Port Gamble S'Klallam Tribe signed a treaty with the United States and is located in Washington State, claimed it had the inherent sovereign authority to exercise criminal jurisdiction over a non-Indian's violation of the Tribe's criminal law occurring on its reservation, an authority that Congress had never taken away. The Supreme Court disagreed. It held that although Indian tribes retain some inherent sovereign powers, by submitting to the overriding sovereignty of the United States, treaty tribes necessarily gave up the power to try non-Indian citizens of the United States. The Court ruled that for a tribe to exercise criminal jurisdiction over non-Indians would require a delegation of such power by Congress

The power of the United States to try and criminally punish is an important manifestation of the power to restrict personal liberty. By submitting to the overriding sovereignty of the United States, Indian tribes therefore necessarily give up their power to try non-Indian citizens of the United States except in a manner acceptable to Congress.

The Court recognized that the Indian Civil Rights Act, which applies to anyone tried in tribal court and the prevalence of crimes committed on reservations might argue for tribal criminal jurisdiction over non-Indians, but those ". . . are considerations for Congress to weigh in deciding whether Indian tribes should finally be authorized to try non-Indians." *Id.* at 12. The Court concluded, however those considerations were irrelevant to the issue of whether tribes retained the inherent power to try and punish non-Indians. Because tribes gave up that power, citizens of the United States who are not Indians cannot be subjected to a tribe's criminal jurisdiction. *Id.*

In *Wheeler*, decided shortly after Oliphant, the Court held a tribe had the inherent power to try and punish a member of the tribe. A tribe's "sovereign power to punish tribal offenders," while subject to congressional "defeasance," remains among those "inherent powers of a limited sovereignty which has never been extinguished." *Wheeler* 435 U.S. at 31 8.4 Later, in *Duro v. Reina*, 495 U.S. 676 (1990), the Court expanded its holding in *Oliphant* to include non-member Indians. It held that "the retained sovereignty of the tribe as a political and social organization to govern its own affairs does not include the authority to impose criminal sanctions against a citizen outside its own membership." *Id.* at 679. The Court affirmed its ruling in *Oliphant* that a tribe's power to criminally prosecute a non-member must be a delegation of that power from Congress and subject to the constraints of the Constitution. *Id.* at 686. The Court ruled, as American citizens, non-member Indians were not subject to the criminal authority of tribes were they could not become full tribal members. *Id.* at 692–93. The ruling was premised on a consent theory. Retained criminal jurisdiction over members is accepted by our precedents and justified by the voluntary character of tribal membership and the concomitant right of participation in a tribal government, the authority of which rests on consent. *Id.* at 694.

Congress immediately responded by overruling *Duro* in 1991. It amended the Indian Civil Rights Act to define tribal powers of self-government to include "the inherent power of Indian tribes, hereby recognized and affirmed, to exercise criminal jurisdiction over all Indians." 25 U.S.C. § 1301(2).

In 2004 the Supreme Court discussed the amendment, sometimes referred to as the "Duro fix", *see, e.g., Lara*, 541 U.S. at 216 (concurring opinion of Justice Thomas). Lara was an Indian charged with assaulting a police officer on the reservation where he lived but he was not a member of the tribe. *Id.* at 196. The tribe prosecuted Lara for the offense. Later, after he served his sentence, the United States government charged him for committing the same crime. Lara argued that double jeopardy barred the federal government from prosecuting him. The Court ruled the "Duro fix" legislation was predicated on Congress' recognition of the "inherent" authority of tribes to prosecute all Indians. The Court determined Congress had the power to remove the restrictions it had previously placed on the tribes' "inherent" power to prosecute nonmember Indians. It held that because Congress affirmed that the tribal authority to prosecute non-member Indians was inherent and was not a delegation of power, under the dual sovereignty doctrine (footnote omitted) the Tribe and the federal government were separate sovereigns and therefore, double jeopardy did not bar Lara's prosecution in both tribal and federal courts. *Id.* at 210.

In concluding Congress removed the restrictions on a tribe's inherent power to prosecute a non-member Indian, the Court retreated from its earlier pronouncements in *Oliphant* and *Duro* that a tribe's criminal jurisdiction over nonmembers could only be exercised if Congress delegated that authority. The Court reasoned its earlier decisions holding tribes did not have the "inherent" power to criminally try a nonmember but retained the "inherent" power to criminally try their own members was judicially made federal common law that Congress could change. *Lara*, at 207. "*Wheeler*, *Oliphant*, and *Duro*, then, are not determinative because Congress has enacted a new statute, relaxing restrictions on the bounds of the inherent tribal authority that the United States recognizes." *Id.*

Generally, "[j]urisdiction to resolve cases on the merits requires both authority over the category of claim in suit (subject-matter jurisdiction) and authority over the parties (personal jurisdiction), so that the court's decision will bind them." *Ruhrgas AG v. Marathon Oil Co.*, 526 U.S. 574, 577 (1999). Subject-matter jurisdiction cannot be forfeited or waived "because it involves a court's power to hear a case." *United States v. Cotton*, 535 U.S 625. 630 (2002). Thus, parties cannot confer subject matter jurisdiction by consent. *California v. LaRue*, 409 U.S. 109 (1972); *Oven Equip. & Erection Co. v. Kroger*, 437 U.S. 365. 377. n. 21 (1978) (quoting *Am. Fire & Cas. Co. v. Finn*, 341 U.S. 6. 17 (1951)).

The requirement that a court have personal jurisdiction, however, flows from the Due Process Clause. U.S. Const. amend. V. The personal jurisdiction requirement recognizes and protects an individual's liberty interest. *Ins. Corp. of Ire. Ltd. V. Compagnie des Bauxiles de Guinee.* 456 U.S. 694. 701 (1982). "As [t]he personal jurisdiction requirement recognizes and protects an individual liberty interest . . . it can, like other such rights, be waived." *D.H. Chemical Co. v. Calderon*, 422 F.3d 827, 831 (9th Cir. 2005) (citations and internal quotation marks omitted). Due process rights can be waived only if the waiver is knowing and voluntary. *D. H. Orermyer Co. r. Frick Co.*, 405 U.S. 174, 175 (1972); *United States v. Navarro-Boltello*, 912 F.2d 31 8. 321 (9th Cir. 1990).

We have found no federal cases, however, squarely addressing the issue of whether a non-Indian can expressly consent to tribal criminal jurisdiction, nor has Congress expressly prohibited a Tribe from exercising its criminal jurisdiction over non-Indian who expressly consents to such jurisdiction. In *Oliphant*, *Duro* and *Lara*, the Court uses the term "inherent" power in the context of a Tribe's criminal jurisdiction. The Court has never explained whether that term means subject matter or personal jurisdiction or something else altogether. If it means subject matter jurisdiction, then regardless of whether Hjert consented, the Tribal court did not have jurisdiction and the trial judge correctly dismissed the cases on that basis. If, however, the Court is referring to personal jurisdiction or something akin to personal jurisdiction, then Hjert could waive his right not to be tried and punished for a violation of the Tribe's criminal laws.

The Court has relied on its judicially made federal common law holding in *Oliphant* in the context of a tribe's civil jurisdiction over a non-Indian. Those decisions restate that a tribal court does not have criminal jurisdiction over a non-Indian, but cast little light on whether the holding in *Oliphant* is based on a tribe's lack of subject matter or personal jurisdiction.

In *Montana v. United States*, 450 U.S. 544 (1981), for example, where the issue was the authority of the Crow Tribe to regulate hunting and fishing by non-Indians on lands within the Tribe's reservation but owned in fee simple by non-Indians, the Court explained its holding in *Oliphant* rested on the "general proposition" that the "inherent sovereign power of an Indian tribe do not extend to the activities of nonmembers of the tribe." *Id.* at 564–567. It concluded, however, there are exceptions to the "general proposition" a tribe has inherent civil adjudicatory jurisdiction when the nonmember enters into consensual relationships with the tribe or its members through commercial dealing, contracts, leases, or other arrangements, or when the nonmember's conduct threatens or has some direct effect on the political integrity, the economic security, or the health or welfare of the tribe. The Court distinguished its decision in *Oliphant* on the ground that *Oliphant* held tribes had no "inherent" authority over non-Indians in criminal matters.

In *Nat'l Farmers Union Ins. Cos. v. Crow Tribe of Indians*, 471 U.S. 845, 854 (1985), the issue was whether in a civil suit non-Indian defendants were required to exhaust their tribal court remedies before the federal court could decide whether to assume jurisdiction. The Court explained that "[i]f we were to apply the *Oliphant* rule here, it is plain that any exhaustion requirement would be completely foreclosed because federal courts would always be the only forums for civil actions against non-Indians." *Id.* at 854.

In *Nevada v. Hicks*, 533 U.S. 353 (2001), another case involving a tribe's civil adjudicatory jurisdiction over a non-Indian. Justice Scalia, the author of the lead opinion, cited *Oliphant* for the general proposition that a tribe's power does not extend to the activities of nonmember. He noted the "limitation on jurisdiction over nonmembers pertains to subject-matter, rather than merely personal jurisdiction, since it turns upon whether the actions at issue in the litigation are regulable by the tribe." 533 U.S. at 367, n. 8. The Court ruled "a tribe's inherent adjudicative jurisdiction over nonmembers is at most only as broad as its legislative jurisdiction." *Id.* at 367.

Although these decisions cite *Oliphant*, they do not identify whether a Tribe's lack of "inherent" authority over non-Indians means a lack of subject matter or personal jurisdiction. Justice Scalia's statement that the limitation on jurisdiction over nonmembers pertains to subject matter jurisdiction is dicta and was made in the context of a tribe's civil jurisdiction. *See Hicks*, 533 U.S. at 358. n. 2 ("Our holding in this case is limited to the question of tribal-court jurisdiction over state officers enforcing state law. We leave open the question of tribal-court jurisdiction over nonmember defendants in general.").

Justice Souter's concurrence in *Hicks*, however, suggests *Oliphant*'s "general proposition" that the "inherent" sovereign powers of an Indian tribe do not extend to the activities of nonmembers is grounded on a lack of personal jurisdiction. "The principle on which *Montana* and *Strate* were decided (like *Oliphant* before them) looks first to human relationships. . . ." *Hicks*, 533 U.S. at 381. Also, in *Oliphant*, the Court relied in part on Judge Isaac Parker's decision in *In Ex parte Kenyon*, 14 Fed. Cas. No. 7.720 (W.D.Ark.I 878) to support the proposition tribes did not have the "inherent" power to try non-Indians, "Judge Isaac C. Parker, who was District Court Judge for the Western District of Arkansas was constantly exposed to the legal relationships between Indians and non-Indians, held that to give an Indian tribal court jurisdiction of the person of an offender, such offender must be an Indian." *Oliphant* 435 U.S. at 200 (citing *Kenyon*, at 355). That holding suggests a tribe has legislative authority to adopt criminal laws, the subject matter, but does not have the jurisdiction to apply those laws to persons who are not Indians (personal jurisdiction). In *Duro*, the Court even recognized the possibility a nonmember might consent to a tribe's criminal jurisdiction. It did not, however, rule on that issue or what would constitute a valid consent. "We have no occasion in this case to address the effect of a formal acquiescence to tribal jurisdiction that might be made, for example, in return for a tribe's agreement not to exercise its power to exclude an offender from tribal lands." *Duro*, 495 U.S. at 689. Although the Court did not rule on the issue, recognizing the possibility a person could consent to a tribe's criminal jurisdiction likewise suggests it is a tribe's lack of personal jurisdiction or something akin to personal jurisdiction that prohibits its criminal jurisdiction over a non-consenting non-Indian.

That Tribes originally had the "inherent" power to preserve order and punish anyone within their territorial borders who violated their rules, which judicially made federal common law has restricted, is without question. "The tribes were self-governing sovereign political communities" but, after "[t]heir incorporation within the territory of the United States," the tribes could exercise their inherent sovereignty only as consistent with federal policy embodied in treaties, statutes, and Executive Orders, *Wheeler*, 435 U.S. at 322–323; *see also*, *McClanahan v. Arizona State Tax Comm.*, 411 U.S. 164, 172 (1973) ("It must always be remembered that the various Indian tribes were once independent and sovereign nations . . ."). "A sovereign nation has exclusive jurisdiction to punish offenses against its laws committed within its borders, unless it expressly or impliedly consents to surrender its jurisdiction." *Wilson v. Girard*, 354 U.S. 524. 528–30 (1957). "Indian tribes therefore necessarily *give up* their power to try non-Indian citizens of the United States except in a manner acceptable to Congress."

It will come as no surprise to Indian law practitioners that federal common law governing a tribe's criminal (as well as civil) jurisdiction is inconsistent and defies a reasoned legal analysis. We find, however, based on our survey of that law, that while it lacks clarity there are some basic principles that lead us to conclude that tribes have subject matter jurisdiction over criminal offenses committed on tribal land, and the "general proposition" that tribes lack the "inherent" power to try and punish non-Indians is referring to personal jurisdiction.

Those principles are summarized as follows: 1. Tribes have the power to adopt laws proscribing criminal activity on tribal lands and as self-governing sovereign political communities had the inherent power to try and punish anyone within their territory who violated those laws, but upon treating with the United States that power was impliedly restricted or given up where the person who committed the violation is a non-Indian: 2. Tribes still retain inherent authority to try and punish members and Indians who violate their criminal laws based on consent: and 3. Tribes retain the inherent power to exclude nonmembers from tribal lands for criminal activity. Thus tribes have authority over criminal activity committed on tribal lands (the category of claim in suit), whether committed by an Indian or non-Indian, and therefore subject matter jurisdiction.

Because a tribe's lack of authority to try and punish a non-Indian for a violation of the tribe's criminal laws is in the nature of its lack of personal jurisdiction and because personal jurisdiction can be waived, the Port Gamble S'Klallam Tribe can exercise criminal jurisdiction over a non-Indian if there is a valid waiver of the personal jurisdiction requirement. We therefore hold "applicable federal law" does not prohibit the Tribe's assertion of criminal jurisdiction over a consenting non-Indian.

The second question is whether the Port Gamble S'Klallam Tribe has vested its Community Court with the authority to assert the Tribe's criminal jurisdiction over a consenting non-Indian. Title 1 of the Port Gamble S'Klallam Tribe Community Court General Rules provides "[t]he Port Gamble S'Klallam Community Court is vested with the fullest personal, subject matter and territorial jurisdiction *permissible under applicable law.*" PGSTC 1.02. There is no Port Gamble S'Klallam Tribal law expressly permitting criminal jurisdiction over a consenting non-Indian.

> There is no statute or code provision that authorizes the Community Court to assert the Tribe's criminal jurisdiction over a consenting non-Indian, or establishes what the Tribe's prosecutor may or may not promise on behalf of the Tribe in exchange for a non-Indian's consent and when and under what circumstances the prosecutor can make any such promises. Given the absence of such affirmative statutes or codes, we find the Tribe has not vested the Community Court with criminal jurisdiction over consenting non-Indians. Such jurisdiction is not permissible under applicable Tribal law.
>
> In addition, even if Tribal law permitted the court to exercise criminal jurisdiction over a non-Indian who consents to jurisdiction in exchange for a benefit, such an agreement is more than a simple common law contract. It concerns fundamental constitutional rights protected under the equal protection and due process provisions of the Indian Civil Rights Act. 25 U.S.C.A. § 1302 (a)(8). The person's waiver of the right to be free from the Tribe's criminal jurisdiction cannot be coerced, induced by misrepresentation, or implied, but must be freely and expressly given, knowing, voluntary, intelligent and case specific (in other words a valid waiver must be obtained each time the Tribe wants to assert criminal jurisdiction). *See Johnson v. Zerbst*, 304 U.S. 458. 464 (waiver means "an intelligent relinquishment or abandonment of a known right or privilege"). The record must show the waiver meets due process and equal protection guarantees under the Indian Civil Rights Act.
>
> ### III. Conclusion
>
> As the Tribe's appellate court, our responsibility is to interpret the Tribe's laws consistent with its Constitution, the intent of the Tribe's legislative body and the Indian Civil Rights Act. It is the Tribe's intent to vest its court with jurisdiction over any person who violates its criminal laws except where prohibited by federal law and as permitted by Tribal law. The Tribe has not specifically permitted its court to exercise criminal jurisdiction over a consenting non-Indian as required under PGSTC 1.02.01. And, even if it had, Hjert's "consent" to the Tribe's criminal jurisdiction does not meet the minimum due process requirements necessary to constitute a valid waiver of his right not to be criminally tried and punished by the Tribe. For these reasons we affirm the trial court's order dismissing the charges in these cases, albeit on other grounds. See PGSTC 7.08.01 (appellate court may reverse, affirm or modify the trial court's decision and take "any other action as the merits of the case and the interest of justice may require.").

Civil Contempt Power

Tribal judges have the inherent power to respond to people who disobey court orders through contempt power. Thus, if a non-Indian disobeys a tribal court order, she may face consequences from the judge.

Ute Indian Tribe's Civil Contempt Power

The following acts or failures to act may serve as the basis for finding an individual or other entity in contempt of court:

1. *Disorderly, contemptuous, or insulting behavior toward a Judge while holding Court, which tends to interrupt the course of the proceedings or undermine the dignity of the Court.*
2. *A breach of the peace, or loud or boisterous conduct which tends to interrupt the course of a judicial proceeding.*
3. *Misbehavior in office, or other willful neglect or violation of duty as a counselor, attorney, or other spokesman, or a clerk, court administrator, police officer or other person appointed, elected, or hired to perform a representative, judicial or ministerial service in connection with the operation of the Court.*
4. *Deceit, or abuse of process or proceedings of the Court by a party or counselor to a judicial proceeding.*
5. *Disobedience to a lawful judgment, order or process of the Court.*
6. *Assuming to be an officer, spokesman or other official of the Court and acting as such without authority.*
7. *Rescuing or taking any person or property from the Court or an officer acting under Court order, contrary to the order of the Court.*
8. *Unlawfully detaining or otherwise interfering with a witness or party to an action while such person is going to or from a Court proceeding or attending Court.*
9. *Disobedience of a subpoena duly served, or refusing to be sworn or answer as a witness.*
10. *Any other interference with the process, proceedings, or dignity of the Court or a Judge of the Court while in the performance of his official duties.*

Ute Indian Tribe Law and Order Code § 1-4-1 (1988).

Exclusion or Banishment of Non-Natives

Tribes generally have the authority exclude or remove any individuals from tribal lands. Tribes often use this power to exclude non-Native criminal offenders to prevent them from repeating criminal behavior and thus protecting. For banishment or exclusion of Native people, please refer to chapter 27.

The following tribal statutes demonstrate the exclusion rules of particular tribes.

Grounds for Exclusion for the Oglala Lakota Tribe

Oglala Sioux Tribe Law and Order Code Ch. 10 § 2 (1996).
Non-members of the Oglala Sioux Tribe may be excluded on one or more of the following grounds:

A. *Commission of a crime, as defined by Federal, State, or Tribal law, including violation of State or Tribal traffic regulations.*
B. *Unauthorized **prospecting**.*

C. Unauthorized trading.
D. Unauthorized mining, timber cutting, or other activity causing physical loss or damage of any nature to property on the Pine Ridge Reservation.
E. Forcible entry into the home or onto the land of any Tribal member without the consent of the occupant or occupants.
F. Interference with or photographing of Tribal ceremonies without the permission of the Tribal members involved.
G. Commission of fraud, confidence games, or usury against Tribal members, or inducing such members into grossly unfavorable contracts of any nature.
H. Recruiting Tribal members for off-Reservation employment without prior permission of the President of the Tribal Council and the Superintendent.
I. Defrauding any Tribal member of just compensation for his or her labor or services of any nature done at the request of the non-member.
J. Breach of the peace or repeated public drunkenness.
K. Contagious disease.
L. Entry of an area on the Pine Ridge Reservation in violation of an order of the President of the Tribal Council and the Superintendent, designating such area as closed because of fire hazard or any other reason.
M. Removal or attempted removal of any Tribal member under the age of eighteen (18) from the Pine Ridge Reservation without prior approval of the Tribal Council, except for the purpose of attending school under a non-sectarian program approved by the Bureau of Indian Affairs. Provided, however, that this ground for exclusion shall not apply in cases where such minor Tribal member is removed from the Pine Ridge Reservation by its adopted parents, or by persons who have received custody of such child pursuant to an order of the Oglala Sioux Tribal Court.
N. Conducting missionary activities without prior authorization from the Tribal Council.
O. Hunting, fishing, or trapping without permits required under State and Tribal laws.
P. Failure or refusal to pay any taxes, costs or other charges justly due the Oglala Sioux Tribe after reasonable notice and opportunity to pay.

Civil Forfeiture Laws

Some tribes also use civil forfeiture laws against non-Natives to regulate their behavior. Civil forfeiture laws authorize a tribe to acquire property that is by its nature illegal (a machine gun), or property that is used in an illegal manner (a boat used for smuggling), or property used as part of a crime (a car used in a robbery). A conviction is not needed for a tribe to acquire property through civil forfeiture, and ownership of the property does not matter. By taking property, such as cars used to transport drugs or alcohol, the tribe can halt illegal behavior without using criminal law. Since the tribe is merely acquiring the property in a civil process, the restrictions on criminal jurisdiction against non-Natives do not apply.

Sault Ste. Marie Civil Forfeiture Law
Proceedings for the civil remedial forfeiture of property shall be instituted by the filing of a complaint in rem against the property in Tribal Court by an enforcing officer. A complaint shall be filed whenever such officer has a reasonable basis to believe that a Tribal Code provision has been breached and that the property is forfeitable under Tribal law.

Sault Ste. Marie Tribal Code § 84.301 (1995).

Red Cliff Band's Civil Forfeiture Code

4.5.1   *All actions to recover forfeitures for violations are civil actions in the name of the Red Cliff Band, and shall be heard in the Red Cliff Tribal Court.*

4.5.2   *A forfeiture action may be commenced either by issuance of a violation notice or by a complaint and summons.*

4.5.3   *Service upon a suspected violator of a violation notice by an enforcement officer in connection with a violation is adequate process to give the Red Cliff Tribal Court jurisdiction over the person, upon the filing of the violation notice with the Court and provided the violation notice states which regulation has been violated and the time and place that a hearing will occur.*

Red Cliff Band Tribal Code § 4.5.1-4.5.3

The following case demonstrates how tribal civil forfeiture law was used to sanction a non-Native drug dealer on the Tulalip reservation:

Tulalip Tribal Court of Appeals
The Tulalip Tribes v. 2008 White Ford Econoline Van (2013)
Respondent in rem Alfred Luongo, Registered Owner and Appellant.
11 Am. Tribal Law 199
PER CURIAM:

Appellant, Alfred Luongo, seeks reversal of the July 6, 2012 Order of the Tulalip Tribal Court in which the Tribal Court ordered that a 2008 Ford Econoline Van owned by Appellant be forfeited to the Tulalip Tribes (hereinafter also "Appellee") under the civil forfeiture provisions of Chapter 2.15 of the Tulalip Tribal Code. This Court holds that the excessive fines clause of the Indian Civil Rights Act applies to civil forfeitures under Chapter 2.15, and we remand this matter to the Tribal Court for a determination of whether the forfeiture of Appellant's van constitutes an excessive fine in this case.

Discussion
Mr. Luongo, a non-Indian and the registered owner of the vehicle that the trial court ordered forfeited in this case, advertised the sale of medical marijuana in

the Tulalip area in an on-line ad on Craigslist.com. An undercover Tulalip police officer noticed the ad and arranged to meet with Mr. Luongo on the reservation to make a purchase. Mr. Luongo met with the officer in a WalMart parking lot on the reservation and showed the officer a bag containing less than one ounce of marijuana, but refused to sell the marijuana to the officer at the time, and instead made arrangements to meet the officer later to complete the transaction. Upon leaving the WalMart, Mr. Luongo was arrested and his vehicle seized by a second Tulalip police officer. In his answer, testimony, notice of appeal, and a letter filed supplementing his notice of appeal, Mr. Luongo, age 68, claims this was his first experience in selling marijuana and that he was misled into believing his selling of medical marijuana was legal. He argues that he was entrapped by the Tulalip Police, that the forfeiture constitutes an excessive penalty, and he pleads for mercy. However, aside from certain details concerning the nature of the sting and arrest, Mr. Luongo does not contest the fundamental factual allegation that he used his vehicle to transport and facilitate the sale of a controlled substance on the Tulalip reservation.

Mr. Luongo's arguments on appeal can be fairly boiled down to (1) he was drawn onto the reservation by Tribal Police and therefore entrapped; and (2) the forfeiture of his van constitutes excessive punishment. The Tribe concedes Mr. Luongo raised both of these claims before the trial court, and they are both clearly articulated in his Notice of Appeal and his brief (though he provides no legal citations to support his rhetoric on either issue). We address each argument in turn below.

II. Entrapment

As the Tribes note, federal courts have "consistently adhered to the view ... that a valid entrapment defense has two related elements: government inducement of the crime, and a lack of predisposition on the part of the defendant to engage in criminal conduct." *Mathews v. United States*, 485 U.S. 58, 62–63, 108 S.Ct. 883, 99 L.Ed.2d 54 (1988) (citations omitted). The Tribes further argue that the defense of entrapment "has been recognized as unique to criminal law" and is therefore not available to Mr. Luongo in this is, a civil in rem proceeding against property. We do not share the Tribes' certainty that the defense of entrapment is "unique" to criminal law and therefore inapplicable to a civil proceeding.

Turning to the facts of this case, the entrapment defense is of no avail to Appellant. The trial court allowed both parties to present evidence in regards to Mr. Luongo's claim that he was entrapped. A printout of an email introduced into evidence by the Tribes establishes that it was Mr. Luongo, not the police, who first suggested a meeting place on the reservation (the food court at the Tulalip Outlet Mall). Mr. Luongo claims he later tried to persuade the undercover officer to meet him at Lake Goodwin, a location which Mr. Luongo testified is about a mile north of the reservation boundary. Ultimately, however, Mr. Luongo agreed to meet the undercover officer at the WalMart on the reservation based on no more than his email and telephone discussions with the officer. The undercover officer testified that during the meeting in the WalMart parking lot, Mr. Luongo asked the officer if he was a police officer and if their conversation was being recorded. Moreover, Mr. Luongo's written answer to the complaint and his testimony under oath establish that the marijuana he sought to sell was from a grow operation that had been left for him at his house as a means to settle a debt, and that his house is within the boundaries of the Tulalip reservation. Thus, regardless of the meeting place for the sale itself, Mr. Luongo himself confirmed that his intent was to transport a controlled substance within the boundaries of the Tulalip reservation.

After observing the witnesses and reviewing the evidence, the trial judge specifically found that the Tulalip Tribal Police did not go out into the state jurisdiction and bring Mr. Luongo onto the reservation for purposes of seizing his vehicle. The judge further found that in asking the undercover officer if he was a cop, Mr. Luongo showed knowledge that his activities might be illegal and that the vehicle was being used for an illegal purpose. This Court defers to the trial court's determination of witness credibility, and the trial court's findings of fact "shall be sustained unless clearly erroneous." TTC 2.20.090. We find no error in the judge's findings of fact. Based on this record, there can be no question that Mr. Luongo was predisposed to transport a controlled substance within the exterior boundaries of the Tulalip reservation in violation of TTC 2.15.010(1)(a)(iv).

Therefore, regardless of any concerns this Court may have regarding the tactics employed by the police in this case, there is no basis for this Court to overrule the trial court's finding that Mr. Luongo was not entrapped.

Because we affirm the trial court's ruling that Mr. Luongo was not entrapped, we need not rule definitively on the question of whether entrapment or entrapment-like defenses are available in TTC 2.15.010 forfeiture proceedings.

III. Excessive Fines Doctrine

The Indian Civil Rights Act (ICRA) provides that no Indian tribe in exercising powers of self-government shall "require excessive bail, impose excessive fines, or inflict cruel and unusual punishments." 8 25 U.S.C. 1302(a)(7)(A). Although the Tulalip Tribes do not appear to have expressly adopted the provisions of ICRA in toto, as have some other tribes (at least in regards to tribal members), 9 various provisions of the Tulalip Code and Constitution do recognize the applicability of ICRA and other aspects of federal law in Tulalip Tribal Court proceedings. See, e.g., TTC 2.05.020(2) (long arm jurisdiction consistent with ICRA); TTC 2.40.010(3) (exclusion power consistent with ICRA); TTC 8.10.310 (hunting violation penalties limited by ICRA); TTC 8.05.380 (fishing violation penalties limited by ICRA); TTC 2.05.030(2) (federal law may be utilized as a guide where no Tulalip Tribal law, ordinance, or custom law can be found); Constitution and

Bylaws for the Tulalip Tribes of Washington, Preamble (exercise of home rule to be not inconsistent with federal laws).

In his Notice of Appeal, Mr. Luongo argues the forfeiture of his van constitutes "excessive punishment, a constitutional protection I am being denied." Similarly, his written brief argues that forfeiture constitutes "undue and excessive punishment." Although we find no explicit reference to ICRA or the excessive fines clause by Mr. Luongo in the trial court proceedings, he did argue during the hearing on the merits that the forfeiture is an "unfair price to pay" for any transgression he might have committed. The "Verifiable [sic] Answer" Mr. Luongo filed with the trial court and his testimony at the hearing described in some detail his purchase of the van, the investments he had made in the van, and the importance of the van to his ability to earn income and as a potential shelter in light of his concerns that he might lose his home. Luongo's Verifiable Answer asserted that "[t]aking my truck ... would be a crushing blow to my struggle for survival." In light of the fact that Mr. Luongo appeared pro se and that TTC 2.20.030(1) commands that the court rules be construed to protect the rights of individuals, secure simplicity in procedure, and secure the just and inexpensive determination of every civil matter; this Court concludes that Luongo's testimony and evidence was sufficient to preserve for appeal the issue of whether the forfeiture constituted an excessive fine.

Although Appellant has not presented the Court with legal authority concerning the excessive fines doctrine, the Tribes have. The Tribes argue that the Tribes' civil forfeiture procedure is a "purely remedial" civil statute, and "not a punitive statute" that would implicate the excessive fines clause of either the Eight Amendment or ICRA. However, the lead case cited by the Tribe, *Austin v. United States*, 509 U.S. 602, 113 S.Ct. 2801, 125 L.Ed.2d 488 (1993), directly contradicts the Tribes' argument. As the Tribes acknowledge, the Austin Court held that where asset forfeiture is at least part punitive, it is subject to analysis under the excessive fines clause. However, the Austin decision goes much further than that. Austin holds that, with the exception of the forfeiture of contraband materials (as opposed to a vehicle used to transport the contraband), virtually all forfeiture statutes are at least partly punitive in nature. The Austin decision also states that this is particularly so for forfeiture statutes that (1) provide for an "innocent owner" defense, and (2) are tied directly to the commission of drug offenses. *Austin*, 509 U.S. at 615–620, 113 S.Ct. 2801. Here, the Tulalip forfeiture statute is, of course, directly tied to drug offenses, and includes an "innocent owner" defense. TTC 2.15.010(1)(e)(2). Thus, under the Tribes' own theory of the case, the excessive fines clause of ICRA is applicable to forfeiture proceedings under TTC 2.15.010.

This Court agrees with the Tribe that TTC 2.15.010 forfeiture proceedings serve "a myriad of public policy objectives that are remedial in nature," including "incapacitating illegal drug sales through removing conveyances used to facilitate the possession or transport of non-prescribed controlled substances." This Court further recognizes that in light of federal law restricting tribal criminal jurisdiction over non-Indians, civil forfeiture statutes are an especially important tool in tribal efforts to incapacitate illegal drug sales by non-Indians. Nonetheless, as the Austin Court stated, "[w]e need not exclude the possibility that a forfeiture serves remedial purposes to conclude that it is subject to the limitations of the Excessive Fines Clause." 509 U.S. at 610, 113 S.Ct. 2801.

[4] Based on the reasoning of Austin, supra, we now hold that the excessive fines clause of the Indian Civil Rights Act, 25 U.S.C. 1302(a)(7)(A) does apply to civil forfeiture proceedings under TTC 2.15.010.

The trial court did not address Mr. Luongo's excessive fines argument in either in its written judgment or its ruling from the bench. As noted above, TTC 2.20.090(7) states the imposition of a forfeiture "shall be reviewed as a discretionary determination of the Tribal Court," while TTC 2.20090(8) provides that "[a] matter which is within the discretion of the Tribal Court shall be sustained if it is reflected in the record that the Tribal Court exercised its discretionary authority, applied the appropriate legal standard to the facts, and did not abuse its discretion." Here, in failing to rule on appellant's excessive fines claim, the trial court did not fully exercise its discretionary authority or apply the appropriate legal standard to the facts in regards to the claim. We therefore remand this matter to the trial court for additional fact-finding as to the value of Mr. Luongo's van and a ruling as to whether the forfeiture of the van was excessive in light of the facts of this case.

Conclusion

Not every tribal nation struggles with crimes committed by non-Indians. However, some statistics suggest that non-Indian violent crime is a problem for many communities. Until Congress reverses the decision in *Oliphant*, tribal governments sometimes need to use other forms of regulation to hold offenders accountable.

Questions

1. Of the examples of addressing jurisdiction gaps discussed in the chapter, what do you think is the best option?
2. In *Eastern Band of Cherokee Indians v. Torres*, what did the Court use as legal authority to support exercising jurisdiction over the defendant? Do you think this legal reasoning would be successful in other tribal courts?
3. In *Means v. District Court*, how did the Navajo Supreme Court use its treaty to establish criminal jurisdiction?
4. In *Port Gamble S'Klallam Tribe v. Michael Hjert*, why did the Court of Appeals decide that consent was insufficient to establish jurisdiction over the defendant?
5. What were the arguments raised by the owner of the van in the Tulalip case? How did the court respond to those arguments?

In Your Community
1. How does your tribe deal with jurisdiction gaps or non-Natives who commit crimes in your tribal community?
2. Does your tribal code include a civil forfeiture statute? If not, do you think this would be an effective way to address some criminal behavior in your community?

Terms Used in Chapter 8
Contempt: An act that obstructs a court's work or lessens the dignity of the court.
Forfeiture: Losing the right to do something or own something because of an offense.
In rem: Latin term meaning "thing." Describes a lawsuit brought to enforce rights in a thing.
Prospecting: To look over; explore or examine something (such as the prospect a district for gold).
Stipulation: A condition or requirement in a contract or agreement.

Suggested Further Reading
Catherine Baker-Stetson, "Decriminalizing Tribal Codes: A Response to Oliphant," 9 *American Indian Law Review* 41 (1981).

Geoffrey C. Heisey, "Oliphant and Tribal Criminal Jurisdiction over Non-Indians: Asserting Congress' Plenary Power to Restore Territorial Jurisdiction," 73 *Indiana Law Journal* 1051 (1998).

Henry S. Noyes, "A Civil Method of Law Enforcement on the Reservation: In Rem Forfeiture and Indian Law," 20 *American Indian Law Review* 307 (1995).

Philip H. Tinker, "In Search of a Civil Solution: Tribal Authority to Regulate Nonmember Conduct in Indian Country," *Tulsa Law Review* (forthcoming 2014).

Hallie Bongar White, Kelly Gaines Stoner, and James G. White, "Creative Civil Remedies Against Non-Indian Offenders In Indian Country" (2008). http://www.swclap.org/uploads/file/d03f27dc405e4a0aa821aedf4bc7bd04/Creative%20Civil%20Remedies%20Against%20Non-Indian%20Offenders%20In%20Indian%20Country.pdf.

Criminal Jurisdiction as Defined by Tribal Courts

Chapter 9

Criminal jurisdiction is a question many tribal courts address every day. The tribal court cases in the following text give examples of the jurisdictional issues addressed by tribal courts. Courts must determine whether the crime occurred in Indian country; territorial jurisdiction; who is an Indian, which often merges personal and subject-matter jurisdiction; status; whether a person can consent to criminal jurisdiction; who must prove Indian; and whether a treaty provides jurisdiction. Treaty jurisdiction and consent are covered in chapter 8.

Did the Crime Occur in Indian Country?

Most tribal courts only exercise jurisdiction over crimes that happen in their territory. As a result, proving that the crime happened in Indian country is one important aspect of a criminal case. The Fort Peck Court of Appeals analyzed territorial jurisdiction in the following case. The case demonstrates how a court can examine their constitution and codes to determine the extent of their jurisdiction.

Fort Peck Court of Appeals
Fort Peck Assiniboine and Sioux Tribes v. Jesse Martell, No. 090 (1990)
OPINION by Arnie A. Hove, Chief Justice, joined by Gary James Melbourne, Associate Justice and Floyd G. Azure, Associate Justice.

On or about April 7, 1989, Martell is alleged to have used coercive methodology to have intercourse with a 14 year old female. Martell is alleged to have transported the 14 year old female to Havre, Montana [outside the reservation] and use alcohol and or drugs in the process to coerce the 14 year old to have intercourse with him. Martell was also alleged to be an adult tribal member.

...

The addendum to the motion contends the tribal court lacks jurisdiction under I CCOJ 106 because the alleged offense did not occur on this reservation. . . .

On November 28, 1989, the tribal court granted defendant's motion to dismiss with prejudice. The reason given for the dismissal was it could not be reasonably argued that any element of the offenses charged were committed on the reservation.

The tribal court's order of dismissal presented several issues and what appear to be statements of law and/or fact. A statement of the issue is, "Whether the Fort Peck Tribes have subject matter jurisdiction of a crime allegedly committed partly off reservation or partly on reservation."

The relevant statements of fact discussed in the order are discussed in the following. It is alleged one or more elements of a certain crime occurred on reservation, while other elements occurred off reservation. The Tribes intend to prove defendant removed the alleged victim from this reservation to have intercourse with her off the reservation and return her to the reservation.

The relevant statement of law is discussed in the following. There seems to be no barrier in Tribal or Federal Law to prosecution in extra-territorial crimes.

The issues to be addressed by this Court are as follows:

1. Whether the tribal court has jurisdiction of a criminal offense where elements of the offense occurred on and off the reservation. . . .

The Fort Peck Tribes' jurisdiction over criminal offenses is set forth in the tribal code at I CCOJ 106. This section reads:

> The Court shall have jurisdiction over all offenses by an Indian committed within the boundaries of the Fort Peck Indian Reservation against the law of the Tribe as established by duly enacted ordinances of the Tribal Executive Board.

In reviewing the briefs and memorandum certain matters are uncontested. There is no barrier in tribal law to the exercise of the Fort Peck Tribes' jurisdiction over criminal offenses where elements of the offense are committed partly within the reservation. From the Indian Law Clinic Memorandum, there is no barrier in federal law to the exercise of jurisdiction by the Fort Peck Tribes over an offense committed partly within the reservation.

In addition, the Fort Peck Tribes' constitution does not prohibit the exercise of criminal jurisdiction over an offense when part of that offense occurred off the reservation. The constitution does not specifically address the issue, however, Article VIII, Section 5 authorizes the Tribal Executive Board to enact a law and order code. This section reads in full:

> To provide, subject to the review of the Secretary of the Interior, or his authorized representative, for the maintenance of law and order and the administration of justice by establishing tribal courts and police force, and defining the powers and duties of same, and to promulgate criminal and civil codes or ordinances governing

the conduct of the members of the tribes and non-member Indians residing within the jurisdiction of the tribes.

In any event defendant was charged with rape under III CCOJ 208. This section reads in applicable part as follows:

A person who engages in a sexual act with another, or who causes another to engage in a sexual act, is guilty of rape if:

(a) the defendant compels the other person to submit by force or by any threat that would render a person of reasonable firmness incapable of resisting; or
(b) the defendant or someone else, with the defendant's knowledge, has substantially impaired the other person's power to appraise or control that person's conduct by administering or employing, without the other person's knowledge, intoxicants, drugs or another similar substance with intent to prevent resistance;

The facts alleged in the complaint charging rape are as follows: (1) The defendant is a tribal member and is an adult over 19 years old. (2) Using coercive methodology the defendant did have intercourse with a 14 year old female. (3) The defendant transported the 14 year old female to Havre, Montana on or about 4-7-89. (4) The defendant did use alcohol and or drugs in the process to coerce the 14-year-old-female to have intercourse with him. (5) The use of alcohol and or drugs was done with the intent to lever [sic] the resistance level of the victim if indeed she was legally capable of resisting. Elements of the offense as charged could have occurred on and off the reservation.

In conclusion, if the facts demonstrate elements of the offenses of rape or statutory rape occurred partly on the reservation, then the tribal court could properly exercise jurisdiction. However, it is recommended that to avoid jurisdiction challenges in situations similar to the instant case, ordinances should be adopted addressing the same.

. . .

The tribal courts motion to dismiss the tribes' complaints against the defendant is reversed. This matter is remanded to tribal court for amendments to the charges and a trial on the merits.

Who Is an Indian? Personal and Subject-Matter Jurisdiction

In addition to establishing territorial jurisdiction, tribal courts must determine whether the defendant in a criminal case is Indian or not, due to the U.S. Supreme Court's decision in *Oliphant*. Although part of tribal sovereignty is the authority to define tribal membership, or define who qualifies for citizenship, questions often arise about people who might not qualify for enrollment but have a relationship with the tribe and whether or not they are "Indian" for the purposes of exercising criminal jurisdiction. There is now a major exception to the *Oliphant* rule that tribes may only exercise criminal jurisdiction over Indians. See chapter 10 for information about the Violence Against Women Act (VAWA) and jurisdiction over non-Indians who commit acts of domestic violence. The cases in this chapter were decided prior to the signing of VAWA.

The following cases include decisions about who qualifies as an "Indian" for the purposes of exercising criminal authority. Courts often address the problem that *Oliphant* created, tying together subject-matter jurisdiction (whether the court has authority to hear a case involving a certain crime) and personal jurisdiction (whether the court has jurisdiction over a non-Native) by looking to tribal citizenship. However, when a person is not an enrolled tribal member or citizen, tribal courts sometimes look to how federal courts define "Indian" for purposes of criminal jurisdiction under the Major Crimes Act. But before determining what evidence may be considered, courts often address whether the tribe must prove the defendant is an Indian or whether the defendant has the **burden** to raise the issue.

Who is an Indian?

The Cherokee Trial Court Qualla Boundary
Eastern Band of Cherokee Indians v. Lambert (2003)
003.NACE.0000003 (VersusLaw)

The Defendant moved to dismiss this case on the grounds that the Court lacked jurisdiction over her, as she is not an enrolled member of any federally recognized Indian Tribe. The parties stipulated to this fact, and to the fact that the Defendant is recognized, politically, by the Tribe as a "First Lineal Descendent" (First Descendent). . . .

The Defendant argues that *Oliphant v. Suquamish Indian Tribe*, et al., 435 U.S. 191 (1978) prohibits this Court from exercising criminal jurisdiction over her. To be sure, in *Oliphant*, the Supreme Court held that Indian tribal courts do not have criminal jurisdiction over non-Indians. Id. at 195. Then, in *United States v. Wheeler*, 435 U.S. 313 (1978), a case decided shortly after *Oliphant*, the Supreme Court reaffirmed Tribal courts' jurisdiction over tribal members. In *Duro v. Reina*, 495 U.S. 676 (1990), the Supreme Court ruled that the Indian Tribes also lacked the authority to prosecute non-member Indians for criminal acts.

Immediately after Duro issued, Congress amended the Indian Civil Rights Act (ICRA). The effect of this amendment was to "revis[e] the definition of 'powers of self-government' to include 'the inherent power of Indian tribes, hereby recognized and affirmed, to exercise criminal jurisdiction over all Indians.'" *United States v. Lara*, 324 F., 3d 635 (8th Cir. 2003) (en banc); 25 U.S.C. §

1302(2). Thus, as amended, ICRA clarifies that Indian nations have jurisdiction over criminal acts by Indians, regardless of the individual Indian's membership status with the charging Tribe.

Having established that the several Tribes are vested with jurisdiction over alleged criminal acts by Indians, the Court next must consider whether the Defendant is an Indian for the purposes of such jurisdiction. The Court concludes that she is.

Pursuant to 25 U.S.C. § 1301(4) an "'Indian' means any person who would be subject to the jurisdiction of the United States as an Indian under section 1153 of Title 18 if that person were to commit an offense listed in that section Indian country to which that section applies." 18 U.S.C. § 1153 does not provide further definition. In *Duro*, the Supreme Court noted that "the federal jurisdictional statutes applicable to Indian country use the general term 'Indian.'" *Duro*, 495 U.S. at 689. Even earlier, the Supreme Court construed such a term to mean that it "does not speak of members of a tribe, but of the race generally, of the family of Indians." *United States v. Rogers*, 45 U.S. (4 How.) 567, 573 (1846). In *Rogers*, the Supreme Court recognized that, by way of adoption, a non-Indian could "become entitled to certain privileges in the tribe and make himself amenable to their laws and usages."

The same concept is true here. By political definition First Descendents are the children of enrolled members of the EBCI [Eastern Band of Cherokee Indians]. They have some privileges that only Indians have, but also some privileges that members of other Tribes do not possess, not the least of which is that they may own possessory land holdings during their lifetimes, if they obtain them by will. During this time, the Government will honor its trust obligations with respect to First Descendents who own Tribal Trust lands. Also, First Descendents have access to Tribal educational funds, with certain limitations, and may appeal the adverse administrative decisions of Tribal agencies. Like members of other tribes, First Descendents may apply for jobs with the EBCI and receive an Indian preference and they may also address the Tribal Council in a similar manner as members of other Tribes. Of course, it almost goes without saying that First Descendents may, as this Defendant has, seek recourse in the Judicial Branch of Tribal Government. Most importantly, according to the testimony of Councilwoman McCoy, First Descendents are participating members of this community and treated by the Tribe as such.

Defendant relies heavily on the fact that she cannot vote or serve in Tribal Government (and presumably, although she did not argue it, serve on a jury in the Cherokee Court) to support her position that she should not be treated as an Indian for the purposes of this Court's criminal jurisdiction. And while it is true that members of other Tribes may participate in their respective governments, membership in a Tribe is not an "essential factor" in the test of whether the person is an "Indian" for the purposes of this Court's exercise of criminal jurisdiction. *United States v. Driver*, 755 F. Supp. 885, 888-89, aff'd, 945 F.2d 1410, cert. denied, 502

U.S. 1109 (1991), accord Rogers, see also, *United States v. Dodge*, 538 F.2d 770, 786 (8th Cir. 1976), cert. denied, 429 U.S. 1099 (1977). Rather, the inquiry includes whether the person has some Indian blood and is recognized as an Indian. Id. The second part of the test includes not only whether she is an enrolled member of some Tribe, but also whether the Government has provided her formally or informally with assistance reserved only for Indians, whether the person enjoys the benefits of Tribal affiliation, and whether she is recognized as an Indian by virtue of her living on the reservation and participating in Indian social life. Id.

Applying this test in this case, the Court can only conclude that the Defendant meets the definition of an Indian pursuant to 25 U.S.C. § 1301(4). Accordingly, the Court has jurisdiction over the Defendant in this case.

Who Must Prove Indian Status?

The two cases below disagree who has the burden to prove Indian status in a criminal case. Examine their reasoning and consider why the Hopi Court disagrees with the Navajo Nation Court.

Supreme Court of the Navajo Nation
Navajo Nation v. Cynthia Hunter (1996)
7NAV. R 194
Before Yazzie, Chief Justice, Austin and Cadman, Associate Justices.
The opinion of the court was delivered by: Yazzie, Chief Justice.

The charges arose out of an incident where a citizen saw drunken activity and also saw individuals put two cases of beer in a vehicle at Waterflow, New Mexico. Upon the citizen's report to a Navajo police officer, the officer followed the reported vehicle and saw it speeding and weaving in and out of traffic. The officer stopped the vehicle within the territorial jurisdiction of the Navajo Nation. Upon inspecting the vehicle, the officer saw packages of liquor and seized forty-seven cans of beer. Upon a proper inquiry about the identity of the passengers, the officer discovered that two were male minors who were 15 and 16 years of age. They were visibly intoxicated.

The district court found culpability in Hunter's role in obtaining the liquor, giving it to the minors, importing it into the Navajo Nation and permitting the minors to participate in the criminal offenses of possession, delivery and consumption of liquor.

Hunter contends that at trial, she made a motion for acquittal on the ground that the Navajo Nation failed to prove, beyond a reasonable doubt, that she was a "person" within the meaning of the criminal law.

The issue is who has the burden of proof to show that a defendant is or is not an "Indian" for purposes of jurisdiction. We will also address the method of proof to be used and the scope of the term "Indian" for purposes of criminal jurisdiction.

II.

. . .

The definition of "person" in the Criminal Code "includes any natural Indian individual." 17 N.T.C. § 208(17). Navajo law does not require affirmative proof of the terms "person" or "Indian" as an element of any crime. The statute which addresses criminal culpability, 17 N.T.C. § 211, provides only as follows: "A person shall not be guilty of an offense unless he acted intentionally, knowingly, recklessly, or negligently as the law may require with respect to each material element of the offense." That section does not require the prosecution to prove personal status as a material element, and the exclusion of it as a condition of culpability evidences the Navajo Nation Council's intent that such, is not required. This section is read with 17 N.T.C. § 206, which requires that each element of the offense must be proved beyond a reasonable doubt. That means each and every material element of the statute which constitutes the offense. In other words, the prosecution need only prove the conduct which is prohibited by the statute (along with the required mental state), as material elements.

This analysis is reinforced further by the territoriality statute, 17 N.T.C. § 203. It provides that the Navajo Nation courts have jurisdiction over "any person" who commits an offense "if the conduct constituting any element of the offense" occurs within the territorial jurisdiction of the Navajo Nation.

. . . The rules give a defendant an opportunity to challenge the court's jurisdiction at any time, but place the burden of proof upon the defendant to show a lack of jurisdiction. The burden was on Hunter to show, by a preponderance of the evidence, that she was not an "Indian" for purposes of 17 N.T.C. § 208(17). (footnote omitted)

A.

It is unreasonable to require the Navajo Nation to prove that an individual is an "Indian" because that information is in the hands of the defendant or more readily obtained by the defendant. It is difficult or impossible for the prosecution to ascertain someone's ancestry or to survey the defendant's community to find its perceptions of his or her personal status. We construe the definition of "person" as being an "Indian" to mean the following:

> Recognizing the possible diversity of definitions of "Indian-hood," we may nevertheless find some practical value in a definition of "Indian" as a person meeting two

qualifications: (a) that some of his ancestors lived in America before its discovery by the white race, and (b) that the individual is considered an Indian by the community in which he lives. Felix S. Cohen, *Handbook of Federal Indian Law*.

We add to the definition that if a non-Navajo individual assumes tribal relations with Navajos or the Navajo Nation in our territorial jurisdiction, as discussed below, that person is deemed to be an Indian for purposes of jurisdiction.

B.

The prosecution may not be able to question a defendant about ancestry due to the privilege against self-incrimination. We do not decide that issue here. The privilege is not jeopardized by the burden we place upon defendants in this case. Rule 26 of the Navajo Rules of Evidence (1978) provides several methods of proof of "Indian-hood" where the availability of the declarant is immaterial. The rule addresses the situation where the declarant cannot be the defendant, if he or she invokes the privilege against self-incrimination. The methods of proof include records of regularly conducted activity (No. 6), absence of entry in records of regularly conducted activity (No. 7), public records and reports (No. 8), absence of public record or entry (No. 10), (footnote omitted) records of religious organizations (No. 11), marriage, baptismal and similar certificates (No. 12), family records (No. 13), and reputation on personal or family history (No. 19).

The last exception, reputation on personal or family history, is also known as pedigree evidence. Where a question of whether a person is an "Indian" arises, testimony about a person's ancestry can be used. In *Hudgins v. Wrights*, 1 Henning & Munford's Rpts. 133 (Va. 1806), the court permitted individuals to testify about their percentage of Indian blood, color and features and the fact they were descendants of a free Indian woman, to obtain freedom from slavery. (footnote omitted) In *State v. Rackich*, 119 P. 843 (Wash. 1911), involving the crime of illegal sale of liquor to an Indian, the prosecution was permitted to put on testimony that the person to whom the liquor was sold was one-half Portuguese and one-half Indian. In *United States v. Mid-Continent Petroleum Corp.*, 67 F. 2d 37 (10th Cir. 1933), the issue was whether parties to an intestate probate of an allotment could testify about their parentage to establish they were "Indian" heirs. The court ruled that "[e]vidence of declarations, tradition, and reputation is admissible to provide facts as to genealogy or pedigree." Id. at 45. In *Ware v. Beach*, 322 P.2d 635 (Okla. 1957), where a husband elected against his wife's will and his ability to inherit was challenged on the ground he was not an "Indian," the court said, "The question here involved is, strictly speaking, race or race-ancestry rather than pedigree. The rule as to proof of race ancestry is not so strict as the rule as to proof of pedigree. Evidence as to the general reputation in the community concerning the race of a member of the community is competent." Id. at 639. Finally, in Matter of R.M.B., 689 P.2d 281 (Mont. 1984), an Indian Child

Welfare Act case, the Montana Supreme Court upheld use of statements by out-of-court declarants under the Montana Rules of Evidence to determine if a child was an "Indian child" within the meaning of that Act.

We approve the use of proof of ancestry and community reputation as an "Indian" under the Criminal Code. We hold that the defendant has the burden, by a preponderance of the evidence, to prove he or she is not an "Indian" for purposes of challenging the jurisdiction of the court.

. . .

The Shiprock District Court judgments are AFFIRMED.

Appellate Court of the Hopi Tribe
In Matter of Certified Question, Case No. 98AC00004 (2001)
3 Am. Tribal 423
Before, Sekaquaptewa, Chief Justice, and Lomayesva and Abbey, Justices

I. Is the Element of "Indianness" Required?
To determine if the element of Indian status is a required element for the prosecution of a crime under Section 3.3.75, this Court looks to the statute itself.

A. Section 3.3.75

Section 3.3.75 states that "[t]he Arizona Act Regulating Traffic on Highways (Arizona Statutes 28-401 et seq.) is hereby incorporated into this Code by reference together with all amendments which have been or which may be made" (footnote omitted) See Ordinance 21, Title 3, Section 3.3.75. Reviewing the Arizona statutes, the term "Indian" is never mentioned in any of the laws. Rather, only the term "person" is used to designate the individuals who can be prosecuted under the law. Reading the statutes literally, since the term "Indian" is not used, it is not an element that the Prosecution has to prove in their case in chief. Further, since Section 3.3.75 only states that the Arizona statutes were incorporated into the Hopi Code without mentioning any changes in the statutes, this Court is to assume that the Tribal Council did not want to change the wording of the statute. With this in mind, it is the conclusion of this Court that the element of "Indianness" is not a required element pursuant to Section 3.3.75.

II. "Indianness" Is a Jurisdictional Issue
Since it is determined that "Indianness" is not an element under Section 3.3.75, the next issue is whether "Indianness" is an issue at all in any trial proceeding.

In Hunter, (footnote omitted) the Navajo Supreme Court held that the issue of "Indianness" was a matter to be considered under the court's criminal jurisdiction.

See *Navajo Nation v. Cynthia Hunter*, [N.L.R. Supp. 429 (Nav. Sup. Ct. 1996)], page 4. The proposition that "Indianness" is a jurisdictional issue is consistent with the Supreme Court's holding in *Oliphant v Suquamish Indian Tribe*, where the Court held that the Indian tribes had no general criminal jurisdiction over non-Indians. See *Oliphant v Suquamish Indian Tribe*, 435 U.S. 191 (1978). This Court similarly holds that the Indian status of the defendant must be determined to establish the tribal court's criminal jurisdiction.

A. Where Does the Burden Fall?

With the determination that "Indianness" is a jurisdictional issue, the more difficult question is with respect to the allocation of the burden of proof.

i. *The Burden Falls on the Defendant.* In its Brief, the Prosecution, citing Hunter, argues that the burden should fall on a defendant to prove the element of "Indianness." See Hopi Tribe's Position on Certified Question of Law, page 2. As reason for their position, the Prosecution asserts that:

"[r]equiring the Tribe to prove that such individuals are Indians for the purposes of establishing jurisdiction puts an undue burden on the Hopi Tribe. This forces the Tribe to attempt to obtain Certificates of Indian blood or enrollment information from Nations across the West, from Arapahoe to Zuni and every Tribe in between. This can be a significant impediment to prosecution when the Tribe in question may not be able to provide the information or worse yet, will not cooperate in releasing said information." Id. at 2.

The Prosecution's position is consistent with the Navajo Supreme Court's decision in *Hunter*. In Hunter, the Supreme Court held that it would be "unreasonable to require the Navajo Nation to prove that an individual is an 'Indian' because that information is in the hands of the defendant or more readily obtained by the defendant." See *Navajo Nation v Hunter*, N.L.R. Supp. 429 (Nav. Sup. Ct. 1996), page 5. In addition, the situation would be further complicated by the fact that the Prosecution may not be able to question the defendant about his or her status due to the privilege against self-incrimination. Id. at 6. See also Ordinance 21, Title II, Section 2.8.5. (footnote omitted)

After considering the Prosecution's argument and the holding of the Navajo Supreme Court in Hunter, we see a number of problems in adopting *Hunter's* holding. First, how would a defendant prove that he or she is not an Indian? Such a task would be difficult, time-consuming and financially burdensome to the defendant. As stated infra, an Indian is defined as "any person who is an enrolled member of any Federally recognized tribe or who has Indian blood and is regarded as an Indian by the society of Indians among whom he lives." See also Ordinance 21, Title III, Section 3.1.1 To prove that he or she is not an Indian, a defendant must first show that he or she is neither an enrolled member of any federally recognized tribe nor has Indian blood. This would require the defendant to produce the roll sheets of every Indian nation associated with the defendant and demonstrate that the defendant is not listed. Further, a defendant must produce his or her lineage to demonstrate that she has no Indian blood—this could possibility [sic] require the defendant to produce numerous generations to prove that he or she has no percentage of Indian blood. This is no simple task even if this Court assumes that a defendant would retain such quality information regarding his or her family tree. Once a defendant has fulfilled this requirement, the defendant must then demonstrate that he or she is not regarded as an Indian by the society of Indians among whom he or she lives. This would seem to be the easier of the two requirements to fulfill since the defendant can easily have neighbors sign affidavits stating that the defendant is not considered an Indian in their community.

Once the defendant demonstrates that he or she is not an Indian, the prosecution would be allowed to rebut the defendant's position. This would lead to another problem that the Prosecution and the Navajo Supreme Court did not seem to consider. Once a defendant has made a case that he or she is not Indian, the prosecution has to present evidence to challenge the defendant's position and persuade the judge that the defendant is an Indian. To present such evidence, the Prosecution must first find the evidence. Thus, the Prosecution has to commit their efforts to finding the defendant's possible enrollment in a tribe or defendant's Indian blood. Further, the prosecution has to interview individuals in defendant's community to determine if he or she is considered an Indian. Consequently, one of the main reasons the Navajo Supreme Court and Prosecution cited for holding that the burden should fall on the defendant is cut down. Regardless of who carries the burden, the prosecution still has to commit to the tough task of finding a defendant's Indian status to either rebut the defendant's position or to carry the burden.

ii. Burden on the Defendant to make a threshold showing and then shift the burden to the Prosecution. To balance the interest of the parties, this Court believes that the burden should first fall on the defendant and then shifts to the prosecution once the defendant has made a threshold showing that he or she is not an Indian. Under this option, the defendant would have to raise the issue and then create a reasonable belief that he or she is not an Indian. Once the defendant fulfills this requirement, the burden will shift to the prosecution to prove beyond a reasonable doubt that the defendant is an Indian.

This position is consistent with the Ninth Circuit Court of Appeal's opinion in *United States v Hester*. (footnote omitted) In *Hester*, the defendant was charged with crimes under the Federal Enclaves Act, 18 U.S.C. § 1152 for sexually related crimes. See *United States v. Hester*, 719 F. 2d 1041, 1042 (9th Circuit, 1983). The Federal Enclaves Act provides for the prosecution of crimes committed in Indian country by non-Indians against Indian. However, the Act also provides that its coverage "shall not extend to offenses committed by one Indian against the person or property of another Indian." See 18 U.S.C. § 1152. (footnote omitted) With respect to this law, the court held that the prosecution did not have to raise the issue of Indian status to determine if the defendant fell into the exception provided by the Act. The court's holding was based on the finding that:

> "[i]t is more manageable for the defendant to shoulder the burden of producing evidence that he is a member of a federally recognized tribe than it is for the Government to produce evidence that he is not a member of any one of the hundreds of such tribes." Id. at 1043

The court went on to hold that "[o]nce the defendant properly raises the issue of his Indian status, then the ultimate burden of proof remains, of course, upon the Government." Id.

The decision in Hester is persuasive in informing this court of the federal position on this issue. However, Hester is unclear on the type of burden the defendant had to carry and the degree of proof the defendant had to show to "raise the issue."

1. Type of Proof and Degree of Proof

The first question this Court has to answer is the type of proof the defendant is required to carry. Reviewing the decisions in Hester, it would be clear that the defendant has the burden of raising the issue. Once the defendant raises the issue, he has the burden to produce sufficient evidence to raise a reasonable belief on the part of the judge that the defendant is not an Indian. Allocating the burden in this manner is justified since the defendant would be the moving party on this issue. Once the defendant has made this threshold showing, the burden then shifts to the prosecution to carry the ultimate burden of proof in persuading the judge that the defendant is an Indian.

This option would be best to balance the interests of both defendants and prosecutors. Further, this arrangement is favorable on the grounds of policy and possession of proof. It is the policy of the law to discourage further litigation. As a result, the party that usually asserts a particular defense or argument is generally assigned the burden. In addition, the task of carrying this burden should be simple for the defendant. He is the party who is mostly likely to have or have access to the evidence needed to prove the fact.

This arrangement will also be favorable for the Prosecution since it will decrease the likelihood that defendants will file frivolous motions raising the issue of jurisdiction and thereby place the burden on the prosecution to prove the defendant's Indian status. Otherwise, the prosecution will be required to prove the Indianness of the defendant in every case it prosecutes under Section 3.3.75. This will not only lead to the further depletion of the prosecution's resources by also the lost [sic] of valuable court resources to maintain such hearings.

The next major issue facing this court is with respect to the degree of proof. For a defendant to shift the burden to the prosecution, the defendant should be required to demonstrate to the judge that there is a reasonable belief that the defendant is not an Indian. This degree of proof is best suited for the situation because of the flexibility that it offers the judge in considering the evidence. Further, the degree is not too burdensome on the defendant to attain and thus, seems fair to possible defendants who do not have the wealth of resources like the prosecution.

In proving his Indian status, the defendant is not limited to the type of evidence he or she is allowed to show. Given the different prongs of the test, the evidence provided to the court will vary from case to case. To create a rigid standard of proof and method to weigh the evidence would run counter to the fluid nature of the evidence. With this reasonable belief standard, the judge is able to weigh the different evidence presented and not require the defendant to prove every prong to a specific standard. Rather, if one source of evidence is very strong then the judge may balance this with the other prongs to determine if there is sufficient proof of the defendant's non-Indian status.

Once the defendant has created a reasonable belief, the burden shifts to the prosecution to persuade the judge that the defendant is an Indian. To sufficiently carry this burden, the prosecution must demonstrate beyond a reasonable doubt that the defendant is an Indian. This burden is consistent with the prosecution's burden throughout the criminal proceedings.

In establishing this standard of proof, this Court referred to *Morrison v. United States*. (footnote omitted) In *Morrison*, the United States Supreme Court, citing to earlier decision in the same case, held "that within limits of reason and fairness the burden of proof may be lifted from the state in criminal prosecution and cast on a defendant." See *Morrison v. California*, 291 U.S. 82, 88. The Court's rationale is based upon a "balancing of convenience or of the opportunities for knowledge the shifting of the burden will be found to be an aid to the accuser without subjecting the accused to hardship or oppression." Id. at 89. In this case, the Supreme Court acknowledge the difficulty the state would face in proving that the person's citizenship since "[i]n all likelihood his life history would be known only to himself and at all times to relatives or intimates unwilling to speak against him." Id. at 88.

II. Definition of "Indian"

The next pertinent question for this Court is what is the definition of an Indian. To define an Indian, this Court will look at Hopi Ordinance 21.

Ordinance 21, Title III, Section 3.1.1 defines "Indian" as "any person who is an enrolled member of any Federally recognized tribe or who has Indian Blood and is regarded as an Indian by the society of Indians among whom he lives."

This definition of "Indian" is consistent with definitions given by federal case law. In *United States v. Driver*, (footnote omitted) the federal court held that the test of whether a person is an "Indian" for criminal jurisdictional purpose turns on whether the person has some Indian blood and whether the person is recognized as an Indian.

Since the Tribal Council has clearly defined "Indian" in Ordinance 21 and the definition is consistent with federal law, this Court will accept the definition of "Indian" under Ordinance 21.

Conclusion

Judges must always determine if they have jurisdiction over an offense and offender prior to hearing the case. As the cases demonstrate, offenders often challenge the court's jurisdiction. In addressing the jurisdiction question, judges will look to federal law's limitations on tribal jurisdiction (discussed in Chapter 7) and their tribal law's grant or definition of jurisdiction.

Questions

Fort Peck v. Martell
1. Did this crime occur in Indian country?
2. How was the Court of Appeals able to justify exercising jurisdiction over the defendant?
3. Do you agree that the tribes should have jurisdiction in this case? Why or why not?

Eastern Band of Cherokee Indians v. Lambert
1. In the *Lambert* case, what reasoning did the Court use to determine that the band has criminal jurisdiction over First Descendants?

Navajo Nation v. Hunter and *In Matter of Certified Question*
1. Which Court do you agree with, Navajo Nation in *Hunter*? Or the Hopi Court in *In Matter of Certified Question*? Explain your reasoning.

In Your Community

1. How does your tribe define "Indian"? Who is required to provide evidence to the court on this matter?
2. Does your nation have an **implied consent** law? If not, how would you write one for the tribal council?
3. Who has the burden of proof for Indian status in your tribal court?
4. How does your tribe define *territorial jurisdiction*?
5. Do any of the treaties between your nation and the United States address criminal jurisdiction? If yes, how is criminal jurisdiction addressed in the treaty?

Terms Used in Chapter 9

Amicus curiae: Latin term meaning "friend of the court"; a person who is allowed to appear in a lawsuit even though the person is not a party to the lawsuit.

Burden: The requirement that to win a point you must show that the weight of the evidence is on your side.

Implied Consent: A presumption or inference, based on signs, actions, facts, or inaction or silence, that consent has been given.

Suggested Further Reading

Lindsey T. Golden, "Embracing Tribal Sovereignty to Eliminate Criminal Jurisdiction Chaos," 45 *U. Mich. J. L. Reform* 1039 (2012).

Kevin Meissner, "Modern Problems of Criminal Jurisdiction in Indian Country," 17 *American Indian Law Review* 175 (1995).

Chapter 10

Tribal Criminal Jurisdiction Reform: The Tribal Law and Order Act and the Violence Against Women Act

Both the Indian Civil Rights Act (ICRA) and the Supreme Court decision in *Oliphant v. Suquamish* have long frustrated tribal leaders who seek to address criminal behavior in their nations. After years of lobbying Congress to address the restrictions on jurisdiction, tribal leaders are beginning to find success in the power of Congress to recognize inherent tribal criminal jurisdiction.

This chapter focuses on two important federal laws passed during the Obama administration: the Tribal Law and Order Act (TLOA) and the 2013 Violence Against Women Act reauthorization (VAWA). These laws were passed, in part, due to the high rates of violent crime in tribal nations. The federal legislation also begins to signal that the restrictions that have been placed on tribal criminal authority are inconsistent with self-government. However, these laws do not fully address all of the criminal jurisdiction concerns of tribal governments. Many tribal leaders and advocates hope that this legislation will become part of a longer era of support for tribal courts. Others are skeptical about the motives or ability of the federal government to address the problem.

Fortunately, the legislation is written in such a way that tribal governments can decide whether or not to comply with the requirements in the statute. In other words, tribes are not automatically bound by the new laws. This is a basic change of framework for federal law in this area. In the past, the federal government **unilaterally** made decisions that affected tribal nations. With these new laws, the federal government may be signaling an era of partnership in which tribal leaders and state and federal leaders work together as equals to address criminal behavior. This chapter covers some of the basic changes in the law that are relevant to tribal courts.

The original 2013 "Special Domestic Violence Jurisdiction" contained a provision that would have prevented most Alaska tribes from exercising the restored jurisdiction. Fortunately, Congress corrected this exemption in a 2015 law, and now Alaska tribes also can exercise special domestic violence jurisdiction, provided they meet all the requirements in the law.

Statistics and History

Beginning in 1999, the U.S. Department of Justice began to release some alarming national data about violent crime committed against Native people. By gathering data from various sources (including victim surveys), the federal government determined that Native people suffer the highest **per capita** rate of violence in the United States. For example, studies have demonstrated that Native women experience the highest rates of domestic violence and sexual assault in the nation.

Many Native people were not surprised by this data because it confirmed the sad reality they had been living with for decades. However, journalists and Congress took notice of the high rates of violence. This did two things. First, it signaled the problem to the public at large. Second, it opened more conversations about violent crime within tribal communities. For decades, these high crime rates had gone largely unnoticed from the outside world.

In 2007, Amnesty International—a global human rights organization—issued a report entitled "Maze of Injustice: The Failure to Protect Indigenous Women from Sexual Violence in the USA." This report brought national and international attention to high crime rates on Indian reservations. Soon thereafter, several legislative initiatives were launched. Two senators in particular, Byron Dorgan and Daniel Akaka, led efforts to document the impact of high crime in tribal nations.

The Senate Committee on Indian Affairs began to hold hearings about the high rates of crime in tribal communities. Tribal leaders and victim advocates were invited to testify in front of Congress about the hardships and triumphs. Tribal leaders communicated directly with Congress about the need for reform. Native women's and children's organizations as well as the National Congress of American Indians raised national awareness about the high crime rates. Specific legislation was proposed to restore authority to tribal courts and provide funding for victim advocacy.

Many (but not all) aspects of the proposed legislation became federal law. When TLOA and VAWA were signed into law, many celebrated with the hope that the inherent sovereignty of tribal nations will be able to respond to more crime and help more victims.

The following sections focus exclusively on the tribal sovereignty components of the new laws. The legislation also includes new rules for the federal government, such as mandatory reports on prosecution rates as well as new funding and training for BIA and tribal law enforcement.

The Tribal Law and Order Act: TLOA

TLOA was signed into law in July 2010. TLOA contained many provisions to reform criminal justice in Indian country. Tribal Court Sentencing (amending ICRA) changed the limits to tribal sentencing authority. The ICRA sentencing limitation now reads as follows:

Excerpts from ICRA as of 2014

§ 1302. *Constitutional Rights: No Indian tribe in exercising powers of self-government shall:*

(a) *In general*—No Indian tribe in exercising powers of self-government shall—
  (7)
  - (A) *require excessive bail, impose excessive fines, or inflict cruel and unusual punishments;*
  - (B) *except as provided in subparagraph (C), impose for conviction of any 1 offense any penalty or punishment greater than imprisonment for a term of 1 year or a fine of $5,000, or both;*
  - (C) *subject to subsection (b), impose for conviction of any 1 offense any penalty or punishment greater than imprisonment for a term of 3 years or a fine of $15,000, or both; or*
  - (D) *impose on a person in a criminal proceeding a total penalty or punishment greater than imprisonment for a term of 9 years;*

(c) *Rights of defendants*
In a criminal proceeding in which an Indian tribe, in exercising powers of self-government, imposes a total term of imprisonment of more than 1 year on a defendant, the Indian tribe shall—
  (1) *provide to the defendant the right to effective assistance of counsel at least equal to that guaranteed by the United States Constitution; and*
  (2) *at the expense of the tribal government, provide an indigent defendant the assistance of a defense attorney licensed to practice law by any jurisdiction in the United States that applies appropriate professional licensing standards and effectively ensures the competence and professional responsibility of its licensed attorneys;*
  (3) *require that the judge presiding over the criminal proceeding—*
    - (A) *has sufficient legal training to preside over criminal proceedings; and*
    - (B) *is licensed to practice law by any jurisdiction in the United States;*
  (4) *prior to charging the defendant, make publicly available the criminal laws (including regulations and interpretative documents), rules of evidence, and rules of criminal procedure (including rules governing the recusal of judges in appropriate circumstances) of the tribal government; and*
  (5) *maintain a record of the criminal proceeding, including an audio or other recording of the trial proceeding.*

(d) *Sentences*
In the case of a defendant sentenced in accordance with subsections (b) and (c), a tribal court may require the defendant –
  (1) *to serve the sentence—*
    - (A) *in a tribal correctional center that has been approved by the Bureau of Indian Affairs for long-term incarceration, in accordance with guidelines to be developed by the Bureau of Indian Affairs (in consultation with Indian tribes) not later than 180 days after July 29, 2010;*

>   (B) in the nearest appropriate Federal facility, at the expense of the United States pursuant to the Bureau of Prisons tribal prisoner pilot program described in section 304(c)[1] of the Tribal Law and Order Act of 2010;
>   (C) in a State or local government-approved detention or correctional center pursuant to an agreement between the Indian tribe and the State or local government; or
>   (D) in an alternative rehabilitation center of an Indian tribe; or
> (2) to serve another alternative form of punishment, as determined by the tribal court judge pursuant to tribal law.
> (e) Definition of offense
> In this section, the term "offense" means a violation of a criminal law.

TLOA requires tribal courts to protect these specific rights of criminal defendants in order to impose a sentence of more than one year:

- Effective assistance of counsel
- Free, appointed, licensed attorneys for indigent defendants
- Law-trained judges who are also licensed to practice law
- Publically available tribal criminal law and rules; and
- Recorded criminal proceedings

Many tribal governments already provide these rights, but some tribal governments may need to update their codes and procedures. TLOA also authorizes the attorney general to deputize tribal prosecutors and other experts in Indian law to serve as special assistant U.S. attorneys to prosecute Indian country crimes in federal court.

Section 201 of TLOA includes a special provision regarding tribes in the six mandatory PL280 states. Champagne and Goldberg explain how the legislation is intended to work:

> [T]ribes can ask the United States to reassume jurisdiction under the two main Indian country criminal statutes—the Indian Country Crimes Act and the Major Crimes Act. The Attorney General is allowed to accept or deny the request. Where such a request is granted, state jurisdiction remains, so there is three-way criminal jurisdiction—tribal, state, and federal. Although this provision does not achieve retrocession of state criminal jurisdiction under Public Law 280, it does open the possibility of greater tribal deputization under special BIA commissions to conduct federal law enforcement activities and greater access to BIA police and court funding. It may also make it easier for tribes to argue in favor of retrocession in the future, at least if the federal government is already assuming significant law enforcement and criminal justice responsibility. Finally, it may provide a partial remedy where tribes have difficulty securing adequate law enforcement and prosecutorial services from state and local governments. This section makes it clear that state duties to provide such services to Indian country under Public

Law 280 are not diminished. Several Public Law 280 tribes have expressed interest in invoking this provision, but it is too early to tell how widely it will be used or what the consequences will be.[1]

VAWA 2013

VAWA was originally passed by Congress in 1994 to address the high rates of gendered violence (domestic violence and sexual assault) throughout the United States. It has been amended several times—in 2000, 2005, and 2013. The 2013 version was a step forward in the restoration of tribal criminal authority over non-Indians.

Most notably, it authorizes tribes to exercise "special domestic violence criminal jurisdiction" over non-Indians. A "participating" tribe is a tribe that has opted to exercise this special domestic violence criminal jurisdiction.

Special Domestic Violence Jurisdiction

Indian Civil Rights Act
25 U.S. Code § 1304—Tribal jurisdiction over crimes of domestic violence

(a) Definitions
  In this section:
  (1) Dating violence
    The term "dating violence" means violence committed by a person who is or has been in a social relationship of a romantic or intimate nature with the victim, as determined by the length of the relationship, the type of relationship, and the frequency of interaction between the persons involved in the relationship.
  (2) Domestic violence
    The term "domestic violence" means violence committed by a current or former spouse or intimate partner of the victim, by a person with whom the victim shares a child in common, by a person who is cohabitating with or has cohabitated with the victim as a spouse or intimate partner, or by a person similarly situated to a spouse of the victim under the domestic- or family-violence laws of an Indian tribe that has jurisdiction over the Indian country where the violence occurs.
  (3) Indian country
    The term "Indian country" has the meaning given the term in section 1151 of title 18.
  (4) Participating tribe
    The term "participating tribe" means an Indian tribe that elects to exercise special domestic violence criminal jurisdiction over the Indian country of that Indian tribe.
  (5) Protection order
    The term "protection order"—
      (A) means any injunction, restraining order, or other order issued by a civil or criminal court for the purpose of preventing violent or threatening acts or harassment against, sexual violence against, contact or communication with, or physical proximity to, another person; and

(B) includes any temporary or final order issued by a civil or criminal court, whether obtained by filing an independent action or as a pendent lite order in another proceeding, if the civil or criminal order was issued in response to a complaint, petition, or motion filed by or on behalf of a person seeking protection.

(6) Special domestic violence criminal jurisdiction

The term "special domestic violence criminal jurisdiction" means the criminal jurisdiction that a participating tribe may exercise under this section but could not otherwise exercise.

(7) Spouse or intimate partner

The term "spouse or intimate partner" has the meaning given the term in section 2266 of title 18.

(b) Nature of the criminal jurisdiction

(1) In general

Notwithstanding any other provision of law, in addition to all powers of self-government recognized and affirmed by sections 1301 and 1303 of this title, the powers of self-government of a participating tribe include the inherent power of that tribe, which is hereby recognized and affirmed, to exercise special domestic violence criminal jurisdiction over all persons.

(2) Concurrent jurisdiction

The exercise of special domestic violence criminal jurisdiction by a participating tribe shall be concurrent with the jurisdiction of the United States, of a State, or of both.

(3) Applicability

Nothing in this section—

(A) creates or eliminates any Federal or State criminal jurisdiction over Indian country; or

(B) affects the authority of the United States or any State government that has been delegated authority by the United States to investigate and prosecute a criminal violation in Indian country.

(4) Exceptions

(A) Victim and defendant are both non-Indians

(i) In general. A participating tribe may not exercise special domestic violence criminal jurisdiction over an alleged offense if neither the defendant nor the alleged victim is an Indian.

(ii) Definition of victim. In this subparagraph and with respect to a criminal proceeding in which a participating tribe exercises special domestic violence criminal jurisdiction based on a violation of a protection order, the term "victim" means a person specifically protected by a protection order that the defendant allegedly violated.

(B) Defendant lacks ties to the Indian tribe

A participating tribe may exercise special domestic violence criminal jurisdiction over a defendant only if the defendant—

(i) resides in the Indian country of the participating tribe;

(ii) is employed in the Indian country of the participating tribe; or

(iii) is a spouse, intimate partner, or dating partner of—

(I) a member of the participating tribe; or

(II) an Indian who resides in the Indian country of the participating tribe.

(c) Criminal conduct
A participating tribe may exercise special domestic violence criminal jurisdiction over a defendant for criminal conduct that falls into one or more of the following categories:
   (1) Domestic violence and dating violence
   An act of domestic violence or dating violence that occurs in the Indian country of the participating tribe.
   (2) Violations of protection orders
   An act that—
      (A) occurs in the Indian country of the participating tribe; and
      (B) violates the portion of a protection order that—
         (i) prohibits or provides protection against violent or threatening acts or harassment against, sexual violence against, contact or communication with, or physical proximity to, another person;
         (ii) was issued against the defendant;
         (iii) is enforceable by the participating tribe; and
         (iv) is consistent with section 2265 (b) of title 18.
(d) Rights of defendants
In a criminal proceeding in which a participating tribe exercises special domestic violence criminal jurisdiction, the participating tribe shall provide to the defendant—
   (1) all applicable rights under this Act;
   (2) if a term of imprisonment of any length may be imposed, all rights described in section 1302 (c) of this title;
   (3) the right to a trial by an impartial jury that is drawn from sources that—
      (A) reflect a fair cross-section of the community; and
      (B) do not systematically exclude any distinctive group in the community, including non-Indians; and
   (4) all other rights whose protection is necessary under the Constitution of the United States in order for Congress to recognize and affirm the inherent power of the participating tribe to exercise special domestic violence criminal jurisdiction over the defendant.
(e) Petitions to stay detention
   (1) In general
   A person who has filed a petition for a writ of habeas corpus in a court of the United States under section 1303 of this title may petition that court to stay further detention of that person by the participating tribe.
   (2) Grant of stay
   A court shall grant a stay described in paragraph (1) if the court—
      (A) finds that there is a substantial likelihood that the habeas corpus petition will be granted; and
      (B) after giving each alleged victim in the matter an opportunity to be heard, finds by clear and convincing evidence that under conditions imposed by the court, the petitioner is not likely to flee or pose a danger to any person or the community if released.
   (3) Notice
   An Indian tribe that has ordered the detention of any person has a duty to timely notify such person of his rights and privileges under this subsection and under section 1303 of this title.

A participating tribe may exercise "special domestic violence criminal jurisdiction" over a non-Indian defendant for acts of domestic violence or dating violence that occur in the Indian country of the participating tribe and violations of protection orders that are violated in the Indian country of the participating tribe.

There are several standards that tribal courts must meet in order to allow federal approval of tribal jurisdiction. In a sense, this federal legislation encourages further assimilation of tribal courts. However, many tribal courts had already been exceeding these standards long before VAWA become law. The requirements are designed to address unsubstantiated concerns that tribal courts may violate fundamental rights without these requirements.

VAWA Requirements When Prosecuting "Special Domestic Violence Jurisdiction"

- All rights from TLOA (see preceding text).
- Protect the rights of defendants under ICRA, which largely tracks some of the U.S. Bill of Rights, including the right to due process.
- Include a fair cross-section of the community in jury pools and not systemically exclude non-Indians.
- Inform defendants ordered detained by a tribal court of their right to file a federal habeas corpus petition.

The following cases represent some of the very first efforts to exercise restored jurisdiction under TLOA and VAWA. As you review the cases, notice how the tribal judges are careful to make a good record of complying with the standards.

Chehalis Tribal Court of Appeals

Confederated Chehalis v. Lyons
No. CHE-CR 12/11-326 (2013)
Note: Confrontation Clause issue deleted so as to focus on TLOA compliance.

I. Background
On February 25, 2013, a jury convicted the defendant on two counts of indecent liberties, two counts of incest, two counts of assault, two counts of battery, and one count of rape. We address only two issues raised in the appeal: whether Mr. Lyons' right to confront witnesses at trial was violated by the admission of a Sexual Assault Report without the opportunity for him to cross-examine the nurse who drafted the Report; and whether the Tribe complied with the federal Tribal Law and Order Act of 2010 (TLOA) by making its criminal laws and rules of evidence available to the public prior to charging Mr. Lyons, and by maintaining a record of

the criminal proceedings, both of which are required under TLOA for Mr. Lyons to be sentenced to more than one year in jail in this criminal proceeding.

According to the testimony at trial of the alleged victim (hereinafter "A.V."), during the early morning hours of December 8, 2011, A.V. was at the Chehalis Tribe's casino gambling and drinking alcohol. When the casino was closing, A.V. and a male companion left to find more alcohol, but the stores were closed. A.V. then made arrangements through text messages to have Mr. Lyons, her cousin, meet her at a bus stop sign on the Chehalis reservation. Mr. Lyons and A.V. then walked to A.V.'s house. As they walked, Mr. Lyons put his arm around A.V. and attempted to touch her breasts, but she pulled away. When they arrived at her house, A.V. could not find her keys, so she called an aunt who had her keys and car to come and unlock her door. At approximately 3:30 a.m., while waiting for her aunt, A.V. and Mr. Lyons went to a shed behind the house. A.V. testified that while she was trying to open the shed, Mr. Lyons groped her, ripped her pants down, and had sexual intercourse with her. Mr. Lyons then sat down on a chair and A.V. sat down on him for sexual intercourse. She started to struggle and Mr. Lyons became angry. When the aunt arrived, they put their clothes back on.

The jury returned a not guilty verdict on this charge of rape and the trial court dismissed an assault charge and battery charge related to this portion of the incident.

According to A.V.'s testimony, after her aunt arrived, A.V. drove her aunt home with Mr. Lyons as a passenger in the car. A.V. then drove Mr. Lyons to a friend's house, and while sitting in the car, he grabbed A.V. around the neck, choked her and tried to kiss her. A.V. then drove back to her house with Mr. Lyons. She ran to her house, but Mr. Lyons followed her and forced his way inside the house. A.V. locked herself in the bathroom, but Mr. Lyons forced his way in. She then went to her bed, where Mr. Lyons then climbed on top of her. He had sexual intercourse with her. She rolled on her side, crossed her legs and said, "no" and "we are cousins." He tried to place her hand on his penis. She further testified that she tried to call her aunt and when that failed she dialed "911." She did not say anything on the 911 call, because at that point Mr. Lyons got up and dressed. She then went to the bathroom and locked the door. The police called back, but she did not answer. When the police called again, they told her they were at the door. She let them in, but by that time Mr. Lyons was gone.

At approximately 1:30 p.m. the same day, A.V. went to a hospital for a sexual assault exam. The exam was conducted by a nurse who recorded her examination and evidence collection on a pre-printed Sexual Assault Report Form. The nurse who prepared the Report was out of state during the trial and did not testify. The Report was admitted into evidence at Mr. Lyon's trial with **hearsay** statements of the victim contained in the Report redacted by the trial judge.

On February 28, 2013, the trial having concluded, the jury rendered the guilty verdicts on the nine counts as noted above. On March 11, 2013, two days prior to sentencing Mr. Lyons, the trial court issued a "Sentencing Order

RE: ICRA Compliance," in which the trial court stated that "the Tribe makes its codes and regulations available for public view at the Chehalis Tribal Court where defendant and counsel have full access to them, as well as being provided to the public defender for their office use." On March 13, 2013, Mr. Lyons received a sentence of one year in jail and a $5,000 fine for each count upon which he was convicted for a total of nine years of jail and $45,000 in fines, with six years jail time to be served and $30,000 in fines due, and three years of jail time and $15,000 in fines suspended.

II. Analysis
[Confrontation clause analysis deleted]

B. Tribal Law and Order Act Compliance and Sentencing

The second dispositive issue concerns whether appellant's sentence conformed to the Tribal Law and Order Act of 2010, 25 U.S.C. 1302 ("TLOA"). Mr. Lyons challenged whether the total consecutive terms of his sentences were in violation of the sentencing requirements of the TLOA, because the Chehalis Tribal criminal laws and rules of evidence used at trial were not available to the public prior to charging, and because the record of proceedings were not properly maintained.

1. Public availability of the Chehalis Tribe's criminal laws. Mr. Lyons was found guilty by a jury on two counts of Indecent Liberties, two counts of Incest, two counts of Assault, two counts of Battery, and one count of Rape. Each of the nine offenses carries a maximum jail term of 365 days under Chehalis Tribal law. He was then sentenced to nine years in jail with three years suspended for a total of six years to be served in jail. The TLOA, 25 U.S.C. 1302 (c)(4) requires:

In a criminal proceeding in which an Indian tribe . . . imposes a total term of imprisonment of more than 1 year on a defendant, the Indian tribe shall prior to charging the defendant, make publicly available the criminal laws (including regulations and interpretative documents), rules of evidence, and rules of criminal procedure (including rules governing the recusal of judges in appropriate circumstances) of the tribal government.

The Chehalis Tribe's Court Procedures were updated on March 8, 2011, and specifically address the availability of copies of the laws as follows

2: Copies of the laws of the Chehalis Tribe shall be available for use of spokespersons and individuals representing themselves before the court of justice. The business committee may establish a fee to cover the cost of copying the laws. CTC 2.1.9.070

It is clear that CTC 2.1.9.070 limits the availability of the criminal laws of the Tribe, which are therefore not publicly available as intended by the TLOA. By the terms of its own code, the Tribe's criminal laws are only available to spokespersons and individuals representing themselves. TLOA does not require that a tribe's criminal laws be available only to the individual being prosecuted, but requires that criminal laws be publicly available to anyone, with no exceptions or limitations.

The prosecutor represented to this Court during oral argument that anyone can obtain a copy of the Tribe's criminal laws by asking the Clerk of Court. TLOA places the responsibility on the Tribe to make its criminal laws publicly available. Court employees do not have the authority to contravene the public policy of the Tribe when the Tribe has clearly set forth in law that the criminal laws are available to only spokespersons and individuals representing themselves. Nonetheless, and notwithstanding the Tribe's own law to contrary, we look to the record of this case for evidence that the Tribe has implemented policies making its criminal laws publicly available.

There is no evidence in the record that the Tribe has implemented policies and procedures to comply with TLOA, 25 U.S.C. 1302 (c)(4), to make its criminal laws publicly available. The record shows that during a December 5, 2012 motion hearing, the relevant portion of the prosecutor's response regarding the Tribe's criminal laws being publicly available was as follows:

Since the beginning of the Tribe as recorded time, it was—all laws are common, known to all individuals by word of mouth. Later when they became documented, they're available to Tribal members, though not exposed to the outside world. Within the Tribal reservation, all they have to do is go to Public Safety or to the Court Clerk of the Tribe and any kind of law is available. Also, if you're a member of the Tribe, you can go on the website and you have a member ID, as far as I know you can also get the laws from there. 12/5/2012 RP 37-38.

In ruling on this issue at the motion hearing, the trial court provided no specific citation to a tribal law or policy making the Tribe's criminal laws publicly available. 12/5/2012 RP 62-64. The trial court added in its oral ruling regarding accessing the tribal laws, "I think even a non-Indian can." This statement shows a lack of certainty on the part of the trial judge that the Chehalis Tribe's criminal laws were in fact publicly available as intended by TLOA, and is certainly not evidence that they were.

On March 11, 2013, the trial court issued a Sentencing Order RE: ICRA Compliance. In its order, the trial court made the following finding in support of the Tribe's compliance with 25 U.S.C. §1302(c)(4): "the Tribe makes its codes and regulations available for public view at the Chehalis Tribal Court where defendant and counsel have full access to them, as well as being provided to the public defender for their office use." The finding by the trial court is consistent with CTC 2.1.9.070, but does not go as far as finding that the Chehalis criminal laws are available to the public as intended by TLOA. A trial court must make specific findings of fact that the Tribe has complied with all enhanced sentencing requirements before a defendant is charged.

Despite the prosecutor's representations to the Court, and despite the trial judge's "belief," there is no evidence in the record establishing whether and to what degree the Tribe's criminal laws are in fact available to the public. Therefore, this Court holds that the criminal laws and rules of evidence of the Chehalis Tribe were not publicly available prior to charging Mr. Lyons as required by 25 U.S.C. §1302(c)(4). The Chehalis Tribe was not in compliance with 25 U.S.C. §1302(c)(4), and therefore cannot impose a total term exceeding one year of imprisonment in these proceedings.

2. *Public availability of the rules of evidence.* Mr. Lyons also raised the issue of the Tribe's rules of evidence not being publicly available as required by the Tribal Law and Order Act of 2010, 25 U.S.C. 1302 (c)(4) for enhanced sentencing. The Tribe has very limited rules of evidence, which are included in the Tribe's Court Procedures ordinance. However, the Tribe's rules of evidence are not publicly available, because, per our discussion above, the rules of evidence are incorporated into the laws of the Tribe that are not publicly available. It is evident that the Tribe's limited rules of evidence are not sufficient to meet the requirements necessary to analyze and manage evidence in a jury trial involving sexual assault related crimes. Mr. Lyons points out that the court found it necessary to analyze evidentiary issues using the Federal Rules of Evidence. Although the Federal Rules of Evidence are publicly available, Mr. Lyons argues there was no prior notice in the Tribe's laws that the trial court could, or would, be applying the Federal Rules of Evidence. Therefore, he argues the use of the Federal Rules of Evidence by the trial court did not comply with the TLOA for enhanced sentencing.

The Congressional intent in enacting the TLOA of 2010 was to encourage the continued development and maturation of tribal courts. Tribes that comply with the requirements of the TLOA are permitted to exercise greater authority in sentencing defendants in criminal cases, provided that those tribes actively accept responsibility for ensuring that their laws are developed and applied in a manner found in justice systems that have developed rules of evidence and have their criminal laws and rules of evidence available to the public. Just as it would not be tolerated in state and federal courts to have minimal procedural rules and rules of evidence that could be supplemented at the discretion of a trial judge during trial, the TLOA of 2010 suggests that Congress also finds such practices unacceptable in tribal courts.

We therefore hold that the incompleteness of the tribes rules of evidence and the inevitable need to supplement rules of evidence in a criminal proceeding with rules of evidence taken from foreign jurisdictions on an ad hoc, case-by-case basis prevents the Tribe from satisfying the public availability requirement imposed by the TLOA of 2010 and therefore limits the authority of the trial court to impose a sentence in these proceedings of greater than one year.

3. Record of proceedings. The Tribal Law and Order Act of 2010, 25 U.S.C. 1302 (c)(5) requires that when an Indian tribe "[i]n a criminal proceeding in which an Indian tribe . . . imposes a total term of Title 2, Chapter 1, Section 2.1.12.010. CHE-CR 12/11-326, et al. imprisonment of more than 1 year on a defendant, the Indian tribe shall maintain a record of the criminal proceeding, including an audio or other recording of the trial proceeding." The Chehalis Tribal Court maintains an electronic recording system for its court proceedings. Here, the criminal proceedings involving Mr. Lyons, including his jury trial, was recorded and then later transcribed. There were gaps in the recording, which may have been due to human error or technical failure. Mr. Lyons does not argue on appeal that the unrecorded testimony was necessary to his defense on appeal, or that he was deprived of his ability to raise an error on appeal.

Therefore, this Court holds that the missing portions of the recording of the jury trial were not prejudicial to appellant's appeal. Even though portions of the electronic recording may have failed during the trial, nonetheless the Chehalis Tribal Court was in compliance with 25 U.S.C. § 1302 (c)(5) during the criminal proceedings involving Mr. Lyons. We further hold that the criminal laws and rules of evidence of the Chehalis Tribe were not publicly available prior to the charging of the defendant in this case as required for the Tribe to exercise the enhanced sentencing authority permitted by the federal Tribal Law and Order Act of 2010.

For the reasons set forth above, it is hereby ORDERED that the judgment and sentences of the trial court on all counts is hereby REVERSED and this case is REMANDED to the trial court for further proceedings consistent with this opinion.
Robert J. Miller, Chief Appellate Judge
Gregory M. Silverman, Judge
Randy A. Doucet, Judge

Pascua Yaqui Court of Appeals
In Re Pascua Yaqui Tribe, Petitioner (2014)
Writ of Mandamus regarding Pascua Yaqui Trial Court in Case No. CR-14-080 and CR-14-081
Opinion

I. Jurisdiction
1. This Court has jurisdiction to hear a writ of mandamus pursuant to PYT Constitution Article VIII , §2 and 3 PYTC §2-3-260.

II. Summary

2. The petition before this Court is unusual in that Petitioner Tribe filed an extraordinary **writ of mandamus** seeking an order to direct the Respondent, the Honorable Judge Stoof, to receive the Defendant's waiver of counsel on the record. "The remedy of mandamus is a drastic one, to be involved only in extraordinary situations." *Bauman v. U.S Dist. Court*, 557 F.2d 650, 654 (9th Cir. 1977) (citing *Will v. United States*, 389 U.S. 90, 95 (1967). Therefore, "only exceptional circumstances amounting to a judicial 'usurpation of power' will justify the in vocation of this extraordinary remedy." Id. "To warrant the court in issuing the writ it must appear that the petitioner has a clear legal right to the performance of the particular duties sought to be enforced and that it has no other plain, adequate and complete method of redressing the wrong or obtaining the relief to which it is entitled so that without the issuance of the writ there would be a failure of justice." See *Kay Ferer Inc. v. Hulen*, 160 F.2d 146, 149 (1947). Even if the Government has no right to appeal, the writ of mandamus should not be used as a substitute for an **interlocutory** appeal. See *Will v. United States*, 389 U.S. 90, 97 (citing *DiBella v. United States*. 369 U.S. 12 I, 130 (1962)). In this case, the Tribe could have sought to have the Tribal Court reconsider the request by way of motion, or alternatively the Tribe could have sought to have this Court rule on the matter by way of an interlocutory appeal. Instead, the Tribe is seeking judicial review, and while the foregoing options present a more suitable way to request a remedy, judicial efficacy requires consideration of the time to re-file under a more appropriate Code section and committing further judicial resources than have already been spent in this matter. This Court is not proceeding on the basis of mandamus; the writ of mandamus is denied. However, we will proceed on the basis of judicial efficacy and will address the issue of waiver of counsel as an interlocutory appeal. The Court of Appeals may suspend any Rules of Appellate Procedure and order proceedings in accordance with its discretion. 3 PYTC §2-3-50.

3. This case revolves around the issue of whether Ms. Molina is lay counsel, which by all accounts she is. In the instant case, the guiding provision this Court focused on, 3 PYTC § 1-4-50, provides that "Lay counsel shall be permitted to practice before the Pascua Yaqui Courts in criminal matters, only when the defendant has waived his right to counsel. Lay counsel shall be certified as provided in Section 20." Since Ms. Molina is lay counsel, and in light of the unique facts underlying this case, this Court is of the opinion that the learned Judge Stoof is required by the Pascua Yaqui Code to obtain the Defendant's waiver of counsel. As a procedural safeguard then, the waiver should be explicit and on the record. This case is remanded to the Tribal Court for compliance with this order.

III. Background

4. On November 18, 2013, Defendant was involved in an altercation with the victim, Ignacio Valenzuela. Defendant knocked the victim onto the ground and kicked him in the head and face. Another individual, Daniel Ramirez, began kicking the victim. The victim was unconscious, but Defendant and Ramirez continued kicking the victim. Defendant and Ramirez escaped in a green vehicle, which was later found with Defendant and Ramirez still inside. Blood was still on their shoes and pants. Defendant was searched and a plastic bag containing 6 small packaged plastic bags containing a white powdery substance, which tested positive for cocaine, were found. Defendant was charged by criminal complaint CR-14-080 with Count 1, assault, a violation of 4 PYTC § 1-130(A)(1); Count 2, aggravated assault, a violation of 4 PYTC § 1-130(8)(4); Count 3, battery, a violation of 4 PYTC § 1-150(A); Count 4, rout, a violation of 4 PYTC § 1-740; and Count 5, disorderly conduct, a violation of 4 PYTC § 1-580(A)(1). He was also charged by criminal complaint CR-14-081 with Counts 1 and 2, narcotics and dangerous drugs, a violation of 4 PYTC § 1-780(C), and Count 3, possession of drug paraphernalia, a violation of 4 PYTC § 1-790(A).

5. On November 18, 2013, Defendant appeared in custody for an initial hearing with his counsel Melissa Acosta, who requested that she be allowed to withdraw representation because of a direct conflict. The court granted Ms. Acosta's request and an arraignment was scheduled for November 27, 2013. On November 26, 2013, Lourdes Salomon Molina entered a Notice of Appearance as Defendant's lay advocate. At the November 27th hearing, the Defendant's decision to retain Ms. Molina was a significant factor that informed the interplay between the Tribe's duty to provide counsel pursuant to the Code on the one hand and the Tribal Law and Order Act (TLOA) on the other.

6. During the Arraignment hearing, the Tribe informed the court that it would seek a sentence in excess of one year under the TLOA. The applicable provisions require that an indigent defendant be provided, at the Tribe's expense, a defense attorney licensed to practice by any jurisdiction in the United States. The Tribe stated that pursuant to TLOA, the Defendant was entitled to a state bar licensed attorney and that a waiver on the record or in writing was necessary in order for Ms. Molina to continue as his counsel. Judge Stoof ordered a five-minute break to allow Ms. Molina to explain the situation with her client with respect to the Tribe's position on sentencing, the TLOA provisions, and the Defendant's entitlement to a state licensed attorney.

7. Once the proceedings came back on the record, the learned Tribal Judge pointed out that 25.U.S.C.§ 1302(c) of the TLOA provides the following:
    (c) RIGHTS OF DEFENDANTS. In a criminal proceeding in which an Indian tribe, in exercising powers of self-government, imposes a total term of imprisonment of more than 1 year on a defendant, the Indian tribe shall—
    (1) provide to the defendant the right to effective assistance of counsel at least equal to that guaranteed by the United States Constitution; and
    (2) at the expense of the tribal government, provide an indigent defendant the assistance of a defense attorney licensed to practice law by any jurisdiction in the United States that applies appropriate professional licensing standards and effectively ensures the competence and professional responsibility of its licensed attorneys.

    Judge Stoof reasoned that according to the provisions of the TLOA, Ms. Molina is qualified to represent a defendant facing over a year in prison because she has been licensed by the Pascua Yaqui Court, which is in a Tribal jurisdiction, has a bar exam and appropriate licensing standards that effectively ensure the competent and effective responsibility of its licensed attorneys. Following the adjournment, neither the Tribe, nor Ms. Molina appear to have raised the issue of the Defendant's explicit waiver on the record with respect to the requirements prescribed by 3 PYTC § 1-4-50. Moreover, the transcript suggests that because the Defendant retained Ms. Molina on a non-indigent basis there was ambiguity insofar as the Defendant was required to submit a waiver in writing, or on the record, and it appears to have been addressed during the five minute adjournment as per Ms. Molina's undertaking. After the adjournment the issue with respect to waiver of counsel, however, appears to have been subsumed with the TLOA and its application to the Pascua Yaqui Tribal courts.
8. On December 30, 2013, the Tribe filed a Writ of Mandamus claiming that the Tribal Court judge violated his duty by failing to obtain an express waiver of counsel on the record. Respondent Judge Stoof filed a Response on January 3, 2014 claiming that there was no duty, statutory or otherwise, that the court failed to follow the federal statue or tribal statutes to appoint a licensed attorney. Petitioner Tribe filed a Reply Brief on January 14, 2014.

IV. Lay Advocate and Attorney

9. The first issue before us is whether Ms. Molina is a lay advocate. Several Tribal Courts have defined a lay advocate as a person who is "a non-lawyer and who has been qualified by the Court to serve as an Advocate on behalf of a party." See Sault Ste. Marie Tribe of Chippewa Indians Admissions to Practice, Rule 87.102 (4), and Bay Mills Tribal Code, Rule I 05.2, Code of Ethical Conduct. Our own Pascua Yaqui Code goes further to distinguish between those who have a state license and those who do not have a state license but are certified by the Tribal Court with 3 PYTC § 1-4-10, which states, "Officers of the Tribal Court include state licensed attorneys and lay counselors who are certified by the Tribal Court." Ms. Molina is not licensed by the State of Arizona. She has been disbarred. Therefore, she is not considered a lawyer within the State. She has complied, however, with the Pascua Yaqui requirements to become a lay advocate. A certified attorney would be one who is licensed with a state and becomes licensed with the Pascua Yaqui Tribe, while a lay advocate will be one who is not licensed with a state, yet he/she completes the requirements to represent individuals in Tribal Courts.

10. The TLOA merely provides that the attorney appointed at the court's expense must be a defense attorney licensed to practice law by any jurisdiction in the United States. Ms. Molina has been retained and is not appointed. This, however, does not change the Pascua Yaqui Tribal Code's definition of whether she is lay counsel or an attorney. The Pascua Yaqui Tribal Code includes certified attorneys and lay counsel as those permitted to practice in the Pascua Yaqui courts. The Tribal Code goes a step further and requires that there be a valid waiver of counsel before a defendant is allowed to proceed with a lay advocate. Although the waiver of counsel is usually in the context of appointed counsel (and not retained lay counsel), the Pascua Yaqui Code does not differentiate between retained and appointed counsel. For further commentary on the issue, see Fortin, Seth, The Two-Tiered Program of the Tribal Law and Order Act, 61 UCLA L. Rev. Disc. 88 (2013); Patton, David, Tribal Law and Order Act of 2010: Breathing Life Into the Miner's Canary, Gonzaga L. Rev. Vol. 47:3 (2012). The Code merely states that if a defendant proceeds in a criminal matter with lay counsel, he has to waive his right to counsel.

11. This situation is peculiar in that Ms. Molina was licensed by the State of Arizona at one point, and although no longer licensed by the State, she has been licensed by the Tribe, has experience in the legal field, and would understand the law more effectively than the average lay counsel. The Tribe's desire to protect a defendant is well-founded, especially

considering the punishment Defendant is facing. Ms. Molina is likely to be more than able to assist Defendant during trial with the same zeal and knowledge as a licensed state attorney, but the Code appears to confine her within the definition of lay counsel, which requires a waiver from Defendant before she is allowed to proceed as his counsel.

V. Waiver

12. Next we consider what constitutes a sufficient waiver. A waiver of defendant's right to counsel must be "knowingly and intelligently" made. *Faretta v. California*, 422 U.S. 806, 835 (1975). A waiver may be implied through a defendant's actions or conduct. See *State v. Hampton*, 92 P.3d 871, 874 (Ariz. 2004) (citing *United States v. Goldberg*, 67 F.3d 1092, 1100 (3d Cir. 1995)). Consistent "disruptive or dilatory conduct by a defendant will support a determination that the defendant 'waived' his right to counsel." Hampton, 92 P.3d at 874. A waiver by conduct may occur only after a court warns the defendant that further disruptive conduct may result in the loss of the right to counsel and explains the consequences of such a waiver. Id.

13. In Hampton, the defendant's waiver was implied from his numerous death threats against each attorney appointed to represent him. Nonetheless, the court was required to inform the defendant of the consequences of waiving his right to counsel. "When lower courts are confronted with misconduct directed toward counsel, they should apprise the defendant, on the record, of the risks and consequences of waiving the right to counsel." Hampton, 92 P.3d at 5 874, fn. 3. The superior court was instructed to warn the defendant of the consequences of his misconduct and that any further misconduct could be considered a waiver of his right to counsel. The Court was also instructed to warn the defendant that representing himself in a capital case without counsel would be difficult and that this could be his final opportunity to challenge his conviction and death sentence. Hampton. 92 P.3d at 875.

14. In the instant case, there is no egregious conduct such as death threats against counsel. The learned Tribal judge's comment concerning "conduct" referred to Defendant's conduct in choosing Ms. Molina as counsel. The judge stated that Defendant's conduct in choosing Ms. Molina was an implicit waiver of counsel. However, the waiver of counsel should be on the record. Hampton provides that even when a defendant's "conduct" is of a serious nature to constitute a waiver of counsel, he must still be informed of the consequences of proceeding without counsel. There is no indication this was done in the case at bar and in particular after the adjournment.

15. "While an accused may waive the right to counsel, whether there is a proper waiver should be clearly determined by the trial court, and it would be fitting and appropriate for that determination to appear upon the record." *Johnson v. Zerbst*, 304 U.S. 458, 465 (1938). The record must show that the defendant waived his right to representation. *U.S. v. Wadsworth*, 830 F.2d 1500, 1504 (9th Cir. 1987). See also *Carnley v. Cochran*, 369 U.S. 506, 516 (1962) ("[p]resuming waiver from a silent record is impermissible"); *United States v. Kennard*, 799 F.2d 556, 557 (9th Cir. 1986) (per curiam) (explicit waiver required for a second trial although defendant waived his right to counsel at his first trial). In *U.S. v. Balough*, the Ninth Circuit stated that "a district court should not grant a defendant's request to waive representation of counsel and serve as his own counsel, without discussing with the defendant, in open court, whether the waiver was knowingly and intelligently made, with an understanding of the charges, the possible penalties, and the dangers of self-representation. This is clearly the preferable procedure and should be followed by district courts in every case." 820 F.2d 1485, 1488 (9th Cir. 1987).
16. Although the cases involving a waiver involve a defendant proceeding pro se, the Pascua Yaqui Code requires a waiver of the right to counsel when a defendant proceeds with lay counsel in criminal matters. One can only assume that this waiver is for a defendant who has been appointed lay counsel, but the Code concerning the waiver does not differentiate between lay counsel who has been appointed or lay counsel who has been retained. Respondent argues that because Defendant retained Ms. Molina, Defendant implicitly waived his right to counsel. Case law appears uniform on waivers implied through the defendant's conduct. Even when a defendant repeatedly threatens counsel's life, the Court must still inform the defendant of consequences of waiving counsel.
17. In this case, Defendant does choose Ms. Molina as counsel even though she is a lay advocate. However, the record shows that Ms. Molina asks for a recess to explain to Defendant the consequences of choosing lay counsel over a state licensed attorney. A short recess was taken where Ms. Molina presumably explained the fact that she is not a state licensed attorney, but since it was off the record, it is unclear whether Defendant truly understood the fact that he was waiving his right to a state licensed attorney.
18. This case is of such a magnitude that Defendant will be facing over a year in prison for a violent crime. He will be utilizing lay counsel; therefore, a waiver should be on the record in this instance. Even in situations where a defendant threatens his attorney and clearly displays (by his conduct)

that he does not want counsel, jurisprudence has held that the court is required to warn Defendant of the consequences of proceeding without counsel. Defendant's conduct was merely in choosing Molina as his counsel. Therefore, a valid waiver and informing Defendant of the nature of the charges, the possible penalties, and the consequences of proceeding to trial with lay counsel should be obtained on the record.

VI. Sanctions

19. Although Petitioner Tribe requested relief through the most extraordinary method instead of a more direct and less resource consuming motion to reconsider or interlocutory appeal, this Court does not find that these particular set of facts merit sanctions on Petitioner Tribe.

VII. Conclusion

20. For the foregoing reasons, this Court holds that Defendant should waive his right to counsel on the record if he is to continue being represented by lay counsel. The case is remanded to Tribal Court for compliance with this order.

So ordered on this 28th day of January 2014.
Chief Justice, James Hopkins

Tulalip Tribal Court of Appeals.

Tulalip Tribes v. Lindy Lee Morris (2014).
Nos. TUL–CR–AP–2013–0406, TUL–CR–DV–2013–0004. May 8, 2014.
Before: Daniel A. Raas, Chief Justice; Elizabeth F.M. Nason, Justice; Jane M. Smith, Justice.
Opinion
Per Curiam:

In this appeal, Defendant/Appellant Lindy Lee Morris challenges his convictions and sentences for violations of Tulalip Tribal Code (TTC) 3.35.180 (violation of a protective order) and TTC 4.25.060 (domestic violence). In regards to his conviction for violation of a protective order, Appellant argues that the protective order he was accused of violating was invalid, and therefore there could be no violation of TTC 3.35.180. In regards to his conviction for domestic violence, Appellant argues that "abuse" is an essential element of that crime, and because the Tribes failed to prove that any abuse had occurred, he was wrongly convicted of domestic violence. Finally, Appellant argues that if he was actually convicted of the offense of a "crime involving domestic violence" as defined by TTC 4.25.050(7), because the elements of that crime as applied to this case are identical to those of violation of a protective order under TTC 3.35.180, his convictions for violations of both TTC 3.35.180 and TTC 4.25.050(7) constitute double jeopardy in violation of the Tulalip Tribal Code and the Indian Civil Rights Act, 25 U.S.C. § 1302(a)(3).

While we apply a somewhat different analytic framework to the issues than that proposed by Appellant, we agree with Appellant that the trial court committed clear error in regards to the domestic violence charge, and therefore Appellant's conviction and sentence for violating TTC 4.25.060 are hereby reversed and vacated. We find no prejudicial error concerning Appellant's conviction for violation of a protective order, and therefore affirm the judgment and sentence for violation of TTC 3.35.180.

Facts

The essential facts of this case are not in dispute. On November 13, 2012, the Tribal Court for the Lummi Nation issued an Order for Protection–Domestic Violence in Lummi Tribal Court proceeding number 2012 CVPD 3185. That protective order prohibited Mr. Morris "from coming near or having any contact whatsoever" with D.J., the petitioner in that proceeding. The Lummi protective order expressly ordered Mr. Morris to "[r]emain 100 yards away from petitioner" for one year. Exactly forty four days later, on December 27, 2012, Tulalip Tribal Police observed Mr. Morris enter the driver's seat of a vehicle occupied by D.J. in the parking lot of the Tulalip Liquor Store, which is within the exterior boundaries of the Tulalip Reservation.

Having determined that Mr. Morris was subject to the Lummi protective order, and upon observing Mr. Morris commit a pair of minor traffic violations, the Tulalip Police stopped him and arrested him for violation of the Lummi protective order.

At no time during this incident did the Tulalip Police observe any physical contact between Mr. Morris and D.J. The Tribes never produced any evidence, nor alleged, that Mr. Morris "abused" D.J. on December 27, 2012.

Violation of a Protective Order

Prior to trial, Mr. Morris moved to have the charge of violation of a protective order dismissed. Mr. Morris argued that the Lummi Tribal Court protective order at issue was invalid because there were defects in the petition that resulted in the issuance of the order. The trial court denied that motion, ruling both that the Lummi order was valid, and that Mr. Morris was collaterally estopped from attacking the validity of the Lummi order in the Tulalip Tribal Court. On appeal, Mr. Morris again argues that the Lummi protective order is invalid because it is based on a defective petition. Mr. Morris does not address collateral estoppel in any of his appellate filings.

This Court may affirm the judgment of a trial court on any ground supported by the record, even if the trial court did not rely on it. See, e.g., *Rupp v. Omaha Indian*

Tribe, 45 F.3d 1241, 1244 (8th Cir.1995), citing *Monterey Dev. v. Lawyer's Title Ins.*, 4 F.3d 605, 608 (8th Cir.1993). Because the trial court was required to give **full faith and credit** to the Lummi Nation protective order under both the federal Violence Against Women Act (VAWA) and Section 4.25.210 of the Tulalip Tribal Code, we need not decide if the trial court correctly applied the collateral estoppel doctrine in this case.

There is no evidence in the documentary record establishing that Mr. Morris was ever served the "permanent" protective order issued by the Lummi Tribal Court on November 12, 2012; However, there is also no claim by Mr. Morris in either his trial court or appellate pleadings that he lacked notice of that order. Moreover, Mr. Morris has not raised lack of notice of the Lummi order as an issue on appeal, and has therefore waived any legal right to claim on appeal that he lacked notice of the issuance of the order. TTC 2.20.030(2).

The Tulalip Tribal Code requires the Tulalip Tribes to accord full faith and credit to the Lummi order. The Tulalip Tribes' Board of Directors adopted TTC 4.25.210 for the express purposes of ensuring "compliance with the full faith and credit provision of the Violence Against Women Act of 1994 (VAWA) as set forth in Title 18 of the United States Code, Section 2265 (18 U.S.C. 2265)," and ensuring that "victims of domestic violence are able to move across State and Tribal boundaries without losing [*sic*] ability to enforce protection orders they have previously obtained to increase their safety."

The requirements for establishing the validity of a foreign protection under TTC 4.25.210 are virtually identical to those set forth in 18 U.S.C. 2265. As the trial court rightly observed, the proper forum available to Mr. Morris for challenging the validity of the Lummi Tribal Court's protective order was the Lummi Tribal Court.

Mr. Morris failed to appear for the hearing upon which the permanent protective order was issued and failed to appeal the issuance of the order. The Lummi order is valid under the terms of the applicable Tulalip and federal laws requiring Tulalip to accord full faith and credit to the Lummi order. Thus, Appellant's argument on appeal that the Lummi order is invalid is without merit.

In addition, the federal VAWA provides that "[a]ny protection order issued that is consistent with subsection (b) of this section by the court of one State, Indian tribe, or territory (the issuing State, Indian tribe, or territory) shall be accorded full faith and credit by the court of another State, Indian tribe, or territory (the enforcing State, Indian tribe, or territory) and enforced by the court and law enforcement personnel of the other State, Indian tribal government or Territory [territory] as if it were the order of the enforcing State, Indian tribe, or territory." 18 U.S.C. § 2265(a). Subsection (b) provides in relevant part:

> (b) Protection order. A protection order issued by a State, tribal, or territorial court is consistent with this subsection if—

(1) such court has jurisdiction over the parties and matter under the law of such State, Indian tribe, or territory; and

(2) reasonable notice and opportunity to be heard is given to the person against whom the order is sought sufficient to protect that person's right to due process. 18 U.S.C. § 2265(b). Mr. Morris has never asserted that the Lummi Court lacked jurisdiction to issue the protective order and the record firmly establishes that the Lummi Court provided Mr. Morris notice and the opportunity to be heard in regards to the issuance of its protective order. The Lummi protective order is consistent with 18 U.S.C. § 2265(b), and therefore the Tulalip Tribes are compelled by federal law, as well as tribal law, to accord it full faith and credit. Appellant's conviction and sentence for violation of a protective order under TTC 3.35.180 are therefore affirmed.

Domestic Violence

The record is consistent only in that the trial court, prosecution and defense each could not parse the Tribal Code sections under which Mr. Morris was charged, tried, convicted or sentenced. Because the Tulalip Tribes has amended its Domestic Violence Code, TTC 4.25, to eliminate the problems present in this appeal, this Court need not plunge into the morass presented by this record.

Instead, our focus is on the rights every defendant is afforded when charged with a crime by the Tulalip Tribes. TTC 2.25.060(2) enumerates these rights, and in particular each defendant has the right "[t]o be informed of the nature of the charges pending against him or her and to have a copy of those charges." TTC 2.25.060(2)(c).

The initial Criminal Complaint against Mr. Morris cites and charges him with "domestic violence" pursuant to TTC 4.25.060, but fails to cite a subsection of 4.25.060. It also recites allegations that together would, it claims, constitute a "crime involving domestic violence" but again cites no subsection of 4.25.060. Without a specification as to which crime in 4.25.060 is being charged, Mr. Morris would be unable to properly defend himself, and his rights would be violated. The Amended Complaint has the same defects.

While further proceedings in a criminal prosecution could clarify the precise crime with which a defendant was charged so a proper defense could be mounted, such clarification apparently did not happen here. Both the Complaint and the Amended Complaint were dismissed during pre-trial proceedings, and a presumed Second Amended Complaint under which Mr. Morris went to trial is not in the record.

The confusion survived the trial and the jury's verdict. Indeed, in a post-trial motion Mr. Morris sought clarification as to which crime the jury had convicted him. The trial judge, in an unsuccessful attempt to harmonize the record, ruled that the two code sections were "coterminous." They were not, nor are they the same crime with the same potential penalties.

> A defendant is entitled to notice of the crimes with which he is charged. A complaint which alleges violation of a general code section which has subsections which do not have the same elements violates a defendant's rights under TTC 2.25.060(2)(c). Mr. Morris' conviction for a "crime involving domestic violence" or, in the alternative, his conviction for "domestic violence," is reversed.
> IT IS SO ORDERED.

Conclusion

Starting in 2006, the federal government began to turn more attention to the criminal justice crisis in Indian country. Changes in federal law pursuant to TLOA and VAWA have slightly changed the structure of the criminal jurisdiction scheme in Indian country. Law reform is a long process, and many tribal leaders and advocates will continue to press for restoration of inherent sovereignty. Because tribal nations have unique circumstances, there is not one specific avenue of reform that will meet the needs of all tribal criminal justice systems.

Questions

1. Why did Congress pass TLOA and VAWA?
2. Why do TLOA and VAWA focus on defendants' rights?
3. Should Congress continue to expand recognition of inherent tribal sovereignty? Why or why not?
4. In *Chehalis v. Lyons*, why did the Court of Appeals overturn the nine-year sentence? What would the tribe need to do in order to comply with TLOA?
5. In *In Re Pascua Yaqui*, why did the tribal prosecutor object to the decision of the trial judge regarding the lay advocate? Does TLOA require defense counsel to be licensed by the state?
6. Why did the Tulalip court affirm the violation of a protection order conviction but reverse the domestic violence conviction?

In Your Community

1. Has your tribal government considered exercising the jurisdiction recognized by Congress in TLOA and VAWA?
2. What changes (if any) would need to be made to your tribal code to meet the standards required by TLOA and VAWA?
3. Would exercising the jurisdiction recognized in TLOA and VAWA benefit your community?

Terms Used in Chapter 10

Full Faith and Credit: Recognition and enforcement of the public acts, records, and judicial proceedings of other sovereigns.

Hearsay: Legal term for an out of court statement, made in court, to prove the truth of the matter asserted. Hearsay is generally inadmissible in a trial.

Interlocutory: A judicial opinion given during an intermediate stage of a case.

Per capita: Per unit of population.

Unilaterally: Performed or undertaken by only one side.

Writ of mandamus: Used by courts of superior jurisdiction to require a lower court to perform a certain act.

Note

1. Duane Champagne & Carole Goldberg, *Captured Justice: Native Nations and Public Law 280* 209 (2012).

Further Reading

Amnesty International, "Maze of Injustice: The Failure to Protect Indigenous Women from Sexual Violence in the USA" (2007), http://www.amnestyusa.org/pdfs/MazeOfInjustice.pdf.

Gregory S. Arnold, *Tribal Law and Order Act and Violence Against Women Act: Enhanced Recognition of Inherent Tribal Sovereignty Creates Greater Need for Criminal Defense Counsel in Indian Country*, Fed. Law. (January/February 2014), at 4.

Seth Fortin, "The Two-Tiered Program of the Tribal Law and Order Act," 61 *UCLA Law Rev. Discourse* 88 (2013).

Shefali Singh, "Closing the Gap of Justice: Providing Protection for Native American Women Through the Special Domestic Violence Criminal Jurisdiction Provision of VAWA," 28 *Colum. J. Gender & L.* 197 (2014).

State and Tribal Court Collaboration

Chapter 11

Introduction

Indian nations have endured many attacks on their sovereignty as federal laws have limited the recognition of their criminal jurisdiction over non-Indians, sentencing authority, and unilaterally imposed concurrent criminal jurisdiction with certain states and the federal government. These legal obstacles, along with lack of justice system resources, have strained relationships between tribes and state governments. Long-standing disagreements over jurisdiction have made it increasingly difficult to address crime on Indian lands. In the last twenty years, however, Indian nations have been collaborating with state and federal partners to address crime problems. These collaborative efforts strive to address jurisdictional gaps while also enhancing respect for tribal authority. Criminal behavior doesn't stop at a particular political boundary. When states and tribes work together on important issues, such as drug trafficking, it enhances the ability for effective crime control since the partners are communicating about their investigations. Many states have used such agreements with other states for decades. Tribal-state cooperative efforts have been highly successful in some areas. The following examples highlight some successful collaborative efforts.

Building Collaborative Bridges

Law Enforcement Cross-Deputization Agreements

Tribal police, as first responders, often are the first to deal with jurisdictional issues. Unable to arrest non-Indians for violations of criminal law, they may only stop, detain, and turn over non-Indians to state or federal authorities, unless the tribe is exercising special criminal jurisdiction under the Violence Against Women

Act (see chapter 10). Sometimes state and county law enforcement refuse to recognize tribal law enforcement's authority, because they disagree with the tribe's exercise of sovereignty. Often the states and tribes have a history of disputes over jurisdiction issues and have built a relationship based on mistrust. In particular, tribes affected by laws like Public Law (PL) 280, or other similar legislation, may resent the intrusion by the state upon their sovereignty. Additionally, for many years, tribal governments subject to laws like PL 280 were not eligible for Bureau of Indian Affairs funding for developing criminal justice systems and thus were forced to rely on the state system to enforce criminal law. Disputes about political boundaries have been very common with regard to treaty rights and other cultural practices. To address these issues, Indian nations enter into cross-deputization agreements with county, state, and federal law enforcement agencies. This can be done in the form of a Memorandum of Understanding or Agreement between the nation and state and/or county.

The agreements can take several forms, and are customized to the particular partnership. Some agreements authorize the tribal police to assist the county in enforcing state law or outright deputize tribal police to enforce state law. Another common feature of these agreements is an authorization for state/county law enforcement officers to enter tribal lands under specific circumstances. Many agreements require tribal police officers to be trained or certified at a particular academy—and receive the same training as state or federal officers. Some states have enacted laws that authorize the designation of tribal police officers as state law enforcement. Such laws also often include the training and certification requirements that tribal officers must meet.

Granting State Peace Officer Status to Tribal Law Enforcement

Duane Champagne and Carole Goldberg, *Promising Strategies: Public Law 280*, 13-14 (2013) Available at: http://www.walkingoncommonground.org/

In 2011, Oregon lawmakers and the state Supreme Court granted tribal law enforcement officers the power to pursue suspects and make arrests off the reservation. Tribal police officers are accorded the same off-reservation policing powers as county and state police officers. The Oregon Legislature and an executive order from the governor in 1996 had already gone on record for recognizing the sovereignty of federally recognized tribal governments and outlined the goal of working cooperatively with tribes on a government-to-government basis. With those policies as a foundational philosophy for working with tribes, the Oregon Supreme Court ruled that tribal police officers are empowered to make an arrest off the reservation if they are giving chase and intending to make an arrest. The case arose from an incident during 2005 in which a Warm Springs Reservation police officer began chasing a suspect within the Warm Springs Reservation but was not able to subdue the suspect within the confines of the reservation. The tribal police officer caught and arrested the suspect in Jefferson County, which is off the reservation. The defendant argued that the Warm Springs police officer did not have authority to make an arrest off the reservation. Further complicating the issue was the fact that the pursuing tribal police officer had not attended a state-approved police academy and was not certified by the sheriff to make arrests in Jefferson County. Most tribal police officers have the same training as nontribal police officers in Oregon.

The Oregon Court of Appeals ruled that tribal police officers did not have arrest authority off the reservation, but the Oregon Supreme Court reversed the decision and ruled that tribal police officers did have authority to make arrests off the reservation. After the Oregon Supreme Court decision, the Oregon Legislature passed legislation to regulate the powers and administration of tribal police officers making off-reservation arrests. This state law grants tribal police limited off-reservation authority and required tribal police officers to obtain certified police training from the Oregon Department of Public Safety Standards and Training. The tribe and tribal police departments must also agree to state-approved rules for insurance, **tort** liability, and evidence. Many, if not most, tribal officers in Oregon already have training equivalent to Oregon State Police training standards. Furthermore, many tribal police departments have procedures for obtaining evidence and maintaining public records, as well as other procedures that are similar to nontribal police departments and in accordance with Oregon law.

The new law gives tribal police officers Oregon state peace officer status. Tribal police are empowered to arrest non-Indians on the reservation for violation of state law and to continue pursuing a suspect onto off-reservation jurisdiction and take action on crimes committed in their presence. The governor supported the bill against opposition that argued that the bill provided enhanced powers to tribal police. The governor, however, argued

> that compatible training was the key issue and not tribal jurisdiction or powers. If the tribal police officers have training that is the same as other Oregon police officers, then they are qualified to enforce state law as long as they are managed by a federally recognized tribal government.

Tribal and State Court Jurisdictional Collaborations

Tribal courts face challenges that are similar to those faced by tribal police. Because of the history of colonization, racism, and oppression from neighboring governments, tribal courts often have a strained or nonexistent relationship with state and federal courts. State and federal courts have sometimes refused to respect a tribal court's authority or court orders, deciding a case that had already been addressed by the tribal court. Like tribal police, tribal courts affected by state authority (through PL 280) have struggled to develop a strong criminal justice system because of limited access to resources.

To address these problems, several tribal courts have begun to work with county courts to transfer offenders from state court into various tribal court dockets and exercise supervisory jurisdiction over the offender. As part of tribal court dockets, rehabilitative services are offered to help the offender address problems that have resulted in criminal conduct. The most common type of this relationship is between a tribal healing to wellness court (drug court) and county criminal court or drug court. The courts work together to develop a process to refer offenders from county court to tribal court. Typically, an offender is placed on probation in county court and as part of his probation the offender is required to complete the rehabilitation process in the tribal healing to wellness court. (See chapter 27 for a discussion on healing to wellness courts.) The tribal healing to wellness court then exercises supervisory jurisdiction over the offender's probation. If the offender fails to progress and complete the healing to wellness court requirements, the tribal court reports back to the county court and recommends appropriate sanction or sentencing.

The preceding description is only one model of courts working together in jurisdictional collaborations. Courts can be and are creative in determining the best way to collaborate. The Leech Lake Band of Ojibwe Tribal Court and Minnesota's Ninth Judicial District developed a mechanism for collaboration that demonstrated tribal and county courts can work together successful, despite a history of mistrust.

Leech Lake Band of Ojibwe Tribal Court and Minnesota's Ninth Judicial District Court for Cass and Itasca Counties

Duane Champagne and Carole Goldberg, *Promising Strategies: Tribal-State Court Relations*, 13-17 (2013). Available at: http://www.walkingoncommonground.org/

The Leech Lake Band of Ojibwe Indians is located in the State of Minnesota, one of the "mandatory" PL 280 states—meaning that in 1953, the federal government gave up most of its Indian Country criminal jurisdiction in that state, and the state received authority to enforce its criminal laws on reservations. As a consequence of PL 280, tribes in that state were denied federal funding to develop their own tribal courts, although tribal court civil and traffic dockets began to grow during the 1980s. Because state jurisdiction was introduced without tribal consent or any federal funds to support it, tribal members have often viewed state criminal justice as culturally inappropriate and inadequately responsive to community safety needs. The result had been mistrust between tribal and state systems. Simultaneously, Leech Lake, like many American Indian communities, was facing dire conditions due to the increasing prevalence of drug and alcohol offenses. Because of PL 280, tribal members were processed in state court, which turned into a revolving door, with offenders cycling in and out of the system. There was a general frustration among tribal members, not only because tribal members were coming back through the system, but because there was a feeling that the state courts were not addressing tribal needs.

In an effort to address these conditions, the Leech Lake Tribal Court entered into two Joint Powers Agreements with two of the four counties that overlap the reservation. In these unprecedented agreements, one in 2006 and the other in 2008, the tribal and county courts pledged to "jointly exercise the powers and authorities conferred upon us as judges of our respective jurisdictions." The agreement with Cass County produced a joint Wellness Court aimed at DWI cases, and the agreement with Itasca County produced a joint Wellness Court that combines drug and DWI cases. Following the Wellness Court model that focuses on rehabilitation rather than punishment, these courts allow qualifying individuals sentenced in the state court system to opt in to the program as an alternative to serving their sentences. In the two courts, judges from both jurisdictions preside together. In Cass County, there is even a videoconferencing system that allows tribal and county courtrooms to be used simultaneously, with the defendant/client choosing the preferred location.

Both of these joint courts incorporate a multidisciplinary, multijurisdictional team that draws up an individualized treatment plan and meets regularly to discuss and monitor each case. Clients report their progress directly to the pair of tribal and county judges. Significantly, both courts employ evidence-based practices that are proven to reduce recidivism, including data-based decision making, identification of offender risk and appropriately targeted treatment interventions, and balancing positive reinforcement with swift imposition of appropriate sanctions for violating conditions. Results have been striking, including a significant reduction in recidivism, coupled with reunification of families, an end to abusive relationships, and securing of employment and valid drivers' licenses. In 2010, the Joint Leech Lake/Cass and Itasca County Wellness Courts were awarded honors by the Honoring Nations program at Harvard University's John F. Kennedy School of Government.

The joint nature of the two Wellness Courts means that criminal proceedings that once would have taken place exclusively within the state court system can now benefit from culturally appropriate tribal resources and involvement. For example, although the state may have access to drug-testing technology, Leech Lake can call on spiritual healers to help participants make cultural connections and work through historical trauma. Additionally, tribal understandings of restorative justice can find their way into the criminal justice process. At the broadest level, the entire concept of authority can be reconceived to comport more closely with tribal conceptions that stress collaboration rather than control or domination.

As Judge Korey Wahwassuck has observed, the day-to-day communications built into the operation of the courts has also enhanced judges' and staff members' awareness and sensitivity to cultural values and cultural differences. She notes, "These cultural values are important to understand because they are part of the makeup of each individual and his or her approach to society."

Furthermore, Ojibwe ceremonies have been used to enhance the cultural legitimacy of the joint Wellness Courts. For example, on the occasion of the signing of the agreement between Leech Lake and Itasca County, a young Nishnabek boy made his way down the line of tribal and state court judges at the county courthouse, smudging each one of the judges with cleansing smoke to clear away any negative thoughts and feelings. The judges proceeded to the courtroom as a youth drum group from the Leech Lake Band of Ojibwe's Bug-O-Nay-Ge-Shig School sang an honor song.

The nation-to-nation nature of the Joint Powers Agreements hearkens back to the treatymaking era, when native nations were dealt with on a basis of mutual consent. At a more practical level, the Leech Lake Band of Ojibwe had played no part in the criminal justice system affecting its people before these agreements were made. Racial tensions were high, and the tribe and state competed for sovereignty, often through litigation. With the new partnerships in place, the Leech Lake Tribal Court participates in sentencing and can shape and supervise appropriate treatment options. Energy that would have been spent on jurisdictional competition can be used to achieve tribal goals, such as family reunification and safer roads.

At a more symbolic level, the Joint Powers Agreements have enhanced the stature and legitimacy of the tribe among outside authorities and citizens. In Cass and Itasca Counties, for example, the Leech Lake flag now flies alongside flags of the state and federal governments. Moreover, this enhanced respect for the tribal court has led to other cooperative initiatives that can extend the reach of tribal authority, including development of a multijurisdictional delinquency court and joint hearings on custody cases not covered by the Indian Child Welfare Act (ICWA).

Significantly, the joint tribal–state court arrangement expanded in 2010 to encompass juvenile and family cases. Under this arrangement, review hearings are held in tribal court, with supervision services provided by the Cass County Probation Department under a crossjurisdictional appointment order. Both systems remain involved, and the reach of tribal authority is extended.

The benefits of intergovernmental cooperation are plainly manifest in the two Wellness Courts created by Leech Lake and the two Minnesota counties. Sharing of resources has made it possible for the justice system to produce positive results in an era of shrinking budgets. Staff positions can be shared, and the judges from each system can cover for each other should scheduling conflicts arise. As Judge Wahwassuck of Leech Lake points out, "The judges have worked so well together that they have become very confident in each other and are comfortable having the other judge handle the proceedings in their absence. This is true even if it means that the tribal court judge takes the bench alone in state court, or that the state court judge takes the bench alone in tribal court."

The Joint Powers Agreements emerged from a mutual realization that the tribe and the counties shared common problems and goals. The problems were high levels of alcohol related crashes on county highways and high levels of drug and alcohol addiction associated with criminal activity and family dysfunction. The common goals included decreasing the number of arrests for DWI, fewer fatalities, and decreased recidivism rates. Once those common goals were identified, it became easier to overcome centuries of mistrust and even animosity.

Open communication and the development of mutual respect were essential to the success of the partnerships. Participants from tribal and county courts learned how to disagree and still reach a desirable result. Jon A. Maturi, Chief Judge of the Ninth Judicial District, has credited the success of the collaborative efforts to "a mutual understanding of our respective sovereignty, but, more importantly, [to] our mutual understanding of what we hold in common and our joint desire to better serve the residents of [the] County, Leech Lake and the Ninth Judicial District."

CASS COUNTY/LEECH LAKE BAND OF OJIBWE WELLNESS COURT SUPERVISION

MEMORANDUM OF UNDERSTANDING

AGREEMENT between the Cass County Cass County Probation Department, Minnesota Department of Corrections, Cass County District Court, and Leech Lake Tribal Court.

The parties to this Agreement endorse the mission and goals of the Cass County/Leech Lake Band of Ojibwe Wellness Court so that participants may eliminate future criminal behavior and improve the quality of their lives. The parties recognize that for the Wellness Court mission to be successful, cooperation and collaboration must occur within a network of agencies.

The parties to this Agreement support the following mission statement:

The purpose of the Cass County/Leech Lake Band of Ojibwe Wellness Court is to reduce the number of repeat substance dependent and DWI offenders by using a team approach in the court system. Upon acceptance, candidates will be provided the opportunity to

Figure 11.1. Cass County/Leech Lake Band of Ojibwe Wellnes Court Supervision

participate in individual treatment programs designed to promote accountability, self-sufficiency and to enhance public safety. Compliance will be accomplished by using an established system of court ordered sanctions/ incentives as well as community and family support systems.

The parties agree that there are ten principles under which the respective agencies will work cooperatively. They are:

1. The wellness court integrates alcohol and other drug treatment services with criminal justice system processing.
2. The wellness court uses a non-adversarial approach, prosecution and defense counsel to promote public safety while protecting participants' due process rights.
3. Eligible participants are identified early and referred to the wellness court.
4. The wellness court provides access to a continuum of alcohol, drug and other related treatment and rehabilitation services.
5. Frequent alcohol and other drug testing monitor's abstinence.
6. A coordinated strategy governs the wellness court responses to the participant's compliance.
7. There is on-going judicial interaction with each wellness court participant.
8. A monitoring and evaluation plan measures the achievement of program goals and gauges effectiveness.
9. Continuing interdisciplinary education promotes effective substance abuse court planning, implementation and operations.
10. Forging partnerships among wellness courts, public agencies and community-based Organizations generate local support and enhance the wellness court's effectiveness.

INDIVIDUAL AGENCY RESPONSIBILITIES AND STAFF COMMITMENTS

Wellness Court Judge

1. The judge will assume the primary role to motivate and monitor the participants of the wellness court program.
2. The judge will ensure a cooperative atmosphere for attorneys, case managers, probation, law enforcement, and treatment providers to stay focused on the task of providing substance abusers with treatment opportunities.
3. The judge will provide the necessary reinforcers when deemed appropriate while maintaining the integrity of the court.
4. The judge will participate as an active member of the staffing team and chairs the Steering Committee.
5. The judge will provide training to new or replacement judges.
6. The judge will act as a mediator to develop resources and improve interagency linkages.
7. The judge will act as a spokesperson to educate the community and peers about the wellness court program.

Wellness court Coordinator

1. A 0.5 FTE coordinator will be assigned to the wellness court program by the Cass County Probation Department, and will participate as an active member of the staffing team and the Steering Committee.
2. The coordinator will provide oversight to the wellness court program.
3. The coordinator will provide a letter of acceptance to the Department of Corrections acknowledging acceptance into the wellness court for felony offenses.
4. The coordinator will notify the wellness court probation officer of acceptance of participants into wellness court.
5. The coordinator will organize events and meetings, compile supporting materials to disseminate to stakeholders and providers of services to maintain linkages, develop marketing strategies, create a press package and act as a media contact person.
6. The coordinator will continuously monitor and evaluate the progress of the wellness court program participants.
7. The coordinator will seek funding sources; respond to grant solicitations; implement and monitor grant funds and provide fiscal, narrative and statistical information as required by the funding source to ensure the ongoing operation of the program.
8. The coordinator will provide or seek continuing training for the wellness court team.
9. The coordinator will provide an annual report setting forth the incidence of recidivism among wellness court graduates.

Figure 11.1. (*continued*)

10. The coordinator will provide leadership and direction to ensure compliance with the National Standards set forth by the National Association of Wellness court Professionals.
11. The coordinator will create court calendars; prepare reports for staffings and assure timely dissemination of compliance information; perform case flow coordination; expedite processes of notification, service placement, rescheduling, and preparation of warrants; collect fees; and monitor compliance.
12. The coordinator will provide training to wellness court team members.
13. The coordinator will negotiate and monitor treatment and ancillary service contracts; conduct site visits; review progress reports and assist in audits and certification monitoring; create and monitor standards for urine collection and compliance reporting; ensure gender, age and culturally specific treatment services.
14. The coordinator will create and maintain a data collection system to monitor client compliance, identify trends and provide a basis for evaluation.
15. The coordinator will notify the district coordinator of wellness court participant hearings and events so that the district coordinator may appropriately enter data into the Minnesota Court Information System (MNCIS).

Minnesota Department of Corrections

1. A representative of the Department of Corrections will participate as an active member of the staffing team and Steering Committee.
2. The Department of Corrections will provide the coordinator with copies of the pre-sentence investigation, chemical dependency evaluation, sentencing minutes and any other documentation required for wellness court participation, upon sentencing of felony participants to wellness court.
3. The Department of Corrections will upload the felony participants into the Statewide Supervision System.
4. The Department of Corrections will notify the wellness court probation officer of violations, arrests, or any positive chemical tests occurring on felony participants.
5. The Department of Corrections will assume full supervision for a period of 12 months upon graduation of a felony participant from wellness court.

Cass County Probation Officer

1. A 1.0 FTE dedicated probation officer will be assigned to provide field supervision of wellness court participants, and will participate as an active member of the staffing team and Steering Committee.
2. The probation officer will provide coordinated and comprehensive supervision and case management so as to minimize participant manipulation and splitting of program staff.
3. The probation officer will monitor suitability of social activities and home environment of the participant.
4. The probation officer will develop effective measures for drug testing and supervision compliance reporting that provide the team with sufficient and timely information to implement sanctions and incentive systems.
5. The probation officer will participate in bi-weekly case reviews with the judge, treatment provider and wellness court staffing team.
6. The probation officer will coordinate the utilization of community-based services such as health and mental health services, victims' services, housing, entitlements, transportation, education, vocational training, job skills training and placement to provide a strong foundation for recovery.
7. The probation officer will provide on-site progress reports to the judge.
8. The probation officer will provide frequent, observed drug testing on a random basis.
9. The probation officer will contribute to the team's efforts in community education and local resource acquisition.
10. The probation officer will contribute to the education of peers, colleagues, and judiciary in the efficacy of wellness courts.
11. The probation officer will provide progress reports on felony participants to the Department of Corrections.
12. The probation officer will provide violation reports on felony participants to the Department of Corrections.
13. The probation officer will notify the Department of Corrections on felony participants should a violation occur that needs referral back to the state.
14. The probation officer will notify the Department of Corrections should a felony participant be terminated from wellness court.
15. The probation officer will notify the Department of Corrections when a felony participant is graduating from wellness court.

Figure 11.1. *(continued)*

In creating this partnership and uniting around a single goal of addressing an underlying problem affecting our community, we are pledged to enhance communication between the courts, law enforcement and treatment programs. Through this linkage of services, we expect greater participation and effectiveness in addressing drug offenders involved in the criminal justice system.

Agreement Modifications

Any individual agency wishing to amend/modify this Agreement will notify the Cass County/Leech Lake Band of Ojibwe Wellness court of the issue(s). The Cass County/Leech Lake Band of Ojibwe Wellness court will address the issue(s) for purposes of modifying/amending the Agreement.

IN WITNESS THEREOF, the parties have caused their duly authorized representatives to execute this Agreement.

Dated:

_____   _____
Judge John P. Smith, Ninth Judicial District Court   Judge Korey Wahwassuck, Leech Lake Tribal Court

_____   _____
Reno Wells, Cass County Probation Department   Victor Moen, Minnesota Department of Corrections

Revised 9/23/10

Figure 11.1. *(continued)*

Tribal State and Federal Court Forums

In 1988 the Conference of Chief Justices of the State Supreme Courts created a Committee on Jurisdiction in Indian Country to study civil conflicts between tribal and state courts. After conducting a national survey about civil jurisdictional conflicts, the Committee convened tribal-state court forums in Arizona, Oklahoma, and Washington to investigate jurisdictional problems. Subsequently, the Conference of Chief Justices held a national conference in 1991 addressing jurisdictional problems that created conflicts between tribal and state courts. This conference generated the Building on Common Ground initiative. Subsequently, Chief Justices of Michigan, North Dakota, and South Dakota created tribal-state forums. And in 1992 the initiative began to include criminal jurisdictional conflicts and include federal courts in the discussion. After another national conference in 1993, a detailed report was issued, "Building on Common Ground: A Nation Agenda to Reduce Jurisdiction Disputes between Tribal, State, and Federal Courts."[1] The initiative developed numerous resources to help tribal and state courts work together including guides to help develop and maintain Tribal Court–State Court Forums.

In 2005, the Building on Common Ground initiative evolved into the "Walking on Common Ground" to focus on incorporating many of the lessons learned from the prior initiative. Since 2005, four national gatherings have been held to foster collaborative relationships between tribal, state, and federal courts. Included in the following text are specific examples of Tribal-State-Federal Court Forums working together to address common problems. Although most of these examples focus on civil jurisdiction or civil law, one can develop a list of recommendations for how these forums could be used to address criminal jurisdiction and criminal law problems shared by tribal, state, and federal courts.

Idaho State/Tribal Court Forum and Idaho State Judiciary—Idaho Tribal Court Benchbook

Duane Champagne and Carole Goldberg, *Promising Strategies: Tribal-State Court Relations*, 23 (2013). Available at: http://www.walkingoncommonground.org/

The Idaho Tribal Court Benchbook was created by the Idaho State/Tribal Court Forum in order to provide judges, lawyers, and litigants with information and a short description of tribal judicial organizations and tribal judicial relationships with other jurisdictions, including citations to additional authorities on these and other related topics. The Idaho State/Tribal Court Forum was first convened in 1994, when the chief justice of the Idaho Supreme Court designated members of the state judiciary to serve and invited the federally recognized tribes in Idaho to send their own representatives. In an effort to alleviate jurisdictional conflicts and enhance mutual respect, the forum recommended development of a tribal court benchbook. As the preface to the publication indicates, the members of the forum set out to create "a benchbook dealing with the laws and customs of the various Tribes, as well as identifying those lawyers admitted to practice before each of the Tribes, which would be helpful to the Judges of the Idaho Judiciary and the Indian Tribes."

The benchbook describes each tribe's judicial organization and supplies names, addresses, and information relating to each of the sovereign tribes existing in the State of Idaho. It also lays out basic principles of federal Indian law that support tribal governmental powers, including judicial powers, and explains the legal framework of tribal, state, and federal jurisdiction, both civil and criminal. The benchbook then proceeds to describe the extent to which tribal and state courts are obliged to recognize and enforce one another's judgments and identifies other important interactions between tribal and state courts, including choice of law questions and the possibility of overlapping proceedings in the two court systems. Where matters remain legally uncertain, the benchbook notes that fact. It also provides Idaho legal authorities on specific topics such as search warrants and the status of traffic infractions.

The benchbook is updated periodically, the latest update having occurred in 2005. A web site was also created that provides easily accessible and more up-to-date information on the tribal courts in Idaho, as well as descriptions of the tribal governments, histories, and web sites of the five federally recognized tribes in Idaho (http://www.isc.idaho.gov/tribal-state/tribalcourt).

New Mexico Tribal-State Judicial Consortium and Cross-Cultural Exchanges

Duane Champagne and Carole Goldberg, *Promising Strategies: Tribal-State Court Relations*, 45 (2013). Available at: http://www.walkingoncommonground.org/

The New Mexico Tribal–State Judicial Consortium was established in 1998 by the joint action of the New Mexico Supreme Court and Colorado–New Mexico Indian Court Judges Association. With 14 members—7 representing state courts and 7 representing tribal courts—the consortium's initial mission was broad: "to address questions of jurisdiction and sovereignty, focusing at first in the areas of domestic violence, domestic relations and custody, child support, child abuse and neglect, and juvenile justice, and perhaps expanding into other areas of law in the future." Expansion has definitely occurred, with domestic violence, law enforcement, and general jurisdictional issues among the topics that have received attention.

Two of the original goals of the New Mexico Tribal–State Judicial Consortium were "to facilitate communication between State and Tribal judicial systems" and "to improve awareness and develop information . . . about the different judicial and legal systems in place in the State and in the various Tribes and Pueblos." In order to further those goals, the consortium has conducted a series of Cross-Court Cultural Exchanges, beginning in 2000. These exchanges, which are typically cohosted by a tribal court and a local state court, have been well attended and well received and have offered an introduction for many participants to tribal court processes and related activities. From these exchanges, workshops have been developed that have focused on issues such as child welfare and cross-jurisdictional issues presented by federal sex-offender registration requirements. The exchanges have also discussed Navajo peacemaker jurisdiction, recognition of judgments, and domestic violence matters.

New York Federal-State-Tribal Courts Forum

Duane Champagne and Carole Goldberg, *Promising Strategies: Tribal-State Court Relations*, 41-42 (2013). Available at: http://www.walkingoncommon ground.org/

The Federal-State-Tribal Court Forum was founded in 2004 through the initiative of Chief Judge Judith S. Kaye of the New York Court of Appeals, who formed a committee in 2002 engaging the tribal nations within the state, as well as federal and state judges, to study the possibility of starting a tribal-state-federal forum in New York State. The forum emerged with three main priorities:

1. To ensure accurate application of ICWA at the federal and state level;
2. To devise a means of achieving full faith and credit for judgments of tribal justice systems and federal and state courts; and
3. To provide judicial education and training, not only about relevant law but also about the cultures and justice systems of nations and tribes indigenous to what is now New York State.

As a means to achieve these goals the forum held its first Listening Conference in 2006, convening state and federal judges and court officials in sessions with tribal judges, chiefs, clan mothers, peacemakers, and other representatives from the justice systems of New York's Indian nations to exchange information and learn about respective concepts of justice. The Listening Conference, a first step in a dialogue and ongoing educational program, included panel discussions of topics such as child welfare, civil and criminal jurisdiction, and native justice systems and concepts of restorative justice. In addition, participants and panelists discussed potential solutions to the problems presented by different coexisting justice systems.

Before the New York Listening Conference, the state court committee involved in development of the forum made visits to the Onondaga Longhouse and the Oneida and Tuscarora reservations to meet with clan mothers, elders, and tribal officials. The visual theme of the conference was inspired by the Two Row Wampum (Guswhenta), a symbol of the principles governing relationships between the Iroquois/Haudenosaunee and the European nations at the time of first contact—two vessels traveling side by side, neither forcing its way into the other or trying to steer the other. A member of the Oneida Nation's Men's Council addressed the conference with an explanation of the Guswhenta. Tribal ceremonies and dances were incorporated into the proceedings, and tribal culture bearers and spiritual leaders were recognized, heard, and given positions of honor. A central goal of the forum is to enhance federal and state court judges' understanding of native cultures and justice systems in order to increase sensitivity to and respect for tribal cultures and tribal courts. The Listening Conference was one of the first steps in developing that understanding and building relationships.

Lessons Learned

Collaboration is not an easy process, particularly when there is a history of colonization, mistrust, and disrespect. As leaders, Indian nations, state courts, and law enforcement agencies have come together to tackle different jurisdictional problems, they have noted the first step is to reach out to partners in the neighboring jurisdictions. As relationships develop, opportunities to collaborate grow. Tribal-State Court Forums have become critical places to develop these relationships to collaborate or simply talk out problems.

Jerry Gardner, Executive Director of the Tribal Law and Policy Institute, developed a list of recommendations to consider in the development of tribal-state court forums. Examine the list and consider whether there are other recommendations that should be added.

Tribal/State Court Forum Dos and Don'ts[2]

(Based on the experience of the members of the Arizona Court Forum as reported by the National Center for State Courts)

Membership
- DO select forum members from diverse perspectives who have demonstrated interest, expertise, or experience in addressing Indian law issues.
- DON'T select forum members based only on their position within the judiciary or elsewhere.

Mutual Respect
- DO acknowledge differences between tribal and state court systems and seek ways of cooperating consistent with those differences.
- DON'T characterize either system as better or worse or more or less sophisticated than the other.

Scope
- DO proceed in phases with predetermined time frames, including a study phase in which issues are identified, before implementing recommendations.
- DON'T devote resources to implementation until a consensus is reached concerning priority issues and recommendations.

Persistence
- DO design a process that invites broad-based participation in identifying issues and making recommendations.
- DON'T be discouraged by lack of participation or lack of progress.

Performance
- DO assign manageable tasks to forum members or subcommittees to be accomplished within established time frames.
- DON'T delay too long before dividing the work of the forum into tasks that can be accomplished within the time frames established.

Solutions
- DO emphasize creative solutions to jurisdictional issues that avoid litigation and are consistent with the rights of the parties, sovereignty, and judicial independence.
- DON'T emphasize jurisdictional limitations.

Communications
- DO emphasize person-to-person communication and education to address jurisdictional issues.
- DON'T seek to address jurisdictional issues solely through large-scale change in the law or legal systems.

Other leaders have shared lessons learned from their experience in developing collaborative strategies. Professors Carole Goldberg and Duane Champagne addressed several lessons learned in their report "Promising Strategies: Tribal-State Court Relations," which contained many of the preceding examples. They noted all of the examples had strong and persistent leadership, followed from sustained educational efforts, and achieved progress when both sides put jurisdictional conflicts aside and focused on common goals.[4] Chief Judge Herne noted the importance of setting aside conflicts in developing the New York Federal-State-Tribal Courts Forum. "This effort is important for state and tribal court systems to begin developing a positive relationship. One of the great things they've done is they've agreed not to talk about issues that would break down a conversation, like land claims and gaming. I think the key is in keeping the lines of communication open and looking for ways to work with state courts."[5]

Conclusion

Tribal, state, and federal justice systems are collaborating to address gaps in jurisdiction, share resources, and address high crime rates. Agreements between sovereign governments typically begin with one person willing to take that initial step to reach out to their counterpart and begin bridging the years of strained relationships, resentment, mistrust, and colonialistic state and federal laws and policies. Through discussions, that often include tribal representatives educating their county, state, or federal counterparts about the history of the tribe's relationship with the county, state, or federal government, relationships are slowly built as solutions to common problems are sought.

Questions
1. What is the purpose of a law enforcement cross-deputization agreement?
2. What are some of the difficulties in developing a cross-deputization agreement?
3. What was the purpose in developing the Idaho Tribal Court Benchbook?

In Your Community
1. What type of collaborative efforts is your tribal government engaged in?
2. What obstacles exist for entering into collaborative agreements with neighboring jurisdictions?

Terms Used in Chapter 11
Cross-deputization: An agreement that facilitates law enforcement to cross borders in criminal cases.

Docket: A list of the legal cases that will be heard in court.
Tort: A civil violation where one person causes damage, injury, or harm to another person.

Notes

1. Matthew L. M. Fletcher, Kathryn E. Fort, and Wenona T. Singel, "Indian Country Law Enforcement and Cooperative Public Safety Agreements," 44 *Michigan Bar Journal* (February 2010).
2. The report may be accessed at http://www.tribal-institute.org/articles/common.htm.
3. Jerry Gardner, "Improving the Relationship between Indian Nations, the Federal Government, and State Governments," http://www.tribal-institute.org/articles/mou.htm.
4. Duane Champagne and Carole Goldberg, "Promising Strategies: Tribal-State Court Relations" (August 2013): iii.
5. Ibid., 42.

Suggested Further Reading

Duane Champagne and Carole Goldberg, "Promising Strategies: Public Law 280," August 2013, http://www.walkingoncommonground.org/promising-strategies.cfm.
Matthew L. M. Fletcher, Kathryn E. Fort, and Wenona Singel, "Indian Country Law Enforcement and Cooperative Public Safety Agreements," 43 *Michigan Bar Journal* (February 2010).
Carole Goldberg and Duane Champagne, "Promising Strategies: Tribal-State Court Relations," August 2013, http://www.walkingoncommonground.org/promising-strategies.cfm.

Overview of Criminal Laws: Statutes and Procedures

Chapter 12

Studying modern criminal law begins with understanding the definitions of crimes and exploring the **elements** that must be proven to establish that a crime has been committed.

After an explanation of how crimes are defined and applied, we will explore defenses to criminal acts and the rules of criminal procedure that police and prosecutors must follow to protect defendants' rights. Throughout these discussions we will address how tribes addressed these issues traditionally and today.

Introduction to Elements and Acts

Elements of a Crime

For every crime there are generally at least two elements:

1. A particular act, often referred to as *actus reus*, which consists of certain conduct, circumstances, omissions, or results that occur during the commission of a crime, and
2. A certain mental state or **intent**, often referred to as *mens rea*, which is the defendant's intent, knowledge, recklessness, or negligence.

Generally, both elements must be present for a crime to exist, unless a court or legislative body that writes the law decides that a mental state or intent is not necessary.

Elements of an Offense—Nez Perce Tribal Code

Nez Perce Tribal Code, Sec. 4-1-1

"Element of the offense" means:

1. the conduct, **attenuated** circumstances or result of conduct included in the description of the forbidden act in the definition of the offense; and
2. the establishment of the required mental state or **culpability** described in the offense, if any; but
3. an *"element of the offense"* shall not relate exclusively to the statute of limitations, jurisdiction, venue or to any other matter similarly unconnected with the harm or evil, incident to the prohibited conduct, or the existence of justification or excuse for such conduct.

The Act

The act, or *actus reus*, generally consists of a voluntary act that causes social harm. An act in a criminal offense can be of three types:

- Physical acts—Striking someone or stealing property are physical acts that might be prohibited by tribal ordinances.
- Verbal acts—Threatening someone with bodily harm or slandering someone's reputation are verbal acts that might be prohibited by tribal ordinance.
- Failure to act—Failing to act where a duty to act is imposed by law might also be prohibited by ordinance. For example, failing to report child abuse might be a violation of the duty to act.

Why is an act required? Without *actus reus*, governments could punish people for thoughts, wishes, or ideas. Imagine a tribal ordinance that prohibited "thinking about starting a fight." A person who is angry at someone could be arrested and convicted for a crime, even if she didn't actually start a fight. In addition, this kind of law would present problems of proof. It would be difficult to prove the content of a person's thoughts.

The U.S. Supreme Court has stated that an "act" is necessary for each crime. To charge someone with a crime that does not include an act is considered cruel and unusual punishment. In other words, a defendant would be punished for his **status**, not an act. It is wrong to send people to jail for something they are, such as a drug addict, instead of for actually using drugs.

Offense in Tribal Law

Nez Perce Tribal Code, Sec. 4-1-9

I. a. A person is not guilty of an offense unless his liability is based on conduct which includes a voluntary act or the omission to perform an act of which he is physically capable.
   b. The following are not voluntary acts within the meaning of this section:
      1. a reflex or convulsion;
      2. a bodily movement during unconsciousness or sleep;
      3. conduct during hypnosis or resulting from hypnotic suggestion;
      4. a bodily movement that otherwise is not a product of the effort or determination of the actor.
   c. Liability for the commission of an offense may not be based on an omission unaccompanied by action unless:
      1. the omission is expressly made sufficient by the definition of the offense; or
      2. a duty to perform the omitted act is otherwise required by this code.

Acts under Traditional Law

Traditionally, tribal nations had different rules and customs about what acts were prohibited or criminal. Certain acts were commonly prohibited by tribes, such as murder, treason, and witchcraft. The Iroquois specifically prohibited wife battering along with murder, treason, and witchcraft.

Other tribes developed laws about preserving their natural resources. As discussed previously, many tribes held cultural beliefs that directed them to care for their community, which included natural resources. Thus they developed laws to protect the environment and ensure everyone could partake of nature's gifts.

The Cup'ik People of the Western Tundra
John Pingayak

Rules for Seal Hunting
Over the years Cup'ik hunters developed a set of rules for hunting seals in the Bering Sea which can be calm and beautiful but which can also be treacherous for the unwary. These rules are vital for anyone who ventures onto sea ice.

   1. Use a legcik when you are walking on sea ice.
      The legcik is a hooked walking stick with an ice pick at the bottom, and it is a necessity for all hunters. Check for thin ice in front

of you, even if you walk only a short distance. The legcik can get you out of the water if you fall in.
2. Avoid thin ice.
    Dark-colored ice is thin; light-colored ice is thicker and safer. If at any time you doubt the strength of the ice, check it with a legcik.
3. When it is windy, avoid going beyond a big crack (aaquqaq) separating the shore-fast ice from the moving ice.
    On calm days it is safe to go beyond cracks that separate the shore-fast ice from the moving ice—these are cracks between the deeper and shallower areas along the shore. Big cracks develop in the ice because it rises and falls when the tide moves in and out.
4. Observe all landmarks in the area—especially the icebergs when you are seal hunting.
    On shallow sandbars, the ice is usually heaved up. These icebergs are called evuneq (large ice that is formed in the shallow parts of the sea). You can use these landmarks to help determine where you are. Be observant everywhere you go!
5. If there is a lot of loose ice during high tide, avoid going too far out at low tide or when the blocked ice opens along the solid shoreline.
    If you are going after the bearded seals when there is a lot of loose ice, go out to the deep waters. Once you catch a bearded seal, cut up the seal and go back as fast you can.
6. If ice blocks your way when you're coming back to shore, wait for the low tide because the ice may open up as the tide flows out.
    If conditions allow you to see when the ice opens, go north to the Kokechik River. The Kokechik usually opens because of high pressure at low tide. Another place to go is Nengqirneq, which is located west of the Aprun River. As long as you get to the solid ice edge, you will be fine. Being on the solid ice edge means being out of danger. But avoid getting in the moving ice during tides, because it can be very dangerous. The moving ice can crush the qayaqs or boats used for seal hunting.
7. If you are offshore without a compass and heavy fog occurs, look for an iceberg.
    Observe the iceberg by going around it. The sunny side will be light and the other side will be in shadow. The deep water is usually clear you can look and determine the shadow side. After finding the

sun's direction, move to the direction of the shore. If you have a radio, move it around until you get the best reception from the Nome area stations (KNOM or KICY), which are to the north. Once you determine the direction of Nome, west will be on your left as you face toward Nome.

8. When there is a lot of ice, do not go into the main channel of the river (kaineq) or into the mouth of a river because of the strong currents, which may be dangerous to boats.

    When there is an abundance of ice, do not go to the main channel of a river, especially during high tide. The strongest current occurs in the main channels.

9. The keys to survival in any dangerous situation are stability and clear thinking.

    This is probably the most important rule. If you panic, it can kill you. Panic causes hunters to make wrong decisions. Such decisions have caused many deaths in the past. Older hunters will usually make wise decisions and young hunters should follow those decisions. If young, less experienced hunters go against the decisions of the Elders, it will often cause accidents or even deaths. Many stories of our forefathers are about such situations.

Is the Failure to Commit an Act a Crime?

In many cultures, people have important responsibilities to one another or to the entire community. In some kinship structures, for example, all clan members are obligated to defend and protect their fellow clan members. A failure to act when harm is occurring would be considered a crime in and of itself.

In the American system, however, there is generally no affirmative duty to *prevent* harm. There is only a duty not to *commit* a social harm. There are some exceptions to this general rule. If there is a legal requirement to act, the *failure* to act becomes the voluntary act or *actus reus*. Most of these requirements arise when there is a preexisting relationship between the victim and the offender.

Some of these relationships include parents and married couples. Parents have a duty to take care of their child. Otherwise they can be charged with child neglect or abuse. The duty to act can be created by a contract, such as a caretaker who is hired to take care of an elderly person. Also, a doctor who fails to report evidence of physical child abuse is guilty of a crime under federal law.

The following case demonstrates the question of abuse and responsibility.

Court of Appeals of the Confederated Salish and Kootenai Tribes

Confederated Salish & Kootenai Tribes v. Burland (2004)
5 Am. Tribal Law 54
Before William Joseph Moran, Chief Judge, Chuck Wall, and Clayton Matt, Associate Justices.
OPINION
MORAN, Chief Judge.

On May 2nd 2002, Defendant Donelda Burland's two year old daughter, [J][1] accompanied by her preschool age sister wandered into the William Harvey Elementary School in Ronan, Montana during the daytime. An anonymous parent found the two young children by themselves playing on the school playground and brought them to a school counselor. At the time of this incident the Defendant was an inpatient in St. Luke's Hospital in Ronan, Montana having left the children to the care of her live in boy friend, Tom Evans. Counselor Amy Griffin observed numerous bruises on the [J]'s face and later she and a school social worker found numerous bruises on the torso of the child giving rise to an investigation of child abuse.

An examining medical doctor was unable to find fractures or to offer his opinion to the investigators as to the cause of the bruises and lacerations on the child's torso and head and shoulders. Further examination two days later by a physician assistant who ordered a radiological examination of the child's arm revealed significant fractures of the child's arm. Both the radius and ulna were fractured. The issue was then, how old were the fractures and to what decree [sic] were they evident to a layperson.

Subsequently the Tribal Prosecutor filed charges alleging defendant violated CSKT Laws Codified § 2–1–509, Criminal Endangerment. § 2–1–509 provides:

"2–1–509 Criminal endangerment.

(1) A person who knowingly engages in conduct that creates a substantial risk of death or serious bodily injury to another commits the offense of criminal endangerment.

(2) For purposes of this Section, 'Knowingly' means that the person is aware of the high probability that the conduct in which he or she is engaging, whatever that conduct may be, will cause a substantial risk of death or serious bodily injury to another.

(3) Criminal endangerment is a Class E offense over which the Tribes have concurrent jurisdiction with the State of Montana."

CSKT Laws as Codified defines serious bodily injury at 2– 1–114(38) as:

> "Serious bodily harm" or "Serious bodily injury" means bodily injury which "creates a risk of death, causes serious permanent or protracted loss or impairment of the function or process of any bodily member or organ, causes permanent disfigurement, or causes a serious mental disorder."

Prosecution alleges in its complaint as follows: "the Defendant . . . knowingly engaged in conduct that created a substantial risk of death or serious bodily injury to her two year old daughter, [J], by allowing her to receive multiple injuries, including bruises over her face and torso, bite marks on her face, abrasion to her face, and a fracture of both her radius and ulna, without taking any measures to stop the injuries or to seek medical attention for them."

At trial a jury returned a verdict of guilty and the trial court judge sentenced Defendant to 365 days in the tribal jail and a $5000.00 fine. The court then suspended 265 day [sic] of the jail term and the $5000.00 and defendant was ordered to meet conditions of release.

Discussion

First, the Appellant argues that the Jury Verdict was not supported by substantial evidence and specifically argues that the jury verdict should be reversed "because no **rational** finder of fact could conclude from the evidence presented at trial" that she knew of any serious bodily injury to [J]. The overwhelming witness testimony elicited at trial was that [J] had numerous bruises, lacerations and abrasion about her face, head, and torso. Witness testimony throughout the record also reveals that [J] exhibited serious pain and tenderness to an arm, later found to be have been fractured in two places. Appellant theorizes that there was not evidence sufficient to support a jury finding that Defendant knew the cause of the injuries. Prosecution argues that the conduct of Defendant was to completely abandon the care normally given to young children by parents complying with the CSKT Law as Codified and in doing so the Defendant created a substantial risk of death or serious bodily injury by specifically not taking measures to stop the injuries or to seek medical attention for them. The jury agreed. The laws established by the tribal council and provided in the Confederated Salish and Kootenai Tribes, Laws as Codified govern this jurisdiction. The specific code section analyzed in the instant matter is a replicate of the Model Penal Code and Montana Code Annotated. In the absence of specific tribal common law clarifying the issues appealed herein, we will look to Montana common law. Appellee argues that *State v. Fuger*, 170 Mont. 442, 554 P.2d 1338 (1976) and *State v. Walsh*, 281 Mont. 70, 931 P.2d 42 (1997) are helpful for our determination of the issue of what constitutes "serious bodily injury." In *Fuger*, extensive bruising and swelling around the face and a broken nose plus a fractured palate satisfied the definition of serious bodily injury. In Walsh the loss of two teeth was sufficient to establish serious bodily harm. We hold that [J] suffered serious bodily injury.

In the case before us the defendant parent lived in and was capable of observing her three children to adequately care and protect them from harm throughout the relevant time frame and she failed in that duty. We hold here that parents do indeed have the duty to protect and care for their minor children living in their household and that duty entails that every effort must be expended towards creating a healthful and safe environment within the parent's means. The defendant did fail to provide reasonable care to her child when she failed to adequately determine the source of [J]'s injuries or to seek medical care for her, and that failure created a substantial risk of death or serious bodily injury to [J].

The jury verdict is affirmed.

Omissions and Traditional Criminal Law

As discussed in previous chapters, many Native nations possess a different set of beliefs based upon spirituality and individuals' duties within their societies. These beliefs create a different and sometimes stronger set of laws or duties than are found in American criminal law.

For example, the Cherokee traditionally had spiritually based laws. The laws involving the spirits forbid omissions of certain acts, such as omissions that violate the general norms of conduct or such rituals as bathing, singing, and eating corn. As a result, the beliefs and laws that regulated behavior were quite different from the U.S. criminal laws, which criminalize very few omissions. American laws impose duties, not on the basis of spiritual beliefs or a community obligation, but rather to help or protect.

Conclusion

In order to convict a person of a crime, the prohibited behavior must be identified in the law itself. Reading statutes carefully and thoughtfully is necessary to ensure that the criminal justice system is fair to everyone. Not every type disrespectful behavior is criminal. Each tribal nation's code should set forth fair standards by which to judge the actions of the accused.

Questions

1. Is it a good idea to require an act or omission and a mental state or intent?
2. Did consumption occur in Condon? Make a case for both yes and no.

3. Do you agree with the Condon court that consumption is a "continuing process"?
4. Should there be an affirmative duty to prevent harm? If a person is drowning in a pool, should there be a law that requires you to save that person? What if you have to leave your two-year-old niece unattended while you save the person and there is a good chance that your niece will wander into the street or water while you're saving the person?

In Your Community
1. If your tribe has a criminal code,
   - Does your nation require an act as an element of every crime?
   - How does your tribal code or tribal court define consumption?
   - Does your tribal code prohibit any "status" offenses?
2. Did your tribe traditionally punish any status offenses?
3. What traditional acts did your tribe engage in to protect individuals, families, property, or resources? What acts would violate this traditional law?
4. How did your nation traditionally deal with omissions? Does your traditional belief system require certain acts? If those acts are not done, what is the punishment?

Terms Used in Chapter 12
Attenuate: To lessen the amount, force, or value, or to reduce the severity.
Culpability: Deserving blame or punishment for violating the law.
Elements: Basic parts. Elements of a crime are the basic parts that are required in order to convict someone of a crime.
Intent: The resolve or purpose to use a particular means to reach a particular result.
Rational: Based on reason.
Status: A basic condition of a person.

Note
1. To protect the identity of the victim, we have replaced her name with an initial.

Suggested Further Reading
Andrew Ashworth, "The Scope of Criminal Liability for Omission," 105 *Law Quarterly Review* 424 (1989).

Michael Corrado, "Is There an Act Requirement in the Criminal Law?" 142 *University of Pennsylvania Law Review* 1529 (1994).

The Mental State   Chapter 13

The second element of almost every criminal offense is a mental state, often referred to as *mens rea*, or a guilty mind. There are four types of *mens rea*: general intent, specific intent, constructive intent, and transferred intent.

Criminal statutes have mental states or intents to make sure accidents are not treated as crimes. Drawing the line between an accident and a crime can be difficult. For example, if someone shoots a gun into the air, that person might not "know" that the bullet may hit someone, but knows the conduct is "reckless" or unreasonable under the circumstances. Thus firing a gun into the air is considered a crime.

But if someone is driving a car down a street, obeying the speed limit and all other traffic laws, and a child runs out into the street and is hit by the car, there was no intent to hit the child and no intent to commit any crime. The driver had no way of knowing the child would run out into the street. However, if a sign indicating a school crossing and announcing a reduced speed was in view and if the driver was not obeying the sign and hit a child, then the driver may be guilty of driving negligently or recklessly.

These intent elements of American law are not necessarily consistent with traditional tribal law, and Indian nations differ as to whether a mental state or intent is considered as part of a wrongdoing. But mental states have found their way into contemporary tribal criminal codes because of the infusion of American law into contemporary tribal criminal justice systems.

General Intent

A general intent crime is one that does not include a specific intent in the statute and when the prosecution proves the act, it is presumed the defendant had the necessary intent or knew that the act was wrong. For example, if the law prohibits firing a gun in a public place, there is no specific intent to cause harm. Only a general intent to fire a gun is required to be guilty of firing a gun in a public place.

Specific Intent

A specific intent crime is one that requires the government to prove a specific state of mind, such as assault with intent to commit rape. Generally six different specific mental states are included in the definition of criminal offenses: intentionally, purposely, knowingly, willfully, recklessly, and negligently.

Intentionally

Intentionality means that the prohibited conduct is a **conscious** objective or that an offender has a desire to engage in the conduct or a conscious objective or desire to cause the result. For example, a battery is intentional if someone struck or applied force to another person and had a conscious objective or desire to injure the person.

Purposely

A person acts purposely with respect to an element of an offense when it is the person's conscious goal to engage in conduct or to cause such a result. Purposefulness may also apply when offenders are aware of facts that allow them to commit a crime and go about the crime using this knowledge.

Knowingly

Knowingness means that the offender is aware of the nature of his or her conduct; the offender is aware or believes that a circumstance exists or the offender is aware or believes that the conduct is substantially certain to cause the result. For example, a tribal ordinance may prohibit the "knowing transportation of liquor" onto the reservation. The statute requires offenders to know that alcohol is present in the car they are driving. If Fred borrows his sister's car, and there is alcohol in the trunk, but he never looks in the trunk and was never told there was alcohol in the trunk, Fred has not knowingly transported the alcohol onto the reservation.

Willfully

Willfulness means an act is done with a bad purpose or evil motive.[1] Willfulness requires that the person committing an act be consciously aware of the risk or consequences of the act.

The following tribal court decisions help illustrate the way in which tribal judges analyze the question of intent.

Proving Knowingly

Colville Confederated Tribes Court of Appeals
Colville Confederated Tribes v. Swan (2003)
31 ILR 6011
Before Dupris, C.J., Nelson, J., and Chenois, J.
The opinion of the court was delivered by: Nelson, J.

1. The Charge

Prior to June of 1999, Deborah Finley-Justus adopted her natural (biological) grandson, Jacob Riley Finley-Justus. Jacob's natural mother was Anastasia Snyder Price, the daughter of Deborah Finley-Justus.

After the adoption, a new birth certificate for Jacob Riley Finley-Justus was issued by the State of Washington. That birth certificate listed the parents as Deborah Finley-Justus and her husband. The birth certificate was sent to the Colville Tribal Enrollment Office "for enrollment purposes." Plaintiff's Exhibit #5. (P#5)

In June of 1999, Deborah Finley-Justus sent an application for enrollment of Jacob Riley Finley-Justus in the Confederated Tribes of the Colville Reservation to the Enrollment-office. The application form, P#8, has a space where the applicant is asked whether the person to be enrolled has been adopted. There are two boxes, "Yes" and "No." Rather than check either of those boxes, Deborah Finley-Justus wrote in the letters "NA."

A few spaces below, there is a box that asks for the names of the natural mother and father "[i]f applicable." Deborah Finley-Justus and her husband's names appear in these spaces.

Deborah Finley-Justus also submitted a Family Ancestry Chart for Jacob Riley Finley-Justus. This listed her and her husband as the parents of Jacob Riley Finley-Justus.

On the basis of the application, the family ancestry chart, and the birth certificate, a recommendation was made to the Tribal Government Committee (also referred to at trial as the Enrollment Committee) to enroll Jacob Riley Finley-Justus. Defendant, Richard Swan was the Chair of that Committee at that time. On July 9, 1999, the Committee agreed to the recommendation by a vote of 10-0.

The Committee's recommendation was brought before the full Council on August 5, 1999. The recommendation passed by a vote of 10-0. Jacob Riley Finley-Justus was then enrolled. Defendant was not present at this Council meeting.

On April 5, 2001, Deborah Finley-Justus was charged with Forgery, Fraud, and Conspiracy to Commit Fraud. After trial and an appeal, she was ultimately convicted of Fraud and Conspiracy. The fraudulent scheme for which she was convicted was the willful representation of her status as the natural mother of Jacob and getting him enrolled based on this misrepresentation and having a per capita payment made in his name.

On July 3, 2002, defendant was charged with Aiding and Abetting Fraud. The complaint reads as follows:

On or about the 9th day of July, 1999, the Defendant, an Indian, did Aid and Abet the commission of the crime of Fraud by Deborah Finley-Justus in the submission of her fraudulent application for enrollment of Jacob Riley Finley-Justus into the Confederated Tribes of the Colville Reservation. Specifically, the defendant, Richard Swan, in his capacity as a member of the Colville Business Council and presiding as Chair of the Tribal Government Committee, recommended approval of the application for enrollment of Jacob Riley Finley-Justus which he knew to contain willful misrepresentations by Deborah Finley-Justus concerning her status as the natural mother; this recommendation by defendant and assurances made by defendant during this Government Committee meeting aided and abetted Deborah Finley-Justus to obtain the enrollment of Jacob Riley Finley-Justus and money or other property by willful misrepresentations or deceit, to wit: a December 3, 1999, per capita payment in the amount of $500.00 for Jacob Riley Finley-Justus. The acts alleged herein took place at the Colville Agency, Nespelem, Washington, within the exterior boundaries of the Colville Indian Reservation; the defendant thereby committed the following criminal offense: Aiding and Abetting the commission of the crime of Fraud, which constitutes a violation of the Colville Tribal Law and Order Code, in particular sections: 3-1-48 and 3-1-232.

Trial was held on October 16 and 17, 2003. The Tribes called four witnesses. Two were members of the Government Committee on July 9, 1999. One, a current member of the Colville Business Council, was the Tribes Enrollment Officer on July 9, 2003. The last witness called was Deborah Finley-Justus. The Tribes then rested.

The defendant made a motion to dismiss for failure of the Tribes to prove its case. The Court granted that motion and the reasoning for that decision is laid out below.

2. *What the Tribes Must Prove*

It is important to spell out what the Tribes had to prove. We need to start with the Tribal Code. As set forth above, defendant was charged with the violation of two code sections, CTS 3-1-48 and 3-1-232.

CTC 3-1-48 states: Fraud Any person who shall, by willful misrepresentation or deceit or by false interpreting or by the use of false weights or measure, obtain any money or other property shall be guilty of Fraud. Fraud is a Class B offense.

CTC 3-1-232 states: Aiding or Abetting Any person who shall counsel, encourage, solicit, request, aid, procure or abet another to commit an offense under this Chapter or under any ordinance or regulation of the Colville Business Council shall be guilty of aiding or abetting. Aiding or Abetting an offense is an offense of the same classification as the offense aided or abetted. (Thus, in this case, a class B offense.)

Reading these two statutes together with the complaint, the Tribes must prove that Richard Swan counseled, encouraged, solicited, requested, aided, procured or abetted Deborah Finley-Justus in committing fraud. They must prove that Deborah Finley-Justus committed fraud. During the trial, the parties agreed to an instruction to the jury that admitted this fact.

That instruction read: You are instructed that Deborah Finley-Justus was convicted of fraud in connection with the application for the enrollment of Jacob Riley Finley-Justus. The attorneys have stipulated to this instruction in order to avoid calling numerous witnesses to establish this. However, Deborah Finley-Justus' conviction of fraud does not in any way establish or prove Richard Swan committed any wrongdoing in and of itself. You are still here to decide, in accordance with the instructions I give you a the end of the trial, whether Plaintiff has proven beyond a reasonable doubt that Richard Swan aided or abetted Deborah Finley-Justus in committing the fraud of which she was convict [sic].

The Tribes must prove that defendant knew the application for membership contained material misrepresentations. In other words, they must prove that he knew that Deborah Finley-Justus was not the natural mother of Jacob Riley Finley-Justus.

The Tribes must also prove that defendant took certain acts. These acts must have been made with the intent to aid and abet Deborah Finley-Justus.

Defendant argued that defendant must have known of and aided in each element of the charge against Deborah Finley-Justus. In this case, that must mean that he knew and aided Deborah Finley-Justus in receiving money as well as knowing of the material misrepresentations in the application.

The Court rejected such an interpretation of the law. If defendant was correct, then a sophisticated criminal group could commit crimes with only one of them being criminally liable. As long as the principal actor never told them that it was a criminal enterprise and as long as they each only knew of one element of the crime, they could not be guilty of aiding and abetting.

In this case, if defendant was proved to have known that the application contained material misrepresentations, then he knew or should have known that a criminal act was being undertaken. If he intended to aid or abet the criminal act, then he would be guilty.

The acts committed by the defendant must be with the intent to aid or abet Deborah Finley-Justus. They did not have to be successful or actually aid and abet. But they must have been taken with the intent to aid or abet.

There was some question about the meaning of "aid and abet." The statute reads "counsel, encourage, solicit, request, aid, procure or abet." Defendant reads this to mean that a person must "counsel, encourage, solicit, request, or procure" another to commit a crime before the person can be guilty. He drops the words "aid" and "abet." Defendant asserts that the statute is entitled "Aiding or Abetting." He concludes that the statute defines "aid" and "abet" and therefore these two words cannot be included in the definition itself.

The title is just that, the name of the crime. The statute itself defines how the crime may be committed. The statute is not an attempt to define the title, but lays out the elements of the crime itself which is called by the name of the title.

Thus, defendant may commit the crime of Aiding or Abetting, if he should "counsel, encourage, solicit, request, aid, procure or abet" another in committing a crime. In its plainest meaning, the statute makes it criminal for one person to help another person commit a crime or to get the other person to commit a crime. The Tribes must prove that when he committed the alleged acts that defendant did so with the intent to help Deborah Finley-Justus commit a crime.

. . .

4. What Was Proved
A. Summary of the Witnesses' Evidence

1. Margie Hutchinson. Ms. Hutchinson is currently on the Colville Business Council. During the period of time important to this trial, i.e., June through August 1999, she was the Enrollment Officer. The Enrollment Officer is the lead person in the Tribal Enrollment Office.

The Enrollment Office received a letter from Deborah Finley-Justus. (P#4). The letter indicated that Ms. Finley-Justus was sending in a birth certificate for Jacob Riley Finley-Justus. The letter indicated this was being done for enrollment purposes. The birth certificate was enclosed. (P#5).

These documents were put into the enrollment file for Jacob Riley Finley-Justus. Ms. Hutchinson then sent a letter to Ms. Finley-Justus (P#6). This letter included an application form for enrollment and an instruction sheet listing what documents would be needed.

The application (P#8) and a family history chart (P#9) were sent back to Enrollment. A cover letter was attached. (P#7).

A letter was sent back from Enrollment to Ms. Finley-Justus. (P#10). This letter indicated that Enrollment had received all necessary paperwork and that the application and the Enrollment Office's recommendation was being presented to the Tribal Government Committee. A copy of the recommendation (approving enrollment) was included. The letter was from Margie Hutchinson and was dated July 8, 1999.

The next step was to take the recommendation to the Enrollment Committee (also known as the Tribal Government Committee). The Committee reviews the recommendation. The Committee then either agrees or disagrees with the recommendation.

Ms. Hutchinson remembers going to the Committee with this recommendation. The Committee met on July 9, 1999. The meeting took place in the Business Council chambers. The defendant, Richard Swan, was Chair of the Committee. The Committee had the whole file including the application.

Ms. Hutchinson was unaware of any minutes of the meeting. At the meeting, Richard Swan initialed and approved the recommendation. (P#11).

The recommendation sheet (P#11) was read out to the full Business Council on August 5, 1999. The minutes of that meeting shows that Richard Swan was not at that meeting. (P#12). The full Business Council approved the enrollment and passed a Resolution stating such. (P#13).

Margie Hutchinson then sent a letter to Ms. Finley-Justus indicating that Jacob was adopted into the Tribes. Ultimately, Jacob was disenrolled.

Richard Swan did not make the application. He never told Margie Hutchinson to push this application through.

Margie Hutchinson did not call Deborah Finley-Justus about putting "NA" on the application where it asks if the child was adopted. Although in her career as the Enrollment Officer she has called and talked with applicants before, she did not do this in this case.

As far as Ms. Hutchinson knew, Richard Swan was not involved in any way prior to the case getting to the Committee. He did not attempt to keep Children and Family Services (CFS) records away from Enrollment. CFS keeps records of adopted children for the Tribes.

Ms. Hutchinson had no knowledge of defendant helping to fill out the application. Defendant was not involved in sending out the July 8, 1999 letter. (P#10).

At the time of the Committee meeting, she does not remember defendant saying to the other Committee members to sign the recommendation sheet. He did not "ram" it through. He did not do anything to force them to approve the recommendation.

In the past, members of the Committee have raised questions and sent the recommendation back to the Enrollment Office. When this happens, the Enrollment Office researches whatever questions have arisen and reports back to the Committee. If questions had been asked in this case, she would have checked on them.

The minutes of the full Council meeting show that no questions were asked. Defendant was not there and was off on tribal business. Margie Hutchinson was also not at the full Council meeting.

The Committee has voted against her recommendations in the past. They are under no obligation to follow her recommendation.

A Committee member can find out what is on a Committee's agenda prior to the hearing. Committee members can go or not to the meetings. It is not very often that the Council will not approve the enrollment if the Committee approves it but it is not automatic.

2. *Louella Anderson.* She is a member of the Colville Business Council. She was on the Enrollment Committee in July of 1999. That Committee hears enrollment application requests.

She remembers this application coming before the Committee. The meeting was at the Council chambers. Richard Swan was the Chair and was present.

The usual process is that each Committee member gets a look at the file. They then ask any questions. They then sign the recommendation sheet.

Ms. Anderson looked over the file. She saw the names of the purported parents. She did not know them personally.

She asked if this was Deborah Finley-Justus from Inchelium. Mr. Swan said: "Yes." Ms. Anderson then said that Ms. Finley-Justus was a little old to be having a baby. Mr. Swan laughed and said: "That's her kid alright." Ms. Anderson said that she was just wondering and thought she would ask. She then signed the recommendation sheet for approval of the application.

She knew that Richard Swan lived in Inchelium. She thought he must know if this was her baby. When he assured her it was, this was why she signed it.

As far as she knows, Richard Swan did not help Deborah Finley-Justus in the application. She is not sure all of the members of the Committee heard her. She assumed that he knew if it was Ms. Finley-Justus' child.

Richard Swan did not cajole Margie Hutchinson. He never asked Ms. Anderson to vote for recommendation.

3. *Jeanne Jarred.* Ms. Jarred is a member of the Colville Business Council. She was a member of the Council and the Government Committee at all times relevant to this case. She voted to approve the recommendation at the time of the Committee hearing.

Richard Swan was the Chair of the Committee at the time and was present at the meeting on July 9, 1999. She believes she sat to the right of Mr. Swan. She was able to hear him.

Ms. Jarred is a distant relative to Deborah Finley-Justus. Ms. Jarred has known her since childhood. She was not aware Deborah Finley-Justus had another baby. She testified that usually when a child is born the family and community hear about it.

She was not aware as to when Deborah Finley-Justus moved to Spokane. She did not know that Deborah Finley-Justus lived in Spokane at the time the application was made. Deborah Finley-Justus recently told Ms. Jarred that Deborah Finley-Justus lived in Spokane.

She believes that Ms. Deborah Finley-Justus has three children. Ms. Jarred believes that the youngest is about three years old.

Ms. Jarred made a comment at the Committee meeting that she did not know that Deborah Finley-Justus had another baby. Mr. Swan said: "Yeah she did" or "Yes she did." He said nothing else directly to her.

Ms. Jarred heard Margie Hutchinson comment that Deborah Finley-Justus was a little old to have a baby. Richard Swan said: "She's a late bloomer."

Richard Swan did not say anything on his own. He only made these remarks in response to comments from Ms. Jarred and Ms. Hutchinson. The recommendation is brought by the Enrollment Officer. Richard Swan did not come to Ms. Jarred to get this application passed.

The Committee gets the full file. They are given the documents, a family history and a recommendation. Enrollment does a background check to see if the person is eligible. The age of the applicant is something for Enrollment to check on.

A birth certificate was part of the documents given to the Committee. This is a required document. If it is not present, then the application should not be processed.

It is not her responsibility to question the birth certificate. It is not Richard Swan's duty to do so either.

Margie Hutchinson made her comment. It was made to no one in particular. There was no general discussion of the issue.

She does not know what others may have known about this incident. She was relying on the documents given to her.

She does not know if Richard Swan met with Deborah Finley-Justus before the application. She believed he knew where she lived because of his political activities.

Because Richard Swan and Deborah Finley-Justus were relatives, she assumed he knew if Jacob Riley Finley-Justus was Deborah Finley-Justus' son. She does not know if in fact he knew.

Even if she did not sign the recommendation sheet it would still have gone to the full Council because there were enough other signatures approving it. Richard Swan was not at the full Business Council meeting where the application was approved. All of those in attendance approved the application.

4. Deborah Finley-Justus. Deborah Finley-Justus was born at Colville, Washington. She was raised in Inchelium, Washington and still has a house there. She is related to Richard Swan. He is her third cousin. Deborah Finley-Justus' mother and Richard Swan's grandmother were sisters.

She is the mother of Anastasia Price. Jacob Riley Finley-Justus is Anastasia's son. Deborah Finley-Justus adopted him from Anastasia.

After Jacob Riley Finley-Justus was baptized, the community knew that he was adopted. It was pretty much a whole family celebration.

She thinks Richard Swan was at a barbeque she held at her house on Easter Sunday 1999 after the baptism. There were a lot of people there coming and going. Richard Swan was probably invited but she did not personally invite him.

Her whole family was at the baptism. Her husband raised Jacob Riley Finley-Justus above his head and said this is the newest member of the family.

There were a total of about fifteen people getting baptized that day. She did not see Richard Swan there. Most of the community did not know until the baptism. Richard Swan did not know about the adoption.

Deborah Finley-Justus was asked about her prior testimony at her own trial. This is contained in P#20 on page 179. While the transcript was not read into evidence, the gist of it was.

The transcript reads as follows:

Q. And was it your understanding that the community knew of the adoption?
A. Oh yes. Everybody knew. We celebrated it. We celebrated it in Inchelium.
Q. And by everybody, who do you mean specifically?
A. My whole family.
Q. Uh-huh.
A. There were Bob Louie, Richard Swan, Lou Stone, Jude Stenskar [sic], there were a lot of other folks that had been in council that aren't in council.
Q. Many of those who were on council at the time . . .
A. Yes. Yes.
Q. And your application for enrollment of Jacob would have been before these people?
A. Yes. Pages 179–80, lines 19–22 and 1–11. Questions by Dan Gargan, spokesperson for Deborah Finley-Justus. Answers by Deborah Justus-Finley.

At the instant trial, Deborah Finley-Justus testified that when she said that the whole family was at the baptism she was not sure if Richard Swan was there. The church was full with about fifteen other children getting baptized. (D#1).

Richard Swan is a cousin. When she said "whole family" she meant her close family. Mr. Swan is not a member of her close family.

She has been in Spokane since 1977. She is a Planner/Grant Writer for the Chehalis Tribe.

She had four children. Now she has five with Jacob Riley Finley-Justus. Her husband is a civil engineer with the Department of Health. She does return to Inchelium. She usually goes to Inchelium Days. She sees her cousins then.

Jacob Riley Finley-Justus was held out as her own son. She was told that according to Washington State law, he was their son as if he was their biological son. She is not required to refer to his adoption.

Richard Swan had no part in the adoption in any way. He had no part in the letter sent to ask that Jacob Riley Finley-Justus be enrolled. He did not know she was going to do that.

She did not know that Richard Swan was on the Government Committee until two days ago. She did not contact any member of that Committee, including Richard Swan, prior to the vote.

No one from Enrollment or the Tribes called her with any questions. She said that she and her husband were the natural parents. She was convicted for fraud because of this.

She did not know the Enrollment process. She did not know Richard Swan's role in an Enrollment. No one told her what happened at a Committee meeting. She did know that it had to go to the full Council.

Richard Swan's name was not on the paperwork she got about the enrollment being approved. He was apparently on travel.

She assumed that Council members knew of the adoption. She does remember seeing Jude Stensgar at the baptism. She does not remember seeing Lou Stone. No one asked at her trial if she actually saw them at the church for the baptism.

She is under oath today. She told the truth.

5. Analysis

Looking at the testimony above, there are problems in proof of both knowledge and intent. Neither of these were proven to the point where a reasonable juror could have found beyond a reasonable doubt that Richard Swan knew that Jacob Riley Finley-Justus was not the natural son of Deborah Finley-Justus nor that Richard Swan had the intent to help, aid or abet Deborah Finley-Justus in her fraud.

A reasonable juror could have found that certain acts were made that could have been in aid of the fraud. These were the statements made by Mr. Swan at the Committee hearing. These statements are not enough on their own.

A. Knowledge

At her trial, Deborah Finley-Justus testified that the whole community knew of the adoption. When asked who she meant specifically she said her whole family and then named several people including Richard Swan.

At this trial, she explained that she did not know if Richard was even there. She also said the term "whole family" meant her close family, not cousins like Richard Swan.

None of the other witnesses could say whether or not Richard Swan knew. They assumed he knew but could not say if he actually knew.

This element is a close one. The jury could have believed Deborah Finley-Justus' first testimony and disbelieved her testimony at the second trial. However, it must be remembered that the jury in the first trial disbelieved her. In addition, she was testifying about how "everyone knew" because if believed it would be hard to say she was being deceitful, an element in her fraud case.

The "everyone knew" testimony is also obviously hyperbole. Surely this cannot mean that literally everyone in Inchelium was proven to have known because of these words.

She did specifically identify Richard as one of the persons who knew. She was never asked at her trial how she knew he knew. When that basic line was inquired into at this trial, she said she did not see Mr. Swan at the church. She did not invite him to her home afterwards but that he may have been there.

There is not enough to say that he knew beyond a reasonable doubt. This element was not proven by the Tribes.

B. Intent

There is even less evidence of intent. While it is clear that the jury could have easily found that he made the statements, there are problems with the proof of intent.

While it is not required, there was no direct proof of intent. The only way intent could have been found was by inference or circumstantial evidence.

Here, the witnesses testified that Richard Swan never came to them before the Committee hearing to ask them to approve this application. The only evidence was that he did not coerce, threaten or otherwise force anyone to approve the application.

The only evidence was that Richard Swan was not involved in making or sending in the application. He never talked with Enrollment prior to the Committee hearing. At the Committee hearing, Mr. Swan did not initiate any statements or discussion of this application. He merely responded to three comments made by persons in attendance.

There is no evidence as to who heard any of the statements except that each member who made a comment heard Mr. Swan's response. In addition, Ms. Jarred said she heard the reply to Ms. Hutchinson's comment.

None of the witnesses could say that all of the members heard the statements. The witnesses were not even sure if anyone other than Mr. Swan heard their comments.

Ms. Jarred testified that the members could rely upon the documents provided by Enrollment. She testified that it was not her, nor Mr. Swan's, nor any Committee member's, duty to question the birth certificate.

There may be many reasons why Mr. Swan made the statements he did. One of those is that he intended to aid Deborah Finley-Justus. But others are equally as likely.

One of those is that he, like Ms. Hutchinson, Ms. Anderson and Ms. Jarred, was merely relying on the documents in front of him. The birth certificate said that this was her child. When a comment was made about whether this was Deborah Finley-Justus' child, he could have merely looked at the birth certificate and said the child was hers alright. When the comment was made that a member did not know she had another child, he could have known what was in the Enrollment file and said yes she did.

While the "late bloomer" comment may have been in bad taste, it may also have been based upon his knowledge of the file. It may not have had anything to do with aiding her fraud.

The lack of evidence is also profound. There is no evidence he helped Deborah Finley-Justus in the application. He did not speak to any Committee members prior to the meeting to get them to approve this application. He put no pressure on Ms. Hutchinson and in fact did not contact her about this prior to the meeting.

He did not raise the issue in the meeting. He made at most three comments. These comprised about a dozen words spoken to three different persons present. He never said the members should vote for this application. He was not at the full Council meeting.

Again, there is not sufficient evidence for a reasonable juror to find beyond a reasonable doubt that Mr. Swan made these statements (all factual based upon the documents in front of the Committee which had been reviewed and approved by Enrollment) with the intent to aid Deborah Finley-Justus in her fraud. This element was not proved by the Tribes.

6. Conclusion

Looking at all of the evidence in the light most favorable to the Tribes, the elements of knowledge and intent were not proved sufficiently to allow this case to go to the jury. Based upon that, the case should have been dismissed at the time the Tribes rested.

7. Order

1. The case is dismissed with prejudice for failure of the Tribes to sufficiently prove the elements of knowledge and intent.
2. Each party will bear their own costs and fees.

Constructive Intent

Constructive intent includes crimes in which the offender did not intend for the end result to happen, but should have known the end result would happen. Often this is defined as having a disregard for other person's safety. Most jurisdictions include recklessly and negligently as constructive intent crimes.

Negligently

People act negligently if they take an unjustifiable risk that harms or endangers another. The risk must be of such a nature and degree that the offender's failure to perceive it, considering the nature and purpose of the conduct and the circumstances known to the offender, involves a great deviation from what a reasonable person would do in the situation.

Recklessly

People act recklessly if they consciously disregard a substantial and unjustifiable risk. For example, a person driving seventy-five miles per hour in front of a school and ignoring the traffic signs that children are present is acting recklessly toward the children that may be hit and injured. The risk must be so great that, considering the circumstances known to the offender, it is something a law-abiding person would never accept.

Many jurisdictions separate negligent and reckless intent according to whether the offender knew of the risk. Negligence requires that the offender should have known about the risk. Recklessness requires (1) that the offender actually knew about the risk but still disregarded it and (2) that the risk was huge.

Transferred Intent

Finally, transferred intent occurs when a person intends to harm a specific person, but ends up hurting another person. The intent to commit the first crime is transferred to the crime that was actually committed. For example, Victor throws a bottle at Ray, but Ray ducks and the bottle hits Sally. Victor's intent toward Ray is transferred to the actual victim, Sally. If the transferred intent rule were not used, Victor would not be held accountable for hitting Sally with a bottle.

Mental States in Tribal Law—Pueblo of Laguna, NM Criminal Code

Section 15-2-2. *Culpability—General requirements.*

A. *A person is not guilty of an offense unless he acted purposely, knowingly, recklessly, or negligently, as the law may require, with respect to each element of the offense; unless his acts constitute an offense involving* **strict liability**.
B. *Culpable mental states. The following definitions apply with respect to the offenses set forth in this title:*
   (1) *"Purposely" means a person acts purposely with respect to an element of an offense:*
      (a) *If the element involves the nature of his or her conduct or a result thereof, it is his conscious object to engage in conduct of that nature or to cause such a result; and*
      (b) *If the element involves the* **attendant circumstances**, *he is aware of the existence of such circumstances; or he believes or hopes that they exist.*
   (2) *"Knowingly". A person acts knowingly with respect to an element of an offense:*
      (a) *If the element involves the nature of his or her conduct or the attendant circumstances, he is aware that his conduct is of that nature or that such circumstances exist; and*
      (b) *If the element involves a result of his or her conduct, he is aware that it is practically certain that his conduct will cause such a result.*
   (3) *"Recklessly". A person acts recklessly with respect to an element of an offense when he consciously disregards a substantial and unjustifiable risk that the element exists or will result from his conduct. The risk must be of such a nature and degree that, considering the nature and purpose of the actor's conduct and the circumstances known to him, its disregard involves a gross deviation from the standard of conduct that a law-abiding person would observe in the actor's situation.*

(4) *"Negligently"*. A person acts negligently with respect to an element of an offense when he should be aware of a substantial and unjustifiable risk that the element exists or will result from his conduct. The risk must be of such a nature and degree that the actor's failure to perceive it, considering the nature and purpose of his or her conduct and the circumstances known to him, involves a gross deviation from the standard of care that a reasonable person would observe in the actor's situation.

(5) *"Strict liability"*. An element of an offense shall involve strict liability only when the definition of the offense or element clearly indicated a legislative purpose to impose strict liability by use of the phrase "strict liability" or other terms of similar import. When so used, no proof of a culpable mental state is required to establish the commission of the element or offense.

C. *When the culpability sufficient to establish an element of an offense is not specifically prescribed by law, such element is established if a person acts purposely, knowingly or recklessly with respect to that element.*

D. *When the law defining an offense prescribes the kind of culpability that is sufficient for the commission of an offense, without distinguishing among the elements thereof, such provision shall apply to all the material elements of the offense, unless a contrary purpose plainly appears.*

E. *When the law provides that negligence suffices to establish an element of an offense, such element is also established if a person acts purposely, knowingly or recklessly. When recklessness suffices to establish an element, such element is also established if a person acts purposely or knowingly. When acting knowingly suffices to establish an element, such element is also established if a person acts purposely.*

F. *When knowledge of the existence of a particular fact is an element of an offense, such knowledge is established if a person is or should be aware of a high probability of its existence, unless he actually believes that it does not exist.*

G. *A requirement that an offense be committed wilfully is satisfied if a person acts knowingly with respect to the material elements of the offense, unless a purpose to impose further requirements appears.*

Strict Liability

Strict liability crimes are offenses or wrongdoings that do not require a mental intent. For examples of strict liability crimes see table 13.1. The law does not require proof of intent or that the defendant knew it was wrong. These are often referred to as *malum prohibitum* crimes, or the government has declared that these acts are criminal, regardless of intent or knowledge of the offender.

To determine whether a crime is a strict liability crime, one must look at the elements contained in the definition of the crime. The difficulty is when intent is not included in the law, the drafters of the law may have consciously made the offense a strict liability crime requiring no mental state or may have inadvertently omitted the required mental state. The Pueblo of Laguna example above requires the drafters of the law to state it is a strict liability crime, otherwise intent is inferred. Other legislatures may not be as clear and the courts will have to interpret the statute to determine if it is a strict liability crime. Generally, the defendant bears the burden of persuading the court that the tribe intended a required mental state as part of the definition of the offense. If the court finds a mental state is required, then the prosecution must prove the existence of the implied mental state in addition to the other elements of the crime. The federal courts and many state courts use a general presumption that a mental intent is required, and therefore implied, by most statutes.[2]

For example, many jurisdictions have a "statutory rape" law prohibiting people from having sexual intercourse with a child, usually under the age of sixteen. If such a statute does not state that the defendant must know that the person was under the age of sixteen, then the statute is not clear about whether the crime is a strict liability crime or comprises an implied mental state. Because the ordinance makes no mention of a required mental state, the defendant bears the burden of persuading the court that knowledge of the child's age is part of the offense. If the court so finds, the prosecution must prove the presence of such knowledge beyond a reasonable doubt to support a conviction of the offense of statutory rape. If the court finds a mental state was intentionally left out of the statute, the crime is a strict liability crime. In other words, the offender is strictly liable for the acts, regardless of his intent.

Examples of Strict Liability Crimes

- Driving without a license
- Selling prohibited beverages to minors
- Public health laws
- Littering

Strict Liability in Tribal Court

Colville Confederated Tribes Court of Appeals
Shane C. Innes v. Colville Confederated Tribes (1992)
1 CTCR 57, 1992.NACC.0000001 (VersusLaw)
Before Chief Judge Bonga, Judge Collins and Judge Miles
The opinion of the court was delivered by: Bonga, C.J.

Discussion
The Appellate Panel finds that . . . the Intoxication statute is an offense of malum prohibitum [a wrong because society prohibits it]. Such statutes are designed to protect and preserve the peace of the citizenry. Intent, or a specific mens rea, is not an element of such an offense, nor does the law require such an element for validity. The prohibited act itself is the crime.

> The Panel further agrees with the appellee position . . . that when a person voluntarily consumes intoxicating beverages, that **volitional** consumption makes the actor liable for the consequences that may occur as a result of his intoxication. . . . The evidence found in the court record supports the jury's finding of guilty.
>
> It is hereby Ordered and Adjudged that the jury decision in this matter is Affirmed.

Traditional Criminal Law and Intent

The mental state element in traditional criminal rules depended upon the tribe and its customs. Among the Yurok, intent was irrelevant. "Intent, ignorance, malice or negligence, are never a factor. The fact and amount of damage are alone considered. The psychological attitude is as if intent were always involved."[3] The Choctaw allowed even accidental killings to be avenged by relatives of the victim, indicating that intent, at least when it involved a death, was irrelevant.[4] Many of the other nations discussed in earlier chapters focus their justice system on atonement or restitution for the act. The amount of restitution depended upon the value of the individual killed or the severity of the crime, which meant that the "crime" did not necessarily include intent, unlike the American system, which often looks first to intent in order to determine the severity of the crime.

The traditional teachings below of the Yup'ik and the Cheyenne illustrate the different role of mental states or intent among different indigenous peoples. The case of Sticks Everything Under His Belt provides an example of a person purposely violating Cheyenne law. "Cheyenne law was built to deal with action, not with intention,"[5] and as a result he was disciplined for his action, not necessarily his intent and the discipline helped restore him to the community. And intent did not play a role in the discipline of Cries Yia Eya. However, the power of one's thoughts plays an important role among the Yup'ik.

The Tribal Ostracism and Reinstatement of Sticks Everything Under His Belt

Karl N. Llewellyn and E. Adamson Hoebel, *The Cheyenne Way*, University of Oklahoma Press, 9-12 (1941).

Once, at a time when all the Cheyenne tribe was gathered together, Sticks Everything Under His Belt went out hunting buffalo alone. "I am hunting for myself," he told people. He was implying that the rules against individual hunting did not apply to him because he was declaring himself out of the tribe—a man on his own.

All the soldier chiefs and all the tribal chiefs met in a big lodge to decide what to do in this case, since such a thing had never happened before. This was the ruling they made: no one could help Sticks Everything Under His Belt in any way, no one could give him smoke, no one could talk to him. They were cutting him off from the tribe. The chiefs declared that if anyone helped him in any way that person would have to give a Sun Dance.

When the camp moved, Sticks Everything Under His Belt moved with it, but the people would not recognize him. He was left alone and it went to his heart, so he took one of his horses (he had many) and rode out to the hilltops to mourn.

His sister's husband was a chief in the camp. This brother-in-law felt sorry for him out there mourning, with no more friends. At last he took pity on his poor brother-in-law; at last he spoke to his wife, "I feel sorry for your poor brother out there and now I am going to do something for him. Cook up all those tongues we have! Prepare a good feast!"

Then he invited the chiefs to his lodge and sent for his brother-in-law to come in. This was after several years had passed, not months.

When the chiefs had assembled, the brother-in-law spoke. "Several years ago you passed a ruling that no one could help this man. Whoever should do so, you said, would have to give a Sun Dance. Now is the time to take pity on him. I am going to give a Sun Dance to bring him back in. I beg you to let him come back to the tribe, for he has suffered long enough. This Sun Dance will be a great one. I declare that every chief and all the soldiers must join in. Now I put it up to you. Shall we let my brother-in-law smoke before we eat, or after?"

The chiefs all answered in accord, "Ha-ho, ha-ho [thank you, thank you]. We are very glad you are going to bring back this man. However, let him remember that he will be bound by whatever rules the soldiers lay down for the tribe. He may not say he is outside of them. He has been out of the tribe for a long time. If he remembers these things, he may come back."

Then they asked Sticks Everything Under His Belt whether he wanted to smoke before or after they had eaten. Without hesitation he replied, "Before," because he had craved tobacco so badly that he had split his pipe stem to suck the brown gum inside it.

The lodge was not big enough to hold all the chiefs who had come to decide this thing, so they threw open the door, and those who could not get in sat in a circle outside. Then they filled a big pipe and when it was lighted they gave it to Sticks Everything Under His Belt. It was so long since he had had tobacco that he gulped in the smoke and fell over in a faint. As he lay there the smoke came out of his anus, he was so empty. The chiefs waited silently for him to come to again and then the pipe was passed around the circle.

When all had smoked, Sticks Everything Under His Belt talked. "From now on I am going to run with the tribe. Everything the people say, I shall stay right by it. My brother-in-law has done a great thing. He is going to punish himself in the Sun Dance to bring me back. He won't do it alone, for I am going in, too."

In another case, the Cheyenne incorporated intent, when they dealt with the length of banishment of a wrongdoer. Typically banishment for murder was five or ten years, but it could be shortened due to the absence of intent. In the case of White Bear, who accidentally killed his mother while drunk, it was decided that because the killing was accidental, White Bear would be allowed to rejoin the community. But it is important to note that although absence of intent might alleviate the type or length of punishment among the Cheyenne, the Cheyenne still had to undergo their cultural ritual of Cleansing the Arrows to remove the sin of any killing, regardless of intent. The Cheyenne also made a distinction between "decent men who happened to kill and mean, bullying men, who in their overbearing conduct kill."[6] This distinction illustrates that the Cheyenne took intent into account when considering reinstating the offender into the community, as they did in the case of Cries Yia Eya, who was a naturally mean man.

Cries Yia Eya Banished for the Murder of Chief Eagle
Karl N. Llewellyn and E. Adamson Hoebel, *The Cheyenne Way*, University of Oklahoma Press, 9-12 (1941).

Cries Yia Eya had been gone from the camp for three years because he had killed Chief Eagle in a whiskey brawl. The chiefs had ordered him away for his murder, so we did not see anything of him for that time. Then one day he came back, leading a horse packed with bundles of old-time tobacco. He stopped outside the camp and sent a messenger in with the horse and tobacco who was to say to the chiefs for him, "I am begging to come home."

The chiefs all got together for a meeting, and the soldier societies were told to convene, for there was an important matter to be considered. The tobacco was divided up and chiefs' messengers were sent out to invite the solider chiefs to come to the lodge of the tribal council, for the big chiefs wanted to talk to them. "Here is the tobacco that that man sent in," they told the soldier chiefs. "Now we want you soldiers to decide if you think we should accept his request. If you decide that we should let him return, then it is up to you to convince his family that it is all right." (The relatives of Chief Eagle had told everybody that they would kill Cries Yia Eya on sight if they ever found him. "If we set eyes on him, he'll never make another track," they had vowed.) The soldier chiefs took the tobacco and went out to gather their troops. Each society met in its own separate lodge to talk among themselves, but the society servants kept passing back and forth between their different lodges to report on the trend of the discussion in the different companies.

At last one man said, "I think it is all right. I believe the stink is blown from him. Let him return!" This view was passed around, and this is the view that won out among the soldiers. Then the father of Chief Eagle was sent for and asked whether he would accept the decision. "Soldiers," he replied, "I shall listen to you. Let him return! But if that man comes back, I want never to hear his voice raised against another person. If he does, we come together. As far as that stuff of his is concerned, I want nothing that belonged to him. Take this share you have set aside for me and give it to someone else."

Cries Yia Eya had always been a mean man, disliked by everyone, but he had been a fierce fighter against the enemies. After he came back to the camp, however, he was always good to the people.

Ann Fienup-Riordan, *Boundaries and Passages: Rule and Ritual in Yup'ik Eskimo Oral Tradition*, Univeristy of Oklahoma, 52-53 (1994).

The Yup'ik Eskimos believed that animals and humans alike shared a common code for conduct, emphasizing personal integrity and respect for others in their interaction. These rules for living marked the crucial boundaries both between and within the human and animal worlds. They were known collectively as qaneryarat (from qaner – to speak, literally "that which is spoken"), and specifically as alerquutet (laws or instructions, from alerqur – to tell to do something, to advise, to command, to order) and inerquutet (admonishments or warnings, from inerqur – to admonish, to tell or warn not to do something). The rules enabled a person to "stand up properly."

As both human and nonhuman persons grew to maturity and gained awareness, they learned a multitude of alerquutet and inerquutet for the proper living of life:

Alerguun [singular] . . . is passed on orally. They tell it so that it is strongly encouraged for people to live by. The alerguun gives strict guidelines for a person to live by.

And inerquun, a warning, which will cause bodily damage to a person that will cause that person to be irritating to others, or cause unfavorable attention to [that person], that is strongly discouraged. (footnote omitted)

The rules for proper living took a lifetime to learn and to fully understand. Three related ideas underlay their detail: the power of a person's thought; the importance of thoughtful action to avoid injuring another's mind, and, conversely, the danger inherent in following one's own mind.

Regarding the power of a person's thought, the message was that people's attitudes were as significant as their actions. Thus, hunters admonished young men to "keep the thought of the seals" foremost in their minds as they shoveled snow, carried out trash, and hauled water. In these acts, by the power of their mind, they "made a way for the seals" they would someday hunt.

Conclusion

Mental states or intent are defined by tribal law, which is interpreted by tribal courts. In criminal law, intent is typically required to ensure accidents are not prosecuted or treated as crimes. The various types of intents often contribute to the seriousness of the offense. Prosecutors will look to tribal law to discern what intent is required to be proven in court. Prosecutors will then present evidence in their case to prove the offender had the required intent to commit the crime. The judge or jury will then determine whether the necessary intent was proven beyond a reasonable doubt. Unless intent is not required, because it is a strict liability crime, failure to prove intent will result in a not guilty verdict.

Questions

1. Do you agree with the Court in *Colville Confederated Tribes v. Swan*? Why or why not?
2. What is a *malum prohibitum* offense? Is it a good idea to have these kinds of offenses? Why or why not?

3. What kinds of crimes do you think should be "strict liability"? Why do you think that intent is not important for these crimes?
4. According to the passages from *The Cheyenne Way*, how did the Cheyenne use intent in dealing with wrongdoers?

In Your Community
1. How did your nation traditionally use intent in dealing with wrongdoers?
2. How does your tribal code define different mental states?
3. Does your tribal code provide for strict liability crimes?

Terms Used in Chapter 13
Attendant circumstances: Facts surrounding an event.
Conscious: Possessing the faculty of knowing one's own thoughts or mental operations.
Strict liability: Guilt even without criminal intention.
Volitional: By a conscious choice or decision.

Notes
1. Joshua Dressler, *Understanding Criminal Law* 127 (Lexis, 2001).
2. *U.S. v. U.S. Gympsum Co.*, 438 U.S. 422 (1978).
3. A. L. Kroeber, *Yurok Law and Custom, the California Indians Source Book* 391 (R. F. Heizer and M. A. Whipple, eds., University of California Press, 1971).
4. Angie Debo, *The Rise and Fall of the Choctaw Republic* 22 (University of Oklahoma Press, 1961).
5. Karl N. Llewellyn and E. Adamson Hoebel, *The Cheyenne Way* 124 (University of Oklahoma Press, 1941).
6. Id. at 137, 144.

Suggested Further Reading
Jeremy M. Miller, "Mens Rea Quagmire: The Conscience or Consciousness of the Criminal Law?" 29 *Western State Law Review* 21 (2001).
Harvey Wallace and Cliff Roberson, *Principles of Criminal Law.* 4th ed. (Pearson, 2008).
Deborah M. Weiss, "Scope, Mistake, and Impossibility: The Philosophy of Language and Problems of Mens Rea," 83 *Columbia Law Review* 1029 (1983).

A Closer Look at Criminal Elements

Chapter 14

Today tribal criminal law includes crimes such as driving while under the influence of alcohol, child abuse, domestic violence, murder, assault, battery, theft, and drugs. Acts that are considered crimes should be part of a written tribal criminal code. Every tribe must continually review its criminal code to ensure it is meeting the needs of the community and protecting the community from acts the community has deemed wrong.

The definition and elements of the crimes of battery, assault, theft, and driving while under the influence of intoxicating liquor or drugs are presented here to illustrate the act and mental-state requirements of a crime. Each general definition is followed by actual criminal offenses taken from various tribal codes. After each example are hypotheticals you can use to test your knowledge. Answers are included at the end of the chapter.

Assault

An assault may be defined in one of two ways: (1) an attempted battery, in which case it is often required that the defendant have a "present ability" to commit the battery which failed (swinging and missing), or (2) a verbal battery, in which case the defendant threatens the victim in some way (e.g., saying "I'm going to get you") with the intent to injure or frighten the victim, resulting in the victim's reasonable **apprehension** of bodily harm. Each sovereign can define assault differently, as tribes did under traditional law.

A. Examples and Hypotheticals: Assault

Sault Ste. Marie Tribal Code Sec. 71.701
Offense: A person commits the offense of assault, if:

- A. *he attempts to commit a battery or an unlawful act that places another in reasonable apprehension of receiving an immediate battery; and*
- B. *he intended either to injure the person or intended to put the person in reasonable fear or apprehension of an immediate battery.*

HYPOTHETICALS

A1. Fred and Barney are having a verbal argument. Fred says to Barney, "I hate you! Get away from me!" Barney is frightened by Fred's words. Has Fred committed an assault?

A2. While Wilma is sitting behind the wheel of her car, Betty slams a baseball bat into the windshield while screaming, "I'm going to get you!" The windshield is shattered. Wilma is not hurt but is afraid of Betty. Has Betty committed an assault?

B. Examples and Hypotheticals: Assault

Oglala Law and Order Code Sec. 62.
Any Indian who shall attempt or threaten bodily harm to another person through unlawful force or violence shall be deemed guilty of assault . . . .

HYPOTHETICALS

B1. While angry, Warren says to Michael, "I'm going to blow you away." Did Warren assault Michael?

B2. Anna and Rachel are arguing. Anna picks up a knife and lurches toward Rachel, who dodges out of the way at the last minute. The knife ends up in the wall. Is Anna guilty of assault?

Battery

Battery is generally considered to be an act committed with the intent to injure and that results in harm to the victim. Each jurisdiction defines what kinds of actions can constitute battery. For example, the "harm" can include any "offensive touching" or injury. Some jurisdictions may decide that battery may be committed even if there is no actual physical injury or even if only the victim's clothing is touched. A battery may also be committed indirectly, such as if a defendant kicks a ladder out from under someone, causing the victim to fall and be injured.

C. Examples and Hypotheticals: Battery

Duckwater Shoshone Tribe Law and Order Code Section 2.02

A person commits the offense of battery if:

    A. He intentionally causes bodily injury to another person without legal justification,
    B. With intent to batter, threaten, **menace**, intimidate, or endanger any person he causes bodily injury to another person,
    C. If he recklessly or by gross negligence causes bodily injury to another person,
    D. Under circumstances manifesting indifference to the value of human life, he intentionally engages in conduct which creates significant risk of injury to a person, and thereby causes bodily injury to another person,
    E. He operates a motor vehicle in a reckless or grossly negligent manner, or while intoxicated, or while under the influence of alcohol, drug, or other intoxicant, and such conduct causes bodily injury to another person.

HYPOTHETICALS

    C1. Joe is walking down the stairs when he trips and falls. As he is falling, Joe's head strikes Tim, who is walking up the stairs. Tim suffers a broken nose because of the collision. Has Joe committed a battery?
    C2. Tim and Joe are known enemies and have been feuding for many years. One night, hoping that Joe will be injured, Tim leaves broken glass outside Joe's front door. The next morning, Joe steps outside with no shoes on and cuts his foot. Is Tim guilty of battery?

D. Nez Perce Tribal Code Sec. 4-1-38.

It shall be unlawful for any person to:

    A. willfully and unlawfully use force or violence to another;
    B. actually, intentionally and unlawfully touch or strike another person against their will; or
    C. unlawfully and intentionally [cause] bodily harm to an individual.

HYPOTHETICALS

    D1. Leslie is angry at Marla and pushes her into a wall. Marla has no physical injuries. Is Leslie guilty of battery?

D2. Marla falls asleep at the wheel of her car and strikes Leslie, causing injury to Leslie. Did Marla commit a battery?

Theft

The crime of theft is generally defined as the taking of property not your own, without permission of the owner, with intent to deprive the owner of the property. Historically, the three crimes of larceny, embezzlement, and false pretenses, which deal with various aspects of the general crime of theft, were treated separately. But the distinctions between these crimes were only technical and confusing, and many tribes simply use the single offense of theft, which includes several different actions. Traditionally, theft was not a common crime among many tribes. For example, stealing outside the tribe was a virtue among the Choctaw, but little theft occurred between tribal members because Choctaw society held falsehood in contempt.[1] Stealing was also rare among the Comanches, so they had little reason to develop methods or mechanisms for dealing with theft.[2]

The Iroquois also experienced very little theft; as with the Choctaw, the consequence of theft was public indignation, which was a severe punishment among the Iroquois.[3]

E. Examples and Hypotheticals: Theft

Sault Ste. Marie Tribal Code Sec. 71.806

Offense: A person commits the offense of theft, if he knowingly obtains or exercises control over anything of value of another, without authorization, or by threat or deception, or knowing said thing of value to be stolen; and he

   a. *intends to deprive such other person permanently of the use or benefit of the thing of value; or*
   b. *knowingly uses, conceals or abandons the thing of value in such a manner to deprive such other person permanently of its use or benefit; or*
   c. *uses, conceals or abandons the thing of value intending that such use, concealment or abandonment will deprive such other person permanently of its use and benefit; or*
   d. *demands any consideration to which he is not legally entitled as a condition of restoring the thing of value to such other person; or*
   e. *having lawfully obtained possession for temporary use of the personal property of another, deliberately fails to reveal the whereabouts of or to return said property to the owner or his representative or the person from whom he has received it, with the intent to permanently deprive such other person of its use and benefit.*

HYPOTHETICALS
>   E1. Bob allows Tom to borrow his power drill for a day. Later, Tom refuses to return the power drill when Bob asks for it. Later, Tom tells his wife, "I'm going to keep this drill. Bob doesn't even use it." Is Bob guilty of theft?
>   E2. While at the tribal health clinic, Barbara accidentally picks up a purse that doesn't belong to her. She takes the purse home without realizing that it is the wrong one. Is Barbara guilty of theft?

Driving While under the Influence of Intoxicating Liquor or Drugs (also known as DWI, DUI)

The statutory definition of driving while under the influence of intoxicating liquor or drugs usually contains the following elements:

1. a definition of the crime itself, that it is unlawful for any person who is under the influence of intoxicating liquor or drugs to drive or be in actual physical control of a vehicle within the territorial jurisdiction of the tribal court;
2. **presumption**s at trial that may exist depending on the amount of alcohol in the person's blood at the time of the alleged offense;
3. the procedure for chemical analysis of the blood of the person charged with the offense;
4. the penalties for conviction of the offense of driving while under the influence; and
5. the procedure to appeal the conviction of driving while under the influence because of the severity of the penalties.

F. Examples and Hypotheticals of Driving While under the Influence of Intoxicating Liquor or Drugs (Also Known as DWI)

Absentee-Shawnee Tribe of Indians of Oklahoma Criminal Code Sec. 605

>   a. *It shall be unlawful to drive or be in actual physical control of any motor vehicle upon any private or public road within the Tribal jurisdiction while under the influence of intoxicating liquor, or controlled dangerous substances or any other drugs, or intoxicating inhalants which impair the ability to control or operate a vehicle.*

b. A person is presumed to be under the influence of intoxicating liquor if there is 0.1% or more of alcohol in the blood by weight, and a person is presumed not to be under the influence if there is less than 0.05% of alcohol in their blood by weight. Between such percentages, results of tests showing such fact may be received in evidence, with other tests or observations, for consideration by the court or jury. A breath or blood test must be administered with the consent of the subject, by a qualified operator using a properly maintained apparatus in order to be admissible, provided, that if any person refuses to take such a test when requested to do so by an Officer having reasonable suspicion that such person may be intoxicated, the person's driving privileges within the Tribal jurisdiction shall be suspended by the Court for a period of six months whether or not such person is convicted of any offense. Such suspension is mandatory.

HYPOTHETICALS

F1. Nathan is pulled over while driving his motorcycle. He was weaving from side to side in a residential area. The tribal police, after their investigation, determine that Nathan had been sniffing paint before he rode the motorcycle. Is Nathan guilty of driving under the influence?

F2. After being pulled over for speeding, Donna blows a 0.03 percent on an alcohol breathalyzer. The tribal police have no other evidence that Donna's driving was impaired. Is Donna guilty of DUI?

Conclusion

Definitions of crimes should give clear guidance to the community about what is acceptable behavior. By defining both the act and the mental state will ensure that the criminal justice system is fair to everyone.

Questions

1. For each crime listed in the hypotheticals in this chapter, identify:
   actus reus
   mens rea
2. Do any of the listed criminal definitions fail to take into account certain actions that should be criminal (i.e., are there loopholes)? If so, how would you strengthen the law(s)?
3. Do you think any of the legal definitions listed in this chapter are too strict? If so, how would redefine the laws?

In Your Community

1. How does your nation define battery?
2. How does your nation define assault?
3. How was assault dealt with traditionally? Was it a crime?
4. How was theft dealt with traditionally?

Terms Used in Chapter 14

Apprehension: Fear.
Menace: To threaten, cause danger.
Presumption: A conclusion or inference drawn.

Answers to Hypotheticals

A1. Under Sault Ste. Marie law, Fred is not guilty of assault. The law requires that Fred "attempt to commit a battery or unlawful act," and words are not unlawful.

A2. Under Sault Ste. Marie law, Betty is guilty of assault. The act of breaking a windshield is a crime, and Betty acted in such a way as to make Wilma afraid she would be injured.

B1. Under Oglala law, Warren would probably be guilty of assault because he has threatened bodily harm to Michael.

B2. Under Oglala law, Anna is guilty of assault because she attempted to harm Rachel.

C1. Under the Duckwater Shoshone Code, Joe is not guilty of battery because he did not act intentionally when he injured Tim.

C2. Under the Duckwater Shoshone Code, Tim is guilty of battery because he intended for Joe to be injured.

D1. Under Nez Perce Tribal law, Leslie is guilty of battery. There is no injury requirement in the Nez Perce law.

D2. Under Nez Perce Tribal law, Marla is not guilty of battery. All elements of the Nez Perce law require that the defendant act willfully or intentionally.

E1. Under Sault Ste. Marie law, Bob is guilty of theft because he won't return the power drill to Bob and he intends to deprive Bob of the drill permanently.

E2. Under Sault Ste. Marie law, Barbara is not guilty of theft because she did not mean to take the purse.

F1. Under the Absentee-Shawnee law, Nathan is guilty of driving under the influence.

F2. Under the Absentee-Shawnee law, Donna is probably not guilty of driving under the influence. Her blood alcohol level was lower than 0.05 percent, and thus she is presumed not to be under the influence. There is no other evidence regarding her possible intoxication.

Notes

1. Angie Debo, *The Rise and Fall of the Choctaw Republic* 23 (1961).
2. Ernest Wallace & E. Adamson Hoebel, *The Comanches: Lords of the South Plains* 240 (1952).
3. Lewis Henry Morgan, *The League of the Iroquois* 324 (1851).

Is Helping a Criminal Act? Preliminary Crimes and Accomplice Liability

Chapter 15

Suppose that someone attempts to commit a crime but fails. The criminal justice system still penalizes the person for their efforts to commit a crime. These crimes are typically referred to as inchoate crimes. Inchoate criminal offenses—solicitation, attempt, and conspiracy—are aimed at giving the police the opportunity to prevent the intended crime. Society has deemed these acts to be prohibited or criminal conduct, even though a completed crime has not occurred. Each offense can be punished even if the harm intended never occurred.

Solicitation

A number of jurisdictions make it a crime for a person to **solicit** another person to commit a crime. Solicitation is a specific-intent crime. To commit solicitation, the individual has to intentionally invite, encourage, command, or hire someone else to commit a crime with the intent that the other person commit the crime. The act occurs when the person invites, encourages, or hires the second person to commit a crime. The crime does not have to take place for the first person to be guilty of solicitation.

For instance, solicitation for bank robbery occurs when Frankie hires Joe to drive the getaway car while Frankie robs the bank. Even if Joe has a heart attack and dies before robbing the bank, Frankie is guilty of solicitation for bank robbery.

When Is Soliciting a Crime?

Nez Perce Tribal Code Sec. 4-1-36

Solicitation

a. It shall be unlawful for any person to promote or facilitate the commission of an offense by enticing, advising, inciting, commanding, encouraging or requesting another person to engage in specific conduct which would constitute an offense.

b. It is no defense to a prosecution for criminal solicitation that the person solicited could not be guilty of the crime proposed due to:
   1. legal incapacity or other exemption;
   2. unawareness of the criminal nature of the conduct solicited or the defendant's criminal purpose;
   3. other factors precluding the mental state required for the commission of the crime in question.

Attempt

In most jurisdictions, an attempt to commit a crime is by itself a crime. The attempt may be a complete or an imperfect attempt; as long as the offender has taken at least one step toward completion of the crime, but not followed through with the remaining steps, it is a crime. In order to be guilty of the crime of attempt, the accused generally must have intended to commit a crime and taken a substantial step toward committing the crime. Mere preparation to commit the crime is not enough. The difficult problem with the crime of attempt is determining whether the actions of the accused were a step toward the actual commission of a crime or mere acts of preparation.

A common example of attempt is the situation in which a person decides to shoot and kill someone but, being a poor shot, misses the intended victim. The person doing the shooting would be liable for attempted murder.

What Is a Substantial Step?

Sault Ste. Marie Tribal Code § 71.202(29) (2013)

"Substantial step" means any conduct, whether act, omission, or possession, which is **corroborative** of the actor's intent to commit the other offense.

What Happens When You Attempt a Crime?

Nez Perce Tribal Code Sec. 4-1-34

Attempt
  a. It shall be unlawful for any person acting with the kind of culpability otherwise required for commission of the crime to:
     1. willfully engage in conduct which would constitute the crime if the attendant circumstances were as he believes them to be;
     2. do or omit to do anything with the purpose of causing or with the belief that it will cause such result without further conduct on his part when causing a particular result is an element of the crime; or
     3. willfully do or omit to do anything which, under the circumstances as he believes them to be, is an act or omission constituting a substantial step in a course [of] conduct planned to **culminate** in his commission of the crime.
  b. Conduct shall not be held to constitute a substantial step under this section unless it is strongly corroborative of the actor's criminal purpose.
  c. No defense to the offense of attempt shall arise:
     1. because the offense attempted was actually committed;
     2. due to factual or legal impossibility of **consummating** the intended offense if the offense could have been committed had the facts been as the actor believed them to be; or
     3. that in attempting unsuccessfully to commit a crime, the person accused actually accomplished the commission of another and different crime.

The following case concerns a conviction for attempted aggravated assault. After reviewing the trial transcript, the Fort Peck Court of Appeals determined that the conviction was justified. Do you agree?

Fort Peck Court of Appeals
Fort Peck Tribes v. William Turcotte (1988)
Fort Peck Court of Appeals No. 054

The Appellant contends the evidence was insufficient to sustain Appellant's conviction for attempted aggravated assault. Appellant's complaint specifically charged a violation of III CCOJ 112, 213.

Title III CCOJ 112 [Attempt] reads in part:

  (a) A person is guilty of an attempt to commit a crime who intentionally does or omits to do anything which, under the circumstances as the defendant believes them to be, is an act or omission constituting a substantial step toward the commission of a crime.

...

(d) The penalty for an attempted crime is the same as the penalty for the completed crime.

Title III CCOJ 213 [Aggravated Assault] reads in full as follows:

Whoever

  a. intentionally causes serious bodily injury to another; or
  b. intentionally causes bodily injury to another with a deadly weapon; or
  c. recklessly causes serious bodily injury to another under circumstances manifesting indifference to the value of human life is guilty of aggravated assault.

Aggravated assault is a felony.

The evidence was sufficient for the jury to find the Appellant took "substantial steps" towards the commission of the offense of aggravated assault. The prosecutor [Ron Arneson] when questioning the victim elicited "substantial steps" in the following testimony:

Ron Arneson: Would you describe briefly his tone of voice?

Linda Turcotte: He was yelling.

Ron Arneson: And his general demeanor? Your perception of that?

Linda Turcotte: Very, very angry.

Ron Arneson: What happened, in the process?

Linda Turcotte: He hit me.

Ron Arneson: Where did he hit you?

Linda Turcotte: I believe, the first time that he hit me was on this side of the face.

Ron Arneson: Let the record show that the witness is showing on the left side of the face.

Linda Turcotte: He struck me and I remember saying, "don't or I will call the cops. I can't really remember the exact sequence of everything but then the next thing I knew, he had a hold of my hair and he had a gun at my head. And He said go ahead and call the cops, they will find a mess when they get here."

Ron Arneson: Okay! Do you recall where you were at the time this was happening? Where were you positioned? Were you on a chair or were you somewhere else?

Linda Turcotte: I was sitting at the dining room table.

Ron Arneson: Okay! When he was holding your hair, were you sitting at the dining room table?

Linda Turcotte: Yes.

Ron Arneson: AT [*sic*] any time, did you end up on the floor, do you recall?

Linda Turcotte: Yes. I really, like I say, I can't really remember the full sequence, you know. Maybe I don't want to . . . I think he pushed me. . . . I can't remember if it was after he let go of me or after he had the gun to my head and he pushed me. I really don't recall how I ended up on the floor. But I was on the floor at one time.

Ron Arneson: Would you describe for us, as best as you can, the circumstances as to his holding your hair and the position of the gun and that particular scene, right at that moment?

Linda Turcotte: I was sitting at the table. He was standing on my right side. He had a hold of this side of my head, grabbed my hair and pulled it towards him with the gun right . . . almost at my temple.

Ron Arneson: Was the gun, as you recall, touching your head?

Linda Turcotte: Yes, it was.

Ron Arneson: Did . . . do you recall some of the feelings that you were experiencing at that moment?

Linda Turcotte: I was very, very frightened. He had in the past, told me more than once, that he would kill me. . . .

Ron Arneson: What went through your head at that time, did you consider that serious, to be serious?

Linda Turcotte: Yeah! More and more, he seem to become . . . he seemed to be losing control where I was concerned. Maybe . . . I don't know why.

Ron Arneson: Would you like to describe some other indicators of why you say that? Other incidents or occurrences?

Linda Turcotte: One morning, we woke up . . . I could tell he was in a very bad mood. Finally on the way to work, I asked him what was the matter, and he said I had a dream last night and you slept with so-and-so. I was catching heck because he had a dream, you know, something that was in his mind. When he put that gun to my head, I didn't know what he was going to do, I was scared. I didn't know what he really was going to do, if he would really pull the trigger. I thought that he would.

Ron Arneson: So you . . . in your mind, you felt that you were really close to death?

Linda Turcotte: Yes. My children were there to see how he is. And that's another thing that I never thought would happen. He would do something like that in front of his kids.

Ron Arneson: Did you see, did you believe the gun to be loaded?

Linda Turcotte: Yes. I didn't know, of course, I really didn't know but yes.

It was a "substantial step" for Appellant to intentionally strike the victim in the face and hold her hair with a gun to her head. The gun, a .22 automatic pistol, was recovered and produced as evidence at the trial. In addition, Appellant told the victim, "go ahead and call the cops, they will find a mess when they get here." Appellant had also told the victim on several occasions he was going to kill her and the victim believed the gun to be loaded.

As for serious bodily injury, the victim was observed with bruises and an abrasion around her face and eye. Testimony was given by Dr. Yutani that the blows to the facial structure had the potential for serious bodily injury.

Appellant took the "substantial steps" contemplated by III CCOJ 112 and committed the crime of Attempted Aggravated Assault, a violation of III CCOJ 213. Therefore, the evidence produced at trial was sufficient to sustain the conviction on the charge of attempted aggravated assault.

Conspiracy

A conspiracy is an agreement between two or more persons to commit a crime. Some jurisdictions require an **overt** act as part of the conspiracy. An overt act does not have to be as significant as an act needed to prove an attempt. The act can be any act that is done as part of the conspiracy.

The charge of conspiracy is designed to prevent crimes and criminal activity by groups, but it is sometimes criticized because it is so vague that a person can be convicted before committing any act that is an element of a crime, and many believe conspiracy is mostly made of mental intentions and is not an actual act.[1]

For an example of conspiracy as a crime, suppose that Dick wants his wife, Jean, killed. Dick asks Bob to commit the murder by poisoning her with cyanide. If Bob agrees to Dick's request and commits an overt act (such as buying cyanide) as part of the conspiracy, then both Dick and Bob could be convicted of conspiracy to commit murder, even if the murder is never attempted or accomplished.

What Is Criminal Conspiracy?

White Mountain Apache Criminal Code Sec. 2.19A

A person is guilty of conspiracy with another person, or persons, to commit a crime if, with the purpose of promoting or facilitating the crime's commission, he agrees to aid such other person(s) in the planning or commission of such crime.

> 1. *No person may be convicted of conspiracy to commit a crime unless an overt act in pursuance of such conspiracy is alleged and proved to have been done by him or by a person with whom he conspired.*

2. *Any person guilty of conspiracy, who knows that a person with whom he conspired has also conspired with another person or persons to commit the same crime, is guilty of conspiring with such other person(s), whether or not he knows their identity.*
3. *If a person conspires to commit a number of crimes, he is guilty of only one conspiracy so long as such multiple crimes are the object of the same agreement or continuous conspiratorial relationship.*
4. *Defense to Conspiracy:* **Renunciation**. *In a prosecution for conspiracy, it is a defense that the defendant, under circumstances manifesting a voluntary and complete renunciation of his criminal intent, gave timely warning to law enforcement authorities of the conduct or result which is the object of the conspiracy, or otherwise made a reasonable effort to prevent such conduct or result.*
5. *A renunciation is not voluntary and complete within the meaning of this section if it is motivated in whole or in part by:*
   a. *A belief that circumstances exist which either increase the probability of immediate detection or apprehension of the accused or another participant in the criminal enterprise, or which render more difficult the accomplishment of the criminal purpose; or*
   b. *A decision to postpone the criminal conduct or to transfer the criminal effort to another victim, place or another but similar objective.*

It Takes Two to Commit a Conspiracy

In the case below, the court addresses that a conspiracy must be an agreement between two people. Why did the court determine a conspiracy was not committed?

Colville Confederated Tribes Court of Appeals
Amundson v. Colville Confederated Tribes (1998)
4 CCAR 62 (1998)
Before Chief Justice Dupris, Justice Bonga and Justice Stewart
The opinion of the court was delivered by: Dupris, C.J.

Statement of Facts

Appellant was charged with conspiracy to distribute a controlled substance. The allegation of facts was that, on April 26, 1996 Appellant attempted to purchase a controlled substance from an undercover police officer. The Affidavit of Probable Cause stated that on April 26, 1996 at about 6:30 PM, Tribal Police Services, with the assistance of Tribal Conservation Officers and Okanagan County Deputy Sheriffs, executed a search warrant upon a residence within the boundaries of the Colville Reservation. Upon entry, all persons in the house were placed in custody.

While the search was being executed a telephone call was taken wherein the male caller said he wanted to come over and buy some cocaine. The search team hid itself when the defendant, an Indian, arrived at the residence with his brother.

The two brothers entered the house and contacted Tribal Police Services Detective D. Garvais, who identified himself as "Jose." The defendant told "Jose" that he wanted to buy $100.00 worth of cocaine, a controlled substance, on credit and would pay for it on his payday.

"Jose" stated that he wanted to make sure that the defendant's brother was not a Narc. "Jose" asked the brother to go outside, which the brother did. After the brother went outside "Jose" gave the defendant a baggie containing a white, powdery substance, which appears similar to cocaine. The defendant took the baggie. The defendant was placed under arrest by Tribal Police Services by Lt. M. Whitney and ultimately transported to the Okanagan County Jail for booking on conspiracy to commit an offense.

Appellant, pro se, moved to dismiss the matter, and the Court ordered the motion to dismiss set for a hearing. (footnote omitted) On November 20, 1998, the Office of Public Defender was appointed to represent the appellant by the Trial Court. On December 6, 1996, Jeff Rasmussen, Public Defender filed a Notice of Appearance in behalf of the appellant with the Trial Court. On January 14, 1997 a Change of Plea Hearing was held but the appellant failed to appear for that hearing. The Trial Court issued a bench warrant for the appellant. A second Change of Plea Hearing was held on February 8, 1997, and the appellant pled guilty to the charge, and, through counsel, appellant stipulated to the Affidavit of Probable Cause. On May 13, 1997 a Sentencing Hearing was held before Trial Court and the Judgment and Sentence was entered on May 27, 1997. The appellant filed a Notice of Appeal on June 5, 1997. (footnote omitted)

. . .

II. An agreement between two persons, where one is an undercover police officer, for sale of drugs is not a conspiracy.

The tribal conspiracy statute, CTC 5.4.03 (now 3-1-122) states:

> Any two or more persons who shall conspire to commit an offense enumerated in this Code against the Tribe or any human being, one or more of whom shall do an act to effect the object of the conspiracy, shall each be guilty of Conspiracy to Commit an Offense.

Conspiracy is an agreement between individuals to commit a crime. This Court finds merit in the discussion by the court in Barboa, supra, which wrote, "A conspiracy is an agreement between two or more people to commit an unlawful act, and there is no real agreement when one 'conspires' to break the law only with government agents or informants. The elements of the offense are not satisfied unless one conspires with at least one true co-conspirator." In this matter the alleged co-conspirator is clearly identified in the pleadings and in appellant's statement on plea of guilty as a tribal police officer.

> III. Agreement to buy drugs is not conspiracy to transfer drugs.
>
> Appellant in the captioned matter agreed to buy drugs from an undercover officer. Rather than charge appellant with conspiracy to possess drugs or attempted possession, appellant was charged with conspiracy to transfer drugs. The Appellate Panel finds merit with the federal court's statement in U.S. v. McIntyre, 836 F.2d 467 (10th Cir. 1990): "proof of the existence of a buyer-seller relationship, without more, is inadequate to tie the buyer to a larger conspiracy. . . . In order for the government to establish a case of conspiracy against the defendant, it must sufficiently prove that the defendant had a common purpose with his co-conspirators to possess and distribute cocaine."
>
> There is no allegation that appellant had such a common purpose in this case. The facts show that the appellant was a common drug buyer and not a conspirator to transfer drugs. It is the position of the Court of Appeals that the facts alleged and admitted to, were not a basis to find appellant had conspired to transfer drugs.
>
> . . .
>
> The guilty plea is hereby Vacated and the matter is Remanded to the Trial Court for dismissal consistent with the Panel's decision.

Accomplice and Accessory Liability

Many tribes also prohibit aiding and abetting crimes, often referred to as accomplice and accessory crimes. The person who actually commits a crime is called the principal (e.g., the person who fires the gun in a murder). An accomplice is someone who intentionally assists another individual to commit a crime. An accomplice who helps another person commit a crime (e.g., the person who drives the getaway car during a bank robbery) may sometimes also be considered a principal to the crime, depending on how a tribe decides to define principle and accomplice.

A person who helps the principal after he has committed the crime but who is not present is known as an accessory. This person is not charged with the original crime but may be charged with a separate crime, such as harboring a fugitive, aiding the principal's escape, or obstructing justice (sometimes called aiding and abetting).

What Is an Accomplice?

Nez Perce Tribal Code Sec. 4-1-13

a. A person is an accomplice of another person in the commission of an offense if:
  1. with the purpose of promoting or facilitating the commission of the offense he:
    A. solicits such other person to commit it;
    B. aids or agrees or attempts to aid such other person in planning or committing it;

C. having a legal duty to prevent the commission of the offense, fails to make proper effort to do so; or
2. his conduct is expressly declared by the code or the definition of the crime to establish his **complicity**.
b. When causing a particular result is an element of an offense, an accomplice in the conduct causing such result is an accomplice in the commission of that offense, if he acts with the kind of culpability necessary for the commission of the offense.
c. A person who is legally incapable of committing a particular offense may be guilty thereof if it is committed by the conduct of another person for which he is legally accountable.
d. A person is not an accomplice in an offense committed by another person if:
1. he is a victim of that offense; or
2. he terminates his complicity prior to the commission of the offense; and
A. wholly deprives it of effectiveness; and
B. gives timely warning to the Tribal Police or otherwise makes proper effort to prevent the commission of the offense.

An accomplice may be convicted on proof of the commission of the offense and of his complicity therein, though the person claimed to have committed the offense has not been prosecuted or convicted, has been convicted of a different offense or degree of offense, has an immunity to prosecution or conviction or has been acquitted.

Traditional Law and Accomplices

The following case excerpt addresses the issue of accomplice liability in the context of tribal fishing traditions. As you read the case, think about how tradition and culture might impact the choices someone makes if a companion is breaking the law. Do you agree with the court's decision? Why or why not?

Upper Skagit Court of Appeals
John C. Bowen v. Upper Skagit Indian Tribe (1990)
1 Northwest Indian Court System 106
IRVIN, Chief Justice:
Was the defendant a "helper"? what about the tribal axiom, used for protection, of "where-you-go-I-go" on the river?

It was argued that the defendant was not fishing but was merely a "helper" and therefore should not bear full responsibility for a fishing violation. Sherman Williams, who initiated the illegal conduct admitted guilty for the violation and has been sentenced for Fishing in a Closed Area. The designation of someone as a "helper" for fishing purposes is subject to regulation by the Tribal Fisheries Code.

If a Tribe chooses to authorize "helpers" under its fisheries, who qualifies to act as a "helper" is defined by the tribal fisheries code. Further, according to that authorization the Tribe issues a "helper's permit" to the authorized person. A person does not ex post facto become a "helper" but is authorized to be such under a legal fishery prior to engaging in the authorized conduct.

Finally, defendant argues that he did not initiate the illegal fishing activity but was a victim of the circumstances and for adhering to the tribal **maxim** for protection on the river of "where-you-go-I-go." According to the defendant's testimony he originally had his boat ported downstream and was intending to fish there. When he got to his boat it had been sunk and his nets cut. His vehicle would not start so, as a last resort, he hitched a ride upriver until he saw Williams' truck parked. He thought he could get a ride from Williams. He didn't know that Sherman Williams was illegally fishing. He stayed with Williams, even though Williams was illegally fishing, to help protect himself from the dangers of being an easy target for those who are hostile to tribal people; or, as his counsel put it, he followed the tribal maxim of "where-you-go-I-go" for his protection. This is offered as a justification for his actions.

Whether the defendant should have been able to surmise that he was illegally fishing from the early morning hour and the location of his truck near what is commonly a closed area is a question left unanswered. However, he did assist Sherman Williams in withdrawing fish and carrying them from a closed area. While it is understood that tribal members are subjected to danger by others on the river and band together for their protection, it does not justify participation in illegal fishing. It is apparent from tribal proceedings that the fact that the defendant did not go to the river initially with any intention of illegally fishing and may have been caught in a circumstantial bind was considered and given some weight in the sentence imposed.

For these reasons the judgment is affirmed.

Conclusion

In most jurisdictions, helping to commit a crime has been deemed a crime, even if the "helper" did not commit the crime. Soliciting, attempting, conspiring, and acting as an accomplice are criminalized to discourage the planning or aiding with crimes and to punish the actors. It can be a challenge to prove an inchoate crime or to demonstrate the offender knew or had the intent, as illustrated by the cases. Reasonable doubt is a high burden that must be met, as it is important innocent people are not convicted, especially with inchoate offenses so innocent bystanders are not caught up in the criminal acts of another.

Questions
1. Is helping a criminal a crime? Why or why not?
2. In *Ft. Peck v. Turcotte*, what actions by the defendant contributed to a finding that he attempted to assault the victim?
3. In *Bowen v. Upper Skagit*, what was the tribal maxim used in the defendant's argument? Do you agree? Why or why not?

In Your Community
1. Does your tribal code include the crime of attempt? What is required to prove attempt?
2. Does your nation criminalize helping a criminal? In what way?

Terms Used in Chapter 15
Complicity: Fact of being an accomplice.
Consummating: Bringing to completion or fruition.
Corroborative: Strengthening or supporting with other evidence; making more certain.
Culminate: To come to completion; end.
Maxim: A saying that is widely accepted.
Overt: Out in the open; not secret.
Renunciation: The process of rejecting, casting off, or giving up something openly and in public.
Solicit: To ask for; entice; strongly request.

Note
1. Joshua Dressler, *Understanding Criminal Law* 423 (Lexis, 2001).

Suggested Further Reading
Candace Courteau, "The Mental Element Required for Accomplice Liability," 59 *Louisiana Law Review* 325 (1998).
Arnold N. Enker, "Impossibility in Criminal Attempts—Legality and the Legal Process," 53 *Minnesota Law Review* 665 (1968).

Criminal Defenses   Chapter 16

This chapter provides an overview of criminal defenses used in tribal courts. In the American system, a defendant is never required to present an official defense at trial. The government must prove the case beyond a reasonable doubt regardless of the defendant's choice.

Criminal defenses are used for two main reasons. First, the defense can result in a not-guilty verdict from the judge or jury. Second, the defenses can mitigate the defendant's guilt, making it more likely that the sentence will be lighter.

Criminal defenses generally deny or reduce the defendant's guilt by refuting, justifying, or excusing the offense. Guilt is refuted by a defense that seeks to prove that the defendant did not do the acts or did not have the mental state required by the definition of the crime. A legal justification also defeats or reduces the defendant's guilt when a crime has been committed. For example, self-defense might be a justification for a use of force against another person that would otherwise be a crime. Legal justifications say, "I did it, but what I did was necessary and proper." Legal excuses say, "I did it, but because of the circumstances, I should not be held responsible." Legal excuses also reduce or defeat guilt. For example, **insanity** or **duress** might excuse an act normally considered a crime. Duress is being forced to commit a crime against one's will, such as by a threat to kill one's relative unless one commits the crime.

Defenses to criminal charges fall into four categories:

> Failure of proof: The prosecution has not proven each of the elements.
> Justification: The defendant's actions were lawful.
> Excuse: The defendant admits the conduct but argues he had just cause for his actions.
> Nonexculpatory defenses: The prosecution violates public policy, such as a statute of limitations.

The Sault St. Marie Tribal Code sets forth a list of affirmative defenses:

Sault Ste. Marie Tribal Code § 71.401 (1995)
Affirmative Defenses
1. *Unless the prosecution's evidence raises an issue of affirmative defense to an alleged offense, the defendant, to raise the issue, must present some credible evidence on that issue. If the issue involved in an affirmative defense is raised, the guilt of the defendant must be established beyond a reasonable doubt as to that issue as well as all other elements of the offense.*
2. *Affirmative defenses include but are not necessarily limited to the following:*
   a. **Alibi.** *The evidence must indicate that the defendant's whereabouts at the time of the crime make it impossible or impracticable to place the defendant at the scene of the crime.*
   b. *Claim of right. The evidence must indicate that the person thought the property to be legally his, and that he was operating under an honest conviction that he was acting under claim of right.*
   c. *Duress. The evidence must indicate that the person engaged in the conduct charged because he was coerced against his will by the use, or the threatened use of, unlawful force against his person or the person of another. The* **coercion** *must be such that a reasonable person would be unable to resist.*
   d. *Protection of self, property or other person. The use of reasonable force towards another person is justified when:*
      i. *the force is directed toward one who is using unlawful force; and*
      ii. *the person using such force reasonably believes that use of force is necessary for the person's protection or that of a third person. The use of reasonable force toward another person is justified if used to prevent the unlawful entry into the dwelling of the person asserting the defense or to prevent the unlawful carrying away of personal property.*
   e. *Those affirmative defenses specified elsewhere in this chapter or another chapter of the Tribal Code.*

Failure of Proof Defenses

Failure of proof defenses are claims that the prosecution has not met its burden of proof in proving all the elements of the crime beyond a reasonable doubt. "Although courts may characterize such claims as defenses, the purpose of the defendants' evidence [for failure to prove defenses] . . . is to raise a reasonable doubt regarding an element of the prosecutor's case-in-chief."[1] For failure of proof defenses or claims, the defendant may introduce evidence or argue that the prosecutor has failed to prove the case.

Prosecutor Failed to Prove the Case

If the prosecutor fails to produce evidence for each element of a crime, the judge must dismiss the case. If the prosecutor has produced evidence for each element, then it is up to the fact finder, which is the judge or jury, to decide whether there is reasonable doubt as to whether the defendant committed the crime.

No Crime Has Been Committed
A defendant can establish innocence by showing that no crime has been committed. For example, the defendant was carrying a gun but had a valid license, or the defendant was cited for driving without insurance, but actually did have insurance at the time.

Defendant Did Not Commit the Crime
Often there is no doubt that a crime has been committed. In this case the question is, Who committed it? In this situation, the defendant can often establish innocence by showing a mistake in identity or by an alibi, which is evidence that the defendant was somewhere else at the time the crime was committed.

Defendant Did Not Have the Necessary Intent
When specific intent (i.e., the intent to accomplish the precise act which the law prohibits) is an element of a crime, then defendants can defeat the charge by demonstrating that they did not have the necessary specific intent. For example, defendants charged with theft can defeat the charge by demonstrating that they thought the property belonged to them; in other words, they had no intent to steal.

Infancy/Age
Minors are treated differently in the criminal justice system based on their young age. For example, children under the age of twelve cannot be charged with a crime in many jurisdictions. Juveniles (ages 13–17) may be held accountable for a criminal act, but the system generally offers a more lenient response. Many tribal justice systems have a juvenile code (sometimes called a children's code or a delinquency code) that is separate from the criminal code. The goal of juvenile criminal justice systems is to help rehabilitate the juvenile and help her correct her behavior by providing counseling and treatment.

Mistake of Fact and Mistake of Law
As a general rule, ignorance of the law does not provide a defense. Imagine a defendant who said "I didn't know that stealing was a crime." If that argument was a successful defense, then individuals would be encouraged to ignore or not learn the law.

Sometimes, genuine ignorance may be part of a defense to show that the defendant lacked the necessary *mens rea* (specific intent) element of the offense. The defense of "mistake of law" is used to show that the defendant did not have the required intent to commit a crime.

In a 1991 Navajo case (*Navajo Nation v. Platero*), the court **exonerated** a defendant who acted as a police officer due to an honest mistake.

NEZ PERCE MISTAKE OF LAW DEFENSE

Nez Perce Tribal Code Sec. 4-1-2

a. *Ignorance or mistake as to a matter of fact or law is a defense if:*
   1. *it **negates** the mental state for the offense; or*
   2. *this code provides that the state of mind established by such ignorance or mistake constitutes a defense.*
b. *Although ignorance or mistake would otherwise afford a defense to the offense charged, the defense is not available if the defendant would be guilty of another offense had the situation been as he supposed.*

Justification Defenses

Justification defenses focus on the act engaged in by the defendant. Although normally the act is criminally prohibited, justification defenses argue that under certain circumstances the criminal act is acceptable and criminal sanctions should not be imposed.

For instance, Tilly's car breaks down at night during a sudden snowstorm. Tilly takes shelter from the storm in an abandoned building overnight. The police give Tilly a ride home the next day but also give her a ticket for trespassing in the abandoned building. Tilly can claim that the storm created a life-threatening emergency and she was justified in trespassing overnight to keep from freezing to death.

The following case discusses a defense of justification. Consider why the defendant's claim is unsuccessful.

Grand Traverse Band of Ottawa and Chippewa Indians Tribal Court

People of the Grand Traverse Band v. Raphael (2000)
MICHAEL PETOSKEY, Chief Judge.

This matter involves an alleged violation of the criminal provisions of the Chippewa–Ottawa Treaty Fishery Management Authority (COTFMA) rules and regulations governing tribal commercial fishing activities in the 1836 Chippewa–

Ottawa Treaty ceded waters. Defendant is charged with damaging or stealing the nets belonging to another fisher in violation of Section 16(A)(6).

Case Analysis and Reasoning

Defendant admits that he cut nets belonging to George (Skip) Duhamel. He argues that Mr. Duhamel set his nets over those of Defendant. Defendant testified that as he was pulling his nets he discovered that Mr. Duhamel's nets were set over his nets. Defendant says that the discovery was such that Defendant's boat was then in danger of becoming entangled in Duhamel's nets. Defendant argues that safety concerns dictated that he cut Mr. Duhamel's nets. However, Mr. Duhamel suspects that Defendant cut his nets because Defendant did not want Mr. Duhamel fishing close to where Defendant was fishing. Mr. Duhamel farther [sic] suggests that Defendant then dragged his nets "into the deep." Mr. Duhamel's suspicions are based upon an alleged previous threat to do so and by the fact that Mr. Duhamel was unable to recover his nets by dragging for them in the area where they were cut.

The fact that Defendant admits that he cut Mr. Duhamel's nets is enough for the Court to find that he damaged the nets of another fisher. Cutting nets under any theory of this case is to damage them.

The Defendant argues that there is legal justification for his actions. Although, Defendant did not present his defense using the terminology of "legal justification" or "necessity," the Court understands that Defendant's argument is that, although he cut the nets, there was a safety necessity for him to do so. A successful defense of legal justification would excuse his actions.

The presentation of a defense of legal justification shifts the burden of proof to the Defendant to prove his actions were a necessity precipitated by concerns for safety. Both parties to this action recognize that commercial fishing is an inherently dangerous occupation and that safety concerns are paramount.

The Court believes that Defendant did maliciously cut Mr. Duhamel's nets and drag them "into the deep" because Defendant was mad that Mr. Duhamel was fishing close to Defendant's nets. The Court further believes that Mr. Duhamel was fishing too close and should have realized that he was flirting with the potential to inflame Defendant's anger. The Court makes these findings based upon all of testimony presented during the Hearing. Defendant and his witnesses were not credible. Defendant was devoid of passion in the presentation of his defense. While he was testifying his eyelids blinked incessantly. The Court simply does not believe his story. The defense witnesses were members of Defendant's crew. The Court does not believe their testimony either because of the employment relationship that each has with the Defendant. The Court believes that Defendant dragged Mr. Duhamel's nets "into the deep" because of Mr. Duhamel's testimony that he

> dragged for the nets in the area where they were cut and if the nets were there he would have been able to recover them.
> FOR ALL OF THE FOREGOING, this Honorable Court:
>
> (1) FINDS DEFENDANT GUILTY; and
> (2) ORDERS the scheduling of a Sentencing Hearing in this matter

Self-Defense and Defense of Property and Others

Many legal systems protect the right of a person unlawfully attacked to use reasonable force to protect himself from **imminent** harm. There are usually three requirements: (1) The attack must be unlawful (not started by the defendant). (2) The harm is imminent. Imminent means immediate in the sense that the attack is happening or about to happen in the next few seconds. (3) The defendant must also reasonably believe that the use of force is necessary to protect herself. Self-defense also recognizes the right of one person to use reasonable force to defend another person from imminent attack; this is often called defense of others.

There are, however, a number of general limitations to these defenses.

A person who reasonably believes there is imminent danger of bodily harm can use only a reasonable amount of force in self-defense. A person cannot use more force than necessary. If, after stopping an attacker, the defender continues to use force, the roles reverse, and the defender can no longer claim self-defense. Also, a person is usually allowed to use nondeadly force in defense of any third person if the third person is entitled to claim self-defense. Reasonable nondeadly force may also be used to protect property.

Deadly force can be used only if one reasonably believes that there is imminent danger of death or serious bodily harm. The defense is not allowed if a reasonable person would not have believed harm was about to occur. Each jurisdiction has different rules about this defense, and not all jurisdictions have the same requirements for the use of deadly force.

When Can I Use Force to Defend Others or Myself?

Nez Perce Tribal Code Sec. 4-1-22

> a. The use of reasonable force upon or toward another person is justifiable when the actor believes it is immediately necessary for the purpose of protecting himself or a third person against the use of unlawful force. The force used must be reasonably necessary to protect the actor or a third person.
> b. The use of force is not justifiable under this section:

1. *to resist or assist another in resisting arrest which the actor knows is being made by a peace officer, although the arrest is unlawful;*
2. *if the actor uses deadly force unless the actor believes that such force is necessary to protect himself or a third person against death, serious bodily injury, kidnapping or sexual intercourse compelled by force or threat;*
3. *if the actor, with the purpose of causing death or serious bodily harm,* **provoked** *the use of force against himself or a third person in the same encounter; or*
4. *if the actor was the aggressor or was engaged in combat by agreement, unless he withdraws from the encounter and effectively communicates to the other person his intent to do so and the other notwithstanding continues or threatens to continue the use of unlawful force.*

The following cases explore self-defense. As you review the decisions, consider how the tribal court describes what is needed to establish a self-defense claim.

Confederated Tribes of the Colville Reservation Court of Appeals
Davisson, et al. v. Colville Confederated Tribes (2012)
No. AP08-001 (June 26, 2012), 39 ILR 6049

Opinion and Order
Appeal to determine whether provisions of the Domestic Violence Code violate provisions of the ICRA and CTCRA by imposing enhanced sentencing and requiring the defendant to prove self-defense by a preponderance of the evidence. We affirm in part and reverse in part.

Procedural History
On June 3, 2004, the Business Council of the Confederated Tribes of the Colville Reservation (hereinafter CBC) amended the Domestic Violence Code, CTC 5-5 et seq., to enhance sentencing for crimes involving domestic violence. The CBC also added a provision that, should self-defense be claimed, the defendant has the burden of proving self-defense by a preponderance of the evidence, rather than the prosecution having to prove the absence of self-defense by proof beyond a reasonable doubt.

The appellants are numerous defendants charged with crimes involving domestic violence who contend their rights were violated under the Indian Civil Rights Act, 25 U.S.C. § 1302 (hereinafter ICRA), and the Colville Tribal Civil Rights Act, CTC 1-5 (hereinafter CTCRA) by the enhanced sentencing requirements. Appellants also contend that requiring a defendant to prove self-defense by a preponderance of the evidence for crimes involving domestic violence violates ICRA and CTCRA in that the tribal prosecutor should have the burden to prove a lack of self-defense beyond a reasonable doubt. They make these arguments on the basis of the trial court's interlocutory order denying defendant's motion to accept proposed jury instructions which supported their position. . . .

Statement of Relevant Facts

The cases before us are similar only in that they involved alleged crimes involving domestic violence. They do, however, present identical issues of law for this court to determine. In order to put the issues in perspective and for purposes of illustration, we set forth the facts alleged in Davisson.

Connie Davisson was charged with willfully striking or otherwise inflicting bodily injury by scratching her former boyfriend on his nose and cheek on October 25, 2004. (Battery) CTC 3-1-4. She is also charged in a separate count of biting him on his chest at the same date and time. (Battery) CTC 3-1-4. She is further charged with entering or remaining in a building without permission with the purpose of committing the above referenced crimes. (Burglary) CTC 3-1-41). And finally, she is charged with possessing a controlled substance. (Prohibited Acts—Possession) CTC 3-1-180.

The first three counts are alleged crimes involving domestic violence. Domestic Violence is defined as "the occurrence of one or more of the following acts by a family or household member but does not include acts of self-defense or culturally appropriate discipline of a child." CTC 5-5-3(d). These include acts "Attempting to cause or causing physical, mental, or emotional harm to another family or household member" (CTC 5-5-3(1) and acts "Attempting to commit or committing any criminal offense under Colville Tribal law against another family or household member." CTC 5-5-3(4). A household member includes "persons who are dating or have dated." CTC 5-5-3(g)(3). It is alleged that Connie Davisson assaulted her former boyfriend.

The complaint charging Ms. Davisson with these crimes noted on its face that the battery and burglary counts were subject to enhanced penalties. The complaint labeled the crimes as "Domestic Violence Battery" and "Domestic Violence Burglary."

The prosecution of Ms. Davisson was without complication until the parties submitted proposed jury instructions. The prosecution/appellee's proposed jury instructions were standard instructions for the crimes of battery and burglary. Additional instructions directed the jurors to determine: 1) whether the defendant committed a crime beyond a reasonable doubt involving domestic violence, and 2) whether, by a preponderance of the evidence, the acts of committing the crime were made by another family or household member. Proposed instructions were also included that provided for the defendant to prove such by a preponderance of the evidence.

The defendants/appellants' proposed jury instructions took a different track. Their proposed instructions contend the amendments to the Domestic Violence Code resulted in the establishment of the new crimes of Domestic Violence Battery and Domestic Violence Burglary. They also included instructions requiring the prosecution to disprove self-defense beyond a reasonable doubt for all criminal offenses charged. The trial court rejected this view and denied the motion to accept the proposed instructions.

The defendants/appellants filed this appeal.

Issues

1. Whether the due process and equal protection rights given criminal defendants under ICRA and the Tribal Civil Rights Act are violated by the provisions of the Domestic Violence Act that require those claiming self-defense to establish it by a preponderance of the evidence;
2. Whether the due process and equal protection rights given criminal defendants under ICRA and the Tribal Civil Rights Act are violated by the provisions of the Domestic Violence Code that allows the prosecution to establish that a crime is a crime of domestic violence by a preponderance of the evidence rather than by evidence beyond a reasonable doubt; and
3. Whether the provisions of the Domestic Violence Code that require those criminal defendants claiming self-defense to establish it by a preponderance of the evidence violate the rights given them under ICRA and the Tribal Civil Rights Act to not be compelled to testify against themselves?

Due Process and Equal Protection

The Colville Confederated Tribes enacted the Civil Rights Act (CTCRA) of the Confederated Tribes of the Colville Reservation which provides that the Tribes shall not "(d)eny any person within its jurisdiction the equal protection of its laws or deprive any person of liberty or property without due process of law." CTC 5-2(h). This court has consistently held the CTCRA requires that every defendant in a criminal proceeding is entitled to basic rights including the protections of due process and equal protection of the law. This has always required, at a minimum, proper notice to the defendant and an opportunity for a fair hearing before an impartial decision maker. *Lezard v. CCT*, 3 CCAR 04, 2 CTCR 11, 22 Indian L. Rep. 6135 (1995), *Louie v. CCT*, 2 CCAR 47, 2 CTCR 05, 21 Indian L. Rep. 6136 (1994), *St. Peter v. CCT*, 2 CCAR 02, 1 CTCR 75, 20 Indian L. Rep. 6108 (1993), *Wiley v. CCT*, 2 CCAR 60, 2 CTCR 09, 22 Indian L. Rep. 6059 (1994). Colville tribal law, with respect to due process and equal protection rights of criminal defendants, has always been protective, if not more protective, than the federal Indian Civil Rights Act and thus any rulings by this court necessarily meet any federal law and federal constitution requirements.

A review of the basic tenets of due process and equal protection of laws may be helpful before examining the issues here.

Due Process of Law

There are two facets to due process of law: procedural due process and substantive due process.

Procedural due process of law. Procedural due process requires at a minimum notice and an opportunity to be heard. *Silver Firs Town Honies, Inc. v. Silver Lake Water Dist.*, 103 Wash. App. 411, 425, 12 P.3d 1022 (2000), review denied, 143 Wash. 2d 1013 (2001). Nothing in the record before us shows the appellants were denied procedural due process at trial.

Substantive due process of law. Substantive due process protects against arbitrary and capricious government action even when the decision to take action is pursuant to constitutionally adequate procedures. *Halverson v. Skagit County*, 42 F.3d 1257, 1261 (9th Cir. 1994). The appellants claim that shifting the burdens of proof and persuasion from the prosecution to the defendants for crimes involving domestic violence violates their right to substantive due process.

When state action does not affect a fundamental right, the proper standard of review is whether a rational basis exists for that action. John E. Nowak and Ronald D. Rotunda, Constitutional Law § 11.4, at 370; § 14.4, at 601 (4th ed. 1991); *United States v. Glucksberg*, 521U.S. 702, 728. Under this test, the challenged law must be rationally related to a legitimate state interest. Id.; *Seeley v. State*, 132 Wash. 2d 776, 795, 940 P.2d 604 (1997); *In re Pers. Restraint of Metcalf*, 92 Wash. App. 165, 963 P.2d 911 (1998), cert. denied, 527 U.S. 1041 (1999). In determining whether a rational relationship exists, a court may assume the existence of any necessary state of facts which it can reasonably conceive in determining whether a rational relationship exists between the challenged law and a legitimate state interest. *Heller v. Doe*, 509 U.S. 312, 320, 113 S. Ct. 2637, 125 L. Ed. 2d 257 (1993); see Seeley, 132 Wash. 2d at 795; Glucksberg, 521 U.S. 702. (Taken generally from *Amunrud v. Bd. of Appeals*, 158 Wash. 2d. 208, 219 (2005).)

Rational basis review applies where there are no factors triggering more intensive scrutiny. *State v. Manussier*, 129 Wash. 2d 652, 673, 921 P.2d 473 (1996), cert. denied, 117 S. Ct. 563, 137 L. Ed 2d 709 (1997). *State v. Wallace*, 86 Wash. App. 546, 553, 937 P.2d 200 (1997).

Intermediate scrutiny is applied to a statute that creates a classification based on a semi-suspect class, where an important right is involved. Heiskell, 129 Wash. 2d at 123. An example is where the right to liberty is implicated and the classification is based on poverty. *State v. Heiskell*, 129 Wash. 2d 113.

State interference with a fundamental right is subject to strict scrutiny. In re Parentage of CA.M.A., 154 Wash. 2d 52, 57, 109 P.3d 405 (2005).

Strict scrutiny applies to a statute that creates an inherently suspect classification. Inherently suspect classifications are those based on race, national origin, or alienage. *Petersen v. State*, 100 Wash. 2d 421,444, 671 P.2d 230 (1983). None of the parties have identified an inherently suspect classification in this matter, however, strict scrutiny is also applied where a party is threatened with deprivation of a fundamental right.

The right to not be compelled to testify against oneself is a fundamental right. Thus we review the due process challenge to the amendments to the Domestic Violence Code under the strict scrutiny standard.

Equal Protection

Equal protection of the law is denied when state officials enforce the law with an "unequal hand or evil eye." *Yick Wo v. Hopkins*, 118 U.S. 356, 6 S. Ct. 1064, 30 L. Ed. 220 (1886). Mere selectivity in prosecution creates no constitutional problems; a defendant must show deliberate or purposeful discrimination based on an unjustifiable standard such as race, religion, or other arbitrary classification. *United States v. Steele*, 461 F.2d 1148 (9th Cir. 1972); *Yakima v. Johnson*, 16 Wash. App. 143, 553 P.2d 1104 (1976).

For purposes of an equal protection analysis, if the legislature creates a classification based on certain characteristics of an offender, we determine whether the appropriate standard of review is strict scrutiny, intermediate scrutiny, or the rational basis test, depending on the nature of the interest affected by the law and the characteristics of the legislatively created class. *State v. Shawn P.*, 122 Wash. 2d 553, 560, 859 P.2d 1220 (1993).

Under the rational relationship test, the law is subjected to minimal scrutiny and will be upheld "unless it rests on grounds wholly irrelevant to the achievement of a legitimate state objective." *State v. Smith*, 117 Wash. 2d 263,277, 814 P.2d 652 (1991) (quoting *State v. Phelan*, 100 Wash. 2d 508, 512). Under the strict scrutiny test, the law will be upheld only if it is shown to be necessary to accomplish a compelling state interest in order to be upheld. Smith, 117 Wash. 2d at 277 (*Citing State v. Schaaf*, 109 Wash. 2d 1, 17, 743 P.2d 240 (1987)); Phelan, 100 Wash. 2d at 512. Under the intermediate or heightened scrutiny test, the challenged law must be seen as furthering substantial interest of the State. Smith, 117 Wash. 2d at 277 (citing Schaaf, 109 Wash. 2d at 17); Phelan, 100 Wash. 2d at 512).

Success under any of the articulated tests requires that the appellants first establish a challenged classification. *State v. Osman*, 126 Wash. App. 575 (2005). The appellants have identified only one fundamental right in their Opening Brief and that is the right of a defendant not to be compelled to testify against himself.

See p. 9. In their Reply Brief, the appellants augment that claim by contending a legal process is flawed which requires defendants in crimes involving domestic violence to prove such by a preponderance of the evidence while defendants claiming self-defense in crimes NOT involving domestic violence are relieved of that burden.

Again, the right to not be compelled to testify against oneself is a fundamental right. We review the equal protection challenge to the amendments to the Domestic Violence Code under the strict scrutiny standard.

Discussion of Issues

All three issues center around self-defense. We re-phrase the issues as follows:

Can the CBC shift the burden of proving self-defense from the prosecution to the defendant without violating tribal and United States statutes guaranteeing the right to due process and equal protection?

If so, can the CBC change the burden of persuasion in criminal cases involving domestic violence from "beyond a reasonable doubt" when self-defense is required to be proven by the prosecution to "by a preponderance of the evidence" when the burden shifts to a defendant?

And, finally, whether shifting the burden of proving self-defense to the defendant in crimes involving domestic violence compels the defendant to testify against himself in violation of tribal law?

1. Can the CBC shift the burden of proving self-defense from the prosecution to the defendant without violating tribal and United States statutes guaranteeing the right to due process and equal protection?

Self-defense is not specifically defined in either Colville tribal law or Colville common law, (footnote omitted) but it is the law that "self-defense justifies an act done in reasonable belief of immediate anger and if an injury was done in justifiable self-defense he can never be punished criminally." *Louie v. CCT*, 2 CCAR 47, 2 CTCR 05, 21 Indian L. Rep. 6136 (1994). This interpretation was sanctioned in the legislative history of the Domestic and Family Violence Code in the section entitled "self-defense provisions." This court has applied the state and federal common law rule that once the defendant has presented evidence of self-defense, the absence of self-defense must be proven beyond a reasonable doubt by the prosecution. To be sure, the defendant must present some evidence to raise the issue of self-defense under this analysis. *Louie, supra*. This does not answer the question of whether the legislature can establish different rules on self-defense which more directly is the question in this case.

Most of the laws enacted by the CBC have been passed without a legislative history attached. The CBC deemed amendments to the Domestic Violence Code of such importance that it included a legislative history. The history sets forth the need for the legislation and the intent of the CBC in dealing with the pervasive problem of domestic violence. The Code itself identifies seriousness of the threat of domestic violence to the Tribes, its families, and that it affects the health, welfare, and political integrity of all Reservation residents. The section of the history concerning shifting the burden of proof and burden of persuasion from the prosecution to the defendant is set forth below in its entirety:

Legislative History:
Self-defense Provision:

In giving direction for the drafting of this chapter, the Colville Business Council made the deliberate choice to favor prosecution of crimes involving domestic violence. This choice was intended as a clear statement that this harmful behavior is not to be condoned nor tolerated and rather, shall receive a strong and certain response by the Tribes' law enforcement and justice system.

Consistent with its decision to favor prosecution, when considering claims of self-defense, the CBC carefully examined existing Colville Tribal case law and decided that a departure from prior precedent was warranted in cases involving domestic violence. The self-defense provision in this chapter has been discussed at great length within the Tribes' law enforcement and justice community as well as with the community as a whole at the 2003 Juvenile Task Force Workshop in Keller. With due deliberation and care, the CBC has decided to place the burden of proving self-defense on the defendant accused of a crime involving domestic violence. The fact that this may be contrary to other jurisdictions' allocation of the burden has been weighed in the deliberations.

At the time this chapter was drafted, Colville case law placed the burden on the Tribes (the prosecutor) to prove the absence of self-defense beyond a reasonable doubt once the defendant introduced evidence in support of self-defense. Under this chapter, the burden never shifts from defendant to prosecutor. In cases where the defendant is accused of a crime involving domestic violence and self-defense is claimed, the defendant has the burden of proving by a preponderance of the evidence that he or she was acting in self-defense. To protect against unjust results, the evidentiary threshold was lowered from beyond a reasonable doubt to a preponderance of the evidence. It should be noted that the underlying principle remains the same as always: "The law of self-defense justifies an act done in the reasonable belief of immediate danger, and if an injury was done by a defendant in justifiable self-defense, he can never be punished criminally. . . ." *Louie v. Colville Confederated Tribes*, 2 CCAR 47, 2 CTCR 05, 21 Indian L. Rep. 6136 (1994).

As in all cases, there are valid concerns that a defendant may be wrongly accused. However, the rule of evidence in Tribal Court should allow all defendants to present all relevant evidence available in support of self-defense. Evidence of past violence by the alleged victim would clearly be admissible to support a claim of self-defense.

That a defendant may choose to testify in support of the claim of self-defense does not amount to compelling the defendant to testify against himself or herself. Such testimony is not testimony against the defendant, nor would any testimony elicited in cross examination necessarily be.

The legislative history sets forth compelling reasons for enhancing sentencing and shifting the burden of proving self-defense from the prosecution to the defense for crimes involving domestic violence. The amendments satisfy the strict scrutiny test.

There is no tribal case law that considers whether placing the burden of proof on a defendant violates tribal or federal statutes. Accordingly, we look to other jurisdictions, state and federal, for guidance. See CTC 1-2-11.

The State of Washington has considered whether shifting the burden of proof is unconstitutional. One court stated:

> It is not a constitutional imperative that a state "must disprove beyond a reasonable doubt every fact constituting any and all affirmative defenses related to the culpability of an accused. Traditionally, due process has required that only the most basic procedural safeguards be observed; more subtle balancing of society's interests against those of the accused have been left to the legislative branch.... Proof of the nonexistence of all affirmative defenses has never been constitutionally required. ..." Patterson v. New York, 432 U.S. 197, 210, 53 L. Ed. 2d 281, 97 S. Ct. 2319 (1977). The state legislatures may define crimes so as to place the burden of proving a defense upon defendant. As noted in Patterson, "The decisions are manifold that within limits of reason and fairness the burden Of proof may be lifted from the state in criminal prosecutions and cast on a defendant." 432 U.S. at 203 n.9, quoting Morrison v. California, 291U.S.82, 88-89,78 L.Ed. 664, 54 S.Ct. 281 (1934). *State v. McCulllum*, 98 Wash. 2d 484, 656 P.2d 1064 (1983).

Another Washington State Supreme Court case that reviewed whether it is constitutionally permitted to shift the burden of proof and persuasion from the prosecution to the defendant is *State v. Carama*, 113 Wash. 2d 631,781 P.2d 483 (1989). That court held a defendant's right to due process was not violated when the legislature shifted the burden of proof of the affirmative defense of consent in a case involving sexual assault from the prosecution to him.

A leading federal case regarding shifting of the burdens of proof and persuasion is *Patterson v. New York*, 433 U.S.197, 201–202 (1997). That court noted that:

> [A]mong other things, it is normally "within the power of the State to regulate procedures under which its laws are carried out, including the burden of producing evidence and the burden of persuasion" and its decision in this regard is not subject to proscription under the Due Process Clause unless "it offends some principle of justice so rooted in the traditions and conscience of our people as to be ranked fundamental." Patterson at 201–202, quoting *Speiser v. Randall*, 357 U.S. 513, 523, 78 S.Ct. 1332, 1341, 2 L. Ed. 2d 1460 (1958), et al.

We see no difference in the issues in Patterson, supra, and Carama. We find the reasoning of both courts persuasive.

The amendments to the domestic violence act offend no principles of justice that are so rooted in the traditions and conscience of our people as to fundamentally deny due process to a defendant in a case involving domestic violence.

We hold the CBC has not violated tribal or federal statutes guaranteeing the right to due process and equal protection by shifting the burden of proving self-defense from the prosecution to the defendant for crimes involving domestic violence.

3. Whether shifting the burden of proving self-defense to the defendant in crimes involving domestic violence compels the defendant to testify against himself in violation of tribal law.

To claim self-defense is a choice made by the defendant. Should he claim self-defense in a Class A offense involving domestic violence, he is obligated to prove it by a preponderance of the evidence. He may prove self-defense through the testimony of witnesses or himself or both. It is his decision whether to testify. He may incriminate himself should he choose to do so, but it is his decision whether to testify. He cannot be compelled to testify, but by voluntarily putting himself on the witness stand, he has made moot his fight not to be compelled to testify against himself. As was stated in a recent Washington State court: "The safeguards against self-incrimination are for the benefit of those who do not wish to become witnesses in their own behalf and not for those who do." *State v. Burke*, 163 Wash. 2d 04. 211 (2008).

The United States Supreme Court preceded Burke when it stated that a defendant faces a dilemma demanding a choice between "complete silence and presenting a defense" which has never been thought an invasion of the privilege against compelled self-incrimination. *Williams v. Florida*, 399 U.S. 78, 84 (1970).

We hold that shifting the burden of proving self-defense to the defendant in Class A offenses involving domestic violence does not compel the defendant to testify against himself. By claiming self-defense he has the burden of proving it by a preponderance of the evidence.

Conclusion

We affirm the trial court's order denying the appellants' motion to accept proposed jury instruction. We reverse the trial court's order approving the appellee's proposed jury instructions to the extent that it accepts those instructions regarding the shifting of the burdens of proof and persuasion from the prosecution to the defendants who claim self-defense for Class B and C offenses involving domestic violence. We remand this matter to the trial court to process these cases consistent with this Opinion.

Done this 19th day of June, 2012.

Colville Confederated Tribes Court of Appeals
Waters v. Colville Confederated Tribes (2004)
4 CTCR 14, 7 CCAR 44, 2004.NACC.0000002<http://www.versuslaw.com>
Before Chief Justice Anita Dupris, Justice Elizabeth Fry, and Justice Theresa Pouley. The opinion of the court was delivered by: Dupris, CJ

Summary of Proceedings
Appellant, Sharon Waters, (Appellant) was charged with Disorderly Conduct by criminal complaint on September 9, 2002. On December 9, 2002, the Trial Court entered an Order From Pretrial which indicated that Appellant intended to raise the issue of self-defense at trial. On February 18, 2003, proposed jury instructions were filed by Appellant which included an instruction for self-defense. On June 2, 2003, the Trial Court entered another order from pretrial which indicated that Appellant intended to raise the self-defense argument. Appellee Colville Confederated Tribes (Appellee) did not raise an objection nor did they ask for a motion hearing on the issue at any of these prior notices.

On September 11, 2003, at the preliminary hearing prior to the jury trial, the Trial Court ruled that the affirmative defense of self-defense could not be raised in a Disorderly Conduct case and distinguished *Louie v. CCT*, 2 CCAR 47, 2 CTCR 05, 21 ILR 6136 (1994). Appellant was granted an interlocutory appeal on the issue by the Court of Appeals. Briefing was conducted and oral arguments were heard on February 20, 2004.

We hold that self-defense is available to a defendant charged regarding the public fighting component of the Disorderly Conduct statute. Louie sets out the burdens of proof required to meet the self-defense argument. The Trial Court is reversed and this matter remanded to the Trial Court for trial.

Issue
May a defendant raise the defense of self-defense to a charge of Disorderly Conduct?

Discussion
Appellant argues that self-defense is an inherent right, and the Trial Court was in error when it ruled that the self-defense argument in Louie only applied to cases where Battery was charged. If a person is being confronted by another, that person has the right to defend himself against attack. Louie states: "The law of self-defense justifies an act done in reasonable belief of immediate danger, and if an injury was done by defendant in justifiable self-defense, he can never be punished criminally."

Appellee asserts a custom and tradition argument that has not been developed at the trial level. Appellee states that the public has the right to have a peaceful place and that the Disorderly Conduct statute reflects that public interest by including the public fighting aspect. The community interest in a peaceful existence carries greater weight than the personal interest in the use of self-defense as an argument. Traditionally, argues the Appellee, the Colville Tribes were peaceful and resisted fighting in most instances. As a general rule we do not consider custom and tradition arguments that have not been developed at the trial level. See *Watt v. CCT*, 4 CCAR 48, 2 CTCR 43, 25 ILR 6027 (1998), and *Smith v. CCT*, 4 CCAR 58, 2 CTCR 67, 25 ILR 6156 (1998). The argument of cultural restriction goes more to the common law history of the statute rather than to the issue of self-defense.

We are compelled to agree with the Appellant regarding the use of self-defense when charged with fighting in public. As a matter of common sense we must recognize there may be times when a person will be in a situation where he is unable to withdraw, and must react first in order to retreat. This reaction could be construed as public fighting. If the Court adopts Appellee's arguments, the defendant would have no alternative but to allow himself to be battered. The Court must strike a balance between the public interest and the personal interest of its people.

Self-defense in a Disorderly Conduct charge is a matter of fact, the proof of which is a matter for the fact-finder, either jury or judge, to decide. Once a defendant has established evidence of self-defense, the burden shifts to the Tribes to show its absence beyond a reasonable doubt. This issue has already been settled by this Court. See *Louie*, supra, at 49.

Conclusion
Based on the foregoing we hold that self-defense may be asserted as a defense against a Disorderly Conduct charge before the Trial Court based on fighting in public, and Louie v. CCT, supra controls regarding the burdens of proof on said defense. The Trial Court's orders to the contrary are REVERSED and this matter is REMANDED to the Trial Court for disposition consistent with this order.

It is SO ORDERED.

Necessity

The defense of necessity is somewhat similar to the defense of duress. Necessity may be a defense to a crime where the defendant acts in the reasonable belief that there is no alternative (but the person may be liable for costs). For example, Sally steals a boat to escape an onrushing flood. This defense is available only when there was no other way to avoid the threatened harm. Mere economic necessity (need for money) is not sufficient to excuse a criminal act. Also, in American law, neither duress nor necessity is a defense in a crime of homicide.

When using the defense of necessity, defendants are saying that the action they committed was necessary to protect themselves or another, that the action was no worse than the crime charged, and the defendants did not recklessly or negligently create the situation.

Take, for example, a defendant who has been drinking at a party. Someone else at the party is injured. The defendant drives the injured person to the hospital at high speed, but along the way, the defendant loses control of the car and kills someone walking along the road. It turns out the defendant was legally intoxicated at the time of the car accident. Many questions arise: Was it necessary for the person to drink and drive? Were there others who could have driven? How badly injured was the person? Was it necessary to speed? How far away was help, in relation to the injury? In this case, it is questionable whether necessity would be a valid defense.

Excuse Defenses

Excuse defenses focus on the defendant more than the act. This type of defense typically argues that the defendant is not guilty because of lack of intent. An excuse defense recognizes that the act caused social harm but that the defendant should not be blamed for the act. Excuse defenses include duress and mental illness.

Duress or Coercion

The defense of coercion or duress is available to defendants when they were threatened with immediate, serious bodily harm (e.g., a threat of death) to themselves or a close relative unless they committed the offense. The keys to this defense are (1) coercion, (2) use or threat of use of unlawful force, (3) inability to resist the coercion, and (4) not having put oneself into the situation in the first place in a reckless or negligent way.

Note that coercion equals the use of unlawful force by another. That force could be a deadly weapon, such as a firearm, or even the use or threat of physical force (e.g., beating) to force someone to commit a crime. The element of inability to resist can be supported by the kind of force that was used and the individual's age, gender, size, strength, and other factors that demonstrate the individual's inability to resist the force used.

When Can I Use the Duress Defense?

Nez Perce Tribal Code Sec. 4-1-16

 a. *It is an affirmative defense that the actor engaged in the conduct charged to constitute an offense because he was coerced by the use of, or a threat to use, unlawful force against his person or the person of another, which a reasonable person in his situation would have been unable to resist.*

b. *The defense provided by this section is unavailable if:*
  1. *the actor knowingly, willfully or negligently placed himself in a situation in which it was probable that he would be subjected to duress;*
  2. *the coerced conduct threatens to cause death or serious bodily harm to some person other than the actor.*

Insanity/Mental Illness

During criminal proceedings, insanity becomes an issue in determining the following: whether the defendant is competent to stand trial; whether the defendant was sane at the time of the criminal act; and whether the defendant is sane after the trial. An insanity defense is concerned only with the defendant's sanity at the time of the criminal act. Insanity or incompetence at the time of trial may delay the proceedings until the accused can understand what is taking place, but insanity during or after the trial does not affect criminal liability.

To prove insanity, the defense must produce evidence of a mental disease or defect. It is an affirmative defense, meaning the defendant has the burden of producing evidence of his or her mental condition at the time of the criminal act. Psychiatrists are usually brought in to give testimony in this regard. Both the defense and the prosecution may have psychiatrists examine the defendant, and their testimony is often in conflict. The decision as to whether insanity is a valid defense then rests with whomever—judge or jury—decides the facts of the case.

Courts agree that a person who, at the time of committing a criminal act, was so mentally ill as to be deemed legally insane is not responsible for the act. However, courts in different jurisdictions disagree over what constitutes insanity. Some courts say that defendants are not responsible for a crime if at the time of the act they did not know what they were doing or if they were aware of what they were doing but did not know the difference between right and wrong. Other courts use the irresistible impulse test. The test requires that an irresistible impulse caused the defendant to lose the power to choose between right and wrong and that the impulse destroyed the defendant's willpower so that his or her actions were beyond his or her control. For example, Joan suffers from schizophrenia and hears voices telling her to steal objects. If she is charged with theft, she will have a valid insanity defense in some courts if she can show that as a result of a mental disorder, schizophrenia, she could not keep herself from stealing.

Voluntary Intoxication

Defendants sometimes claim that at the time of a crime, they were so drunk on alcohol or so high on drugs that they did not know what they were doing. As a general rule, voluntary intoxication is not a defense to a crime. However, remember that some crimes require proof of a specific mental state. For example, John attacks his wife, Jenni, and Jenni runs away and calls the police. John is charged with assault with intent to kill, but John claims he was drunk and did not intend to kill Jenni when he attacked her. If he can prove that he was too drunk to form the intent to kill, intoxication is a valid defense because it negates the specific mental state (i.e., intent to kill) required to prove the crime. John can still be convicted of assault, however, because specific intent is not required to prove that crime. If John decided to kill Jenni before he got drunk, or if he got drunk to get up enough nerve to commit the crime, then intoxication would not be a defense because the required mental state existed before the drunkenness.

Voluntary intoxication is not a defense to a crime where recklessness is the required mental state.

Is Intoxication a Defense?

Sault Ste. Marie Tribal Code § 71.403 (1995)

Intoxication of the defendant is not a defense to the charge of a criminal offense, but in any prosecution for an offense, evidence of intoxication of the defendant may be offered by the defendant whenever it is relevant to negate the existence of a specific intent, if such intent is an element of the crime charged.

Involuntary Intoxication

People are involuntarily intoxicated if they are forced to take an intoxicating substance against their will or if they take it without knowledge or reason to know it will intoxicate them. Involuntary intoxication can be used as a defense in any case in which a voluntary intoxication defense may be used to negate the intent requirement. Involuntary intoxication may also be used similarly to an insanity defense. A valid defense exists if the involuntarily intoxicated person could not distinguish right from wrong.

In the following case, how does the court distinguish between the insanity defense and the intoxication defense?

Swinomish Tribal Court

Swinomish v. Fornsby (2009)
WL 9125779 (Swinomish Tribal Ct.)
Mark W. Pouley, Chief Judge.

This matter came on before the Court on Defendant's Motion to establish the legal standards of the "insanity defense." The Court having heard the testimony of experts, the argument of counsel and considered the pleadings filed issues the following opinion.

The Defendant is charged with multiple counts of assault, malicious mischief, and criminal contempt. The alleged facts of the complaints are not immediately relevant to the decision of this court. During the pendency of these proceedings, counsel for the defense has raised concerns regarding the mental capacity of his client, both as to his competency to assist in his defense and as to his mental capacity at the time of the alleged incidents. As a result of these questions, the Defendant has undergone multiple mental health evaluations. The specific details of these evaluations and opinions regarding the Defendant's mental condition are also, not immediately relevant to the matter before the court.

At issue in this motion, and the subject of this opinion, is what legal standard should be applied, and how should a jury be instructed, if a Defendant raises his alleged insanity as a defense to criminal charges. To be clear, the motion presented and this opinion addresses exclusively the issue of "insanity" as a complete defense to criminal conviction. This is distinct from the concept of "diminished capacity"; the argument that a defendant, at the time of an alleged incident, lacked the mental capacity to form a required specific intent to commit the charged crime. See, *State v. Jamison*, 94 Wash.2d 663, 665, 619 P.2d 352 (1980).

Historically, in western jurisprudence a person could not be held legally responsible for any act committed by him while he was "insane." The issues that flow from this are the various definitions of "insane" and how it may be proved. One of the earliest standards of the defense, The McNaughten test, required proof the defendant suffered "a defect of reason, from disease of the mind" such that he did not, at the time of the alleged incident, understand the nature and quality of his actions or did not know right from wrong. See, 8 Eng. Rep 718 (H.L.1843). The "insanity defense" has long been a common law defense created and defined by the inherent authority of the courts. See, *State v. Strasburg*, 60 Wash. 106, 110 P. 1020 (1910). Overtime, the specifics of the defense, including definitions of insanity and the burdens of proof/persuasion have been codified and become the subject of state and federal statutes. See, R.C.W. 9A.12.10 and R.C.W. 10.77.030; 18 U.S.C. §§ 4241–4247.

The Swinomish Rules of Criminal Procedure contemplate application of the insanity defense; STC 3–03.270(B)(13) obligates the Defendant to disclose reliance on the defense if requested by the prosecuting attorney. The Swinomish Tribal Code and remainder of the procedural rules are otherwise silent as to the legal requirements and application of the insanity defense. Lacking specific statutory guidance, the Court must exercise inherent authority to develop definitions and rules for the application of the insanity defense to be used in the Swinomish Tribal Court. In exercising this inherent authority, however, it is appropriate and advisable to examine, where possible, the history and culture of the Swinomish community, and any guidance provided by other statutory language. The court is statutorily directed, where helpful and equitable, to inquire as to the customs and usages of the tribe, STC 4–01.070(A) and matters not covered by our codes or rules, to the common law developed by other courts. STC 4–01.070(B).

The asserted facts of the Defendant's mental condition, as they relate to the proposed instructions are these: all of the mental health experts agree that the Defendant may have underlying mental defects or disease that, alone, would not likely be sufficient for a finding that the defendant was insane at the time of the commission of the alleged acts. The forensic physiologist testifying for the defense alleges, however, that Defendant's severe intoxication at the time of the incidents, when added to these mental disabilities, rendered him unable to control his allegedly criminal behaviors to the point he should be considered insane. It is further argued that Defendant's mental disabilities and the history of cultural trauma caused by alcohol and drug use renders substance abuse an involuntary act. With these arguments, the Defense asks the court to instruct the jury to consider if the Defendant's overall mental condition at the time of the incidents, including the effects of his severe intoxication, rendered him unable to appreciate the wrongfulness of his conduct or to conform his conduct to the requirements of the law, and therefore render him "not guilty" of the charged offenses.

In support of his arguments the Defendant presented testimony from the cultural resource officer of the tribe and a forensic psychologist. The tribe presented testimony from a tribal elder and educator and head of the Swinomish Family services department. Each witness offered testimony about the role of drugs and alcohol in the Swinomish Community and the broader native community as well as the interplay of substance abuse, mental disabilities and criminal responsibility.

The testimony provided by the cultural resource officer clearly established that the concept of "healing" individuals and the community is a traditional and cultural cornerstone of Swinomish jurisprudence. The community's response to wrongdoing focuses less on punishment for the unacceptable act, and more on putting things right with the wrongdoer, the victim and the community. It is also clear that alcohol abuse is inconsistent with cultural traditions and the Swinomish people are victims of the introduction of alcohol to the native community. Many community members are so victimized they become impaired in their ability to conform to accepted cultural norms. The overriding community response to such an individual is to help them heal and overcome the impairment. While it is undoubtedly true that the community embraces a therapeutic emphasis, this is not mutually exclusive of the concept of accountability.

The testimony was that making mistakes is part of the learning process, but that it was wrong to repeatedly make the same mistakes. The community does not "just accept" wrongs, but expects "payment" to the community and/or the victim to correct the wrong. If a person fails to take responsibility for the wrongs they commit, it creates tensions within the community. Most significantly, it is not culturally acceptable for a person to deny responsibility for a wrongful act because they were intoxicated. This is inconsistent with Swinomish cultural values and "violates universal human values." Recognizing the role of the judicial system in the modern native community, the cultural resource officer recommended a "two prong approach" with the western methods encouraging people toward cultural remedies. The tribe's witnesses support these conclusions as well. The witnesses highlighted the impact of drugs and alcohol on families and the community, and the use of community resources to help these individuals heal. The influence of the court is included in the healing process by requiring strict accountability for one's acts to motivate individuals to seek and/or utilize the community healing resources.

The forensic psychologist, examining the language of the various legal standards for the "insanity defense" applied by the many jurisdictions offered his opinion that no jurisdiction adequately addresses substance use as it relates to mental incapacity. It was suggested that for some people, alcohol use is involuntary and some people have no capacity to avoid drinking. He suggests this is true because of underlying mental defects or a lack of substantial cognitive abilities which is exacerbated in native communities where one's ability to resist alcohol abuse is overcome by additional severe social pressures to consume. While this opinion opens the door to a much broader, and potentially controversial, argument about alcohol abuse and addition, the court does not find it appropriate to weigh in on the persuasiveness or efficacy of this opinion. It is clear this opinion is inconsistent with the great weight of testimony of the elders and cultural representatives and is at odds with the legion of community and governmental efforts to stem the tide of trauma caused by the abuse of drugs and alcohol. If the expert's opinion gains transaction in the community, the Court expects the legislative and policy making bodies can form tribal law and programs accordingly. It is not the province of the court to blaze the trail on a theory that appears so contrary to custom and tradition and the clearly stated policies and goals of the community.

More fairly, the testimony of the all of the witnesses supports the implementation sentencing options that recognize the underlying causes of unacceptable behavior and that adopt therapeutic rather than punitive models. This is supported by the expert's testimony that it may be more appropriate to find individuals "guilty but impaired" rather than "not guilty by insanity." This is also consistent with interests of therapeutic justice already adopted by the Swinomish court in its sentencing and probation review decisions. See, *SITC v. James* CrCo–2006–0213 (Swinomish Tribal Ct. July 13, 2007).

The Defense does not argue, nor do any of the facts support, that defendant is suffering a "fixed or settled insanity" caused by long-term voluntary or involuntary intoxication, which is an acceptable insanity standard in some jurisdictions. See,

> *State v. Wicks*, 98 Wash.2d 620, 657 P.2d 781 (1983). Instead, the Defense argues he was insane at the time of the alleged incidents as a result of the combination of his severe intoxication and his underlying mental defects, but lasting only during the period of his intoxication. This is not an accepted standard of insanity in any jurisdiction cited to the court, and it is inconsistent with the cultural history presented in testimony. The court will not, therefore, adopt this standard lacking express statutory authority or direction to do so.
>
> Based upon the testimony presented and a review of the law of other jurisdictions the court holds that to establish the defense of insanity, the defendant must prove by preponderance of the evidence that, at the time of the commission of the offense, as the result of mental disease or defect, the mind of the defendant was affected to such an extent that he was unable to perceive the nature and quality of the act with which he is charged OR he was unable to tell right from wrong with reference to the particular act charged.
>
> No condition of the defendant's mind that is proximately induced by the voluntary act of the defendant, including severe voluntary intoxication, shall constitute the defense of insanity. This ruling is consistent with the statutory and common law defense of insanity as it has been established in Washington State, and is consistent with the rule of law and customs and traditions of the Swinomish community.
>
> Further, the court holds that it is judicial error to instruct the jury on the defense of insanity absent substantial evidence to support the theory. *Wicks*, at 625, 657 P.2d 781. At best, the evidence suggests the combined effects of underlying mental illness and severe intoxication may impair the defendant's ability to refrain from unlawful conduct, but absent evidence of the effects of his voluntary severe intoxication, there is insufficient evidence to support instructing the jury on the defense of insanity in this matter.

Other Defenses

Entrapment

Entrapment is a defense used to argue that the police convinced the defendant to commit the crime. Police are permitted to present an opportunity to a person to commit a crime (e.g., an undercover **sting**). However, the targeted person must be predisposed or ready and willing to commit the crime. The police cannot use trickery, persuasion, threats, or fraud to induce the person to commit the crime. If the person would not have committed the crime without the police's inducement, the person has a valid entrapment defense.

Entrapment is usually raised as a defense in drug cases involving undercover narcotics officers or other kinds of sting operations where law enforcement officers try to get someone to commit an offense in their presence. The entrapment defense is not usually successful. However, there might be rare instances when a law enforcement officer falsely makes someone believe that the given act is not a crime, for example by telling someone, "It is all right to grow marijuana for medical purposes, so sell me some because I have glaucoma." The person must have been unwilling to commit the crime before the officer's statements, and this unwillingness is very difficult to prove.

Conclusion

Defendants can argue many kinds of defenses when accused of a crime. The ultimate goal of a criminal case is to hold people accountable for their actions. Most tribal laws recognize that there are some situations in which the defendant should not be convicted. This chapter has discussed some of the basic principles of criminal defenses. Consult your own tribal code and case law for other potential defenses.

Questions

1. Are the criminal defenses described in this chapter consistent with tribal traditions of accountability?
2. In *Grand Traverse v. Raphael*, why did the judge express skepticism about the defendant's justification defense?
3. Do you think that force can ever be justified as self-defense? How would you define this in a law?
4. In *Colville v. Davisson* and *Colville v. Waters*, what did the defendants claim was their justification for self-defense? How does the court response to these claims?
5. Do you think that intoxication ever excuses criminal actions? Why or why not? In *Swinomish v. Fornsby*, how did the court describe traditional law and custom in response to the defendant's claims?

In Your Community

1. Find out what your tribal laws say about criminal defenses.
2. Are any defenses codified? If so, compare them to the possible defenses in this chapter. Are any defenses missing from your tribal laws?
3. Do you think they should be added?
4. How does your community respond to people with drug or alcohol problems who commit crimes? Should the courts be more lenient with defendants who have addictions? Why or why not?

Terms Used in Chapter 16

Alibi: Evidence that a defendant was in a different place during the commission of a crime.

Coercion: Compulsion or force; making a person act against free will.

Duress: Unlawful pressure on a person to do what he or she would not otherwise do.

Exonerated: Cleared of a crime or other wrongdoing.

Imminent: Just about to happen; threatening.

Insanity: A legal word regarding a person's mental capacity—sometimes invokes mental illness. It has different meanings in different court systems.

Negate: To make ineffective or invalid; nullify.

Provoked: Acted in a way that triggered a reaction of anger or rage in another person.

Sting: An operation organized and implemented by undercover law enforcement to apprehend criminals.

Note

1. For a more detailed discussion *see* Joshua Dressler, *Understanding Criminal Law* 201-204 (2001).

Suggested Further Reading

Seth Diamond, "Criminal Law: The Justification of Self-Defense," *Annual Survey of American Law* 673 (1987).

Albin Eser, "Justification and Excuse," 4 *American Journal of Comparative Law* 621 (1976).

The Burden of Proof — Chapter 17

Individual rights exist to protect people from the abuse by the government. The Indian Civil Rights Act (ICRA) prohibits a government from depriving of life, liberty, or property without due process of law. One aspect of "due process" is the presumption of innocence. When a person is charged with a crime, the person is presumed innocent until proven guilty. The U.S. Supreme Court has interpreted this right to mean that the burden of proof is on the government, or the prosecution. The burden or standard of proof in a criminal case is **beyond a reasonable doubt**.[1] Due process during trial is discussed in more detail in chapter 24.

Tribal codes and constitutions, as well as ICRA, also provide individuals with a right to due process of the law before losing life, liberty, or property. Tribal courts may also look to federal law and the U.S. Supreme Court for guidance on due process and the standard of reasonable doubt. However, remember federal law is not binding on tribal courts. Thus tribal courts will look to their tribal laws, which often provide a **presumption of innocence**, place the burden of proof on the prosecution, and require the tribal court to use the reasonable doubt standard in criminal cases.

There are two types of burdens. One is the **burden of production**, or presenting the evidence. The other is the **burden of persuasion**, or convincing the judge or jury of the defendant's guilt.

The Burden of Production

The prosecutor, representing the government, charges a person with a crime with a document called a **complaint** or **information**. The prosecutor is required to present, or produce, evidence in trial to prove the crime alleged in the complaint. Thus, the prosecutor has the burden of production for each element of the crime.

A defendant is presumed innocent until proven guilty beyond a reasonable doubt, so the defendant is not required to produce evidence of innocence. Defendants also cannot be required to testify against themselves. If the prosecution fails to produce evidence for any one element of an offense, the court can and should dismiss the case after the prosecution finishes presenting its evidence.

The Burden of Persuasion

The burden of persuasion focuses on how convinced the trier of fact, the judge or jury, must be to convict the defendant. The burden of persuasion in a criminal case is beyond a reasonable doubt. The U.S. Supreme Court requires this burden in criminal cases, but has failed to define reasonable doubt. Tribes may provide a definition in their tribal laws or simply require the prosecution to prove every element of the crime beyond a reasonable doubt. Generally courts and scholars agree that reasonable doubt is "doubt that prevents one from being firmly convinced of a defendant's guilt, or the belief that there is a real possibility that a defendant is not guilty."[2] A high standard of proof is required because the defendant is facing imprisonment or losing his liberty. Due process of law requires a high level of confidence that the defendant committed a criminal act.

Presumption of Innocence and Reasonable Doubt

Sault Ste. Marie Tribal Code § 71.405 (2008)

1. *Every person is presumed innocent of any offense with which he is charged until proven guilty.*
2. *No person shall be convicted of any offense unless his guilt, as to each material element, is proven beyond a reasonable doubt.*

In *Commonwealth v. Webster* (59 Mass. 295, 320 [1850]), the U.S. Supreme Court gave some guidance as to the definition of reasonable doubt stating it is "not merely possible doubt; because everything relating to human affairs, and depending on moral evidence, is open to some possible or imaginary doubt."[3] And that reasonable doubt "leaves the minds of jurors in that condition that they cannot say they feel an abiding conviction to a moral certainty, of the truth of the charge."[4]

Reasonable Doubt

Nez Perce Tribal Code Sec. 4-1-7

No person may be convicted of an offense unless each element of such offense is proven beyond a reasonable doubt. In the absence of such proof the defendant shall be acquitted.

Proving Beyond a Reasonable Doubt in Tribal Court

Reasonable doubt arises because not enough evidence has been produced to prove the defendant committed the acts included in the definition of the crime. The following two tribal court cases explore the concept of reasonable doubt and whether the prosecutor met that burden.

Colville Confederated Tribes Court of Appeals
Condon v. Colville Confederated Tribes (1996)
3 CCAR 48
Before Presiding Justice Collins, Justice Bonga and Justice Miles.
The opinion of the court was delivered by: Collins, P. J.

Factual and Procedural Background

During the late evening hours of June 24, 1994, Condon and his companions gathered to play basketball on an outdoor court located in the Moccasin Flat HUD Housing Area in Omak, Washington, which is located within the Colville Indian Reservation. Condon and his friends were then under age 21. Members of the group were consuming beer while they were playing basketball.

At approximately 2:00 a.m. on June 25, 1994, the Colville Tribal Police were called to the Moccasin Flat Housing Area in response to a reported fight involving a carload of juveniles. The police stopped a car occupied by Condon and his friends. After the occupants exited the vehicle, the police officers discovered that members of the group exhibited telltale signs of consuming alcoholic beverages.

At trial, Sgt. William Evans testified that he detected the odor of alcohol on Condon and that "he appeared to have been drinking." Evans testified that he recognized Condon and knew him to be under 21 from previous contacts. Evans testified that the other members of the group appeared intoxicated. Condon and his companions were arrested and taken to the Omak Police Station where they were individually interviewed. Both Sgt. Evans and Officer Rotter, who interviewed Condon, testified that they smelled alcohol on his breath.

Although Condon denied consuming alcohol, he testified that members of the group drank beer while playing basketball and that containers of beer were in the car at the time of the stop. Both the police and Condon testified that the containers of beer found in the car were unopened. The record does not reflect which member of the group owned the car.

Among the instructions given to the jury, the Court gave the following:

> You are instructed that possession may be either actual or constructive. Actual possession means possession in person, upon the person, and within his actual physical control, of the substance involved. Constructive possession means such dominion

and control over a place where the substance was found so as to give a person in possession of such a place the right to complete access to, or disposition of, the substance found. Jury Instruction No. 5.

The Panel has repeatedly reviewed the taped record from trial. From our review the Panel concludes that defense counsel did not object on the record to any of the jury instructions given by the Tribal Court, including Instruction No. 5.

The jury found Condon guilty and he was sentenced to pay a fine of $600.00, with $400.00 conditionally suspended upon his compliance with conditions of sentencing.

I. *Issues*

There are two primary issues raised on this appeal. The first is whether there was sufficient evidence adduced at trial to for the jury to convict Condon of the offense. . . .

II. *Discussion*

A. *The Offense*

The required elements to be support Condon's conviction for Possession of an Alcoholic Beverage by a Person Under 21 are: 1) that Condon was under the age of 21 at the time of the offense; 2) that he possessed, purchased, consumed, obtained or sold an alcoholic beverage; 3) that the offense occurred within the Reservation. CTC 5.5.13. Thus, the prohibited conduct encompassed by the statute includes more than mere possession of alcohol.

B. *Sufficiency of Evidence to Support a Conviction*

We have previously had an opportunity to review criminal cases in which reversal was sought on grounds that there was insufficient evidence adduced at trial to support a conviction. In *Cora L. Pakootas v. Colville Confederated Tribes*, AP92-15148, [1 CTCR 67, 1 CCAR 65], we held that the Court will not reverse a conviction, based upon sufficiency of evidence, unless "after reviewing the evidence in a light most favorable to the prosecution, no rational trier of fact could have found the essential elements of a crime beyond a reasonable doubt." Id. at 4. All reasonable inferences from the evidence must be drawn in favor of the prosecution and interpreted most strongly against the defendant. Simply stated, on appeal the appellant must show that, from the evidence at trial, no reasonable jury would have found that he possessed or consumed an alcoholic beverage in violation of the statute.

It is unchallenged that Condon was under age 21 when the offense occurred. It is also unchallenged that the offense took place within the Reservation. Thus, our inquiry is whether there was sufficient evidence presented that any reasonable jury could have found that Condon "possessed, purchased, consumed or sold an alcoholic beverage."

From the facts of this case, the relevant prohibited conduct under CTC 5.5.13 concerns whether Condon "possessed" or "consumed" alcohol. Although there was conflicting testimony at trial as to whether Condon consumed alcoholic beverages prior to his arrest, two police officers testified that they detected the odor of alcohol on Condon's breath and body at the time of arrest and during questioning at the Omak Police Station.

The officers testified that they were in a position to detect the odor of alcohol and to observe the defendant, and it appeared to them that Condon had been drinking. The police officers also testified that there was beer in the automobile in which Condon was riding and that Condon's companions were intoxicated.

The officers' testimony was partially corroborated by Condon, who testified that there was beer in the car when it was stopped. The officers' testimony was further corroborated by Condon's companions, who testified that they had beer in their possession and had been consuming beer.

While there were certain discrepancies in the officers' testimony, we find that their testimony concerning the material points in this case was consistent. The evidence presented at trial was not such that a reasonable jury should have concluded that the officers' testimony lacked credibility and that it should have been given less weight than needed to support a conviction.

Although defense witnesses came forward with testimony that Condon had consumed no alcohol during the night in question and was not generally known to consume alcohol, there was also testimony presented that Condon had, on at least one occasion, consumed alcohol. In addition, there was no evidence presented to show that Condon was an unwilling participant in the group's activities, which included drinking beer, or that he attempted to leave the group when his friends began consuming alcoholic beverages.

C. Consumption

Although the defense witnesses denied that they saw Condon consume alcoholic beverages, there was evidence presented that he had done so. In *Colville Confederated Tribes v. Terry Dean Fry*, Case Nos. 80-3351, 80-3352, 80-3353, [1 CTCR 02] (Colv. Tr. Ct. 1981), the Tribal Court determined that "consumption" is a continuing process which begins when alcohol is swallowed and ends when the substance has been fully metabolized. There is record evidence, from the police officers' testimony, that the smell of alcohol was detected on Condon's breath. Thus, a reasonable inference can be drawn, based on the reasoning in *Fry*, that Condon was then in the process of consuming alcohol. There was also evidence presented that beer could have been made available to Condon and that he was present when his friends were consuming alcohol. We therefore conclude that the evidence adduced at trial was such that a reasonable jury could have found, beyond a reasonable doubt, that Condon consumed alcohol, as well as the remaining elements of the offense.

. . .

For the reasons stated above, it is Ordered that the judgment of the Tribal Court is Affirmed and the matter is remanded to the Tribal Court.

Fort Peck Court of Appeals

Fort Peck Tribes v. Joseph Harold Jones (1992)
Fort Peck Court of Appeals No. 148
Held: Appellant's conviction of DUI [Driving Under the Influence], a violation of IX CCOJ 107 is reversed.

Facts

The facts as we are able to determine from the transcripts are as follows:

On October 12, 1991, at approximately 9:30 o'clock P.M., Appellant Jones was arrested and charged with DUI, a violation of IX CCOJ 107 and refusal to submit to a chemical blood, breath or urine test, a violation of IX CCOJ 108.

The charge stemmed from an event earlier that day in which a white car traveling west of Wolf Point, Montana, on Highway No. 2 "ran a school bus in the ditch" TR., November 26, 1991, Page 2. The officer making the arrest testified that he had been advised that . . . "Mr. Jones owns the same type of car, so I pulled into his residence, just to check out his car. When I pulled in, I found Mr. Jones passed out in the front seat of his car, keys in the ignition." Appellant Jones testified that he was not in the car at the time of the officer's arrival, but rather in his house. There was no other evidence offered at trial linking Appellant's vehicle with that involving the school bus incident, or any evidence indicating that Mr. Jones had been operating a motor vehicle on the day in question.

Issue

The basic issue before the Court is as follows:

Whether the prosecution met its burden of proof which was that defendant was in actual physical control of a vehicle upon the highways or roads of the reservation while he could not safely operate a vehicle.

Discussion

. . . The Appellant was found guilty of violation IX CCOJ 107. This statute reads in part as follows:

> (a) It is unlawful and punishable for any person who is under the influence of intoxicating liquors, under the influence of any drug, or under the combined influence of alcohol and any drug, to a degree **which renders him incapable of safely driving a motor vehicle to operate or be in actual physical control of any motor vehicle upon the highways or roads of the Reservation.** (emphasis made)
>
> Pursuant to II CCOJ 103, the Tribe has the burden of proof in proving violations of the Tribal code. This section reads:
>
> (a) The Tribes have the burden of proving each element of an offense beyond a reasonable doubt.
> (b) Whenever the defendant introduces sufficient evidence of a defense to support a reasonable belief as to the existence of that defense, the Tribes have the burden of disproving such defense beyond a reasonable doubt, unless this Code or another ordinance expressly requires the defendant to prove the defense by a preponderance of evidence.
>
> In applying the law to the facts of this case, the record is clear that Appellant Jones was at the time of his arrest at his private residence (or the driveway thereof). There is no indication in the record that Mr. Jones was at any time on the day in question "in actual physical control of a motor vehicle upon the highways or roads of the Reservation" IX CCOJ 107. The only testimony offered at trial linking Mr. Jones' car to that involved with the bus incident was this testimony:
>
>> Officer DeCoteau: "Well, I was looking for a white car. I received a call about 20:00, looking for a white car that ran a school bus in the ditch earlier that evening. I was informed that Mr. Jones owns the same type of car, so I pulled into his residence, just to check out his car. When I pulled in, I found Mr. Jones passed out in the front seat of his car, keys in the ignition. And, I then arrested him for DUI."
>
> The Tribes here have the burden of proving each element of an offense beyond a reasonable doubt. III CCOJ 103.
>
> We find that the burden of proving that Defendant was in actual physical control of a vehicle upon the highways and roads of the Reservation was simply not met here.
>
> Accordingly, we reverse the decision of the Court.

Self-Defense and the Burdens of Production and Persuasion

Some defenses raised by defendants will shift the burdens of production and/or persuasion. If a defendant decides to raise a defense he is typically required to produce evidence of a defense he wishes to raise in a trial. The prosecution is not required to produce evidence that defenses did not occur. However, in limited situations, the burden of persuasion may also shift to the defense but jurisdictions will differ. For example, to defend against a murder charge, the defense may produce evidence self-defense. Some jurisdictions will then place the burden of proving self-defense on the defendant, while other jurisdictions, will require the prosecution to prove the killing was not committed in self-defense.

The following cases explore the burdens of production and persuasion in self-defense. What are the differences between the courts' decisions?

Confederated Salish and Kootenai Tribes Court of Appeals
Confederated Salish and Kootenai Tribes v. Daniel Felix Finley, (2000) 27 Indian L. Rep. 6161

Background
This case presents the question of the burden of proof that a criminal defendant must meet in raising self-defense and whether the trial court committed error in rejecting the claim of self-defense. This Court finds that no error was committed by the trial court in ruling on the claim of self-defense. We affirm.

This case involves a domestic dispute that arose in the early morning hours of October 22, 1998, between Daniel Finley and Shannon Hewankorn. The verbal dispute escalated into a physical altercation wherein Mr. Finley bit Ms. Hewankorn twice on the neck. At trial, Mr. Finley claimed that the biting was an act of self-defense. He alleges that the biting was in self-defense to Ms. Hewankorn grabbing his hair at the top of the head and pulling down. Because of an accident that occurred seven months previous resulting in frontal damage to his skull, and related medical treatment, Mr. Finley testified that he was afraid the hair grabbing could result in serious injury to him. He alleges he bit Ms. Hewankorn in self-defense to prevent this form of serious injury to himself.

The trial court heard evidence on whether the biting occurred before or after the alleged hair pulling. . . .

Analysis
Our analysis begins with the Tribal Law and Order Code. Section 2-3-101 states:

> A person is justified in the use of force or threat to use force against another when and to the extent the person reasonably believes that such conduct is necessary to: a) defend herself or himself or another against the offender's imminent use of unlawful force; . . .

Section 2-3-102 also provides that:

> Self Defense is not available to a person who:

2. Knowingly or purposely provokes the use of force against herself or himself unless:
    a. Such force is so great that the person reasonably believes there is imminent danger of death or serious bodily harm and the person has exhausted every reasonable means to escape such danger. . . .

The defendant alleges that the burden rests with the prosecution to disprove self-defense beyond a reasonable doubt. Under defendant's theory, all the defendant need do is bring forward "any evidence" that he acted in self-defense, then the burden shifts in its entirety to the prosecution to disprove self-defense beyond a reasonable doubt.

The United States Supreme Court provides some clear guideposts on this matter. The Supreme Court, in the case of *In the Matter of Samuel Winship*, 397 U.S. 358 (1970), held that the reasonable doubt standard of criminal law has constitutional statute grounded in the Due Process Clause. Referring to the reasonable doubt standard, the Winship Court states:

> This notion—basic in our law and rightly one of the boasts of a free society—is a requirement and a safeguard of due process of law in the historic, procedural content of due process. 397 U.S. at 362 (quoting Justice Frankfurter)

. . . The Supreme Court in *Martin v. Ohio*, 480 U.S. 228 (1987), upheld Ohio law requiring a defendant to prove by a preponderance of the evidence that the defendant was acting in self-defense. The Court noted that all but two of the states have abandoned the common law rule (which places the self-defense burden on the defendant) and required the prosecution to prove the absence of self-defense when it is properly raised by the defendant. In Martin the Supreme Court affirmed that there is no constitutional due process requirement that the prosecution must bear the burden to disprove the self-defense. Therefore, this leaves considerable discretion in the states and tribal governments to allocate this burden. . . .

With these Supreme Court guideposts in mind, this Court is left to decipher the burden of proof allocation in the Salish-Kootenai Tribes' self-defense statute which is silent on the question. As discussed above, the Supreme Court has determined that there is no violation of constitutional due process if a state places a burden on a defendant to prove by a preponderance of the evidence that an affirmative defense (or mitigating circumstances) exists. . . .

In the absence of the Tribal Code providing guidance as to the burden of proof in self-defense matters, Judge Tanner's opinion indicates that she concluded that the defendant did not produce "sufficient evidence" regarding the claim to self-defense to raise a reasonable doubt in the judge's mind.

We believe Judge Tanner reasonably applied the burden of proof standard given the lack of direction in the Tribal Code. Importantly, she first concluded that

> the prosecution had met its burden in proving beyond a reasonable doubt every element of the crime of assault. . . .
>
> The "sufficient evidence" standard applied by Judge Tanner lies somewhere between the "any evidence" standard argued for by the prosecution and the "preponderance of evidence" standard which the Supreme Court has affirmed. . . . Therefore it does not offend the Due Process Clause and it is a reasonable interpretation of the tribal self-defense code.
>
> The trial court's rejection of the claim of self-defense is also independently supported by the trial court's conclusion that the defendant failed to establish that he had exhausted every reasonable means to escape the alleged danger. This factual finding, standing alone, strips the defendant of a claim to self-defense.
>
> For the [foregoing] reasons, the decision of the lower court in this matter is unanimously Affirmed.

Conclusion

When a person comes before the court in a criminal case, he is presumed innocent until proven guilty beyond a reasonable doubt. The government is required to present evidence to the judge or jury that demonstrates or proves the defendant committed the acts with the required mental state. The evidence must prove this beyond a reasonable doubt. Legislatures and courts are reluctant to give a strict definition to "beyond a reasonable doubt." It is the judge or jury's job to assess each case and determine whether the government has proven their case.

Questions

Condon v. Colville Confederated Tribes
1. What evidence proved the defendant's guilt beyond a reasonable doubt?
2. Do you agree with the court, and why or why not?

Ft. Peck v. Jones
1. Was the defendant operating or in actual physical control of a motor vehicle? Why or why not?
2. If you were the judge in this case, how would you have decided it and why?

In Your Community

1. Are there exceptions to the burden of proof rule in your tribal code or in tribal court decisions?

2. Does your tribe use the reasonable doubt standard? If yes, how does the court define it? If no, what standard of proof does the court use in criminal trials?
3. Traditionally, what was your nation's standard of proof? What was required in order for a person to be found guilty?

Terms Used in Chapter 17

Beyond a reasonable doubt: The level of proof required to convict a person of a crime.

Burden of persuasion: The requirement of obligation of a party to convince the judge or jury.

Burden of production: The requirement of obligation of a party to present the evidence.

Complaint: A formal document charging a person with a crime.

Information: A formal accusation of a crime made by a prosecuting attorney.

Presumption of innocence: The rule that all persons are innocent until proven guilty.

Notes

1. *In re Winship*, 397 U.S. 358.
2. *Black's Law Dictionary*, 2nd ed., 584.
3. *Commonwealth v. Webster*, Mass. 295, 320 (1850).
4. Id.

Suggested Further Reading

Ronald J. Allen, "Burdens of Proof, Uncertainty, and Ambiguity in Modern Legal Discourse," 17 *Harvard Journal of Law and Public Policy* 627 (1994).

Miller W. Shealy Jr., "A Reasonable Doubt about 'Reasonable Doubt,'" 65 *Oklahoma Law Review* 225 (2013).

Rights of Criminal Defendants

Chapter 18

"Criminal procedure" refers to the rules and methods that apply during the various stages of a criminal case to ensure a fair trial. Prior to beginning a discussion of criminal procedure, one must understand what rights are to be protected. This chapter will introduce laws protecting the rights of criminal defendants. This chapter offers an introduction to the American conception of individual rights and also examines how tribal governments define civil rights in tribal law.

In American law, a right is a power or privilege protected by law. There are many different forms of rights, but in criminal law and procedure, rights refer to rights that protect us from governmental oppression or intrusion on our liberty, our right to be free. These rights limit the power the government has over us during the investigation, trial process, and sentencing. Civil rights are designed to provide fundamental fairness to defendants when the government is investigating a crime or taking us away to jail. In the following chapters we will discuss rights and criminal procedures, particularly during arrest, interrogation, search, and court proceedings. The flowchart in Chapter 1 (figure 1.2) illustrates the criminal procedural process. In this text, we do not fully discuss pretrial and trial procedures, jury trial procedures, postconviction relief, or criminal appeals.

Tribes varied as to the role of rights in their societies. Some tribes, such as the Iroquois, focused on group rights or duties while others focused on the individual. Navajo traditional or common law values both individual and group rights, as explained by James W. Zion:

> What is a "civil right" in the Navajo context? I believe that rights develop as expectations arise and are eventually accepted. When there is a hitch, dispute, grievance, or trouble, what are the individual and group expectations about how it will

be resolved? I suggest that the core of the Navajo concept of civil rights lies in the maxim, "It's up to him." It states a Navajo base value of individualism whereby no one and no institution has the privilege to interfere with individual action unless it causes an injury to another or group. Another way the maxim is stated is that "What is good for me is good for everyone else, but what is good for everyone else is also good for me." That more specifically relates the interaction between a high degree of Navajo individualism and reciprocal obligations to and from the group. It's up to me to decide what is good for me, but I look to the group's sense of what is right and "good," and "bad" or prohibited, to guide my actions.[1]

Native societies' rights often conflict with American notions of rights because of the idea of group rights. In many traditional Native governments, distinctions between political communities were not necessary, partly due to respect. As a result, a legal or political institution was not necessary to enforce rights. Mohawk scholar Taiaiake Alfred explains the conflict in this way:

> The concept of "rights," especially in the common Western sense, leads nowhere for indigenous peoples because it alienates the individual from the group. By contrast, the tension between individual and collective rights is a mainstay of discussions about justice in Western societies, which conceive of rights only in the context of a sovereign political authority because the law that defines and protects them depends on the existence of a single sovereign. Native people respect others to the degree that they demonstrate respect. There is no need, as in the Western tradition, to create political or legal uniformity to guarantee respect.... Internally, instead of creating formal boundaries and rules to protect individuals from each other and from the group, a truly indigenous political system relies on the motif of balance; for the Native, there is no tension in the relationship between the individual and the collective. Indigenous thought is based on the notion that people, communities, and the other elements of creation coexist as equals. The interests and wants of humans, whether as individuals or as a collective, do not have a special priority in deciding the justice of a situation.[2]

With the introduction of American law's focus on individual rights into tribal law and institutions, many tribes have adopted written laws and procedures to protect defendants. Further, the introduction of American models of police, jails, and more coercive governmental power has required tribal governments to protect individuals from overbearing governments and intrusions upon their liberty.

There are a number of provisions in the Bill of Rights of the U.S. Constitution that are designed to protect individual liberties and property rights from governmental interference. These constitutional provisions have been interpreted by the U.S. Supreme Court as requiring federal and state governments to follow certain rules during all stages of criminal proceedings (e.g., arrest, search and seizure, interrogation, and trial). The rules prevent the federal and state governments from infringing on individual civil rights. State courts have also interpreted provisions of state constitutions to require state governments to follow certain criminal procedures. In addition, federal and state governments have adopted statutes and rules to guide governments through the criminal process and protect individual rights.

However, the provisions in the federal and state constitutions that prevent the federal and state governments from interfering with individual civil rights do not apply to Indian tribes. In addition, federal and state rules of criminal procedure do not apply to tribal courts unless the tribe has enacted laws or rules adopting the federal or state rules of criminal procedure.

Tribal definitions of civil rights and tribal rules of criminal procedure that protect these rights are found in tribal codes and constitutions, tribal court rules, the Indian Civil Rights Act of 1968 (ICRA), and tribal court decisions applying tribal civil rights and ICRA.

Although the federal case law interpreting the U.S. Bill of Rights is not binding on tribal governments, some tribal courts refer to this case law when they examine and apply ICRA. This is not simply because tribal courts are trying to mirror American courts but because it may be an issue of first impression, meaning the court has not addressed the issue raised by the defendant. The courts will generally assess whether the federal courts' interpretation of the right complies with their tribal unwritten and written tribal law. If it does not conflict, sometimes the court will choose to adopt the federal courts' interpretation. The court may also note how the federal courts' interpretation is supported by their tribal law.

Tribal Protections for Civil Rights

Many tribes contain provisions within their codes and constitutions that protect civil rights of defendants. Some tribes specifically list in their codes or constitutions every right that is granted to tribal members, and others include a more generic statement about civil rights. Included in the following text are four examples of civil rights protections.

The Constitution of the Native Tribe of Huslia, Alaska
Article 12—Rights of Members
Section 3. Indian Civil Rights. The Tribal shall provide to all persons within its jurisdiction the rights guaranteed by the Indian Civil Rights Act of 1968, as amended. In summary, the Tribal Government shall:

1. *Not prohibit the free exercise of speech, press, religion or rights of the people to assemble peacefully or file grievances against the tribal government.*

2. Not allow unreasonable search and seizure or issue search warrants without probably [sic] cause.
3. Not try anyone for the same offense twice.
4. Not make any person testify against himself in a criminal matter.
5. Not take private property for public use without paying the owner the fair market value.
6. Not deny a person the right to a speedy public trial. A speedy public trial is generally assumed to be a trial within ninety (90) days or less. The accused person must be informed of the nature of the crime he is accused of, told about the witnesses against him, be allowed to have witnesses testify in his favor and be allowed a lawyer at his own expense.
7. Not impose excessive bail or fines, nor impose cruel or unusual punishments. Tribal courts cannot impose a penalty greater than $5,000 or one (1) year in jail, or both for the one offense.
8. Give all persons equal protection under tribal laws.
9. Not pronounce anyone guilty of a crime or civil violation without a fair trial. The tribal government shall not pass an ordinance or change penalties, after an incident (**ex post facto**).
10. Provide anyone accused of an offense punishable by jail time the right to a trial by jury of no less than six persons.

Nez Perce Tribal Code

Chapter 2-1: Rules of Criminal Procedure
Rule 3. Rights of Defendant
   In a criminal action the defendant is entitled:

a. to a speedy and public trial;
b. to be informed of the nature of the charges against him and to have a written copy of the charges;
c. to appear and defend in person or by an attorney at the defendant's expense;
d. to not be twice placed in jeopardy for the same offense by the Nez Perce Tribe;
e. to not be compelled in a criminal action to be a witness against himself;
f. to confront and cross examine all witnesses against him;
g. to be subjected before conviction to no more restraint than is necessary to insure his appearance to answer the charge and/or to protect the public;
h. to compel by subpoena the attendance of witnesses in his own behalf;
i. to a trial by jury unless expressly waived;
j. to appeal in all cases.

Poarch Band of Creek Indians Code of Justice

9-1-3 Defendant's Rights in all Criminal Proceedings
In all criminal proceedings, the defendant shall have the following rights:

1. The right to be present throughout the proceeding and to defend himself in person, provided defendant conducts himself with proper **decorum**, or at his own expense to be represented by an attorney who is licensed to practice law in the Tribal Court of the Poarch Band of Creek Indians.
2. To know the nature and cause of the charges against him.

3. The right to confront all witnesses who testify against the defendant and to cross-examine the same.
4. The right to **compulsory process** through subpoena to obtain testimony of witnesses and physical evidence.
5. The right to speedy, public trial by an impartial judge and jury.
6. The right to refuse to testify in his own behalf and said refusal cannot be held against the defendant nor commented on by the prosecution.
7. The right to appeal to the Supreme Court.
8. The right to not be put in jeopardy or tried twice by the Tribal Court for the same offense.
9. All other rights and protections which the Tribal Court may find to have been conferred upon the defendant by the Indian Civil Rights Act of 1968, 25 USC 1301, et seq., or rights and protections conferred upon the defendant by the Constitution of the Poarch Band of Creek Indians.
10. Upon being arrested a defendant shall be advised that he is under arrest and the charge or offense for which the arrest is being made.

Salish and Kootenai Criminal Procedures, Codified

2-2-104. Rights of defendant.

1. In all criminal proceedings, the defendant shall have the following rights:
   a. to be released from custody pending trial upon payment of reasonable bail;
   b. to appear and defend in person, by Tribal Defender, by tribal member, or by private counsel obtained at defendant's own expense, as provided in Section 2-2-504.
   c. to be informed of the nature of the charges pending against her or him and to have a copy of those charges;
   d. to confront and cross examine all prosecution or hostile witnesses;
   e. to compel by subpoena:
      i. the attendance of any witnesses necessary to defend against the charges; and
      ii. the production of any books, records, documents, or other things necessary to defend against the charges;
   f. to have a speedy public trial by judge or a jury, unless the right to a speedy trial is waived or the right to a jury trial is waived by the defendant, as provided in Section 2-2-1001;
   g. to appeal any final decision of the Tribal Court to the Tribal Court of Appeals;
   h. not to be twice put in jeopardy by the Tribal Court for the same offense; and
   i. not to be required to testify.
2. No inference may be drawn from a defendant's exercise of the right not to testify.

Habeas Corpus in Tribal Courts

A writ of habeas corpus (Latin for "you may have the body") is used to ask a court to address whether a person is being detained illegally.

Persons incarcerated by tribal governments may file a writ for habeas corpus to challenge the legality of their detention. ICRA (discussed in the following text) allows defendants detained by a tribal government to file a habeas corpus action in federal court. However, federal courts most often require exhaustion of tribal remedies or that the defendants initially challenge their detention in tribal courts.

A detained person may file a petition or complaint for a writ of habeas corpus at any time while he is during his incarceration. Often it is used pretrial to challenge the court's decision to not grant bail or postconviction to challenge the length of a sentence. If the allegations establish an illegal detention, the court will issue a writ ordering the person or entity detaining the defendant, generally the tribal or Bureau of Indian Affairs jail, to produce the defendant at a hearing and show cause why the defendant should not be released. If the petition filed by the defendant fails to establish an illegal detention, the writ is denied by the court. At the hearing, the government must provide proof that defendant is not being held illegally. Below is a summary of the habeas corpus process for the Navajo Nation.

Navajo Nation Supreme Court
Thompson v. Greyeyes (2004)
No. SC-CV-29-04

We now lay out the proper procedure for incarcerated criminal defendant writs. A petitioner does not have to pay a filing fee, but only needs to file the petition with the Supreme Court. NRAP 14(b). The respondent to a habeas corpus petition is not the court who ordered the detention, (footnote omitted) but the "person having custody of the person." Id. That person is the Director of the Department of Corrections (Director). The Chief Justice reviews the petition, and may issue the writ if "in proper form." Id. The writ of habeas corpus itself does not order the release of the petitioner, but merely directs the Director "to appear in the [Supreme Court] on a certain date and bring the detained person with him [or her] and show cause why the person should not be released." Id. In other words, the writ is the equivalent of an order to show cause, and the Director must bring the petitioner with her and respond to the petition by demonstrating that the petitioner is lawfully detained. The burden of proof in a habeas case therefore shifts once the Chief Justice issues the writ. The petitioner initially has the burden to establish facts showing his illegal detention. In re Application of Johnson, 6 Nav. R. 186, 187 (Nav. Sup. Ct. 1990). Once shown, the petition is in "proper form," and when the Chief Justice Issues the writ the Director must show that the petitioner's detention is legal. (footnote omitted)

Federal Protections for Civil Rights: The Indian Civil Rights Act of 1968

In 1896, the U.S. Supreme Court ruled that tribal governments are not subject to the Bill of Rights in *Talton v. Mayes*. ICRA was enacted in 1968 to protect individual rights from intrusion or violation by tribal governments by requiring tribal courts to abide by language similar to that seen in the Bill of Rights. Before ICRA, restrictions on tribal governments were based on tribal law.

Congress passed ICRA after seven years of hearings and field investigations regarding the civil rights of Native people. Although many witnesses testified about the abuses Native people suffered at the hands of federal and state law enforcement, Congress focused on alleged abuses of individual rights by tribal governments.

The first sentence of ICRA begins, "no Indian Tribe in exercising powers of self-government shall," which prohibits tribal governments from certain actions. Thus, ICRA has nothing to do with how Indians or Indian governments may be treated by the state or federal governments. The U.S. Constitution provides protections in those circumstances. ICRA defines "Indian Tribe" as all federally recognized tribes. Note that the act applies to *all tribal government activities* and that it limits how those activities may be carried on. So all government entities, including tribal councils, courts, police, administrative offices, social agencies, and so forth, all have to comply with the requirements of ICRA.

Many tribal nations view ICRA as an infringement on the right to self-governance and believe the federal government should not dictate how to protect their members and visitors within the boundaries of reservations. Moreover, as discussed previously, some tribal cultures are centered on community-based values or rights. For these tribes, preservation of the rights of the community has traditionally been more important than protecting individual rights. The imposition of an individualistically based civil rights law was met with suspicion and clashed with some tribal cultures. Some tribal leaders argued that ICRA was merely another attempt to destroy tribal cultures and force tribes to adopt individualistic Western values. Other Natives, however, welcomed the protection of many rights held sacred by their cultures: respect for individuals, freedom of the press, and freedom of religion.

Since its enactment in 1968, ICRA has been amended four times.

> 1986 Amendments: It was first amended in 1986 to increase the sentencing limitations in section 1302(7). This provision originally limited tribes to imposing sentences for a single offense to no greater than six months' imprisonment or a fine of $500 or both. In 1986, it was amended (as part of a federal drug and alcohol prevention act) to "in no event impose

for conviction of any one offense any penalty or punishment greater than imprisonment for a term of one year or a fine of $5,000 or both."
- 1991 Amendments: ICRA was amended again in 1991 in order to overturn the U.S. Supreme Court decision in *Duro v. Reina*, 495 U.S. 676 (1990). The *Duro* decision held that tribal courts did not have criminal jurisdiction over nonmember Indians. The U.S. Congress overturned the *Duro* decision (with the so-called congressional *Duro*-fix; see Chapter 7) by adding "and means the inherent power of Indian tribes, hereby recognized and affirmed, to exercise criminal jurisdiction over all Indians" to the definition of "powers of self-government." The congressional *Duro*-fix restored tribal criminal court jurisdiction over all Indians, members and nonmembers.
- 2010 Amendments: Tribal Law and Order Act (TLOA): ICRA was amended to authorize a sentence of up to three years per offense and nine years total for a criminal incident. (See Chapter 10, TLOA)
- 2013 Amendments: Violence Against Women Act: ICRA was amended to authorize criminal jurisdiction over non-Indian people accused of domestic violence.

As of 2014, ICRA reads as follows:

The Indian Civil Rights Act (2014 version)

25 U.S. Code § 1302

(a) *In general*
  No Indian tribe in exercising powers of self-government shall—
  (1) make or enforce any law prohibiting the free exercise of religion, or abridging the freedom of speech, or of the press, or the right of the people peaceably to assemble and to petition for a redress of grievances;
  (2) violate the right of the people to be secure in their persons, houses, papers, and effects against unreasonable search and seizures, nor issue warrants, but upon probable cause, supported by oath or affirmation, and particularly describing the place to be searched and the person or thing to be seized;
  (3) subject any person for the same offense to be twice put in jeopardy;
  (4) compel any person in any criminal case to be a witness against himself;
  (5) take any private property for a public use without just compensation;
  (6) deny to any person in a criminal proceeding the right to a speedy and public trial, to be informed of the nature and cause of the accusation, to be confronted with the witnesses against him, to have compulsory process for obtaining witnesses in his favor, and at his own expense to have the assistance of counsel for his defense (except as provided in subsection (b));

(7)
- (A) require excessive bail, impose excessive fines, or inflict cruel and unusual punishments;
- (B) except as provided in subparagraph (C), impose for conviction of any 1 offense any penalty or punishment greater than imprisonment for a term of 1 year or a fine of $5,000, or both;
- (C) subject to subsection (b), impose for conviction of any 1 offense any penalty or punishment greater than imprisonment for a term of 3 years or a fine of $15,000, or both; or
- (D) impose on a person in a criminal proceeding a total penalty or punishment greater than imprisonment for a term of 9 years;

(8) deny to any person within its jurisdiction the equal protection of its laws or deprive any person of liberty or property without due process of law;

(9) pass any bill of attainder or ex post facto law; or

(10) deny to any person accused of an offense punishable by imprisonment the right, upon request, to a trial by jury of not less than six persons.

(b) *Offenses subject to greater than 1-year imprisonment or a fine greater than $5,000*
A tribal court may subject a defendant to a term of imprisonment greater than 1 year but not to exceed 3 years for any 1 offense, or a fine greater than $5,000 but not to exceed $15,000, or both, if the defendant is a person accused of a criminal offense who—
   (1) has been previously convicted of the same or a comparable offense by any jurisdiction in the United States; or
   (2) is being prosecuted for an offense comparable to an offense that would be punishable by more than 1 year of imprisonment if prosecuted by the United States or any of the States.

(c) *Rights of defendants*
In a criminal proceeding in which an Indian tribe, in exercising powers of self-government, imposes a total term of imprisonment of more than 1 year on a defendant, the Indian tribe shall—
   (1) provide to the defendant the right to effective assistance of counsel at least equal to that guaranteed by the United States Constitution; and
   (2) at the expense of the tribal government, provide an indigent defendant the assistance of a defense attorney licensed to practice law by any jurisdiction in the United States that applies appropriate professional licensing standards and effectively ensures the competence and professional responsibility of its licensed attorneys;
   (3) require that the judge presiding over the criminal proceeding—
      (A) has sufficient legal training to preside over criminal proceedings; and
      (B) is licensed to practice law by any jurisdiction in the United States;
   (4) prior to charging the defendant, make publicly available the criminal laws (including regulations and interpretative documents), rules of evidence, and rules of criminal procedure (including rules governing the recusal of judges in appropriate circumstances) of the tribal government; and
   (5) maintain a record of the criminal proceeding, including an audio or other recording of the trial proceeding.

(d) *Sentences*
In the case of a defendant sentenced in accordance with subsections (b) and (c), a tribal court may require the defendant—

(1) to serve the sentence—
    (A) in a tribal correctional center that has been approved by the Bureau of Indian Affairs for long-term incarceration, in accordance with guidelines to be developed by the Bureau of Indian Affairs (in consultation with Indian tribes) not later than 180 days after July 29, 2010;
    (B) in the nearest appropriate Federal facility, at the expense of the United States pursuant to the Bureau of Prisons tribal prisoner pilot program described in section 304(c) [1] of the Tribal Law and Order Act of 2010;
    (C) in a State or local government-approved detention or correctional center pursuant to an agreement between the Indian tribe and the State or local government; or
    (D) in an alternative rehabilitation center of an Indian tribe; or
  (2) to serve another alternative form of punishment, as determined by the tribal court judge pursuant to tribal law.
(e) Definition of offense
  In this section, the term "offense" means a violation of a criminal law.
(f) Effect of section
  Nothing in this section affects the obligation of the United States, or any State government that has been delegated authority by the United States, to investigate and prosecute any criminal violation in Indian country.

Federal Court Review of Tribal Criminal Cases

During the ten-year period between the passage of ICRA in 1968 and the *Martinez* decision in 1978, federal courts heard approximately eighty cases involving the application of ICRA. These cases covered many subjects, including tribal election disputes, reapportionment of voting districts on Indian reservations ("one man, one vote"), tribal government employee rights, land use regulations and condemnation procedures, criminal and civil proceedings in tribal courts, tribal membership and voting, tribal police activities, conduct of tribal council members and council meetings, and standards for enforcing due process of law and equal protection of the laws in tribal settings.

During this period, the federal courts devised rules of interpretation, including the following:

1. While ICRA is generally patterned after the Bill of Rights, the same language does not necessarily have to be interpreted in the same way;
2. ICRA does not require that Indians and non-Indians always be treated identically by tribal governments; that is, different treatment is permitted and justified in certain circumstances (e.g., tribal membership requirements);
3. Tribal customs, traditions, and culture must be considered in interpreting and applying ICRA; and

4. Tribal remedies must first be **exhausted** before a dispute can be heard in federal court.

Allowing federal courts to review tribal court decisions for alleged ICRA violations proved to be problematic. Any defendant who felt that their rights had been violated could ask for a review from a federal judge. Thus, federal courts were reviewing a high volume of cases from tribal courts. Federal judges are often not in the position of assessing whether tribal governments adequately protect rights under ICRA. Tribal judges are usually the best arbiter of such accusations.

Santa Clara Pueblo v. Martinez

Santa Clara Pueblo is located in northern New Mexico and has about 1,200 members living on it along with about 150 to 200 nonmembers. In 1939 the tribal council of the Pueblo adopted an ordinance that extended tribal membership to the children of male members who married nonmembers but denied membership to children of female members who married nonmembers. The tribe justified the ordinance on the basis of its patriarchal traditions plus the economic need to restrict tribal enrollment.

Julia Martinez, a full-blooded member of the Pueblo, married a Navajo. Even though their children were raised in the Pueblo, spoke the Tewa language, and continued to live there, because of the 1939 ordinance they were denied membership in the tribe. After unsuccessfully attempting to get the Pueblo to change the ordinance, Mrs. Martinez sued the tribe and its governor in federal court. She claimed that the ordinance denied her and her children equal protection of the laws as guaranteed by ICRA.

The issue before the U.S. Supreme Court was whether ICRA prohibits an Indian tribe from setting membership criteria that discriminate against women. It is a difficult question: equal rights for women on one side, a tribe's right to set membership criteria on the other side.

The Supreme Court, in *Martinez*, never actually decided the **merits** of the case.

It disposed of the case on a jurisdictional basis; that is, that ICRA does not give federal courts broad jurisdiction to review tribal government actions in Indian country. Thus, Mrs. Martinez's challenge to the tribal ordinance could not go forward. In reaching this conclusion, the Court noted that Congress had two purposes in mind in enacting ICRA:

1. Protection of individual civil rights in Indian country. It did this by prohibiting tribal governments from taking actions that might interfere with individual freedoms.

2. Encouragement of tribal self-government. It did this by implicitly recognizing the importance of tribal governments on reservations, reaffirming the idea of sovereign immunity as applied to Indian tribes, and giving tribal institutions the principal responsibility for resolving disputes over civil rights.

The Supreme Court interpreted ICRA as not giving the federal court any power to review all complaints of ICRA violations by a tribal government except those arising as writ of habeas corpus actions—complaints of unlawful detention raised by individuals being held in tribal custody. The decision held that violations of all the other rights guaranteed under ICRA, including freedom of speech and equal protection rights, fell under tribal jurisdiction and thus could be brought only in tribal court.

ICRA (as interpreted by the U.S. Supreme Court in *Martinez*) was a compromise that guaranteed tribal governments would respect civil rights with little interference in tribal culture and tradition by the federal government. This compromise resulted in allowing only one federal court remedy for ICRA violations: habeas corpus. All other remedies must be sought in tribal court, where tribes can apply custom and tradition in interpreting ICRA and tribal civil rights.

For example, if tribal police arrest Joe for DWI, he might bring a writ of habeas corpus that he is being held illegally because he is non-Native and the Court has no criminal jurisdiction over non-Natives. Under ICRA, a writ of habeas corpus is the only claim a defendant may bring under ICRA in federal court. Thus, if a tribal court denies a defendant's motion to suppress evidence seized in violation of ICRA, the defendant cannot challenge or appeal this ruling in federal court. The defendant can only challenge his detention or incarceration by the tribal government in federal court. A writ for *habeas corpus* may raise many different issues, such as a claim that the defendant was sentenced improperly, was not granted bail, or denied access to effective representation.

However, if the defendant is not detained all other ICRA claims can be heard only in tribal court. However, at least one federal court found that banishment by a tribe impacted the defendant's liberty severely enough to support a habeas corpus claim in federal court. Banishment is covered in more detail in chapter 27.

Most federal courts require the defendants to exhaust their tribal remedies prior to examining the illegality of the detention. Thus defendants should raise their challenges to detention through a tribal writ of habeas corpus or through the tribal appellate court after their conviction.

What happens when a tribal government is accused of violating a criminal defendant's civil rights? It depends on the type of violation. If a defendant claims a violation of the right to be free from unreasonable search and seizure, the defendant would file a claim in tribal court claiming the evidence should not be allowed in court because it was acquired in violation of rights protected by tribal law and ICRA. Judges can suppress evidence that was gathered unfairly. This result is referred to as the "exclusionary rule" which is covered in chapter 22.

Conclusion

Chapters 19-24 will describe the various components defendants' rights, often referred to as civil rights, under tribal law. Law enforcement officers, prosecutors, judges, and defense attorneys need to have a full understanding of civil rights in order to ensure that the entire process is fundamentally fair.

Questions

1. What civil rights are protected by the tribal codes and constitutions in this chapter?
2. Would all tribal governments include the civil rights if not required by ICRA?
3. Do any of the civil rights required by the American interpretation of ICRA contradict tribal custom and tradition?

In Your Community

1. What civil rights are protected by your tribal codes and constitution?
2. What civil rights are protected by traditional law?

Terms Used in Chapter 18

Compulsory process: Official action to force a person to appear in court as a witness.

Decorum: Appropriate behavior or conduct.

Ex post facto: After the fact.

Exhausted (in reference to tribal remedies): Tribal courts are given full opportunity to make the initial determination of all claims raised in the case.

Merits: The substance or real issues of a lawsuit, as opposed to the form or legal technicalities it involves.

Notes

1. James W. Zion, "Civil Rights in Navajo Common Law," 50 *Kansas Law Review* 523, 525 (2002).

2. Taiaiake Alfred, *Peace, Power, Righteousness: An Indigenous Manifesto* (Oxford University Press, 1999), 140–1.

Suggested Further Reading

Matthew L. M. Fletcher, "Indian Courts and Fundamental Fairness: Indian Courts and The Future Revisited," 84 *University of Colorado Law Review* 59 (2013).

Christian M. Freitag, "Putting Martinez to the Test: Tribal Court Disposition of Due Process," 72 *Indiana Law Review* 465 (1998).

Elmer R. Rusco, "Civil Liberties Guarantees under Tribal Law: A Survey of Civil Rights Provisions in Tribal Constitutions," 14 *American Indian Law Review* 269 (1988/1989).

James W. Zion, "Civil Rights in Navajo Common Law," 50 *University of Kansas Law Review* 523 (2002).

The Law of Arrest　　　　　Chapter 19

An arrest is the taking of a person into **custody**, or a seizure of a person, by law enforcement. A person taken into custody and not free to leave is considered to be under arrest regardless of whether the person has actually been told that he or she is under arrest.

The Indian Civil Rights Act (ICRA) and many tribal laws require that a seizure or arrest of a person must be either reasonable or pursuant to a warrant based upon probable cause. Some tribal codes or constitutions impose requirements concerning arrest procedures that are stricter than the requirements of ICRA. Thus, it is important to examine ICRA and the law of the Indian Nation where the seizure or arrest occurred to understand the legal requirements for an arrest or seizure.

The Indian Civil Rights Act

Section 1302(2)
No Indian tribe in exercising powers of self-government shall (2) violate the right of the people to be secure in their persons, houses, papers and effects against unreasonable search and seizures, nor issue warrants, but upon probable cause, supported by oath or affirmation, and particularly describing the place to be searched and the person or thing to be seized.

There is a vast body of U.S. constitutional law interpreting the provisions of the U.S. Bill of Rights, after which ICRA was patterned. It is important to remember that law interpreting the U.S. right to be free from unreasonable seizures is only a guide in Indian country, not the law. Furthermore, the tribal court cases discussed are binding only on their particular tribe. An invalid arrest is not a defense against the crime. However, the **validity** of an arrest is often crucial in determining the admissibility of evidence that is obtained from the accused at the time he or she is taken into custody.

Arrest Warrants

An arrest warrant is a written court order, signed by a judge or magistrate, that commands that the person named in the warrant be taken into custody. A warrant is obtained by filing a sworn complaint before a judge. Although the person requesting the warrant is generally a police officer, it may also be a victim or a witness. The complainant (the person filing the complaint) must set out and swear to the facts and circumstances of the alleged crime. Arrest warrants are the preferred procedure for arresting a person as this allows a neutral person, a judge, to review the facts and determine whether probable cause exists. This review ensures that police do not abuse their powers to arrest or act irrationally in the heat of solving a crime. It protects the right of an individual against a seizure by requiring the police to demonstrate to a judge there is probable cause for an arrest.

ICRA requires that arrest warrants be based on probable cause. Probable cause exists when "the facts and circumstances within [the arresting officers'] knowledge and of which they had reasonably trustworthy information [are] sufficient in themselves to warrant a man of reasonable caution in the belief that"[1] an offense has been or is being committed.

If a police officer believes there is probable cause that a crime has occurred, the officer can apply to the tribal court judge for an arrest warrant. The judge will review the information from the officer and issue an arrest warrant if, the judge finds probable cause:

1. to believe that an offense has been committed; and
2. that the accused committed it.

An arrest warrant may also be issued when the prosecutor issues a criminal complaint charging a defendant with a crime. Regardless of when the warrant is obtained, it must be based on a showing of probable cause.

Probable cause is needed to obtain an arrest warrant. There is no exact formula for determining probable cause. The arresting officer must use his or her own judgment as to what is reasonable under the circumstances of each case. In all cases, probable cause requires more than a mere suspicion or a hunch. There must be some facts that indicate that the person arrested has committed a crime. Probable cause may be based on the officer's personal observations or knowledge of criminal conduct or entirely upon hearsay (tips from others) if the hearsay is reasonably **corroborated** by other information within the officer's knowledge. The information must be sufficiently trustworthy and enough to create probable cause.

Probable cause asks not whether it is possible that the facts are true or that an individual has committed a crime but whether it is probable that the crime was committed by a certain individual. Moreover, probable cause is based on what the officer or judge knows prior to the arrest or issuing the warrant and not what the officer or judge learns after the arrest.

What Is Probable Cause?

"Probable cause" exists under this chapter when an officer or the Tribal Court has substantial objective basis for believing that a person has committed an offense. In determining whether probable cause exists, the officer or tribal judge may take into account all information which a prudent officer or judge would deem relevant to the likelihood that an offense has been committed and that the person charged has committed it. Nez Perce Rules of Criminal Procedure Rule I(b)

Table 19.1. Sources of Probable Cause for Law Enforcement

Source of Probable Cause	Description
Observation Expertise	Information the officer obtains via the senses: sight, smell, hearing, etc. Things a police officer is specially trained in, such as gang awareness, burglar tools, and ability to read graffiti.
Circumstantial evidence	Evidence that points the finger away from other suspects and, by a process of elimination, toward the probable conclusion that a particular person is involved in a crime.
Information	Informants and statements by witnesses and victims.

Arrests without Warrants

There are many occasions when police do not have time to get a warrant. ICRA allows reasonable seizures of a person. And many tribal laws have exceptions to the warrant requirements, which provide guidance as to what is reasonable under tribal law. Typically laws for warrantless arrests require the crime must have occurred in the presence of a police officer or there are reasonable grounds to believe a crime has been committed by the person outside the officer's presence.

Some jurisdictions impose restrictions on the types of offenses for which warrantless arrests are allowed. Some only allow a warrantless arrest for an alleged crime that has occurred out of the officer's presence when it is a felony.[2] Thus, if the crime was only a misdemeanor and it was not committed within the officer's presence, the officer would need to obtain a warrant before making an arrest. Some jurisdictions are now allowing warrantless arrests for misdemeanors that occur outside the presence of an officer if there are reasonable grounds to believe it was committed by the suspect. One reason this has developed is to allow police officers to arrest for domestic violence misdemeanor crimes that occur outside the officer's presence.

Ute Indian Tribal Court
Of The
Uintah And Ouray Reservation

The Ute Indian Tribe,
        Plaintiff,
Vs.

                                        Warrant of Arrest

LEO GOMEZ
        Defendant,

Warrant No. **02 CR 16**

Greetings: To The Ute Indian Tribal Police Or Any Police Officer Of The United States Indian Service.

WHEREAS, A complaint has been filed in the above-entitled Court charging that the offense of **BURGLARY OF A VEHICLE** in violation of Section **13-4-27** of the Ute Law and Order Code, has been committed and accusing the above-named Defendant thereof, you are hereby commanded to arrest and bring the said defendant before a Judge of the Ute Indian Tribal Court to answer said complaint.

Date: **AUGUST 12, 2002**

                                        Les Staub
                                        Judge of the Tribal Court

Received the within Warrant on the _____ Day of _____ 19___ and executed the same on the _____ day of _____ 19___

By arresting the within named defendant at _____ and now have him or her before the Court as commanded.

_____
Officer's Signature

_____
Title

Figure 19.1.   Sample Warrant

Warrantless Arrests: Violation Must Occur in Presence of an Officer

Gila River Tribal Code Sec 208
No member of the Gila River Community Police or other peace officer acting under the authority of the Gila River Indian Community shall arrest any person for any offense defined by these ordinances or for violation of the laws of the United States except when such violation shall occur in the presence of the arresting officer or the officer shall have a warrant issued upon probable cause, ordering him to apprehend such person.

Warrantless Arrests: Reasonable Cause

Salt River Pima-Maricopa Indian Community, Civil and Criminal Procedure, Article III Section 5-33(a)
An office of the Salt River Department of Public Safety or of the Bureau of Indian Affairs shall have the authority to arrest any person for any violation of an ordinance of the Salt River Pima-Maricopa Indian Community or a federal law when such offense shall occur in the presence of the arresting officer, when the arresting officer shall have reasonable cause to believe that person has committed such offense or when the officer has a warrant commanding him to append such person.

Review the following tribal court cases involving arrests by tribal law enforcement. Think about ICRA's arrest requirements and determine if you think the arrests were lawful.

Court of Appeals of the Navajo Nation
Eugene Lamone v. Navajo Nation
No. A-CR-02-81 (1982)
Before Chief Justice Nelson J. McCabe and Associate Justices Marie F. Neswood and Homer Bluehouse
Opinion
Reversed, charge dismissed.

This is an appeal from the conviction of Eugene LaMone for the crime of trespass with force. The arrest, trial and conviction of the defendant were all connected with the occupation of the Consolidated Coal Mine site at Burnham, Navajo Nation (New Mexico) during July of 1980.

The events and facts of this case are somewhat confusing due to the state of the record, but the Court will attempt to set them forth in a logical fashion before discussing their legal aspects. This appeal was not heard upon the full record of the case in the trial court for reasons which will be discussed below, and the factual basis for this appeal is founded upon the files of the matter, such as they are.

The property of the Burnham Consolidated Coal Mine was occupied by demonstrators, and the defendant was arrested without warrant by the Navajo Police Department. He was then charged with the crimes of criminal entry into the property (Case no. SR-CR-7527-80), criminal damage to property at the site (Case no. SR-CR-7526-80), unauthorized use of a motor vehicle (SR-CR-7765-80), unlawful imprisonment (SR-CR-7766-80) and trespass with force (SR-CR-7767-80). The first three charges were washed out by the motion of the prosecutor withdrawing them. The file shows the defendant was acquitted of the charge of unlawful imprisonment, so only the charge of trespass with force remained. . . .

The contentions raised by the defendant in his appeal are: 1) There was an illegal warrantless arrest. . . .

The Need for a Warrant in Demonstration Situations

The defendant has briefed his case very well, particularly with regard to the law of illegal arrest. The court does not have the benefit of a brief on the part of the prosecution so it will rely upon facts contained in the defendant's brief. (We would have thought the prosecution would be well-prepared to brief a case with such importance as this case has.)

The arresting officer did not see the crime of trespass with force committed in his presence and made the arrest upon the statement of another officer who also did not see any illegal events, the defendant's brief states.

Our arrest statute, 7 NTC Sec. 1804, indicates an arrest can be made by a Navajo Police Officer 1) where the offense occurs in the presence of the arresting officer, 2) where the arresting officer has "reasonable evidence that the person arrested has committed an offense," or 3) where the officer has an arrest warrant. Arrest upon the commission of an offense in the presence of the officer is the most obvious, and since the facts to support the main charge merge with the justification for the arrest, that ground for arrest is usually adjudicated at trial and does not become the subject of a pretrial motion. The other ground we are concerned with is an arrest on reasonable evidence the individual has committed an offense. The test for this ground for officers is:

> "Whether at the moment the facts and circumstances within their knowledge and of which they had reasonably trustworthy information were sufficient to warrant a prudent man in believing that the petitioner had committed or was committing an offense." *Beck v. Ohio*, 379 U.S. 89, 91 (1964).

The standard under our statute is not "probable cause"—it is "reasonableness." When the arresting officer makes his arrest, can he satisfy the judge there was enough evidence to believe the individual had committed an offense or was in the act of committing an offense? This judgment is to be made on all the facts the officer had before him and not on the basis of picking out and pooh-poohing an individual element of an offense.

[The Court found that although the arresting officer did not see an offense being committed, he could have had sufficient information to have reasonable evidence and the trial judge's determination that reasonable cause for arrest existed was not overturned. However, the defendant's conviction was reversed on other grounds.]

Northern Plains Intertribal Court of Appeals
Devils Lake Sioux Tribe[3] *v. Frederick* (1994)
21 Indian Law Reporter 6137

Adrian Frederick appealed from judgment of conviction entered upon jury verdict finding him guilty of assault and battery.

We affirm.

At about 11:30 P.M. on December 30, 1993 police officers Peltier and Laducer responded to a call to the police department from Carletta Walking Eagle requesting that the appellant Frederick be removed from her mother's residence. Upon arriving at the Walking Eagle residence at Crowhill on the Fort Totten Indian Reservation, the officers found appellant, Adrian Frederick, and Carletta Walking Eagle and Carletta's nine-month-old minor child and Carl Walking Eagle, Jr. present in the home. Officer Peltier ascertained that Frederick had been drinking alcoholic beverages. Officer Laducer removed the defendant from the Walking Eagle residence.

Officer Peltier proceeded to interview Carletta Walking Eagle. She told him that she had been slapped and pushed by Frederick, prior to the arrival of the police officers. Neither officer personally observed any physical contact.

Frederick was arrested without a warrant and charged with assault and battery. A six-person jury returned a verdict of guilty on the charge.

Frederick appeals to this court raising four issues. Frederick argues that a warrantless arrest for an alleged offense not committed in the presence of a police officer was unlawful and thus the trial court lacked jurisdiction over him. . . .

1) Frederick accurately points out that the "general rule" has been a police officer cannot make a misdemeanor arrest unless he or she has a warrant or the offense was committed in the presence of the officer. However, the governing body of the Devils Lake Sioux Tribe has enacted legislation that is not as restrictive as the "general rule" or North Dakota law. Devils Lake Sioux Law and Order Code Sec. 3-2-104(2) authorizes a police officer to make arrests when "the officer shall have probable cause to believe that the person to be arrested has committed such offense."

> Devils Lake Sioux Law and Order Code Sec. 3-7-161(3) states as follows:
>
> A law enforcement officer shall arrest a person, anywhere, with or without a warrant, including at the person's residence, if the officer has probable cause to believe:
>
> a. that an assault has occurred;
> b. an assault has occurred and has resulted in bodily injury to the victim whether the injury is visible to the officer or not;
> c. that any physical action has taken place with the intention of causing another person reasonably in all probability serious bodily injury or death, and the victim is the person's family member, household member or former household member.
>
> That statute is similar to recent laws that have been enacted through this country in many states and on many Indian reservations to help combat domestic violence. The Devils Lake Sioux Tribe, through legislation, has authorized police officers to make warrantless arrests based on probable cause (especially for domestic assaults) for offenses that they do not actually witness.
>
> Under the set of facts presented to the trial court the police officer acted within his lawful authority and the arrest was proper. . . .
>
> Affirmed.

What Is the Difference between an Arrest Warrant and a Summons?

If an arrest is not necessary to preserve the peace at the scene of a crime or the defendant is not considered a danger to the community, an officer can issue a **summons**. A summons is a court order to appear in court on a particular date for arraignment. A summons serves the same purpose as an arrest warrant, that is, it requires the person to appear before the court. However, a person served with a summons is not immediately incarcerated. Instead, the accused remains free at least until his arraignment. Therefore, a summons is far less intrusive than an arrest warrant.

The most common type of case in which a summons is used is in traffic cases. A summons procedure, however, should generally be used in all instances in which there is no danger to the community or the accused if the accused is left at large rather than being arrested.

Probable cause still applies to a summons to appear in court. When the individual appears in court, the judge makes a determination, based on the summons and complaint, as to whether the person is properly before the court, that is, whether probable cause existed to issue the summons and complaint.

Arrests in a Private Home

The U.S. Supreme Court has held that state and federal police must have an arrest warrant to enter a suspect's home to arrest the suspect.[4] The only exceptions are when the officer obtains the consent of an occupant of the residence or when some special circumstances exist (see the following section on warrant exceptions) that allow a warrantless entry.[5] The reasoning behind the warrant requirement is that "physical entry of a home is the chief evil against which the wording of the Fourth Amendment is directed."[6] This reasoning may also be used by tribal courts when applying ICRA to determine whether tribal police may enter a suspect's home to arrest him.

This requirement also applies when police want to enter the home of a third party to arrest someone who does not live there. Generally, unless consent is given or emergency circumstances exist, the police must obtain a warrant to search a person's home for the guest or individual the police want to arrest.[7]

Additionally, under federal, state, and some tribal laws, an officer must, before using force to enter a home to make an arrest, announce his authority and purpose (e.g., "Open up. It's the police. We're here to arrest Victor Rising Star.").[8] Failure to make the announcement generally makes the arrest illegal. There are, however, some limited situations in which the announcement may be omitted, such as when police officers reasonably believe that any announcement would place them in danger, significantly increase the possibility of a suspect's escape, or permit the destruction of evidence.[9]

The warrant requirement also applies to temporary residences, such as motels.[10] An important distinction exists between public and private property. A warrant is required when an officer would have to enter a private home, but the officer is not required to obtain a warrant to make the same arrest in a public place, such as the street, as long as the officer has probable cause.[11]

Review the following case regarding entry into a private home. Determine if you think the facts were sufficient to justify a warrantless entry.

Colville Confederated Tribes Court of Appeals
John Manuel v. Colville Confederated Tribes (2001)
3 CTCR 31, 5 CCAR 39
The opinion of the court was delivered by: Bonga, J.

History
About 5:00 A.M. on a Saturday in October 1997, Tribal Police officers responded to a complaint of battery in HUD Housing, Nespelem, Washington. The officers

contacted the victim, Amelia Tatshama, who had fled to a house across the street from her residence. She was visibly upset and crying. She was observed to have a swollen lip, dried blood, and stretched clothing. She was also holding her right arm and lower jawbone.

She stated that the Appellant, John Manuel, had been consuming alcohol and when they arrived home, he had called her names and beat her. She then fled the home and called CTPS. She stated that the Appellant was still in the residence. An inquiry prior to her transport to the hospital revealed that the Appellant had a loaded rifle in the home, which he kept next to his bed.

The officers attempted to gain entry to the home, but there was no response. Near a window of a bedroom both officers heard snoring. The officers again contacted the victim. They obtained information that the residence was being rented by both the parties, each paying an equal share of the rent. The victim authorized the officers to enter the residence to arrest the Appellant. Emergency Services arrived and transported the victim to the local hospital for x-rays of her injuries.

When the officers approached the residence, they noted that there was now a light on in the window where they had previously heard snoring. They knocked on the front door and announced that they were police officers several times. They received no response. The officers then entered the unlocked residence, located the Appellant, and arrested him for Battery and Resisting Arrest.

Appellant filed a Motion to Suppress Evidence on January 29, 1998 alleging that the officers made an illegal entry into his home and made an unlawful arrest. Appellant requested that all evidence of his Resisting Arrest violation be suppressed. Appellant alleged that the officers could not enter his home without his consent as he was present and had refused to open the door.

On May 1, 1998, the Appellant pled guilty to the offense of Battery and was sentenced. The guilty plea was conditional on a ruling from the Court of Appeals on the Motion to Suppress.

Issue #1: Can a Third Party Give Consent to Authorities without a Warrant to Conduct a Valid Search of a Place?

Prosecution may justify a warrantless search of a place by proof of voluntary consent by a third party who possesses common authority over or other sufficient relationship to the premises sought to be inspected.

"[T]he consent of one who possess [*sic*] common authority over premises or effects is valid as against the absent, non-consenting [*sic*] person with whom that authority is shared", *U.S. v. Matlock*, 415 U.S. 164, 170.

In the case at bar the facts indicate that the victim and Appellant resided together in a spousal-type relationship and both shared costs for the home. Neither party objected to those facts or additional factors supporting the spousal-type relationship between the parties.

"... [W]hen the prosecution seeks to justify a warrantless search by proof of voluntary consent, it is not limited to proof that consent was given by defendant, but may show that permission to search was obtained from a 3rd party who possessed common authority over ... the premises ... to be inspected." Id. At 250.

Under the rule established by Matlock the government/prosecution in this case made the requisite showing that the victim had common authority over the house involved. Therefore, one can easily conclude that the victim had authority to give consent to law enforcement to validate entry into the house for arrest of the Appellant for an alleged criminal act of abuse.

Issue #2: Is a Warrantless Entry to Arrest a Suspect Consented to by a Third Party Not Present Authorized If the Subject of the Arrest Is Present and Refuses to Answer the Door?

The rule is that warrantless entry by authorities is valid if the entry was consented to by a party not present but who possessed common authority over the premises.

In this case the Appellant was present in the house, but that fact was unclear to the officers at the time of entry. The Appellant had the ability to object to entry by the officers, but chose not to by not answering the door.

The officers had a valid consent to enter the house from the victim and did so. As a result of the valid entry they found the Appellant and arrested him.

Appellant argues that he is protected by the Fourth Amendment of the U. S. Constitution which prohibits unreasonable searches and seizures. He goes on to cite the Washington State Constitution which provides that "No person shall be disturbed in his private affairs or his home invaded, without authority of law." A quote from *Illinois v. Rodriguez*, 497 U.S. 177 (199) is appropriate here:

> What Rodriguez is assured by the trial right of the exclusionary rules, where it applies, is that no evidence seized in violation of the Fourth Amendment will be introduced at trial unless he consents. What he is assured by the Fourth Amendment itself, however, is not that no government search of his house will occur unless he consents, but that no such search will occur that is "unreasonable." U. S. Constitution, Amendment 4 ...

The fundamental objective that alone validates all unconsented government searches is, of course, the seizure of persons who have committed or are about to commit crimes, or of evidence related to crimes.

In this case the officers had evidence of probable cause to arrest the Appellant and the officers had consent to search the house for him.

> *Conclusion*
> The Panel finds that the Trial Court did not err in denying Appellant's Motion to Suppress Evidence and Dismiss the case and affirms the March 16, 1998 Order in this matter. This case is remanded to the Trial Court for execution of the Judgment and Sentence of May 1, 1998.
> It is SO ORDERED.

Exigent Circumstances

A warrant to enter a person's home is not required during some circumstances, commonly called exigent or emergency circumstances.

Warrantless entry of a home is allowed when a police officer is in hot pursuit of an alleged felon.[12] For example, if Officer Sam sees Victor steal Mary's purse at knife point and then chases Victor down the street to catch him, and Victor runs into his own house, Officer Sam can pursue Victor into the house without waiting to get a warrant because he was in hot pursuit of a fleeing felon. Also, if Officer Sam had to wait for a warrant, Victor might destroy any evidence of the crime.

The U.S. Supreme Court has indicated that other exigencies may exist that justify a warrantless entry into a private home if the officers have probable cause to believe the evidence will be destroyed, the suspect will escape, or harm will occur to the police or others inside or outside the home.[13] Many tribes also recognize **exigent circumstances** and allow police to enter private homes without a warrant if the officer has probable cause to believe an exigent circumstance exists.

Is a Stop Always an Arrest?
The Law of the Stop and Frisk

Courts have ruled that police officers may temporarily detain and even "pat down" individuals without a warrant or probable cause if police officers see unusual conduct that leads them to believe that criminal activity is afoot. As the stop is a seizure of a person, without a warrant, it is subject to the reasonableness requirement of the Fourth Amendment in federal and state courts and ICRA in tribal courts. If, after making the stop, the officer has a reasonable belief that the person is armed, the officer may also **frisk**, or pat down, the person's outer clothing. Because of *Terry v. Ohio*, a U.S. Supreme Court decision allowing this action, this type of stop is often called a Terry stop.[14]

As stated, neither an arrest warrant nor probable cause is necessary for an investigatory field stop or Terry stop. The police officer need have only some objective basis for believing that the person had been engaged, or was about to engage, in criminal activity. The officer, however, must be able to cite particular facts that formed the basis for the inference that the individual was armed.

When a police officer has grounds to detain a person suspected of criminal activity, the officer may ask for some identification and for an explanation of the suspicious behavior. If asked specific questions about a crime in which he may be involved, the individual does not have to answer. A refusal to cooperate, however, may result in further detention. In some cases it may provide sufficient additional information to result in a valid arrest. For example, suppose a police officer has reason to suspect someone of a crime and the suspect refuses to answer the officer's questions or attempts to flee when approached by the officer. This conduct, when considered together with other factors, might provide the probable cause necessary to arrest.

What is the difference between an arrest and a stop? Generally a stop must be brief,[15] the individual is not moved to the police station or another location,[16] and the investigative methods are of less intrusive means than an arrest.[17] When assessing these factors, a court may decide that the stop was in reality so intrusive that it was an arrest and that probable cause was necessary. And if probable cause was not present for the arrest, any evidence found as a result of the stop or arrest may not be allowed in court.

The following cases are examples of the ways some tribal courts have analyzed the tribal and federal laws in this area. In each case, decide whether the officers' actions were justified.

Tulalip Tribal Court of Appeal
The Tulalip Tribes v. Merle K. Johnny (2006)
2006 WL 6357124
Before Jane M. Smith, Chief Justice; Edythe Chenois, Justice; Daniel A. Raas
Opinion by Raas, J.

Facts
This discussion incorporates and relies upon facts found by the trial court. The Tulalip Tribe advanced different facts in its briefing. However, we hold that a party challenging Findings of Fact entered by the trial court must clearly identify the Findings of Fact with which it disagrees and provide specific citations to the record in order properly to present such a challenge. (footnote omitted) This the Tulalip Tribe has not done.

Defendant Merle K. Johnny was stopped on the afternoon of August 11, 2004, on the Tulalip Reservation by Snohomish County Deputy Sheriff Sanders for driving with a cracked windshield. Deputy Sanders requested and received defendant's

Washington driver's license. The defendant volunteered that his license was suspended, he had no insurance and that the car he was driving was not his. Deputy Sanders took his driver's license, returned to his patrol vehicle, verified that the car was registered to a woman and that it was not reported stolen.

The deputy put on latex gloves and returned to defendant's car. He asked the defendant to step from the car, which he did. Mr. Johnny was nervous and fidgety. Deputy Sanders asked defendant to give him permission to search the car, which Mr. Johnny refused. For approximately the next ten minutes, the deputy aggressively asked for permission to search the car, and Mr. Johnny continued to deny such permission.

In one of those fortuitous happenstances that occasionally occur, Tulalip Chief of Police Goss then drove up. After a short conversation with Deputy Sanders, Chief Goss approached Mr. Johnny and asked if the reason that he would not allow a search of the car was that drugs were in the car. Mr. Johnny replied it was, and reached inside and handed Chief Goss a McDonald's Restaurant bag containing scales and at least two baggies of marijuana. Chief Goss arrested Mr. Johnny and charged him with a drug offense.

Deputy Sanders never checked the status of defendant's license, wrote a citation for the cracked windshield, or impounded the car.

The Trial Court suppressed the seized drugs and drug paraphernalia. The Tulalip Tribe appealed.

Discussion

The activity at the side of the road has two distinct phases. The first begins with the observation of the cracked windshield and continues through the initial questioning of the defendant regarding his license and the ownership of the car, through Deputy Sanders' return to the patrol car, and ends with the check on the status of the vehicle Mr. Johnny was driving. The second begins when Deputy Sanders dons the latex gloves and ends with the defendant's arrest by Chief Goss. Putting on the gloves is a sign that the deputy had decided to search the car. To conduct such a search requires probable cause. We conclude that the decision to search the car was without probable cause, and that therefore the fruits of the search must be suppressed.

The initial stop was valid. Driving with an obstructed windshield is an infraction under Tulalip law. Tulalip Tribal Ordinance 49, Section 3.3.1 incorporates RCW 46.37, which, in RCW 46.37.410(2), prohibits driving a motor vehicle with any nontransparent material on the front windshield. A cracked windshield is an infraction under Tulalip law, and stopping the offending vehicle and its driver is appropriate.

So was the initial investigation of the infraction, where Deputy Sanders sought information regarding Mr. Johnny's license status, car ownership, and insurance status. The difficulty with the stop arises when Deputy Sanders determined that a search of the car was needed.

Tulalip Tribal Code, Ordinance 49, § 2.2.5, requires that a search may be made, and contraband seized when a search is made, either with a search warrant or "in accordance with federally judicially recognized exceptions to the warrant requirement." § 2.2.5.2. TTC, Ordinance 49, § 2.2.14 permits investigative stops of persons or vehicles "in circumstances that create a particularized suspicion that the person or occupant has committed . . . an offense." And TTC, Ordinance 49, § 2.2.17 provides that the duration of a stop under §2.2.14 "may not last longer than is necessary to effectuate the purpose of the stop."

Here, Deputy Sanders had all the information he needed to complete the investigation of the cracked windshield when he took the defendant's driver's license back to his patrol car.

But the Deputy did not stop there. He retained the defendant's license and spent ten minutes seeking permission to search the car. In order to search the vehicle, Deputy Sanders required a "particularized suspicion" that an offense had been committed. Ordinance 49 § 2.2.14. The only objective evidence the Deputy cited as raising his suspicions was that the defendant was nervous and fidgety.

Every search or seizure must be reasonable. *Indianapolis v. Edmond*, 531 U.S. 32, 121 S.Ct. 447, 148 L.Ed.2d 333 (2000), 25 U.S.C. § 1302(2). Even a detainee's "extreme nervousness" during a traffic stop, without more, does not justify further detention or an expansion of an otherwise justified stop. *United States v. Chavez–Valenzuela*, 268 F.3d 719, 726 (9th Cir.2001). Deputy Sanders was not justified in holding the defendant in order to search his car, nor was Chief Goss justified in continuing the inquiry. Without the particularized suspicion required by § 2.2.14, the continued detention was unlawful. Without a lawful stop, the contraband recovered from defendant must be suppressed.

Other tribal courts have reached similar conclusions. *Fort Peck v. Vondall*, 2 Am. Tribal Law 139 (Fort Peck, 07/29/1999) (Objective evidence which would support a reasonable suspicion that criminal activity had taken place needed to justify investigatory stop), *Maho v. Hopi Tribe*, 1 Am. Tribal Law 278 (1997) (warrantless search must be based on reasonable or probable cause), *Navajo Tribe v. Todecheene*, 1 Nav. R. 67 (Navajo 09/18/1973) (warrantless search of automobile incident to arrest is limited to instrumentalities of crime for which individual was arrested, weapons, or means of escape).

The Trial Court is affirmed.

Colville Confederated Tribes Court of Appeals
Colville Confederated Tribes v. Peter P. George
3 CTCR 01, 1 CCAR 132, 1990.NACC.0000001 (VersusLaw) (1985)
Before Chief Judge Baker, Judge Chenois and Judge Naff.
The opinion of the court was delivered by: Baker, C.J.

Statement of Facts
The relevant facts in this matter as disclosed from the taped record of the arraignment are:

1. The arresting officer was on routine patrol on 3/5/85 at 4:00 P.M. in East Omak in an area believed by the officer to be a high crime area.
2. No crimes had been reported in the recent past in the area in question.
3. The officer observed a young male walking.
4. The officer did not recognize the young male as local.
5. The officer stopped the defendant and asked him to identify himself.
6. Upon stopping defendant, the officer noticed the defendant was slightly unsteady, had disheveled clothing and had an odor of intoxicants about him.

The issue at bar is: Was the "stop" permissible?

In analyzing the issue, the Court addresses each citation of authority given by plaintiff.

First, plaintiff, in his discussion, cites Colville Tribal Code § 4.1.11, Applicable Law. Since a "stop" is a seizure, federal and state criminal law are looked to for authority.

Plaintiff argues that the facts in the case at bar justified a Terry stop. A Terry stop is justified by "reasonable suspicion" (less than probable cause but more than a hunch). *Terry v. Ohio*, 392 U.S. 1 (1968). In Terry, the officer had observed defendants go through a series of acts, each of them perhaps innocent in itself, but which taken together and along with the officer's training, raised a reasonable suspicion that criminal activity was afoot and thus the situation warranted further investigation and a limited intrusion whereby the officer properly conducted a "stop and identify," i.e. he stopped the defendants and required them to identify themselves and state their business. Chief Justice Warren, speaking for the Court in Terry, and laying down the requirement for articulable facts, said, "This demand for specificity in the information upon which police action is [based] is the central teaching of this court's Fourth Amendment jurisprudence." Id. at 21, n. 18. . . .

Plaintiff also relies on *United States v. Cortez*, 449 U.S. 411, 101 S.Ct. 690, 66 L.Ed.2d 621 (1981). . . . [T]his is search and seizure law applied in the customs arena but moreover demands that two elements be present before a stop is permissible: (1) Assessment must be based upon all of the circumstances with various objective observations, such as police reports of modes or patterns of operations of certain kinds of lawbreakers, and (2) Assessment of the whole picture must yield a suspicion that the particular individual being stopped is engaged in wrongdoing. Neither of these elements exists in the case at bar. . . .

Plaintiff lastly cites *State v. Belanger*, 36 Wn. App. 818 (Div. II, 1984), a case in which the officer based the stop on the prior activity of Huddleson, a known transient, who upon seeing police approaching, hurriedly handed over a sleeping bag to the defendant and walked away. This activity, coupled with the officer's prior acquaintance with Huddleson, alerted the officer to further inquiry. This case is readily distinguishable from the case at bar, since the officer here had no prior acquaintance with the defendant.

We see no justification for the officer's intrusion upon the defendant in stopping him on the public street. Accordingly, we find that the Trial Court correctly dismissed the case, and it is now, therefore Ordered that the decision of the Trial Court be, and it hereby is, Affirmed.

Appellate Court of the Hopi Tribe
The Hopi Tribe v. Beauford Dawahoya (1995)
1995.NAHT.0000012 (VersusLaw)
Before Sekaquaptewa, Chief Justice, and Lomayesva and Abbey, Justices

Opinion and Order
Factual and Procedural Background

The Hopi Tribe appeals dismissal of a wrongful possession of alcohol charge against defendant, Beauford Dawahoya. On June 21, 1991, the Hopi Police Department dispatcher received an anonymous telephone tip that defendant was transporting an unknown quantity of alcohol in his red Ford pickup truck and was traveling northbound from Winslow on Highway 87. The arresting officer, Howard Sakiestewa, stopped defendant's vehicle on Highway 87, advised him of the report received, and asked him if he was transporting alcoholic beverages. The defendant answered, "The beer might belong to my son." The officer asked if he could search the vehicle. Defendant replied, "Sure, go ahead and look." The officer found a total of 33 unopened cans of Budweiser beer behind the driver's seat.

The Hopi Tribe charged defendant with wrongful possession of alcoholic beverages. Defendant filed a motion to dismiss the charge with prejudice because the officer did not have a reasonable suspicion to stop the vehicle. After a hearing on September 2, 1992, the Tribal Court granted defendant's motion to dismiss.

On September 3, 1992, the Hopi Tribe filed an appeal with this Court. The Hopi Tribe argues that the trial court erred in dismissing the case with prejudice because: (1) Officer Sakiestewa was entitled to stop and search Dawahoya's truck based on reasonable suspicion; and (2) the automobile exception to the warrant requirement excused Officer Sakiestewa from obtaining a search warrant.

Discussion

This Court reviews the grant of a motion to dismiss for clear **abuse of discretion**.

For reasons we will explain, we hold that the trial court did not abuse its discretion when it granted defendant's motion to dismiss the case after determining that Officer Sakiestewa did not have a reasonable suspicion to stop defendant's vehicle. Because Officer Sakiestewa did not have a reasonable suspicion to stop appellant's vehicle, we do not reach the Tribe's argument that the automobile exception to the warrant requirement excused the search in this case.

The applicable standard for determining whether a police officer's investigatory stop of a vehicle is justified is "reasonable suspicion." *Hopi Tribe v. Sockyma*, No.0669/87. In *Berkemer v. McCarty*, 468 U.S. 420, 439 (1984), the Court held that the usual traffic stop is analogous to a so-called "Terry stop." An officer has reasonable suspicion if he can "point to specific and articulable facts" sufficient to give rise to a reasonable suspicion that an individual has committed or is committing a crime. *Terry v. Ohio*, 392 U.S. 1, 21 (1968).

In the present case, the anonymous telephone tip did not exhibit sufficient **indicia** of reliability to provide reasonable suspicion for the investigatory stop. An anonymous tip exhibits sufficient indicia of reliability when it contains "a range of details relating not just to easily obtained facts and conditions existing at the time of the tip, but to future actions of third parties ordinarily not easily predicted." *White*, 496 U.S. 325, 332 (1990) (quoting *Illinois v. Gates*, 462 U.S. 213, 245 (1983)).

The Supreme Court has held that an anonymous telephone tip, if corroborated independently by police, could exhibit sufficient indicia of reliability to provide reasonable suspicion for an investigatory stop. *White*, 496 U.S. at 330, 331. However, "if a tip has a relatively low degree of reliability, more information will be required to establish the requisite quantum of suspicion than would be required if the tip were more reliable." Id. at 329. Whether the informant's tip is reliable enough to give rise to the required reasonable suspicion is to be determined by the totality of the circumstances. Id. at 330.

In the present case, the tipster stated only information that anyone could have known at the time of the call. In contrast to the information in White, this information does not lead to the inference that the informant had reliable access to inside information about defendant's illegal activities. The fact that defendant was driving northbound on Highway 87 in a red Ford pickup truck was easily obtainable by any roadside observer and did not require "inside information."

The amount of information provided in this anonymous tip was even less than that provided in *Arizona v. Bullington*, 165 Ariz. 11, 795 P.2d 1294 (Ct. App. 1990), where the court found that an anonymous tip did not justify an investigatory stop of defendant's van. In Bullington, an anonymous informant called the police and told them that four people in town from Ohio were attempting to purchase $24,000 to $26,000 of marijuana. Id. The informant named the four people, their hotel room, the color and license plate number of their van. Id. The police were not able to independently verify this information. The court held that they lacked reasonable suspicion to stop the van even though they observed the van driving erratically. Id. at 1296.

In this case, the anonymous informant only described respondent's vehicle, the direction the vehicle was traveling in, and its location at a specific time. Anyone could have obtained this information. The anonymous informant did not provide any information about defendant's itinerary that was not readily available to anyone who happened to observe the truck driving northbound on Highway 87. Therefore, this information was not enough to give the police the reasonable suspicion necessary for them to stop the vehicle.

The decision of the trial court is AFFIRMED.

Conclusion

An arrest, a seizure of a person by the government, must be reasonable or done with an arrest warrant based on probable cause. An arrest without a warrant is generally only reasonable if the offense occurs in front of the officer or the officer has reasonable or probable cause to believe the person committed a crime. There are exceptions, such as a Terry stop, which allow an officer to temporarily stop an individual. An arrest warrant, which protects against police abuse, is the preferred procedure to arrest a person, as it requires a neutral person, a judge, to review the facts to determine if probable cause actually exists.

Questions

Lamone v. Navajo
1. Did the arresting officer in this case see the defendant commit a crime?
2. According to the Navajo appellate court, when can a warrantless arrest be made?

Devil's Lake v. Frederick
1. Did the arresting officer in this case see the defendant commit a crime?
2. According to the Northern Plains Intertribal Court of Appeals, what standard should police officers use in determining whether a misdemeanor arrest should be made?
3. Do you agree that it is important for officers to be able to arrest on probable cause in cases of domestic violence? Why or why not?

Manuel v. Colville Tribes
1. In this case, who gave the tribal police officers permission to enter the house where Mr. Manuel was?
2. According to the Colville Appellate Court, when can police make a warrantless entry of a home to make an arrest occur?

Tualalip Tribes v. Johnny
1. Why was the initial stop valid?
2. Why was the officer not justified in holding Johnny after the investigation of the cracked windshield was completed?

Colville Tribes v. George
1. Why do you think the officer stopped Mr. George in this case? Do you think the stop was justified?
2. What decision did the court come to as the justification for stopping Mr. George?

Hopi v. Dawahoya
1. Why did the tribal police stop Mr. Dawahoya's truck?
2. According to the Hopi appellate court, why was the tip not sufficient to justify stopping Mr. Dawahoya's truck? Do you agree with the decision?

In Your Community
1. When does your nation require an arrest warrant? What are the rules for obtaining an arrest warrant?
2. How does your tribal court define probable cause for arrest?
3. Under your law, when can a warrantless arrest be made?
4. Does your nation allow warrantless entries into people's homes? Under what circumstances? Do you think this is a good policy? Why or why not?

5. Does your nation allow Terry stops? What test does the court use to determine if the stop was reasonable? Does your tribal court allow anonymous tips to justify a Terry stop?

Terms Used in Chapter 19

Abuse of discretion: A failure to use sound, reasonable judgment when a person is under a legal duty to do so.

Corroborate: Add to the likely truth or importance of a fact; give additional facts or evidence to strengthen a fact or assertion.

Custody: A suspect is "in custody" for purpose of determining necessity of Miranda warnings if police, by word or by conduct, have expressed to the suspect that he is not free to leave.

Exigent circumstances: Situations that demand unusual or immediate action.

Frisk: A superficial running of hands over a person's body to do a quick search, usually for weapons.

Indicia: Latin term meaning indications; pointers; signs.

Summons: A formal written notice to show up in court.

Validity: Legal sufficiency.

Notes

1. *Carroll v. United States*, 267 U.S. 132, 162 5 (1925).
2. *United States v. Watson*, 423 U.S. 411 (1976).
3. Devil's Lake Sioux Tribe is now known as Spirit Lake Sioux Nation.
4. *U.S. v. Karo*, 468 U.S. 705, 714–715 (1984).
5. *Illinois v. Rodriguez*, 497 U.S. 177, 182 (1990); *Warden, Md. Penitentiary v. Hayden*, 387 U.S. 294 (310) (1967).
6. *Payton v. New York*, 445 U.S. 574, 585–586 (1980).
7. *Steagald v. United States*, 451 U.S. 204 (1981).
8. *Wilson v. Arkansas*, 514 U.S. 927 (1995).
9. *Richards v. Wisconsin*, 520 U.S. 385 (1997).
10. *Illinois v. Rodriguez*, 497 U.S. 197 (1990).
11. *U.S. v. Arvizu*, 534 U.S. 266 (2002).
12. *Warden, Md. Penitentiary v. Hayden*, 387 U.S. 294, 310 (1967).
13. *Minnesota v. Olson*, 495 U.S. 91 (1990).
14. *Terry v. Ohio*, 392 U.S. 1 (1968).
15. *United States v. Sharpe*, 470 U.S. 675 (1985).
16. *Dunaway v. New York*, 442 U.S. 200 (1979).
17. *Florida v. Royer*, 460 U.S. 491 (1983).

Suggested Further Reading

Michael L. Barker, *Policing in Indian Country* (Harrow and Heston, 1998).

David M. Blurton and Gary D. Copus, "Administering Criminal Justice in Remote Alaska Native Villages: Problems and Possibilities," 11 *The Northern Review* 118 (1993).

Jerold H. Israel and Wayne R. Lafave, *Criminal Procedure Constitutional Limitations in a Nutshell*, 7th ed. (Thompson West, 2006).

Eileen Luna-Firebaugh, *Tribal Policing: Asserting Sovereignty, Seeking Justice* (University of Arizona Press, 2007).

Otwin Marenin and Gary Copus, "Policing Rural Alaska: The Village Public Safety Officer (VPSO) Program," 10 *American Journal of Police* 1 (1991).

Stewart Wakeling, et al., "Policing on American Indian Reservations," A Report to the National Institute of Justice (2001).

Chapter 20

Interrogations and Confessions: The Right to Remain Silent

When trying to solve a crime, police officers often interview suspects—both before and after an official arrest. Sometimes people confess they committed a crime during these interviews (also called **interrogations**). These confessions are then used as evidence at the trial of the accused.

Throughout American history, there are many examples of state and federal law enforcement officers abusing suspects during interrogation in order to get a confession. The abuse can be physical or psychological. Sometimes, innocent people will confess to a crime because of the abusive actions of police. However, interrogation, when done correctly, is also an important tool for law enforcement in solving crimes and holding perpetrators accountable for their actions. Since the questioning of suspects usually takes place behind closed doors at police stations, there is little solid evidence of what goes on in the course of interrogation. Therefore, disagreements constantly arise as to whether the police violated the rights of the suspect.

Courts have struggled to find a balance between the needs of law enforcement and the rights of individuals. Because police interrogation has resulted in some controversial confessions, courts have ruled that certain protections must be provided to the suspect. The American system has recognized the "right to remain silent" as a critical component of the Fifth Amendment.

This book focuses on how cultural values of tribal nations inform criminal law, and this is particularly important in the area of interrogations and confessions. Some Native cultures foster the belief that people should be honest about their actions and that the "right to remain silent" is inconsistent with tribal values. For example, lying was despised among the Mohawk, and it included attempting to deny or minimize one's behavior. A third offense for lying would result in banishment. Thus, there was no true right to remain silent but rather a cultural requirement of full disclosure, which was the first step toward rehabilitation and reintegration into the community.[1] These cultural values clash with the American justice system, which supports the right to remain silent. As a result, these cultural values can lead to a high rate of guilty pleas rather than to forcing the prosecutor to prove a case beyond a reasonable doubt, as required by the American justice system.

Defending Native people against criminal charges may present special challenges for defense attorneys and advocates. As discussed earlier, Native cultures often clash with an adversarial philosophy of American justice. Native cultures tend to value restoration and healing over proving guilt or innocence. Thus, many Native people are taught that when they commit a crime they must offer restoration and compensation—and not challenge their accusers. However, American defense lawyers typically encourage their clients to plead "not guilty" so that the prosecutor has the burden of proving the case.

A non-Native lawyer among the northwestern tribes in Canada noted several cultural customs that clashed with the Canadian court system. Avoiding eye contact was common among the Ojibway this lawyer defended in court. A sign of respect among the Ojibway, avoiding eye contact is a sign of guilt or shame in Anglo-American culture.[2] The implications of this cultural difference are immense. For example, when a client must testify before a jury, attorneys often counsel the client to look at the jurors; for Native people, looking at the jurors would violate cultural norms and be disrespectful, but non-Native jurors view the refusal to look at them as a sign of guilt.

Dr. Clare Brant, a Native psychiatrist, observed that among many Native cultures, confrontation or testifying against someone, even if that person harmed you, violates cultural norms. In many Native societies, interference is forbidden regardless of mistakes a person may make. Dr. Brant says, "We are very loath to confront people. We are very loath to give advice to anyone if the person is not specifically asking for advice. To interfere or even comment on their behavior is considered rude." To stand up in front of a judge and jury and testify against someone is very confrontational and difficult for many Natives.[3] Thus, Natives' refusal to testify does not mean an event did not occur but that their culture is directing them to address the harm in a different way.

A related cultural belief among some Natives is the duty not to point out the errors of others or "show them up." The non-Native lawyer in Canada gives another example of a young girl who was confronted by police with a summons. She signed the summons in the name of the accused and came to court with the police despite the fact that she was not the accused. Her rationale was that the police thought she was the other girl and eventually would figure out the error on their own. To point it out to them would have been rude. These cultural beliefs can have a large impact on interrogations and confessions by Natives: some Natives may simply agree they committed certain acts because that's what the police want them to say.[4]

The following passage illustrates how cultural and language differences may play a role in the response of a defendant to law enforcement and court systems. As you read the passage, think about your own tribal traditions and beliefs and how they may or may not clash with the American justice system.

A Sociolinguistic Mismatch: Central Alaskan Yup'iks and the Legal System

Phyllis Morrow, "A Sociolinguistic Mismatch: Central Alaskan Yup'iks and the Legal System," 10 *Alaska Justice Forum* 2 (1993)

Legal professionals working in the Central Alaskan Yup'ik region of Southwest Alaska commonly observe relatively high rates of confession and guilty pleas among Yup'ik clients. In 1991, a research team which included a trial lawyer (Galen Paine, Public Defender's Office, Sitka), a cultural anthropologist (Phyllis Morrow, University of Alaska Fairbanks), and a linguist (Betty Harnum, First Languages Commissioner of the Northwest Territories, Canada) isolated a number of cultural and linguistic factors which contribute to this pattern. This research reveals significant differences between prevailing legal and Yup'ik **sociolinguistic** norms, shows how miscommunication commonly builds in this setting, and suggests that when indigenous people like the Yup'iks find themselves enmeshed in the conventions of EuroAmerican legal institutions, unequal justice is likely to result.

The data for this study were gathered through observation, interviews, and linguistic analysis of courtroom discourse in Bethel, Alaska. For two months, researchers observed open court proceedings and had access to audiotapes of these proceedings. The majority of the data came from routine interactions such as plea entry or change, jury **voir dire**, and third party custodian assignment and from a few trials conducted during this period. While most of those undergoing proceedings were Yup'ik, as is consistent with the demography, non-Yup'iks ("Kass'aqs," as people originating in the Lower 48 and Europe are locally known) also appeared as defendants, jurors, and custodians, allowing for a comparative perspective. Interviews were conducted with both Yup'iks and Kass'aqs within the court system and related agencies. In addition, an informal sense of the concerns of inmates and their perceptions of the legal system was obtained by holding a series of workshops on legal procedures at the regional correctional center.

Analysis of these data revealed certain cross-cultural miscommunication patterns that are particularly critical in the administration of justice. The patterns centered around the process of interrogation, where differences in cultural expectations concerning questions and answers were tied to different expectations about conflict resolution. In particular, lawyers, judges, and law enforcement personnel, following the norms of legal discourse, tend to structure frameworks for questioning that cue a compliance response from many Yup'iks.

This compliance pattern was strong among Yup'iks who had little day-to-day interaction with Western bureaucratic systems, was evident in even the least inherently coercive court routines, such as the voir dire, and contrasted in significant ways with the responses of Kass'aqs and other Yup'iks who had more extensive daily involvement with EuroAmerican institutions, such as the workplace. While virtually all individuals, both Yup'iks and legal professionals, regardless of their familiarity with cross-cultural settings, employed a variety of communicative strategies in an attempt to repair the more obvious miscommunications, their strategies were often unsuccessful. This was partially because speakers differed in terms of language use and degree of understanding of the legal system, but also because Yup'ik and EuroAmerican strategies were based on fundamentally different approaches to the management of speech and interpersonal relationships. In fact, attempts on both sides to repair miscommunication often merely compounded it.

It is a clue to Yup'ik perceptions that the court is called "a place to be made to talk" (qanercetaarvik), rather than, for example, "a place where one brings problems for resolution" or "a place where justice is administered to wrongdoers." Clearly, the courts are, to some extent, intended to be intimidating: the solemnity of judicial discourse and garb and the formality of proceedings are meant to convey a sense of seriousness. Nonetheless, if a high proportion of Yup'iks feel coerced beyond this intended level, and if their response to this perceived coercion is to respond more compliantly to questioning than do other groups, then there are serious implications for justice. First, and of most obvious interest to legal professionals, such a communicative interplay can affect legal outcomes by increasing rates of confession and guilty pleas (and, by extension, rates of conviction) and by affecting rates of those excused from serving on juries. Given the present data, it seems likely that such imbalances occur. Second, and at another level, the courtroom can be seen as both a microcosm of intersocietal conflicts and a setting where such tensions are exacerbated. This is of critical importance to legal practitioners because it calls into question the basic efficacy of the legal system in bilingual/bicultural settings, which are becoming increasingly common throughout the country.

The Applicable Law

Many tribal governments have included rights pertaining to interrogation in their contemporary tribal codes.

Salish and Kootenai Criminal Procedures, Codified

2-2-405. Notice of rights prior to interrogation.

1. *Prior to questioning any person in custody, a law enforcement officer must inform the person in clear and unequivocal terms of the following rights:*
   a. *that the person has the right to remain silent;*
   b. *that anything said by him or her can and will be used against the person in any subsequent court proceedings;*
   c. *that the person has the right to legal counsel or representation as provided in Sections 2-2-503, prior to answering any questions; and*
   d. *that if, at any point during questioning, the person indicates that she or he wishes to remain silent the questioning will cease.*
2. *Any statement obtained in violation of these rights may not be admitted into evidence.*
3. *The fact that a person chooses to remain silent cannot be used against her or him in any subsequent criminal proceedings.*

The Indian Civil Rights Act (ICRA) includes several provisions to protect the right to remain silent or protect against incriminating yourself:

First is the right to due process, found in ICRA 1302 (8): "No Indian tribe in exercising powers of self-government shall deprive any person of liberty or property without due process of law."

The second is the privilege against **self-incrimination**, which is found in ICRA 1320(4): "No Indian tribe in exercising powers of self-government shall compel any person in any criminal case to be a witness against himself."

The third is the right to an attorney, which is found in ICRA 1320 (6): "No Indian tribe in exercising powers of self-government shall deny to any person in a criminal proceeding the right . . . at his own expense to have the assistance of counsel for his defense."

If the tribal code or constitution imposes procedures that are stricter than the provisions of ICRA, the interrogation and confession procedures, to be valid, must comply with both ICRA and the tribal code or constitution.

Was the Confession Voluntary?

One of the first questions a court may ask when determining whether a confession can be used in court is whether it was voluntary. The Fifth and Fourteenth amendments to the U.S. Constitution provide that no person shall be deprived of life, liberty, or property without due process of law. ICRA also provides the same rights.

Federal law prohibits the use of involuntary confessions in court. Involuntary confessions are confessions obtained by physical force—such as torture or beatings—or psychological coercion. In order to use a confession or other self-incriminating statement against a criminal defendant, it must first be shown that the statement or confession was made voluntarily. With very few exceptions, involuntary or coerced confessions may not be used in the prosecution of criminal defendants in U.S. courts. See chapter 22 for more information about the exclusionary rule.

Over the years, the U.S. Supreme Court has developed a test for determining the voluntariness of statements and confessions. This test of voluntariness is whether, considering the totality of the circumstances surrounding the statement, the accused's statement or confession is the product of a free and rational choice.

The factors that have been considered most important in determining the totality of the circumstances include the following:

1. Physical abuse,
2. Threats,
3. Extensive questioning,
4. **Incommunicado** detention,
5. Denial of the right to consult with counsel,
6. The age of the accused,
7. The intelligence and experience of the accused, and
8. The emotional stability of the accused.

Right to Counsel during Interrogation

Chapter 23 focuses on the right to counsel (attorney or lay advocate) during a trial. However, there also is a right to have counsel at interrogation/questioning. The following case explores this issue.

Swinomish Tribal Court
Swinomish Indian Community v. Vincent Lee Reid (2011)
11 Am. Tribal Law 179
MARK W. POULEY, Chief Judge.

THIS MATTER came on before this Court on Defendant's MOTION TO SUPPRESS statements he made during a custodial interrogation by the Swinomish Tribal Police. The issue before the court is whether the Defendant requested to consult with an attorney during the interrogation, whether the police violated such a request and if so, whether subsequent statements made by the Defendant should be suppressed. The court finds that the Defendant made a request for counsel that was disregarded by the police and the Motion to Suppress all statements made subsequent to the request is GRANTED.

The Defendant was charged with multiple counts of drug possession and conspiracy to deliver drugs and other charges. The Defendant was arrested at his home and transported to the Swinomish Tribal Police station for questioning. It is undisputed that the Defendant was subjected to custodial interrogation and prior to that interrogation he was properly advised of the rights afforded to him by the Indian Civil Rights Act and the Swinomish Tribal Code. During the initial interrogation, the Defendant appears to admit to personal use of non-prescribed pain killers, but consistently denies any involvement in the sale or distribution of drugs. The conversation also covers the Defendant's history of drug use, disputes with his family, and particular concerns about his children's welfare. Approximately thirty minutes into the interview, the interviewing officer begins to explore the amount of drugs the Defendant purchased and used over a given period of time. At this point the following exchange occurs:

> D(efendant): Look, I've got this problem. I need to get it fixed. No time for shining here. I'm gonna wait for a lawyer. You know, I screwed up. I know it.
>
> O(fficer): You're gonna wait for a lawyer for what? To get—, for your—, I don't understand what you just said.
>
> D: You told me that, you know, to wait for a lawyer, you read me my Miranda rights.
>
> O: Right.
>
> D: We all know we screwed up. I gotta fix it.
>
> O: O.K. Are you wanting to talk to me or do you want to talk to a lawyer. Are you saying you don't want to talk to me?
>
> D: Well, you're trying to construe everything and get me to say sh*t. Not cool man.
>
> O: I'm trying to get you to explain, to clarify.

D: Yah, so you can build up this big frickin' ordeal and make it worse.

O: Hold on bud, don't put that on me, the ordeal is already here. I'm trying to— actually what I'm trying to do is to minimize.

D: You're trying to get a collar man, you know.

O: I already got that bud, you're already under arrest.

D: What do you need?

O: First of all, do you want to talk to me, or are you telling me you want a lawyer?

D: Yah sure, I'll talk to you.

O: O.K. I told you before hand, Vincent Reid, the first guy I met here, can't be all that bad. O.K. What I'm trying to do is give you a chance to explain your side of this. To explain your side of what we know. Are you a big drug dealer or is it just a couple of times a month?

The interview continues from there.

While Federal and State court decisions regarding right to counsel during custodial interrogation are not controlling in this court, they can be instructive in developing a rule of law that is consistent with the precedents of this court and the jurisprudence of the tribal community. In *Miranda v. Arizona*, 384 U.S. 436, 86 S.Ct. 1602, 16 L.Ed.2d 694 (1966) the Supreme Court established the rule that if an accused indicates in any manner and at any stage of the process that he wishes to consult with an attorney before speaking, there can be no further questioning. This rule preserves the Defendant's right against self incrimination. Upon making an unambiguous request for counsel, all interrogation must cease. *Edwards v. Arizona*, 451 U.W. 477 (1981). The tribe argues that the Defendant's initial statement, "I'm gonna wait for a lawyer," is **ambiguous**, in which case the officer is permitted to ask questions to clarify if the Defendant is seeking to invoke his right to counsel. See, *State v. Smith*, 34 Wash.App. 405, 661 P.2d 1001 (1983). The tribe also argues that the Defendant continues talk and therefore initiates further communication with the officer, which is also a recognized exception to the rules announced in Miranda and Edwards. While the Court agrees with this line of case law, it does not provide for an exception under the facts of this case.

The tribe argues that the Defendant's initial statement was ambiguous because, given the context the many personal problems that the Defendant already discussed, it was unclear for what reason the Defendant wanted to wait for an attorney. Assuming arguendo that this first statement is ambiguous, following the officer's first attempt to clarify, the Defendant was clear and unambiguous when he referenced the officer reading him is [sic] Miranda rights and that he could "wait for a lawyer." At this point, all interrogation should have immediately ceased. But the conversation continued, and ultimately the Defendant agreed to speak to the officer without the presence of an attorney and the interrogation proceeded.

It is true that even after invoking his right to counsel a suspect can waive his right to counsel by knowingly and voluntarily reinitiating conversations with the police. For such an action to be valid, however, the police may not engage in any tactics which may tend to coerce the suspect to change his mind. See, *State v. Smith*, at 409, 661 P.2d 1001; *State v. Pierce*, 94 Wash.2d 345, 618 P.2d 62 (1980). Custodial interrogation is inherently coercive and the court must adopt rules that will prevent the police from badgering a defendant into waiving his previously asserted rights. See, *Michigan v. Harvey*, 494 U.S. 344, 110 S.Ct. 1176, 108 L.Ed.2d 293 (1990). Admittedly, this is an extremely close case, and the interviewing officer engaged in no offensive tactics, but it is clear from the context that the conversation centered more upon how the Defendant could help his own case by continuing the interview, and by implication, not waiting for an attorney. The court is unable to conclude that the Defendant made a free and voluntary waiver of his previously asserted right to counsel, nor did he willfully reinitiate the interview with the officer after having so asserted his rights.

The conversation continues without a clear break, and the tribe argues from this that the officer was merely trying to clarify the ambiguity and that the Defendant continued to talk and ultimately reinitiated the interview. Close review of the interview does not support this interpretation of the events. After the officer asks the Defendant a second time if he wants to talk to him or wait for a lawyer, the Defendant accuses the officer of "trying to construe everything" and "make him say sh*t." In this statement the Defendant is not demonstrating a willingness to speak, but instead expressing distrust in the direction of [*sic*] the conversation was going. While the officer then says he is trying to "clarify" it is obvious from the context that the officer is not saying he is trying to clarify the ambiguous statement about a lawyer, but he is trying to get the defendant to explain and clarify the events. The officer says he wants to help the Defendant "minimize" the situation. In this portion of the conversation, it does not appear that the officer has misunderstood the Defendant's request for an attorney, but is attempting to explain to the Defendant why he may not want or need an attorney.

The Court finds that the Defendant made a clear and unambiguous request for a lawyer and all interrogation should have immediately ceased. The officer continued to engage the suspect in conversation apparently intended to encourage the Defendant to continue the interview without the assistance of counsel. The Court GRANTS the motion and all statements made by the Defendant following his request for counsel must be suppressed at trial. Dated this 24th day of October, 2011.

Advisement of the Right to Not Incriminate Yourself (Miranda Warnings)

Even if a confession or incriminating statement is found to be voluntary, there are further protections against a defendant's right not to incriminate himself or herself, including the right to remain silent under the Fifth Amendment to the U.S. Constitution and under ICRA. The U.S. Supreme Court developed rules to protect this right in *Miranda v. Arizona*, 384 U.S. 436 (1966). Although *Miranda* is binding only on state and federal courts, many tribes have adopted laws that are similar to *Miranda* or that explicitly follow *Miranda*.

The Facts: *Miranda v. Arizona*

Ernesto Miranda was accused of kidnapping and raping an eighteen-year-old woman. The woman testified that she was on her way home from work when a man grabbed her, threw her into the back seat of a car, and raped her. Ten days later, Miranda was arrested, placed in a lineup, and identified by the woman as her attacker. The police then took Miranda into an interrogation room and questioned him for two hours. At the end of the two-hour questioning, the police officer obtained a written and signed confession. This confession was then used as evidence at trial, and Miranda was found guilty.

Miranda later appealed his conviction to the U.S. Supreme Court, arguing that he had not been warned of his right to remain silent under the U.S. Constitution and that he had been deprived of his right to counsel. He did not suggest that his confession was false or brought about by coercion but rather that he would not have confessed if he had been advised of his right to remain silent or of his right to an attorney.

After considering all of the arguments, the U.S. Supreme Court ruled that Miranda's confession could not be used at his trial because it was obtained without informing him of his constitutional rights. As a result of the *Miranda* decision, statements or confessions obtained from an accused during custodial interrogation—before or after formal charges are filed, and regardless of voluntariness—are not admissible unless certain procedural safeguards are observed. Specifically, police are now required to clearly inform persons accused of a crime of the following so-called Miranda rights before questioning begins:

> You have the right to remain silent. Anything you say can be used against you in court. You have a right to a lawyer and to have a lawyer present while you are being questioned. If you cannot afford a lawyer, one will be appointed for you before any questioning begins.

The rationale behind the Miranda warnings is that in-custody interrogations are coercive by their very nature and require very careful protection of an accused's civil rights (such as the privilege against self-incrimination and the right to counsel). Therefore, the prosecution must show that these rights were carefully protected whenever the prosecution seeks to use any statements obtained from the accused during such interrogations.

Sault Ste. Marie Tribal Code § 70.106 (1995)
Upon arrest, the suspect shall be advised of the following rights:

1. *That he has the right to remain silent.*
2. *That any statements made by him may be used against him in court.*
3. *That he has the right to obtain counsel at his own expense.*

What Does "In Custody" Mean?

The Miranda rules apply when the accused is in custody. The Miranda rules, however, do not apply when the police are asking general questions about the facts or when someone volunteers a statement. It should also be noted that the Miranda rules apply only to interrogations by the police or persons acting on behalf of the police. Therefore, incriminating statements made by the accused to friends or cellmates while in custody are admissible regardless of Miranda.

The following scenarios explain common rules on the question of custody for Miranda rights.

- Vickie Two Horses is arrested at her home for criminal child abuse. She is in custody—that is, she is no longer free to go. Therefore, she must be informed of her rights before any questioning begins—even if the questioning takes place in her home rather than at the police station.
- Victor Smith is arrested for criminal assault and battery and taken to the police station for interrogation. He must be informed of his rights before the questioning begins.
- Police come upon the scene of a fight and ask Robert Young, one of the people involved in the fight, what happened. The police in this situation are not required to inform Robert of his rights because this is just general on-the-scene questioning. Robert is not in custody.

Waiver of Miranda Rights

An accused may waive (give up) his or her Miranda rights. The prosecution, however, bears a "heavy burden" of demonstrating that the waiver was knowledgeable, intelligent, and voluntary. In the words of the *Miranda* decision, if the accused "indicates in any manner, at any time prior to or during any questioning, that he wishes to remain silent, the interrogation must cease." In addition, if the accused "states that he wants an attorney, the interrogation must cease until an attorney is present."

In some jurisdictions, the Miranda warnings are given orally, and the police officer or investigator reads the warnings from a card. Other jurisdictions use written warning forms that the suspect is encouraged to sign in order to demonstrate a knowing waiver of Miranda rights. A written form signed by the suspect helps to establish a waiver, but it does not constitute an absolute waiver because there is no guarantee the accused understood the form. The court may have to make an additional inquiry to ensure that the rights of the accused are carefully guarded. The prosecution must show that there was a knowing, intelligent, and voluntary waiver of Miranda rights.

Once warnings have been given and the defendant invokes the right to remain silent or to have an attorney present, questioning must cease. Questioning may resume, but the defendant's rights must be "scrupulously honored,"[5] normally by reading Miranda to the defendant a second time. Also, once the defendant requests an attorney, questioning must cease until the accused has had an opportunity to speak with the attorney, unless the defendant initiates further conversations with the police.[6]

In the following two cases, the tribal courts use tribal custom and tradition to support the concept of giving warnings to suspects.

Crow Court of Appeals
Crow Tribe v. Lance Big Man
2000 Crow 7
Before Stewart, C.J., Gros-Ventre, J., and Watt, J.

Opinion
This is an appeal by Defendant Lance Big Man from his conviction by the Tribal Court (Stovall, S. J.) for driving under the influence of alcohol under Crow Tribal Code Section 13-3-302 ("DUI"). On appeal, Mr. Big Man argues that the Tribal Court erred in not dismissing the charge against him because the arresting officer failed to read him his Miranda rights, and he did not waive his Miranda rights to allow the officer to conduct sobriety tests.

For the reasons explained below, we affirm the Tribal Court's conviction.

A. Facts and Course of Proceedings

At approximately 10:00 P.M. on March 2, 2000, Crow Tribal police officers responded to a complaint from two Tribal members about a dark-colored van, possibly being driven by Lance Big Man, almost running their pickup off the road. Officers Eastman and Stops drove to the Appsalooka Heights area in Crow Agency, where they saw a blue van drive over a curb as it entered the highway. When the officers turned on their overhead lights to stop it, the van accelerated, drove through a borrow pit, and sped through the residential area. The officers followed the van until it parked in the driveway of the Defendant's residence.

When Mr. Big Man got out of his vehicle, Officer Eastman smelled alcohol on his breath, and observed that his speech was slurred and he was not steady on his feet. Officer Eastman placed him under arrest for reckless driving, but did not inform Mr. Big Man of his Miranda rights. After Officer White Hip arrived in another patrol car, he assisted Officer Eastman with handcuffing Mr. Big Man. At that time, Officer White Hip gave Mr. Big Man his Miranda rights. Officer White Hip then transported Mr. Big Man to the Crow jail. Officer White Hip testified that on the way to the jail, Mr. Big Man asked about the charges against him and was offered a breathalyzer test, but refused.

At the booking area of the jail, Officer Eastman administered several field sobriety tests on Mr. Big Man, including the "one leg stand," "walk and turn," and "ABC's." When Mr. Big Man was not able to successfully perform any of the tests, Officer Eastman advised him that he was being charged with DUI, and Mr. Big Man was booked and jailed.

At the bench trial conducted by Special Judge Stovall on March 21, 2000, Defendant Big Man was represented by the Tribal public defender Cloyce Little Light. The original complainants testified, as did all three officers involved in Mr. Big Man's arrest and booking. At the conclusion of the trial, the public defender asked the court to dismiss the charges because Mr. Big Man was not informed of his Miranda rights by the Officer Eastman, the arresting officer, but the Tribal Court denied the motion.

The Tribal Court found Mr. Big Man guilty of violating the Tribal DUI statute "Persons Under the Influence of Alcohol or Drugs," Section 13-3-302, Crow Tribal Code. Although the Tribal Court did not enter written findings of fact and conclusions of law to support its judgment of conviction, Judge Stovall explained his findings and reasoning to Mr. Big Man in open court. The public defender filed Mr. Big Man's notice of appeal that same day.

On March 23, Judge Stovall sentenced Mr. Big Man to 5 days in jail (with credit for one day already served) and 90 days supervised probation, including a substance abuse evaluation. Pursuant to Rule 6 of the Crow Rules of Appellate Procedure, Judge Stovall granted Mr. Big Man's request to stay his jail sentence pending the outcome of this appeal.

B. Issues on Appeal

In this appeal, Defendant Big Man does not challenge the officers' reasons for stopping him and arresting him for reckless driving. Mr. Big Man also does not argue that Officer Eastman lacked probable cause to arrest him for DUI, or that the evidence heard at trial was not sufficient to convict him on that charge.

Rather, Mr. Big Man argues on appeal that Officer Eastman, the "arresting officer," never read Mr. Big Man his Miranda rights, thereby violating Rule 8(f) of the Crow Rules of Criminal Procedure.

Mr. Big Man further argues that as a result of this alleged violation, together with the fact that Officer Eastman initially informed him only that he was being arrested for reckless driving, Mr. Big Man could not have made a knowing and intelligent waiver [of] his Miranda rights in order to permit Officer Eastman to perform the field sobriety tests that provided the evidence for Mr. Big Man's conviction.

Therefore, Mr. Big Man argues, the Tribal Court erred by not dismissing the charge against him on either one of these grounds.

The facts behind Mr. Big Man's legal arguments are not disputed. This case raises pure issues of law as to the scope of the protections guaranteed by Rule 8(f) of the Crow Rules of Criminal Procedure, the Indian Civil Rights Act, and the Miranda law developed by the federal courts. This court will conduct an independent or de novo review of these questions of first impression.

C. Applicable Law

The United States Supreme Court's landmark decision in *Miranda v. Arizona*, 384 U.S. 436 (1966), with its requirement for "reading a defendant his rights," was only recently reaffirmed as a constitutional principle.

In the Miranda case, the Court held that in order for a suspect's statements made while he was in custody to be admissible against him, he must first receive certain warnings about his constitutional rights. Those four warnings are "that he has the right to remain silent, that anything he says can be used against him in a court of law, that he has the right to the presence of an attorney, and that if he cannot afford an attorney one will be appointed for him prior to any questioning if he so desires." *Miranda*, 384 U.S. at 479. . . .

Of course, Miranda does not apply directly here, because Tribal governments are not subject to the Bill of Rights or the Fourteenth Amendment of the United States Constitution. However, by enacting the Indian Civil Rights Act of 1968, 25 U.S.C. §§ 1301—1303 (the "ICRA"), Congress exercised its plenary power over Indian Tribes to grant similar (although not identical) protections to persons subjected to Tribal government actions.

1. THE INDIAN CIVIL RIGHTS ACT. In the present case, the pertinent provisions of the ICRA are its prohibitions against compelling a person to be a witness against himself, and against depriving any person of liberty or property without due process of law. 25 U.S.C. § 1302(4) and (8). The wording of these provisions is nearly identical to the Fifth Amendment. However, in view of the legislative history of the ICRA, and subsequent court interpretations, it is not certain how closely this court is bound to apply federal constitutional law in interpreting these rights.

In its only case devoted to interpreting the ICRA, the Supreme Court in *Santa Clara Pueblo v. Martinez*, 436 U.S. 49 (1978), held that federal-court remedies for violations of the ICRA were limited to the one expressly provided by Congress, i.e., the writ of habeas corpus "to test the legality of [any person's] detention by order of an Indian tribe." 25 U.S.C. § 1303. Thus, in Martinez, the federal courts lacked jurisdiction of a mother's civil action to enforce the equal protection clause of the ICRA against a Tribal law that denied membership to children of female members who married outside the Tribe.

Instead, the Court stated:

> Tribal forums are available to vindicate rights created by the ICRA . . . which these forums are obliged to apply. Tribal courts have repeatedly been recognized as appropriate forums for the exclusive adjudication of disputes affecting important personal and property interests of both Indians and non-Indians. (*Martinez*, 436 U.S. at 65)

The legislative history of the ICRA, as described by the Martinez Court, supports a view that Tribal courts have some flexibility in interpreting the specific provisions of ICRA. The Court in Martinez clearly recognized the competing Congressional purpose manifest in the ICRA, that of promoting Tribal self-government. *Martinez*, 436 U.S. at 62. In view of this competing purpose, Congress decided that restricting federal-court review of alleged violations "would adequately protect the individual interests at stake while avoiding unnecessary intrusions on tribal governments." Id. at 67; see also, id. at 68 (quoting Edison Real Bird's objections on behalf of the Crow Tribe to a previous version of the bill that would have required the U.S. Attorney General to investigate alleged violations).

Congress may also have considered that ICRA's interpretation "will frequently depend on question of tribal tradition and custom which tribal forums may be in a better position to evaluate than federal courts." *Martinez*, 436 U.S. at 71. Finally, the Court agreed with the district court that "efforts by the federal judiciary to apply the statutory prohibitions of § 1302 in a civil context may substantially interfere with a tribe's ability to maintain itself as a culturally and politically distinct entity." Id. at 72 (citing in a footnote the importance of a Tribe being able to define its own membership).

The above-quoted language from Martinez echoes an earlier Ninth Circuit opinion that summarized some of the federal appeals courts' views of how ICRA should be interpreted: We note in passing that the courts have been careful to construe the terms "due process" and "equal protection" as used in the Indian Bill of Rights with due regard for the historical governmental and cultural values of an

Indian tribe. As a result, these terms are not always given the same meaning as they have come to represent under the United States Constitution. (*Tom v. Sutton*, 533 F.2d 1101, 1104-05 n.5 [9th Cir. 1976] [footnotes omitted] [due process right does not entitle indigent defendant to appointed counsel]).

In a later criminal case in which the Ninth Circuit reversed the district court's grant of habeas corpus relief, the court stated: "The procedures that the Tribal Courts choose to adopt are not necessarily the same procedures that the federal courts follow. Federal courts must avoid undue or intrusive interference in reviewing Tribal Court procedures." *Smith v. Confederated Tribes of Warm Springs*, 783 F.2d 1409, 1412 (9th Cir. 1986), cert. denied, 479 U.S. 964 (1986) (citations omitted) (deferring to Tribal interpretation of when Tribal prosecution commenced under Tribal law).

On the other hand, the Ninth Circuit has stated that when Tribal court procedures and rights parallel those found in Anglo-Saxon society, "federal constitutional standards are employed in determining whether the challenged procedure violates the Act." *Randall v. Yakima Nation Tribal Court*, 841 F.2d 897 (9th Cir. 1988) (emphasis added). In Randall, the court concluded that the appellate procedures provided under Tribal law "parallel exactly those employed by the United States courts," and the requirement for paying a $60 appeal filing fee had nothing to do with Tribal custom and tradition. Id. at 902. The Randall court therefore held that a criminal defendant's procedural due process rights under the ICRA were violated when her appeal was dismissed for failing to pay the filing fee within 10 days because the Tribal court had neglected to rule on her pending motion to waive the fee.

In the present case, as further explained below, the Tribe has adopted a requirement for Miranda warnings that appears to parallel the requirement under current federal constitutional law. The requirement for these warnings is not grounded in Tribal custom or tradition—nor is the rest of the adversarial criminal prosecution process set out in the Crow Rules of Criminal Procedure.

Under Randall, then, it is arguable that the ICRA gives this court no choice but to apply federal constitutional law. However, this approach is extremely rigid, and could lead us down the wrong path when the Tribal Council has adopted a protection for criminal defendants that the U.S. Congress and the federal courts have sought to deny to other American citizens. See, e.g., discussion of Dickerson and Section 3501, above.

Thus, consistent with Martinez and Smith, rather than deciding this appeal based on the ICRA, we believe it is more appropriate to look to the intent of the Tribal Council in enacting the requirement for Miranda warnings under Tribal law.

CROW TRIBAL LAW. The Crow Rules of Criminal Procedure, adopted in 1978, provide in pertinent part:

> Arrest Procedure. Unless exigent circumstances exist, when arresting an individual, Police Officers shall use the following procedure:

- (b) Officer shall inform the individual that he is under arrest;
- (d) Officer shall inform the arrested party of the charges against him;
- (e) Officer shall inform the arrested party of his various rights including the right to remain silent, the right to have his attorney present during questioning, and if he cannot afford an attorney, the right to be represented by the Tribal Defender unless that position is vacant at any time during the court of proceedings against him;
- (g) Officer shall transport defendant to the closest Tribal detention facility. (Rule 8, Crow Rules of Criminal Procedure [Title 6, Crow Tribal Code]).

A preliminary analysis of this language in the context of Appellant's arguments will assist in determining the scope of the protections that the Council intended to provide when it enacted the Rule.

Appellant argues that Rule 8(f) requires that the defendant be given his Miranda rights by the "arresting officer." The phrase "arresting officer" is not used in Rule 8. Rather, the Rule refers to procedures that "Police Officers shall use," except in emergency situations, "when arresting an individual[.]" The language in the body of the Rule does not clearly state that the same officer who informs the defendant that he is under arrest must also be the one who informs the defendant of his Miranda rights. It is possible, though, that the use of the singular term "Officer" in subparagraphs (b), (d) and (f) implies that it is supposed to be the same officer. Subparagraph (e) also uses the term "Officer," so under the interpretation urged by Mr. Big Man, only Officer Eastman as the arresting officer would have been allowed to transport the defendant to the "closest Tribal detention facility."

Such an interpretation goes much too far. When a team of police officers is on the scene of an arrest, rigid legal restrictions on which officer Mirandizes the defendant, and which officer transports him to jail, would unnecessarily interfere with the officers' ability to perform their work efficiently while not advancing any substantial rights of the defendant. We do not believe that was the intent of the Tribal Council when it enacted Rule 8.

Instead, we believe that the Tribal Council intended to make it clear that criminal defendants are entitled to Miranda protections when they are prosecuted in the Crow Tribal Court. Except for the right to appointed counsel as modified by Rule 8(f), the Tribal Council intended to provide Crow Tribal members and non-member Indians who may be subject to Tribal criminal prosecution with the same Miranda rights enjoyed by all other Americans, as recognized and developed in the Supreme Court's decisions. . . .

There can be no question that this holding provides at least the minimum protections required by the ICRA. Any concern on the part of law enforcement that this holding goes further than the minimum protections required by the ICRA is best addressed by Chief Justice Rehnquist's recent observation that the Miranda rule actually simplifies the prosecution's burden of showing that statements were voluntary, and only in rare cases can the defendant show that his confession was involuntary despite the fact that police adhered to Miranda. Dickerson, 120 S.Ct. at 2336.

Rule 8 provides a sound, specific guide for proper police procedure in making an arrest. However, we do not believe that the Tribal Council intended for this court to create new remedies for technical violations of the arrest process set forth in Rule 8 that would greatly expand upon the Miranda rights recognized by the Supreme Court. In any event, no violation of the arrest procedures specified in Rule 8 occurred in this case, when the Defendant was given his rights and transported to the Crow jail by an officer who was present at the scene of the arrest. Therefore, consistent with the Tribal Council's intent, this court will determine Mr. Big Man's claims of error with reference to the rules developed by the Supreme Court in Miranda and subsequent cases.

D. *Resolution of Issues under Miranda*

Compared to the popular misconception that any violation of a defendant's Miranda rights will allow him to "get off on a technicality," the scope of the Miranda rule is quite limited.

In essence, the Miranda rule only prohibits the prosecution from using in its "case in chief" any statements made by the defendant after he was in police custody or otherwise significantly deprived of his freedom. *Miranda*, 384 U.S. at 444. Confessions are the main type of statements with which Miranda is concerned, but it also applies to exculpatory statements. Id. However, regardless of whether or not Miranda warnings were given, statements made by the defendant can be used to **impeach** contradictory testimony given by the defendant if he chooses to testify in the defense case. *Harris v. New York*, 401 U.S. 222 (1971).

When the police fail to give a Miranda warning at the time of arrest, the defendant's remedy is not to have the charges automatically thrown out. Rather, the defendant's exclusive remedy is to suppress his statements—that is, to obtain a ruling by the court that any statements made while in custody and before the defendant was read his Miranda rights may not be introduced into evidence as part of the prosecution's case. If the prosecution's case depends on these "unwarned" statements to show guilt, then the prosecution will lose and the failure to give Miranda rights will have the effect of throwing the case out. However, if the prosecution is able to prove the defendant's guilt without using the inadmissible unwarned statements, the failure to give a Miranda warning will not affect the outcome of the trial.

In the present case, under Miranda, the mere undisputed fact that the "arresting officer" failed to give Mr. Big Man his rights does not by itself entitle Mr. Big Man to dismissal of the charge. Granting the dismissal requested by Mr. Big Man would stretch Miranda far beyond any form of relief ever discussed by the Supreme Court, and beyond what the Tribal Council intended when it adopted Crow R.

Crim. P. 8(f). The Defendant's sole remedy is to exclude evidence of statements or confessions that were obtained in violation of Miranda.

We thus turn to Mr. Big Man's second argument—that he could not have knowingly and intelligently waived his Miranda rights to allow Officer Eastman to perform field sobriety tests at the jail, when Big Man had not yet been informed that he was under arrest for suspected DUI.

Under Miranda, "[o]nce warnings have been given, the subsequent procedure is clear." *Miranda*, 384 U.S. at 474. "If the individual indicates in any manner, at any time prior to or during questioning that he wishes to remain silent, the interrogation must cease." Id. at 473–74. If the individual requests legal counsel, the questioning must cease until the defendant's counsel is present, unless the defendant himself "initiates further communication, exchanges or conversations with the police." *Edwards v. Arizona*, 451 U.S. 477, 485 (1981).

The defendant's other alternative after receiving his Miranda rights is to waive those rights, "provided the waiver is made voluntarily, knowingly and intelligently." *Miranda*, 384 U.S. at 444. The prosecution has the burden of proving any waiver.

In this regard, the Supreme Court has specifically addressed the situation where the defendant does not know what crime he is going to be questioned about when he waives his Miranda rights. In *Colorado v. Spring*, 479 U.S. 564 (1987), the suspect was arrested for illegal trafficking in stolen firearms, but after he waived his Miranda rights, the police questioned him about a murder. The Court held that "the suspect's awareness of all possible subjects of questioning in advance of interrogation is not relevant to determining whether the suspect voluntarily, knowingly, and intelligently waived his Fifth Amendment privilege." Id. at 577 (emphasis added).

Therefore, Mr. Big Man's second argument, that he was not informed he was under investigation for suspected DUI, even if supported by the record, would not be relevant in determining whether Mr. Big Man knowingly and intelligently waived his rights.

In the present case, there is no evidence that the defendant stated that he wished to remain silent, or that he requested legal counsel. On the other hand, there is also no evidence that Mr. Big Man made any waiver, knowing or otherwise, of these rights. Therefore, in the absence of an effective waiver, any statements or confessions covered by Miranda were not admissible. The only remaining question in this case is whether Mr. Big Man's conviction was based on any such statements or confessions.

It is important to understand that the Fifth Amendment's prohibition against compelling a defendant be a witness against himself only covers so-called "testimonial" evidence, i.e., the content of verbal and written communications by the defendant. As the Supreme Court explained shortly after issuing its Miranda decision:

> [B]oth federal and state courts have usually held that it [the privilege against self-incrimination] offers no protection against compulsion to submit to fingerprinting,

photographing, or measurements, to write or speak for identification, to appear in court, to stand, to assume a stance, to walk, or to make a particular gesture. *Schmerber v. California*, 384 U.S. 757, 764 (1966) (defendant may be compelled to supply blood samples in DUI case). Because these other forms of "nontestimonial" evidence are not protected by the Fifth Amendment's protection against self-incrimination, they are not subject to Miranda warnings and waivers.

The Crow Traffic Code, which establishes the crime of DUI for which Mr. Big Man was convicted, does provide greater protections for defendants in this area than would be required under Schmerber and federal constitutional law. It prohibits the police from taking chemical tests of blood, breath or urine without the defendant's consent. Crow Tribal Code § 13-3-303(3). If the defendant refuses, the tests may not be given, but the defendant's driving privileges may be suspended, and the fact of his refusal may be used against him in court. Id.; § 13-3-305(2). Interpreting a similar Tribal DUI code provision, the Court of Appeals of the Confederated Salish and Kootenai Tribes has held that when the police forced the defendant to submit to a blood test, the results of the blood test must be suppressed and excluded from evidence. See *Tribes v. Conko*, Cause No. AP-96-1066-CR (CS&K Ct. App. 1998).

In the present case, the sobriety tests administered by Officer Eastman at the jail did not involve any chemical tests that required Mr. Big Man's consent under Section 13-3-303(3). The Traffic Code, Section 13-3-305(3), specifically states that it is not intended to limit the introduction of "other competent evidence" such as these types of test results. The results of these sobriety tests (and Mr. Big Man's unsteadiness and slurred speech observed by the officers at the time of his arrest) fall within the above list of recognized non-testimonial evidence. They are not the type of statements or confessions that are subject to Miranda, and the Defendant could be forced to submit to the tests without any Miranda warning or waiver.

Because Mr. Big Man's conviction was based entirely on those test results, there is no basis under Miranda, and therefore no basis under Tribal law, for overturning his conviction.

E. Specific Warnings Required

In view of this court's adoption herein of the Supreme Court's Miranda [case law], it is important to clarify some ambiguous wording in the Tribal Rule 8(f) about the warnings that must be given.

The language of Rule 8(f), with its use of the word "including," does not purport to be a complete list of the warnings that must be given. For example, it omits a specific warning held to be essential in Miranda: "The warning of the right to remain silent must be accompanied by the explanation that anything said can and will be used against the individual in court. This warning is needed in order to make him aware not only of the privilege, but also of the consequences of forgoing it." *Miranda*, 384 U.S. at 469.

Furthermore, although the Rule properly states Tribal law (that the arrested party may be represented by the public defender "unless that position [is] vacant"), the defendant is entitled under Miranda to know precisely what kind of legal assistance may actually be available to him if he cannot afford an attorney. See *Miranda*, 384 U.S. at 473.

Therefore, consistent with Miranda, and with adaptations for the more limited right to counsel under Tribal law and the ICRA, criminal defendants prosecuted under Crow Tribal law are entitled to the following warnings:

1. You have the right to remain silent.
2. Anything you say can and will be used against you in a court of law.
3. You have the right to hire an attorney or lay counselor at your own expense to be present during questioning.

If the office of Tribal public defender is filled at the time of the arrest, a fourth warning must be given, depending on how that office is filled:

4. If you cannot afford an attorney, a non-attorney lay counselor [or "attorney" if one is available] from the Tribal public defender's office will be appointed for you prior to questioning, if you so desire.

The above warnings are the minimum requirements for satisfying Miranda and Rule 8(f) of the Crow Rules of Criminal Procedure. This court does not express an opinion on any other warnings or advice of rights that may be required or desirable under Tribal law or the ICRA.

By setting out these warnings, and confirming Tribal defendants' Miranda rights under Tribal law, the court does not intend to imply that Tribal police officers have ever done anything differently. To the contrary, if the present case is any guide, Tribal law enforcement officers have consistently respected defendants' Miranda rights, and will continue to do so.

F. Conclusion

This court holds that the protections guaranteed to individual criminal defendants under Rule 8(f) of the Crow Rules of Criminal Procedure are co-extensive with those guaranteed under the Fifth and Fourteenth Amendments by the Supreme Court's current Miranda jurisprudence, as affirmed in *Dickerson*, 120 S.Ct. 2326 (2000). The only exception is that indigent Tribal defendants must be informed that they are entitled to free legal counsel only to the extent that the Tribe funds the public defender's office.

A criminal defendant's right to relief under Miranda has always been limited to suppressing unwarned statements or confessions, so as to prevent them from being used in the prosecution's case in chief. Miranda and the Fifth Amendment have never prevented the police from forcing a defendant to submit to tests that did not involve "testimonial" evidence, and using that evidence against the defendant.

In the present case, Mr. Big Man's conviction was not based on any testimonial evidence covered by Miranda or Rule 8(f) of the Crow Rules of Criminal Procedure. Mr. Big Man was not entitled to dismissal of the charge against him merely because the arresting officer failed to inform him of this [sic] Miranda rights.

For the foregoing reasons, the judgment of the Tribal Court is affirmed.

Pursuant to Rule 16 of the Crow Rules of Appellate Procedure, this court's Mandate will issue automatically ten (10) days from the date of this decision, unless a motion for rehearing is filed and granted before that time. Mr. Big Man is directed to contact the public defender on or before that time so that arrangements can be made to serve the remainder of his jail time that was stayed pending this appeal. This case is remanded to the Tribal Court for execution of the sentence.

Navajo Nation Supreme Court
Navajo Nation v. Rafael Rodriguez (2004)
5 Am. Tribal Law 473, 8 Nav. R. 604
Before FERGUSON, Acting Chief Justice, and HOLGATE, Associate Justice (by designation).

Opinion
This case concerns the admissibility of a confession in a criminal case. Based on our review, we vacated the conviction and released Appellant in a previous order. Our reasons are set out below.

I

The relevant facts are undisputed. The Navajo Nation police arrested Appellant Rafael Rodriguez ("Rodriguez") following a shooting at a trailer park in Kayenta. While in custody, Investigator Kirk Snyder ("Investigator Snyder") of the Kayenta Police District interviewed Rodriguez. Investigator Snyder began the interview by stating to Rodriguez that his alleged actions could put in him in federal prison for up to sixty years and could result in a fine of a million and a half dollars. Investigator Snyder then produced an "advice of rights" form, a document laying out several purported rights, apparently based on the United States Supreme Court's ruling in *Miranda v. Arizona*, 384 U.S. 436, 86 S.Ct. 1602, 16 L.Ed.2d 694 (1966). The form was in English, and there is no evidence that Investigator Snyder explained each of those rights in English or Navajo. Rodriguez signed a waiver on the bottom of the form, and then proceeded to write out a lengthy confession implicating himself as the shooter.

The Navajo Nation filed a criminal complaint against Rodriguez in the Kayenta District Court seeking a conviction for the offense of Aggravated Assault. The Navajo Nation submitted the advice of rights form and the Confession during the testimony of Investigator Snyder. After hearing objections from Rodriguez, the court admitted both into evidence. After hearing the witnesses and reviewing the evidence the Kayenta District Court found Rodriguez guilty, and sentenced him to one year in jail. Rodriguez then filed this appeal.

We initially remanded the case to Kayenta District Court in light of our opinion in *Navajo Nation v. Badonie*, 5 Am. Tribal Law 416, 2004 WL 5658159 (Nav.2004), for the court to include findings of fact and conclusions of law. After the court did that, Rodriguez re-filed his appeal, and both sides submitted briefs.

This Court heard oral argument on October 22, 2004. We issued an order of release on October 26, 2004 vacating the conviction and requiring the Department of Corrections to immediately release Rodriguez. We stated that an opinion giving reasons would follow. We now issue that opinion.

II

The issues in this case are (1) whether a criminal defendant must be present at an appellate hearing, (2) whether a coerced confession may be used in a criminal proceeding to establish the truth of the allegations in the criminal complaint; and (3) whether the provision of an English language form informing a person in custody of his or her rights, and a signed waiver by that person on the form, without more, is sufficient for a confession to be voluntary.

III

As a threshold matter, we dispose of an argument made by Rodriguez's counsel concerning his absence from the oral argument. She argued that the Navajo Rules of Criminal Procedure required the Navajo Nation to bring him to the appellate hearing. The Navajo Nation conceded this point, and claimed that he was "in route" from the Tuba City Detention Center. Despite this claim, Rodriguez never appeared. Though his counsel did not cite a rule, she presumably was referring to Rule 16 which requires that "the defendant shall be present at the arraignment and at every stage of the trial, including the impaneling of the jury and return of the verdict, and at the imposition of sentence." Nav.R.Cr.P. 16(a).

This rule does not require the presence of the defendant at the appellate oral argument. The key word in this rule is "trial." The rule clearly requires the defendant's presence only at the lower court trial through the sentencing phase. The rule does not mention the appellate process. Further, the Rules of Criminal Procedure do not apply to appeals, which are covered by the Rules of Appellate Procedure. The appellate rules contain no requirement that the defendant be present. Therefore, there was no requirement that Rodriguez attend, and no prejudice to his case because he was not there. His counsel was there, and represented his interests at the hearing. Though the defendant's attendance is not required, we encourage the parties to agree that he or she may attend, so that he or she may observe and provide guidance to his or her counsel. We now turn to the main issue in this case: the admissibility of Rodriguez's statement to the police.

IV

Rodriguez argues that the District Court wrongly allowed the Confession into evidence for the truth of the allegations in the criminal complaint. He contends that Investigator Snyder coerced the statement through threats and other pressure. He also contends that, even if there was no coercion, the "advice of rights form" itself is insufficient, as applied to him, as a waiver of his right not to give a statement to the police. At oral argument the Navajo Nation conceded that there was a "degree of coercion" by Investigator Snyder, but that the confession was nonetheless valid because Rodriguez signed the advice of rights form, thereby waiving his right not to make the statement.

The Court makes a preliminary observation concerning the oral argument. Neither side was prepared to discuss the confession admissibility issue. Rodriguez's brief contains no citation to any statute, case law, or Navajo common law or principle concerning confessions, and his counsel did not submit any at the oral argument. When asked about the Indian Civil Rights Act, the Navajo Bill of Rights, and the possible application of *Miranda v. Arizona*, 384 U.S. 436, 86 S.Ct. 1602, 16 L.Ed.2d 694 (1966), his counsel admitted having no knowledge of any of these sources of law. The Navajo Nation, though showing knowledge of these laws, admitted having no knowledge of the actual facts in this case to apply them, asserting that she was not the attorney who presented the case to the lower court. Ordinarily, we rely on the parties, especially the appellant, to argue their points and provide us with guidance on the relevant law and its application to the record in the case. We would be severely limited in our discussion if we were to rely on the parties in this case. Because the issues are of such importance to the Navajo Nation, we cannot limit ourselves to the arguments made by the parties.

A. 2 Section 8 of our Navajo Bill of Rights protects criminal defendants from being "compelled . . . to be a witness against themselves." 1 N.N.C. § 8. This provision is almost identical in language to the equivalent section of the Indian Civil Rights Act, 25 U.S.C. § 1302(4) (Indian tribe cannot "compel any person in a criminal case to be a witness against himself"), and the Fifth Amendment to the United States Constitution (no person can be "compelled in any criminal case to be a witness against himself"). In *Navajo Nation v. McDonald*, we recognized that the right against self-incrimination under our Bill of Rights is fundamental. 7 Nav. R. 1, 13 (Nav.Sup.Ct.1992). A person cannot give information for his or her own punishment unless there is a "knowing and voluntary decision to do so." Id. We interpreted the English words in our Bill of Rights in light of the Navajo principle rejecting coercion. Id. We said that "others may 'talk' about a Navajo, but that does not mean coercion can be used to make that person admit guilt or the facts leading to a conclusion of guilt." Id.

We reiterate these principles today. Our Navajo Bill of Rights, as informed by the Navajo value of individual freedom, prohibits coerced confessions. We expand upon McDonald by applying these principles to a person in police custody. The police department is an arm of the Navajo government, and as such must recognize a person's rights in much the same ways, and to the same extent, as must our courts. Therefore, in this case, the right against coerced self-incrimination attached not when Rodriguez first appeared before the district court, but when he was placed in police custody and was interviewed by Investigator Snyder.

Based on the Navajo Nation's concession that the police coerced Rodriguez, we have no choice but to conclude that coercion occurred. The Navajo Nation did not dispute that the investigator threatened Rodriguez by indicating to him the possibility of sixty years of federal jail time and a fine of one and a half million dollars before Rodriguez reviewed and signed the advice of rights form. Though the Navajo Nation referred to a "degree of coercion" without defining "degree," we do not see how coercion can be measured by degrees. Either the police coerced Rodriguez or it did not. The parties agree that Rodriguez was coerced, and we find that any degree of coercion is in violation of the Navajo Bill of Rights.

B. The coercion itself may be enough to vacate Rodriguez's conviction, however we also consider the Navajo Nation's argument that his waiver on the advice of rights form was enough for his confession to be admissible. As discussed above, the right against self-incrimination in the Navajo Nation includes the requirement that a confession be "knowing." *McDonald*, 7 Nav. R. at 13. Even if no coercion occurred, we must decide what rights Rodriguez had when he signed the waiver. The main question is whether the protections recognized in the United States Supreme Court's decision in Miranda apply on the Navajo Nation, or whether this Court should apply some other approach.

In giving meaning to the right against self-incrimination, this Court does not have to directly apply federal interpretations of the Bill of Rights. In interpreting the Navajo Bill of Rights and the Indian Civil Rights Act, as with other statutes that contain ambiguous language, we first and foremost make sure that such interpretation is consistent with the Fundamental Laws of the Dine. Navajo Nation Council Resolution No. CN–69–02 (November 1, 2002). That the Navajo Nation Council explicitly adopts language from outside sources, or that a statute contains similar language, does not, without more, mean the Council intended us to ignore fundamental Dine principles in giving meaning to such provisions. *Cf. Fort Defiance Housing Corp. v. Lowe*, 5 Am. Tribal Law 394, 399, 2004 WL 5658062, *3 (Nav.2004) (statute adopted from outside source is not illegitimate, but must be carefully interpreted consistent with Navajo values). Indeed, Navajo understanding of the English words adopted in statutes may differ from the accepted Anglo understanding. Further, the Indian Civil Rights Act does not require our application of federal interpretations, but only mandates the application of similar language. Federal courts have declined to blindly apply federal interpretations of an equivalent constitutional provision in certain circumstances when tribal cultural values dictate a different outcome. See, e.g., *Randall v. Yakima Nation Tribal Court*, 841 F.2d 897, 899–900 (9th Cir.1988) (quoting with approval Handbook of Indian Law statement that interpretation "is not an easy process because [ICRA] concepts are not readily separated from their attendant cultural baggage"); *Janis v. Wilson*, 385 F.Supp. 1143, 1150–51 (D.S.D.1974) (interpreting equal protection provision in ICRA "with recognition of the Oglala's Sioux Tribe's unique cultural heritage, their experience in self government, and the disadvantages or burdens, if any, under which the defendant tribal government was attempting to carry out its duties").

While we are not required to apply federal interpretations, we nonetheless consider them in our analysis. We consider all ways of thinking and possible approaches to a problem, including federal law approaches, and we weigh their underlying values and effects to decide what is best for our people. We have applied federal interpretations, but have augmented them with Navajo values, often providing broader rights than that provided in the equivalent federal provision. See, e.g., *Duncan v. Shiprock District Court*, 5 Am. Tribal Law 458, 464–65, n. 5, 2004 WL 5658109, *4, n. 5 (Nav.2004) (applying federal definition of "equitable proceeding" but declining to apply Seventh Amendment historical test on right to jury trial); *Lowe*, 5 Am. Tribal Law at 398–99, 2004 WL 5658062, **2–3 (recognizing that Navajo Due Process protects a greater scope of "property" than federal due process). Our consideration of outside interpretations is especially important for issues involving our modern Navajo government, which includes institutions such as police, jails, and courts that track state and federal government structures not present in traditional Navajo society. See, e.g., *Mitchell v. Davis*, 5 Am. Tribal Law 434, 435–38, 2004 WL 5658158, **1–3 (Nav.2004) (using federal interpretations of civil procedure rules as part of analysis for interpreting Navajo court rules adapted from federal rules).

We hereby interpret the right against self-incrimination to require, at a minimum, clear notice by the police in a custodial situation that the person in custody (1) has the right to remain silent and may request the presence of legal counsel during questioning, (2) that any statements can be used against him or her, (3) the right to an attorney, and (4) the right to have an attorney appointed if he or she cannot afford an attorney. These are the rights already recognized by the Kayenta

Police District in their advice of rights form, and we confirm here that they apply across the Navajo Nation. Essentially, we adopt the minimum requirements from Miranda as consistent with our Navajo values. We have previously suggested, without explicitly holding, that this is appropriate. See In re A.W., 6 Nav. R. 38 (Nav.Sup.Ct.1989) (referring to "Miranda rights" required to be given in Navajo Children's Code); *Navajo Nation v. McCabe*, 1 Nav. R. 63, 64–65 (Ct.App.1971) (indicating Miranda rights not necessary without explicitly adopting standard).

However, we add the following. The mere giving of a standardized "advice of rights" form to a person in custody is not enough. The relationship between the Navajo Nation government and its individual citizens requires the same level of respect as the relationship between one person to another. In our Navajo way of thinking we must communicate clearly and concisely to each other so that we may understand the meaning of our words and the effect of our actions based on those words. The responsibility of the government is even stronger when a fundamental right, such as the right against self-incrimination, is involved.

In Miranda, the U.S. Supreme Court recounted the source of the constitutional protection against self-incrimination. Miranda, at 442–443, 86 S.Ct. 1602 (quoting *Brown v. Walker*, 161 U.S. 591, 16 S.Ct. 644, 40 L.Ed. 819 (1896)). Reminiscing about the English criminal procedure, the Court stated that

> if an accused person be asked to explain his apparent connection with a crime under investigation, the ease with which the questions put to him may assume an inquisitorial character, the temptation to press the witness unduly, to browbeat him if he be timid or reluctant, to push him into a corner, and to entrap him into fatal contradictions . . . made the system so odious as to give rise to a demand for its total abolition.

Id. With such inequities impressed upon the minds of American colonists, "a denial of the right to question an accused person . . . became clothed in this country with the impregnability of a constitutional enactment." Id.

We are not guided in our own criminal jurisprudence by a legacy of internal oppression. Nevertheless, the U.S. Supreme Court's discussion reminds us of our Navajo principle of hazhó'ógo. Hazhó'ógo is not a man-made law, but rather a fundamental tenet informing us how we must approach each other as individuals. When discussions become heated, whether in a family setting, in a community meeting or between any people, it's not uncommon for an elderly person to stand and say "hazhó'ógo, hazhó'ógo sha'áłchíní." The intent is to remind those involved that they are Nohookáá Diné'é, dealing with another Nohookáá Diné'é, and that therefore patience and respect are due. When faced with important matters, it is inappropriate to rush to conclusion or to push a decision without explanation and consideration to those involved. Áádóó na'níle'dii éí dooda. This is hazhó'ógo, and we see that this is an underlying principle in everyday dealings with relatives and other individuals, as well as an underlying principle in our governmental institutions. Modern court procedures and our other adopted ways are all intended to be conducted with hazhó'ógo in mind.

Considering the means by which Rodriguez's confession was obtained and the use of the advice of rights form, we now stand and say "hazhó'ógo." The transaction between Rodriguez and Investigator Snyder, and the way that the advice of rights form was presented to Rodriguez does not conform with the ways that people should interact. We must never forget that the accused is still Nohookáá Diné'é, and that he or she is entitled to truthful explanation and respectful relations regardless of the nature of the crime that is alleged. Likewise, a police badge cannot eliminate an officer's duty to act toward others in compliance with the principles of hazhó'ógo.

We therefore hold that the police, and other law enforcement entities and agencies, must provide a form for the person in custody to show their voluntary waiver. They must also explain the rights on the form sufficiently for the person in custody to understand them. Merely providing a written English language form is not enough. The sufficiency of the explanation in a Navajo setting means, at a minimum that the rights be explained in Navajo if the police officer or other interviewer has reason to know the person speaks or understands Navajo. If the person does not speak or understand Navajo, the rights should be explained in English so that the person has a minimum understanding of the impact of any waiver. Only then will a signature on a waiver form allow admission of any subsequent statement into evidence.

In this case, there is insufficient evidence that the Navajo Nation police explained each of the rights on the form to Rodriguez. Consequently, even if there was no preceding coercion, there was not a "voluntary" waiver of his rights.

V. The remaining question is the effect of the improper admission of the confession on the conviction. We questioned both sides at oral argument whether, despite the inadmissibility of the confession, there still was sufficient evidence to maintain the conviction. In reviewing the order of the District Court, we conclude that the confession was a significant part of the evidence used by the court to reach its ruling. To parse out the confession from the rest of the evidence at this level and speculate on what the District Court would have done if the confession was never admitted at trial would be improper. Given the importance of the fundamental right of the defendant against self-incrimination, and the difficulty, if not impossibility of retroactively reviewing a case as if that evidence never entered into the court's decision, the vacating of the conviction and release of the defendant was proper.

We did not come to this decision lightly. The crime which Rodriguez was accused of committing is a serious one. However, the seriousness of the crime does not excuse the conceded violation of the defendant's rights. Therefore, though we had significant reservations, we decided the only proper remedy was to vacate the conviction and release the defendant.

VI. Based on the above, we vacated the conviction and released Rodriguez.

Nonverbal Evidence

The privilege against self-incrimination protects a defendant from being compelled to testify against himself or otherwise provide evidence of a testimonial or communicative nature (e.g., police interrogations, testimony at trial). However, the privilege against self-incrimination does not prevent the government from:

1. Drawing a blood sample from an unwilling accused;[7]
2. Making the accused give handwriting samples;[8]
3. Making the accused appear before witnesses for possible identification;
4. Fingerprinting suspects; or
5. Making the accused repeat certain words or gestures or give voice samples.[9]

However, there are other rights that must be considered and protected.

When lineups and photo identifications occur, the defendant's right to due process must also be protected. All identification procedures must not be "so impermissibly suggestive as to give rise to a very substantial likelihood of **irreparable** misidentification."[10] If the identification procedure is unfairly suggestive, then it is a denial of due process, and state and federal courts must exclude the identification at trial.

In determining whether an identification procedure was so unfair as to deny due process of the law, it is necessary to consider all of the circumstances surrounding the identification. Some of the factors that are relevant to the fairness of a particular identification include the witness's opportunity to view the criminal at the time of the crime, the witness's degree of attention at the time of the crime, the accuracy of any prior description given by the witness, the length of time between the crime and identification, and any suggestiveness in the identification procedure.[11]

Conclusion

Because of the serious consequences for breaking the law, all suspects should have information about their rights before they begin answering questions. Tribal courts have used both persuasive case law from the federal courts as well as their own tribal customs and values to establish the type of warnings that must be provided to suspects. These warnings are intended to protect the fundamental rights of defendants, and tribal courts have the authority to require law enforcement to abide by these fundamental principles.

Questions

1. Why are Miranda warnings required in federal and state courts?
2. Should tribal courts consider cultural values of honesty and respect when reviewing whether warnings are required under tribal law?

3. In *Swinomish v. Reed*, what aspect of the conversation did the court rely upon to make the ruling that the interrogation violated the defendant's rights?
4. In *Crow v. Big Man*, did the Crow Court of Appeals treat the *Miranda* case as binding or persuasive? Did Mr. Big Man waive his rights? How do we know?
5. In *Navajo v. Rodriguez*, how does the Navajo Supreme Court use traditional Navajo common law to consider the Miranda warnings?

In Your Community
1. Does your nation require law enforcement to provide warnings to suspects before questioning them?
2. Has your tribal court provided any guidance for law enforcement and prosecutors seeking to use "nonverbal" evidence against defendants?

Terms Used in Chapter 20
Ambiguous: Having more the one reasonable interpretation.
Impeach: To show that a witness is being untruthful.
Incommunicado: A condition in which a person accused of a crime does not have the right to communicate with anyone other than the custodian.
Interrogation: The questioning by police of a person suspected of a crime.
Irreparable: Impossible to repair, rectify, or amend.
Self-incrimination: Anything said or done by a person that implicates herself in a crime.
Sociolinguistic: Pertaining to the study of relationships between language and the social and cultural factors that affect it.
Voir dire: The preliminary in-court questioning of a potential juror to determine that person's suitability to decide a case.

Notes
1. Rupert Ross, *Dancing with a Ghost: Exploring Indigenous Reality* (Octopus, 1992), 13–14.
2. Ibid., 4.
3. Ibid., 12–13.
4. Ibid., 22–26.
5. *Michigan v. Mosley*, 423 U.S. 96 (1975).
6. *Edwards v. Arizona*, 451 U.S. 477 (1981).
7. *Schmerber v. California*, 384 U.S. 757 (1966).
8. *Gilbert v. California*, 388 U.S. 263 (1967).
9. *Schmerber v. California*, 384 U.S. 757, 764 (1966).
10. *Simmons v. U.S.*, 390 U.S. 377 (1968).
11. *Neil v. Biggers*, 409 U.S. 188 (1972).

Suggested Further Reading

Floralynn Einesmann, "Confessions and Culture: The Intersection of Miranda and Diversity," 90 *J. of Crime, Law and Criminology* 1 (1999).

Sheri Lynn Johnson, "Confessions, Criminals and Community," 26 *Harvard C.R.-C.L.L. Review* 327 (1991).

Search and Seizure   Chapter 21

The Indian Civil Rights Act (ICRA) protects against unreasonable searches and seizures. While many Native cultures have some traditional expectations of privacy, tribal cultures have not always divided the public and private sphere into distinct and separate entities. For example, among some tribal cultures, most property was considered communal property, people used each other's property, and only a careless use of property would result in a sanction.[1] Nevertheless, as tribal nations have developed contemporary tribal justice systems, they have simultaneously developed legal protections, in addition to ICRA, that protect people from unreasonable search and seizure.

The provisions of ICRA which apply to searches and seizures are sections (2) and (8):

> No Indian tribe in exercising powers of self-government shall—
>
> (2) *violate the right of the people to be secure in their persons, houses, papers, and effects against unreasonable search and seizures, nor issue warrants, but upon probable cause, supported by oath or affirmation, and particularly describing the place to be searched and the person or thing to be seized;*
> (8) *. . . deprive any person of liberty or property without due process of law*

A search is any government intrusion upon a person's reasonable and justifiable expectation of privacy. A seizure is the exercise of **dominion** or control by government over a person or thing. Search and seizure procedures involve balancing the individual's right to privacy against the government's need to gather information or collect evidence against criminals and protect society against crime.

In applying ICRA, courts must determine whether a defendant has exhibited an expectation of privacy and that this expectation of privacy is considered by society to be reasonable. Generally, abandoned property such as trash and abandoned vehicles do not fall under the protection of ICRA, as it is not a search because as abandoned property a person does not have an expectation of privacy. Property in the public domain would not fall under the scope of ICRA, either.

ICRA does not provide an absolute right to privacy, nor does it prohibit all searches. It only prohibits unreasonable searches. In deciding if a search is reasonable, the courts look at the facts and circumstances of each individual case. In general, however, a search or seizure is reasonable only if it is made under a valid search warrant or there is legal exception for the search or seizure without a search warrant.

As with an arrest warrant, the purpose of a search warrant is to regulate the activity of the police. A neutral and detached judge reviews an application for a warrant and makes an independent and neutral determination of whether there is probable cause to issue the warrant. The judge is not involved in the actual determination of guilt when considering the application for a warrant and the approval by a judge provides protection for people's privacy and civil rights. The judge is not influenced by incriminating evidence found subsequent to the search. Furthermore, many believe that the warrant requirement prevents police from abusing their powers or engaging in unlawful actions. However, it is important to note that nongovernmental searches and seizures are not covered by ICRA.

Applicable Law

In order for a search or seizure to be valid in Indian country, the police must comply with both the applicable tribal law and the provisions of ICRA. There is a vast body of U.S. constitutional law interpreting the provisions of the U.S. Bill of Rights, on which ICRA was patterned. In fact, some of the relevant U.S. Supreme Court cases are discussed in this textbook. But remember that the federal and state court cases interpreting rights are only a guide in Indian country, not the law. The tribal court cases discussed are the law for their particular tribe but can be a guide for other tribal courts.

Procedures concerning searches and seizures must also comply with the provisions of the applicable tribal code or constitution. If the tribal code or constitution imposes procedures that are stricter than the provisions of ICRA, the search and seizure procedures must comply with both ICRA and the tribal code or constitution in order to be valid.

In state and federal court systems and in many tribal courts, any evidence obtained from an invalid search or seizure is not admissible at the defendant's trial, which is referred to as the exclusionary rule. When the evidence is admitted in violation of the exclusionary rule, the conviction may be reversed upon appeal.

Also, for ICRA to apply, the person challenging the search or seizure must have **standing**, or the legal right to go into court and challenge the conduct of the police. The standing question arises in many cases, but with regard to criminal procedure, the question arises over whether a person owned or possessed the property that was seized and is being used against that person in court. Generally, only people who owned or possessed the property seized can object to its being used against them in court. So someone could not accuse police of unreasonable search and seizure of property seized in someone else's house.

Search Warrants

A search or seizure is presumed reasonable under ICRA if it is made under a valid search warrant or there is some special justification for the search or seizure. Similar to an arrest warrant, a search warrant is a written court order obtained from a judge and commands the police to search a specified dwelling or area. A search warrant must be based upon probable cause, be supported by an affirmation or an oath, and describe in detail the place to be searched and the person or thing to be seized. Many tribal codes specify search warrant requirements.

Ute Indian Tribal Code

Rule 31. Search and Seizure

1. *A search warrant authorized under this rule may be issued by a Tribal judge on a request of a Tribal police officer, or any police officer or law enforcement officer of the federal, state or municipal government.*
2. *A warrant may be issued under this rule to search for and seize any*
    a. *Property that constitutes evidence of the commission of a crime;*
    b. *Contraband, the fruits of crime, or things otherwise criminally possessed;*
    c. *Property designed or intended for use or which is or has been used, as the means of committing a criminal offense.*
3. *A warrant shall issue only on an **affidavit** sworn to before a Tribal judge and establishing grounds for issuing the warrant. If the judge is satisfied that grounds for the application exist or that there is probable cause to believe that they exist, he shall issue a warrant identifying the property and naming or describing the person or place to be searched. The finding of probable cause may be based on hearsay evidence either in whole or in part. Before ruling on a request for a warrant, the judge may require the affiant to appear personally and be examined under oath. The warrant shall be directed to any police or law enforcement officer or official and shall command such person or persons to search, within a specified period of time not to exceed 10 days, the person or place named for the property specified. The warrant shall be served in the daytime unless the issuing judge otherwise authorizes on the warrant. The warrant shall be returned to the judge after service or at the end of the 10-day period.*

4. The officer taking property under warrant shall give the person from whom or from whose premises the property was taken a copy of the warrant and a receipt for the property taken or shall leave the copy and receipt at the place from which the property was taken. The return to the issuing judge shall be made promptly and shall be accompanied by an **inventory** of the property taken.
5. A person aggrieved by an unlawful search and seizure may move the Tribal court for the return of the property on the ground that he is entitled to lawful possession of the property illegally seized. The judge may receive evidence on any issue of fact necessary to the decision of the motion. If the motion is granted, the property shall be returned and shall not be admissible at any hearing or trial.
6. No law enforcement officer shall search or seize any premises, property or person without a search warrant unless he knows or has reasonable cause to believe that the person in possession of such property is engaged in the commission of an offense or such is done incident to a lawful arrest or under such other circumstances in which it would not be reasonable to require the obtaining of a warrant prior to the search.

[Section 7 omitted]

8. The term "property" is used in this rule to include documents, books, papers, and any other tangible object. The term "daytime" as used in this rule shall mean the hours from 6:00 o'clock A.M. to 10:00 o'clock P.M., according to local time.

Probable Cause

Probable cause for a search warrant is the same for probable cause for an arrest warrant, as discussed in chapter 19. There is no exact formula for determining probable cause. Judges issuing a search warrant must use their own judgment as to what is reasonable under the circumstances. In all cases, probable cause requires more than a mere suspicion or a hunch. There must be some facts that indicate that a search is justified. These facts must be sufficient to enable judges to make their own independent evaluation of whether probable cause for the search exists.[2]

The Oath or Affirmation

ICRA requires that the facts and information presented to the judge be supported by oath or affirmation. This is usually done in the form of affidavits (sworn statements) or sworn testimony. The affidavits or sworn testimony must contain more than mere conclusions by the police officer. Instead, the affidavits or sworn testimony must allege facts showing that seizable evidence will be found in the place to be searched. The judge must determine that these facts are accurate and relevant.

However, a judge may find evidence reliable enough to support a search warrant even if that evidence would not be admissible at trial. A search warrant may still be valid even if it is based on affidavits that are entirely hearsay (such as when a police officer swears to facts reported by victims, witnesses, or police informers).[3] The court will examine the warrant for probable cause using a **totality of the circumstances** test, which includes the reliability of the informant and whether the information was obtained in a manner justifying reliance upon the information.[4] The totality of the circumstances test is a legal test that allows judges to examine anything they deem relevant to their decision.

It is important to note that probable cause for a search warrant does not depend on whether seizable evidence is found. Instead, the primary question in determining the validity of search warrants is whether the judge acted properly in issuing the warrant.

In the following case, the criminal defendant argues that the search warrant used to find evidence against him was unfair. Read the decision and identify why the court upheld the search warrant.

Puyallup Tribal Court
Puyallup Tribe v. Darrell Keating (2000)
No. CR-00-123, 2000.NAPU.0000002 (VersusLaw)
The opinion of the court was delivered by: Lawrence Numkena, Chief Judge

Order Denying Defendant's Motion to Suppress
This matter came before the court on the defendant's motion to suppress.

Arguments of the Defendant
The defendant argues that the evidence should be suppressed by virtue of the information submitted for the March warrant being "stale and deficient."

The defendant is protected under the Indian Civil Rights Act, 25 U.S.C. § 1302.

There was no affidavit filed in support of the warrant, but merely a motion and order for warrant, and the defendant has not been provided with any affidavit in support of said search warrant.

The defendant cites Aguilar/Spinelli (*Aguilar v. Texas*, 378 US 108, 12 L.Ed. 2d 723 (1964), *Spinelli v. US*, 393 US 410, (1969)), as the standard for search warrants.

Further that there were hearsay statements that Diane Keating may or may not have made, and she could not have been legally on the premises because of protection orders.

Arguments of the Plaintiff
The plaintiff argues that evidence was lawfully obtained under a search warrant that was issued after a finding of probable cause. A defendant does not have an

absolute right and is not necessarily entitled to a copy of the affidavit supporting a search warrant.

The Puyallup Tribal Code does not require **notarization** of an affidavit.

There is no connection between the existence of a restraining order against Diane Keating and the validity of the search warrant. The Aguilar/Spinelli two-pronged test was overturned by *Illinois v. Gates*, 462 US 213 (1983), and that a "totality of circumstances" standard applies.

Findings

The court having considered the arguments, briefs, and review of the record finds:

1. On March 9, 2000 the prosecutor formally applied to the court for a search warrant of 1201 Goldau Road East, by a motion.
2. The court went on record for hearing on the application for search warrant and the tribe submitted supplemental information regarding "heavy trafficking activities," a Fire Incident Report citing a possible meth [methamphetamine] lab, and a second Fire Incident Report regarding a statement of Diane Keating, pursuant to Title 4, Rule 41(3).
3. The warrant #00-123 was executed on March 10, 2000 and an inventory was returned of items seized.
4. The defendant is protected under the Indian Civil Rights Act § 1303 (2), against unreasonable search and seizures.
5. Title 4, Rule 41 (3) states:

    The finding of probable cause may be based upon hearsay evidence in whole or in part.

6. The standard in Aguilar/Spinelli was overturned by Gates. Under Gates it states:

    The rigid "two pronged test" . . . is abandoned, and the "totality of the circumstances" approach . . . is substituted in its place.

    Further:

    The task of the issuing magistrate is simply to make a practical, common-sense decision whether, given all the circumstances set forth in the affidavit before him, there is a fair probability that contraband or evidence of a crime will be found in a particular place.

    In regard to probable cause the Court stated:

    . . . it is clear that "only the probability, and not a prima facie showing, of criminal activity is the standard of probable cause."

7. As to the issue of statements that may or may not have been made by Diane Keating, the Court also under Gates states:

> We agree . . . that an informant's "**veracity**," "reliability" and "basis of knowledge" are all highly relevant in determining the value of his report. We do not agree, however, that these elements should be understood as entirely separate and independent requirements to be rigidly exacted in every case. . . . Rather . . . they should be understood simply as closely intertwined issues that may usefully illuminate the commonsense, practical question whether there is "probable cause" to believe that contraband or evidence is located in a particular place.

8. Under Title 4, Rule 41, there is no requirement that the Tribe provide an affidavit for a search warrant to a defendant. The rule does provide that upon request a copy of the inventory be provided to the person from whom property was taken.
9. The court finds that the search warrant was issued pursuant to a finding of probable cause from a determination based on the "totality of circumstances."

IT IS ORDERED that defendant's motion to suppress is denied.

Search Warrants Must Be Precise

A search warrant must be specific as to the area to be searched and the items to be seized. The area to be searched must be described so that there is no ambiguity concerning which premises are to be searched. The items to be seized must be described with enough detail and particularity that the police officer executing the warrant will have little discretion as to what may be seized.

Colville Court of Appeals
Julie R. Swan v. Colville Confederated Tribes (2007)
34 ILR 6110

Opinion and Order
Julie R. Swan appeals her criminal conviction because a search warrant was issued on insufficient information and that the evidence obtained by law enforcement issuing the warrant are "fruit of the forbidden tree," was stale, and should have been excluded from her jury trial. We agree that the search warrant should not have been issued. Her conviction is Vacated.

Summary

A tribal police officer was approached by a private citizen and was informed that he had driven her sister to Julie Swan's residence; Swan's sister went in to Swan's residence and came back with cocaine. He then drove Swan's sister to his residence where she proceeded to "cook" the cocaine and then smoke it. The tribal officer drafted an Affidavit and approached a tribal court judge with his information and requested a search warrant. The judge reviewed the Affidavit [and] approved the issuance of a search warrant. The warrant was executed on Julie Swan's residence where drugs were found and she was arrested. Before trial, she filed a Motion to Suppress the evidence seized as a result of the search warrant, alleging staleness and other grounds. The trial court denied the motion. A jury trial was held and Appellant was found guilty of possession of drugs.

Discussion

Swan's argument revolves around unreliable hearsay and stale information. The informed citizen that approached the tribal police officer voluntarily described the details of an alleged drug buy by Appellant's sister. Appellant argues that the officer relied on information that was stale, and that there was no independent verification that either the informant was reliable or that potential drug activity was being conducted at Appellant's residence. Neighbors were not interviewed about any suspicious activity, a "sting" operation was not conducted by an undercover officer, nor did officers indicate that any additional investigation was done independent of the notification by the private citizen. The Tribes argue that information provided by a known citizen should be given more weight in veracity than an unnamed informant.

The eradication of drugs on our Reservation is a high priority for both the Tribe and its community members. We seldom question a magistrate's judgment when substantive facts presented for a warrant is sought by law enforcement in pursuit of that effort. However, a higher priority is placed on the individual right to be secure in our homes from unreasonable searches and seizures. The Colville Tribal Civil Rights Act, Chapter 1-5 of the Colville Law and Order Code, states, in part:

> The Confederated Tribes of the Colville Reservation in exercising powers of self-government shall not: . . . (b) Violate the right of people within its jurisdiction to be secure in their persons, houses, papers, and effect against unreasonable search and seizures, nor issue warrants, but upon probable cause, supported by oath or affirmation, and particularly describing the place to be searched and the person or thing to be seized.

We have only limited material information before us in this matter. However, a close look at the affidavit and the search warrant that were issued reveals that neither meet minimum standards that should be used for the issuance of warrants on the Colville Indian Reservation.

I. Affidavits for Search Warrants

Privacy and the presumption of innocence is a right of the people and the use of a search warrant is a powerful weapon that must not be misused when dealing with the sanctity of people's homes.

To obtain a search warrant, an officer must provide sufficient information to a magistrate to make an independent determination that probable cause exists that the search will result in discovery and seizure in the warrant application. *Edenshaw v. M IC*, 5 NICS App. 156, 159 (1999), citing *Illinois v. Gates*, 462 U.S. 213 (1983). The search warrant must be specific as to the place searched, and the items to be seized must be described with adequate precision so that the officer can recognize them. Edenilhaw, id., citing *Maryland v. Garrison*, 480 U.S. 79 (1987).

There must be probable cause to enter a home and to seize evidence. In the instant case, the Affidavit for Search Warrant consisted, in part, of two short paragraphs which described Appellant and the information by which the officer concluded that a violation of the laws had occurred. Paragraph 4(a) named Appellant, listed her date of birth and gave her residence address verified by H.U.D.

Paragraph 4(b) is a short narrative by the officer of being contacted by a citizen saying that he took the Appellant's sister to the Appellant's residence; that the Appellant's sister went into the residence and came out with cocaine that she had purchased from the Appellant. The citizen then returned with the Appellant's sister to his residence where she proceeded to "cook" the cocaine after asking for some specific materials (penny, soda powder, teaspoon and water).

A close look at the affidavit does not reveal any date or time given for when the alleged incident took place. It could have happened the day that the informant talked with the police officer or it could have happened any other day, possibly months before. There is no information that could give the independent magistrate any idea of the staleness of the information. The officer gives sufficient data as to his qualifications and knowledge, but does not remotely elaborate on any qualifications or experience of the informant citizen. The Court is left with too many unanswered questions. Has this informant been used before? Where did he obtain his knowledge of the "processing" of the alleged drugs? Was he a prior user? What was his relationship to either the sister or the Appellant? Could this voluntary information be based upon a potential grudge on the part of the informant against the Appellant? Police should not rely solely upon a citizen's allegations without some corroboration. The officer did corroborate that the residence was in the appellant's name, but apparently went no further with any additional investigation or independent corroboration of informant's information.

The final paragraph in the affidavit asks that the search warrant be issued because the officer submits that there is probable cause to believe a crime has been committed, that a search of the residence should be allowed so that the Appellant can be found. Nowhere does the affidavit request that paraphernalia or drugs be included in the search and seizure.

The law requires that when searches are conducted, the warrant must specify, in detail, the areas to be searched. The precision of the search and seizure procedures were instituted so that "fishing expeditions" would not be conducted at the expense of an individual's basic rights. It would follow then, that in order for the warrant to specify what and where to search, that the affidavit must also state, with specificity, what is to be searched for and where.

Moreover, the affidavit only requests that the officers be allowed to enter the specified residence to search for the Appellant. The warrant, however, expands the search to include the residence, attached sheds, out buildings or storage sheds and open places where a person could reasonably hide. The Officer's Affidavit mentions that a person could hide in various places, (footnote omitted) but the Affidavit does not ask to be allowed to search those places. The warrant allows seizure of all illegal narcotics, paraphernalia and items related to manufacture and sale of the illegal narcotics. It also allows the seizure of "all persons involved in the sale, distribution and manufacture of said illegal narcotics."

There is a great difference between what was requested in the affidavit and what was included in the warrant. This is the very type of discrepancy that the judiciary must be wary of.

An independent magistrate must make every effort to make sure that the information on the affidavit matches what is contained in the warrant, and that both are as specific as necessary to ensure that both sides receive a fair and independent judicial decision.

II. Minimum Requirements

What is the minimum information that should be contained in an affidavit? Each affidavit must be evaluated on a case-by-case basis, but there are some minimum standards that can apply to most affidavits.

The magistrate must be assured that a criminal act has occurred or is going to occur very soon without intervention by the police. There must be a time and place indicated when the violation is to have occurred or will occur. There must be some independent verification of the violation, or the veracity of the informant must be specified in order that the magistrate can make an independent assessment of the truthfulness of his allegations. The standard "who, what, where, when, why and how" should be addressed in every affidavit or at least a mention of why it is not included or doesn't apply before issuance of any type of warrant is issued. This should not mean that each affidavit will need to be a 10-page document. It just means that the magistrate should not have to "fill in the blanks" in order to determine that a warrant should be issued.

In the instant case, a simple explanation that the police had verified suspicious activity through their observation or interviews with neighbors would have bolstered their case. Also, information that the informant had a successful history as a drug informant or had other training that would qualify him as a drug expert, and that he had no malicious intent to point his finger at Appellant would have helped. What relationship the informant had with Appellant's sister and why she wanted him to take her to Appellant's residence might have supported the affidavit more. The Appellee argues that the informant is reliable because he used drug terminology and lived in the area, therefore the magistrate should have been able to determine that the informant was knowledgeable and was being truthful. While, by itself, this might have not been an issue in another warrant, combined with the utter lack of supporting information in this affidavit, this argument fails.

III. Search Warrant vs. Arrest Warrant

Was the affidavit in question requesting a search warrant or an arrest warrant? If we look at the plain language of the affidavit, it appears that the police officer is only requesting to search a residence for a specific person, the Appellant. An arrest warrant would issue for a person who is accused of committing a crime, which appears to be the case here. Yet, the magistrate issued a search warrant and expanded the search beyond what was requested in the affidavit, that is, to the person, paraphernalia and other items related to the sale, distribution and possession of narcotics. Again, magistrates need to be sensitive to not allowing law enforcement to go into people's homes and conduct unreasonable searches. Law enforcement must be specific in what they are looking for, where they want to look and it must all be reasonable to do so. If they want an arrest warrant to arrest a particular person, then that is what they must ask for. If they want to search a particular place for specific tools of a crime, then they must ask for that. If they want both, they need to ask for both. The Court should not authorize a search beyond what is requested in the affidavit unless there is a very good reason for it. If and when it does, there should be a sound basis for it along with a brief explanation in the search warrant or some other part of the record.

IV. Totality of the Circumstances

Appellee argues that this Court should look to *U.S. v. Leon*, 468 U.S. 897, 104 S. Ct. 3405 (1984). The Leon case seems to excuse law enforcement when they "in good faith" rely on a warrant properly issued by a judge. We can distinguish this case from the Leon case. The difference between that case and this is the information contained in the affidavits. The affidavit in Leon was extensive in listing the investigation done prior to requesting a search warrant. Here, no investigation seems to have been done, except for verifying that the residence was in Appellant's name. Where an affidavit is so deficient in the basic information, a judge should not issue a warrant, and if the warrant is issued, law enforcement should not be able to hide behind a "good faith" argument. The evidence seized in such a manner must be excluded.

Conclusion

The community loses when law enforcement fails to take even the simplest of steps when investigating and seeking a search warrant. As much as the Court dislikes vacating a conviction when all other procedures and trial are unquestioned, it cannot tolerate the ignorance or misuse of the safeguards that provide our members their constitutional entitlement to be secure in their homes.

There is a right way and a wrong way for government to exercise its police powers. Law enforcement cannot act with less than minimal information in seeking a search of a person's home and the judiciary cannot act with less than objectivity in the issuance of a warrant notwithstanding personal knowledge of the same to the community caused by drug use and activity. An unbiased judiciary is a key element of the Tribe's constitutional guarantees to its members.

There were no exigent circumstances described in the affidavit which would allow deviation from the basic requirements being met. Judges are well aware that drug activity is a constantly changing activity and what is here today may not be here tomorrow. However, that doesn't justify cutting corners when it comes to issuing search warrants that are not properly obtained and used in violation of a person's right to privacy and to be secure in his or her home.

Decision

The evidence gathered by law enforcement under a warrant and submitted at Julie Swan's trial was not lawfully obtained. Appellant's conviction is Vacated and this matter is remanded to the court for proper action consistent with this Order.

It is So Ordered.

Serving the Search Warrant

There are two other important conditions relating to search warrants. Generally police serving search warrants must follow the following guidelines:

1. Search warrants must be executed during daylight hours unless night searches are specially designated;
2. Search warrants must be served within a limited period of time after the warrant is signed by the judge (usually ten days); and
3. Officers serving a search warrant may force their way into a dwelling only after the officers have announced their authority and purpose and have been refused entrance. However, exceptions are allowed for these when to protect the officers' safety.

The Scope of the Search

Finally, the search and seizure must not exceed the scope of the search warrant.[5] The police do not have the power to obtain a search warrant and then make a general search. Instead, the search is limited by the specifics of the search warrant. The search may not exceed the premises described in the warrant. In addition, the search must be limited to locating the items described in the search warrant (e.g., a search warrant that authorized a search for a stolen twenty-inch television would not justify a search through three-inch desk drawers).[6] However, the police may seize any evidence of illegal acts that is in plain view during a valid search (such as illegal drugs lying on a table or a stolen car in the garage).

Appellate Court of the Hopi Tribe
Elmo Nevayaktewa and Emily Verna Mutz v. The Hopi Tribe (1998)
No. 97AC000004
Before Sekaquaptewa, Chief Justice and Lomayesva and Abbey, Justices.

Opinion and Order
In this appeal, the defendants challenge their arrests and convictions for the possession of marijuana pursuant to Hopi Ordinance 21 § 3.3.55. They raise a number of issues on appeal, including that: . . . (4) the evidence was obtained in violation of their rights to be free of unreasonable searches and seizures; (5) the police engaged in certain misconduct during the search; . . . .

Factual and Procedural Background
This case revolves around the discovery of sixteen marijuana plants at a trailer owned by Leroy Lewis. On August 19, 1997, defendant Elmo Nevayaktewa was residing at the trailer because Lewis requested that Nevayaktewa be responsible for the guarding, care, and preservation of it. On that evening, defendant Emily Verna Mutz was visiting Nevayaktewa. Sergeant Bennett Chatter received two reports indicating that the defendants were growing marijuana plants in ice chests and cans in the last bedroom of the trailer.

Sergeant Chatter telephoned the Honorable Delford Leslie to request a warrant to search the trailer for marijuana. Judge Leslie found that probable cause existed to believe that marijuana was present in the trailer and authorized Sergeant Chatter to sign his name on the original warrant that authorized the search of the trailer, a grey GMC pickup truck with New Mexico plates, and a red and white Chevrolet pickup truck.

Sergeant Chatter and Officers Emerson Ami and Selanhongva McDonald proceeded to the trailer and served the search warrant upon Nevayaktewa. Sergeant Chatter escorted the defendants to the front room while the other officers ascended to the second floor and found marijuana plants in the last bedroom. Officer McDonald secured the front room and watched the defendants while Sergeant Chatter went into the room where the marijuana was found. He saw fourteen marijuana plants in a white ice chest and two more plants in a large plastic container. All sixteen plants were confiscated. A subsequent search of the grey Chevrolet pickup truck with New Mexico license plates and the red and white GMC pickup truck parked in front of the trailer did not yield any new evidence. Officer Ami used a personal video camera to record the search.

The defendants were arrested for the possession of marijuana in violation of Hopi Ordinance 21 § 3.3.55. Both defendants entered a plea of "not guilty" at their arraignments. On August 28, 1997, the actions were consolidated. The Hopi Tribe filed a Motion for Change of Judge for Cause, asserting that the defendants could not receive a fair and impartial trial because Judge Leslie had issued the search warrant and was also prepared to sit at trial. Evidently, the motion was denied. The trial was conducted and the defendants were convicted of possession of marijuana and each was sentenced to ninety (90) days in jail and a $1,000 fine. The defendants promptly appealed their convictions. . . .

Issues Presented on Appeal

The defendants assert that: . . . (4) the evidence was obtained in violation of their rights to be free of unreasonable searches and seizures.

Discussion

[Points 1–3 omitted]

IV. The Sixteen Marijuana Plants Were Not Obtained as the Result of an Unreasonable Search or Seizure

The defendants also argue on appeal that the search of the trailer and the trucks and the seizure of the marijuana plants violated their right to be free from unreasonable searches and seizures under the Indian Civil Rights Act of 1968. Like the Fourth Amendment, the Indian Civil Rights Act creates a preference for the use of the warrant procedure. The warrant procedure is the favored approach because it creates an orderly procedure whereby a neutral and detached magistrate may make an informed and deliberate decision regarding probable cause. Moreover, this [before-the-search] procedure is preferred to ex post determinations because it helps prevent judicial biases that may arise after incriminating evidence has been obtained, and it also helps prevent police perjury because [before the search] it is more difficult to fabricate a story.

Hopi Ordinance 21 permits defendants to suppress evidence that has been unlawfully obtained. In this case, the police did obtain a warrant. Despite the fact that the warrant procedure is favored, defendants can still challenge the legitimacy of a facially sufficient search warrant. As this court articulated in *Hopi Tribe v. Randolph*, the defendant bears the burden of production and the burden of persuading the court by a preponderance of the evidence that evidence obtained pursuant to a warrant nonetheless was illegally obtained. The defendants assert three reasons why the search warrant was invalid and the evidence illegally seized: (1) the judge did not personally sign the warrant; (2) the warrant should have been served upon the owner of the trailer, Leroy Lewis, rather than upon the defendants; and (3) the warrant did not particularly describe the places to be searched. None of these arguments have merit.

First, the defendants rely upon the definition of the term "search warrant" contained in Hopi Ordinance 21 §2.4.1. for the proposition that the issuing judge must personally sign the search warrant. The defendants protest because Judge Leslie issued a telephonic search warrant and allowed Sergeant Chatter to sign the judge's name. The defendants ignore the fact that the term "signed" is broadly defined in Hopi Ordinance 21. (footnote omitted) More importantly, the defendants are attempting to circumvent the holding in *Hopi Tribe v. Miguel*, 93CR001527 (1993), that telephonic search warrants are permitted in Hopi courts. See also ARIZ. REV. STAT. ANN. §§ 13-3914(c), 13-3915(c) (1997): Comment. 24 WILLIAMETTE L. REV. 967 (1988) (on Oregon practice); *State v. Lopez*, 676 P.2d 393 (Utah 1984); *State v. Lindsey*, 473 N.W.2d 857 (Minn. 1991); *State v. Valencia*, 459 A.2d 1149 (N.J. 1983); FED. R. CRIM. P. 41 (c)(2) permitting oral search warrants in other jurisdictions. How else can a telephonic search warrant be signed? Therefore, the defendants' argument lacks merit. Second, the defendants contend that the search warrant should have been served upon the owner of the trailer, Leroy Lewis. However, "[w]hat is generally required is that the officer give appropriate notice of his authority and purpose to the person . . . in apparent control of the premises to be searched." In this case, the defendants were in apparent control of the trailer. Presenting the search warrant to the defendants served the purposes of the notice requirement. Specifically, the notice requirement serves to decrease the potential for violence because there will be no unannounced breaking and entering into the house, protects privacy interests because it minimizes the chances that the wrong premises will be searched, and prevents the physical destruction of property because no breaking and entering will be necessary. Therefore, the warrant was served upon the proper parties in this case.

Finally, the defendants assert that the search warrant failed to particularly describe the places to be searched in violation of Hopi Ordinance 21 § 2.4.2 and the Indian Civil Rights Act of 1968. Specifically, the defendants object on two grounds. First, the search warrant provided that a grey GMC pickup truck with New Mexico plates and a red and white Chevrolet pickup truck could be searched while the police officers actually searched a grey Chevrolet pickup truck and a red and white GMC pickup truck with New Mexico plates. Second, the defendants object because the warrant authorized the search of the entire house even though the police only had probable cause to believe that the marijuana was located in one room. With regard to the description of the trucks, the colors of the trucks had been reversed and the plates had been reversed. What the defendants fail to recognize is that the most important information in the warrant was the location of the trailer. When the police arrived at the trailer and saw the two trucks on the premises, it was easy to recognize that a minor error had occurred in the search warrant. It was still clear which trucks were to be searched. Moreover, none of the marijuana was found in the trucks. Therefore, the defendants suffered no injury even if the trucks were not particularly described. With regard to the trailer, the defendants assert that the warrant was overbroad because it permitted the police to search too much of the trailer. However, when police have probable cause to believe that contraband is contained within a home or trailer, it is appropriate to allow the police to search anywhere in the trailer or home where the contraband may be contained. If this search were not permitted, defendants could move the contraband when the police arrived and render it outside the scope of the warrant. This is an absurd result that would incredibly reduce the effectiveness of law enforcement without any corresponding benefit to legitimate privacy interests because the police already have probable cause to believe that contraband is on the premises. Therefore, the defendants' challenges to the validity of the search are unfounded. . . .

Order of the Court
For the foregoing reasons, the judgment of the trial court is affirmed and the case is remanded to the trial court for execution of the judgment.

Searches without Search Warrants

The general rule under federal law is that any government search or seizure without a valid search warrant is unreasonable, unless one of the exceptions exists, and therefore a violation of the U.S. Constitution. Some tribes may interpret ICRA in the same way. But recall that tribes are not bound by federal civil rights case law when interpreting ICRA. There are a number of exceptions to the warrant requirement in state and federal courts, and tribal courts may elect to allow these exceptions. Each of these exceptions involves some special factor or special circumstances that justify the governmental intrusion. The following exceptions to the search warrant requirement are recognized by courts:

- Plain view searches,
- Consent searches,
- Searches incident to a lawful arrest,
- Searches incident to "stop and frisk,"
- Automobile searches, and
- Emergency searches justified by "exigent" or emergency circumstances. Exigent circumstances include hot pursuit of dangerous suspects, imminent destruction of evidence, preventing an escape, and risk of harm to police or others.

Plain View Searches

If an object connected with a crime is in plain view and can be seen by an officer from a place where the officer has a right to be, it can be seized without a warrant. The theory is that no search is really necessary to reveal the evidence. There is no search when a police officer keeps his eyes open while in a place he has a right to be, even when the "view" is into private premises, such as the defendant's home or place of business. For instance, if the police are called to a home to investigate a burglary, the owner invites them into the house, and the police see drugs on the kitchen counter, the police can seize the drugs because they are in plain view. Therefore, if the objects are seizable evidence and the evidence is actually in plain view, the officer may seize the objects without a search warrant.

The plain view doctrine only covers evidence that can be seen from a place where the officer has a right to be. If a police officer sees evidence in plain view after gaining entry by trespass into a suspect's home or place of business without a warrant or other justification, then the intrusion is an unreasonable search not covered by the plain view doctrine. An officer could be in a home to arrest an individual pursuant to an arrest warrant, and anything in plain view would be seizable. Also, anything in plain view during a search pursuant to a search warrant is seizable even if it is not listed on the search warrant. An officer may also be conducting a search pursuant to one of the warrant exceptions and seize an item that is in plain view.

Plain View?

While a police officer is issuing a routine traffic ticket to Christina Colby, the officer sees a sawed-off shotgun on the seat of Christina's car. The officer may seize the gun without a search warrant since the gun was in plain view and the officer had a right to be where he was when he saw the gun.

Although the police often attempt to use the plain view doctrine to justify warrantless searches, the scope of the plain view doctrine is limited. Police are not allowed to search everywhere. They are limited to the items that are out in the open and in areas they are legally allowed to be. The following tribal court opinion illustrates some of the issues involved in applying the plain view doctrine.

Court of Appeals of the Navajo Nation
Navajo Nation v. Marie Franklin (1977)
1 Nav. R. 145
Before Kirk, Chief Justice, Bencenti and Bluehouse, Associate Justices
The opinion of the court was delivered by: Kirk, Chief Justice

This case came on appeal from a conviction of defendant-appellant of the charge of selling liquor in violation of 17 N.T.C. [Navajo Tribal Code] 561.

We are aware that the appellant took the stand in her own behalf at her trial and made statements that tend to support her conviction. However, there are important issues presented by this case which the Court of Appeals wishes to discuss and therefore we do not choose to uphold the conviction on that basis.

The questions presented by this case are:

1. Under what conditions may the police conduct warrantless searches when it is clear that they could have gotten a search warrant in advance?
2. What is the scope of the "plain view" doctrine under Navajo law?

Neither counsel for the appellant nor counsel for the government focused clearly on these two issues in their briefs and oral argument.

The facts, as best we can determine them from the incomplete record presented to us, are the following:

1. Acting on a tip from an informer, on March 7, 1976, the police, dressed in plainclothes, went to the home of Marie Franklin to purchase liquor.
2. When they knocked on her door, Marie Franklin opened it and, after some discussion, sold the police officer liquor in violation of 17 N.T.C. 561.
3. Upon being sold the liquor, the police arrested Ms. Franklin, entered her home, and conducted an extensive search, seizing an unspecified quantity of liquor, said by counsel for the [Navajo] government to have been in plain view of the opened door at which the purchase was made.

In any situation in which the police have information in advance of a planned operation sufficient to establish probable cause to obtain a search warrant, they must obtain such a warrant. To allow any other practice would in effect negate the substantive protections of Title 1, Section 4 of the Navajo Tribal Code. This is the "search and seizure" section of the Navajo Bill of Rights.

The situation in this case is confused by the fact that apparently the government is claiming that probable cause developed only at the scene and therefore a search warrant was not needed. We are not satisfied, upon examining the District Court record and after hearing oral argument, that such was the case. Even if liquor was in fact in plain view at the time of the arrest, the questions surrounding the search remain.

At the time Marie Franklin was arrested, her entire house was extensively searched. The plain-view doctrine as we apply it only permits the seizure of the thing actually in plain view, the theory being that no "search" was really necessary to reveal the evidence seized. Therefore, once the police gain access to a place to seize something they have seen while outside, they can only seize the object which was already visible and any other materials that then are in plain view of the thing being seized.

Obviously, then, the plain-view doctrine has limits. It does not authorize the police to open doors, drawers, and cabinets. Nor does this doctrine allow police to enter and search areas not within plain view of the thing being seized. The overreaching search in this case was indefensible. However, the record is not clear as to what evidence was seized in the illegal portion of the search and whether such evidence was material to the conviction.

Therefore, this case is remanded to the District Court with instructions to hold a hearing on the following issues:

1. Whether the Navajo Division of Law Enforcement had probable cause to obtain a search warrant in advance of the search;
2. Whether liquor was in plain view of the officer making the purchase; and
3. Whether any evidence seized in the illegal portion of the search was material to the conviction.

If it is determined by the District Court that the police could have gotten a search warrant but did not, or that no liquor was in plain view of the arresting officer, or that evidence seized illegally was material to the conviction, then Marie Franklin's conviction shall be reversed.

It is so ordered.

BECENTI, Associate Justice, concurring in the judgment:

> I agree with the decision but I think that we should make it absolutely clear that the police would be barred from using any evidence they get from a search conducted without a warrant when they could have gotten one ahead of time.
>
> Under our decision today, we are leaving open the possibility that the police can simply deny that they had probable cause far enough in advance to get a search warrant. I think the burden of proof should be squarely on the government in this matter. Otherwise, this issue will constantly come up in just about every criminal case.

> BLUEHOUSE, Associate Justice, concurring in the judgment:
>
> I also concur in the result but I do want to express my strong feeling that we should avoid putting our Navajo Division of Law Enforcement in a straightjacket.
>
> I can understand the dangers that lie in judicial approval of warrantless searches after they have happened. But that is a responsibility we judges must face up [to]. Of course, it is up to the government to establish probable cause and I think it will be very seldom that they could establish probable cause for searching a house without a warrant. It is not often that a policeman will spot contraband through an open door.
>
> There are many exceptions to the requirement of a search warrant. They are all based either on the concept of "exigent" circumstances or on the notion of what is "reasonable" in a given situation, because the Fourth Amendment to the Constitution, and Clause 2 of 25 U.S.C. 1302 by reference, requires a search warrant to protect people against unreasonable searches.
>
> This case is a bad one to use to clarify these issues because the facts were so poorly developed. That is why I agree with the opinion of the Chief Justice remanding this case to the District Court.

Consent Searches

The police may conduct a search without a warrant and without probable cause when a person voluntarily agrees or consents to the search. When the police claim consent, however, three factors must be established:

1. The person consenting must have authority to consent.
2. The consent must be voluntary.
3. The search must be limited to the scope of consent given.

THE PERSON MUST HAVE AUTHORITY TO CONSENT. A person may grant permission to search only his own belongings or property. Obviously a person in sole control of the property or belongings has the right to consent to a search of the property or belongings. A third party may also consent to the search of belongings and property if the third party has common authority or a relationship with the property.[7] The consent is valid even if the other party objects to the search. Also, if an individual reasonably appears to have authority to give consent and gives the police consent to search, and it subsequently turns out the individual did not have authority, the search is valid as long as the police reasonably believed the individual had common authority.[8]

Authority to Consent?

A landlord usually does not have the right of access to the tenant's apartment and cannot give effective consent to a search of the apartment. Similarly, a hotel clerk cannot give valid consent to the search of a guest's room.

THE CONSENT MUST BE VOLUNTARY. The consent to a search must be voluntary. A search will most likely be found unreasonable and in violation of ICRA if the consent of the accused was obtained by duress, coercion, or misrepresentation. The police cannot claim to have authority to search to obtain the person's consent. A police officer can deceive the person about the officer's identity, for example if the officer is undercover, but the officer cannot deceive the person about the purpose of the search.

The burden is on the prosecution to demonstrate that the consent of the accused to a warrantless search was voluntary. Whether the subject of a search knows of the right to refuse consent is a factor in determining the voluntariness of the consent, but it is not an absolute prerequisite to valid consent. Therefore, it is not essential that the police inform a person of the right to refuse consent to a search.[9]

THE SEARCH MUST BE LIMITED TO THE SCOPE OF THE CONSENT. A search that is conducted pursuant to consent must not exceed the scope or the area officers are given consent to search. The search is considered reasonable only if officers search just the areas they are given consent to enter. Furthermore, consent to a search may be revoked, and once the consent is revoked, the search must stop.

Searches Incident to a Lawful Arrest

Searches incident to a lawful arrest are one of the most common exceptions to the search warrant requirement. This exception allows the police to search a lawfully arrested person and the area immediately around that person for hidden weapons or for evidence that might be destroyed.

There are two important considerations in determining the validity of a search incident to a lawful arrest. First, the arrest must be lawful (i.e., it must be based on a valid arrest warrant or be a valid warrantless arrest). Because the search is based on the arrest, probable cause to search is not necessary. However, probable cause to seize the item must be present, meaning it must be an item related to the crime or a person who represents danger. Second, the search must be limited in scope.[10] Only areas within the arrestee's immediate control can be searched. When the suspect is arrested at home, the closets and spaces adjoining the place where the arrest takes place may be searched. But the search is only for individuals or weapons that could be used in a surprise attack on the officer.

The reasoning behind this exception is the risk to the officer. The suspect being arrested has an incentive to resist or flee and destroy or conceal evidence. Also, when the arrest takes place at the suspect's residence, there may be others within the home who could inflict harm on the officer. Thus, a search to ensure the officers' safety from weapons or other individuals and to preserve evidence is necessary.

Searches Incident to "Stop and Frisk"

As previously discussed, a police officer may stop and question an individual under certain limited circumstances. A police officer has the right to detain and question a person in the field if the officer has a reasonable belief—in light of the officer's own experience—that "criminal activity is afoot." If, after making the stop, the officer has a reasonable belief that the person is armed, the officer may also frisk, or pat down, the person's outer clothing. Only if the frisk reveals a "weapon-like lump" may the officer reach inside the suspect's clothing to locate and remove a weapon.[11] Where the "weapon-like lump" turns out to be other seizable evidence (e.g., burglar's tools or contraband), the search is probably still valid. This exception to the search warrant requirement was created to protect the safety of police officers and bystanders who might be injured by a person carrying a concealed weapon.

Automobile Searches

Police officers may stop and search an automobile that is actually moving on the highway or temporarily stopped if they have probable cause to believe it contains items that are subject to seizure.[12] This does not mean that the police have the right to stop and search any vehicle on the streets. The right to stop and search must be based on probable cause. The theory behind this exception is that an automobile on the highway, in contrast to an automobile parked at a person's home, is a "fleeting target," that is, it can move out of the jurisdiction before the police can obtain a search warrant.[13]

The area of automobile searches is a very important and controversial subject in both tribal courts and state and federal courts. There have been many recent U.S. Supreme Court cases concerning automobile searches. The general trend of these decisions seems to be in the direction of allowing more police flexibility concerning automobile searches. For instance, the U.S. Supreme Court, in *United States v. Ross*, held that police who have probable cause for a vehicle search under the automobile exception may search, without a search warrant, every part of that vehicle and its contents (including closed containers) that may conceal seizable evidence.[14]

If the police have probable cause to stop and search a vehicle on the highway, they also have the power to detain the vehicle until a search warrant is obtained or, where reasonable, to take the vehicle to the police station and search the vehicle there.

When police lawfully impound a vehicle, they may conduct a routine inventory search of the vehicle without a search warrant or probable cause. This is considered by state and federal courts to be reasonable to protect the owner's property, to protect the police against a claim that the owner's property was stolen while impounded, and to protect against vandals' finding firearms or contraband.[15]

Finally, in cases in which the police do not have what the U.S. Supreme Court has called an "**articulable** and reasonable suspicion" that a motorist is engaged in unlawful conduct, state and federal courts have held that the U.S. Constitution prohibits random stopping of vehicles to check the driver's license and vehicle registration. However, spot-check measures such as questioning all traffic at roadblocks or DUI checkpoints are permitted.[16]

Emergency Searches Justified by "Exigent Circumstances"

The police may enter a building without a search warrant to search for a dangerous suspect when they are in "hot pursuit" of the suspect and have reason to believe that the suspect is in the building. Once inside the building, the police may continue their search, including determining whether any potentially threatening person in the building is armed. Furthermore, any evidence within the "plain view" of the police is also seizable on the theory that the police had a right to be there during the sweep for dangerous people and the police officers were in the middle of their work when they saw the evidence.[17] Courts have also held that a warrantless search may be justified when there are reasonable grounds to believe that the delay in obtaining a search warrant would endanger the physical safety of the police officers or third persons or allow the destruction or removal of seizable evidence.[18]

Review the following cases regarding warrantless searches. In each case, identify the reasons that the court finds as to whether there was a valid search.

Hopi Tribal Court
Hopi Tribe v. Kahe (1994)
21 Indian Law Reporter 6079
Before Talayumptewa, Judge

Opinion/Order
Facts

Defendant, Thomas E. Kahe, is a member of the Hopi Tribe and First Mesa Village. On July 30, 1993 at 12:28 p.m., within the territorial confines of the Hopi Indian Reservation on SR 264 at M.P. 395.5, Thomas E. Kahe was pulled over by Criminal Investigator Alphonso Sakeva after receiving a telephone call from a person identifying herself as Mr. Kahe's daughter.

Mr. Kahe's daughter had telephoned the Hopi Police Department asking to check to see if it was her father's car she saw traveling towards the police station because he had not come home the night before. As Officer Sakeva was leaving the police station, he saw a vehicle which matched the description of Mr. Kahe's heading westbound on SR 264. Based solely on his concern due to Ms. Kahe's call, Officer Sakeva turned on his "wigwag lights" to stop the vehicle. Following the stop, Officer Sakeva recognized the driver as Thomas Kahe. However, he still asked for his driver's license. He detected a "faint odor of alcohol" on Mr. Kahe and noticed that his eyes were red. He asked Mr. Kahe to step out of the vehicle, which he did without any difficulty. Meanwhile, Sergeant Bennett Chatter arrived at the location and while he also recognized Mr. Kahe, the sergeant also asked for Mr. Kahe's driver's license. Mr. Kahe could not produce a driver's license. At that point Mr. Kahe was informed that he was being cited and arrested for driving while license suspended/revoked.

Mr. Kahe's daughter was notified to come and pick up Mr. Kahe's vehicle. Sergeant Chatter conducted an "inventory" search of the cab and trunk of Mr. Kahe's vehicle and confiscated an ice chest which contained twenty-five (25) 12 ounce cans of Bud Light Beer from the trunk. Sergeant Chatter neither sought nor received permission to search defendant's vehicle. Furthermore, Sergeant Chatter did not have any type of search warrant. After the "inventory" search, Mr. Kahe was also cited for possession of alcoholic beverages. When Ms. Kahe arrived at the scene, the vehicle was released to her.

Defendant argued that the stop was unreasonable and that any evidence seized as a result of the unreasonable stop must be suppressed. The police were merely responding to a request for a welfare check on Mr. Kahe. In responding to the request the police did not observe any law violations from the time Mr. Kahe's vehicle was seen and observed until it was stopped. Both officers recognized Mr. Kahe. Mr. Kahe was not cited for intoxication.

The Hopi Tribe argued that in a small community, such as the Hopi Reservation, welfare checks, when requested by the family of a person, are a common practice for law enforcement officers. Vehicle stops made by police officers to make welfare checks pursuant to the request of concerned family members are reasonable. The tribe also argued that defendant's "red, bloodshot" eyes and the faint odor of alcohol on Mr. Kahe's person was sufficient to constitute probable cause to search Mr. Kahe's vehicle without a search warrant. The court agrees with the former argument but remains unconvinced of the latter.

Findings/Discussion

The court finds that this court has jurisdiction over this matter, pursuant to Hopi Ordinance 21, section 1.7.2, Criminal Jurisdiction. The court further finds that the "welfare" check stop of Mr. Kahe's vehicle is reasonable for the following reasons.

The court considered the special circumstances of this case, including the telephone call from Mr. Kahe's daughter, her concern because her father had not come home the night before, and her concern for Mr. Kahe's welfare. The court also took into consideration customary and traditional ways of the Hopi people. Because of the extended family system, Hopi people look out for and take care of each other. It is Hopi to be concerned about the welfare of your family and neighbors and to make sure that they are okay. Therefore, when someone makes a request of the police to check on the well-being of a person it is expected that police officers have the responsibility and obligation to make the welfare check. Likewise, this court wants to encourage the principle behind welfare stops, it does not want to discourage calls from concerned family members with the threat that those individuals will be subject to arrest. Based on the information given, the stop to make a welfare check on Mr. Kahe is reasonable and permissible.

However, because the Hopi Reservation is considered to be a relatively small community, many people are related to or know one another. In this instant case, Mr. Kahe and Officer Sakeva are both members of the First Mesa Village. Mr. Kahe is a well-known person within his community, having served as tribal council representative from First Mesa Village as well as taking part in community related activities. Therefore, asking for Mr. Kahe's driver's license for identification in this situation was not necessary when identification was immediate. At this point, the purpose of this particular welfare stop was satisfied. The inquiry should not have gone any further.

When Officer Sakeva stopped Mr. Kahe's vehicle, the officer observed a "faint odor of alcohol" on Mr. Kahe and that his eyes were "red." However, when asked to exit his vehicle, Mr. Kahe did so without any difficulty. There was no evidence of alcoholic beverages in plain view anywhere inside the vehicle. The Hopi Tribe argued that there was probable cause to search his vehicle due to Mr. Kahe's appearance and the fact that he did not come home the night before. The Hopi Tribe further argued that, because probable cause existed, a search warrant was not necessary. However, the court finds that the Hopi Tribe's argument is without merit. The warrantless search of the cab and trunk of Mr. Kahe's vehicle was unreasonable and unlawful.

Orders

It is hereby ordered that the stop to make a welfare check on Mr. Kahe was reasonable and lawful.

It is further ordered that henceforth following shall be the procedures which law enforcement officers shall follow in making welfare stops.

1. Upon a request from an identified caller, whether family member or neighbor, to Hopi Law Enforcement regarding concern for the welfare of

a person, Hopi Law Enforcement officers are hereby authorized to make stops of motor vehicles to make welfare checks.
2. The law enforcement officer shall inform that occupant of the vehicle the purpose of the stop and advise the occupant to check with the person making the call to locate the occupant.
3. Because the Hopi Reservation is considered to be a small community, when a motor vehicle is stopped for a welfare check, if the driver or persons in the vehicle are identified by the officer making the stop, no further identification is necessary. If identification is not readily made, request for identification shall be made of the persons for identification purposes.
4. If in the course of making the welfare stop, the officer observes any obvious law violations, it is his duty and responsibility to respond to the law violation.
5. If a person is arrested after a welfare check, the calling party shall be notified of the arrest and advised to pick up the vehicle. If no response is received from the calling party or owner of the vehicle, the vehicle shall be impounded until such time as the vehicle can be released to the owner. At this point, an inventory search to secure the vehicle and its contents is proper and lawful. If there is probable cause to believe that contraband may be in the trunk of the vehicle, absent permission of the driver or owner to search the trunk, a search warrant must be obtained to make a lawful search of the trunk.

It is further ordered that all evidence confiscated as a result of this stop is hereby suppressed.

It is further ordered that driving while license suspended/revoked, 24412, is hereby dismissed with prejudice.

It is further ordered that possession of alcoholic beverages, 1402/93, is dismissed with prejudice.

Eastern Band of Cherokee Tribal Court

Eastern Band of Cherokee Indians v. Cruz (2007)
No. CR-06-1571-72
The opinion of the court was delivered by: J. Matthew Martin, Judge

Order

. . .

Finding of Facts
1. At approximately 10:34 p.m. on December 28, 2006, Officer Brian Kirkland of the Cherokee Indian Police Department (CIPD) received a call about a suspicious vehicle in a motel parking lot on the Qualla Boundary.

2. Officer Kirkland responded and found a vehicle matching the description given to him in the area indicated in the call he received.
3. Officer Kirkland observed the occupants of the car behaving suspiciously, by moving furtively within the vehicle.
4. Officer Kirkland explained that some drug addicts use the relative privacy of motel parking lots to smoke controlled substances.
5. When he approached the vehicle Officer Kirkland identified the Defendant as the operator of the car.
6. Officer Kirkland observed a quantity of steel wool and a pair of scissors on the front passenger part of the car in plain view. Officer Kirkland knew that drug abusers who smoke crack cocaine and methamphetamine use glass pipes packed with steel wool for the delivery of the drugs to the lungs.
7. After ordering the Defendant and his companion out of the vehicle, Officer Kirkland determined that he had probable cause to search the automobile.
8. A search ensued and allegedly controlled substances and paraphernalia were discovered.
9. Officer Kirkland did not seek a warrant from the Magistrate.

Discussion

The Court is called on to determine, apparently for the first time, whether the so-called "automobile exception" to the warrant requirement of the Constitution applies within Indian Country. The Court concludes that it does. C.C. § 7-2(d) provides that, where no Cherokee law is applicable, the Court is to look to federal law. In particular in C.C. § 15-7, the Tribe has adopted the protections of the Indian Civil Rights Act 25 U.S.C. § 1301, et seq. (1968).

This Court has previously found that the right to be free from unreasonable searches and seizures applies on Indian reservations. *EBCI v. Reed*, 3 Cher. Rep. 126, 128, 2004 N.C. Cherokee Ct. LEXIS 572, 7 (2004). More importantly for this inquiry, this Court has also found that "[t]he limitations imposed by 25 U.S.C. § 1302(2) are identical to those imposed by the 4th Amendment." Id.

The "automobile exception" to the warrant requirement of the Fourth Amendment can seem counterintuitive at times. The requirement has its origins in the doctrine established in *Carroll v. United States*, 267 U.S. 132, 45 S.Ct. 280, 69 L.Ed. 543 (1925) and *Chambers v. Maroney*, 399 U.S. 42, 90 S.Ct. 1975, 26 L.Ed.2d 419 (1970) in which the Supreme Court of the United States explained that the easily movable nature of automobiles makes them special for the purposes of the Fourth Amendment, where they, unlike dwellings and structures, can swiftly secret the fruits of criminal activities. This doctrine was linked in *California v. Carney*, 471 U.S. 386, 105 S.Ct. 2066, 85 L.Ed.2d 406 (1985) with the legal concept that as a part of being readily movable, vehicles have a reduced expectation of privacy. Probable cause to search for evidence of crimes, not necessarily a warrant, is all that is required to search a readily movable vehicle.

Thus, the Supreme Court of the United States has not hesitated to reverse lower courts who required a warrant to search a vehicle in the absence of exigent circumstances. See *Pennsylvania v. Labron*, 518 U.S. 938, 116 S.Ct. 2485, 135 L.Ed.2d 1031 (1996); *Maryland v. Dyson*, 527 U.S. 465, 467, 119 S.Ct. 2013, 2014, 144 L.Ed.2d 442, 445 (1999) (reversing a lower court which erroneously held "that the 'automobile exception' requires a separate finding of exigency in addition to a finding of probable cause").

The test therefore involves a two part analysis: whether the car was readily mobile and did probable cause exist to believe it contains contraband? In this case the answers to both of these questions is yes, and the Defendant's Motion must be denied.

Conclusions of Law
1. The Court has jurisdiction over the subject matter and the parties to this case.
2. The Defendant has standing to contest the search of the vehicle in question.
3. The Defendant's vehicle was readily mobile.
4. Probable cause existed for Officer Kirkland to believe the Defendant's car contained contraband.

ACCORDINGLY IT IS HEREBY ORDERED that the Defendant's Motion to suppress the search of his vehicle on December 28, 2006 by Officer Brian Kirkland of the CIPD is DENIED. This case is returned to the trial calendar and the Clerk is directed to set it on Officer Kirkland's next Court appearance date.

Three Affiliated Tribes of the Fort Berthold Reservation Tribal Court
Three Affiliated Tribes v. Crow Flies High (1991)
19 Indian Law Reporter 6009
Before Strate, Associate Tribal Judge

Memorandum Opinion
This matter came before the court on December 14, 1990 at which time the defendant made a motion to suppress evidence and statements obtained as a result of a November 11, 1990 joint state of North Dakota/Three Affiliated Tribes mandatory game check stop. Following testimony from Robert Baker, Tribal Game Warden; Gerald Fox, BIA Police Captain; and Jeff White, Tribal Ranger, each party submitted briefs on the suppression motion.

The evidence establishes that the defendant was stopped on Highway 23 within the boundaries of the Fort Berthold Reservation as part of a game check operation being conducted by state and tribal officers. The defendant's vehicle was stopped on the highway by a state officer and directed to an area where tribal officers were conducting game checks of vehicles which were operated by persons who appeared to be tribal members. The testimony established that all vehicles were being stopped at this game check regardless of any suspicion or belief on the part of the officers that a game or fish violation had occurred, whether state or tribal.

Tribal Game Warden Robert Baker testified that the purpose of the game check was to check for valid hunting licenses and to determine whether any harvested animals had been properly tagged. There was no evidence presented indicating this particular game check was implemented to obtain biological data on the Fort Berthold deer population as contemplated by the 1990 Tribal Hunting Proclamation.

Mr. Baker also testified that it was the state game wardens who initially pointed out the presence of game animals in the defendant's vehicle. Therefore, the discovery of any game animals in the defendant's vehicle by Tribal Game & Fish Officers was not **inadvertent**.

The defendant contends that the motion to suppress should be granted as the game check constituted a warrantless search and did not fall within any of the categories of warrantless search authorized by Rule 18 of chapter 6 of the Tribal Code. The plaintiff responded that this warrantless search is permissible as either a consensual search, the consent being the tribal hunting license, or as a search incident to a lawful arrest, arguing that the court should expand the definition of a search incident to a lawful arrest to include a search and seizure for contraband inadvertently discovered during a mandatory and valid game check. Finally, the plaintiff argued that the Game, Fish and Recreation Code (chapter 18-2) expanded upon the permissible warrantless searches beyond those in chapter 6, Rule 18.

The court declines to expand the definition of a search incident to a lawful arrest as urged by the plaintiff. In this case, the search was not inadvertent nor was it pursuant or incident to a lawful arrest. In fact, the search occurred prior to any arrest of the defendant. Accordingly, this search cannot be justified as a warrantless search incident to a lawful arrest.

The court also rejects the argument that the application for and receipt of a hunting license constitutes a written consent to a warrantless search contemplated by Rule 18(2). In this case, the search was conducted prior to the officers determining whether the defendant had a hunting license. Also, there is nothing in the hunting license application specifically authorizing warrantless searches or indicating an acknowledgment of and compliance with the tribal codes regulating hunting. The hunting proclamation sections dealing with game checks speak of road checks being implemented to obtain biological data on the Fort Berthold deer population. It is clear that this was not the purpose of the particular game check involved in this case. Accordingly, under the circumstances in this case, the application for and receipt of a hunting license does not constitute a valid written consent to a warrantless search pursuant to chapter 6, Rule 18 of the Tribal Code. In order to constitute a valid written consent to a warrantless search, the application, at a minimum, would have to contain a statement of compliance with tribal hunting codes and regulations, or, to avoid any questions, a specific consent to searches conducted under the tribal code or regulations.

Finally, the plaintiff urges that the motion to suppress should be denied as the Game, Fish & Recreation Code authorizes warrantless searches. However, the sections cited by the plaintiff all contain an element of probable cause as the basis for any search. Section 18-2-4(10)(a) speaks of a "reasonable basis for believing that a person stopped was hunting or fishing." Section 18-2-6(2) deals with the inspection of fish and game once an officer is aware such are in a person's possession. Section 18-2-6(3) requires probable cause that a fish and game offense has been committed to justify a warrantless search of a vehicle. Similarly, section 18-2-6(5) authorizes warrantless searches by tribal rangers when they have reason to believe that game or fish are held or possessed contrary to the tribal code. Although it may be that the court, when faced with a different case, may find that the warrantless searches authorized by chapter 6, Rule 18 are expanded by the provisions of the Game, Fish & Recreation Code, the authorization for warrantless searches in the Game, Fish & Recreation Code [does] not apply to the instant case.

As the search of the defendant's vehicle does not come within any of the provisions authorizing warrantless searches by chapter 6, Rule 18, the defendant's motion to suppress is granted.

Eastern Band of Cherokee Indians Supreme Court
Eastern Band of Cherokee Indians v. Reed (2004)
No. CR-04-1094-1103

Memorandum Order

. . .

The Court makes the following Findings of Fact:

1. The parties stipulated that the Defendant has standing to make this Motion to suppress evidence seized as a result of a search of his home.
2. The Defendant and his wife, Gerri Lynn Smith Reed, live on the Qualla Boundary in the Rough Branch community.

3. The Defendant's home consists of two travel trailers, approximately 12' × 20' and 10' × 16' connected by plywood and tarpaulins, creating additional space between the two.
4. In July, 2004, the Defendant's wife, Gerri Lynn Smith Reed, was placed on probation by the Honorable Monica Leslie, District Court Judge in the North Carolina's 30th Judicial District.
5. A condition of Mrs. Reed's probationary Judgment calls for her to submit to warrantless searches by her probation officer of her premises at reasonable times and in her presence.
6. Officer Glen Weeks, a Probation and Parole Officer of the North Carolina Department of Community Corrections was assigned as Mrs. Reed's Probation Officer.
7. Initially, Mrs. Reed failed to report for office visits, and thus Officer Weeks visited at the Reed residence.
8. In that capacity, Mr. Weeks came to Mr. and Mrs. Reed's home in July, 2004, and inquired about the whereabouts of Mrs. Reed.
9. Mr. Weeks was told by someone present at the home that Mrs. Reed was not there, however, the Defendant appeared and indicated that Mrs. Reed was in the shower and would be out shortly. Mrs. Reed did appear and met with Mr. Weeks at that time.
10. On August 6, 2004, Sergeant Julius Taylor and Officer Jose Rodriguez of the Cherokee Indian Police Department received information regarding a stolen, blue mini-motorcycle from a craft store on Highway 441 North on the Reservation.
11. Information obtained during their investigation led to suspicion that the stolen motorcycle might be located at the Reed residence.
12. Thinking that the State Probation officer could enter the Reed residence without seeking a search warrant, CIPD Officer John Nations contacted Mr. Weeks and asked that he join the CIPD officers at the Reed residence. Mr. Weeks agreed to participate in searching Mrs. Reed.
13. The CIPD officers also suspected that illegal drugs were present at the Reed residence, and for this reason, narcotics Officer Frankie Bottchenbaugh accompanied Officers Rodriguez and Nations and Mr. Weeks. Officer Bottchenbaugh was told by other officers that, because Mrs. Reed was on probation, the party did not need a search warrant.
14. Upon arriving at the Reed residence, Officer Nations and Mr. Weeks approached the door. Officers Rodriguez and Bottchenbaugh acted as backup. In light of their previous dealings with the Reeds and, considering the remote location of the residence as well as the nature of the information the officers had regarding controlled substance offenses,

all officers present, including Mr. Weeks, were wearing flack [sic] jackets, and Officer Bottchenbaugh was armed with an AR-15 rifle.
15. Officer Weeks knocked at the front door of the Reed residence. Mr. Reed answered the door, in his hand a hose with water running out of it. When Officer Weeks asked if Mrs. Reed was in, Mr. Reed replied that she was at her brother's home, and offered to call her on his telephone.
16. During the conversation with Mr. Reed, Officer Weeks could observe a blue mini-motorcycle on the floor behind Mr. Reed. Officer Weeks remarked to Officer Nations, "There's your motorcycle."
17. At that point, Mr. Reed was taken into custody and he was immediately "handed over" to Officer Rodriguez, who guarded him and ultimately placed him in restraints and into his patrol vehicle.
18. Officer Nations and Officer Weeks then began what they characterized as a "protective sweep" of the home. Mr. Reed protested the search and argued that the officers had no warrant to go into his residence.
19. Almost immediately, in the same area as the blue mini-motorcycle, the officers found a .22 rifle with some sort of device on the end of the barrel.
20. Moments later, a pit bull terrier jumped out from behind some furniture, and Officer Nations drew his weapon, however, the dog then curled up on the ground.
21. Officer Nations then called out, "Right here's a meth pipe." Moments later, "Here's some baggies," and then, "Let me look here."
22. Officer Nations was looking at a black soft zippered bag with the letters ETW printed on it. Officer Nations opened the ETW bag and found what he thought were drugs in it.
23. Officer Bottchenbaugh believed that Officers Nations and Weeks were searching for Mrs. Reed. They then called him into the house and he commenced to search for drugs, testing some of the seized items, including material in the ETW bag, for the presence of methamphetamine, and obtaining positive field results.
24. Ultimately, the officers seized the blue mini-motorcycle, the .22 rifle, a baggie with controlled substance residue on it, the FTW bag with what tested positive as methamphetamine in it, two pipes, other baggies, a digital scales and rolling papers.

Discussion

The right to be free from unreasonable searches and seizures applies on Indian Reservations. 25 U.S.C. § 1302(2). The limitations imposed by 25 U.S.C. § 1302(2) are identical to those imposed by the 4th Amendment. *United States v. Strong*, 778 F.2d 1393, 1397 (9th Cir. 1985).

The first question the Court must confront is whether the Officers had any lawful business even coming onto Mr. Reed's property. "Just as other punishments for criminal convictions curtail an offender's freedoms, a court granting probation may impose reasonable conditions that deprive the offender of some freedoms enjoyed by law-abiding citizens." *United States v. Knights*, 534 U.S. 112, 119, 151 L. Ed. 2d 497, 505, 122 S. Ct. 587 (2001) (quoting *Wyoming v. Houghton*, 526 U.S. 295, 300, 143 L. Ed. 2d 408, 414, 119 S. Ct. 1297 (1999)). The State of North Carolina, and the Tribe, in this case have a concern, "quite justified, that [Mrs. Reed, the probationer] will be more likely to engage in criminal conduct than an ordinary member of the community." Id. at 121. Thus, "[C]onditional releasees enjoy severely constricted expectations of privacy relative to the general citizenry—and . . . the government has a far more substantial interest in invading their privacy than it does in interfering with the liberty of law-abiding citizens." *United States v. Kincade*, ___ F. 3d. ___, ___ (9th Cir. August 18, 2004) (Slip Op. at 56) (upholding searches of probationers without suspicion as long as they are reasonable under the totality of the circumstances).

Inasmuch as Mrs. Reed lives with Mr. Reed, she diminished his right of privacy in their marital premises, while she was present, by being a conditional releasee. Officer Weeks and the other Officers therefore, were justified in going onto the Reed property to conduct a search of Mrs. Reed and her residence.

However, giving full faith and credit to the Judgment of Judge Leslie, this diminishment of rights, as well as the right of the Probation Officer to search, only applies in the presence of Mrs. Reed. C.C. § 25-5(a). In this case, Mrs. Reed was not present.

When the Officers arrived, Mr. Reed informed them that Mrs. Reed was not home, but rather was at her brother's house. On a previous occasion, he corrected someone who told Officer Weeks that Mrs. Reed was not present at the marital residence, and made arrangements for Mrs. Reed to meet Mr. Weeks outside the residence. No evidence was submitted to the Court which gave any indication that Mr. Reed was not being truthful about the whereabouts of Mrs. Reed. No evidence was submitted to the Court that any other person was present at the Reed residence, either.

At this point, the encounter began to change. When Officer Weeks told Officer Nations, "There's your motorcycle," Mr. Reed was taken into custody and a full blown search of the Reed residence began. The Officers who testified indicated that the blue mini-motorcycle was "in plain view," directly behind Mr. Reed in the doorway. A seizure based upon the "plain view" exception to the warrant requirement "is legitimate only where it is immediately apparent to the police that they have evidence before them. . ." *Coolidge v. New Hampshire*, 403 U.S. 443, 466, 91 S.Ct. 2022, 29 L.Ed.2d 564 (1971). While the officers could not be certain that the mini-motorcycle behind Mr. Reed was, in fact, the one they were seeking, it nevertheless was a blue mini-motorcycle matching the description of the one reported stolen and it was located where they expected to find it. The privacy rights of a person of whom police observe evidence in plain view are not violated because the officers had a right to be where they could see it. Id. Thus the observation was not a search. Id. Accord, C.C. § 15-1(e)(providing that no CIPD officer "shall search or seize any property without a warrant unless he shall have reasonable cause to believe that the person in possession of such property is engaged in the commission of an offense under the Code of Federal Regulations or under Tribal law."), cf., *Arizona v. Hicks*, 480 U.S. 321, 107 S.Ct. 1149, 94 L.Ed.2d 347 (1987) (suppression ordered when officers not looking for stolen stereo moved component to determine whether it was evidence of another, unrelated crime). Therefore, the seizure of the mini-motorcycle was lawful. The officers could make a limited entry into the home to secure it.

In doing so, they would have encountered the .22 rifle. Seizure of it was valid, as well under the plain view doctrine.

However, the officers actually entered the home to conduct what they characterized in Court as a "protective sweep." At least one of the search party, Officer Bottchenbaugh swore before the Magistrate and testified before the Court that they were, in fact, "searching for Mrs. Reed." The Court will take these search parameters up in reverse order.

First, there was no lawful authority to search the Reed home for Mrs. Reed. Any such search, beyond asking Mr. Reed if she was home, would have required a warrant. (footnote omitted) The Tribe has not submitted any authority which would indicate that there was any justification for searching the Reed home for Mrs. Reed. The Court can find none, either.

In *Maryland v. Buie*, 494 U.S. 325, 110 S.Ct. 1093, 108 L.Ed.2d 276 (1990), the Supreme Court considered protective sweep searches. The Court held that "there must be articulable facts which, taken together with the rational inferences from those facts, would warrant a reasonably prudent officer in believing that the area to be swept harbors an individual posing a danger to those on the arrest scene." Id. at 334. No such evidence exists in this case. There was a weapon noticed by the officers, the .22 rifle, but it was seen only after they began their protective sweep. The officers were wearing their [sic] flack jackets, but they did not articulate what kind of danger they thought they might face, or from whom it might emanate. They offered no evidence that anyone else was in the Reed home, including Mrs. Reed. Indeed, there was no one else home.

Furthermore the Supreme Court held that, "[t]he protective sweep must be aimed at protecting the officers and must extend only to a cursory inspection of places where a person may hide." *State v. Wallace*, 111 N.C. App. 581, 588, 433 S.E.2d 238, 242 (1993), disc. rev. denied, 335 N.C. 242, 439 S.E.2d 161 (1993). In this case Officer Nations went well beyond these restrictions by stating "Let me look here," and opening the FTW bag.

The evidence strongly suggests that Officer Nations, and Officer Bottchenbaugh were searching for drugs, not for persons. In particular, the scope and duration of the search went far beyond searching for persons. The Supreme Court held that the protective sweep should take no longer than is necessary to dispel the reasonable suspicion of danger. Id. The further search of the Reed home, beyond that needed to seize the blue mini-motorcycle and the .22 rifle was unlawful.

The Police are cautioned against taking shortcuts around the warrant requirement. When officers embark on an operation, as here, intending to conduct a search, the detour to the Magistrate's office is minimal and uncomplicated and is always preferred. As a general rule, most warrantless searches are presumed by the law to be unreasonable. While the warrantless search provision of a conditional release may appear relatively simplistic on the surface, as can be seen in this case, complications can always arise. To be on the safe side, to guard against unreasonable intrusions into rights of the public, and to avoid suppression in the future, if the Police wish to search, they should, if possible, always seek a warrant.

Conclusions of Law

1. The Court has jurisdiction over the parties and the subject matter of this case.
2. The Defendant has standing to make his Motion to suppress evidence seized as a result of the search of his premises.
3. The Officers had a valid right to be on the Reed property and to inquire of the whereabouts of Mrs. Reed.
4. The seizure of the blue mini-motorcycle and .22 rifle were lawful.
5. The further search of the Reed residence was unlawful and violated Mr. Reed's rights to be free from unreasonable searches and seizures.
6. Except for the seized blue mini-motorcycle and the .22 rifle, the evidence seized as a result of the search of the Reed residence must be suppressed.

ACCORDINGLY IT IS HEREBY ORDERED that the Defendant's Motion to suppress the blue mini-motorcycle and the .22 rifle is DENIED. The Defendant's Motion to suppress all other evidence seized as a result of the search and seizures of the Reed residence is GRANTED. IT IS FURTHER ORDERED that the Defendant's bond is modified to one thousand dollars ($1,000.00) secured with per capita garnishment.

Conclusion

Searches and seizures conducted by government must be done pursuant to a warrant based on probable cause or be conducted reasonably pursuant to one of the legal exceptions to the warrant requirement. Like arrest warrants, search warrants prevent police abuse by requiring a judge to make neutral determination whether probable cause exists. Reasonable searches that may be conducted as an exception to the warrant requirement are plain view searches, searches incident to lawful arrest and stop and frisk, along with automobile searches. Evidence discovered in violation of the search warrant requirement may be prohibited from being used in court, as discussed in chapter 22.

Questions

1. Do you agree that obtaining a warrant should be favored over any other approach to searches? Why or why not?
2. Should hearsay statements be allowed in an application for a search warrant?

Puyallup Tribe v. Keating

1. What did the defendant argue in terms of the legality of the search warrant in this case?
2. How did the court explain the requirements of probable cause in issuing a search warrant? Do you think the analysis is fair to defendants? Why or why not?

Swan v. Coleville Confederated Tribes

1. Why was the warrant not obtained lawfully?
2. What did the police officer need to do differently?

Nevayaktewa et al. v. Hopi

1. Who was present in the trailer when the law enforcement officers served the warrant in this case?
2. According to the Hopi appellate court, was the warrant precise enough? Why or why not?

Navajo Nation v. Franklin

1. Did the police have a search warrant before they went to Ms. Franklin's home?

2. How did the police justify their search of Ms. Franklin's home? What did the Navajo appellate court say about the extent of the search?

Hopi v. Kahe
1. Why did law enforcement stop the car driven by Mr. Kahe in this case?
2. What did the Hopi appellate court say about the need for law enforcement to conduct "welfare checks"?
3. What did the Hopi appellate court rule in regard to the evidence seized?

Eastern Band of Cherokee Indians v. Cruz
1. Why did the court rule the search was valid?

Three Affiliated Tribes v. Crow Flies High
1. Why was the car driven by the defendant stopped in this case?
2. Why did the court rule that the warrantless search was not justified? Do you agree with the decision?

Eastern Band of Cherokee Indians v. Reed
1. Why did the defendant have standing to make a motion to suppress?
2. Why was the seizure of the blue mini-motorcycle and .22 rifle valid?
3. Why was the remainder of the search unlawful?

In Your Community
1. How does your nation define probable cause for search warrants?
2. How does your tribal court determine whether the information is sufficient to issue a search warrant?
3. Traditionally, did searches ever occur in your nation? Was there any sort of standard prior to allowing a "search"?
4. Is a warrant needed to search schools in your community?
5. Does your tribal court allow plain view searches? What are the limits?
6. Does your tribal court allow automobile searches? When are they allowed?
7. Does your tribal court allow any exceptions to the warrant requirement? What are they?

Terms Used in Chapter 21
Affidavit: A written statement, usually about the truth of a set of facts, sworn to before a person who is officially permitted by law to administer an oath.

Articulable: Capable of being articulated; expressed easily.
Dominion: Legal ownership plus full actual control.
Inadvertent: Without intention; especially, resulting from heedless action.
Inventory: A detailed list of articles of property.
Notarization: Certification of or attestation to.
Standing: The right of a person (or party) to bring (start) or join a lawsuit because they are directly affected by the issue raised.
Totality of the circumstances: Test used to determine the constitutionality of various search and seizure procedures. The standard focuses on all the circumstances of a particular case rather than just one factor.
Veracity: Truthfulness; accuracy.

Notes

1. Vine Deloria Jr. and Clifford Lytle, *American Indians, American Justice*, 162 (University of Texas Press, 1983).
2. *Franks v. Delaware*, 438 U.S. 154, 165 (1978).
3. *McCray v. State of Illinois*, 386 U.S. 300, 311 (1967).
4. *Illinois v. Gates*, 462 U.S. 213, 230–231 (1983).
5. *Horton v. California*, 496 U.S. 128, 140 (1990).
6. *United States v. Ross*, 456 U.S. 798, 824 (1982).
7. *United States v. Matlock*, 415 U.S. 165, 171 (1974).
8. *Illinois v. Rodriguez*, 497 U.S. 177, 186 (1990).
9. *Schneckloth v. Bustamonte*, 412 U.S. 218 (1973).
10. *Chimel v. California*, 395 U.S. 752 (1969).
11. *Terry v. Ohio*, 392 U.S. 1 (1986).
12. *Carroll v. United States*, 267 U.S. 132, 153–54 (1925); *California v. Carney*, 471 U.S. 386, 392–394 (1985).
13. *Carroll v. United States*, 267 U.S. 132 (1925).
14. *United States v. Ross*, 456 U.S. 798, 820–21 (1982).
15. *South Dakota v. Opperman*, 428 U.S. 364 (1976).
16. *Delaware v. Prouse*, 440 U.S. 648 (1979).
17. *Warden v. Hayden*, 387 U.S. 294 (1967).
18. *Vale v. Louisiana*, 399 U.S. 30 (1970).

Suggested Further Reading

Pat Hanley, "Warrantless Searches for Alcohol by Native Alaskan Villages: A Permissible Exercise of Sovereign Rights or an Assault on Civil Liberties," 14 *Alaska Law Review* 471 (1997).

James B. Jacobs and Nadine Strossen, "Mass Investigations without Individualized Suspicion: A Constitutional and Policy Critique of Drunk Driving Roadblocks," 18 *U.C. Davis Law Review* 595.

The Exclusionary Rule: Remedies for Civil Rights Violations

Chapter 22

When a defendant's civil rights are violated, how should the courts respond? What happens when tribal police officers are accused of abusing their power? The text U.S. Constitution and the Indian Civil Rights Act (ICRA) are silent as to a remedy for violations of civil rights. Over the years, the U.S. Supreme Court has developed what is known as the **"exclusionary rule"** for constitutional violations. Many tribal courts have also adopted the exclusionary rule.

A simple example of the basic exclusionary rule:

Suppose Officer Joe decided to walk into Susan's home without a warrant. He sees marijuana plants in a bedroom and arrests her for growing marijuana. The prosecutor will not be able to introduce the plants into evidence because they were obtained by violating Susan's rights.

The exclusionary rule was created for two main reasons. First, the rule should discourage police officers from violating civil rights because they will not be able to secure a conviction. Second, the rule supports the integrity of the courts. If a court allowed this evidence in, it would be endorsing a constitutional violation.

The exclusionary rule applies to any governmental action, arrest, interrogation, or search and seizure that violate someone's civil rights. The exclusionary rule does not necessarily guarantee that a defendant will be acquitted—it merely excludes the evidence associated with the civil rights violation. There may be other evidence the prosecutor can introduce to prove guilt.

In subsequent years, the U.S. Supreme Court has narrowed the exclusionary rule and indicated it is a "judicially created remedy" for constitutional violations by law enforcement. Because a judicially created remedy can also be judicially modified, this development leaves the door open for the Supreme

Court to weaken or abandon the exclusionary rule—or for Congress to pass legislation abolishing it.

The following court case is an example of the way one tribal court has chosen to analyze and apply the exclusionary rule.

Lower Elwha Klallam Tribal Appeals Court
Lower Elwha Klallam Tribe v. James L. Bolstrom and Russell N. Hepfer (1991)
1 Northwest Indian Court System 127
Before: Chief Justice Elbridge Coochise, Associate Justice Calvin E. Gantenbein, and Associate Justice John L. Roe.

Opinion and Order
Per Curiam

This appeal presents two issues for review. First, should the trial court have allowed the defendants to make their motion for dismissal after the trial had begun? Secondly, is dismissal of criminal charges the proper remedy for an officer's failure to advise a defendant of his Miranda rights?

Facts
Both defendants are enrolled members of the Lower Elwha Klallam Tribe. On December 22, 1990, at approximately 7:40 in the morning, Fisheries Enforcement Officer Zeller observed the defendants drift net fishing on the Elwha River. Tribal fishing regulations in effect at this time only allowed for fishing by set nets and hook and line fishing. Officer Zeller requested other officers and arrested the defendants a short time later. Both defendants were transported to jail, where they were advised of their Miranda rights. Neither defendant made any incriminating statements. From the time of arrest to the advisement of rights, approximately one hour had elapsed.

On March 1, 1991, this matter came for trial before the Tribal Court. Each defendant had been charged with one count of fishing by an unlawful method. During cross examination of Officer Zeller, the defendants moved to dismiss the charges against them under Rule "O" of the Lower Elwha Klallam Tribe's Court Procedures Code. The defendants alleged that the officer violated Section 40.20 of the Tribal Fishing Ordinance by not immediately informing them of their rights, and that, therefore, the charges should be dismissed. The trial court agreed with the defendants and dismissed the charges. The Tribe appeals.

Conclusion
The Tribal Appeals Court, having heard the oral arguments of the parties, having read all court documents and reviewed other documents pertinent to the case,

and having considered all exhibits introduced into evidence, now makes the following conclusions.

The appellate court finds that the evidence does not support the Tribe's assertion that the trial court committed error in entertaining the defendant's motion after the trial had started. Rule "O" allowed the trial court discretion as to when motions can be raised. The defendants are both laymen and were without the assistance of legal counsel and should be afforded wider latitude by the court. The trial court's failure to apply strict procedural time limits so as to bar the defendants' motion for dismissal was not error.

The appellate court finds, however, that the trial court did err when it granted the motion for dismissal based on the officer's failure to advise the defendants of their rights immediately after their arrest. Section 40.20 of the Fishing Ordinance is essentially a statutory listing of the decision in *Miranda v. Arizona*, 384 U.S. 436 (1966). The Miranda decision provides that prior to any questioning of a person in custody, he must be advised that he has the right to remain silent and that any statements made can and will be used as evidence against him. Failure to advise a defendant will generally bring sanctions by the court. These sanctions are in the form of the exclusionary rule. The exclusionary rule is used to suppress any evidence that is gained prior to the defendants having been given their rights.

The Tribal Appeals Court agrees with the Tribe that the purpose of Section 40.20 is to adopt the policy of Miranda. This being a **case of first impression**, there is no Lower Elwha Klallam statutory or case law prescribing a remedy for failing to give Miranda warnings in a timely fashion. However, this court finds that the exclusionary rule conforms to the spirit of fundamental fairness inherent in Lower Elwha Klallam law. Neither of the defendants in this case made any statements to the officer and were therefore not harmed by the officer's failure to advise. If they had made incriminating statements, then those statements would not have been allowed as evidence.

Dismissal of charges should only be used when the defendants' rights have been so prejudiced that their right to a fair trial is materially affected. There has been no evidence in this case that the rights of the defendants have been prejudiced, and therefore dismissal of the charges was inappropriate.

Order

It is hereby ordered, adjudged and decreed as follows:

1. The trial court's order of dismissal is reversed.
2. This case is remanded to the trial court to continue the trial.
3. The defendants are ordered to appear before the trial court on the twenty-first day of June, 1991, at 10:00 A.M.
4. Costs will not be awarded to either party.

Another type of possible remedy for constitutional violations during search and seizure is a tort (injury) action, in which the individual files a civil action against the police for compensation.

Generally, tribal governments have sovereign immunity from suit. This means that tribal law must explicitly allow for lawsuits against the government. Many tribal codes have limited waivers of immunity for business contracts and other noncriminal matters. In addition, individual police officers also have something called "qualified immunity" if they were acting in the scope of their job duties.

Other possible remedies are criminal prosecution of officers who purposely violate the rights protected by tribal codes and ICRA, class action suits, injunctive relief, police review boards that can discipline or fire officers who commit civil rights violations, and statutes that implement procedures preventing violators from being employed by other police departments.

What kinds of police actions can lead to the application of the exclusionary rule?

Search and Seizure Violations

If the tribal court has adopted an exclusionary rule, then evidence obtained from an unreasonable search or seizure is not admissible at the defendant's trial. Unreasonable searches or seizures are those conducted without a valid search warrant or without any special justification for the search or seizure. When evidence is admitted in violation of the exclusionary rule, the conviction might be reversed on appeal.

One particular problem concerning the exclusion of evidence from unreasonable searches and seizures is the question of who can object to an unreasonable search or seizure. Generally, only the following people are considered to have standing, or the legal right, to object to an unreasonable search or seizure:

- The person who was seized;
- The person possessing the evidence that was seized;
- The person who owns the evidence seized and who is charged with a crime; and
- The person who owns or controls the premises where the seizure occurred and who is charged with a crime.

In order for one to have standing to challenge a piece of evidence, not only must one possess or own it, but one must be charged with a crime and be subject to having the evidence used against one in court. For example, Bob's radio is seized as evidence of a burglary charge against Frank. Although Bob owns the radio, he cannot challenge the use of the radio in court because he is not charged with a crime. The radio is being used as evidence against Frank.

Involuntary Statements

An involuntary or coerced statement is one that the police have forced the defendant to make. Coercion covers a range of illegal activities. Coercion includes things as obviously wrong as torture, beating, or death threats. But coercion can also include more subtle things, such as threats to expose humiliating facts or blackmail. Police are often allowed to use trickery to get confessions from criminal suspects, but they cannot beat a confession out of someone. Defining exactly what coercion is and is not is a case-by-case process because police investigations and interrogation techniques are often ambiguous.

There are several reasons to exclude or prohibit the use of involuntary statements or confessions:

- Involuntary confessions are untrustworthy;
- The police are enforcing the law and should also obey the law;
- Involuntary confessions are offensive to the criminal justice system;
- The criminal justice system and government should not press the mind of a criminal defendant so much that the defendant confesses involuntarily;
- A person should not be convicted on the basis of a confession unless it is given freely; and
- Exclusion deters police misconduct.

In federal and state courts, involuntary or coerced statements and confessions cannot be used in any way, either in the prosecution's case-in-chief or as impeachment of the defendant's testimony (i.e., to challenge statements made by the defendant at trial). The accused has a right to a hearing before the jury hears the statement or confession, and the prosecution has the burden of proving voluntariness by a preponderance of the evidence. If an involuntary or coerced confession is presented to a jury, the conviction might be overturned (unless the introduction of the confession was a harmless error).

Miranda Violations

Suspects in criminal cases sometimes complain that they were not read their Miranda rights and, therefore, that the entire case should be dropped and charges dismissed. Failure to give Miranda warnings, however, does not affect the validity of the arrest or the prosecution in general. At most, failure to give Miranda warnings means that the statements or confessions cannot be used against the defendant. (In fact, in his second trial, Miranda was convicted on other evidence.)

In state and federal courts, statements or confessions obtained in violation of a defendant's Miranda rights must be excluded from trial as evidence of guilt. However, the statement or confession can generally be used to challenge or impeach the defendant's testimony on the witness stand at trial.

For example, Victor is accused of stealing Mary's purse. At his criminal trial, Victor testifies that he was at the movies when Mary's purse was snatched. However, he admitted to the police when they arrested him that he had snatched her purse. Victor's statement to the police can be used against him in cross-examination, even if the statement was given in violation of Miranda, because it is used to impeach him (i.e., show that he is lying).

The accused has a right to a hearing before the jury hears the statement or confession, and the prosecution has a heavy burden of demonstrating a proper confession.

"Fruits of the Poisonous Tree"

The exclusionary rule prohibits use of evidence that is the direct result of a government's illegal search or seizure, and indirect evidence, called "fruits of the poisonous tree."

For example, a police officer receives a tip that Rebecca is selling drugs out of her home. Without first obtaining a warrant or Rebecca's consent, the officer enters the home and finds some drugs. The officer also finds a list of names of people Rebecca has sold drugs to and the amounts of money they have paid Rebecca. The officer then arrests Rebecca. The people on the list are contacted and agree to testify against Rebecca in court. The illegal search of Rebecca's home is the poisonous tree. Obviously, the drugs would be excluded in court. But what about the testimony of the people she sold drugs to? The officer would not have found the names but for the illegal search, so that evidence is a product (the fruit) of the illegal search. State and federal courts routinely exclude the fruits of an unconstitutional search or seizure.

There are three exceptions or conditions that will allow "fruits of the poisonous tree" to be used in court. First, if the prosecution can show the evidence was found through an independent source or some way other than the unconstitutional search or seizure, it may be used. The second exception is the inevitable discovery rule, meaning that even if there was an unconstitutional search, the police would have discovered the evidence eventually by lawful means. The third exception is the attenuated connection principle. Under this exception, evidence may be introduced into court if the relationship between the evidence and the unconstitutional search is attenuated, which lessens the taint on the evidence.

Review the following tribal appellate case and identify the reasons the Court ruled that the evidence was inadmissible.

Confederated Salish and Kootenai Tribes Court of Appeals
Confederated Salish and Kootenai Tribes v. William Conko (1998)
25 Indian Law Reporter 6157
Ford, Justice

Factual Background
This case arises from a two car accident in Ronan in November of 1996. Defendant William Conko Camel ("Conko") was allegedly driving eastbound on Terrace Lake Road. The road was icy. His car went into the westbound lane and hit another car head-on. The driver of the westbound car, Sandy Drollman, was badly hurt. Her four minor passengers were also injured.

Conko was cited by tribal police, and later formally charged by the tribal prosecutor, for driving a motor vehicle while under the influence of alcohol or drugs ("DUI"); driving while his license was suspended or revoked; driving without proof of liability insurance; and four counts of negligent vehicular assault.

At the scene of the accident, tribal police allegedly observed signs of alcohol consumption by Conko. They apparently arrested Conko there and then took him to the hospital, intending to test his blood for alcohol content. Conko refused the test. The tribal police then instructed the doctor to take the blood forcibly, and the test was performed over Conko's objections.

The defendant moved the tribal court to suppress all evidence obtained as a result of the forcible blood testing. Judge Yellow Kidney granted the motion, and suppressed the results of the blood test. The Tribes appeal.

Issue on Appeal
The issue before this court is whether Judge Yellow Kidney correctly suppressed the results of the forcible blood testing, done over the clear objection of the defendant.

Applicable Law
The Confederated Salish and Kootenai Tribes have exclusive jurisdiction over misdemeanor crimes committed by Indians, under the Retrocession Agreement of 1993. The Tribes' Law and Order Code, Section 2-8-401, Traffic Violations,

adopts a Montana statute, M.C.A. 61-8-402, as tribal law. That statute provides that anyone operating a motor vehicle on a public road

> (1) ... is considered to have given consent, subject to the provisions of 61-8-401, to a test ... of the person's blood ... for the purpose of determining any measured amount or detected presence of alcohol or drugs in the person's body if arrested by a peace officer for driving or for being in actual physical control of a vehicle while under the influence of alcohol, drugs, or a combination of the two. The test ... must be administered at the direction of a peace officer who has reasonable grounds to believe that the person has been driving or has been in actual physical control of a vehicle ... while under the influence of alcohol, drugs, or a combination of the two. The arresting officer may designate which test or tests are administered.

Thus, under tribal statute, the tribal police had the authority to request and administer the blood test, so long as the defendant did not object. The blood test would have been admissible in evidence at any subsequent criminal proceeding.

However, this particular defendant did object and refused to submit to the test requested by the officer. Subpart (3) of the same statute governs the situation in this case:

> If a driver under arrest refuses upon the request of a peace officer to submit to a test or tests designated by the arresting officer as provided in subsection (1), a test may not be given, but the officer shall, on behalf of the department, immediately seize the person's driver's license. The peace officer shall immediately forward the license to the department, along with a sworn report noting that the peace officer had reasonable grounds to believe that the arrested person had been driving ... while under the influence of alcohol ... and noting that the person refused to submit to the test or tests upon the request of the peace officer.... Upon receipt of the report, the department shall suspend the license ...

Subpart (7) specifically deals with the tribal-state relationship in the case at bar:

> The department may recognize the seizure of a license of a tribal member by a peace officer acting under the authority of a tribal government or an order issued by a tribal court ... if the actions are conducted pursuant to tribal law or regulation requiring alcohol or drug testing of motor vehicle operators and the conduct giving rise to the actions occurred within the exterior boundaries of a federally recognized Indian reservation in this state.

Discussion

This tribal statute is clear. When the defendant objects, the test may not be given. The issue we face is what happens if, despite the clear language of the law, the police do forcibly give the test anyway.

The Confederated Salish and Kootenai Court of Appeals has never ruled on this issue. Montana has construed its identical statute in a series of cases cited by the defendant, which basically hold that the test results are not admissible at trial. In the state of Montana, blood samples drawn in violation of the statute are inadmissible in prosecutions for driving under the influence, and inadmissible in prosecutions for negligent vehicular assault. However, another case held that Section 61-8-402 does not apply to negligent homicide prosecutions, and a blood test taken over the objection of the defendant is admissible in such cases.

At the time of the blood test in this case, it is clear that defendant had been arrested. Defense counsel contended at oral argument that the arrest was for driving under the influence and lack of insurance only, and that the citations for negligent vehicular assault were not issued until sometime after the blood test. The prosecution for which the blood test is offered is for both DUI and negligent vehicular assault. No one died as a result of Conko's accident; there is no prosecution for negligent homicide. Thus, under Montana law, the blood test would clearly be inadmissible and the motion to suppress would be granted.

The Montana cases construing the state statute are persuasive but not binding on this court. As a matter of tribal sovereignty, this court has the power to adopt the construction of the tribal code provisions which the court finds best-reasoned. The Montana cases do not explain clearly why Montana holds that the penalty for violating the statute and taking the blood over the defendant's objection is suppression of the evidence. It seems, though, that the rationale must be that any other result would provide an incentive to law enforcement to ignore the clear language of the statute. If law enforcement obeyed the statute and did not take the blood test, it would not have had any test results to **buttress** its case at trial. In effect, violating the statute adds evidence to the tribes' case. Suppressing the evidence puts law enforcement in the same position it would have been in if it had obeyed the statute.

On the other hand, the tribal prosecutor contends, suppressing the evidence would deprive the court, whether judge or jury, of important information about the defendant's condition at or near the time of the accident. The tribes' code reflects a clear policy against driving while intoxicated, which arguably would not be served by letting a defendant frustrate law enforcement's attempt to gather relevant evidence by refusing the blood test.

Having considered all of the arguments in favor of the parties' position, this Court finds that the exclusion of the results of any forcibly obtained blood test in any subsequent prosecution for driving under the influence or for negligent vehicular assault will best serve the Tribes, and so holds. The rule we announce today is clear and unambiguous, and fairly balances the rights of the tribes and individual defendants.

Other Options Open to Law Enforcement

The Court adamantly opposes driving under the influence of alcohol or drugs, as well as vehicular assault and homicide resulting from such influence. Today's decision does not deprive law enforcement of the ability to convict perpetrators of these crimes. It does ensure that law enforcement follow both the spirit and the letter of the implied consent blood testing law in accumulating evidence for a prosecution, and it deters potential overreaching at the expense of defendants' rights.

In this case, when Conko objected to the test, the tribal police had two legal courses of action open to them. First, they could have moved the court for the issuance of a search warrant, authorizing the blood test. The search warrant route provides the defendant with additional protection beyond the investigating officer's individual judgment as to whether probable cause existed.

Search warrants are ordinarily required for searches of dwellings, and absent an emergency, no less could be required where intrusions into the human body are concerned. The requirement that a warrant be obtained is a requirement that the inferences to support the search "be drawn by a neutral and detached magistrate instead of being judged by the officer engaged in the often competitive enterprise of ferreting out crime." *Schmerber v. California*, 384 U.S. 757, 770 (1965).

The second course of action open to the tribal police appears in the statute itself: forego the blood test but penalize the defendant for refusing to cooperate by seizing his or her driver's license and sending it back to the state with appropriate certification. The state would then suspend the license. The tribes could continue with their prosecution for DUI and any related charges, but without the blood test. This ruling does not affect the tribes' ability to present other types of evidence, such as eyewitness testimony, videotapes of the defendant, and field sobriety tests, any one of which alone might suffice as a basis for conviction.

The tribal council, in adopting the statute, clearly stated that tribal police officers should not forcibly take blood when the defendant objects and established the license suspension penalty for that objection. Allowing the police to act directly contrary to this statute and then reap the reward for that violation in the form of enhanced evidence against the defendant would defeat the council's purpose. If the tribal prosecutors believe that police should be empowered to forcibly test blood of defendants in DUI and other related cases, they should convince the tribal council to change the statute. As it is presently written, the statute is quite clear and our holding comports with its apparent legislative intent. Thus, we affirm the decision of the tribal court judge and suppress the blood test results in this case, regardless of whether the prosecutor proceeds on the basis of driving under the influence or negligent vehicular assault.

Who Has the Burden of Proof?

If a defendant objects to introducing certain evidence, the prosecutors will need to prove that evidence was seized legally. This is normally done in response to a **motion to suppress evidence** filed by the defendant in a hearing prior to the trial. The following cases offer an analysis of the exclusionary rule from a tribal perspective.

Fort Peck Court of Appeals
Fort Peck Tribes v. Victor and Patti Grant (1990)
Fort Peck Court of Appeals No. 106
Opinion delivered by Gerard M. Schuster, Gary James Melbourne and Debra Johnson, Justices by unanimous opinion.
Held: Order suppressing evidence obtained in warrantless search [of] appellants' house is sustained.

Facts

Prior to the search of the Grant residence, a vehicle was seen leaving the Grant residence by officers while they were conducting a surveillance of the residence. The vehicle was stopped and the occupant was arrested after the officers determined that the driver was in possession of what they believed to be marijuana cigarettes. The person was taken to the Bureau of Indian Affairs [BIA] Detention Center where she was interviewed. The information gained from the interview was that the marijuana was allegedly purchased from Victor Grant. Officers then proceeded to the Grant residence where a search of the home was conducted and resulted in the confiscation of several articles which the Prosecution contended were illegal drugs and contraband. Several people were arrested after the search.

This incident occurred shortly after noon on September 15, 1989, during normal Court business hours.

It is abundantly clear from the transcript presented in this matter that the statements given by the female arrested and taken to the BIA Detention center could have provided probable cause for the issuance of a search warrant to search the Grants' home.

The record is completely lacking in facts which show that exigent circumstances existed at the time of this search which would allow the officers to search a residence around midday when the Court was in session, without a warrant.

Title II, Section 303 CCOJ provides:

> No Law Enforcement Officer shall conduct any search without a valid warrant except:
>
>   1. When he/she is making a lawful arrest; or
>   2. With the voluntary consent of the person being searched or the person entitled to possession of property being searched; or
>   3. When the search is of a moving vehicle and the officer has probable cause to believe that it contains contraband, stolen property, or property otherwise unlawfully possessed.

The lawful arrest of the female witness may have provided an opportunity to establish probable cause for issuance of a search warrant, but that fact does not meet the criteria of Section 303 for a warrantless search.

Further, the test set forth in *United States vs. Winsor* 816 F. 2d 1384 (9th Cir., 1987) must be met by the prosecution. This test is two-fold.

(1) It must show probable cause to search the residence, and
(2) It must show the evidence of exigent circumstances to excuse the lack of a warrant.

The record here shows that the officers had ample opportunity and probable cause to request a search warrant. The Grants' house had been under surveillance; there were numerous reports from citizens regarding the suspected drug activity at the Grants' home; a female leaving the home in her automobile was in possession of substance believed to be marijuana; the officer had reason to believe this suspected marijuana was obtained at Grants' home; an interview indicated that the marijuana joints had been purchased from Victor Grant at the Grant home.

The test set forth in *Winsor*, supra, is clearly not met. Here, with all of the above information available to the officers during normal Court business hours, a search warrant could have been easily obtained.

Therefore, it is the unanimous conclusion of this court that the order suppressing evidence issued by the court is sustained and upheld.

Appellate Court of the Hopi Tribe
Timothy Randolph v. The Hopi Tribe (1997)
1997.NAHT.0000019 (VersusLaw)
Before Sekaquaptewa, Chief Judge, and Lomayesva and Abbey, Judges.

Opinion and Order
In this appeal, the appellate court must address the proper allocation of the burden of proof in a motion to suppress evidence that has been allegedly illegally obtained during an improper car search. . . .

Factual and Procedural Background
Officer William Coochyouma was employed as a police officer for the Hopi Tribe. On July 18, 1995, Officer Coochyouma was traveling west on State Route 264 when he noticed appellant Timothy Randolph driving east. Coochyouma estimated that the car was traveling at an excessive speed and decided to turn on the radar device that he had been issued earlier in the day. The police department had a policy of checking the calibration of the radar device with tuning forks and taking any defective radar devices out of service. When directed toward Randolph's car, the radar device

registered 55 miles per hour. The posted speed limit was 45 miles per hour. As the car passed, Coochyouma recognized Randolph as a known drug dealer.

Coochyouma turned his car around, stopped Randolph, and asked him for his license and registration. As Randolph produced his license and registration in his mother's name, Coochyouma smelled alcohol and asked Randolph to step out of the car. As Randolph exited the car, Coochyouma saw a few beer cans in the back seat and asked Randolph if he would consent to a car search. Randolph agreed.

During Coochyouma's search of the passenger area, he found three cans of beer. After this finding, the facts are in doubt. At one point during the suppression hearing, Coochyouma testified that he asked Randolph if he could open the trunk. At another point during the hearing, Coochyouma testified that Randolph offered to open the trunk for him. In any event, Coochyouma proceeded to search the trunk, but he did not find anything. After completing the trunk search, Coochyouma asked to search the passenger area of the car again. During the search, Coochyouma found another can of beer and a fanny pack. Coochyouma admits that at this point he was searching for a plastic bag that he had seen earlier in the encounter. Coochyouma squeezed the fanny pack and noticed that it was soft. He asked Randolph what was in the fanny pack and Randolph responded that it was his stuff. Coochyouma opened the fanny pack and found marijuana.

At this point, Coochyouma arrested Randolph for possession of alcohol in violation of Hopi Tribal Ordinance 21 § 3.3.83 and possession of marijuana in violation of § 3.3.55. Randolph moved to suppress the evidence pursuant to Hopi Tribal Ordinance 21 §§ 2.7.7 and 2.4.8.

At the conclusion of the hearing, the Tribal Court concluded that defendants bear the burden of proof on motions to suppress. Because Randolph had not produced any evidence, the Tribal Court denied his motion without considering the merits.

Randolph filed a motion for reconsideration. The Tribe indicated that it had no objection to the court entering its decision based upon the evidence. The Tribal Court issued another order finding the car stop valid and concluding that the search was also therefore valid. Randolph pled guilty, but reserved his right to appeal the denial of his motion to suppress. The Tribal Court sentenced Randolph to 365 days in jail and a $1,500.00 fine for possession of marijuana and a fine of $40.00 and court costs of $25.00 for possession of alcohol. Two hundred seventy-five days of the prison term were suspended for one year of supervised probation. Randolph promptly appealed his conviction.

Issues Presented on Appeal

The court will proceed to settle the proper allocation of the burden of proof in a motion to suppress evidence.

Discussion

In resolving the issues in this case, it is necessary to consult legal authorities in the proper precedential order. Hopi Tribal Resolution H-12-76, Section 2 enumerates seven categories of legal authority. As interpreted in *Hopi v. Mahkewa*, AP-002-92 (1995), the Hopi Constitution and By-laws, the Ordinances of the Hopi Tribal Council, the Resolutions of the Hopi Tribal Council, and the customs, tradition, and culture of the Hopi Tribe are mandatory authority. Federal law, Arizona law, and the common law may be consulted to help fill in the interstices in the mandatory authority. Therefore, relevant Hopi legal authorities will be consulted before introducing legal authorities from other jurisdictions.

[Sections I and II omitted]

III. The Trial Court Erred in Allocating the Burden of Proof to the Defendant during a Hearing to Suppress Evidence That Had Been Allegedly Illegally Obtained

In this case, the trial court, observing that the burden of proof is ordinarily allocated to the moving party, placed the burden of proof on the defendant to prove that the search was unreasonable. The allocation of the burden of proof is judged by due process standards. . . . [T]his court considered another appeal after the denial of a motion to suppress and stated that "since the police did not obtain a warrant the prosecutor must show that the search conducted by the police was a legal exception to the warrant requirement." This would indicate that the prosecutor bears the burden of proof during a suppression hearing when the police did not obtain a warrant. However, this precise issue was not presented on appeal and the court did not analyze the origins of this rule. Therefore, we are not precluded from analyzing this issue in this case because of the doctrine of stare decisis [the legal principle that past cases should be given respect in deciding cases in front of the court].

The burden of proof in any case is really composed of two distinct elements: 1) the burden of production, and 2) the burden of persuasion. The burden of production refers to which party must produce evidence. The burden of persuasion refers to which party must convince the trier of fact regarding the truth of the matter. These burdens are usually on the same party, but that is not inevitably true.

In other jurisdictions, the general rule regarding the burden of persuasion and the burden of production in a motion to suppress creates a distinction between those situations involving a warrant and those where no warrant was issued. As a noted commentator has explained "[w]ith respect to the issue which is usually central in a motion to suppress hearing—the reasonableness of the challenged search or seizure—most states follow the rule which is utilized in the federal courts: if the search or seizure was pursuant to a warrant, the defendant has the burden of proof, but if the police acted without a warrant the burden of proof is on the prosecution." 5 WANE R. LAFAVE, SEARCH AND SEIZURE: A TREATISE ON

THE FOURTH AMENDMENT § 11.2(b)(3d ed. 1996). This **dichotomy** is normally justified on the grounds that: (1) the warrant represents an independent determination of probable cause by a magistrate that gives rise to a presumption of legality; (2) without a warrant, the facts surrounding the search or seizure are usually within the knowledge and control of the arresting agencies; and (3) without the rule, there is little reason to obtain a warrant.

However, this rule has not been universally adopted. At least three states always place both burdens on the prosecution. See, e.g., *People v. Hoskins*, 101 Ill.2d 209, 78 Ill. Dec. 107, 461 N.E.2d 941 (1984). The reason usually advanced for this rule is that the state is the party seeking to use the evidence and ought to bear the burden of proving that it was lawfully obtained. At least one state places the burden of production on the prosecutor and the burden of persuasion on the defendant. See, e.g., *People v. Whitehurst*, 25 N.Y.2d 389, 306 N.Y.S.2d 673, 254 N.E.2d 905 (1969). This forces the prosecutor to produce the evidence that is usually more available to the police and forces the defendant to persuade the court that probative evidence should be excluded. At least one jurisdiction has placed the burden of persuasion on the prosecutor and the burden of production on the defendant. See, e.g., *United States v. Mueller*, 902 F.2d 336 (5th Cir. 1990). Finally, some jurisdictions always place both burdens on the defendant. See, e.g., State v. McKenzie, 186 Mont. 481, 608 P.2d 428 (1980). At least four states have moved away from this position and accepted one of the other standards, but it is still utilized by at least one state. The rationale for placing both burdens on the defendant is that the burden is on the moving party, there is a presumption of regularity attending the actions of law enforcement officials, the general rule that relevant evidence is admissible, and to deter spurious allegations wasteful of court time. However, this allocation places the defendant in a most disadvantageous position because it is difficult for a defendant to prove the illegality of the search until he knows on what the government relies to establish its legality.

This court must determine which allocation of the burden of proof comports with Hopi public policy. The trial court cited In the Matter of SS, 95JC000030, a juvenile matter, for the proposition that "the burden rests with the moving party to support his motion by proof." While this is the general rule, and this opinion casts no doubt upon its continuing validity, motions to suppress evidence are fundamentally different from most other motions.

In general, the burden of proof is allocated to one party or the other for reasons of convenience, fairness, and policy. During a motion to suppress evidence, these factors weigh heavily in favor of allocating both the burden of production and the burden of persuasion upon the prosecutor when the police did not obtain a warrant. In terms of fairness, it is unreasonable to expect the defendant to be able to produce evidence regarding the validity of the stop. The reasons for the stop and other information are more readily available to the police officers and the prosecutor. Moreover, in terms of policy, it is preferable for police officers to obtain a warrant whenever practical. The detached magistrate who issues the warrant will not be influenced by the same motives that may influence the police and will not be as involved in the investigation. A rule that places the burden of proof upon the prosecutor in the absence of a warrant and the burden of proof on the defendant when the police did obtain a warrant will further this policy. Finally, the convenience factor is neutral in this analysis. As long as it is clear which party has the burden of proof, the facts will be developed and the court will be able to determine whether the evidence was obtained illegally. Therefore, those factors weigh in favor of placing both the burden of production and the burden of persuasion on the prosecutor to establish the legality of the search when the police have obtained evidence without a warrant. In short, we adopt the **majority rule** that the prosecutor bears both the burden of production and the burden of persuasion when the police failed to obtain a warrant and that the defendant bears the burden of production and the burden of persuasion when the police did obtain a warrant.

However, this does not end our inquiry. It is also appropriate to consider the proper burden of persuasion during a motion to suppress. The general rule is that the party with the burden of persuasion must convince the court by a preponderance of the evidence. In determining the appropriate burden of persuasion, it is important to balance the public's privacy interest with the necessity for efficient and effective law enforcement. The majority rule is justified because: (1) it is inappropriate to deter police from making arrests and searches where they can subsequently only establish by a preponderance of the evidence that they acted properly and (2) it would be difficult for police to both respond quickly and compile all the necessary evidence to prove that the action was justified beyond a reasonable doubt. For these reasons, the party bearing the burden of persuasion must convince the court by the preponderance of the evidence.

In this case, the police did not obtain a warrant. Therefore, both the burden of production and the burden of persuasion should have been allocated to the prosecutor. This means that the prosecutor should have been required to prove by a preponderance of the evidence that the police had sufficient justification to stop Randolph's car. Even assuming that the police had sufficient justification to stop Randolph's car, the prosecutor must also prove by a preponderance of the evidence that the police satisfied an exception to the warrant requirement before searching Randolph's car. Because the trial court did not allocate the burden of production and the burden of persuasion to the prosecutor, this case must be remanded to the trial court for further proceedings consistent with this opinion.

Order of the Court
For the foregoing reasons, Randolph's conviction is REVERSED and this case is REMANDED to the Tribal Court for a new suppression hearing with proper burdens applied.

Exceptions to the Exclusionary Rule

The Good Faith Exception
Sometimes law enforcement officers make mistakes. The U.S. Supreme Court has created a "good faith" exception to the exclusionary rule. If the court believes that a reasonably well-trained officer would have believed the actions to be lawful, then the court may allow the evidence.

Impeachment
Sometimes illegally obtained statements or evidence may be used to challenge or impeach the defendant's testimony if the defendant testifies at trial. The rationale for this exception is that one cannot be allowed to knowingly **perjure** oneself, or lie under oath when testifying, and then claim the protection of the previously suppressed statements or evidence.

Another exception is that evidence obtained in violation of a person's civil rights may often be used in court for the purposes of impeachment. If a defendant takes the stand and testifies to having been out of town when the crime was committed, the prosecutor can ask questions about the statement the defendant gave to the police claiming to have been in town during the crime, even if the statement was taken in violation of the defendant's constitutional right to remain silent or was made subsequent to an unlawful arrest.

Conclusion
Many tribal courts have adopted a version of the exclusionary rule for the same reasons that state and federal courts have adopted it. Tribal law and ICRA both place limitations on government actions, and the exclusionary rule is a very common way to enforce those limitations. When government actors violate individual rights, they cannot benefit from the outcome of that illegal behavior.

Questions
1. Do you think the exclusionary rule is a useful remedy for constitutional violations?
2. Should the exclusionary rule be used in tribal court?
3. Do you think tribal police should be allowed to force a suspect in a DUI case to submit to a blood test? Why or why not? What should happen to the evidence if the police force the defendant to take the test?
4. What rule do state and federal courts follow for burden of production in motions to suppress evidence? Why?
5. Why do some state courts always place the burden of proof on the prosecution?

Lower Elwha Klallam v. Bolstrom
1. Why did the trial court dismiss the charges in this case?
2. What did the appellate court say should be the appropriate remedy in this case?

Fort Peck Tribes v. Grant
1. Why was the evidence in this case suppressed?
2. Who has the burden of proof to show that the evidence was lawfully obtained?

Randolph vs. Hopi
1. What evidence was seized by law enforcement in this case?
2. What rule did the Hopi Tribe adopt regarding the exclusionary rule and why?

In Your Community
1. Does your tribal court use the exclusionary rule?
2. Does your nation use any of the other possible remedies for constitutional violations?

Terms Used in Chapter 22
Buttress: Make stronger or defensible.
Case of first impression: A new case; a case that presents an entirely new issue or problem to the court.
Dichotomy: A division or the process of dividing into two mutually exclusive or contradictory groups.
Exclusionary rule: Statements or evidence obtained in violation of a person's civil rights are not admissible in criminal prosecutions against the defendant as proof of the defendant's guilt.
Majority rule: In an appellate court case, the decision of the majority of the justices becomes law.
Motion to suppress evidence: Usually brought by the defendant in a criminal case, the motion asks the judge to disallow certain evidence that was obtained illegally.
Perjure: To lie while under oath, especially in a court proceeding.

Suggested Further Reading

Craig M. Bradley, "The Emerging International Consensus as to Criminal Procedure Rules," 14 *Michigan Journal of International Law* 171 (1993).

Dallin H. Oaks, "Studying the Exclusionary Rule in Search and Seizure," 37 *University of Chicago Law Review* 665 (1970).

The Right to an Attorney/Advocate

Chapter 23

Being arrested and charged with a crime means being under the control of the government. Civil rights exist to protect people from abuse of government power by ensuring the process is fair, and the right to an attorney is an important part of a fair process. The right to an attorney is guaranteed by the Sixth Amendment to the U.S. Constitution but also is found in many tribal constitutions, tribal laws, and the Indian Civil Rights Act (ICRA). In addition, some nations apply traditional tribal law methods to protect the individual and to assist him when he is faced with allegations of committing a wrongdoing.

A Defendant's Right to an Attorney under ICRA

No Indian tribe in exercising powers of self-government shall—(6) deny any person in a criminal proceeding the right to . . . at his own expense to have the assistance of counsel for his defense (25 U.S.C. §1301(6)).

ICRA provides a right to an attorney at the accused's own expense unless the offender is charged with an offense that fails under the special criminal jurisdiction recognized in Violence Against Women Act (see Chapter 10). However, many tribal governments have adopted legislation that requires court-appointed attorneys in criminal cases when a person cannot afford an attorney. Some tribes also protect the right to an attorney in tribal constitutions and/or tribal laws. ICRA provides for the basic right, whereas tribal law defines this right. Tribal laws define when the right attaches, or begins, and how the right can be waived. A defendant cannot exercise her rights if she does not know or understand them. Thus, many laws require that a judge inform the defendant of his rights. This is especially important prior to a defendant waiving his right to an attorney. A defendant cannot truly waive or give a right that he does not understand. Thus a judge must ensure the defendant understands his rights.

The Supreme Court has ruled the Sixth Amendment right to an attorney attaches whenever an accused is facing a jail term.[1] As a result, in federal and state courts, attorneys are provided to criminal defendants who cannot afford to pay for an attorney in any criminal offense involving the possibility of six months' or more incarceration. The Sixth Amendment has been interpreted by the U.S. Supreme Court to mean the right, not just to have an attorney, but to have effective legal representation.[2]

Because tribal governments have limited resources, they are often unable to provide defense attorneys for indigent defendants who cannot pay for an attorney. Thus many tribal governments allow and encourage the use of lay advocates. A lay advocate is a nonlawyer who acts as the defendant's counsel. A well-trained advocate can be as effective as an attorney in tribal court. Often advocates are very familiar with tribal customs and modern tribal law, which a nonmember attorney may not know. When a defendant elects to use an advocate, it is often required by the court to waive his right to an attorney.

Included in the following text is an example of one tribal nation's law that provides and protects the right to an attorney. Compare it to your nation's laws to determine whether there are any differences.

The Right to an Attorney

Mashantucket Pequot

a. *Defendants who are demonstrably indigent are entitled to an attorney at the Tribe's expense.*
b. *Defendants who are tribal members and who are or may be eligible for a distribution under the Tribe's incentive program or other tribal per capita payment plan shall not be considered indigent for purposes of this Law.*
c. *Defendants who are tribal members and who are or may be eligible for a distribution under the Tribe's incentive program or other tribal per capita payment plan shall, at their request, have an attorney appointed by a judge from a list of approved attorneys established by the tribal court. Such appointments shall be paid for by the Tribe, provided that the cost of any attorney appointed and paid for by the Tribe shall be deducted from any future tribal distribution or payment to tribal members.*
d. *Consistent with the provisions of this Law, the tribal court may develop rules regarding the provision of attorneys which shall be effective upon approval by the Tribal Council.*

The following court opinions address the right to counsel. As you read the cases, pay close attention to the court's analysis of the defendant's rights. What must a court do to make sure a person can exercise this right? What is required when a defendant wishes to waive this right?

Quileute Tribal Court of Appeals
Quileute Indian Tribe v. Valerie LeClair (1989)
1 Northwest Indian Court System 50
Before: Rosemary Irvin, Chief Justice; John Roe, Associate Justice; and Elbridge Coochise, Associate Justice.
Memorandum Opinion and Order
IRVIN, Chief Justice:

This matter is on appeal by the Defendant, Valerie LeClair, who was found guilty of Driving While Under the Influence of Intoxicating Liquor at the close of a jury trial during which she was unrepresented by counsel. She was sentenced to a $500 fine and 90 days jail time. The Defendant made a Motion for a New Trial, which was denied by the trial court. The Defendant appealed. . . .

I. Was the Defendant Valerie LeClair Properly Advised of Her Right to Counsel, as Well as Other Rights Guaranteed by the Quileute Law and Order Code to a Defendant Appearing in the Quileute Tribal Court?

On April 4, 1989 the defendant was arraigned. The transcript of that proceeding is as follows:

> The Judge has read the criminal complaint to the defendant that had happened on 3-12-89.
>
> Judge: Is this your first appearance in court?
>
> Valerie: Yes.
>
> Judge: Okay, do you have an attorney or spokesperson or wish to have one?
>
> Valerie: Yeah? . . . I don't never had my license I don't know how it could have been suspended.
>
> Judge: Well, it's not your license wasn't suspended; it's your privilege to drive that is suspended.
>
> Valerie: Oh.
>
> Judge: That's what the actual charge is.
>
> Valerie: Oh, it's not like what he said, he said on the computer it came up that I had my license and . . . ?
>
> Judge: I beg your pardon?
>
> Valerie: He said that he checked my name on the computer and it came up that I had license suspended.
>
> Judge: Well, the way the law reads, that it is your license OR your privilege to drive. So if you hadn't had a license they can suspend your right to drive, whether you have a license or not.

K. L. Lewis: The way the former charge reads, your Honor, the privilege to drive suspended.

Judge: Comments to Court Clerk on last case.

Judge: Okay, are you ready to enter a plea to the charge or do you want to wait until you get a spokesperson? Who's going to be the spokesperson? Are you going to do it Mrs. Penn?

Mrs. Penn: No, I am not taking them anymore, only on rare cases.

Valerie: Don't I get a prosecuting attorney?

Judge: The prosecutor is here, he represents the Tribe, so if you want to get an attorney you have to get your own attorney. You have to pay your own attorney or get a spokesperson. I don't know anyone that does it down here, at this point no one is? We have allowed a spokesperson to come from Neah Bay to represent people, but that would be your responsibility, so . . . .

Valerie: Well, there is someone that said that they would talk for me, so I can get somebody.

Judge: All right that person has to pay the admission fee to tribal bar and they have to certify that they read the code. So, just let them know ahead of time, the $10.00, right, still $10.00?

Clerk: Wasn't it $5.00?

Mr. Harrison: It's $5.00, I think.

Judge: It's only $5.00, but they have to have read the tribal code and understand the court procedures.

Valerie: Uh huh.

Judge: Okay. The paralegal or the clerk has those, who's going to do?

Valerie: Butch Sampson said he was going to ask Arnie Black.

Judge: Well, if he is willing to do it. I'm sure he would be able to understand the procedures. Mr. Black's been in court enough to know what happens in court. You make sure. How are you going to plead? Guilty or not guilty?

Valerie: Not guilty.

Judge: To all three charges?

Valerie: Well, driving without my license; I guess that's guilty.

Judge: Well, there are three charges, actually. Driving While Intoxicated. How do you plead to that?

Valerie: Guilty.

Judge: Okay, Driving While Suspended?

Valerie: Oh, I want to plead not guilty to everything, I guess.

Judge: Okay, there are actually two charges. It is written, looks like one, but it is really two different charges.

Valerie: Yeah.

Judge: And Assault?

Valerie: Oh, that's not guilty.

Judge: Okay, you're going to have a jury trial or a trial to the court?

Valerie: Jury trial.

Judge: Do you want to have any witnesses subpoenaed or can you bring your own witnesses?

Valerie: No, I don't have no witnesses. . . . ?

Judge: Okay, it will be May 2, at 10:00 A.M.

Valerie: Okay, for both of them?

Clerk: All three charges?

Judge: Yes, all three charges. All at the same time, basically, and the same place. So maybe not at the same time. But close enough. Okay, then if you're going to get Mr. Black then I want him to contact the court clerk by a week from today, so we can make sure that he is going to agree to that date.

Valerie: Okay.

The following rights are guaranteed to a defendant under the Quileute Law and Order Code: Section 11.03 Rights of Defendant

In all criminal prosecutions, the defendants shall have the following rights:

a. The right to be present throughout the proceeding and to defend himself in person or by a spokesman.
b. The right to know the nature and cause of the charge and to receive a copy of the complaint.
c. The right to meet the witnesses against him face to face.
d. The right to compulsory process to obtain the testimony of witnesses in his behalf and physical evidence.
e. The right to a speedy public trial by an impartial jury or judge.
f. The right not to testify. The failure of the defendant to testify shall not be construed against him or be commented upon by the prosecution.

Several facts become immediately apparent upon examination of the trial transcript of the Appellant's arraignment. First, this was the first time the Defendant had appeared in Quileute Tribal Court. Secondly, the Defendant clearly wanted counsel to represent her. And finally, it was unclear to the Defendant of the charges being brought against her. The arraignment was not continued and the Defendant, by default, represented herself at that proceeding.

Procedural due process which is fair, is fundamental to the operation of any tribal court. Defendants not only have rights guaranteed to them but they must reasonably understand those rights and have reasonable opportunities to exercise those rights. Because most defendants appearing before tribal court are without representation initially and frequently throughout all proceedings resultant from charges which are lodged, the onus is on the tribal court to duly explain the defendant's rights to him or her and afford the defendant clear opportunities to exercise those rights.

Here the Defendant was not clearly informed by the Complaint of the nature of the Driving While Intoxicated charge.

The charge appeared on the Complaint as:

R.C.W. 46.20.342, 46.61.502, 46.61.515
Driving While Intoxicated
(Suspended)

At arraignment it is questionable whether the Defendant understood the nature of the charges against her, and the penalties which might be imposed for each offense should she be convicted were never explained to her. She indicated several times during the arraignment that she wished to have someone represent her. The judge never explained to her that she had the right against self-incrimination, the right not to testify, and proceeded to ask about witnesses she wished to subpoena and whether or not she wished a jury trial. The decisions as to how a defendant should plead to charges, whether they should testify, whether to try the case to the judge or a jury, and what witnesses to call are all determinations that can be postponed until after a defendant has had the opportunity to consult a tribal court advocate. Knowing the gravity of the penalties which may be imposed should a defendant be convicted of a charge is fundamental to their decision whether to engage in the effort and expense to secure an advocate. Since the right to counsel is not guaranteed expense-free to defendants in tribal court, the tribal court is obligated to provide to a defendant before it the information necessary for him or her to make an informed decision whether to secure counsel or waive the right thereto. . . .

Order

For the above reasons the Motion to Dismiss the Appeal is denied, the ruling of the Tribal Court denying the Appellant's Motion for a New Trial is reversed and the case is remanded to the Trial Court for retrial on the charges of Driving While Intoxicated and Driving While Privilege to Drive is Suspended with the following instructions:

The Trial Court is to rearraign the Defendant on the charges for the purpose of fully advising her of the nature of the charges against her, the potential penalties which may be imposed if she is convicted of the charges and all of her rights as guaranteed by the Quileute Law and Order Code and the Indian Civil Rights Act. Further, she shall be advised of her right to counsel and given a reasonable opportunity to secure counsel, if she so chooses, prior to entering a plea on the charges and making decisions consequential to entering a plea.

Appellate Court of the Hopi Tribe
Ami v. Hopi Tribe (1996)
No. AP-003-89
Before Sekaquaptewa, Chief Justice, and Lomayesva and Abbey, Justices.

. . .

Factual and Procedural Background
The Hopi Appellate Court consolidated three cases on appeal in order to consider them at the same time: *Ami v. Hopi Tribe, Gishey v. Hopi Tribe,* and *Pavatea v. Hopi Tribe*.

In *Ami v. Hopi Tribe*, Emerson Ami was arrested and charged with wrongful possession of alcoholic beverages on 29 April 1989 in violation of Hopi Ordinance 21, Section 3.3.83. On 1 May 1989, Ami was presented with a Legal Rights Form in which he indicated that he waived his right to counsel. Without an advocate, Ami was arraigned and entered a plea of guilty to wrongful possession of alcoholic beverages. Upon entering his plea, Ami was sentenced to a $500.00 fine and 180 days in jail. Ami appeals his sentence on the grounds that: (1) The trial court erred when finding that he knowingly waived his right to counsel and (2) the trial court erred by failing to appoint counsel for him as it had done for similarly situated defendants in the past.

In *Gishey v. Hopi Tribe*, on 21 May 1989, Ronald Gishey was involved in a head on collision on State Road 264. According to the police report filed by Officer Bennett Chatter, Gishey was driving a truck while under the influence of alcohol. He allegedly crossed the double yellow line and struck another truck. When Chatter arrived at the scene, he observed Gishey with eyes bloodshot, face flushed, and emitting a very strong odor of alcohol. Because of the injuries sustained in the accident, no field sobriety test was administered. Gishey was charged with Driving While Under the Influence of Intoxicating Liquor (DUI), driving left of center, passing in a no passing zone, and failing to have a valid operator's license in violation of Hopi Ordinance 21, Section 3.3.75. (footnote omitted) On 23 May 1989, Gishey was presented with a Legal Rights Form in which he waived his right to counsel. The trial court proceeded with the arraignment. Without an advocate, Gishey entered a plea of guilty to DUI, driving left of center, and passing in a no passing zone. He entered a plea of not guilty to failing to have a valid operator's license. Upon entering his plea, Gishey was sentenced to a $200 fine and 30 days in jail for the DUI, $50 fine for driving left of center, $30 fine for passing in a no passing zone, and a fine of $25 for court costs. Gishey appeals the judgment on the grounds that: (1) the trial court erred by finding that he knowingly waived his right to counsel and (2) the trial court erred by accepting his guilty plea while he was under medication and suffering from physical injuries.

In *Pavatea v. Hopi Tribe*, on 3 April 1988, Calvin Pavatea was involved in an altercation at Virginia Tootsie's residence, and he allegedly threatened someone with a rifle. He was arrested and charged with disorderly conduct in violation of Hopi Ordinance 21, Section 3.3.21. On 4 April 1988, Pavatea was presented with a Legal Rights Form in which he waived his right to counsel. The trial court proceeded with his arraignment and Pavatea entered a plea of guilty to the charge of disorderly conduct. Upon entering his plea, Pavatea was sentenced to forty days in jail. Pavatea appeals this judgment on the ground that the trial court erred in finding that he knowingly waived his right to counsel.

Issues Presented on Appeal

These appeals raise very important issues about the proper criminal procedure in Hopi Trial Courts. This court must address: (1) what are the standards in Hopi Trial Courts for the valid waiver of the right to counsel; . . . . (3) were these standards met in the cases before this court.

Discussion

On these appeals, the Hopi Appellate Court is asked to interpret the scope of . . . [the] fundamental . . . the right to counsel. These are fundamental rights because they protect the defendant against the power of the Tribe. For example, the right to counsel provides the defendant with a valuable assistant who can help the defendant prove his innocence. The advocate is an important source of pre-trial investigation. He has the skill and connections to obtain police records, research points of law, and interview witnesses. In these ways, the advocate can build a defense while the defendant is in custody.

Moreover, the qualified advocate has knowledge of criminal procedures and skill at presenting evidence to a fact finder. This allows the advocate to present the best possible defense and protect innocent defendants against the Tribe's authority. . . .

1. In order to accept a criminal defendant's waiver of the right to counsel, the judge must advise the defendant about the desirability of counsel, disclose the maximum consequences of the plea, and inform the defendant about the availability of the public defender.

When deciding matters of law, Hopi Trial Courts must consult authorities in their proper precedential order. The suggested order of authority for the Hopi Tribe is: (1) the Hopi Constitution and By-laws; (2) Ordinances of the Hopi Tribal Council; (3) Resolutions of the Hopi Tribal Council; (4) the customs, traditions and culture of the Hopi Tribe; (5) federal law; (6) Arizona law; (7) the common law. Hopi Resolution H-12-76. Federal law, Arizona law, and the common law are merely persuasive, not mandatory, authority. *Tribe v. Mahkewa*. Therefore, in determining the proper scope of the right to counsel and the right to enter a guilty plea, it is important to consider these authorities in this order.

On the issue of the waiver of counsel, the Ordinances of the Hopi Tribal Council suggest that the Tribe requires a knowing waiver of counsel. Under Ordinance 21, at the time of arrest, the officer must inform the defendant, "[T]hat he has the right to counsel unless he voluntarily waives such right." Hopi Ordinance 21, Section 2.3.4. Additionally, "Lay counsel shall be permitted to practice before the Hopi Tribal Courts in criminal matters only when the defendant has knowingly waived his right to counsel." Hopi Ordinance 21, Section 1.9.3. If the defendant must knowingly waive his right to counsel before he can obtain the assistance of lay counsel, the defendant should have to knowingly waive the right to counsel before receiving no assistance and proceeding alone. Therefore, the Ordinances of the Hopi Tribal Council require a defendant to knowingly waive his right to counsel. Nonetheless, the term "knowing" is not defined in the ordinance.

In an effort to provide judges with a more explicit standard, it will prove helpful to review federal law on this issue. Although federal law is not necessarily binding in Hopi courts, a review of federal law will provide an example of a standard that this Court can modify to meet the needs of the Hopi Tribe.

The Supreme Court of the United States has recognized that because the assistance of counsel is a right belonging to the criminal defendant, the defendant is entitled to waive this right. As the Supreme Court explained,

It [the Sixth Amendment] speaks of the "assistance" of counsel, and an assistant, however, expert, is still an assistant. The language and spirit of the Sixth Amendment contemplate that counsel . . . shall be an aid to a willing defendant— not an organ of the state interposed between an unwilling defendant and his right to defend himself personally. *Faretta v. California*, 422 U.S. 806, 820 (1975).

Despite this pronouncement, courts are reluctant to allow a defendant to waive his right to counsel because of the significant dangers associated with self-representation. The average criminal defendant does not have enough knowledge of the criminal justice system to protect himself against an experienced prosecutor.

Johnson v. Zerbst, 304 U.S. 458, 465 (1938). The fear is that the average defendant simply does not have knowledge about the possible defenses to a charge and the rules of procedure to present an adequate defense. In fact, courts have feared that in the absence of counsel, defendants may plead guilty to crimes that they never committed. Pleading guilty may appear to be an attractive alternative to the defendant so that he can avoid the publicity of trial, secure a break at the sentencing stage, or just get the whole complex and confusing process completed and return to his normal life. *Molignaro v. Smith*, 408 F.2d 795 (5th Cir. 1969).

In order to protect defendants who are not aware of these dangers, "Courts indulge every reasonable presumption against waiver of fundamental constitutional rights." *Johnson*, 304 U.S. at 464 (quoting *Aetna Insurance Co. v. Kennedy*, 301 U.S. 389, 393 (1937)). The Johnson court proceeded to require that the defendant "knowingly and intelligently" waive these rights. Johnson, 304 U.S. at 464. However, courts have not construed this knowing waiver of counsel to require the defendant to know the intricacies of the criminal justice system. In other words, defendants do not have to have a technical knowledge of voir dire and the rules of procedure. *Faretta*, 422 U.S. at 835.

Instead, defendants must have knowledge about the dangers associated with proceeding **pro se**. To this end, courts have required that defendants know the charges against them, the range of allowable punishments, possible defenses to the charges, and factors in mitigation of the charge. *Von Moltke v. Gillies*, 332 U.S. 708, 724 (1947); Aiken v. United States, 296 F.2d 604 (4th Cir. 1961); *Cherrie v. United States*, 179 F.2d 94 (10th Cir. 1949); Birch v. United States, 359 F.2d 69 (8th Cir. 1966); *Stroetz v. Burke*, 268 F.Supp. 912 (E.D. Wi. 1967). It is essential for the judge to ensure that the defendant has all of this information and makes a knowing waiver of counsel.

To discharge his duty properly in light of the strong presumption against waiver of the constitutional right to counsel, a judge must investigate as long and as thoroughly as the circumstances of the case before him demand. The fact that an accused may tell him that he is informed of his right to counsel and desires to waive his right does not automatically end the judge's responsibility.... A judge can make certain that an accused's professed waiver of counsel is understandingly and wisely made only from a penetrating and comprehensive examination of all the circumstances under which such a plea is tendered. Von Moltke, 332 U.S. at 723–724

This comprehensive investigation should include a consideration of the defendant's education and mental condition. It should also include an examination of the existence of promises or threats that may have been proffered in an effort to induce the plea. Moreover, the examination should ensure that the defendant understands the function of counsel and the aid that he is choosing to forego. *Colwell v. Rundle*, 251 F.Supp. 118 (E.D. Pa. 1966). Courts consider this investigation to be so important that many have suggested that the examination should appear in the trial court record. Johnson, 304 U.S. at 465; *Carnly v. Cochran*, 369 U.S. 506 (1962); *United States ex rel. Slebodnick v. Commonwealth of Pennsylvania*, 343 F.2d 605 (3d Cir. 1965). Moreover, if the trial court accepts a guilty plea after a defendant waives counsel without this knowledge, the guilty plea is not valid and will be overturned upon appeal. *Brady v. United States*, 396 U.S. 809 (1970); *McConnell v. Rhay*, 393 U.S. 2 (1968); *Arsenault v. Massachusetts*, 393 U.S. 5 (1968).

Because these federal court cases have been interpreting the Constitution, Arizona state courts are required to abide by these same interpretations. Indeed, decisions of the Arizona state courts are in accord with the federal interpretation. The waiver of counsel must be made knowingly and intelligently. *State v. Lee*, 689 P.2d 153, 142 Ariz. 210 (1984); *State v. DeNistor*, 694 P.2d 237, 143 Ariz. 407 (1985). Furthermore, the waiver is not sufficient unless the defendant is warned of the dangers of self-representation and asked if he wishes to proceed pro se. *State v. Jones*, 705 P.2d 955, 146 Ariz. 278 (1985).

This court has reviewed the current Legal Rights Form to ensure that it adequately informs defendants of their rights. This court recognizes that the current Legal Rights Form does contain information about many of a defendant's rights. For example, the Legal Rights Form contains information about the representation of counsel, the disadvantages of not acquiring counsel, and maximum fines and sentences.

However, this court is convinced that the Legal Rights Form does not convey all of the information that a defendant should have. For example, the current form does not contain such vital information as the criteria to qualify for representation by a public defender. A defendant should have access to this information. In addition, the current form states that a defendant has the right to be represented by "legal counsel." It would be more informative if the defendant learned that he could be represented by an attorney or advocate.

Moreover, the form should be revised in order to simplify the presentation of some important information. For example, the Legal Rights Form states, "If you decide to represent yourself you are advised that self representation is unwise and you will be at a disadvantage as you will follow the same rules as the Tribal Prosecutor and who is trained in law." This is a complex sentence. The idea could be more clearly expressed as, "Proceeding without counsel is unwise because of the Tribal Prosecutor's knowledge of the law and procedure."

Because of our review of the Legal Rights Form, we are persuaded that this form must be amended to conform with minimum requirements to protect a criminal defendant's rights. At a minimum, the form must state that the defendant has the right: (1) to be represented by a public defender when the defendant qualifies (the form should also provide an outline of the criteria for eligibility); (2) to be represented by an attorney or an advocate at one's own expense; and (3) to represent one's self without counsel. In addition to enumerating these rights, the form should also outline the consequences of representing one's self without counsel. Hence, the defendant should be warned: (1) that advocates understand the law and procedure better than the defendant; (2) that the defendant will be at a disadvantage without counsel; and (3) the possible maximum fines or sentences. Finally, this court is concerned that the waiver of the right to "counsel" is ambiguous. It is unclear whether the term only refers to attorneys or whether it encompasses attorneys and lay advocates. In order to ensure that defendants are not confused by this ambiguity, the form must ask a defendant to waive both the right to an attorney and the right to a lay advocate separately.

Although defendants are presented with the Legal Rights Form prior to trial, a defendant's signature is not sufficient to waive one's rights. The Legal Rights Form is not a substitute for an active inquiry by the trial judge. Federal courts have held that a written waiver of counsel is not **dispositive** on appeal. *United States v. Steese*, 144 F.2d 439, 441 (3d Cir. 1944); *United States v. Washington*, 341 F.2d 277 cert. denied 382 U.S. 850 rehearing denied 382 U.S. 933 (1965). These courts have reasoned that even though the waiver is in writing, there is no guarantee that the defendants understood the consequences of waiving their rights. In fact, it is dangerous to force defendants to read their rights because they may be illiterate, have difficulty comprehending what they are reading, or not speak English as a first language.

Comprehension is especially difficult because they are in a novel, frightening, and stressful situation. Under these circumstances, they may have difficulty concentrating on the Legal Rights Form. Moreover, the Legal Rights Form provides so much information that it is probably overwhelming to most defendants. Finally, provisions of the Legal Rights Form are only explained upon a defendant's request. Many defendants may be too embarrassed or frightened to admit that they do not understand something. Because of these fears, we hold that signing the Legal Rights Form is not presumptively enough to waive one's rights.

Instead, the trial judge must make a comprehensive investigation in order to ensure that the defendant has made a knowing waiver. During this investigation, the judge must ensure that the defendant had the capacity to make a knowing, intelligent, and voluntary waiver. The facts of each individual case will reveal those factors that a judge must stress. However, in all cases, the judge will: (1) tell the defendant that an advocate or attorney knows the law and the procedures better than the defendant and that the defendant will be at a disadvantage without counsel; (2) mention the possible maximum consequences in fines or sentences; (3) inform the defendant of the availability of a public defender and ask him if he wishes to pursue this option; (4) ensure that the defendant has the capacity to understand the judge (including level of education, ability to understand English, and mental capacity);

(5) tell the defendant that the court will require the same level of legal skill from the defendant that it requires from attorneys; (6) ensure that the defendant was not coerced into making the plea; (7) explain the charges and possible defenses to the charges; and (8) ask the defendant if he knowingly waives the right to obtain an attorney or lay advocate at his own expense. These minimum requirements must be made in all cases. This standard will not be applied retroactively to cases that have already reached their final disposition.

. . .

III. In the present cases, appellant Gishey did not validly waive his right to counsel and the Appellate Court cannot uphold the other appellants' convictions because the Court does not have an adequate record of the proceedings.

A. *Gishey v. Hopi Tribe*

In the case of *Gishey v. Hopi Tribe*, the appellate court has a copy of the transcript of the trial court proceedings. This court has reviewed the transcript in an effort to ensure that appellant Gishey entered a valid guilty plea and knowingly waived his right to counsel. (footnote omitted)

In evaluating appellant Gishey's guilty plea, this Court recognizes that the trial judge complied with many of the procedural requirements outlined in this opinion. Specifically, the judge must read the complaint to the defendant, give the complaint to the defendant, explain the charge, describe the penalties, advise the defendant of his rights, ensure that there is a factual basis for the plea, determine that the plea was voluntarily made, and make a complete record of the proceedings available to the parties. In this case, it appears that the defendant had a copy of the complaint. (Gishey transcript (hereinafter "G.T.") at 1:10-19). Moreover, the judge explained the consequences of the plea. (G.T. at 3:11-18). The judge also ensured that the plea was not coerced (G.T. at 3:19 to 4:23) and allowed the prosecutor to explain the factual basis for the plea (G.T. at 5:28 to 7:5). Finally, the judge also informed the defendant that he was waiving his right to trial by jury (G.T. at 4:24 to 5:1), right to have witnesses testify on his behalf (G.T. at 5:2-4), right to cross-examine witnesses (G.T. at 5:5-8), and right against self-incrimination (G.T. at 5:9-13).

Despite the meticulous detail followed by the judge in these matters, the judge did not address other important points. The judge did not read the complaint to the defendant. Moreover, the charges were never explained to the defendant and the defendant was not advised of his right to counsel. This court is concerned by the fact that there was no evidence in the transcript that the trial judge told the defendant that an advocate or attorney knows the law and procedures thereby placing a defendant who has waived counsel at a disadvantage at trial. Moreover, the trial judge never asked the defendant if he knowingly waived his right to obtain an attorney or lay advocate at his own expense. Instead, in investigating appellant Gishey's waiver of counsel, the trial judge asked, "Okay now I take it somebody explained it [the Legal Rights Form] to you and you understand everything in it. Do you want an attorney for this proceeding or not?" (G.T. at 1:21-23). When the defendant responded, "I'll just take care of it on my own," (G.T. at 1:26) the trial judge merely concluded that the defendant waived his right to counsel and did not make any further inquiries on this issue (G.T. at 1:27-28). It is important to notice that the court did not warn Mr. Gishey about waiving his right to assistance before this exchange and made no inquiry into his understanding after the waiver. Later in the transcript, Mr. Gishey commented that he did not know if he had the right to an attorney and the court interrupted, "Well all I'm asking you now is did anyone promise you anything?" (G.T. at 3:25-28). Finally, Mr. Gishey suggested that he was pleading guilty so that he could put the whole experience behind him and fulfill his other obligations. (G.T. at 20-24). This would suggest that he did not have a proper understanding of the possible punishments. If this is true, he did not knowingly waive his right to counsel. However, the court interrupted him to say, "I need to find out for me that you're making a knowledgeable and voluntary plea of guilty" (G.T. at 4:10-11). In light of these facts, this court is concerned that appellant Gishey did not knowingly waive his right to counsel or enter a valid guilty plea. Accordingly, we reverse appellant Gishey's conviction. (footnote omitted)

. . .

Order of the Court

It is hereby ORDERED that the convictions in all three of the consolidated cases, *Ami v. Hopi Tribe*, *Pavatea v. Hopi Tribe*, and *Gishey v. Hopi Tribe* are REVERSED and the cases are REMANDED to the trial court for proceedings consistent with this Opinion.

The Right to Effective Representation

The right to an attorney includes having an effective attorney. Effective representation can include representing the client's interests, keeping in touch with the client, and exploring all aspects of the case,[3] along with following all the other aspects of the law and rules of professional responsibility. The tribal court cases below address alleged ineffective assistance of an attorney and describe the standard a defendant must meet to prove ineffectiveness.

Appellate Court of the Hopi Tribe
Nathan J. Navasie v. The Hopi Tribe (1999)
No. 98AC000015
Before Sekaquaptewa, Chief Judge, and Lomayesva, and Abbey, Judges

Opinion and Order
Opening Statement

Appellant seeks reversal of his conviction for abduction and child molesting. The issue addressed on this appeal is whether appellant was denied a fair trial due to ineffective counsel.

Factual and Procedural Background

Appellant Nathan Navasie, a Hopi Indian, was a volunteer wrestling coach at Hopi Junior/Senior High School. Appellant drove alleged victim, aged 14 years, and four other children home after school in his private vehicle on February 6, 1998. Appellant drove past the alleged victim's home after dropping off the other children at their homes. The alleged victim claims that appellant drove past where she had directed him to stop and parked in a remote location known as the old dump. . . . She claims that when she attempted to leave the vehicle, appellant reached around her and locked the car door, detaining her without her consent. She alleges that appellant then grabbed her around the waist, pulled her to him, and kissed her lips and neck, despite her asking him to stop. Appellant allegedly caused a blemish known as a hickie to appear on the alleged victim's neck. The alleged victim stated that appellant had often commented on her figure and asked her personal questions, and that he was always nice to her, trying to be her friend. She said she had heard that he was "that kind of person," always talking to girls. The alleged victim also testified that she told appellant where she lived and had discussed with him one of her neighbors, who appellant claimed to know personally.

Appellant denies these charges. He claims that he did not know where the alleged victim lived, and that when he asked her repeatedly she responded only with, "over there." Appellant claims that when he stopped to get directions, the alleged victim talked to him in the car about problems she was having. Appellant claims that he gave her a support hug; and a kiss on the forehead. He claims that she knew the gesture was for support and didn't resist or become upset. Appellant claims that at about 5 P.M. he dropped the alleged victim off by the kiva area and went to pick up his girlfriend at her work. Appellant says children at the school talk to him about their problems, and that the alleged victim had written him notes about her problems before. Appellant and the alleged victim were the only eyewitnesses to the events composing the alleged crime.

Appellant was charged with the crimes of abduction, Hopi Ordinance 21 §3.3.2, and child molesting, Hopi Ordinance 31 § 3.3.13. The prosecution made its case before the trial judge on August 25, 1998, presenting several witnesses who testified as to the version of events related to them by the alleged victim. The trial was then recessed until September 8, 1998, when the defense presented its case, offering appellant as its sole witness. The trial court found appellant guilty as charged. On October 1, 1998, the trial court sentenced appellant to 365 days in jail for each count (time to be served concurrently) and ordered him to pay $100 in court fees. The appellant subsequently withdrew his counsel Richard George, a lay advocate, and substituted Joe Washington, a member of the Hopi Bar.

In compliance with Rule 37(c) of the Hopi Rules of Civil and Criminal Procedure, appellant filed a timely notice of appeal on October 21, 1995, within 20 days of the trial court's final order issued on October 1, 1998. The Hopi Appellate Court has jurisdiction to hear this appeal because appellant was sentenced to more than thirty days imprisonment. Hopi Ordinance 21 § 1.2.5.

Issues Presented on Appeal
Appellant appeals the trial court's judgment on the grounds that he was denied effective counsel in violation of the Indian Civil Rights Act.

Discussion
I. Appellant Was Denied a Fair Trial Due to Ineffective Counsel

. . .

B. APPELLANT HAD INEFFECTIVE COUNSEL AT TRIAL. Appellant argues that his lay advocate Richard George failed to provide effective assistance of counsel at trial. Appellant points to a number of incidents demonstrating his advocate's incompetence:

George did not move to **sequester** prosecution witnesses when given the opportunity; he had hearing problems that inhibited his ability to cross-examine witnesses; he did not object to the unusual recess and delay of the trial, which resulted in the prosecution calling new rebuttal witnesses and essentially reopening its case; he failed to call an important defense witness; he made no remarks in consideration of sentencing; he was unprepared for trial, as opposing counsel himself pointed out; he did not investigate or produce evidence regarding the "hickie" appellant was alleged to inflict; and he made a late and unnecessary effort to suppress a statement by appellant, confusing the trier of fact. At least some of these allegations are sufficiently supported by the record and sufficiently **egregious** to warrant reversal of the appellant's conviction due to ineffective counsel.

The issue of ineffectiveness of counsel is one of first impression for the Hopi Courts. It is therefore appropriate to consult federal and Arizona state law for guidance on the matter, bearing in mind that Hopi courts retain the discretion to adopt, reject, or modify such law according to the needs of the Hopi community. Hopi Resolution H-12-76 § 2.

Under federal law, a criminal defendant bears the burden of proving ineffective assistance of counsel by a preponderance of the evidence. *Strickland v. Washington*, 466 U.S. 668 (1984). An appellate court reviews the issue of effectiveness of counsel de novo, since it raises mixed questions of law and fact. *Crandell v. Bunnell*, 144 F.3d1213 (9th Cir. 1998). Furthermore, appellate review of a counsel's strategic decisions is highly deferential, so that a reversal is not obtained simply because hindsight reveals an unsuccessful defense. *United States v. Appoloney*, 761 F.2d 520. 525 (9th Cir. 1985).

In order to demonstrate ineffective counsel, federal law requires that an appellant satisfy a two-pronged test. First, the appellant must show that his counsel's actions were unreasonable under the circumstances in light of prevailing professional norms. Second, appellant must demonstrate a reasonable probability that, absent counsel's unprofessional errors, the result of the proceedings would have been different. In other words, the counsel's conduct must have so undermined the proper functioning of the adversarial process that the trial cannot be relied on as having produced a just result. This strict standard means that the appellant must overcome a strong presumption that his counsel's conduct fell within the wide range of reasonable professional assistance.

The Arizona state courts have adopted the Strickland test. *State v. Nash*. 694P.2d 222. 227 (1985). Arizona case law also comports with federal law in requiring a high degree of deference to counsel's trial strategy. In *State v. Lucas*, an Arizona appeals court ruled that matters of trial strategy will not support a claim of ineffective counsel, provided the challenged conduct had some reasoned basis. 794 P.2d 1353 (1990). In Nash the court also required that the appellant specify acts or omissions that show ineffective counsel. *Nash* at 227.

The appellant in this case has specified acts and omissions by his lay advocate that demonstrate ineffective counsel under the Strickland test. Appellant alleges that his counsel failed to request the sequestration of the prosecution's witnesses when given the option by the court. These witnesses testified as to the story related to them by the alleged victim. Because the witnesses were allowed in the courtroom prior to taking the stand, each witness could hear the testimony of the witnesses preceding him or her. Thus each witness could simply have reiterated what was said by other witnesses. Hopi law does not contain a provision mandating the sequestration of witnesses. However, since this case hinged in large part upon the "corroboration" of the alleged victim's testimony, the defense advocate's failure to seek exclusion of witnesses so that they could not hear each other's testimony was a major omission and constitutes irresponsible and ineffective representation.

Appellant also alleges that his lay counsel had severe hearing problems that resulted in ineffective representation. Appellant contends that these hearing problems impeded his counsel's ability to conduct cross-examination of witnesses. This contention is supported by the transcript, which reveals several instances where defense counsel could not hear witnesses. Since witness testimony constituted the sole evidence in this case, competent cross-examination was essential to an adequate defense. Obviously, counsel cannot effectively question witnesses in order to challenge their version of events if he cannot hear their testimony in the first place. Inability to handle cross-examination goes beyond a mere mistake in trial strategy; it constitutes a serious breach of professional norms of criminal defense, thus satisfying the first prong of the Strickland test. The second prong of the test is also satisfied, because the outcome of the case may well have been different if counsel's hearing had afforded him the opportunity to counter witness testimony. Such testimony likely formed the basis for appellant's conviction since it was the only evidence against him. If appellant's counsel had poked holes in this testimony, it is reasonably probable that the trier of fact would have sustained reasonable doubt, preventing conviction.

An essential fact testified to by witnesses in this case was the "hickie" the alleged victim claimed appellant put on her neck. A police officer testified for the prosecution that he observed a light blemish on the alleged victim's neck on the day of the incident. In his police report, however, he noted that the blemish was "too light to show up in a Polaroid photograph." This essential evidence was never elicited by appellant's counsel for the Court's consideration. Moreover, counsel failed to investigate the "hickie" allegation prior to trial or to call any witnesses that might refute or otherwise shed light upon it. A light blemish that could not be photographed could be evidence of an old "hickie" rather than a new one. In fact, a supplemental police report by the above police officer recounting an interview with appellant stated that appellant told police that the alleged victim had hickies on her neck "all the time." Defense counsel also failed to elicit this evidence. Federal Rule of Evidence § 412 forbids admission of evidence of sexual behavior by the alleged victim, but an exception to the rule is made for evidence offered to prove that a person other than the accused was the source of the injury, so long as this evidence is not based on reputation or opinion. Under this exception, appellant or other witnesses could have testified that they had previously seen such blemishes on the alleged victim, planting a reasonable doubt regarding its source. Defense counsel's failure to mount any attack whatsoever on the "hickie" evidence seriously hindered his client's defense, and could reasonably be said to be both an unprofessional and a dispositive [i.e., critical] error.

The above errors meet the Strickland test for ineffective counsel. They are not merely strategic shortcomings; they are clear violations of the prevailing norms for professional conduct of defense counsel, and they likely affected the outcome of the trial. However, since this standard comes from a foreign jurisdiction, Hopi courts should consider whether it is suited to the Hopi community before adopting it. Representation by lay counsel has distinct advantages for Hopi litigants, including affordability and cultural familiarity, that merit preservation. Nonetheless, lay counsel should not be permitted to practice without basic competency in law and procedure. The Strickland test, in assessing the effectiveness of counsel by what is reasonable under the circumstances, allows competency to be evaluated in light of Hopi norms. It strikes an appropriate balance between the need to protect defendants from inept counsel and the need to take into account the relevant cultural context, and thus can be applied to both lay advocates and attorneys. Since appellant's lay advocate provided ineffective counsel under the Strickland test, his conviction is reversed.

Order of the Court

Because appellant did not meet the Ami and Harvey requirements for a knowing waiver of his right to counsel under the Hopi Ordinance, and because he had ineffective counsel under the Strickland test hereby adopted, his conviction by the Trial Court is REVERSED.

Appellate Court of the Hopi Tribe

Taylor v. Hopi Tribe (2000)
No. 00AC000002
Before Sekaquaptewa, Chief Justice and Lomayesva and Abbey, Justices.

. . .

Factual Background

Linda Taylor and Max Taylor are Hopi. They were married in 1982 but separated two years prior to the instant action. They have three minor children in common and an 18 year old son.

On July 27, 1999, at approximately 8:10 P.M. Appellant Linda Taylor went to Rachel Maho's home with three of her children. Lowell Talashoma Jr. and Ira Jolly, friends of the Maho's, were at the house at the time. Shortly afterwards, Mrs. Maho's daughter returned home.

Subsequently Rachel Maho and Mr. Taylor returned to the house and an altercation began. The police, having been previously called, arrived and broke up the hostilities. Sergeant Bennett Chatter placed Mrs. Taylor in the patrol car and interviewed the witnesses. (See Criminal Complaint No. 99CR000999 of Sergeant Chatter.) After the interviews Mrs. Taylor was arrested and later charged with disorderly conduct in violation of Hopi Ordinance 21, 5 3.3.21(A).

Procedural History

The Appellant was arraigned in accordance with Ordinance 21, §§2.6.1-3. The trial was conducted on November 3, 1999, Associate Judge Delfred Leslie presiding. The five witnesses who were present at the house the night of the incident all were called as witnesses and testified. Sergeant Chatter was not called to testify by either party. The Appellant did not testify. The Appellant was found guilty as charged.

Sentencing was postponed until a pre-sentencing report was compiled, which recommended a ten-day sentence. The recommendation was not adopted and on January 14, 2000 the Appellant was sentenced to thirty days in jail. The Appellant filed a timely notice of appeal and a motion to stay judgment on January 21, 2000. The motion was granted, along with a motion granting withdrawal of counsel on January 24, 2000. Brief for Appellant was filed with the Appellate Court on February 22, 2000, within the 30-day statutory requirement.

. . .

Discussion

. . .

II. THE FAILURE OF THE DEFENSE COUNSEL TO CALL SERGEANT CHATTER TO TESTIFY DID NOT ESTABLISH INCOMPETENCY.

A. Standard for the Determination of Competency of Counsel.

The appellant has cited a leading case regarding the Constitutional requirement for effective counsel, *Strickland v. Washington*, 466 U.S. 668 (1984), which involves a two-prong test. The first prong requires a determination of whether counsel acted within the range of competence demanded of attorneys in criminal cases, and the second prong requires an Appellant to show that counsel's deficient performance prejudiced the defense so as to deny the Appellant a fair trial. Additionally, in order to show prejudice, the petitioner must satisfy the difficult "but for" test; that is to say, but for counsel's error the trial would likely have had a different outcome. Id. at 675. This Court has adopted the Strickland rule in *Navasie v. The Hopi Tribe*, 98AC000015. Hopi Ordinance 21, §2.8.5 calls for the right of a criminal defendant to counsel, albeit at his or her own expense. The right to counsel implies effective counsel. If an attorney's performance in representing an accused is such as to amount to no representation at all, the accused has clearly been deprived of effective representation. Success in the outcome of a criminal prosecution is not to be regarded as the sole determinant of effectiveness, and that the quality of representation should not be judged solely by hindsight, but is to be determined in the light of the circumstances of the individual case. 21 Am. Jur. 2d, Criminal Law § 752.

Federal and Arizona courts impose the burden of proof of ineffectiveness upon the Appellant. "The burden of establishing ineffective assistance of counsel is on the Appellant, and proof of ineffectiveness of counsel must be a demonstrable reality rather than a matter of speculation." *State v. Meeker*, 143 Ariz. 256, 692 P.2d 911 (1984).

"In making a claim that the attorney provided ineffective assistance with respect to trial preparation or at the time of trial, a[n] Appellant must generally overcome the presumption that under the circumstances the action which Appellant challenges might be considered sound trial strategy. That is, counsel's trial tactics and strategic decisions not only are entitled to great deference when reviewed on a claim of ineffective counsel, but they typically cannot be the basis upon which to find ineffective assistance." *Holloway v. Arkansas*, 435 U.S. 475 (1978).

The decisions made by defense counsel during the trial were "tactical and strategic decisions." As noted above, such decisions cannot be used to question counsel competency. Additionally, the actions of counsel must be assumed to represent the decisions of the Appellant. To hold otherwise would open every adverse verdict to questions and allegations of incompetence. Therefore it is proper that the burden to prove ineffectiveness lies with the Appellant.

In summary, the proper standard used to judge effectiveness of counsel is the two pronged test of reasonableness and the "but for" requirement, with the burden on the Appellant to establish the existence of both prongs.

B. The Appellant Has Failed to Meet the Strickland Test.

Before going to the question of counsel effectiveness the Appellant must show that the outcome of the trial would have been different. It is not at all obvious that Chatter's testimony would have affected the verdict. Chatter did not observe the events that resulted in conviction. Appellant has not produced an affidavit from Sergeant Chatter with regards to possible exculpatory testimony. A review of the arrest report reveals nothing obviously beneficial to the defendant. The court is not required to indulge in speculation as to what possible testimony Chatter might have given. The evidence must be more than "a matter of speculation." *State v. Meeker*, 143 Ariz. 256, 692 P.2d 911 (1984).

Additionally, the Prosecution called five percipient witnesses and took extensive testimony from those witnesses as to the events that took place. Appellant's counsel cross-examined each witness in turn. The Trial Court found on the basis of that testimony that the Prosecution had met its burden of proving guilt beyond a reasonable doubt.

The burden of proof as to ineffective counsel lies with Appellant. The Sergeant's testimony might well have been detrimental rather than favorable. The Appellant has therefore not met its burden of proof that the Trial Court would reasonably have come to a different verdict had Sergeant Chatter testified. It is therefore unnecessary to evaluate the effectiveness of counsel.

...

Order of the Court

...

The decision of the Trial Court is affirmed.

When the Right to Counsel Begins

In state and federal courts, an accused has a right to counsel at all critical stages of the proceedings,[4] such as a police lineup and interrogation when the police are seeking a confession or incriminating statements. The defendant is not always entitled to an attorney during photo lineups, even after criminal proceedings have been initiated.[5] Specifically, there is no right to the presence of counsel at any of the following pretrial identification and lineup procedures:

1. Police lineups held before the accused is formally charged with a crime,
2. Taking a blood sample from the accused,
3. Obtaining a handwriting sample from the accused,
4. Pretrial display of photographs to witnesses in order to identify the accused, and
5. Pretrial interviews of witnesses.

ICRA provides a right to an attorney, but it is up to each tribe to interpret this right in accordance with tribal law and determine when the right attaches.

Appellate Court of the Hopi Tribe
Sinquah v. Hopi Tribe (2000)
No. 99AC000012
Before Sekaquaptewa, Chief Justice and Lomayesva and Abbey, Justices.

Opinion and Order

...

Factual and Procedural Background
On July 1, 1994 the defendant was charged with sexual conduct with a minor, violating Hopi Ordinance 21, section 3.3.11. On July 10, 1996 the Hopi Tribe

and defendant signed a plea agreement and defendant was ordered to spend 365 days in jail and pay $25.00 court costs. He was given credit for having served 137 days. The remaining 228 days were suspended in lieu of twelve months supervised probation.

After the sentence was imposed, the attorney of record filed two motions to withdraw as counsel. The first was denied because the term of probation had not expired and the second was denied because a warrant for arrest of the defendant was outstanding. After allegedly violating the conditions of his probation, the Prosecutor filed a motion for revocation of the probation on April 29, 1997. Arraignment was set for December 17, 1997. Although counsel was present at that hearing, defendant failed to appear on time.

The arraignment was rescheduled and did not occur until January 12, 1999. At that time, defendant appeared without the counsel he had retained. Counsel swore, through affidavit, that he was expecting to be notified in the event that his client turned himself in or was arrested. At that arraignment, the defendant entered a guilty plea and the Trial Court sentenced him to serve the balance of the 228 days remaining under his suspended sentence under Ordinance 21, Section 2.13.2.

A motion to substitute counsel was filed and granted on February 8, 1999. A Notice of Appeal was filed on August 11, 1999. Grounds for appeal were the Trial Court's denial of defendant's right to assistance of counsel and acceptance of an invalid guilty plea. According to the Appellant, the Trial Court violated the Hopi Constitution, the United States Constitution, the Indian Civil Rights Act, Hopi Ordinance 21, *The Hopi Tribe v. Ami*, Gishey & Pavatea, AP-002-89, AP-003-89, AP-004-89 (1996), and *Harvey v. The Hopi Tribe*, AP-001-89 (1997) by allowing the hearing to proceed without defendant's counsel and accepting his guilty plea.

Discussion

On appeal, this Court is asked to interpret the scope of the fundamental right to counsel and the procedures necessary to waive that right. The right to counsel given to a criminal defendant comes from several different legal authorities. Hopi Tribal Counsel Resolution H-12-76 instructs the Hopi Courts to look at seven authorities when deciding on substantive and procedural matters of law. Under Section 2(a) of Resolution H-12-76, the Hopi Constitution and By-laws, Ordinances of the Hopi Tribal Council and the custom, traditions and culture of the Hopi Tribe are mandatory authorities. See *Tribe v. Mahkewa* AP-008-93, p. 4. Federal, State and common law are merely persuasive authority. The Hopi Courts have the discretion to apply Federal law, State law, a combination of both, or neither, when Hopi law and custom is not on point. See Mahkewa.

1. Right to Counsel

Under the Indian Civil Rights Act and Hopi Ordinance 21, a criminal defendant is entitled to counsel at his own expense. The issue on appeal is whether the

Trial Court, by conducting a hearing without defendant's known counsel present at arraignment violated Hopi Ordinance 21.

The Hopi Constitution, Hopi Indian Rules of Civil and Criminal Procedures and Hopi Ordinance 21 do not explicitly answer the question of whether the presence of known counsel at arraignment is part of the right to counsel. The legal history of the ICRA leads one to the conclusion that the purpose and scope of ICRA is similar, but not identical to that of the United States Constitution. While ICRA guarantees almost all the fundamental rights enumerated in the U.S. Constitution, a tribe is not obligated to provide legal counsel free of charge to a criminal defendant. Under ICRA, defendants in criminal proceedings have the right to counsel at their own expense. Hopi Ordinance 21 provides a nearly identical right. Thus, a criminal defendant's right to counsel is similar to but not identical to a criminal defendant's right to counsel under Federal and State law.

Under federal law, the presence of counsel is not required when the defendant insists on representing himself. In Tom v. Sutton, the Court denied the defendant right to appointed counsel because defendant insisted on representing himself despite the warnings of the trial judge. Defendant was denied appointed counsel and forced to abide by the consequences of his own informed actions. See *Tom v. Sutton*, 9th Cir., 1976, 533 F.2d 1101.

Under federal law, the presence of counsel at arraignment is not required in tribal court either. In *United States v. Ant*, a Northern Cheyenne Tribal Court convicted a defendant after he plead [sic] guilty to the offense without counsel to represent him. The right to counsel at the Northern Cheyenne Tribe is a right provided at one's own expense. The Court held that an uncounseled guilty plea, made in tribal court, is in accordance both with tribal law and the ICRA. See *United States v. Ant*, 882 F.2d 1389 (9th Circuit, 1989).

Under Hopi law, a criminal defendant may waive his right to counsel. In *Ami v. Hopi Tribe*, this court established the procedures necessary for a defendant to do so. These procedures are binding where a defendant wishes to waive his right to counsel and the burden lies with the Court to ensure that these standards are met.

The Appellant had counsel at trial and at sentencing for the original offense. His counsel was also present at the first scheduled hearing for the probation violation. The next step is to determine whether the right to counsel includes the right to presence of known, or in other words retained, counsel at critical stages in criminal proceedings. In this case, the criminal defendant appeared without counsel at a probation violation hearing.

The Hopi Constitution and By-Laws, Hopi Ordinance 21, Hopi Indian Rules of Civil and Criminal Procedure and ICRA do not explicitly answer the question of whether the right to counsel at one's own expense includes the right to counsel at a probation violation hearing. The Constitution of Arizona's Declaration of Rights and State Rules of Criminal Procedure provide the accused in criminal prosecution with the right to counsel at critical stages in criminal proceedings. See *State ex rel. Webb v. City Court of City of Tucson, Pima County*, 25 Ariz. App. 241 (1975); See *State v. Edge*, 96 Ariz. 302, (1965). It has been held that a hearing on revocation of probation is a critical state in a criminal proceeding, at which the accused is entitled to counsel. See State v. Lindsay, 5 Ariz. App. 516 (1967). However, a defendant in Arizona court may waive his right to counsel and appear at arraignment without counsel. See *State v. Edge*, 96 Ariz. 302 (1965).

Under Hopi Law, it is clear that a defendant has the right to counsel at his own expense. This right to counsel is not extinguishable merely because the proceeding at issue is a hearing on revocation of probation. The standards set forth in Ami still apply to such hearings.

2. Waiver of the Right to Counsel

The issue of denying defendant his right to counsel was raised in *Ami v. Hopi Tribe*, AP-003-89 (1996). This Court held that if the defendant did not properly waive his right to counsel the conviction must be reversed since the right to counsel is essential to achieve substantial justice in criminal proceedings. This court set forth explicit standards for a valid waiver of a defendant's right to counsel. If the Trial Court met the standards of Ami, its decision will be upheld. If it did not, its decision will be reversed.

Under Ami, Hopi Ordinance 21 requires that the trial court implement procedures to ensure that a defendant make a "knowing, intelligent and voluntary" waiver of right to counsel. Ami relied upon federal and state interpretations to establish that a valid waiver required that:

I. The defendant must signify understanding of the right by completing the Legal Rights Form.
II. The Trial Court must conduct an "active inquiry" to explain the legal effect of waiving the right, describe available options to retain an attorney, lay counsel or to act pro se, and finally determine if he understands the significance of the action.

The Legal Rights Form must state that the defendant has the right: (1) to be represented by a public defender when the defendant qualifies; (2) to be represented by an attorney or an advocate at one's own expense; and (3) to represent one's self without counsel. In addition to these rights, the form should also outline the consequences of representing one's self without counsel. The defendant should be warned: (1) that advocates understand the law and procedure better than the defendant; (2) that the defendant will be at a disadvantage without counsel; and (3) the possible maximum of fines or sentences. The defendant's signature on the Legal Rights Form does not presumptively establish a valid waiver of the right to counsel. See Ami P. 9. The absence of that form in the record is enough to cause this court to reverse the defendant's conviction.

However, the Legal Rights Form is not a substitute for "active inquiry" by the trial judge. An "active inquiry" is necessary to insure that the defendant understand the questions. The trial judge must make a comprehensive investigation during which the trial judge can insure that the defendant had the capacity to make a knowing, intelligent and voluntary waiver.

In this "active inquiry" the judge will: (1) tell the defendant that an advocate or attorney knows the law and the procedure better than the defendant and that the defendant will be at disadvantage without counsel; (2) mention the possible maximum consequences in fines or sentences; (3) inform the defendant of the availability of a public defender and ask him if he wishes to pursue this option; (4) ensure that the defendant has the capacity to understand the judge; (5) tell the defendant that the court will require the same level of legal skill from the defendant that it requires from an attorney; (6) ensure that the defendant was not coerced into making the plea; (7) explain the charges and possible defenses to the charges; and (8) ask the defendant if he knowingly waives the rights to obtain an attorney or lay advocate at his own expense. These requirements must be met in all cases. See Ami, p.10.

The Court's records should show proof that an "active inquiry" was conducted. Without proof on the records of such an inquiry, the Hopi Court of Appeals will presume that the right was improperly waived. See *Harvey v. Tribe*, 1259/88, AP-001-89 (1997).

The Trial Court conducted the arraignment without presence of defendant's known counsel. Defendant was represented by counsel and two motions filed by counsel to withdraw were denied by the Trial Court. The Trial Court was aware of defendant's representation by counsel and counsel had intentionally not been relieved from his duty to represent defendant. Under such circumstances, the Court must take special care in conducting an "active inquiry" to insure that the defendant fully understands the consequences of his decision to waive his right to counsel and the consequences of that decision.

Defendant in this case claimed in his motion to vacate sentence and dismiss criminal charges that his right to counsel was violated by the Trial Court. The Trial Court did not send any notice to defendant's known counsel about the probation revocation hearing. There is no written record in the Court's file indicating whether defendant waived his right to counsel. The Legal Rights Form used to accept a defendant's waiver of counsel is absent from the file. However, the "active inquiry" made by the Trial Court in order to insure that the defendant understood that both the nature and the consequences of his waiver of his right to counsel was sufficient to meet the standards under Ami.

Under the Ami standard, the judge needs to be assured that the defendant understands the waiver of right to counsel. The judge needs to be assured that the defendant understands each of the eight prongs set forth under Ami. In this case, the defendant's original counsel was a public defender. Thus, the requirement under an "active inquiry" that the defendant be informed of the availability of a public defender had been met even though the judge did not inform the defendant at hearing of that right. The judge does not need to ask questions already answered by the defendant's conduct and answers at trial. In this case, the defendant requested that he be allowed to serve his sentence 2 to 1. Testimony of Defendant, Court Transcript. Under Ami, the judge may draw reasonable conclusions from the testimony of the defendant in conducting an "active inquiry." Thus, in this case it is sufficient for the judge to explain that the maximum possible sentence was 228 days and leave it at that because the defendant clearly understood the full implications of that sentence as indicated by the transcript. However, mere recitation of the sentence is not always sufficient to meet the "active inquiry" standard. The judge may draw conclusions about the sophistication of the defendant from the history of the case and observations of the defendant in determining how to conduct an "active inquiry" that will meet the Ami standard. The only inquiry that the Trial Court made during the hearing consisted of a series of questions.

The minimum standard of waiver that the Court has established is that a waiver of an attorney or lay counsel must be made knowingly and intelligently. Simply asking defendant whether the defendant gives up their right to counsel is not always sufficient nor is it always insufficient. In determining whether an "active inquiry" was made, this court will look to the totality of the record. An "active inquiry" is designed to assure that the defendant understands those consequences of his waiver of his right to counsel. The Trial Court must insure that defendant understands those consequences. In some cases, that must be accomplished by reading all eight questions under the "active inquiry" standard. In others, the Trial Court may skip those questions that the judge is sure that the defendant already understands as observed from the record or the defendant's conduct at trial.

The Hopi Court of Appeals established the standards for a valid waiver in Hopi Tribe v. Ami. A valid waiver requires that defendant signifies understanding of the right to counsel by completing the Legal Rights Form and the trial Court must conduct an "active inquiry" to explain the legal effect of waiving the right, describe options to retain an attorney, lay counsel or to act pro se, and finally determine if he understands the significance of the action.

Defendant in this case had known and retained counsel. The Trial Court was aware of defendant's representation and allowed him to dismiss that counsel. By conducting a probation violation hearing without defendant's counsel present, the Trial Court assumed the burden of conducting an "active inquiry." In order to fulfill that burden, the Trial Court must insure that all eight factors of the active inquiry were fully understood by the defendant. In doing so, the Trial Court need not explicitly ask question but may draw inferences from the record and the conduct of the defendant. However, the absence of the Legal Rights Form is reversible error.

Order of the Court
The Hopi Court of Appeals hereby reverses the conviction of the appellant.

Conclusion

The right to an attorney is a critical individual right that protects against abuse by the government. When charged with a crime, the defendant faces a tremendous burden. The government possesses many more resources to move the prosecution forward. The prosecutor typically possesses much more knowledge about the laws and the procedures than the defendant. To stand alone, without an advocate in front of a judge or jury, and face criminal charges would place the defendant at an enormous disadvantage. Judges are tasked with ensuring a defendant is aware of this right and understands the right before he gives it up or waives it. Part of this right is the right to effective representation, not simply the right to have an attorney or advocate stand beside you. As the cases illustrated, the advocate must be effective in his representation and a defendant may challenge his conviction based on ineffective assistance by his attorney.

Questions

1. In *Quileute v. LeClair*, did the defendant knowingly waive her right to an attorney?
2. According to *Ami v. Hopi*, what factors does the judge need to talk with the defendant about to make sure the defendant makes a knowing, intelligent, and voluntary waiver?
3. According to *Navasie v. Hopi*, what is the federal test for whether an attorney is ineffective? Why did the Hopi Tribal Court decide to use the federal test?
4. Did the advocate in *Navasie* provide ineffective assistance of counsel? Why or why not?
5. Did the defendant in *Taylor v. Hopi Tribe* prove his attorney was ineffective? Why or why not?

In Your Community
1. Is the right to an attorney a right protected by your tribe? How does your tribe interpret that right? How can a person waive that right?
2. Traditionally, did individuals ever have someone represent or help them prosecute or defend a claim of wrongdoing?

Terms Used in Chapter 23
Dispositive: Relating to or having an effect on disposition or settlement, especially of a legal case or will.

Egregious: Conspicuously bad or offensive.

Pro se: Latin term meaning "for oneself"; applied to the actions of a person handling his or her own case in court without a lawyer.

Sequester: To isolate, hold aside, or take away. For example, to sequester a jury is to keep it from having contact with the outside world during a trial.

Notes
1. *Gideon v. Wainwright*, 372 U.S. 335 (1963); *Argersinger v. Hamlin*, 407 U.S. 25 (1972).
2. *Strickland v. Washington*, 466 U.S. 668 (1984).
3. Joshua Dressler, Understanding Criminal Procedure (3rd ed., LexisNexis 2002) 530–1.
4. *United States v. Cronic*, 466 U.S. 648, 659 (1984).
5. *United States v. Ash*, 413 U.S. 300 (1973).

Suggested Further Reading
Robert T. Anderson, "Criminal Jurisdiction, Tribal Courts and Public Defenders," 13 *Kan. J.L. & Pub. Pol'y*, 139 (2003).

Barbara Creel, "The Right to Counsel for Indians Accused of Crime: A Tribal and Congressional Imperative," 18 *Michigan Journal of Race & Law* 317 (2013).

Vincent C. Milani, "The Right to Counsel in Native American Tribal Courts: Tribal Sovereignty and Congressional Control," 31 *American Criminal Law Review* 1279 (1994).

Defendant Rights at Trial   Chapter 24

Prior chapters have focused a defendant's rights during investigation. In addition, there are several rights that protect a defendant during the court process. In the American justice system, prosecuting a defendant is considered to be one of the most powerful actions of the government. A defendant's rights during trial serve to protect him from abuse by the government. Tribal courts recognize and enforce defendant's rights for the same reason. These rights are designed to help ensure that the process is fair.

What Is Due Process?

The Indian Civil Rights Act (ICRA) prohibits any tribal government from depriving any person of liberty or property without due process of law.[1] Due process of law is an important right that often arises during a criminal investigation and prosecution because of the possibility of denying a person's liberty. Due process ensures "that all persons coming before the Court will be treated fairly,"[2] and requires that proceedings within the justice system are fair and protect a person's rights. Procedural due process focuses on the procedures in place to provide a fair trial, which include being advised of the criminal charges, having an opportunity to be heard, having a right to be represented by counsel, and calling witnesses. Substantive due process is a check on the power of the government and examines whether the process is fair and reasonable and not arbitrary.

What Does Due Process Include?

Due process can be difficult to define in simple terms The Fort Peck Court of Appeals provides a good overview of the "due process" concept:

Where life and liberty are involved, due process requires that a criminal trial must proceed according to the established procedure or rules of practice applicable to such cases. . . . Failure to accord a fair hearing violates even minimal standards of due process and constitutes a denial thereof. Since fair hearing requires an opportunity to prepare, due process may be violated by an overhasty trial. And since it is basic to due process that the accused have a fair opportunity to tell his story in a fair trial, reasonable notice of the charges and an adequate opportunity to defendant against them are basic elements of due process in a criminal proceeding.[3]

Tribal courts look to their own laws and customs to define due process, but sometimes tribal courts may look to federal courts' definition of due process as they analyze new issues. Below the Hopi Court addresses what due process means when determining whether bail, a restriction on a person's liberty, should be imposed.

Appellate Court of the Hopi Tribe
Norris v. Hopi Tribe (1988)
No. 98-AC-000007 (Hopi 11/23/1998), 1998.NAHT.0000020

Under Hopi law, the primary purpose of bail is to insure the presence of the accused at trial. See Hopi Tribal Ordinance ("H.T.O.") 2.5.1. All Indian defendants are bailable before conviction as a matter of right. H.T.O. 2.5.1. The judge will set bail upon the showing of probable cause by the prosecutor or complainant. H.T.O. 2.5.4. The amount and form of bail will be fixed in the sum, which, in the judgment of the court, will assure the defendant's presence at future court proceedings. H.T.O. 2.5.4. The court also has the discretion to release a defendant on his own recognizance at arraignment. H.T.O. 2.5.10.

The question of whether due process requires the court to impose a bail bond only if necessary to assure the defendant's presence at trial presents an issue of first impression. Under the Indian Civil Rights Act, "[n]o Indian tribe in exercising the powers of self-government shall: . . . deprive any person of liberty or property without due process of law." 25 U.S.C. 1302(8). Under Hopi Resolution H-12-76, the Hopi courts retain discretion to apply the tribe's interpretation of due process. *Tribe v. Mahkewa,* (1995).

Although the Hopi Tribe is not constrained by the due process guarantees in the United States Constitution, the courts have discretion to apply either federal or state standards to the extent that they are consistent with Hopi notions of fairness. In order to provide the trial court with more explicit standards governing the due process limitations upon bail, it might be helpful to review federal and state law on the issue. See *Tribe v. Ami*, AP-003-89 (1996). Under the federal courts' interpretation of due process, a restriction upon a defendant's liberty before trial must be regulatory, and not punitive.

The courts have found that assuring the defendant's presence at trial represents a legitimate and compelling regulatory interest sufficient to justify the deprivation of some amount of liberty. See *Stack v. Boyle*, 342 U.S. 1, 4 (1952). The practice of requiring admission to bail balances the individual's liberty interest with the government's interest in preventing the risk of flight. Id. Any restriction upon the defendant's liberty which is greater than the amount necessary to provide reasonable assurance of appearance at trial is inherently punitive. *Pugh v. Rainwater*, 572 F.2d 1053, 1057 (5th Cir. 1978).

The Hopi notion of due process encompasses the idea that bail should not be punitive. Fundamental fairness requires the court to restrict an individual's liberty interest before trial no greater than the extent necessary to advance the regulatory goals of the Hopi bail scheme. Because assuring the presence of the accused in court remains the central concern of the bail system, a trial judge should impose a bond as a condition of pre-trial release only after determining that the defendant is not likely to appear at trial.

Due Process Protection against Vague Statutes

Due process requires that a person be on notice or informed about what a law forbids. This means that statutes should be clear and descriptive. When a person's life or liberty is at stake, he is not required to speculate as to what the statute or law requires. Statutes should be clear. The following case addresses the vagueness of a statute.

Fort Peck Court of Appeals
Fort Peck Assiniboine and Sioux Tribes v. Stiffarm (1987)
No. 019 (Fort Peck 08/31/1987)

On March 13, 1986, Officer Andrew Azure signed a complaint alleging Appellant did commit the crime of Carrying a Concealed Weapon, a violation of Title III, Chapter 4, Section 401 of the Comprehensive Code of Justice of the Assiniboine and Sioux Tribes (hereinafter CCOJ). On that date Officer Azure received a call from the Tribal Office concerning an incident where Appellant was alleged to have pulled a weapon on Councilman Weeks and Councilman Culbertson. Officers Osgood and Azure investigated this incident and asked Jonny Lee Stiffarm if she had a gun. Appellant admitted having a gun and pulled it out of her coat and showed it to the officers. When asked if she had a license to carry the gun the Appellant stated she did not need a license under the code.

. . .

Appellant was found guilty of Carrying a Concealed Weapon by a five to one vote of the jury.

. . .

II. Whether the Concealed Weapons statute contained in the Comprehensive Code of Justice of the Fort Peck Assiniboine/Sioux Tribes is vague to the point of being unconstitutional on its face.

The Appellant was found guilty of violating III CCOJ 401, Carrying Concealed Dangerous Weapon. This statute reads:

> Sec. 401. Carrying a concealed dangerous weapon.
>
> Whoever carries, concealed about his or her person, any of the following weapons, unless they are carried with specific governmental approval, is guilty of carrying a concealed dangerous weapon:
>
> (a) any blackjack, billy, bludgeon, metal knuckles, or any knife with a blade over six (6) inches long or other sharp or dangerous instrument usually employed in the attack or defense of a person; or
>
> (b) any gun or dangerous firearm, whether loaded or unloaded.

Appellant contends that the above statute is unconstitutionally vague and indefinite. Appellant argues and states, "the criminal statute in question, as it stands, while it may afford the Defendant some idea as to why and [sic] accusation is made, it does not leave the defendant with the knowledge necessary to know how to comport her actions to avoid the penalty of this vague statute." This Court disagrees with Appellant's contention.

In deciding whether this statute is unconstitutionally vague, Appellant recommends that this Court adopt the test contained in *State v. Huffman*, 612 P.2d 630 (1980), which is set forth as follows:

> The test to determine whether a criminal statute is unconstitutionally vague and indefinite is whether its language conveys a sufficiently definite warning as to the conduct proscribed when measured by common understanding and practice. A statute which either requires or forbids doing of an act in terms so vague that persons of common intelligence must necessary guess at its meaning and differ to its application is violative of due process. 612 P.2d 630 at 636.

This Court has not formally adopted a test to determine whether a criminal statute is unconstitutionally vague and indefinite. The test in *State v. Huffman* is basically the test used in all jurisdictions to determine whether a criminal statute is unconstitutionally vague and indefinite. Therefore, this Court will follow Appellant's recommendation and adopt the test in *State v. Huffman*.

It has been established that whenever a challenge on the basis of vagueness is made to a criminal statute, and that statute does not involve First Amendment freedoms it must be examined in the light of the facts of the case at hand. *United States v. National Dairy Products Corp.*, 372 U.S. 29, 83 S.Ct. 594 (1963).

The facts of this case are that Appellant pulled a hand gun from her jacket pocket and pointed it at Councilman Culbertson and told him, "Don't f*ck with me." Appellant then put the gun back in her pocket and pointed her finger at Councilman Weeks and stated, "Don't ever f*ck with me or screw with me, you're next if you ever mess with me." Officers Osgood and Azure entered the Tribal Executive Council Board's chambers and Appellant showed the Officers the hand gun. When Officer Azure asked Appellant if she had a license, she informed them she did not need a license to carry a gun under the code.

An underlying principle of criminal law is that all are entitled to be informed as to what the state commands or forbids and no one should be required, at peril of life, liberty, or property, to speculate as to the meaning of penal statutes. Fundamental fairness requires that no person be held criminally responsible for conduct which he could not reasonably understand to be proscribed. 21 Am Jur 2d, Section 16, Page 128 et seq. III CCOJ 401 is clear in that it informs all Indians on the Fort Peck Indian Reservation that they are forbidden to carry concealed weapons specifically described therein. The only exception to this statute is the Indian that carries the concealed weapon with "specific governmental approval."

A criminal statute may be challenged as indefinite where the uncertainty has to do with what persons are within the scope of the act, what acts are prohibited, or what acts are excepted from the prohibition. Similarly, uncertainty as regards the penalty may make a criminal statute unenforceable. 21 Am Jur 2d, Section 17, Pages 128–129 et seq.

In the present case, the persons within the scope of III CCOJ 401 are Indians living on the Fort Peck Indian Reservation. (See I CCOJ 106.) The acts prohibited are the carrying of concealed weapons described in III CCOJ 401 without specific governmental approval. The acts excepted are the carrying of those concealed weapons described in III CCOJ 401 with specific governmental approval. The only governments one could reasonable [sic] infer that could give such approval would be the Tribe and the [Bureau of Indian Affairs] BIA for the purposes of law enforcement. Furthermore, the Tribal Executive Board could adopt a system for the issuance of permits to Indians on the Fort Peck Indian Reservation and has not adopted such a system. Therefore, III CCOJ 401 is not indefinite or vague on its face.

As stated above, Appellant argued that III CCOJ 401 does not leave Appellant with knowledge necessary to know how to comport her actions to avoid the penalty of this vague statute. The analysis above demonstrates Appellant's argument is without merit in that Appellant, an enrolled member of the Fort Peck Indian Reservation, should not have been carrying the concealed hand gun without specific governmental approval.

> III. Whether the application of the Concealed Weapons statute contained in Comprehensive Code of Justice of the Fort Peck Assiniboine/Sioux Tribes is a violation of the Defendant's Due Process rights guaranteed by the Indian Civil Rights Act of 1968.
>
> Appellant's Issue No. 2 was actually addressed in this Court's discussion of Issue No. 1. III CCOJ 401 is not vague on its face to the point of being unconstitutional. Therefore, it is the opinion of this Court that the application of III CCOJ 401 to Appellant is not a violation of Appellant's Due Process rights guaranteed by the Indian Civil Rights Act of 1968.

Due Process and Notice

Due process requires that person be provided with details of the crime with which she is charged. A person cannot adequately prepare a defense to a crime if she is unsure of the offense to be proven at trial. The case *Louie* in the following text provides guidance as to what is required to be included in a criminal complaint to provide due process. However, due process does not only require notice of the crime a person is charged with, it also requires notice that a court hearing will occur. *Fort Peck Tribes v. Morales* highlights the duty courts have to ensure fairness by providing notice to defendants of contested hearings.

> ### Colville Court of Appeals
> *Louie v. Colville Confederated Tribes* (1994)
> 2 CCAR 47 (Colville Confederated 10/28/1994)
>
> #### 1. Due Process Concerns
> The facts of this case illustrate that specific details stated in the Complaint are essential for adequate notice to a criminal defendant. Without specificity a defendant's right to due process is endangered. In this case the Complaint states that:
>
>> On or about the 25th day of April, 1993 and about the time of 2100 hours . . . the defendant did the following specific acts: struck Avis Villegas; at the following location: HUD #1136, Malott, Washington.
>
> The Affidavit of Probable Cause states:
>
>> On 25 April 1993 at approximately 18:59 hours, Tribal Officer D. Garvais was dispatched to possible criminal activity in progress at the residence of Avis Villegas, HUD No. 1136, Malott, Washington . . . Officer Garvais made contact with Ms. Villegas at HUD No. 188.

At trial Officer Garvais testified that he was dispatched on April 25, 1993 for an assault in progress at Malott HUD 1136. The officer further testified that he contacted Ms. Villegas, who was at the home of her nephew at Malott HUD house 188. Ms. Villegas told him that the defendant Louie had hit her and that defendant Louie was in her home at HUD 1136, Malott. Officer Garvais further testified that he was informed "later on" by Ms. Villegas that the battery had occurred in a car returning from the Nespelem rodeo.

The evidence at trial was to the effect that an altercation between Louie and Ms. Villegas occurred during a trip from Nespelem. No evidence was presented at trial as to the amount of time that was required to travel from the Nespelem rodeo to Malott. However, judicial notice can be taken of the fact that the time must have been considerable as the distance from Nespelem to Malott is known to be over 50 miles. The altercation in the vehicle and the alleged incident of the Complaint and Affidavit, which purportedly occurred in Malott, were not continuous, therefore, involved separate events. We conclude that the facts adduced at trial concerning the events which occurred in Malott will not support a conviction as to the offense alleged in the Complaint, as the following analysis will demonstrate.

The Colville Business Council was clear and direct regarding formal requirements of criminal complaints at CTC 2.2.01(2) Contents which states:

> 2.2.01(2) Contents. The Complaint shall be in writing and shall set forth:
>
> a. the name of the Court;
> b. the title of the action and the name of the offense charged;
> c. the name of the person charged; and
> d. the offense charged, in the language of the statute, together with a statement as to the time, place, person, and property involved to enable the defendant to understand the character of the offense charged.

The Panel reads CTC 2.2.01 as a directive by the Tribal Council to provide specific details of an offense charged in the complaint itself, so that a defendant will have an opportunity to formulate a defense.

In this case the insufficiency of the Complaint could not have given the defendant adequate notice of the crime he supposedly committed. In effect the defendant would have been required to prepare for two trials in order to present an effective defense.

The Complaint filed herein charged one time and place of occurrence, while the proof offered at trial dealt with an entirely different time and place. We conclude that this discrepancy falls far short of the Tribes' requirements of stating clearly in the Complaint the time and place of the offense as provided in CTC 2.2.01(2) and accordingly violates the due process requirements of CTC

56.02(f) by failing to give proper notice to defendant for the offense charged. *Auburn v. Brooks*, 19 Wn.2d 623 (1992), 41 Am.Jur.2d Indictments and Information, 269; 75 Am.Jur.2d Trials, 551.

. . .

Conclusion

We conclude that the evidence in this case did not justify a conviction of the offense charged in the Complaint. We further note that the inadequacy of the complaint cannot be cured by "bootstrapping" the deficient complaint with the allegations in the probable cause affidavit. The charge must, therefore, be dismissed. (*CCT v. Stensgar*, 1 CTCR 66 [Trial Court, 1993], Auburn v. Brooks, 119 Wn.2d 623 91992).

. . .

Fort Peck Court of Appeals
Fort Peck Tribes v. Morales (2000)
No. 307 (Fort Peck 07/28/2000)

Procedural History

Cerafin John Morales (Morales) was charged with a violation of Title III CCOJ §215 (simple assault) on January 29, 1998. A jury trial was held on September 2, 1998, the Honorable Georgia Dupuis, presiding. The jury returned a verdict which was announced by Judge Dupuis as "not guilty." Later that same day Tribal Prosecutor Chris Manydeeds filed three separate motions: one for mistrial (based upon the mistaken announcement of the judge that the verdict [4 to 2 for "not guilty"] resulted in "not guilty"), one for retrial assuming the grant of the motion for mistrial, and one for the appointment of a special prosecutor to be assigned for retrial, based upon the fact that Morales was a member of the Tribal Executive Board and sat on the Law and Justice Committee which, according to the Prosecutor, effectively controls the judiciary. All three motions were granted by Judge Dupuis. On September 4, 1998, an addendum to his Motion for Mistrial, based upon alleged juror misconduct, was also filed by the Prosecutor and was granted by Judge Barry Bighorn on the same day. The defendant appealed from the grant of these motions on September 4, 1998, citing a denial of due process and equal protection pursuant to 25 USC §1302 (8) (commonly referred to as the "Indian Civil Rights Act.") . . .

Brief Factual Background

On January 10, 1998, Morales and various members of his family were celebrating the marriage of his sister at the V.F.W. Club in Wolf Point, MT. According to the complaint, Morales walked up to the bar where William (Bill) White Head and Randy Nordwick were sitting. After White Head introduced Morales to Nordwick, Morales is alleged to have walked over to Nordwick and, without comment or provocation, assaulted Nordwick, knocking him to the floor. According to affidavits filed with a Motion to Dismiss, members of Morales' party stated that one or more of them were with Morales the entire evening and that no such assault took place.

After several delays occasioned by motions to continue by both sides, Morales was tried by a jury on September 2, 1998. The jury verdict form that was delivered to the Judge reflected a tally of four jurors in favor of "not guilty," and two jurors in favor of "guilty." The record is not clear as to whether Judge Dupuis misinterpreted the form when she declared the verdict as "not guilty." The Court did not poll the jury, nor did the Tribal Prosecutor move the court to do so. Thus, the jury was dismissed without objection of either party and without any indication from the jury panel that the verdict was anything other than "not guilty." Later the same day, realizing the possibility of an error, the Prosecutor immediately filed motions for mistrial, retrial, and for a special prosecutor. Judge Dupuis granted the motions without notice to defendant and without benefit of a hearing.

Issues Presented

Morales contends that the Tribal Court violated due process rights afforded him under the Indian Civil Rights Act (25 USC §1302 (8)), in that the court improperly declared a mistrial based on the ex parte motion of the Prosecutor. . .

Discussion

Due process of law is a broad concept and involves many aspects of an individual's rights, both procedurally and substantively. The Fourteenth Amendment to the United States Constitution provides that no State shall "deprive any person of life, liberty, or property, without due process of law." The Indian Civil Rights Act of 1968 contains a similar provision limiting Tribal governments: "No Indian Tribe in exercising powers of self-government shall . . . deny to any person within its jurisdiction the equal protection of its laws or deprive any person of liberty, or property without due process of law." 25 USC §1302 (8). Federal case law varies as to whether the "federal due process rights" are applicable to Indian Tribes. *Groundhog v. Keeler* (1971, CA10 Okla) 442 F2d 674 holds that 25 USCS § 1302 does not make applicable to Indian tribes the due process clause of the Fifth Amendment, equal protection and due process clauses of Fourteenth Amendment and provisions of Fifteenth Amendment. In accord is *Johnson v. Frederick* (1979, DC ND) 467 F Supp 956 which holds that "powers of tribal government are constrained only by provisions of Indian Civil Rights Act (25 USC §1302) and not by parallel provisions of (US) Constitution." However, *Red Fox v. Red Fox* (1977, CA9 Or) 564

F2d 361 holds that due process under Indian Civil Rights Act is same as that in the federal constitution. Our holding today does not attempt to address this conflict, but rather, will focus solely on our opinion of the requirements of due process under the Indian Civil Rights Act.

First and foremost, we believe that basic principles of fairness impose the duty on our Tribal Court Judges to protect the rights and privileges of all persons appearing in their courts, no matter what the nature of the crime or who the person may be. At a minimum, this duty requires that all parties have "notice" when their liberty or property is at risk and an opportunity to make their own claims or defense. Thus, we agree with the principle set forth in *Twining v. New Jersey*, 211 U.S. 78, 111 (1908) which holds that notice and a reasonable opportunity to be heard to present one's claim or defense have been fundamental conditions prescribed in all systems of law by civilized countries. We also subscribe to the notion that, "Procedural due process rules are meant to protect persons not from the deprivation, but from the mistaken or unjustified deprivation, of life, liberty, or property," *Carey v. Piphus*, 435 U.S. 247, 259 (1978). In essence, the "concept of due process exists to protect individuals against arbitrary action by their government." Berry v. Arapahoe & Shoshone Tribes (1976, DC Wyo) 420 F Supp 934.

This Court, in previously addressing the issue of ex parte orders, has stated, ". . . in obtaining an ex parte order to disqualify a judge under I CCOJ §307 without notice to the other party and the tribal court's failure to make specific findings and give the Tribes an opportunity to be heard, was error, and violated the code of ethics, and denied basic due process of law, and equal protection under the law to the Tribes." *Fort Peck Tribes v. Azure*, FPCOA #081, p. 5 (1989). In Azure we quoted from the Fort Peck Tribal Court Code of Judicial Conduct and find it equally compelling here:

> A judge should accord to every person who is legally interested in a proceeding, or his lawyer or advocate, the full right to be heard under the code, the Indian Civil Rights Act, and any other relevant source of law. Except as authorized by law, the judge shall not initiate nor accept any written or oral communication concerning a pending case, either from a party to the case or from any other person, without either the presence or agreement of all parties. The judge shall not meet with any party to a case, or accept any communication from a party without either the agreement or presence of all other parties. Canon 3 A (4).

Recently we held that the Tribal Court violated principles of due process of law when it dismissed the third party defendant United States on its own Motion, without giving the defendants, who had previously obtained Tribal Court permission to file a third party complaint against the United States, an opportunity to be heard. Jackson v. Grainger, FPCOA #287 (2000). In our opinion, ex parte communications and orders are the natural enemies of the principles of due process and should be used only when the circumstances warrant and such communications and orders are expressly authorized. In the case before us, the circumstances did not warrant, nor were ex parte communications expressly authorized.

Conclusion

We find that the granting of the motions by Judge Dupuis, were a violation of defendant's right to due process of law. It is also obvious that Judge Dupuis did not acquit the defendant on her own volition, but rather, misinterpreted the jury form, and that the Prosecutor's failure to assure that the jury was properly polled contributed to the error. This combined with the jurors failure to dissent or object to the verdict announced by Judge Dupuis, leaves this Court with no alternative but to reinstate the original "announced" verdict of not guilty, rendering all other issues related to this appeal moot.

Accordingly, the order of the Tribal Court granting a mistrial is reversed.

Due Process and Guilty Pleas

Before a court can accept a person's guilty plea, the court must ensure the defendant understands all their rights that they're giving up by pleading guilty to a criminal charge. In Chapter 23 the *Ami* case from the Hopi Tribal Court illustrated the right to an attorney. It also addresses the procedures that must be in place for a court to accept a person's waiver of his rights to protect his right to due process, which includes a right to an attorney, prior to the court accepting a guilty plea.

Appellate Court of the Hopi Tribe
Ami v. Hopi Tribe (1996)
No. AP-003-89 (Hopi 03/29/1996), 1996.NAHT.0000005 (VersusLaw)

. . .

Issues Presented on Appeal

These appeals raise very important issues about the proper criminal procedure in Hopi Trial Courts. This court must address: (1) what are the standards in Hopi Trial Courts for the valid waiver of the right to counsel; (2) what are the standards in Hopi Trial Courts for a valid guilty plea; and (3) were these standards met in the cases before this court.

. . .

II. In order to accept a valid guilty plea, the trial court must comply with the procedural requirements of Hopi Ordinance 21, ensure that there is a factual basis for the plea, and determine that the plea was voluntarily made.

The acceptance of guilty pleas in Hopi trial courts is governed by Title II, Chapter 6 of Hopi Ordinance 21. This provides, in part,

> 2.6.1 ARRAIGNMENT—Defined. The arraignment must be made in open Court, and consists in reading the complaint to the defendant, and delivering to him a true copy thereof and of the endorsements thereon, and asking him whether he pleads guilty or not guilty to the offense charged in the complaint.
> 2.6.2 PROCEDURE AT ARRAIGNMENT. Arraignment shall be conducted in open Court, and consists of the following:
> a. Reading the complaint to the accused.
> b. Stating to him the substance of the charge and the language of the law establishing the offense and fixing the penalty.
> c. Advising him of his rights to counsel at his own expense, if he so desires.
> d. Calling on him to plead to the charges.
> 2.6.3 PLEAS. The defendant may plead 'guilty,' [or] 'not guilty'. . . . If the defendant wishes to plead 'guilty,' he may be sentenced immediately or within a reasonable time thereafter. A plea made to the Court must be made in open Court with the defendant himself in Court. Hopi Ordinance 21, Sections 2.6.1–2.6.3.

The plain language of this ordinance describes the procedures for arraignment proceedings in Hopi Trial Courts. According to this ordinance, the judge should: (1) read the complaint to the defendant; (2) give the complaint to the defendant; (3) explain the charge to the defendant; (4) describe the penalties to the defendant; (5) advise the defendant of his right to counsel; and (6) ask the defendant to plead the charges.

This conclusion is consistent with the ICRA [Indian Civil Rights Act of 1968]. The ICRA does not prescribe a set procedure for arraignment proceedings. However, some of its provisions bear on the acceptance of a valid guilty plea. Specifically, "[n]o Indian tribe in exercising the powers of self-government shall: . . . (8) deprive any person of liberty or property without due process of law." 28 U.S.C. 1302 (8) (1968). An inappropriate standard for the guilty plea could deny the defendant of the due process of law.

This Court will always interpret the ICRA with due regard for the historical, governmental, and cultural values of the Tribe. *Ramos v. Pyramid Tribal Court*, 621 F.Supp. 967 (D. Nev. 1985). Nonetheless, it is appropriate to consider federal case law interpreting this provision and the analogous provisions of the federal Constitution. The analogous provisions of the United States Constitution provide, in pertinent part, "No person . . . shall . . . be deprived of life, liberty, or property, without due process of law," and "[i]n all criminal prosecutions, the accused shall enjoy the right . . . to be informed of the nature and cause of the accusation." U.S. CONST. amend. V and VI. This language requires a knowing, intelligent, and voluntary plea. *Machibroda v. United States*, 368 U.S. 487 (1962). Here we find the ICRA also requires a knowing, intelligent, and voluntary plea.

Although Hopi Ordinance 21 provides some requirements for a valid guilty plea, this Court recognizes that an appropriate standard is essential to the fair and efficient administration of the criminal justice system. Guilty pleas are valuable to the Tribe because they conserve judicial resources on less complex cases in which a defendant admits his guilt and allow the Tribe to punish these defendants. However, defendants may plead guilty for a variety of reasons besides actual guilt. Defendants may feel that it will be easier and faster to plead guilty, they may be apprehensive about the unfamiliar criminal process, they may think that the evidence is too strong against them, or they may want to avoid the publicity and costs of going to trial. If an innocent defendant pleads guilty, he waives many other rights like the right to a jury trial and the right to confront witnesses. Moreover, the Tribe does not have to prove its case. The innocent defendant is punished. This is unfair to the innocent defendant and undermines the credibility and integrity of the criminal justice system. Hence, it is important to adopt a feasible and fair standard.

Because of these concerns, it is useful to review the standards for the entrance of valid guilty pleas in other jurisdictions. In federal courts, the judge must: (1) address the defendant personally; (2) inform the defendant about the nature of the charges; (3) warn the defendant about the possible consequences of the plea; (4) ensure that the defendant knows the rights that he is waiving; (5) determine the voluntariness of the plea; (6) determine that there is a factual basis for the plea; and (7) make a record of the proceedings. FED. R. CRIM. P. 11. In Arizona state courts: (1) the defendant must personally make the plea in open court; (2) the plea must be voluntarily and intelligently made; (3) the judge must make a complete record; (4) the judge must ensure that the defendant understands the nature of the charges, the range of sentences, and his constitutional rights; and (5) the judge must ensure that there is a factual basis for the plea. ARIZ. REV. STAT. ANN. RULES CRIM. PROC. 17.1–17.3 (1986). Finally, another tribal court requires the judge to advise the defendant about: (1) his constitutional rights; (2) the nature of the crime; and (3) the maximum penalty. Furthermore, this information must appear in the record. *Devils Lake Sioux Tribe v. Ironhawk*, 18 Indian L. Rep. 6088 (N. Plns. Intertr. Ct. App., 1990).

This Court recognizes important differences between Ordinance 21 and the federal and Arizona approaches to guilty pleas. Specifically, in addition to the requirements of Ordinance 21, both the federal and Arizona courts require that the judge: (1) advise the defendant of all of his rights (not just his right to counsel); (2) create a complete record of all of the proceedings; (3) ensure that there was a factual basis for the plea; and (4) determine that the plea was voluntarily made. All of these requirements serve to protect the rights of defendants and ensure that innocent defendants are not punished. We will consider each additional requirement in turn.

Hopi Ordinance 21 compels a judge to advise a defendant of his right to counsel. Although this is a very important right, it is not the only right that a defendant waives by pleading guilty to the charges. The defendant also waives his right to confront witnesses, compel witnesses to testify on his behalf, and right to a trial by jury. These are also fundamental rights and a defendant should be advised of these rights as well. All of this information is required in order to make a knowing, intelligent, and voluntary plea. Hence, a Hopi trial judge must ensure that the defendant knows these rights before accepting a plea.

Moreover, the federal and Arizona approaches require that the judge develop a complete record of the proceedings. Hopi courts are also courts of record. Hopi Resolution H-12-76. For this reason, it is also appropriate for Hopi trial courts to make a tape recording of the entire proceeding and make transcriptions of these tape recordings available to this Court at the expense and request of one of the parties. This will require the Tribe to label all tapes and keep them in a secure place so that they will be available at the request of one of the parties. Moreover, these tapes must be preserved (labeled and kept in a secure place) while the case is pending on appeal.

It is also appropriate to ensure that there is a factual basis for the plea. Requiring the judge to ensure that there are facts to support the defendant's plea will help ensure that tribal courts do not impose punishment on innocent defendants. Although this is not required by the plain language of Hopi Ordinance 21, it is not foreign to our courts. Indeed, the Legal Rights Form specifically requires that the judge indicated that there was a factual basis for the plea. Moreover, in *Gishey v. Hopi Tribe*, the trial judge did ensure that there was a factual basis for the plea. For the foregoing reasons, this Court holds that trial judges must also ensure that there is a factual basis for the plea before accepting a defendant's guilty plea.

Finally, federal and Arizona procedures require that the judge determine that the plea was voluntarily entered. Guilty pleas must also be voluntarily entered in Hopi trial courts. It is appropriate to require that the trial judge in the first instance ensures that this requirement is met. Therefore, this Court also adopts this requirement.

To summarize, a judge may accept a guilty plea after: (1) reading the complaint to the defendant; (2) giving the complaint to the defendant; (3) explaining the charge to the defendant; (4) advising the defendant of his rights; (5) creating a complete record of the proceedings; (6) determining that there is a factual basis for the plea; (7) determining that the plea was voluntarily made; and (8) asking the defendant to plead to the charges. Because it is so important to comply with each of these steps, this Court will be reluctant to uphold convictions on appeal when the judge has not complied with each of these steps. See *McCarthy v. United States*, 394 U.S. 459, 472 (1969); United States v. Allard, 926 F.2d 1237, 1244-45 (1st Cir. 1991); United States v. Del Prete, 567 F.2d 928 (9th Cir. 1978). Nonetheless, minor deviations from this standard will be permitted if the defendant still entered a knowing, intelligent, and voluntary guilty plea.

. . .

Order of the Court

It is hereby ORDERED that the convictions in all three of the consolidated cases, *Ami v. Hopi Tribe, Pavatea v. Hopi Tribe,* and *Gishey v. Hopi Tribe* are REVERSED and the cases are REMANDED to the trial court for proceedings consistent with this Opinion.

Due Process and Sentencing

The right to due process does not end when a guilty plea is entered by a defendant. A convicted defendant still has a right to a fair hearing at sentencing. Sentencing is covered in-depth in Chapter 26. The following Colville case focuses on due process rights during the sentencing hearing.

Colville Court of Appeals

Sam v. Colville Confederated Tribes (1994)
2 CCAR 37 (Colville Confederated 03/08/1994), 2 CTCR 04, 21 ILR 6040, 2 CCAR 37, 1994.NACC.0000002 (VersusLaw)

We have been asked to review the sentencing procedure and sentences imposed by the Tribal Court in these cases to determine whether the appellant's civil rights were violated under the Indian Civil Rights Act (ICRA), 25 U.S.C. 1301-1303 and the Colville Tribal Civil Rights Act (CTCRA), CTC 56.02 et seq. Specifically, the appellant alleges that he was denied due process of law in sentencing pursuant to ICRA, 25 U.S.C. 1302 (8) and CTCRA, CTC 56.02(h)...

I

The procedural history of the above cases is as follows: In AP92-15379 and AP92-15380, Sam was convicted at bench trial, on March 4, 1993, Fry, J., presiding, of

Driving While Intoxicated, CTC 9.1.01 and Driving While License Suspended, CTC 9.1.05. The Court ordered a presentence investigation and on April 26, 1993 Sam was sentenced to a jail term of 360 days, with credit for four days served, and a fine of $2,500.

In cases AP92-15414 and AP92-15415, Sam was convicted at bench trial on January 15, 1993, Fry, J., presiding, of Driving While Intoxicated, CTC 9.1.01 and Driving While License Suspended, CTC 9.1.05. The Court ordered a presentence investigation and on March 8, 1993, Sam was sentenced to a jail term of 360 days, with credit for 55 days served, to be served concurrently with any current incarceration. The court also imposed a fine of $2,500 which was conditionally suspended. The appellant preserved the same issues for appeal as in AP92-15379 and AP92-15380.

Our review of the record at sentencing in cases AP92-15379 and AP92-15380 reveals that Sam's counsel objected to the validity of some of the criminal convictions shown in the Presentence Investigation Report (PSIR) and the sentencing judge's finding that Sam had eight previous DWI convictions. Although counsel admitted that Sam had been previously convicted of five DWI's, he argued that at least some of the convictions were constitutionally invalid because Sam was not represented by counsel. The record does not show which of Sam's past convictions were challenged for purposes of sentencing.

. . .

III

. . .

We have held that a criminal defendant has a due process right to be sentenced on the basis of accurate information. St. Peter, at 6111. In order to prevail on a due process challenge, the defendant must show that misinformation of a constitutional magnitude was given to the court and that such information was given specific consideration by the sentencing judge. Id. The defendant must show that the information relied upon by a sentencing judge lacks "some minimal indicum of reliability beyond mere allegation." See *United States v. Matthews*, 773 F.2d 48, 51 (3rd Cir. 1985). See also *United States v. Monaco*, 852 F.2d 1143, 1149 (9th Cir. 1988).

. . .

IV

. . .

We have previously held that, as a matter of due process, a criminal sentence may not be based upon prior unrepresented convictions where the defendant was not advised of his right to counsel or was improperly denied his right to counsel. St. Peter at 6111. A criminal defendant's right to due process is not violated simply because uncounseled criminal convictions are used by the court in sentencing. Id. It is the Appellant's burden to bring to the sentencing court's attention the additional, specific grounds why uncounseled convictions were unconstitutionally obtained and should not be used in sentencing. Where the defendant had an opportunity to examine and correct controverted information in sentencing, and request an evidentiary hearing, but failed to do so, the error is counsel's and not the court's. See *United States v. Barnhart*, 980 F.2d 219, 226 (3rd Cir. 1992), citing *United States v. Matthews*, 773 F.2d 48, 51 (1975).

In view of our holding in St. Peter, we find that the Tribal Court did not error in using uncounseled criminal convictions in sentencing. The appellant has made no showing that the criminal convictions relied upon by the sentencing judge were improperly obtained pursuant to tribal law. The appellant has not shown, for example, in the convictions used in sentencing that the Court failed to inform him of his right to counsel or improperly denied his right to counsel.

From our review of the record, the Panel holds that the sentencing judge's denial of Appellant's motion to continue sentencing did not deprive him of a fair opportunity to rebut or explain the information being considered by the Court for imposing sentence. Appellant did not request an evidentiary hearing to prove the information contained in the PSIR concerning his criminal history was inaccurate. Rather, Appellant advanced a procedural argument, based upon state law, that certain criminal convictions referenced in the PSIR were constitutionally invalid because he was unrepresented. Moreover, the appellant has not shown that he was denied a fair opportunity to review information contained in the PSIR or other information brought before the Court. Accordingly, we also hold that the appellant did not carry his burden of rebutting the accuracy of information considered by the Court in sentencing.

. . .

VI

We find that the remaining issues raised in these appeals have been squarely addressed in St. Peter, supra, and those principles are applicable here. For the reasons stated above the Judgments and Sentences of the Tribal Court are Affirmed.

Double Jeopardy

The U.S. Constitution, ICRA, and many tribal codes and constitutions provide a right against double jeopardy (being prosecuted for the same crime twice). This right protects a person from harassment by the government. Note, however, that prosecutions for the same offense by two separate sovereigns, for instance the federal government and a tribal government, are not barred.

The law of double jeopardy can be confusing. It is clear that if a defendant is acquitted or found not guilty of a crime, then that person cannot be charged with any crime for the same conduct again by the same sovereign. If someone is convicted of a crime, appeals, and wins the appeal, then that person cannot be charged with an offense for the same conduct if that offense carries a greater penalty than the offense for which the defendant was convicted the first time. An appeals court can order that a new trial be held on the same issue, however.

Yet it can be confusing whether a defendant is charged twice with the same offense in a criminal complaint. Sometimes more than one offense applies to a given situation, and the less serious ones are referred to as lesser-included offenses. For example, in the case of a battery on someone, the battery can also be considered disorderly conduct. If someone pleads guilty to disorderly conduct by fighting and is later charged with battery for the same conduct, some jurisdictions would classify the situation as double jeopardy. A prosecutor is permitted to claim that a defendant committed more than one crime in the course of one criminal act, but only if the elements of the two crimes are different.

The following court opinion illustrates a tribal perspective on the doctrine of "double jeopardy." As you review the case, think about the importance of maintaining a fair process for the defendant.

Appellate Court of the Hopi Tribe

The Hopi Tribe v. Marlon Huma (1995)
1995.NAHT.0000013 (VersusLaw)
Before Sekaquaptewa, Chief Judge, and Lomayesva and Abbey, Judges.

Opinion and Order

Factual and Procedural Background

On November 25, 1991 the defendant was exiting a house of a known "**bootlegger.**" The arresting officer saw him exiting the house and "circled back" to see if he was the member of the household who had an outstanding arrest warrant. He was not. The defendant was carrying a brown paper bag under one arm. The officer asked the defendant what was in the bag. The defendant replied, "Nothing." The officer then reached out and touched the bag, felt "the shape and feel of 375 ml glass wine bottles," and heard the "slosh of a liquid." He placed the defendant under arrest on the charge of wrongful possession of alcoholic beverages, a violation of Hopi Tribal Ordinance No. 21, Section 3.3.83. He then searched the bag and found four bottles of "Thunderbird" wine.

The Tribe presented the wine, the bag, and chain of custody at the trial. The defendant did not object to the evidence. The arresting officer testified to the above fact, and the defendant did not object. At the end of trial, the judge held that the officer did not have an **articulable suspicion** of wrongdoing prior to making the stop. The defendant was found "not guilty of any law violation."

The Tribe appeals on two grounds. First, the judge erroneously found that the officer did not have a reasonable articulable suspicion of criminal activity. Second, the evidence was not objected to by the defendant and it is not within the purview of the court to ignore it. We do not reach these issues, however. Before arriving at these issues, we must determine if the doctrine of double jeopardy exists in Hopi criminal jurisprudence, and if so, whether an appeal in the instant case [constitutes] double jeopardy. We conclude that double jeopardy doctrine does apply to Hopi criminal cases [and] that an appeal of an acquittal would violate that right. We therefore dismiss the appeal.

Discussion

We hold that the double jeopardy doctrine applies in a Hopi criminal case.

Neither the Hopi Constitution or Ordinance 21 refers to double jeopardy. However, the Indian Civil Right Act of 1968 (ICRA) established that no Indian tribe may "subject any person for the same offense to be twice put in jeopardy." This language mirrors that of the United States Constitution. It has not been established that the Hopi Courts are bound by ICRA. The Hopi Tribe did not write or adopt ICRA. Rather, it was the United States Congress which passed the legislation to ensure that Indians on reservations were afforded similar liberties as those granted to United States Citizens through the Constitution and the Bill of Rights. While Hopi has not directly accepted ICRA, neither has it rejected it.

The double jeopardy doctrine is an elemental principle of the United States criminal law. No "person shall be subject for the same offense to be twice put in jeopardy of life or limb". . . . The "most fundamental rule" of double jeopardy jurisprudence is that a "verdict of acquittal [can] not be reviewed, on error or otherwise" because it would place the defendant in jeopardy twice. Thus, a verdict of not guilty is not appealable in the United States courts.

The purpose of double jeopardy is to protect both the society and the defendant. "At the heart of this policy is the concern that permitting the sovereign freely to subject the citizen to a second trial for the same offense would arm Government with a potent instrument of oppression." The doctrine insures that the members of the Tribe rely on a verdict of "not guilty." For the Tribal Courts to maintain their status as arbitrators of justice, the people of the Tribe must know that the courts' pronouncements are valid.

The double jeopardy doctrine also protects defendants. It prohibits multiple attempts to convict a defendant and "thereby subjecting him to embarrassment, expense and ordeal and compelling him to live in a constant state of anxiety and insecurity." Id. The doctrine thus serves the purpose of allowing the general population to feel secure from government oppression, increases confidence in the courts, and provides a form of finality to individual defendants.

ICRA applies the Double Jeopardy doctrine to the Tribe. The Hopi Tribe has not created a provision for the Tribe to appeal an acquittal or expressly rejected the doctrine. Double jeopardy is a basic component of the United States legal doctrine and serves goals that will protect the Hopi people and increase the Hopi confidence in the courts.

The Hopi Trial Court did not hold a pretrial hearing to decide the admissibility of the evidence.... Instead, the Hopi Trial Court suppressed the evidence and granted a judgment of acquittal at the end of his trial on the merits. This is the most basic type of bar against retrial. The doctrine of double jeopardy can be complicated, but no court allows the retrial after acquittal, no matter how "mistaken" the trial court may have been.

The Tribal Prosecutor asserts that if "the trial court has neglected its duty, it certainly cannot hold such failure against the Tribe." This gets at the heart of the matter. It is the Tribe which has the duty to prove the defendant guilty. It is the Tribe which has the burden of establishing and running the courts. If, through error, the defendant is found not guilty, it is the Tribe which must bear the burden. In no circumstances can a failure of the courts of prosecution be held against the defendant.

We hold that the principle of Double Jeopardy does not allow a retrial of the defendant upon acquittal. The Tribe cannot appeal. The appeal is DISMISSED.

Statutes of Limitation

A statute of limitations provides the time period within which a criminal or civil action must be brought in court. A statute of limitations means that once a crime has been committed, a prosecutor has a certain time in which to charge the accused. For example, suppose someone reported a theft that happened thirty years ago. The statute of limitations would not allow prosecution for that crime.

Once the specified time period has elapsed, the individual is not subject to criminal prosecution. Many tribal codes include statutes of limitation. Most criminal offenses have a time limit of one to five years, although some major offenses, such as homicide, have no statute of limitations. Some criminal offenses may modify the statute of limitations such that the time does not begin until the crime is discovered. Some governments have laws that the time frame for child abuse cases does not begin until the child turns eighteen.

The prosecution is considered to have commenced when a criminal complaint is filed with the court or when an arrest warrant, for example, is issued. What happens if a crime is committed but not discovered within three years or if the person who committed the crime is not discovered or found within three years?

For example, a body is found three years after death, but the identity of the murderer is not discovered within three years, or it takes more than three years to find the killer. There is a doctrine in some jurisdictions that the time limitation begins upon the discovery of a crime but that it is suspended if the defendant is a fugitive from justice, that is, on the run.

Statute of Limitations

All criminal actions must be brought within one year from the date the offense was committed. For purposes of determining whether the statute of limitations has expired on a criminal charge a criminal action shall be considered brought within the time period if the warrant of arrest has been issued within one (1) year from the date on which the offense was committed. Any criminal action not brought within the time period set forth above shall be forever barred in the Tribal Court.

Poarch Creek Code of Justice Sec. 5-1-2(a)

Speedy Trial

A right to a speedy trial means that the prosecutor cannot delay in charging a defendant with a crime. Once criminal charges have been filed, the tribe has a duty to bring the defendant to trial in a timely manner. Some tribes have dismissed cases for violating a defendant's right to a speedy trial, but only if the delay in the trial prejudiced the defendant. In other words, the delay must have harmed the defendant through the loss of witnesses or memory about the events of the alleged crime. Some tribes have found that a delay longer than six months from the filing of the complaint is a violation of the defendant's right to a speedy trial. Some jurisdictions accept that argument, but others do not.

Appellate Court of the Hopi Tribe

Augustine Komalestewa v. The Hopi Tribe (1996)
1996.NAHT.0000008 (VersusLaw)
Before Sekaquaptewa, Chief Judge, and Lomayesva and Abbey, Judges.

Opinion and Order

Factual and Procedural Background

Because dates are important to the alleged speedy trial claim, the facts will be presented in a manner that best illustrates the chronological order (all events occurred in 1990).

February 12. Augustine Komalestewa, appellant [defendant], was driving on Highway 264 toward Polacca Village when he was stopped by a police officer. Appellant was the driver and sole occupant of the car at the time. The officer searched the car trunk and found 48 bottles of Thunderbird wine. Appellant was arrested for wrongfully possessing (transporting) alcoholic beverages in violation of former Hopi Ordinance 21, section 3.3.83. Appellant claims there was no evidence offered at trial to indicate appellant owned the car or was aware of the contents of the trunk, and respondent [the Tribe] does not say appellant was the registered owner of the car.

February 13. Appellant was arraigned. Appellant claims he was not released on his own recognizance, but respondent claims he was. The pre-trial hearing was set for March 21, [1990], but the trial court then changed the pre-trial date to April 11 . . .

April 11. The parties stipulated to a postponement until April 24.

April 25. Pre-trial was held. Appellant requested the case be tried no earlier than the third week of August 1990. The next day, the appellant filed a motion for a jury trial on August 21. On July 3, the trial court set the case for a bench trial on September 11.

September 11. The trial court recognized that a bench trial was inappropriate given appellant's previous request, and it set the case for a jury trial on October 4.

October 4. After jury selection, respondent moved for a mistrial because it was discovered that three of the selected jury members had lied during the questioning. Appellant objected to a mistrial and moved for dismissal. Respondent's motion was granted. A new trial was set for October 25.

October 25. Before the jury questioning began, the tribal prosecutor made repeated comments the judge found unfairly prejudicial. Appellant moved to have the potential jury members dismissed and the trial judge agreed. A new trial was set for November 13.

November 13. A jury trial was conducted and appellant was found guilty.

Discussion

[Section I omitted]

II. Speedy Trial

Under the Hopi Tribal Code, "the [criminal defendant] shall have the right to . . . a speedy . . . trial. . . ." Hopi Ordinance 21, § 2.8.5. The right to a speedy trial is also found in the Indian Civil Rights Act, which says that "[n]o Indian Tribe . . . shall deny to any person in a criminal proceeding the right to a speedy . . . trial. . . ." 25 U.S.C.A. § 1302(6). However, neither the Hopi Ordinance nor the Indian Civil Rights Act (nor the Sixth Amendment to the U.S. Constitution for that matter) says just how "speedy" the process needs to be. Because this court has not ruled on what constitutes a violation of a defendant's right to a speedy trial either, there is no number of days this court can use to recognize the violation of the speedy trial right.

Under our decision in Hopi Tribe v. Mahkewa, if Hopi written laws or rules are not on point, we will consider first Hopi custom and tradition. If no custom or tradition is on point, then we will turn to foreign law, and we will first consider either federal or Arizona state law, or both. Hopi custom speaks to fairness, but it does not provide specific guidance for defining when the right to a speedy trial has been violated. Therefore, we will consider foreign law and apply it to the extent it is consistent with our customs, traditions and culture.

The generally accepted purpose of a speedy trial right is to: (1) ensure the defendant is not in jail too long before his trial; (2) minimize the length of time a defendant is anxious about an impending criminal trial; and (3) limit the possibility that a delay will impair a defendant's ability to defend himself. To the extent a delay would disadvantage a defendant, the tribe has a duty of fairness to not "stack the deck" against the defendant by delaying the trial so long that the defendant has a more difficult time developing a reasonable defense to the charges. In some cases, however, a delay in a trial may work to the defendant's benefit when prosecution witnesses become either unavailable, or a little less certain of what they observed. Therefore, although most jurisdictions offer a speedy trial "right," violation of that right may not always hurt the defendant.

A. FEDERAL LAW. The federal courts use a balancing test that was handed down by the Supreme Court in Barker v. Wingo. Under this test, a court will weigh four factors against each other to determine if the delay violated the right to a speedy trial. The four factors are:

i. Length of delay;
ii. Reason for the delay;
iii. Defendant's assertion of his right to a speedy trial; and
iv. Prejudice to the defendant

i. Length of delay. The first factor is a threshold matter: if the delay reflected "customary promptness," then there was no violation of the right to a speedy trial. *Doggert v. United States*, 505 U.S. 647, 652 (1992). If the delay was "presumptively prejudicial," however, then the other three factors have to be considered.

In this case, the respondent conceded that the nine month delay from time of arrest (in February 1990) to time of trial (in November 1990) was "sufficient to trigger analysis of the remaining factors. . . ." This does not mean that a nine-month delay will always trigger this analysis, but we suspect it is sufficiently long to probably prejudice any criminal defendant in his or her preparation for the trial. We agree and therefore review the other factors.

ii. Reason for the delay. It is not enough to say that defendant suffered a prejudicial delay without looking into the reasons for the delay—some of which might be inexcusable and others quite reasonable. See Barker (noting that "[a] deliberate attempt [by the government] to delay the trial in order to hamper the defense should be weighed heavily against the government"). The Supreme Court noted that "a more neutral reason such as neglect or overcrowded courts should be weighed less heavily but nevertheless should be considered since the ultimate responsibility for such circumstances must rest with the government rather than the defendant."

In the chronology of this case, the eight week delay from February 13 (arraignment) and April 11 (scheduled pre-trial) was due to court delays, but there is no evidence of a deliberate attempt to prejudice appellant. The seventeen week period from April 11 to August 21 (requested trial date) was either by stipulation of appellant or because counsel for appellant wanted to take the New Mexico Bar Examination. The three week delay from August 21 to September 11 (first attempted trial), is probably due to court scheduling delays. The three week delay from September 11 to October 4 (second attempted trial) was the result of the trial court scheduling a bench trial after a jury trial had been requested. The three week delay from October 4 to October 25 (third attempted trial) is probably neutral because the delay was necessary to ensure the defendant received a fair trial. See Hopi Ord. 21, § 2.9.2. The two week delay from October 25 to November 13 (final trial) should probably weigh heavily against the government. Although we do not have a record of the circumstances, it is appropriate to presume any questions in this regard in favor of the appellant.

Therefore, of the thirty-six week delay, seventeen weeks can be attributed to appellant and do not count against the Hopi Tribe in determining whether appellant's speedy trial right was violated. Fourteen weeks of the delay are attributed to court delays; three of which are the fault of the trial court for erroneously scheduling a bench trial when a jury trial had been requested. Even if the trial court's error was unintentional, such delays are the very kind the speedy trial right is designed to protect against. The two week delay caused by the tribal prosecutor because of his prejudicial remarks during jury selection on October 25 weigh[s] against the government. The remaining three weeks are more neutral in that they resulted from a mistrial granted to protect appellant's rights to a fair and impartial jury.

Against the three-and-one-half month delay attributed to respondent [The Tribe], the five week delay counted against the government is not significant in comparison. Thus, the primary reasons for the delay is appellant's own requests for delays and stipulations to continuances.

iii. Assertion of the speedy trial right. While a defendant does not have to constantly raise the speedy trial right to the court, "[t]his does not mean, however, that the defendant has no responsibility to assert his right." The defendant waived the speedy trial right at the pre-trial hearing on April 24 when he requested a delay until at least August 21. The next time he raised the right was not until October 4—nearly eight months after appellant's arrest. The speedy trial objection was raised in connection to the delays caused by the mistrial and not by those caused by invalid reasons. These facts suggest that appellant did not vigorously assert his speedy trial right.

iv. Prejudice to the defendant. This is also a threshold concern in that unless appellant suffered some prejudice from the delay, there is no violation of the speedy trial right in federal courts. United States v. Griffen, 464 F.2d 1352, 1354 (9th Cir. 1972), cert. denied 409 U.S. 1109 (1972). Appellant does not allege any prejudice caused him by the delay in prosecution. He needs to point to some prejudice because it is equally possible that the delay may have worked to his favor. While this may be unlikely, it would be wrong for us to speculate on how this delay prejudiced appellant at trial or during his pre-trial preparations.

One of appellant's arguments to show why his speedy trial right was violated concerns the trial court's alleged failure under Hopi Ordinance 21, section 2.8.7, to say why the September 11 trial had to be rescheduled. Appellant claims that absent such a showing, this Motion to Dismiss on speedy trial grounds should have been granted.

Appellant is very aware of why the trial had to be rescheduled: the trial court erroneously scheduled a bench trial . . . on September 11, and there was no jury available to hear appellant's case. Short of dismissing the case, which was not called for, or conducting a bench trial, the case had to be rescheduled to obtain a jury, as appellant had required. As to appellant's alleged motion, we believe he did not raise a speedy trial objection at that time. Even if he had, appellant still failed to provide any reason why the delay caused by rescheduling the trial until October 4 somehow prejudiced his preparation for trial.

Conclusion

The above analysis of the four Barker factors shows that while there was a lengthy delay from arrest to trial, Hopi Ordinance 21, section 2.8.5 would not have been violated under federal law, because much of that delay was at appellant's own request and he failed to assert the speedy trial right until very late in the process. He has also been unable to show why the delay caused any prejudice to his case. The facts of this case suggest appellant did not seriously believe his right to a speedy trial was being violated.

The Right to Compulsory Process and to Confront Witnesses

ICRA and many tribal codes protect a defendant's right to compulsory process and to confront the prosecution's witnesses. Compulsory process refers to the ability to summon witnesses into court to testify on the defendant's behalf. As a result of this right, defendants have the power to issue subpoenas, which are court orders, to bring witnesses into court. This is usually done through the court by its defense advocate, depending on the local court rules. The right to confront witnesses is the right to cross-examine witnesses who are called to testify against the defendant. This is important because if the defendant were not allowed to ask witnesses questions or to cross-examine them, the prosecution would be able to present a one-sided story. By allowing the defendant to ask questions, usually done by the defendant's advocate, the court makes sure the jury and judge hear all the facts and any reasons why a witness might not be telling the truth.

As you read the following case, focus on facts that would support the defendant's arguments that her due process rights were violated.

Northern Plains Intertribal Court of Appeals
Turtle Mountain Band of Chippewa v. McGillis
18 ILR 6128 (1991)
Before Fitzsimmons, Gotland and Johnson, Judges
Fitzsimmons, Judge

Deborah McGillis appealed from a bench conviction for contributing to the delinquency of a minor, alleging, among other issues, denial of her statutory right to have compulsory process (subpoenas) issued by the court for obtaining witnesses on her behalf, see Turtle Mountain Tribal Code § 1.1205.

We reverse the conviction.

On May 3, 1990, Carol Patnaude filed a criminal complaint with the Turtle Mountain Tribal Court alleging the defendant and appellant, Deborah McGillis, committed the offense of contributing to the delinquency of a minor. The complaint contended that McGillis stopped her vehicle and allowed her son to attack the complaining witness's son resulting in an injury to the alleged victim's spleen.

On June 16, 1990, the appellant was arrested on the charge and released upon posting a bond. On June 19 the appellant appeared for arraignment before Judge F. Morin. She entered a plea of not guilty to the charge and requested a "Judge Trial." According to McGillis, at the time of her arraignment, she requested subpoenas for witnesses for her defense. McGillis further contended that the court denied her request and told her to bring whatever witnesses she needed to the court on the trial date. Since the Turtle Mountain Prosecutor's Office did not submit a brief or dispute McGillis' account of the arraignment request for subpoenas, this court has no choice but to accept the McGillis version as accurate and truthful.

The court set September 7, 1990 as the trial date and McGillis was released pending trial. However on September 6, 1990, McGillis was arrested and charged with contempt of court stemming from another matter. From September 6 until the time of her trial on the contributing charge, McGillis was held in the Turtle Mountain Correctional facility in Belcourt.

At the beginning of her trial, McGillis requested the court to reschedule the trial because she was unable to round up her witnesses due to her incarceration. Judge Morin denied the motion and ordered the trial to proceed. McGillis was eventually found guilty and sentenced to pay a $180 fine, $25 court costs, serve 60 days of a 90-day jail sentence, provided she undergo an alcohol evaluation, and one year's probation. She was also placed under a restraining order prohibiting contact with the Carol Patraude [sic] family.

McGillis now contends that she was denied a fair trial because the court refused her request to issue subpoenas for the witnesses she wanted to call in her defense. We agree.

In Chapter 1.12 of the Tribal Code of the Turtle Mountain Chippewa Tribe we find specific procedures set forth for criminal trials conducted in the tribal court. Section 05 deals with the rights of the accused: "In all criminal prosecutions, the accused Indian shall have the right to defend himself in person or by counsel, to demand the nature and cause of the accusation against him; to have a copy thereof; to meet the witnesses against him face to face; to have compulsory process served for obtaining witnesses in his behalf; . . . ."

A review of the advisement of rights form provided to McGillis at her arraignment shows that it contains the following statement:

> 4. You have the right of compulsory process or subpoenas served for obtaining witnesses on your behalf. Although, you will need to serve them yourself.

Although there seems to be a conflict between the Code and the advisement of rights form with regard to whether the court must serve the subpoenas or that responsibility was with the defendant—it is crystal clear from both documents that a defendant has the right to have subpoenas issued by the court for his or her defense witnesses.

In the instant case, appellant McGillis requested the issuance of subpoenas at her arraignment. The court failed to comply with the request and directed the appellant to bring her witnesses to her trial. Failing to issue subpoenas when requested violated the rights of the appellant under tribal law and denied her right to a fair trial.

The practical effect of this denial is especially clear in the instant case. McGillis was unable to bring her witnesses to court because she was in jail on the day of the trial. Statutory rights of criminal defendants cannot be ignored because of budget constraints or individual practices of judges. Statutory rights of criminal defendants are what separate tribal, state and federal governments in America from the military **juntas** in Latin America or the dictatorships in Asia. . .

Because the appellant was denied her right to compulsory process (subpoenas) we reverse the judgment of conviction and remand this matter to the Turtle Mountain Tribal Court with instructions to hold a new trial.

The Right Not to Testify

Recall from Chapter 18 that many tribal codes and ICRA prohibit a tribe from compelling defendants to testify against themselves. This right stems from the American doctrine that is related to the right to remain silent as developed after the *Miranda* decision.

Since the burden of proof (see chapter 17) is on the tribal government to prove a defendant's guilt beyond a reasonable doubt, defendants are not required to prove their innocence—and thus can choose not to testify in a trial.

Moreover, most tribal courts will not allow a defendant's choice not to testify to be used against the defendant in deciding guilt. For example, the National American Indian Court Judges Association provides the following statement to be read by tribal court judges to a jury in criminal trials: "The fact that the defendant did not testify may not be considered as any evidence that he is guilty" (*Criminal Court Procedures Benchbook*, 1980).

Conclusion

Due process of law is multifaceted right. It is often considered by the courts along with other civil rights, as illustrated by the cases. With regard to criminal law and procedure, due process protects a defendant's right to a fair process as he proceeds through the court system. Due process requires a person receive notice about what crime with which he is charged, notice to hearings so he may be present and be heard, a right to have an attorney and call witnesses. And the right to due process does not end after a conviction. Sentencing hearing, probation or parole hearings, and appeal all may be places where a defendant might raise a violation of his right to due process. With this important right in hand, defendants can raise these challenges to ensure the government is fair in its prosecution of crime.

Questions

1. Describe various categories of due process.
2. What is a "statute of limitations"?
3. Why do defendants have a "right to a speedy trial"?
4. In *Hopi v. Huma*, how does the appellate court describe double jeopardy?
5. In *Komalestewa v. Hopi*, why was the trial delayed? What rule did the court develop for determining whether the defendant's rights were violated?
6. In *Turtle Mountain v. McGillis*, why wasn't the defendant able to contact her witnesses and tell them to come to court?

In Your Community

1. Does your nation protect citizens against double jeopardy? If so, how is double jeopardy defined?
2. Does your nation have a statute of limitations for bringing criminal complaints?
3. How does your tribal court determine whether the right to a speedy trial has been violated?

Terms Used in Chapter 24

Articulable suspicion: The officer can articulate (explain) what raised suspicion about a person's behavior.

Bootlegger: Someone who makes or sells illegal liquor.

Junta: A closely knit group united for a common purpose and usually meeting secretly.

Notes

1. 25 U.S.C. § 1302(a)(8)

2. *Stead v. Colville Confederated Tribes*, 2 CCAR 27 (Colville Confederated 12/14/1993), 1993.NACC.0000003, 7.

3. *Fort Peck Assiniboine and Sioux Tribes v. Linda Clark*, No. 36 (Fort Peck 09/30/1987), 1987.NAFP.0000010, 6.

Suggested Further Reading

B. J. Jones, "Tribal Courts: Protectors of the Native Paradigm of Justice," 10 *St. Thomas Law Review* 87 (1997).

Robert Lawrence, "Dominant-Society Law and Tribal Court Adjudication," 25 *New Mexico Law Review* 1 (1995).

Victims' Rights Chapter 25

The rate of violent crime in Indian country and tribal communities is higher than in most other communities.

- American Indians and Alaska Natives are 2.5 times as likely to experience violent crimes and at least two times more likely to experience sexual assault or rape than other races.[1]
- Sixty-one percent of American Indian and Alaska Native women have been assaulted in their lifetimes.[2]
- Thirty-four percent of American Indian and Alaska Native women will be raped in their lifetimes.[3]
- Seventeen percent of American Indian and Alaska Native women reported being stalked in their lifetimes.[4]

Why are American Indians and Alaska Natives at a higher risk for victimization? There are several factors contributing to the high rates of crime in Indian country. The jurisdictional and sentencing limitations adopted by Congress and imposed on tribal courts have resulted in a higher rate of crime because the justice system response and penalties are often lenient. Historical oppression and trauma, including the attempted destruction of indigenous cultures, also contributes to the high rate of violence and criminal activity perpetrated against Native people. High rates of poverty and alcoholism in some tribal communities also contribute to higher crime rates. Additional research needs to be done in order to develop a true understanding of the reasons contemporary Native people experience such a high rate of victimization.

Victims of crime in Indian country can be of any age and any economic or political status. The trauma resulting from victimization may have short-term as well as long-term effects. Violence, abuse, and tragedy affect individuals, families, and sometimes an entire community. Acts in which an individual perpetrates violence or abuse against another may include the following: child abuse and neglect, child sexual abuse, elder abuse, sexual abuse, domestic violence, homicide, physical and psychological abuse, and, more recently, acts of spiritual abuse. Assistance to victims is critical at many stages of the trauma and healing process. Crisis intervention, support, advocacy, financial and logistical support, and healing opportunities may allow victims to begin a healing process directed toward finding harmony and balance with themselves and their surroundings once again. There are many culturally specific ways that victims in Indian country receive support and assistance. It is important that these services be designed for each specific community based on its values, beliefs, and practices, and that services be delivered in a manner that respects the individual and the community. Most tribal governments have strong traditions concerning the protection and healing of people who have been hurt. As these governments continue to develop their contemporary justice systems, some have chosen to codify victims' rights laws.

This chapter touches on just a few of the ways that contemporary tribal court systems can protect and secure the rights of crime victims. The examples in this chapter do not include all mechanisms and steps that a tribal government may enact to protect the rights of victims. Examine your tribe's law and look for examples of laws that protect victims' rights. If your tribal law does not contain these protections, think about changes that could be made to provide these protections.

Traditional Victim Response

Criminal procedure affects more than just the individuals accused of crimes. Crime victims are also involved in the criminal justice process because they often must testify against the defendant. In addition, crime victims and their families often suffer long-lasting trauma and pain as a result of being victimized. The traditional American legal system has not always taken into account the needs and rights of crime victims and their families. Most tribal traditions, however, have ways of providing for a sense of healing and support for people who have been hurt. The following story illustrates how one victim of abuse was able to find support from her family, community, and the animals. As you read these passages, consider how your own tribal traditions support the safety and protection of victims of crime.

Domestic Violence in a Cheyenne Story

E. Adamson Hoebel, *The Cheyennes: Indians of the Great Plains*, Holt, Rinehart & Winston, 24-26 (1960).

Brave Wolf was jealous of his wife's good looks. He would hear people remarking, "There is a woman who has two children and still holds her looks." These were children she had had by her former husband, Highbacked Wolf, who had been killed by the Crows. Angered one day, Brave Wolf whipped his wife, Corn Woman, and when the camp moved, he left her behind. Brave Wolf's nephew, Sun's Road, then a single man, came by and heard her weeping. He went to his lodge to get his horse to bring the woman along. He brought her into the main camp that evening. Brave Wolf heard that she was there and came over to take up where he had left off. He began whipping her in the face.

Digging Bear, his niece, watched for her chance. She struck his arm with a club and numbed it as he raised it to swing his whip. He cried out, "Wait until my arm stops hurting! I'll fix you." Digging Bear told Corn Woman to get into the lodge. Brave Wolf got over his hurt and followed her into the lodge to whip her some more.

His niece started cracking his shins with a club.

"It's funny," Brave Wolf said, "that you children are taking the part of a woman not any relation to you. I am your uncle."

"Well, if you hadn't thumped our mother, we would not have done so." (Brave Wolf was their father's cousin and hence called "father"; his wife was therefore their classificatory "mother," even though not a genetic relative.) Brave Wolf then took Corn Woman home, but the next morning he was thumping her again, so she ran away to hide in a gulch, covering herself with grass. Brave Wolf went riding up and down looking for her, with no success. When she thought she was safe, she went out and hid in a patch of boulders. The camp moved on in time, and she was left alone there starving.

After some time, a big wolf came up and asked her what was the trouble (he could speak good Cheyenne).

"My husband has been beating me, and I ran away." "Well," the wolf told her, "I'll get you back safely."

He brought her meat, and warned her when a bear came by, so that she got safely up in a tree and could stay there until the bear went away. An elk came and talked to her, too. He gave her elk power.

Meantime, Brave Wolf went into mourning for her. Everyone in the camp thought she had committed suicide. Brave Wolf also joined the Contraries (a small group of recklessly brave men, who do everything backwards). He got a Contrary lance made by High Forehead. Only single men have such a lance, but when Corn Woman left Brave Wolf, he was single again. He tried to get himself killed in battle, but Contrary lances are very lucky and this one carried him safely through battles. He could not get himself killed.

After a long time, the wolf led Corn Woman back to the Cheyenne camp. The wolf and the woman sat on a high hill overlooking the camp. "Over there is the camp," said the wolf. "A man will come out to look for you. You can't see him. Now I leave you. From now on, always put out some meat for me each morning." For the rest of her days, Corn Woman made an offering to the wolf who had saved her; he was her guardian spirit. When the wolf left her, she "came to." Later, she told people she thought she had almost turned into a wolf herself.

Now she started down the hill through a gulch, and she met a young man. He saw her in her disheveled condition. No clothes but a small piece of blanket for covering. No hair comb. Her hair in a mess. She was weak and emaciated from lack of proper food. The sight of him made her weaker. She staggered. The young man was so sorry for her that he wept in pity. She tried to, too. But no tears or voice would come.

"You stay right here," he said. "Your brother is hunting right over there. I'll bring him."

He found Crazy Head, her brother, and told him, "Your sister is right over here."

Crazy Head and the hunters rushed over and found her. They carried her back to the camp on a horse, so weak she could hardly stay on it.

Brave Wolf heard the news. He came in, his hair cut in mourning style. He ran up and started to hug his former wife. She bit his arm.

That made Crazy Head mad. He wanted to kill Brave Wolf, because he had made his sister remain away for so long. Then Corn Woman's mother came up and started to beat Brave Wolf. All the people began beating him. When they got back to camp, all the women beat him.

Brave Wolf was infatuated with Corn Woman. He wanted her back. He kept sending horses for her, but Crazy Head's people would throwv sticks at them and drive them away. Corn Woman's mother would insult the women who brought them. When Brave Wolf came around, Corn Woman's sister would strike him on the forehead and taunt him, saying "You look more like a mountain sheep than a man." He made no effort to protect himself, but would only drop his head and take the blows.

Brave Wolf was a great fighter, not then a chief, though he was later. He had a fine black war pony that everyone wanted, but he would not trade it or give it away.

> On the warpath, he took to cooking for Sun's Road, Corn Woman's brother. He did everything for him, just as though he were a servant.
>
> One time, when Crazy Head was leading a war party, Brave Wolf brought Sun's Road a nice roast. He was leading the famous bob-tailed black. "You know I have ridden this horse in war. You know this horse's qualities as well as I do," he told Sun's Road. "Now I want you to have him to ride in war. What is more, I want you to have my Contrary lance, if you will take it." These were his greatest possessions.
>
> When they were back from the war party, Sun's Road spoke to his mother, "You know that when a man is leading a war party he is apt to go pretty hungry so that his men will have enough to eat. Brave Wolf has done all these pitiful things for me. I have known all the time what he wants. He wants my sister back. You had better put up an extra lodge. My sister will go back to him. You tell her to get ready."
>
> When her mother told her what Sun's Road had said, Corn Woman wept. "I never thought I would marry that man again, but if my brother says I must go, I must. My brother is a great fighter. If I say, 'No,' he'll probably get himself killed in the first fight (a protest suicide). Then I'll think how I caused it."
>
> When they were together again, she told Brave Wolf, "Don't you ever try to beat me again. If you do, I'll fight you with whatever is at hand. I don't care if you kill me."
>
> From that time on, he was her slave.
>
> This case history was told by Calf Woman and confirmed by High Forehead.

Among California's Yurok Indians, "crossers" facilitated help for victims. When an aggrieved Yurok felt he had a legitimate claim, he engaged the services of two non-relatives from a community not his own. Similarly, the accused could employ the services of non-relatives from another community. These men were called "crossers" because they mediated impartially between the victim and the accused. After hearing and considering all the evidence, the crossers rendered a decision for damages according to a well-established scale that was known to all. A crosser usually received a piece of shell currency, called a "moccasin," for his labor.[5]

Contemporary Victim Response

As tribal governments rebuild their organizations, including justice systems, in a contemporary context, many are developing victim programs and are finding ways to meet victims' needs by including in modern tribal laws various traditions that restore the victim. Many tribal jurisdictions have developed their own versions of victims' rights legislation. A few tribes have passed ordinances specifically for the protection of victims. Many tribes have promulgated domestic violence statutes that provide extra protection to the victims of this domestic abuse and assign responsibilities and duties to law enforcement and the tribal prosecutor.

For example, the White Mountain Apache Tribal Code contains a Victim's Bill of Rights. This Bill of Rights was created "to preserve and protect victims' rights to justice and due process." It provides various rights such as speedy disposition, right to be heard, and the right "to be treated with fairness, respect and dignity."

As you review the White Mountain Victim's Bill of Rights, determine whether you think these rights should be included in your own tribal constitution (if they are not already).

White Mountain Apache Criminal Code
Section 7.1 Victim's Bill of Rights
A. To preserve and protect victims' rights to justice and due process, a victim of crime has a right:
   1. To be treated with fairness, respect, and dignity, and to be free from intimidation, harassment, or abuse, throughout the criminal justice process.
   2. To be informed, upon request, when the accused or convicted person is released from custody or has escaped.
   3. To be present at and, upon request, to be informed of all criminal proceedings where the defendant has the right to be present.
   4. To be heard at any proceeding involving a post-arrest release decision, a negotiated plea, and sentencing.
   5. To refuse an interview, **deposition**, or other discovery request by the defendant, the defendant's attorney, or other person acting on behalf of the defendant.
   6. To confer with the prosecution after the crime against the victim has been charged, before trial or before any disposition of the case and to be informed of the disposition.
   7. To read pre-sentence reports relating to the crime against the victim when they are available to the defendant.
   8. To receive prompt restitution from the person or persons convicted of the criminal conduct that caused the victim's loss or injury.
   9. To be heard at any proceeding when any post-conviction release from confinement is being considered.
   10. To a speedy trial or disposition and prompt and final conclusion of the case after the conviction and sentence.
   11. To have all rules governing criminal procedure and the admissibility of evidence in all criminal proceedings protect victims' rights and to have these rules be subject to amendment or repeal by the Tribal Council to ensure the protection of these rights.
   12. To be informed of victims' constitutional rights.

B. A victim's exercise of any right granted by this section shall not be grounds for dismissing any criminal proceeding or setting aside any conviction or sentence.

C. *"Victim" means a person against whom the criminal offense has been committed or, if the person is killed or incapacitated, the person's spouse, parent, child or other lawful representative, except if the person is in custody for an offense or is the accused.*

D. *The Tribal Council, or the people by initiative or referendum have the authority to enact substantive and procedural laws to define, implement, preserve and protect the rights guaranteed to victims by this section, including the authority to extend any of these rights to juvenile proceedings.*

E. *The enumeration in the constitution of certain rights for victims shall not be construed to deny or disparage others granted by the tribal council or retained by victims.*

History and Philosophy of the White Buffalo Calf Woman Society (WBCWS)

Our Organization

Since 1977, when WBCWS, Inc. was founded as a non-profit organization, WBCWS has been working with women, men, and children on the Rosebud Reservation and surrounding areas. In October of 1980, the WBCWS established the first women's shelter on an Indian reservation in the United States. To this day, it continues to serve victims of domestic violence and sexual assault and it has become more than just a shelter, but also a resource of information for our community.

Our Mission Statement

The White Buffalo Calf Woman Society, Inc. (WBCWS) recognizes that violence against women is not a random state but is, in fact, a system of behaviors and tactics used to maintain power and control over women, whether that is as individuals or as a group.

The WBCWS believes that violence against indigenous/Lakota women is not traditional to our culture and life way teachings. We believe it has its roots in an imposed and institutionalized system that was designed to maintain control over us as a People after genocide failed.

We do not define violence against indigenous women as a problem within a relationship or as the pathology of an individual perpetrator. Again, it is perpetrated and maintained through society and institutions and is the same dynamic that perpetrates other forms of oppression, i.e. racism, classism, ageism, homophobia, able-bodyism, adultism, etc.

We are committed to providing shelter and advocacy for individuals victimized by violence. We recognize the necessity of a multi-faceted approach—the need to develop an effective response to systems in our community such as health, criminal justice, and other institutions that minimize violence against woman. We also believe it is necessary to raise community awareness by naming what has happened to us as indigenous women.

At the same time, we recognize that responding to systems may or may not make significant institutional changes that will stop violence against women. Therefore, we are also dedicated to exploring and creating actions that will move us toward a social transformation that will allow equity for women. We actively seek methods and processes that will facilitate nonviolent human interactions.

We have internalized our oppression. It is also the mission of the WBCWS to support each other in our exploration of ourselves and our attachment to beliefs that justify our own oppressions and the oppressions of others. As we work to transform the world into a circle of peace and harmony, individual responsibility and self-growth is essential.

As indigenous women, we have survived and held on to much of our tradition. In keeping with our woman culture we are expected to conduct ourselves ethically, and there is an expectation that WBCWS members and employees interact with one another in the spirit of unity and mutual support.

Our Philosophy

Many winters past (a waken woman), the White Buffalo Calf Woman, gave the sacred pipe to the Lakota people. The pipe represents the unity of all people and all things of the universe. Through the pipe, peace may come to all who understand and follow its meaning. The understanding would be in both their minds and their hearts.

The White Buffalo Calf Woman Society, Inc. strives to follow the teaching of the White Buffalo Calf Woman. The goals are peace, understanding, and quality of life for all people. Only if there is peace and strength within each of our hearts can we hope to share this with others.

By learning more and caring deeply about ourselves and others, through yearning for and working toward growth, by giving and receiving knowledge, concern and inspiration, the vision of the White Buffalo Calf Woman may become the path of all the people.[6]

The Right to Be Safe

The right to be safe is rooted in the concept that no one deserves to be physically battered or attacked. For example, the Haudenosaunee or Six Nation's Great Law of Peace teaches that abuse is contrary to human nature. The Great Law teaches "[h]uman beings whose minds are healthy always desire peace, and humans have minds which enable them to achieve peaceful resolutions of their conflicts."[7] And the government's role is to prevent abuse by cultivating "a spiritually healthy society and the establishment of peace."[8]

Today, some tribal governments have developed laws and policies to protect victims' rights, including a variety of different laws that serve to protect a victim from future harm. From the immediate aftermath of the crime to safe places in the courthouse to notification of the probation or parole proceedings, these kinds of laws provide protection and notification for victims and their families so that they can participate in the criminal justice process without fear that they will be victimized again.

Review the following statutes from the Sault Ste. Marie Tribe of Chippewa Indians and the Fort McDowell Yavapai Nation. Determine whether and how these laws provide additional safety for victims.

Sault Ste. Marie Tribal Code Crime Victims' Rights
75.105 Notice of Pretrial Release
(1) Not later than 24 hours after the arraignment of the defendant for a crime, the law enforcement agency having responsibility for investigating the crime shall give the victim notice of the availability of pretrial release for the defendant, the phone number of the sheriff, and notice that the victim may contact the sheriff to determine whether the defendant has been released from custody.

(2) Based upon the victim's affidavit asserting acts or threats of physical violence or intimidation by the defendant or at the defendant's direction against the victim or the victim's immediate family, the prosecuting attorney may move that the bond or **personal recognizance** of a defendant be revoked.

75.107 Separate Waiting Area
The court shall provide a waiting area for the victim separate from the defendant, defendant's relatives and defense witnesses if such an area is available and the use of the area is practical. If a separate waiting area is not available or practical, the Court shall provide other safeguards to minimize the victim's contact with the defendant, defendant's relatives and defense witnesses during Court proceedings.

Fort McDowell Yavapai Nation
Article I. Sec. 5-2(2)(o)
Victim protections. The court shall provide appropriate safeguards to minimize contact between the victim and the accused. The protection extends to witnesses and family and covers the defendant's family and witnesses as well. The victim can petition to revoke the bond of the accused if he is harassing her or her immediate family. The victim has the right to refuse an interview with the defendant or his attorney or to set limits on the interview. After charges are filed, defense initiated requests to interview the victim shall be communicated to the victim through the prosecutor. The victim's response to such requests shall also be communicated through the prosecutor. At any interview or deposition to be conducted by defense counsel, the victim has the right to specify a reasonable date, time, duration and location of the interview or deposition, including a requirement that the interview or deposition be held at the victim's home, at the prosecutor's office, or in an appropriate location in the courthouse. The victim does not have to divulge her address, phone number, employment or other locating information in court.

The Right to Have a Voice in the Process
Traditional tribal law in many cultures required that the community listen to the thoughts and feelings of the victimized person and his or her clan or kinship group. The community, attempting to resolve a dispute or criminal act, considers

the impact and results of the crime by hearing the truth as experienced by the victim or the victim's family. Sault Ste. Marie Tribal laws include several protections for victims in this regard.

Sault Ste. Marie Tribal Code Crime Victims' Rights

75.111 Right to Be Present
The victim has the right to be present throughout the entire trial of the defendant, including juvenile hearings, unless the victim is going to be called as a witness. If the victim is going to be called as a witness, the Court may, for good cause shown, order the victim to be sequestered until the victim first testifies.

75.114 Impact Statement for Sentencing
The victim has the right to submit or make a written or oral impact statement to the probation officer for use by that officer in preparing a presentence investigation report concerning the defendant. A victim's written statement shall, upon the victim's request, be included in the presentence investigation report.

75.115 Right to Make Statement at Sentencing
The victim shall have the right to appear and make an oral impact statement at the sentencing of the defendant.

The Right to Have a Victim's Advocate

In Chapter 23, we explored the right to have an attorney/advocate for criminal defendants. Victims of crime often need a support person in the aftermath of a crime.

What can advocates do for victims? Many times, the criminal justice system can be intimidating and emotionally painful for victims and their families. If the crime involves sensitive matters, such as sexual assault or sexual abuse, it may be especially difficult for a victim to feel confident and strong in the courtroom. Victim advocates can provide many different services throughout the criminal justice process, from emergency response to probation hearings.

Some advocates work for independent nonprofit organizations. Other advocates work for a government agency (e.g., tribal social services, tribal police department). Many advocates are not paid for their work; they serve as volunteers because of their commitment and passion for justice.

In protecting the right of a victim to work with an advocate, some tribes have enacted laws that protect the confidentiality of communication between a victim and an advocate. These confidentiality laws ensure that a victim can speak freely to an advocate without worrying that the information will be used in court.

Excerpts from Advocacy by Brenda Hill
Bonnie Clairmont, et al, eds. *Sharing Our Stories of Survival: Native Women Surviving Violence*, Alta Mira, 196-7 (2008)

Advocates are the biased supporters of women who have been battered. There is no other job or position that allows for this stance. Advocates are 100 percent of the time about the sovereignty of women. We are accountable to the women with whom we work, and there should be no conflict of interest.

Being an advocate is powerful in the best sense of the word. Advocates are afforded the challenge and opportunity to make a difference in the lives of our sisters, other relatives, and societies. This work provides an opportunity to reclaim the connections and relationships devastated by colonization and oppression. Advocacy includes providing the following services to individual women:

- Twenty-four-hour crisis line;
- Shelter;
- Food and clothing;
- Transportation and accompaniment to court and other services;
- General, legal, and medical advocacy;
- Consciousness-raising/support groups;
- Information and referrals;
- Assistance with rent and utilities;
- Childcare and crisis intervention;
- Men's re-education groups;
- Probation departments; and
- Children's programming.

Advocacy includes being an agent of social change and providing leadership for coordinated community responses and national initiatives to end violence against women. The list above can be lengthened to include anything a woman needs to be safe and get her life back.

As Native advocates, we can use our knowledge about kinship and relations as a model for our work with women. We can take the time to visit with our relatives who have been battered or raped, respectfully listen and believe what we are told, validate their expertise, and then take action. Advocates assist sisters and other relatives to accurately define their experiences and proactively work to end violence in individual women's lives and in our communities and societies. Advocates focus on women's safety, accountability, and social change—not the faults of women.

Nez Perce Tribal Code

*7-2-16 Advocate-victim **privilege** applicable in cases involving domestic violence.*

a. Except as otherwise provided in subsection "b," a victim of domestic violence may refuse to disclose, and may prevent an advocate from disclosing, confidential oral communication between the victim and the advocate and written records and reports concerning the victim if the privilege is claimed by:
   1. The victim; or
   2. The person who was the advocate at the time of the confidential communication, except that the advocate may not claim privilege if there is no victim in existence or if the privilege has been waived by the victim.
b. The privilege does not relieve a person from any duty imposed pursuant to 5-1-9 of the Nez Perce Tribal Code. Person may not claim the privilege when providing evidence in proceedings concerning child violence.
c. As used in this subsection, "advocate" means an employee of or volunteer for a program for victims of domestic violence who:
   1. Has a primary function of rendering advice, counseling, or assistance to victims of domestic violence; supervising the employees or volunteers of the program; or administering the program;
   2. Has undergone 30 hours of training; and
   3. Works under the direction of a supervisor of the program, supervises employees or volunteers, or administers the program.

Special Rights for Child Victims

Cases involving child abuse and neglect can be particularly difficult for courts. Oftentimes, the testimony of the child victim is needed in order to secure a conviction and hold the offender accountable. However, children who have been victimized may be traumatized by having to recount the abuse in a public forum, in front of the perpetrator. Some tribal governments have enacted special laws that provide an alternate form of testimony for such children.

Review the following statutes from the Mashantucket Pequot Tribal Nation, Yankton Sioux Tribe, and Coquille Tribe. Determine whether and how these laws provide additional safety for child victims, especially child victim witnesses.

Mashantucket Pequot Tribal Nation, Tribal Laws and Rules of Court

Rule 802. Hearsay Rule; Child's Statements

b. In any proceeding before the court wherein it is alleged that a child is the victim of child abuse or neglect, the court may admit and consider oral or written evidence of out-of-court statements made by the child and rely on that evidence to the extent of its probative value.

Yankton Sioux Tribal Code
Title 5, Chapter IX

Sec. 5-9-16 Minor Victim's Treatment

Anyone convicted under Secs. 5-9-1, 5-9-2, or any sexual assault crime defined in the Criminal Code, may be required as part of the sentence imposed by the Court to pay the cost of any necessary medical, psychological or psychiatric treatment of the minor resulting from the act or acts for which the defendant is convicted.

Sec. 5-9-17 Videotape of Victim's Testimony Use at Trial

If a defendant has been charged with a violation of Secs. 5-9-1, 5-9-2, or any sexual assault crimes defined in the Criminal Code, if the victim is a person eighteen years of age or less, the prosecuting attorney may apply for an order that the victim's testimony at the preliminary hearing be stenographically recorded, audio recorded and preserved on videotape, and allowed to be used at trial in place of the victim's live testimony. The scope and manner of the examination shall be such as would be allowed at the trial.

The application for the order shall be in writing and made at least three (3) days before the preliminary hearing.

Upon timely receipt of the application, the court shall order that the testimony of the victim given at the preliminary hearing be taken and preserved on videotape. The videotape shall be transmitted to the Clerk of the Court in which the action is pending.

If at the time of trial the court finds that further testimony would cause the victim emotional trauma, or that the victim is otherwise unavailable within the meaning of Rule 804 (a) of the Federal Rules of Evidence, or that such testimony would in the opinion of the court be substantially detrimental to the well-being of the victim, the court may admit the videotape of the victim's testimony at the preliminary hearing as former testimony under Rule 804 (b) of the Federal Rules of Evidence.

Sec. 5-9-18 Statement of the Sex Crime; Victim under Age Twelve

A statement made by a child under the age of twelve (12) describing any act of sexual abuse performed with or on the child by the defendant, not otherwise admissible, is admissible in evidence in proceedings under this Section in the courts of the Yankton Sioux Reservation if:

- A. The Court finds, in a hearing conducted outside the presence of the jury, that the time, content and circumstances of the statement provided sufficient indicia of reliability, and;
- B. The child either:
  1. Testifies at the proceedings; or
  2. Is unavailable as a witness.

However, if the child is unavailable as a witness, such statement may be admitted only if there is corroborative evidence of the act.

Sec. 5-9-19 Minor's Testimony as to Sexual Offense Involving Child; Closed Hearing

Any portion of proceeding under this Section at which a minor is required to testify concerning rape of a child, sexual abuse of a child, child abuse involving sexual abuse or any other sexual offense involving a child may be closed to all persons except the parties and officers of the court.

Coquille Tribal Evidence Code Rule 803—Hearsay Exception; Availability of Declarant Immaterial

25. Testimony of Child Under 10 Years of Age Concerning Sexual Conduct.

Notwithstanding the limits contained in subsection (19) of this section, in any proceeding in which a child under 12 years of age at the time of trial, or a person with developmental disabilities as described in subsection (19) of this section, may be called as a witness to testify concerning an act of child abuse, as defined in CITC 640.015(5), or sexual conduct performed with or on the child or person with developmental disabilities by another, the testimony of the child or person with developmental disabilities taken by contemporaneous examination and cross-examination in another place under the supervision of the trial judge and communicated to the court room by closed circuit television or other audiovisual means. Testimony will be allowed as provided in this subsection only if the court finds that there is a substantial likelihood, established by expert testimony, that the child or person with developmental disabilities will suffer severe emotional or psychological harm if required to testify in open court. If the court makes such a finding, the court, on motion of a party, the child, the person with developmental disabilities or the court in a civil proceeding, or on motion of the tribal attorney or tribal prosecutor, the child or the person with developmental disabilities in a criminal or juvenile proceeding, may order that the testimony of the child or the person with developmental disabilities be taken as described in this subsection. Only the judge, the attorneys for the parties, the parties, individuals necessary to operate the equipment and any individual the court finds would contribute to the welfare and well-being of the child or person with developmental disabilities may be present during the testimony of the child or person with developmental disabilities.

Victim Restitution

Many victims of crime suffer financial loss as a result of the crime. Victims may lose material goods, such as stolen or damaged property. Many victims have medical bills from being physically attacked. Emotional/spiritual harm may result from the harm. Many tribal nations have strong, traditional laws regarding the obligation that an offender or offender's clan has to restore a victim to wholeness. Such sentences are referred to as restitution. The imposition of a sentence of restitution is not limited by federal law. Restitution is a concept that is not necessarily limited to a single victim. Many tribal traditions consider the entire community to be a victim of a criminal act.

The following two cases demonstrate how tribal courts have applied restitution law.

District Court of the Navajo Nation (Crownpoint District)
In the Matter of the Interest of D.P., a Minor (1982)
3 Nav. R. 255
The opinion of the court was delivered by: Honorable Marie F. Neswood, Judge presiding

Note on Opinion
Initials are used for the caption of this case in order to protect the privacy of the minor involved and in furtherance of the policy that juvenile matters should be closed proceedings.

Situation before the Court
On February 28, 1982 this minor was found to have violated criminal law as a juvenile and to have committed what would otherwise have been the offenses of armed robbery, unlawful use of a deadly weapon and unauthorized use of an automobile had he been adult. The order of the same date ordered that the juvenile "make restitution to the victim in the amount of One Thousand Dollars ($1,000.00) and no/100." That order was appealed, and on August 6, 1982 the Court of Appeals dismissed the appeal for failure to comply with the Rules of Appellate Procedure.

When the case was returned to this court the child asked that the amount of restitution be reduced due to his unemployment and the failure of the victim to prove the amount of damage. On October 20, 1982 the deputy prosecutor moved the court to leave the victim to collect his damages through a separate civil action. Finally, on November 22, 1982 both the counsel for the child and the Navajo Nation entered into a stipulation asking that this action be dismissed because of unknown damage amounts, the fact restitution was not requested by the prosecution, that the amount of restitution is unreasonable and unsubstantiated and that the rules of court and the law of the Navajo Nation do not allow for restitution in juvenile cases.

Whether Restitution in Juvenile Cases Is Permitted by Law
The question of whether restitution is permitted in juvenile cases is easily answered, and counsel should be ashamed to execute a stipulation agreeing there is no such law. NTC Sec. 1191(6) clearly authorizes the court to "order that the child be required to make restitution for damage or loss caused by his wrongful acts." While the statute does say that the obligation to make restitution is only that of the child, it is clear the court has the power to order it.

It is of no consequence whatsoever that the prosecutor did not ask for restitution to the victim in this case. The court has the independent right and duty to do justice and to order whatever relief is appropriate and fits under the circumstances.

9 NTC Sec. 1191. As is noted below, restitution in criminal and quasi-criminal cases is also a matter of Navajo custom, and this court will require it whenever and wherever it is appropriate to the circumstances.

Whether the Amount of Restitution Was Unascertained or Improper

The fixing of an amount to be paid in order to make restitution to a victim is not a civil action for damages. There need not be the quantity and kind of evidence required in normal civil actions. It is sufficient that the court have a reasonable estimate of the injury suffered by the victim and that the juvenile be given the opportunity in a disposition hearing to contest the estimate.

Again, this is not a damage action or a civil action on the part of the victim. It is a disposition by the court to properly deal with a child, and as long as the court has a reasonable basis for the disposition with an opportunity for the child to dispute the amount awarded as restitution, that is sufficient.

As to the amounts to be awarded, our statute is unlike the Federal probation statute which requires that only actual damages or loss can be the subject of a restitution order. 18 USC Sec. 3651. The order may be broad under our statute, and at the very least our law means that any identifiable damage done to the victim can be ordered paid, including medical expenses, pain and suffering, loss of wages, orthopedic devices, dependent support and even "damages in general."

Restitution is simply a "making good for loss or damage." This court has made a determination, subject to comment by the juvenile, that $1,000 is a reasonable sum of restitution to be made to the victim in this case, and the order shall stand.

The Ability of the Juvenile to Pay

The child has shown the court nothing about his ability or inability to pay. As a general matter, the court should consider the child's ability to pay prior to entering an order. Since 9 [Navajo Tribal Code] Sec. 1191(6) does not place the financial burden of paying the victim's damages upon the child's parents, it is the child who should be examined, and the court should consider his ability to pay. The child here has only indicated he is unemployed and that, of itself, does not undermine the court's original order because the child has had an opportunity to address ability to pay.

If a court finds that a child in fact does not have the means of obtaining the money to repay the victim of the wrongful acts, then at the very least the court can consider some sort of community work to show the victim that action will be taken and to teach the child that the penalty for injuring people is that the community must be paid back. The child could also be ordered to serve the victim by personal work until the value of $1,000 in services are rendered.

Courts should not make ineffectual orders, especially in juvenile cases. There are a number of ways the statute permitting restitution by the child can be satisfied, and those ways will be explored in detail in juvenile cases.

Restitution under Navajo Common (Custom) Law

In general Anglo-European history, the victims of crime lost their right to be paid back for a crime by the offender. Some Anglo historians argue that this was because of the need of European governments to build social unity and stop revenge, the desire of kings to take all powers to themselves and the practice of kings of taking money in the form of fines as payment to protect the wrongdoers from the vengeance of the victim. Id. This ridiculous trend, which thankfully is being slowly replaced by concern for the victim of crime, is totally the opposite from the traditional Navajo way.

Under Navajo tradition, all offenses (with the exception of witchcraft) were punished by payments to the victim or the victim's immediate family and clan. In this case, robbery with injury would be punished by a payment of "blood money" to the immediate family, plus a multiple payment for any property taken. Theft would be punished by a multiple payment to the victim of immediate family group.

The Navajo tradition recognized that the central ideas of punishment were to put the victim in the position he or she was before the offense by a money payment, punish in a visible way by requiring extra payments to the victim or the victim's family (rather than the king or state), and give a visible sign to the community that wrong was punished. The offender was given the means to return to the community by making good his or her wrong. Surely this is a far better concept of justice than to leave the victim out of the process of justice and leaving the victim with no means of healing the injury done.

Therefore this court finds that not only is restitution permitted under Navajo custom law, but indeed it was so central to Navajo tradition in offenses that it should be presumed to be required in any juvenile disposition.

Orders

Based on these considerations, the court rejects the stipulation entered into by the parties, reaffirms its prior order requiring restitution and grants the child leave to make further specific motions addressed to the amount of payment, ability to pay or other disposition.

The court also orders that no further consideration will be given to a modification of the prior disposition of the court unless the victim is given notice of any proposed modification and is permitted to be present in court to comment upon any such proposed modification.

Ute Mountain Ute Court of Appeals
Ute Mountain Ute Tribe v. Mills
10 Indian Law Reporter 6046 (1981)
Before DAWES, Appellate Judge

Defendant-appellant, Rutherford Mills (hereinafter referred to as defendant) was convicted of injury to public property in violation of ch. 6 § 19 of the Ute Mountain Ute Law and Order Code and assault and battery in violation of ch. 6 § 2 of the Ute Mountain Law and Order Code, in the tribal court below. As a result of that conviction, the tribal judge sentenced defendant on March 19, 1981, to a 30-day jail sentence, including a work program for the benefit of the tribe; restitution to the police department in the amount of $900.00 to be paid monthly at $100.00/month for nine and one half months; alcohol counseling for six months; and defendant was ordered to have no further violation of the law and order code within six months. Initially, defendant appealed those portions of the order relating to restitution and probation. By order dated July 16, 1981, the tribal court modified defendant's probation, terminating it on March 4, 1981. The tribal court did not modify the restitution requirement. It is from that portion of the sentence that defendant currently maintains his appeal.

On appeal, the defendant contends, first, that the tribal court exceeded its authority under the tribal code by ordering defendant to pay restitution to the tribe. Secondly, defendant contends that the amount of restitution exceeds the limitations of 25 U.S.C. § 1302(7), the Indian Civil Rights Act, in that the restitution exceeds the limitations imposed by the Act on penalty or punishment. . .

In his first argument, defendant argues that the applicable portion of ch. 5 § 1 of the Ute Mountain Ute Law and Order Code limits restitution by an offender to individuals and that the tribe is not an individual within the meaning of the section. The applicable portion of ch. 5 § 1 of the Ute Mountain Ute Law and Order Code provides:

In addition to any sentence, the Court may require an offender who has inflicted injury upon the person or property of any individual to make restitution or compensate the party injured, through the surrender of property, the payment of money damages, or the performance of any act for the benefit of the injured party.

The defendant contends that the principles of criminal law require that that particular portion of the ordinance be strictly construed in favor of the defendant.

The restitution in this case relates to damage done by the defendant to a tribal police car. In particular, the defendant shot three bullet holes into the police car causing the complained of damage. On oral argument, the parties agreed that the vehicle in question is owned by the Ute Mountain Ute Tribe. Further, on oral argument, the defendant conceded that the Ute Mountain Ute Tribe is a collection of individuals: enrolled members of the tribe. Individual members of the Ute Tribe have an interest in the collective assets of the tribe.

In accordance with the general rules of statutory construction, the use of the word "individual" singularly does not exclude the plural of that term.

There can be no question that when the ordinance was approved by the tribal council, the tribal council did not exclude, necessarily, more than one individual when granting authority to the tribal court to order restitution. Thus, if more than one individual were injured, the tribal court has authority to require restitution to all individuals injured. Since the Ute Tribe is a collection of individuals, there can be no doubt that the ordinance allows restitution to the collective group of individuals.

Taking the entire cited section as a whole, it would appear that the intent of the tribal council when adopting the ordinance was to grant authority to the tribal court "to compensate the injured party." Whenever possible the intent of an ordinance should be followed.

In this case, the tribal court ordered restitution to the tribal police department. The vehicle in question is owned by the Ute Mountain Ute Tribe. Accordingly, the order should be modified to require defendant to make restitution to the Ute Mountain Ute Tribe which is the injured party.

The second portion of the defendant's first argument is that ch. 5 § I of the Law and Order Code provides that the maximum punishment for this offense is 30-days at labor and that the tribal court has no authority to impose an additional penalty of restitution. The defendant contends that the tribal court exceeded tribally imposed limitations on its power.

Insofar as the defendant is alleging that the tribal Law and Order Code has restricted the authority of the tribal council to 30-days' labor, it is clear that is not the case. The ordinance specifically provides that in addition to the 30-days' sentence at labor, the court has the authority to order restitution.

Inherent in the previous argument of defendant and stated in defendant's last argument is the contention by defendant that restitution is punishment. Defendant argues in his last argument that the Indian Civil Rights Act limits any penalty or punishment to a term of six months or a fine of $500.00, or both. Defendant conceded in oral argument that if restitution is not penalty or punishment then neither the restrictions of the tribal law and order code nor the Indian Civil Rights Act apply. It might also be pointed out that the defendant has offered no authority that restitution is a penalty or punishment.

Strictly speaking, the tribal court's order was an order of reparation. In general, most jurisdictions do not distinguish between the concepts of reparation and restitution. However, restitution normally refers to the return of something of value to the victim, while reparation is defined as repairing or restoring the damage caused to a victim. Restitution or reparation is generically distinct from a fine. A fine is a penal extraction. Since restitution or reparation is not a penalty or punishment and is clearly authorized by the Law and Order Code of the

> Ute Mountain Ute Tribe, the court below does have authority to impose such a requirement as a condition of sentence. . .
>
> The Indian Civil Rights Act does not impose any conditions on tribes with respect to restitution or reparation. The limitations therein apply only to sentence. Accordingly, the court holds that the Indian Civil Rights Act does not limit the tribal court from ordering restitution or reparation as a condition of sentence. Additionally, since the Law and Order Code of the Ute Mountain Ute Tribe imposes no restrictions on restitution or reparation, none exist. It is, therefore, within the sound discretion of the tribal court to order restitution or reparation. Since there is apparently no question in this case that the damage was inflicted by the defendant, such order by the court was appropriate. . .
>
> Having considered defendant's appeal, it is the decision of this court that the tribal trial court's order shall be modified to require the defendant to pay the restitution or reparation to the Ute Mountain Ute Tribe. In all other respects the tribal court order is affirmed.

Conclusion

In many ways, the American criminal justice system was not created with victims in mind. However, most tribal justice systems made the victim and her family the priority in any resolution to the crime. Today's tribal court systems can serve as leaders in the effort to provide respectful support for the many victims in our communities.

Questions

1. Do you think that the codes provided in this chapter serve to provide additional safety to victims of crime? Why or why not?
2. Why might it be important for crime victims to have an advocate? Why is it important to ensure that communication between victims and their advocates is confidential?
3. Why might it be important to have special protections for child victims?
4. Do you think that victims' rights can ever infringe on defendants' rights? If so, how? How can victims' rights be protected while minimizing any potential infringement on defendants' rights?

In Your Community

1. What victims' rights, if any, are protected in your tribal laws?
2. Do you think that victims should have additional rights in the tribal justice system?
3. Would these victims' rights have been provided in some manner in your community's traditional justice system?

Terms Used in Chapter 25

Deposition: The process of taking a witness's sworn, out-of-court testimony.

Personal recognizance: Permission to go free before trial without putting up a bail bond.

Privilege: The right and duty to withhold information because of some special status or relationship of confidentiality.

Notes

1. National Congress of American Indians Policy Research Center, "Policy Insights Brief: Statistics on Violence Against Women," February 2013.
2. Id.
3. Id.
4. Id.
5. Carol Chiago Lujan and Gordon Adams, "U.S. Colonization of Indian Justice Systems: A Brief History," 19 *Wicazo Sa Rev.* 9 (2004).
6. http://www.wbcws.org/
7. *Basic Call to Consciousness* 10 (Akwesasne Notes ed. 1991).
8. Id.

Suggested Further Reading

Sarah Deer, "Toward an Indigenous Jurisprudence of Rape," 14 *Kansas Journal of Law and Public Policy* 121 (2004).

Sherry Hamby, "Walking with American Indian Victims of Sexual Assault: A Review of Legal Obstacles and Legal Resources Affecting Crime Victims in Indian Country," *Family & Intimate Partner Violence Quarterly* 1(4): 293, 305 (2009).

Gloria Valencia-Weber and Christine P. Zuni, "Domestic Violence and Tribal Protection of Indigenous Women in the United States," 69 *Saint John's Law Review* 69 (2009).

"Victim Services: Promising Practices in Indian Country." Washington, DC: U.S. Dept. of Justice, Office of Justice Programs, Office for Victims of Crime, 2004.

Bonnie Clairmont, et al, eds. *Sharing Our Stories of Survival: Native Women Surviving Violence,* Alta Mira (2008).

Important Organizations

National Indian Child Welfare Association
National Congress of American Indians (NCAI)
NCAI Task Force on Violence Against Women
National Indigenous Women's Resource Center
Native American Child Alliance
Southwest Center for Law and Policy
Unified Solutions
Tribal Law and Policy Institute

Sentencing: Fines and Incarceration

Chapter 26

What Is a Sentence?

A sentence is a legal consequence or sanction for a finding of guilt in a criminal case. Sentences are usually imposed by a tribal judge after a guilty plea or a finding of guilt after a trial.

"A law without penalty is only advice." *Laurie Watt v. Colville Confederated Tribes*, 25 Indian L. Rep. 6027 (1998).

Common sentences from the American system include incarceration (jail time/prison time) and fines (monetary payments to the government). Many tribal governments also rely on incarceration and fines, although tribes are not required to use these forms of punishment. This chapter focuses on incarceration and fines. Chapter 27 explores traditional and alternative sentencing.

Tribal Sentencing Laws

Many tribal governments that exercise criminal jurisdiction have sentencing provisions in their criminal codes. Tribal judges are bound by these sentencing laws to determine the appropriate punishment for a particular crime. Tribal codes provide sentencing procedure and sentencing options and limits. Some tribal codes allow tribal judges to consider federal or state law as persuasive authority, although many tribal courts strive to implement tribal sentencing law based on customs, traditions, and values.

Tribal sentencing policy is often informed by the fact that a convicted person is a member of a large, extended family and will often return to the same community where the wrongdoing occurred. In this sense, tribal nations have an incentive to ensure that convicted people receive treatment and/or rehabilitation so that they can rebuild their lives as contributing members of society.

Some tribal codes require the development of a "Pre-Sentence Investigation Report" (often called a PSIR) that provides the judge with information about the person's criminal history, drug/alcohol problems, and other relevant information.

Tribal sentencing laws can be mandatory (requiring the imposition of a specific sentence) or discretionary (allowing a tribal judge to make a decision that best fits the circumstances).

Sentencing Options/Types of Sentences

There are a variety of types of sentences that can be imposed. Depending on the tribal code, a tribal judge may have the option of crafting a sentence that addresses the unique needs of the convicted person and the tribal community.

- Incarceration: The judge may impose jail time. The length of the sentence depends on the seriousness of the crime, the defendant's criminal history, and other factors proscribed by the tribal code. A few tribal courts operate their own jails/prisons. Other tribes work with the Bureau of Prisons or local state facilities for incarcerating offenders.
- Fines: The defendant must pay money to the tribe as ordered by the court.
- Suspended Sentence: The sentence is ordered, but the jail sentence is not imposed if the defendant obeys certain requirements. The requirements could include completing drug/alcohol treatment or counseling, not committing any new crimes for a year, or other conditions deemed necessary by the court. If the defendant fails to meet the requirements, then she will have to serve the jail sentence.
- Deferred/Delayed Sentence: Similar to the suspended sentence, the sentence is delayed/deferred for a specific period of time. If the defendant obeys certain requirements, then the criminal charge will be dismissed.
- Treatment, Counseling, Rehabilitation: These requirements are sometimes imposed instead of a jail term or in combination with another sentencing option. (See chapter 27 for more alternative sentencing.)
- Community Service: The defendant is required to provide services to the community. Such services often include manual labor (cleaning buildings, picking up litter, mowing lawns).
- Work Release: The defendant serves time in jail, but is allowed to leave jail daily for employment reasons.
- Restitution: Restitution is used to help address harm to the victim(s). The defendant is required to compensate the victim and her family directly for loss or injury. Compensation may be in the form of monetary payments, material goods, or ceremonial duties (covered in chapter 25).
- Probation: The defendant is released to the supervision of a probation officer and agrees to follow certain conditions, such as keeping a job,

avoiding drugs/alcohol, and staying in the community for supervision. A violation of the terms of probation can result in additional penalties.

Public Apology: The defendant is ordered to apologize to the victim, the victim's family, and/or the entire nation. The apology may be written or spoken; the judge may order the time and place for the apology.

Cultural Sanctions: Some tribal courts refer to traditional law and impose certain ceremonial requirements that are unique to that culture.

Example of a Tribal Sentencing Law

EXCERPTS FROM Salish and Kootenai Criminal Procedures, Codified

Part 12 Sentence and Judgment

2-2-1201. Rendering Judgment and Pronouncing Sentence

(1) This Part controls all sentencing in all circumstances. Changes in Montana Law do not apply unless expressly adopted by Tribal Council.
(2) The judgment shall be rendered in open court.
(3) If the verdict or finding is not guilty, judgment shall be rendered immediately and the defendant shall be discharged from custody or from the obligation of his or her bail bond.
(4) (a) If the verdict or finding is guilty, sentence shall be pronounced and judgment rendered within a reasonable time.
   (b) When the sentence is pronounced, the judge shall clearly state for the record his or her reasons for the sentence imposed.

2-2-1202. Sentencing Considerations

(1) Sentences imposed upon those convicted of crime must be based primarily on the following:
   (a) the crime committed;
   (b) the prospects of rehabilitation of the offender, including the possible resources and needs of the offender's dependents, if any;
   (c) the circumstances under which the crime was committed;
   (d) the criminal history of the offender; and
   (e) alternatives to imprisonment of the offender.
   (f) the ability of the defendant to pay a fine.

2-2-1203. Imposition of Sentence

(1) No sentence shall be imposed until:
   (a) the offender and the offender's counsel have had an opportunity to examine any presentence report and to cross-examine the preparer of such report on the basis for any sentencing recommendations contained in the report;
   (b) the prosecution and defense have had an opportunity to present evidence, witnesses, and an argument regarding the appropriateness of a sentencing option; and

(c) the offender has had the opportunity to speak on his or her own behalf and to present any information likely to mitigate the pending sentence.
(2) Sentencing shall be imposed on all offenses pursuant to Tribal law. To the extent that any Montana statute incorporated into Tribal law provides a penalty that conflicts with Tribal sentencing law, Tribal sentencing law will control.
(3) An offender found guilty of an offense may be sentenced to one or more of the following penalties:
   (a) deferred imposition of sentence with reasonable restrictions and conditions monitored by the Tribal Probation Officer, and with the following characteristics:
      (i) the record of the offense shall be expunged upon satisfactory performance by the offender of the restrictions and conditions of deferral for a period not to exceed one year for Class A, Class B, Class C, and Class D offenses and three years for a Class E offense, and
      (ii) imposition of sentence will occur immediately upon violation of a restriction or condition of the deferral;
   (b) suspended **execution** of all or part of a sentence for one year for Class A, Class B, Class C, and Class D offenses and three years for a Class E offense, with the offender being placed on probation under reasonable restrictions and conditions for the period of suspension, and with a violation of a restriction or condition resulting in execution of the suspended portion of the sentence;
   (c) imprisonment for a period of time not to exceed the maximum permitted for the offense;
   (d) a fine in an amount not to exceed the maximum permitted for the offense;
   (e) community service;
   (f) any diagnostic, therapeutic, or rehabilitative measures, treatments, or services deemed appropriate;
   (g) restitution to a victim of an offense for which the offender was convicted; or
   (h) a person may be allowed to serve home arrest at the person's expense, but will not be eligible for parole under Section 2-3-302.
(4) The court may impose any or all of the following restrictions or conditions as part of a sentence, suspended or otherwise, or a deferred imposition of sentence, for rehabilitative purposes or to protect the Reservation community:
   (a) prohibiting the offender from owning or carrying a dangerous weapon;
   (b) restricting the offender's freedom of movement;
   (c) restricting the offender's freedom of association;
   (d) requiring the offender, if employed, to remain employed and, if unemployed, to actively seek employment; and
   (e) any requirement or limitation intended to improve the mental or physical health or marketable skills of the offender.
(5) Unless the Tribal Court otherwise directs in its pronouncement of sentence, all sentences stemming from offenses occurring in the same transaction or course of conduct shall run concurrently and not **consecutively**.
(6) Any monies paid to the Tribes or to the victim of an offense as a result of this provision shall be paid through the Clerk of Court.
(7) Where the Court in its discretion deems it appropriate, a form of traditional punishment may be imposed in addition to or in place of any punishment provided in this Code.

2-2-1204 Execution of Sentence
(1) If the offender is sentenced to imprisonment, the court shall deliver a Detention Order or Judgment outlining the specific requirements of detention to the Tribal law enforcement officers serving as Tribal jailers. The offender shall be discharged from custody by the Tribal law enforcement officers after satisfactorily fulfilling the conditions of the imposed sentence or upon earlier order of the court.
(2) If judgment is rendered imposing a fine only, the offender must be discharged after making acceptable arrangements to pay the fine within the period of time specified by the court. The Tribal Court may also allow the offender to perform community service to offset any fine or allow the offender to be imprisoned until the fine is satisfied, applying $50.00 for every day served, unless a different amount is otherwise established by Tribal Council. If no such permission is included in the sentence, the fine shall be paid prior to formal release.
(3) If judgment is rendered imposing both imprisonment and a fine, the offender shall be discharged after fulfilling the requirements of subsections (1) and (2) of this section.
(4) The Court may in its discretion grant temporary release from custody under any conditions the Court deems appropriate.

2-2-1205. RESTITUTION

(1) When restitution is ordered, the court shall specify the amount, method and payment schedule imposed upon the offender. Before restitution may be ordered, the defendant shall receive notice of the amount and terms requested and shall be entitled to a hearing upon his or her timely request.
(2) The fact that restitution was ordered is not admissible as evidence in a civil action and has no legal effect on the merits of a civil action.
(3) Except as otherwise provided in this subsection, restitution paid by an offender to an injured person must be deducted from any monetary award granted to said injured person in a civil action arising out of the facts or events which were the basis for the restitution. The court trying the civil action shall determine the amount of any reduction due to payment of restitution by an offender under this section.

However, in the event that criminal and civil actions against an offender arising from the same transaction or events are heard in courts of different jurisdictions, one of which is the Tribal Court, the Tribal Court shall adjust offender's payments within its jurisdictional control for restitution or otherwise to assure that an injured party does not recover twice for the same harm.
(4) An offender may petition for modification of sentence imposing restitution and request a hearing on the matter. The injured person shall be given notice by the offender of any proposed modification and afforded an opportunity to be heard on the proposed modification.

2-2-1206. Payment of Fines and Restitution
(1) All monies collected as the result of a fine imposed by the Tribal Court shall be paid through the Clerk of Court. Upon receiving the monies, the Clerk shall:
 (a) issue a receipt to the paying person;
 (b) credit the account of the offender, noting whether the fine is paid in full or what balance, if any, remains due; and

(c) transfer the monies to the general fund of the Tribes, unless otherwise specifically directed by a provision of this Code.
(2) All monies collected for restitution shall be paid through the Clerk of Court. Upon receiving the monies the Clerk shall:
(a) issue a receipt to the paying person;
(b) credit the account of the offender, noting whether the restitution is paid in full or what balance, if any remains due; and
(c) transfer the monies to the person to whom restitution is to be paid.

2-2-1207. Revocation of Parole or Suspended or **Deferred Sentence**

(1) If a petition requesting revocation has been filed and a revocation hearing held, the Tribal Court may **revoke** a defendant's parole or suspension or deferral of sentence if a preponderance of the evidence shows the imposed conditions of the parole, or suspension, or deferral of sentence have been violated.
(2) A petition seeking revocation of a parole or a suspended sentence or imposition of a sentence previously deferred must be filed during the period of parole, suspension or deferral, or within 5 days after the period of parole, suspension, or deferral ends if the offender's violation of a condition of parole or probation occurred within the final 48 hours prior to the end of the period. Expiration of a parole or the time ordered under a suspended or deferred sentence prior to a hearing for revocation does not deprive the Tribal Court of jurisdiction to rule on the revocation petition.
(3) This is the exclusive remedy for violation of a condition of parole, or suspended or deferred sentence.

2-2-1208. Dismissal and Expungement after Deferred Sentence

Whenever the court has deferred the imposition of sentence and after expiration of the period of deferral and after the defendants successful completion of any conditions of deferral, upon motion by the court, the defendant, or the defendant's counsel, the court shall allow the defendant to withdraw his or her plea of guilty or strike the verdict or judgment expunging the court records of all record of the proceedings by entering an order of dismissal of charges and expungement, inscribing each record of the proceedings with the word "Expunged" and sealing the file.

2-2-1209. Failure to Pay a Fine

(1) If a defendant sentenced to pay a fine or restitution fails to make payment as ordered, the Court or the Prosecutor may move that the offender show cause why the offender's nonpayment should not be treated as contempt of court. Notice of a show cause hearing on the contempt charge shall be served on the offender by law enforcement officers at least five days prior to the date set for hearing. Notice shall also be served on the victim if the show cause was issued for failure to pay restitution.
(2) Unless the offender shows that the nonpayment was not attributable to an intentional refusal to obey a Tribal Court order or the offender's failure to make a good faith effort to make the ordered payments, the Tribal Court may find the offender in contempt and order the person incarcerated until the fine is satisfied. Time served shall be credited against the fine at the rate of $50.00 per day unless otherwise set by the Tribal Council.

(3) *If the Court determines that the offender's nonpayment does not constitute contempt, the Court may modify the original sentence, judgment, or order, allowing the offender additional time to pay the fine or restitution or reducing the amount owed.*

2-2-1210. Credit for Time Served

If a defendant has served any of the defendant's sentence under a commitment based upon a judgment that is subsequently declared invalid or that is modified during the term of imprisonment, the time served must be credited against any subsequent sentence received upon a new commitment for the same criminal act or acts. This does not include time served pursuant to Section 2-2-610(1)(c).

2-2-1211. Credit for Incarceration prior to Conviction

(1) *Any person incarcerated on a bailable offense and against whom a judgment of imprisonment is rendered must be allowed credit for each day of incarceration prior to or after conviction, except that the time allowed as a credit may not exceed the term of the prison sentence rendered. This does not include time served pursuant to Section 2-2-610(1)(c).*

(2) *Any person incarcerated on a bailable offense who does not supply bail and against whom a fine is levied on conviction of the offense must be allowed a credit for each day of incarceration prior to conviction, except that the amount allowed or credited may not exceed the amount of the fine. The daily rate of credit for incarceration is $50.00 per day unless otherwise set by the Tribal Council. This does not include time served pursuant to Section 2-2-610(1)(c).*

The following tribal case imposes a suspended sentence and restitution:

Makah Tribal Court
Makah Tribe v. Jonathan Greene (2002)
2002.NAMK.0000002 (VersusLaw)
The opinion of the court was delivered by: Iris K. Shue, Chief Judge.

Amended Judgment and Sentence Order

This Court amends its Judgment and Sentence Order issued on November 20, 2001, for clarification purposes only. This Order does not change any requirement that was ordered on November 20, 2001, which was entered on court record with the Defendant present.

A. *The Offenses Are Determined to Be Alcohol and/or Drug-Related*

This determination was made after Defendant Greene entered a guilty plea on all charges at his November 15, 2001 arraignment. Knowing the Defendant was not apprehended soon after the burglaries, the Court asked the parties if these offenses were alcohol related. The Court judge expressed concern that if the incidents were alcohol related and the problem is not addressed; then the Defendant will likely continue to have the same type of legal problems.

Acting Prosecutor Gilje responded in the affirmative, adding that he had learned that from comments made in interviews; including with the Defendant. The prosecutor added that in the second set of incidents (10/13/01), the Defendant could not even remember details due to having smoked marijuana the night before. The Court informed Defendant Greene about Wellness Court and asked if he would be interested in going, which he stated he was.

At the November 20, 2001 sentencing hearing, prosecutor Gilje recommended consolidation of sentences, with 48 months [in jail] suspended; a $4,000 fine suspended; and 1,000 hours of community service. Also recommended was a 2-year probation term including requirements that Defendant go through Wellness Court, have no similar violations, and pay restitution, the amount undetermined at that time.

Having been informed the Defendant was still residing in Forks, Washington, the Court thereafter ordered the Defendant receive a chemical dependency evaluation from MCDP [Makah Chemical Dependency Program], which has authority to recommend a client for Wellness Court if it was determined that would be the best treatment program for him.

B. *The Defendant's Sentences Are Consolidated As Follows*

445 days jail time w/415 suspended; $2,000 fine w/$2,000 suspended. 500 hours community service to be served.

ALL SUSPENDED JAIL TIME AND SUSPENDED FINES ARE CONDITIONED UPON FULL COMPLIANCE WITH THE FOLLOWING PROBATION TERMS:

1. Defendant shall commit no similar violations.
2. Defendant shall pay restitution of: the total costs/damage divided by the number of persons convicted for the same offense/s.
3. Defendant shall serve 500 hours of community service.
4. Defendant shall report to the Adult Probation Officer [APO] as she schedules and follow recommendations.
5. Complete a chemical dependency evaluation through the Makah Chemical Dependency Program or any certified CD agency within 14 days of release from jail and comply with all recommendations of the counselor.
6. Abstain from consuming alcohol or mind-altering drugs not prescribed by a physician, and submit to random testing through urinalysis or breathalizer tests.
7. Obtain a Baseline test upon release and/or incarceration.
8. Sign any Release of Information forms needed to document compliance.

9. Provide documentation of all compliance to the APO.
10. Notify the Court in writing of any change of address.
11. Defendant may request a restitution hearing if there is a dispute of the amount owed.
12. Time accredited for the 20 days served. Therefore, Defendant has 10 remaining (non-suspended) days of jail time left to serve.

C. The Ordered Fourteen (14) Day Time Line for Defendant to Get a Chemical Dependency Evaluation Begins to Be Counted upon Defendant's Release from Jail

Spokesperson Cindy Renteria who was present on the Defendant's behalf, asked whether Defendant Greene's evaluation would be required while he was serving his jail sentence or if instead the standard 14 day time would apply after his release from jail. The Court clarified that the time is counted from the day of release from jail.

D. A Sixty (60) Day Time Line Is Set for the Restitution Amount to Be Determined from Defendant's Proportionate Share of Total Costs with Respect to Others, If Any, Who Are Also Found Liable

The Court noted two things must be known to ascertain Defendant Greene's restitution amount: 1) the total amount of value of both: the remaining stolen items (prosecutor estimated 90–95% of goods retrieved) and the costs of repairing damage to the premises that were burglarized; and 2) the number of any co-defendant who is [sic] convicted of the respective offense/s. A sixty (60) day time line was set. The Court's expectation is that by that time, there will be documentation (e.g. invoice/s) of costs of un-retrieved stolen goods; damage; and knowledge of the outcome of pending proceedings of co-defendants.

Due to the uncertainty of the restitution amount at that time, the Court noted that the Defendant could request a restitution hearing if a dispute arises as to the amount he is required to pay.

The Order does not state the monthly restitution amount that will be made once the total restitution owed is determined. The standard monthly payment of $50.00 per month (except in extreme circumstances whereby $25.00 monthly is permitted) is required. The restitution is to be paid in full no later than November 21, 2003, which is the end of the 2-year probation period.

Probation requirements of restitution and chemical dependency evaluation recommendations, if any, that are not completed by the end of the probation period will result in extension of the probation period for cause, upon notice from the APO who monitors compliance.

SO DONE, this 31st day of January, 2002.

The following case illustrates the link between tribal sovereignty and the ability of tribal courts to punish defendants. Review the case and determine whether you agree with the outcome.

Colville Confederated Tribes Court of Appeals
Henry Pakootas v. Colville Confederated Tribes (1997)
24 Indian Law Reporter 6113
Before Presiding Justice Miles, Justice Bonga and Justice McGeoghegan
Unanimous Panel

Background
On August 12, 1993, Henry L. Pakootas appeared before the Colville Confederated Tribal Court. Mr. Pakootas was initially charged with Attempted Criminal Homicide. The Tribes made a Motion to Reduce The Charge To Assault, the Court granted the Motion.

Mr. Pakootas entered a guilty plea to the offense of Assault and was sentenced to: (1) $1,000.00 fine with $750.00 suspended conditionally, and the balance payable by February 12, 1994; (2) Ninety (90) days jail with thirty (30) days suspended; fifty-eight (58) days credit for time served, with him serving the remainder of the jail time immediately. Conditions of the suspensions were: (1) file an alcohol and substance abuse evaluation from TCCS by October 12, 1993, and follow recommendations for one year, (2) file progress reports from TCCS on November 12, 1993; February 12, 1994; May 12, 1994; and final compliance report due prior to the Pre-Dismissal Hearing on July 25, 1994. (3) If the defendant is cited for any offenses in any court, he may be brought before this Court to show cause; and (4) $5.00 court costs.

On August 24, 1994, a Show Cause Hearing was set to determine whether the appellant violated the conditions of the suspended portion of the August 12, 1993 Trial Court Order. Mr. Pakootas testified he had pled guilty to Simple Assault in the Federal Court and served a ninety (90) day jail term. He further stated that the federal conviction was only for threatening to beat up Ben Marchand Jr. and this stemmed from the same incident as the Tribal Court matter. On cross examination, Mr. Pakootas further testified that the federal conviction was not related to having a firearm.

The prosecution moved to continue the hearing in order to obtain evidence to contradict Mr. Pakootas' statement regarding the federal matter, the Court denied the prosecution's request.

Following the testimony of Mr. Pakootas, Appellant moved the Court to credit his tribal jail sentence with time he served while in federal custody. The Court denied the motion and reinstated the suspended $750.00 fine, to be paid by August 24, 1995 and imposed a thirty (30) day jail term to be served on weekends. The appellant appeals the Order of August 24, 1994.

Conclusion

In *U.S. v. Wheeler*, 435 U.S. 313 (1978), the Supreme Court stated, "When an Indian Tribe criminally punishes a Tribal member for a violation of Tribal Law, the tribe acts as an independent sovereign."

Being an independent sovereign, the Tribal Court has the inherent power to administer appropriate punishment for any violation of Tribal law. This Court must determine if the Trial Court acted accordingly as prescribed by Tribal law and did not abuse [its] discretion.

Upon review of applicable Tribal laws, this Court finds its Tribal Code and Tribal statutory laws are silent on this matter. Therefore, this Court must rely on CCT 1.5.05 which states:

> When jurisdiction is vested in the court, all the means necessary to carry into effect are also governing; and in the exercise of this jurisdiction, if the course of proceedings is not specified in this Code, any suitable process or mode of proceeding may be adopted which appears most conformable to the spirit of Tribal Law.

It is the opinion of the Court that in order to maintain independence as a sovereign nation; the Tribal Court must strive to protect Tribal interest. In this instance the Tribal Court determined it was not in the best interest of the Tribes to give the defendant double credit for time served while in federal custody. The appellant has not shown any abuse of discretion by the Tribal Court, nor does this Court find any.

For the reasons stated above, the decision of the Tribal Court is Affirmed.

Vacating a Sentence

Persons who are sentenced in tribal court have specific rights that are protected by tribal and federal law.

The sentencing procedure must be fair. Due process and sentencing is covered in Chapter 24. In addition, the sentence must not impose harsh or inhumane punishments (protection against cruel and unusual punishment).

If a tribal court imposes a sentence that fails to follow the procedure outlined in tribal law, the convicted person can usually appeal that sentence to the tribal appellate court. In the following case, the defendant claims that the sentence imposed by the tribal court was unfair. Review the facts of the case and identify the principles that the Colville Tribal Court of Appeals uses to vacate the sentence.

Colville Confederated Tribes Court of Appeals
Joseph Sweowat v. Colville Confederated Tribes (2001)
2001.NACC.0000002 (VersusLaw)
Before Chief Justice Dupris, Associate Justice McGeoghegan and Associate Justice Stewart
The opinion of the court was delivered by: McGEOGHEGAN, J.

Introduction
The appellant was charged with the offenses of Possession of Drug Paraphernalia and Escape. At sentencing, the Court accepted the appellant counsel's Motion for a Deferred Sentence and accepted the appellant's guilty pleas to Possession of Drug Paraphernalia and Escape. The Court ordered the appellant's sentence on both charges deferred for a period of one year. The defendant failed to appear for his Pre-Dismissal Hearing. Following a Show Cause Hearing the Court revoked the appellant's deferred sentence. The Appellant was sentenced to the following:

1. The defendant shall pay a fine in the amount of $4500.00, with $3500.00 suspended conditionally, the unsuspended $1000.00 due and payable immediately.
2. The defendant shall serve 360 days in jail, with 300 days suspended conditionally. Defendant is credited for 22 days already served. The remaining 38 days shall begin immediately.
3. The defendant shall pay $25.00 court costs due and payable immediately.

Conditions of Suspension
1. The defendant shall file a drug and alcohol substance abuse evaluation within 60 days from release from jail and follow the recommended treatment for one year. The defendant shall also file with the Court his quarterly progress reports and a final progress report to be filed no later than the pre-dismissal hearing.
2. The defendant shall not commit any further criminal offenses in any jurisdiction for a period of one (1) year, i.e., until October 2, 1998. If the defendant is cited for any criminal offenses before any court he may be brought before this court to show cause why he should not be found in violation of this court order.

3. The defendant shall notify the Court of any mailing and/or physical address change for one year, i.e., until October 2, 1998.
4. Within 24 hours of release from jail the defendant shall immediately contact the Colville Confederated Tribes Probation and Parole Department for supervision of compliance in this case and vocational rehabilitation of the defendant.
5. The defendant shall fully comply with all orders of the court.

On October 2, 1997, the Appellant filed a Notice of Appeal, and the Appellant filed a Motion for Stay for the execution of the Judgment and Sentence. On October 3, 1997, Judge Eldemar granted the appellant's motion and ordered the Judgment and Sentence stayed upon the appellant posting a $1,025.99 bond until a final order is ordered by the Tribal Court of Appeals.

The Judgment and Sentence set a Pre-Dismissal Hearing for September 14, 1998. The sentencing Judge did not issue formal written findings and the audio record of the sentencing proceedings are not available for review.

Issues on Appeal

The issues before the Appellate Panel are: 1) Whether a Sentencing Court Judge is required to express findings of fact in writing to support or justify a criminal sentence when the sentence is within the statutory limits. 2) Whether the Court below abused its discretion in sentencing the Appellant to the maximum sentence within statutory limits. 3) Whether the Court **arbitrarily and capriciously** sentenced the Appellant to the maximum allowed under the limits of the statute. 4) Whether the Court used **erroneous** information at the time of sentencing the Appellant.

Discussion

At the time of the appellant's sentencing, the former Tribal Code section dealing with sentencing CTC 2.6.07, applied and reads:

CTC 2.6.07 Sentencing
> A sentence shall be imposed at once or, in the discretion of the judge, at a later date not to exceed 60 days from the day of judgment. The judge may suspend all or any part of the fine or sentence imposed by him upon a person found guilty of violating any of the provisions of this Code as provided in section 3-1-263. Pending sentence, the judge may commit the defendant to jail or continue the bail. Before imposing sentence, the judge shall allow a spokesman or the defendant to speak on behalf of the defendant and to present any information which would help the judge in setting the punishment. Amended 08/17/89, Resolution 1989-612.

The language of the last sentence of the statute clearly requires the Court to allow a spokesman or the defendant to present any information to help the Judge in setting the punishment and sentence for the defendant. The implication is that the Court uses discretion in sentencing the defendant. Where there is a claim by the defendant that the Court abused its discretion in sentencing, the reviewing court must look to the record to determine whether the Court abused its discretion. Where the record shows that the Court properly evaluated the facts and information presented at the time of sentencing, this Court will not disturb the lower Court's sentence. The record must show by clear and convincing evidence that the Judge did abuse his or her discretion in sentencing the defendant. Where there is no substantial record, either written or oral, fairness dictates that the defendant's sentence must be **vacated** and the case **remanded** to the lower Court for re-sentencing. A claim of abuse of discretion requires us to freely review the facts in the record of the Court below.

Although Federal case law and the Federal Rules of Criminal Procedure are not authority over the Colville Tribal Court System, they may be analyzed for advisory value.

In *United States v. Barnhart*, 980 F.2d 219 (3rd Cir. 1992), Judge Garth, speaking for the Third Circuit Court of Appeals, said the following:

> Moreover, under the pre-Sentencing Guidelines law, a district court is not obligated to give its reasons for imposing a specific sentence, *United States v. Felder*, 744 F.2d 18, 20 (3rd Cir. 1984) (citing *United States v. Del Piana*, 593 F.2d 539, 540 (3rd Cir.), cert. denied, 442 U.S. 944, 99 S.Ct. 2889, 61 L.Ed. 2d (1979)), although a district court judge who sentences a defendant under the Sentencing Guidelines must state in open court the reasons for imposition of a particular sentence. *United States v. Georgiadis*, 933 F.2d 1219, 1222–23 (3rd Cir. 1991). *U.S. v. Barnhart*, 980 F.2d at 225.

In *United States v. Georgiadis*, 933 F.2d 1219 (3rd Cir. 1991), the Third Circuit Federal Court of Appeals speaking through Judge Nygaard stated the following about sentencing statements at sentencing hearings:

> We reject Georgiadis' contentions. We hold instead that a sentencing court does not commit **reversible error** under the Sentencing Reform Act by failing to state expressly on the record that it has considered and exercised discretion when refusing a defendant's requested downward departure from the Guidelines.
>
> The statute controlling judicial sentencing statements, 18 U.S.C. §3553, (footnote omitted) does not require the statements Georgiadis seeks. Section 3553(c) defines the only statements a district court must make during sentencing. The section requires that at the time of sentencing a judge shall 'state in open court the reasons for its imposition of the particular sentence.' 18 U.S.C. §3553(c). (footnote omitted) This general requirement is satisfied when a district court indicates the applicable Guideline range, and how it was chosen." United States v. Georgiadis. 933 F.2d at 1222–23.

It is clear from U.S. v. Georgiadis, 933 F.2d 1219 (1991) that the federal Sentencing Reform Act does not require that district court judges make formal written findings of fact at sentencing hearings but only need to make statements on the record required by 18 U.S.C. §3553. These cases may be distinguished in that the Colville Tribal Trial Court is not bound by Sentencing Guidelines, and exercises more discretion in sentencing under tribal laws.

In United States v. Morgan, 942 F.2nd 243 (4th Cir. 1991), the Fourth Circuit Court of Appeals held that where the defendant challenged the accuracy of information contained in the pre-sentence report, the district court is required by Federal Rules of Criminal Procedure 32(c)(3)(D) to make a finding with respect to each objection a defendant raises to facts contained in a presentence report before it may rely on the disputed fact in sentencing. The Court of Appeals said that required finding by the district court may be made in several ways. The district court may separately recite its finding as to each **controverted** matter. Alternatively, the district court may expressly adopt the recommended findings contained in the pre-sentence report.

Apparently such findings are made on record as there was no mention of any requirement for formal written findings of fact.

Further, the United States Supreme Court, in Dorszynski v. United States, held that "once it is determined that a sentence is within the limits set forth in the statute under which it is imposed, appellate review is at end." In this there is no need for formal written findings of fact to support the appellant's sentence where the Sentencing Court Judge sentenced the appellant to a sentence within the statutory limits of the penalty for Possession of Drug Paraphernalia and Escape.

It is clear from the above federal case law that sentencing court judges do not need to make formal written findings of fact to support their sentences of criminal defendants in federal courts because of the statutory limits placed on their sentences in federal sentencing guidelines, which are mandatory.

Appellee argues that Colville Confederated Tribes v. David St. Peter clearly holds the Sentencing Judge is not required to make formal findings of fact to support or justify a criminal sentence. In St. Peter we stated in **dicta** the sentencing judge was not required to state specific reasons for the sentences imposed. Dicta does not constitute a ruling of the Court. In St. Peter the Court was presented with the issue of due process in the particular sentence of the Defendant/Appellant. We examined the trial record and found sufficient indicia on record to support the trial judge's sentence. Sam is not **inapposite**. The ruling in Sam supports the proposition that a sentencing judge has discretion, within the statutory limits of what punishment may be imposed.

In Sylvester Sam v. Colville Confederated Tribes, 21 ILR 6040 (1994), we said: "A criminal sentence imposed within statutory limits is generally not reviewable by an appellate court. A particular sentence imposed within the limitations imposed by statute and the Constitution is within the discretion of the court."

> To the extent that the Appellee argues that no reasoning is required in the record, we disagree and thus modify the holdings in St. Peter and Sam to the better and more prudent ruling that absent a statute mandating a specific punishment, findings and conclusions must be expressed in the record, either orally or in writing, which reflect the Court's discretion in sentencing a defendant. When a Court deviates from a stipulated recommended sentencing and the defendant requests written findings at sentencing, the Court must express on the record its reason for denying such a request. In this way defendants can rely on their Courts having in place methods and procedures which establish and preserve fairness and reliability while meeting the expectations of the community subject to this judicial system.
>
> *Conclusion and Order*
> Absent mandatory sentencing by statute for a particular crime, the Court uses its discretion to determine appropriate punishment for a defendant. Discretion requires the Court to analyze and evaluate favorable and unfavorable information about the defendant and announce findings on the record which justify the punishment imposed upon the defendant by the Court. Where the record below fails to provide such findings, either orally or in writing, the Appellate Court is unable to determine whether the defendant's sentence was imposed using erroneous information or imposed arbitrarily and capriciously. The defendant's sentence must be vacated. This case is remanded to the Court below for re-sentencing under the guidance of this opinion.

Limitations on Tribal Sentencing Authority

The Indian Civil Rights Act (ICRA) limits the sentencing authority of tribal courts. The original law, passed in 1968, limited tribal sentencing authority to six months in jail and/or a $500 fine. In 1984, the limitations were changed to a maximum of one year in jail and/or a $5,000 fine. The Tribal Law and Order Act (TLOA), discussed in Chapter 10, authorizes tribal governments to impose a maximum of three years per offense as long as certain protections are provided to the defendant.

Such sentencing limitations are objectionable for many tribes because they deny the tribal government the inherent sovereignty to select the punishments that best meet the needs of their nations. Even if someone is found guilty of a particularly violent crime (such as murder or child sexual abuse), the maximum penalty that tribal courts have been able to impose is one year per offense. Many tribal leaders have been concerned that one year is not a sufficient punishment for a dangerous, violent person. One way of addressing such concern is to impose separate, one-year sentences for each separate violation of law. Such sentences are known as "stacked" or "consecutive." Many tribal courts have upheld the imposition of such sentences. TLOA authorizes consecutive sentences up to nine total years for multiple offenses.

The following tribal cases consider the fairness of consecutive sentences.

Colville Confederated Tribes Court of Appeals
David L. St. Peter v. Colville Confederated Tribes (1993)
1993.NACC.0000013 (VersusLaw)
Before Chief Judge Collins, Judge Baker and Judge Bonga
The opinion of the court was delivered by: Collins, C.J.

This matter was brought before the Appellate Panel seeking review of five maximum sentences imposed by the Trial Court in the above cases. In her Memorandum Opinion; Judgment And Sentence, dated February 2, 1993, Judge Elizabeth Fry imposed maximum jail sentences for two counts of Disorderly Conduct, Assault, Trespass To Buildings, and Resisting Arrest, and specified that each sentence would run consecutively to any other incarceration.

The appellant alleges that the Trial Court erred by imposing excessive sentences which are arbitrary and capricious and constitute cruel and unusual punishment, and claims his rights were violated under the Indian Civil Rights Act, 25 U.S.C. Sections 1301–1303 (ICRA) and the Colville Tribal Civil Rights Act, Title 56.01 et seq. (CTCRA). Appellant raises various issues in support of his Assignment Of Error concerning sentencing by the Trial Court. These issues will be addressed by the Panel.

[Section I Omitted]

II

We next turn our attention to review of sentences imposed upon the appellant and the sentencing procedures used by the Trial Court. Appellant contends his right to due process and right to be free from cruel and unusual punishment were **contravene**d under the Indian Civil Rights Act, 25 U.S.C. Sec. 1302 (7),(8) and the Colville Tribal Civil Rights Act, Title 56.02 (g),(h). Because the appellant claims a violation of his civil rights based upon Tribal and federal statutes, our review will necessarily include principles of Tribal and federal law. In Trial Procedure set forth in Chapter 2.6 of the Tribal Code provides as follows: "All accused persons shall be guaranteed all civil rights secured under the Tribal Constitution and federal laws specifically applicable to Indian tribal courts" (CTC 2.6.09).

We interpret CTC 2.6.09 to mean that a reviewing court must apply the Tribal Constitution, Tribal statutory and common law, and the Indian Civil Rights Act. We will also examine principles applied by the federal courts in sentencing review under the United States Constitution. The federal law principles for sentencing review cited infra, are not "specifically applicable to Indian tribal courts," CTC 2.6.09, supra. They are based upon the federal constitutional standards, and not on the Tribal Constitution or the Indian Civil Rights Act. Therefore, we consider such principles to be advisory only.

[Section VI omitted]

VII

We next address whether the Trial Court abused its discretion by sentencing David St. Peter to five maximum consecutive jail terms. The appellant contends that the Trial Court abused its discretion by imposing sentences which were arbitrary and capricious and violated the prohibition against cruel and unusual punishment. The appellant advances a number of theories in support of these contentions.

The Colville Tribal Business Council has established a broad range of criminal penalties for offenders who are convicted of violating criminal statutes enumerated in the Code. These criminal misdemeanor statutes are divided into three classes, and the penalty range for a given offense is governed by the class to which the particular crime was assigned. A person convicted of "Class A" offenses "shall be sentenced to imprisonment for a period not to exceed 360 days, or a fine not to exceed $5,000, or both the jail sentence and the fine." CTC 5.7.01. "Class B" offenses carry a maximum jail term of 180 days, or a maximum fine of $2,500, or both. CTC 5.7.02. "Class C" offenses carry a maximum penalty of 90 days imprisonment, or a maximum fine of $1,000, or both. CTC 5.7.03. The Code is silent as to whether the sentences for offenses arising from the same transaction may be imposed consecutively.

The appellant was convicted of Disorderly Conduct, CTC 5.5.04, Assault, CTC 5.1.03, and Trespass To Buildings, CTC 5.2.18 which are "Class C" offenses, and Resisting Arrest, CTC 5.4.17, a "Class B" offense. Thus, the maximum consecutive penalties for all offenses is 540 days in jail, $6,500 in fines, or both. The appellant, having received credit for 10 days of jail time served, was sentenced to a jail term of 530 days. Although the trial court imposed maximum jail sentences on the appellant, she did not impose the maximum penalty available for the offenses.

The language chosen by the Tribal Business Council in CTC 5.7.01 et seq. limits the Trial Court's discretion in sentencing. The various offenses enumerated in the Code have been graded into classes for purposes of sentencing. These statutes prohibit the trial judge from imposing a greater sentence for a crime than provided for the class within which the offense falls. Further, all criminal offenses set out in the Code are classified as misdemeanors, which, by definition cannot result in imprisonment for more than one year. In addition, the Congress has restricted sentencing authority of the Tribal Court by placing an upper sentencing limit of one year imprisonment and a fine of $5,000 on the court. 25 U.S.C. Sec. 1301 et seq.

We note that the sentences imposed upon St. Peter by the trial judge were within statutory limits. It is evident that the Tribal Council has delegated considerable latitude to the Trial Court in sentencing criminal offenders within the statutory limits set out in the Code. Because the sentences fall within statutory limits, the Appellate Panel will review only the process by which punishment is determined rather than make an unjustified incursion into the province of the sentencing judge.

X

In conducting this limited review, we emphasize that the due process principles reflected in the cases cited above are federal constitutional standards which cannot be applied without great difficulty to Tribal law. Further, the question before us is whether the appellant's due process rights under Tribal law were contravened. We believe that such a finding must precede any determination that the appellant's due process rights were violated under the Indian Civil Rights Act, 25 U.S.C. Sec. 1302 (8). Therefore, we adopt a flexible standard of review, utilizing the above principles, to determine whether the appellant was afforded due process under Tribal law.

XI

An examination of the record shows that while David St. Peter was given maximum jail terms for each of five sentences, additional charges of Battery and Resisting Arrest were dismissed as part of a plea bargain agreement. Appellant's Opening Brief, Page 1. In addition, the Presentence Investigation Report indicates that St. Peter has an extensive background of prior offenses and a history of alcohol-related incidents with the Tribes. Further, St. Peter has undergone alcohol treatment on four separate occasions.

The record does not show that the trial judge stated her reasons for the sentences she imposed, and we do not believe she was required to do so. It is clear that the trial judge was made aware of the appellant's criminal history and that she considered, at least, Tribal convictions in sentencing. In response to the appellant's objections to use of a United States Government computer printout showing his criminal history, the trial judge indicated that she would not rely on state convictions reflected in the printout, but would refer to the printout for a record of Tribal convictions.

From the preceding discussion, it is clear that the trial judge balanced the value of deterrence in sentencing with St. Peter's likelihood of alcohol rehabilitation and adult educational training as part of probation. It is equally clear that the trial judge determined that rehabilitation was not an appropriate sentencing goal in this instance. In light of St. Peter's past alcohol treatment and continued criminal conduct, we believe the trial judge did not abuse her discretion in reaching that conclusion. From this and the information before the Court, we conclude that the trial judge did not mechanically sentence St. Peter. We hold that the trial judge had sufficient information to meaningfully exercise her sentencing discretion and that she exercised her discretion by sufficiently individualizing sentencing so that the punishment fit not only the offenses, but the individual.

XII

We are not aware of any provision under Tribal law that requires a trial judge to make a finding that a defendant would derive no benefit from rehabilitation before imposing a maximum jail sentence. From our reading of the Code it is clear that the Tribal Business Council delegated broad sentencing discretion to the trial judge, and imposed no such restrictions on the Tribal Court.

The appellant invites the Panel to adopt a similar sentencing standard as did the Congress in enacting the Federal Youth Corrections Act, 18 U.S.C. Sec. 5005, et seq., which has significantly restricted the sentencing authority of federal trial court judges. Under that statute the trial court must make a finding that a youthful offender would derive "no benefit" from rehabilitation before sentencing such offenders under other applicable penal statutes. *Dorszynski v. United States*, 424 U.S. at 442. See also United States v. Wardlaw, 576 F.2d at 936–37.

We believe that placing a "no benefit" requirement on the Trial Court before it can sentence offenders to a maximum jail term would amount to a legislative act by the Court and an impermissible incursion in to the province of the trial judge. This practice . . . would seriously impair the meaningful exercise of the trial judge's sentencing discretion by, in effect, requiring exhaustion of rehabilitative measures before deterrent sentencing could be considered.

We do not accept the appellant's argument that the Trial Court erred by not adopting sentencing standards. The Tribal Business Council has adopted sentencing standards by enacting statutes which limit the punishment which may be imposed for specific offenses. We consider the sentencing limitations found in CTC 5.7.01, 5.7.02 and 5.7.03 to be a reflection of legislative intent to restrict the Trial Court's sentencing discretion. Although the Tribal Business Council has delegated the Trial Court considerable discretion in sentencing, that discretion is circumscribed by the language in the sentencing statutes. Id. The appellant has not challenged the sentencing statutes as being an unlawful delegation of authority to the Court. We believe that imposition of additional sentencing standards by the Panel on the Trial Court, acting within the scope of the Tribal Constitution and the boundaries of its statutorily delegated authority, is a legislative function which should be left to the Tribal Business Council, and not the Appellate Panel.

XIII

The appellant relies on Randall v. Yakima Nation Tribal Court, 841 F.2d 897 (9th cir. 1988) as controlling in this case. Randall stands for the principle that once a tribe has adopted certain procedures, the tribal court must, as a matter of due process follow those procedures. In Randall, the Court stated:

> "Where the tribal court procedures under scrutiny differ significantly from those commonly employed in Anglo-Saxon society . . . courts weigh the individual right to fair treatment against the magnitude of the tribal interest in employing those procedures." However, where tribal court procedures parallel those found in Anglo-Saxon society, the court will not engage in a complex weighing of interests. In that latter instance, the court will "[h]ave no problem of forcing an alien culture, with strange procedures on these tribes."

Thus, where the Yakima Nation had adopted certain procedures governing an appellant's perfection of her right to appeal, and the tribal court deprived the appellant of that right by failing to comply with established court procedure, the Ninth Circuit Court of Appeals had no difficulty applying principles of federal constitutional law and finding that a litigant had been denied due process. Id at 901. We do not believe that Randall is applicable to this case for the reason that the Colville Confederated Tribes have not adopted detailed sentencing procedures such as found in the Federal Rules of Criminal Procedure, and we have not found that the Trial Court abused its discretion in sentencing. We do not find that the procedures followed by the Tribal Court parallel those found in Anglo-Saxon society. The Panel rejects the appellant's view that by adopting procedures similar to those used by the federal or state courts, the Tribes have somehow come within the full reach of the Bill of Rights. This view, which would expand the application of Randall to an area where the Tribal Business Council has delegated considerable latitude to the Tribal Court, runs counter to the clearly enunciated purpose of ICRA, which affords constitutional protection to litigants while fostering tribal self government and cultural autonomy. We view the Tribal Business Council's delegation of broad discretion to the Tribal Court as a statement of policy that the Tribal judge is aware of Tribal norms and is in a position to apply the law consistent with those values.

The Panel also rejects the notion that the doctrine set out in Randall, with its harsh result, should apply where the Tribal Court has adopted procedures designed to provide consistency and accountability in Court proceedings. Even if the Court should follow the Federal Rules of Evidence or the Business Council should adopt specific court rules which parallel the federal criminal rules, this does not mean that the Tribal culture, tradition and autonomy has been abandoned. Nor does it mean that the Tribal Court has taken on such an Anglo-Saxon character that the Bill of Rights should be applied. Following this illogical rule would discourage the Tribal Business Council and the Tribal Court from adopting written, uniform procedures, including those based upon Tribal tradition and cultural standards, or other measures which could improve operation of the Court.

This does not mean that we believe the reasoning in Randall should not be applied in an appropriate case in which the Panel finds that established procedural rules have been violated and the prejudice shown is of a nature where no balancing of tribal and individual interests is required. This is not the nature of the case before us. The Panel finds that neither the Colville Confederated Tribes nor the Tribal Court have adopted procedures which, under the rationale of Randall, bring the instant matter under the federal review standards of the Bill of Rights.

XIV

The appellant argues that the sentences imposed by the Trial Court constitute cruel and unusual punishment in violation of the Colville Tribal Civil Rights Act, CTC 56.02 (g) and the Indian Civil Rights Act. 25 U.S.C. Sec. 1302 (7)....

We have found that the Trial Court imposed sentences on St. Peter that were within statutory limits. Under federal law we do not believe that those sentences were "so arbitrary and shocking to a sense of justice" as to violate the prohibition against cruel and unusual punishment or that the trial judge "manifestly or grossly abused her discretion" by imposing the sentences. Similarly, we have found no support for the appellant's argument under Tribal law.

[Section XV omitted]

The judgments and sentences are Affirmed.
IT IS HEREBY ORDERED.

Cherokee Court of the Eastern Band of Cherokee Indians

Eastern Band Cherokee v. Crowe (2010)
9 Am. Tribal Law 27

The Defendant, Jon Nathaniel Crowe, was convicted by a jury on June 27, 2008 and sentenced by the Court in case # CR07–1373 to a term of incarceration of twelve months, followed by a consecutive sentence of incarceration in case # CR07–1375 of twelve months, followed by a third consecutive sentence of incarceration in case # CR07–1376 of twelve months. Defendant was credited 6 months towards judgment for case # CR07–1373 for time already served. Mr. Crowe has now filed a Motion for Appropriate Relief pursuant to Cher. R.Crim. P. 20(d), asserting that the consecutive sentences imposed by the Court violated 25 U.S.C. § 1302(a)(7) of the Indian Civil Rights Act (hereafter the ICRA) and that he is entitled to discharge from custody.

The Motion came on before the Court for hearing on May 26, 2010. Mr. Crowe was represented by Robert Saunooke, Esquire and, through counsel, waived his right to be present for this hearing, which the Court allowed. The Tribe was represented by Roy Wijewickrama, Esquire, the Tribal Prosecutor. Inasmuch as the original jury trial was presided over by Judge Martin, and the Motion was set before Judge Saunooke, the Court agreed to hear the case en banc. The Court has reviewed the file and heard the argument of counsel.

The issue presented is purely a legal one and no testimony was adduced. Nevertheless, the Court, taking judicial notice of its own records, makes the following:

Findings of Fact

1. The Defendant, Jon Nathaniel Crowe, is an enrolled member of the Eastern Band of Cherokee Indians.
2. On January 16, 2003, Defendant, Jon Nathaniel Crowe, was charged with Domestic Violence (hereafter DV) assault in the 1st degree in case number CR–03–98.
3. On May 2, 2003, the Defendant, Jon Nathaniel Crowe, was convicted of DV assault in the 1st degree in case number CR–03–98.
4. On August 26, 2003, the Defendant, Jon Nathaniel Crowe, was charged with DV communicating threats in case number CR–03–1360.
5. On September 20, 2004, the Defendant, Jon Nathaniel Crowe, was convicted of DV communicating threats in case number CR–03–1360.
6. On August 5, 2005, the Defendant, Jon Nathaniel Crowe, was charged with DV assault on a female in case number CR–05–1010.
7. On September 2, 2005, the Defendant, Jon Nathaniel Crowe, was convicted of DV assault on a female in case number CR–05–1010.
8. On September 28, 2007, the Defendant, Jon Nathaniel Crowe, was charged with DV assault on a female in case number CR07–1373.
9. On September 28, 2007, the Defendant, Jon Nathaniel Crowe, was charged with habitual assault in case number CR07–1374.
10. On September 28, 2007, the Defendant, Jon Nathaniel Crowe, was charged with simple possession of marijuana less than one-half ounce in case number CR07–1377.
11. On September 28, 2007, the Defendant, Jon Nathaniel Crowe, was charged with possession of drug paraphernalia in case number CR07–1378.
12. On September 28, 2007, the Defendant, Jon Nathaniel Crowe, was charged with DV false imprisonment in case number CR07–1375.
13. On September 28, 2007, the Defendant, Jon Nathaniel Crowe, was charged with resisting lawful arrest in case number CR07–1376.
14. On June 27, 2008, the Defendant, Jon Nathaniel Crowe, was convicted by a jury of DV assault on a female in case number CR07–1373.
15. On June 27, 2008, the Defendant, Jon Nathaniel Crowe, was convicted by a jury of DV false imprisonment in case number CR07–1375.
16. On June 27, 2008, the Defendant, Jon Nathaniel Crowe, was convicted by a jury of resisting lawful arrest in case number CR07–1376.

17. At trial, testimony was adduced to show that at the time and place alleged, the Defendant viciously beat [V.P.]¹, held her down and prevented her from fleeing the premises where the beating occurred and then resisted arrest upon the arrival of law enforcement personnel. Additional testimony demonstrated that the Defendant attempted to coerce control over Ms. [P] by violence.
18. Additional testimony indicated that the Defendant may have coerced Ms. George into withdrawing her incriminating statement and substituting a false statement before the United States Magistrate Judge in a federal prosecution stemming from the same incident in order to obtain a more favorable plea bargain arrangement, possibly in violation of 18 U.S.C. § 1512(a)(2) and (c).
19. Finally, other testimony demonstrated that, on a prior occasion, Mr. Crowe dug a grave in the woods and forced Ms. Parker to view it, while he made statements that it was for her and that he once poured kerosene down Ms. Parker's throat and threatened to set her afire.
20. The Chief Justice of this Court, William Boyum is a Phi Beta Kappa graduate of the University of North Carolina at Chapel Hill and has a J.D. from the UNC School of Law. Chief Justice Boyum is a former Assistant United States Attorney and State Court prosecutor.
21. The founding Chief Justice of this Court, Harry C. Martin holds an undergraduate degree from the University of North Carolina at Chapel Hill, a law degree from Harvard Law School, and an L.L.M. from the University of Virginia School of Law. Chief Justice Martin, who continues to serve this Court as a Temporary Justice, is a retired member of the Supreme Court of North Carolina, and is the retired Chief Circuit Mediator for the United States Court of Appeals for the Fourth Circuit. Chief Justice Martin has received numerous national awards in honor of his lengthy legal career including: The American Bar Association's Franklin Flaschner Award, the North Carolina Bar Association's John J. Parker and Liberty Bell Awards and the University of North Carolina's Distinguished Alumni Award.
22. Associate Justice Brenda Toineeta Pipestem is a graduate of Duke University and has a J.D. from Columbia University. Justice Pipestem has worked both in the Bureau of Indian Affairs as well as the Justice Department. In addition to serving this Indian Nation, she sits as a member of the highest Courts of two other Indian Tribes.
23. Judge Kirk G. Saunooke has sat on this Court since its inception. Prior to the creation of this Court in the year 2000, he served for several years as a jurist for the Court of Indian Offenses, which this Court succeeded.

Judge Saunooke is a graduate of Western Carolina University and has a J.D. from the UNC School of Law.
24. Judge J. Matthew Martin holds a B.A. with Honors in History from the University of North Carolina at Chapel Hill, and is a graduate of the UNC School of Law. Judge Martin also has a Master's Degree in Judicial Studies from the University of Nevada. Judge Martin is Board Certified by the North Carolina State Bar as a Specialist in Federal and State Criminal Law and Criminal Appellate Practice by the North Carolina State Bar. In the 1991 Term of the Supreme Court of the United States, he argued *Wade v. United States*, 504 U.S. 181, 112 S.Ct. 1840, 118 L.Ed.2d 524 (1992) for the Petitioner.
25. Judge Steven E. Philo is a graduate of the United States Military Academy and served in Vietnam. Judge Philo is a graduate of the Wake Forest School of Law. Judge Philo is recognized across the State of North Carolina for his dedication to improving the lives of lawyers who struggle with the disease of addiction. Judge Philo presides over the Eastern Band of Cherokee Indians' Drug Court.
26. All of the Judges of the Judicial Branch of Tribal Government are Bar licensed attorneys, as are all members of the Tribal Bar.

Discussion

The ICRA states that an Indian tribe may not "impose for conviction of any one offense any penalty or punishment greater than imprisonment for a term of one year." U.S.C § 1302(a)(7). I Although the Defendant did not argue this, it is worth noting that the protections of the ICRA have been adopted by the Tribal Council and are the law of this jurisdiction, independent of the Act of Congress. C.C. § 15–7.

Defendant argues that "any one offense" is an ambiguous term that has been interpreted by some courts as meaning any criminal acts arising from a single criminal transaction.

Under this interpretation, any criminal acts arising from a "common nucleus of facts" would be within a single criminal transaction.

Defendant claims that his criminal acts arose under a single criminal transaction, thus the ICRA prevents this Court from imposing a sentence in excess of one year incarceration, no matter how many crimes were committed within the so called single criminal transaction. The Eastern Band of Cherokee Indians (hereafter the Tribe) contends that this is not the correct interpretation of the term "any one offense." The Tribe argues that the term "any one offense" is interpreted as any discrete violation of the criminal law. This interpretation allows for consecutive sentences of incarceration to exceed one year so long as the judgment for each individual offense is not in excess of one year.

The rules of statutory construction "require [a court] to presume that the legislature says in a statute what it means and means in a statute what it says there." BedRoc Ltd., LLC v. United States, 541 U.S. 176, 183, 124 S.Ct. 1587, 158 L.Ed.2d 338 (2004). When using statutory construction, the analysis "begins with the statutory text, and ends there as well if it is unambiguous." Id. When specific terms are used in a statute they must be read using their "ordinary meaning . . . at the time Congress enacted [the law]." Id. Moreover, when Congress adopts or uses a term, the Court "must infer, unless the statute otherwise dictates, that Congress means to incorporate the established meaning of th[at] ter[m]." NLRB v. Town and Country Elec., Inc., 516 U.S. 85, 94, 116 S.Ct. 450, 133 L.Ed.2d 371 (1995). Therefore, the meaning of the phrase "any one offense" at the time the ICRA was adopted by Congress must be accepted and applied by the Court.

The Supreme Court of the United States has continually taken the position that the term "offense" is a reference to a discrete criminal violation. In *Ebeling v. Morgan*, 237 U.S. 625, 35 S.Ct. 710, 59 L.Ed. 1151 (1915), the defendant, during a "single criminal transaction," cut and tore multiple mail bags. Even though the mail bags were cut or torn during a single transaction, the Supreme Court held that "successive cutting into the different bags constitute[d] different offenses" so a complete and distinct offense was committed every time an individual bag was cut or torn. Id. at 628, 35 S.Ct. 710.

Furthermore, in *American Tobacco Co. v. United States*, 328 U.S. 781, 66 S.Ct. 1125, 90 L.Ed. 1575 (1946), the Supreme Court affirmed that a single act can be an offense against two different statutes. This reasoning allowed offenses to be distinct in law, no matter how factually related. Because the term "offense" at the time of the ICRA's adoption had a common and accepted meaning, and because there was no special definition for the term included in the ICRA, "any one offense" is not an ambiguous term and the ordinary and accepting meaning must be adopted and applied by the Court according the rules of statutory construction. Therefore, since the common and accepted meaning of "offense" at the time of the enactment of the ICRA was "any distinct violation of a criminal statute," the Court has the authority to impose a one-year maximum term of imprisonment for each distinct violation of a criminal statute in this jurisdiction.

Defendant's arguments rely heavily on *Spears v. Red Lake Band of Chippewa Indians*, 363 F.Supp.2d 1176, 1178, 1181 (D.Minn.2005), a case in which the United States District Court for the District of Minnesota found the term "any one offense" to be ambiguous and interpreted the term to mean that "separate violations form a 'single criminal transaction' when they are factually or legally intertwined." Under this interpretation, a tribal court does not have the authority to impose a sentence of incarceration greater than one year if all criminal acts arise under a single criminal transaction, i.e. criminal acts that spring from a nucleus of common facts.

Defendant also cites the United States District Court for the District of Arizona's decision in *Miranda v. Nielson*, 2009 U.S. Dist. Lexis 122933 and Bustamante v. Valenzuela, 2010 WL 1337131, 2010 U.S. Dist. LEXIS 32238 (D.Ariz., Feb. 3, 2010), a Magistrate Judge's Report and Recommendation filed in the United States District Court for the District of Arizona. However, The Report and Recommendation filed by the Magistrate Judge was not followed by the District Court and thus was effectively overruled by *Bustamante v. Valenzuela*, 715 F.Supp.2d 960, 2010 U.S. Dist. LEXIS 32236 (D.Ariz., Apr. 1, 2010). The Defendant's reliance on the Magistrate's Report and Recommendation is misplaced as Bustamante supports the Tribe's position. On the other hand, *Miranda* is grounded exclusively upon *Spears* and a discussion of *Spears* negates the need to analyze *Miranda* specifically.

In Spears the court found that "any one offense" is an ambiguous term contained within both the Fifth and Sixth Amendment of the United States Constitution. The Spears court suggested that the Fifth Amendment's prohibition on multiple prosecutions "for the same offense" is ambiguous and could be interpreted as either preventing consecutive prosecutions for offenses arising out of the "same evidence," or offenses arising out of the "same transaction." U.S. Const. Amend. V.; Spears at 1178. Since the term "for the same offense" in the Fifth Amendment is ambiguous, the Spears court concluded the term "any one offense" used in the ICRA is equally ambiguous and subject to multiple interpretations.

Similarly, the *Spears* court found that an ambiguity within the context of the Sixth Amendment right to a jury trial mirrored the ambiguousness of the term "any one offense" in the present context. The right to a jury trial does not extend to "petty offenses" (an offense carrying a maximum prison term of 6 months or less) so it is possible that a person convicted of multiple "petty offenses" may be subject to a lengthy prison sentence without having the right to a jury trial. In *Codispoti v. Pennsylvania*, 418 U.S. 506, 94 S.Ct. 2687, 41 L.Ed.2d 912 (1974), the Supreme Court of the United States held that several petty offenses were in effect a single, "serious offense." Therefore, at certain times under the Sixth Amendment, multiple offenses have been interpreted as only one "serious offense," i.e. a single criminal transaction. Thus only one sentence was available per that one transaction. The *Spears* court suggests that this same issue exists in the ICRA's use of the term "any one offense."

This Court rejects the findings in *Spears* and agrees with the U.S. District Court of Arizona's recent decision in *Bustamante v. Valenzuela*, 715 F.Supp.2d 960, 2010 WL 1338125, 2010 U.S. Dist. LEXIS 32236 (D.Ariz., Apr. 1, 2010). In *Bustamante*, the District Court rejected the "single criminal transaction" theory. The *Bustamante* court held that "any one offense" is any distinct violation of a criminal statute and that "Indian tribes may impose a one-year term of imprisonment for each criminal violation." *Bustamante* at 968, 2010 WL 1338125 at *7, 2010 U.S. Dist. LEXIS 32236 at 11–12, 21.

The *Bustamante* court also rejected both *Spears* arguments that the term "serious offense" is ambiguous. Regarding the Fifth Amendment interpretation, *Spears'* use of statutory construction seems misguided. For Constitutional purposes, the Supreme Court of the United States has never adopted the "same transaction" meaning and "to claim the word 'offense' is ambiguous based on a theoretically possible meaning . . . is not a proper method of statutory construction." *Bustamante* at 965, 2010 WL 1338125 at *4, 2010 U.S. Dist. LEXIS 32236 at 13–14.

Moreover, there are two main flaws in the Sixth Amendment analysis. First, any theoretical ambiguities presumed in this sole example of Sixth Amendment jurisprudence occurred after the passage of the ICRA in 1968. Statutory interpretation requires examining the term at the time the statute was passed, and not based upon subsequent developments in legal theory. *Bustamante* at 966, 2010 WL 1338125 at *5, 2010 U.S. Dist. LEXIS 32236 at 15 (citing *BedRoc Ltd.*, 541 U.S. at 183, 124 S.Ct. 1587). Second, the ambiguities arising from Codispoti and the Sixth Amendment are for the terms "serious offenses" and "petty offenses" only. Neither of these terms are used in the ICRA. According to *Bustamante*, "ambiguities arising from a judicially created term of art should not be relied upon to render ambiguous a statute not using that term of art." Bustamante at 966, 2010 WL 1338125 at *5, 2010 U.S. Dist. LEXIS 32236 at 15. The present case concerns the term "any one offense," not "petty offenses" or "serious offenses." Theoretical ambiguities in the Fifth and Sixth Amendment do not provide a reasonable basis upon which to conclude that the term "any one offense" is an ambiguous term justifying relegation to the scrap heap in favor of a new interpretation which limits the exercise of Tribal judicial power.

The *Spears* court also suggests that Congress did not intend to allow tribal courts to impose lengthy prison sentences for fear that these long periods of incarceration would occur despite the fact that defendants did were not represented by counsel. Spears at 1181. The *Spears* Court uses the example that an individual stealing "a rare coin worth $101 . . . faces up to 6 months in jail." Id. at 1179.

Continuing the hypothetical, the *Spears* Court reasoned, if the term "any one offense" of the ICRA did not prohibit consecutive sentences exceeding one year in length, then an individual who stole a whole collection of coins, each of which are each worth $101, would face one count of theft, or possession for each coin stolen and be facing a maximum term of imprisonment of multiple 6-month jail sentences which could be served consecutively without ever having a right to counsel. Id.

The basis of this argument is flawed. First, the provision in question of the ICRA, even if ambiguous, does not prevent Tribal courts from imposing consecutive sentences which cumulatively exceed one year of incarceration. Under Spears' analysis, the ICRA would only prevent Tribal courts from imposing sentences exceeding one year in length if the crimes were factually intertwined. However, it is still possible that the Tribal court could impose a lengthy sentence for a single defendant at the conclusion of a single trial. Using a similar example to that in *Spears*, if an individual stole the same 10-coin collection, albeit this time a single coin was stolen every day for 10 days, there would be 10 separate counts of theft. Although these counts do not arise in a single criminal transaction, it is likely that each of these 10 counts would be joined for trial. See, e.g. Cherokee R.Crim. P. 7(d)(1)(A). If the defendant is convicted of all 10 counts, a Tribal judge would be free to impose a 12 month sentence for each count, resulting in a 10 year sentence without the defendant ever having a right to counsel. Had Congress intended to prevent Indian tribes from imposing a cumulative set of sentences exceeding one year in prison, there would be language expressly prohibiting the practice.

Also, even though the *Spears* court was "convinced" that Congress did not intend to allow Tribal courts to have the authority to impose lengthy prison terms upon defendants that do not have the right to publicly funded counsel, this alone does not prevent a Tribal court from imposing a sentence that exceeds one year. *Spears* at 1181.

In *Romero v. Goodrich*, 1:09–cv–232 RB/DJS, (D.N.M. March 9, 2010)(slip OP.), a case arising from the Pueblo of Nambe Tribal Court, the defendant was unrepresented by counsel and was convicted in the Tribal Court after a bench trial by a Tribal Judge on 12 counts: 2 counts of battery (including one count against a household member); 4 counts of assault (including one count against a household member and another on a peace officer); 3 counts of false imprisonment; and 1 count each of criminal damage to property, interference with communications, and criminal trespass. For each count the defendant was sentenced to 365 days incarceration. Four of these sentences ran concurrently with others resulting in total sentence of 8 years of incarceration.

A similar situation occurred in *Miranda v. Nielson*, 2009 U.S. Dist. Lexis 122933. In *Miranda* the defendant, also without counsel, was found guilty in a bench trial, and subsequently sentenced to two one-year sentences for separate assault charges and sentenced to other shorter terms of incarceration for charges of endangerment and disorderly conduct. The total sentence to be served consecutively was 910 days.

At the trial level in *Spears*, the defendant was represented by counsel but plead guilty to four separate charges: negligent homicide; driving under the influence of alcohol, failing to take a blood, breath, or urine test, and failing to stop at the scene of a crime. The Chippewa Tribal Court imposed a one year sentence for the negligent homicide and 6 months apiece for the DUI, sobriety test, and failure to stop offenses.

The fact that the Defendant in *Spears* was represented by counsel is some indication that the concern of both the District Court in Miranda and the Magistrate Judge in Romero over the right to counsel in Tribal Courts is likely a mere shibboleth. The Court does not cast the concerns of these Courts aside cavalierly. Indeed, in his book, *Broken Landscape*, Professor Pommersheim underscores the fact that the failure of Congress to include a right to counsel in the ICRA creates a structural weakness in the Tribal Court systems of this country that impedes perceptions of their legitimacy and can, in the absence of Congressional action, only be cured, as has been done in this jurisdiction, by a Tribal guarantee of the right to counsel or by a Constitutional amendment.

But the right to counsel is only a part of the story. The larger concern, reflected not only in *Miranda* and *Spears* but also in such cases as *Oliphant v. Suquamish Tribe*, 435 U.S. 191, 98 S.Ct. 1011, 55 L.Ed.2d 209 (1978), *Nevada v. Hicks*, 533 U.S. 353, 121 S.Ct. 2304, 150 L.Ed.2d 398 (2001), *Montana v. United States*, 450 U.S. 544, 101 S.Ct. 1245, 67 L.Ed.2d 493 (1981), *Strate v. A–1 Contractors*, 520 U.S. 438, 117 S.Ct. 1404, 137 L.Ed.2d 661 (1997), and most recently *Plains Commerce Bank v. Long Family Land and Cattle Co.*, 554 U.S. 316, 128 S.Ct. 2709, 171 L.Ed.2d 457 (2008) is a distrust of Tribal Courts themselves, a distrust of the very existence of extra-Constitutional Court systems within the United States only partially controlled by Congress and, by extension, a distrust of the very sovereignty of the Indian Nations themselves. However, to base a Federal Court judgment on the premise that Tribal courts are somehow defective or jurisprudentially inferior is a gross misunderstanding of the system of Tribal courts. For a Defendant to suggest the same is likewise unavailing.

A Cherokee Tribal Court exercised criminal jurisdiction in this territory as early as 1823. Martin, "The Nature and Extent of the Exercise of Criminal Jurisdiction by the Cherokee Supreme Court: 1823–1835," 32 N.C. Cen. Law Rev. 27 (2009). The right to counsel and to a jury trial in this jurisdiction likewise dates to the early 1820s. Id. This Court is staffed with highly professional, Bar licensed Judges, who have attended some of the finest law schools in the country and who have a wide variety of professional and academic achievements and a wealth of jurisprudential experience. By adopting the argument of those who would restrict Tribal courts the Defendant, in essence, seeks to call into question the very legitimacy of this Court. Adopting an argument, which has, at its bedrock, a concern as to the legitimacy of the Court is no guarantor of success.

Congress has plenary authority in the affairs of Indians and Indian Tribes. *Lone Wolf v. Hitchcock*, 187 U.S. 553, 23 S.Ct. 216, 47 L.Ed. 299 (1903). In the exercise of that authority, Congress enacted the ICRA. Subject to the ICRA and C.C. § 15–7, this Court has the authority to impose a maximum sentence of imprisonment of 12 months for each distinct criminal violation committed by a defendant in this jurisdiction. These sentences may run consecutively with one another.

The Defendant received a jury trial before a Bar licensed Judge and with the assistance of a Bar licensed attorney, appointed by the Court. The trial was fair and no suggestion of error was made by the Defendant.

At the end of the day, this Court is not about the business of undertaking a sea change in Supreme Court jurisprudence or even of studying whether this Court is perceived as legitimate. It can only pass on the cases before it. And in this case, the

Judgments, and the Jury's verdict which preceded them, were fair and the products of due process and equal protection.

Jon Nathaniel Crowe has engaged in a pattern of coercive control domestic violence on the person of Vickie Parker over a period of years. The lethality factors in this situation are extremely high. In light of his danger to the community in general and specifically to Ms. Parker, a substantial sentence of incarceration was called for. The consecutive sentences imposed by the Court addressed the Defendant's status as a recidivist, coercive control batterer, took into consideration all of the circumstances of the crimes for which he was convicted by the jury and were reasonable and necessary under the circumstances. In light of the extent to which sentencing in this case was constrained by the ICRA, the interests of justice have been served. Had the Defendant been sentenced for these crimes under the Advisory Guidelines in Federal Court, no doubt a greater sentence of imprisonment would have been imposed.

Based upon the foregoing Findings of Fact, the Court makes the following:

Conclusions of Law

1. The Court has jurisdiction over the parties and the subject matter of this Motion.
2. The imposition of consecutive sentences in this case did not violate the ICRA.

ACCORDINGLY, IT IS HEREBY ORDERED that the Defendant's Motion to vacate his consecutive sentences is DENIED.

KIRK G. SAUNOOKE, Cherokee Court Judge

J. MATTHEW MARTIN, Cherokee Court Judge

Pascua Yaqui Tribal Court of Appeals
Pascua Yaqui v. Miranda (2009)
No. CA-08-015

Opinion
Appeal of a decision of the Pascua Yaqui Tribal Court in Case No. CR-08-119, the Honorable Cornelia Cruz presiding.

Affirmed
I. Statement of the Facts

On the evening of January 25, 2008, Beatrice Miranda, by all accounts wandering around, drunk, came across [M.V.][2], a minor Yaqui teenager. Miranda seems to have thought someone was laughing at her; she pulled a knife, screaming obscenities, and began chasing the girl across the reservation. [M] made it home, just ahead of this woman, and ran inside, where she was able to alert her sister, [B], that Miranda was in their yard, yelling and waving a knife around. [B] went outside to investigate. Miranda threatened to kill the girls, brandishing the weapon. They called the police, and she ran off.

Miranda was picked up, based on their description, near the Valenzuela home. With some difficulty, they were able to restrain and arrest her. She was searched, pursuant to this arrest; the police found a folding knife on her person, later confirmed to be the weapon used in the assault.

On January 26, 2008, the Tribe filed a criminal complaint against Miranda, charging her with two counts of endangerment, two counts of threatening and intimidating, two counts of aggravated assault, and two counts of disorderly conduct, one count each for each victim. At her initial appearance, Miranda, without counsel, was advised of her rights, and declared that she was waiving them:

> The Court: The Pascua Yaqui Tribal Court is now in session in the matter of Pascua Yaqui Tribe versus Beatrice Miranda. Docket number CR-08-119. . . . Let me see, I now will advise you of your rights. You have the right to remain silent. Anything you say may be used against you. You have the right to counsel at your own expense, and you have the right to (inaudible) probable cause in this phase of the proceedings. Do you understand your rights?
>
> Miranda: Yes.

The court found probable cause and set bail at $1500.00.

On February 4, 2008, Miranda appeared at her arraignment, without counsel. She was again advised of her rights, and again waived them:

> The Court: I will advise you of your rights. You have the right to remain silent. Anything you say will be used against you. You have the right to legal counsel at your own expense. You have the right to (inaudible). Miss Miranda, you have the right to cross-examine witnesses and evidence presented by the Tribe, and the right present witnesses and evidence in your behalf. You have the right to know the charges against you, and you have the right to appeal to the Pascua Yaqui Court of Appeals. Do you understand your rights?
>
> Miranda: Yes.

She then attempted to plead guilty to all charges. The court intervened, finding an insufficient factual basis, at that time, to substantiate her pleas, entered not guilty pleas on her behalf, and set a pre-trial hearing date, March 12, 2008. At pre-trial hearing Miranda appeared, was again advised of her rights, and again waived them:

> The Court: I will advise you of your rights. You have the right to remain silent. Anything you say may be used against you. You have the right to legal counsel at your own expense. You have the right to a hearing and to a jury hearing. You have

the right to cross examine the witnesses, and (inaudible) about the Tribe, and the right to examine witnesses in advantage on your behalf. You have the right to know the allegations against you, and you have the right to appeal to the Pascua Yaqui Court of Appeals. Do you understand your rights?

Miranda: Yes.

No motions were made by either party, the case was set for trial on April 12, 2008.

March 12, 2008, the parties submitted a negotiated plea agreement, signed by Miranda. The agreement detailed her rights explicitly, and explicitly waived them:

> I have read and understand the above. I understand I have the right to discuss this case and my civil rights with a lawyer at my expense. I understand that by pleading guilty I will be giving up my right to a trial by jury, to confront, cross-examine, and compel the attendance of witnesses, and my privilege against self-incrimination. I agree to enter this plea as indicated above on the terms and conditions indicated herein. I fully understand that if I am placed on probation as part of this plea agreement, the terms and conditions of probation are subject to modification at any time during the period of probation in the event that I violate any written condition of my probation.

It was accepted by the court; change of plea hearing set for April 12, 2008. March 14, 2008, Miranda sent the court a written request to withdraw from the plea agreement. The court vacated the change of plea hearing, set the matter for trial, April 12, 2008.

April 12, 2008, Miranda appeared pro se. She was advised of her rights, again, and apparently declared that she was waiving them:

> The Court: I will advise you of your rights. You have the right to remain silent. Anything you say may be used against you. You have the right to you own counsel at your own expense. You have the right to a hearing. You have the right to cross examine witnesses and evidence presented by the Tribe, and the right to present witnesses and evidence in your behalf. You have the right to know the charges against you, and you have the right to appeal to the Pascua Yaqui Court of Appeals. Do you understand your rights?
>
> Miranda: (No audible response).

The tribe presented testimony from arresting Officer Jose Montano, [B.V.] and [M.V.] as well as entering the knife recovered from Miranda on arrest into evidence. Miranda presented no evidence or witnesses, did not testify, and did not cross-examine any witnesses offered by the prosecution. The court found her guilty on all counts.

While Miranda requested immediate sentencing, the Tribe asked for a pre-sentence investigative report (to be filed by the Office of Probation and Parole), and the court granted this request. Sentencing was scheduled for May 19, 2008.

At sentencing, Miranda was again advised of her rights:

> The Court: I will advise you of your rights. You have the right to remain silent. Anything you say may be used against you. You have the right to legal counsel at your own expense. You have the right to a hearing. You have the right to cross examine witnesses and evidence presented by the Tribe, and the right to present witnesses and evidence in your behalf. You have the right to know the charges against you, and in the sentencing matter, you have the right to appeal to the Pascua Yaqui Court of Appeals. And the consequences, uh, in the revocation matter may include you being found in violation of you conditions of probation, your probation term being revoked or extended, and any suspended days being imposed. Do you understand your rights?
>
> Miranda: Yes.

The pre-sentence investigative report filed by the Office of Probation and Parole revealed that Miranda was on probation (for conviction in CR-07-064) when she perpetrated her assault against the Valenzuela sisters.

Miranda stated, contrary to her assertions in Appellant's Opening Brief, that she received a copy of the pre-sentence investigation report:

> The Court: And we will first proceed with the sentencing hearing, uh, CR-08-119. And in that matter the pre-sentence investigation report has been filed by The Court or with The Court rather by the Probation Office. And did you receive a copy of that, Ms. Miranda?
>
> Ms. Miranda: Yes.

Her probation was revoked. After hearing the recommendations of the Probation officer, Miranda requested that all of the sentences "run concurrent." Sentence was imposed, with some of the terms running concurrent:

> The Court: At this time, the Court will enforce sentence as follows, after hearing from the probation officer and the Tribe regarding the history of the Defendant. And the Court does find that the Defendant does have a history of failures to comply, failures to appear, uhm, and failure to comply with the conditions of probation and other orders set by the court. The Court will set sentencing as follow: Count One, three-hundred and sixty-five days in jail; Count Two, three-hundred and sixty-five days in jail; Count three, Endangerment, Count Four, uh, sixty days in jail; Count Four, sixty days in jail; Count five, ninety days in jail; Count Six, ninety days in jail; Count Seven, Seven, I'm sorry, thirty days in jail; Count Eight, thirty days in jail. Counts One and Two are to be served immediately for a total of seven-hundred and thirty days in jail; counts Five and Six will be served consecutive to Counts One and two for a total of one-hundred and thirty days in jail; Counts Five and Six will be served consecutive to Counts One and Two for a total of one-hundred and eighty days; Sentencing, Counts Three, Four, Seven and Eight are

concurrent with One, Two, Five and Six for a total of nine-hundred and ten days in jail. The Defendant is restrained for a period of two years from the victims, and Defendant will not possess any type of weapons, for a period of two years.

Miranda requested credit for time served and her request was granted, reducing the sentence going forward by one hundred and fourteen days. Miranda's criminal history informed the sentencing recommendations made the court by the Probation Office and the final sentence imposed.

It is unclear in the record why Miranda chose not to retain the services of the Public Defender's Office in this case; she had ample familiarity with them from past experience, as attested to above. The Pascua Yaqui Public Defender entered its notice of appearance on behalf of Miranda on June 10, 2008. Miranda's Notice of Appeal was filed on June 26, 2008. Oral argument was heard on this appeal on March 17, 2009.

II. Statement of the Issues
  6. Did the sentence imposed by the court violate the Indian Civil Rights Act?

III. Opinion
  [EDITED TO FOCUS ON SENTENCING]
  6. The sentence imposed by the court of nine hundred and ten (910) days did not violate the Indian Civil Rights Act.

Under the Indian Civil Rights Act, 25 U.S.C. § 1302(7), and the Constitution of the Pascua Yaqui Tribe, Art. I, § 1(g) PYT Const., the court may not impose a sentence exceeding one year's imprisonment for conviction of any one offense. Appellant contends that these statutory limitations act to bar any sentence exceeding one year's imprisonment, period, even if a defendant is convicted of multiple offenses, provided those offense are part of "the same criminal transaction" or "course of conduct." Appellant's contention is a misstatement of law and flies in the faces not only of the plain language of the statute in question (which restricts the sentences for "any one offense" not the sentencing of "all offenses" cumulatively) but also the law as it has been construed and applied in Indian Country universally since the passage of the Indian Civil Rights Act in 1968.

Contrary to Appellant's assertion, the phrase "any one offense" is not ambiguous and the purported standard she offers to interpret it is neither controlling on this court nor a correct statement of law as applied within the United States at either the Federal or State level. Appellant puts forth a "same transaction" test to make the claim that the language "any one offense" must be read to mean that no more than one offense may be charged against a defendant, however many crimes she commits, if those crimes are part of a "single criminal episode." She cites Spears v. Red Lake, 363 F.Supp. 2D 1176, 1178 (D. Minn. 2005), which is not binding on this court, and a concurrence, Ashe v. Swenson, 397 U.S. 436, 449-54 (1970) (Brennan, J., concurring), which is not binding on any court, to support this theory.

What Appellant does not cite is the law that is binding in Arizona, and the United States generally, as articulated by the Arizona Supreme Court, *State v. Barber*, 133 Ariz. 572, 576, 653 P.2d 29, 33 (App. 1982), *State v. Eagle*, 196 Ariz. 188, 190, 994 P. 2d 395, 397 (2007), and the United States Supreme Court, *Blockburger v. United States*, 284 U.S. 299, 304, 52 S. Ct. 180, 182 (1932). While decisions of the Arizona and United States Supreme Courts are not controlling authority in this court, they are highly persuasive, particularly when they reflect the majority, or unanimous, legal opinion regarding construction of a disputed term or phrase substantially similar to the term or phrase under examination. Indeed, the authority of the United States Supreme court is particularly instructive here, as Appellant purports to base her argument upon a construction of the Indian Civil Rights Act, a statute enacted by the United States Congress. The presumption that language in such a statute was intended to have the meaning accorded similar language by the Supreme Court is difficult to overcome, and was not overcome by Appellant in her attempt to impose an alternate, unique, construction.

Under *Blockburger*, as restated in *State v. Barber, State v. Eagle*, and drawn from a venerable understanding of the meaning of the phrase "same offense" given expression in *Morey v. Commonwealth*, 108 Mass. 433, 434 (1871), a single act may be an offense against two statutes; and if each statute requires proof of an additional fact which the other does not, an acquittal or conviction under either statute does not exempt the defendant from prosecution and punishment under the other.

The construction of the phrase "same offense" given in *Blockburger* is the construction that is nearly universally controlling now and the construction that controls interpretation of that phrase within the Indian Civil Rights Act, namely, that so long as conviction of one statutory crime requires proof of at least one additional element not required to be convicted of a different crime, the two crimes are separate offenses. *Blockburger v. United States*, 284 U.S. 299, 304, 52 S. Ct. 180, 182 (1932). As separate offenses, a defendant may be properly charged with both, convicted of both, and sentenced separately for both. While Appellant could not have been sentenced to a term of more than one year for any one offense, she was not convicted of one offense, but eight, and sentenced separately for each.

Appellant attempts to circumvent this construction through a purported recitation of the statutory history of the Indian Civil Rights Act, the balance it supposedly struck between federal and Indian jurisdiction over crimes, and the "absurd result" that would, in her claim, be the product of using the Blockburger test to interpret its language, offering her own "single criminal transaction" test as the "clear" expression of Congressional intent, even though that test never appeared anywhere in the legislative history of the Indian Civil Rights Act, was not the meaning accorded the phrase "same offense" under federal law when the statute was enacted, and has only been applied by one court, in *Spears*, since that statute went into effect. See *United States v. Dixon*, 509 US 688, 704, 113 S Ct 2849, rejecting this interpretation of "same offense," "That test inquires whether each offense contains an element not contained in the other;" further "but there is no authority, except *Grady* [overturned], for the proposition that it has different meanings in the two contexts. That is perhaps because it is embarrassing to assert that the single term 'same offense' (the words of the Fifth Amendment at issue here) has two different meanings—that what is the same offense is yet not the same offense." 125 L Ed 2d 556(1993) and *Carter v. McClaughry*, 183 US 367, 394-395; 22 S Ct 181; 46 L Ed 236 (1901) further "Having found the relator to be guilty of two offenses, the Court was empowered by the statute to punish him as to one by fine and as to the other by imprisonment. The sentence was not in excess of its authority. Cumulative sentences are not cumulative punishments, and a single sentence for several offenses, in excess of that prescribed for one offense, may be authorized by statute. Citing *In re De Bara*, 179 U. S. 316; *In re Henry*, 123 U. S. 372. Finally, *Ramos v. Pyramid Lake Tribal Ct.*, 621 F. Supp. 967, 970 (D. Nev. 1985), examining consecutive sentences under the ICRA,

> This Court could find no cases holding that the imposition of consecutive sentences constitutes cruel and unusual punishment. Indeed, the imposition of consecutive sentences for numerous offenses is a common and frequently exercised power of judges. Ramos was found guilty by the Pyramid Lake Tribal Court and sentenced accordingly to those findings of guilt. He may be unhappy with the sentence he received, but there was no violation of his right against cruel and unusual punishment and, thus, no habeas relief lies.

Appellant cites Griffin v. Oceanic Contractors, 458 U.S. 5644, 575 (1982). Interpretation of a statute which would produce absurd results are to be avoided if alternative interpretations consistent with the legislative history are available. No interpretation would be more absurd in this case than one that reversed the meaning the law had for four decades and straight jacketed Indian courts, reducing them to one year, maximum, sentences of imprisonment, however many crimes an Indian offender has committed against Indians on Indian land, whenever, as is usually the case, those crimes were part of a "course of conduct," "criminal episode," or "criminal transaction." Such a ruling would reduce Indians to life on reservations where their own courts cannot maintain order and federal courts will not. I reject that interpretation, and choose instead to follow the essential principles of the Blockburger test.

Furthermore, I recognize that Indian courts have wider discretion to apply this test then federal or state courts, discretion derived both from their status as separate sovereigns (whose sovereignty antedates the existence of the United States) and from compelling, particular interests they have in maintaining order and the rule of law in Indian country. The reality, as long recognized by federal courts, is that Indian courts have primary responsibility to dispense justice to Indian victims of crimes perpetrated by Indians on Indian land. While the Federal Government of the United States curtailed much of the sovereign authority of Indian courts through the Major Crimes Act, 18 U.S.C. § 1153, and the Indian Civil Rights Act, it did not destroy that authority, or abrogate the fundamental responsibilities of those courts. *United States v. Montana*, 450 U.S. 544, 564 101 S. Ct. 1245 (1981) citing *United States v. Wheeler*, 435 U.S. 313, 323-326 (1978). Indeed, the federal government has manifested a general unwillingness to take jurisdiction over crimes committed by Indians in Indian country, which leaves Indian courts as the sole effective guarantors of safety, order and justice for Indians living on Indian land. To fulfill that crucial role, Indian courts are, and must be, accorded greater discretion to charge criminals and mete out sentences than federal or state courts operating more simply within the confines of the Blockburger test.

Accordingly, I find that the court acted properly, under *Blockburger*, and within the wide latitude Indian courts have to charge and sentence criminal defendants, by hearing the charges filed against Appellant, convicting her, and imposing the sentence she received. Each charge heard against Appellant required that sufficient additional facts be proven to satisfy the expansive form of the Blockburger test I am applying. Further, Appellant was not convicted of eight separate charges against one victim, as her Brief implies, but of four sets of charges against two separate victims, making the sentences actually handed down particularly appropriate.

When making this sentence, the court took notice of her prior criminal record, the fact that she was on probation when the crimes occurred (for conviction in CR-07-064), and the possible future threat she might pose to the continued safety of the victims in this case; it then gave her credit for time served, reducing the actual sentence imposed considerably (subtracting one hundred and fourteen days from the sentence to be served) and ran several of the sentences concurrently, further moderating their impact (Counts Three, Four, Seven and Eight, subtracting 240 days from the actual sentence). The trial courts judgment on all counts is affirmed.

Temporary Stay

On this portion of my decision I am issuing a temporary stay effective until April 30th, 2009, as questions regarding the breadth of discretion given to the Pascua Yaqui Courts to hear multiple charges and confer sentence are fundamentally political in nature. The legislative drafters of the Constitution of the Pascua Yaqui Tribe made a deliberate effort to harmonize Art. I, § I(g) PYT with its counterpart in the Indian Civil Rights Act, 25 U.S.C. § 1302(7). Both inform the reader that the court may not impose a sentence exceeding one year's imprisonment for conviction of any one offense. And yet, the Appellant's interpretation leads one to conclude that these statutory limitations act to bar any sentence exceeding one year's imprisonment, period, even if a defendant is convicted of multiple offenses, provided those offenses are part of "the same criminal transaction" or "course of conduct."

Questions regarding the interpretation and breadth of discretion conferred upon the Pascua Yaqui Courts by the Constitution to hear multiple charges and confer sentence are fundamentally political and reside within the domain of the Legislative branch. Moreover, the culture, traditions, and separate sovereign structure of the Pascua Yaqui Tribe make it appropriate that questions of significant policy be decided by the legislative than the judicial branch of our government. Accordingly, I am submitting to the Attorney-General the question as to (1) whether or not Art I, I(g) of the Pascua Yaqui Constitution is to be interpreted in harmony with the Indian Civil Rights Act; and (b) whether the two must be interpreted—and thus applied—by the Pascua Yaqui Courts pursuant to the Appellant's more formalistic construction.

Given Appellant's declaration at oral argument (March 17, 2009) that she intends to use this Court's disposition to perfect her filing of a habeas corpus petition in federal district court, I consider it of paramount importance that the legislative branch of the Yaqui government make a concrete determination of these disputed points of policy before our order concerning them is given full effect. The impact of the delay resulting from the stay will be minimal as counsel for the Appellant, Mr. Fontana, has made it abundantly clear that he intends to file a writ of habeas corpus in federal district court. And yet, during the March 17 hearing it was apparent that the decision sought by the Appellant will have far reaching public policy implications for offenders convicted in the Pascua Yaqui Courts. Thus, before the Appellant moves to pierce the veil of tribal sovereignty at federal district court, the Pascua Yaqui Court of Appeals will continue to hold jurisdiction over the matter until the stay expires in light of the constitutional issue.

At first blush, this may not appear to be a conventional remedy in the Pascua Yaqui Tribal Courts—despite being employed by Appellate Courts in other jurisdictions. And yet, by close analogy matters before the Tribal Courts where the Tribe is not a party and tribal sovereignty is at issue the Constitution prescribes clear notice requirements pursuant to Section 20, PYTC 2-5-20. In sum, I consider it to be of paramount importance that the legislative branch of the Yaqui government make a determination of the disputed points of policy before my order concerning them is given full effect.

IV. Conclusion

The Tribal Court's decision is affirmed on all counts. A temporary stay with respect to the foregoing issue will be in effect until April 30, 2009. As I have already ruled on every issue, absent a response by the legislative branch removing the stay will simply affirm my decision that has already made—not reverse it.

Filed this 29th day of March 2009.

Inter-Tribal Court of Appeals of Nevada
Hardin v. Reno Sparks Indian Colony (2005)
ITCN/AC-CR-05-007

Hardin raises numerous issues related to his convictions of two counts of assault. We affirm the convictions but set aside the sentence and remand for further sentencing proceedings.

Procedural History

Hardin was charged with three counts of assault, a violation of Title 5, Section 50–040, Reno–Sparks Indian Colony [RSIC] Law and Order Code. A bench trial was held on January 18, 2005. Hardin was convicted of two counts of assault and acquitted of a third count on January 24, 2005. A sentencing hearing was held on February 28, 2005. There is no transcript of the sentencing hearing in the record, although at oral argument the party's counsel described some of what transpired. The trial court entered a sentence imposed a jail sentence of 120 days on each count, to run consecutively. A stay of execution of sentence was granted pending appeal.

Facts

This case arose out of a confrontation between various individuals, including Hardin, within Indian Country at the Reno–Sparks Indian Colony on October 27, 2004. During the confrontation, Hardin pointed a toy gun at the victims. The toy gun was part of a Halloween costume he was wearing. He also unsuccessfully tried to discharge the weapon. The would-be victims thought the gun was real and that they were in mortal danger.

Hardin alleged he acted in self defense to what he reasonably perceived to be a growing threat of violence by a group of individuals each of whom were bigger than he was and who were acting in a threatening manner. No one was injured in the confrontation and Hardin eventually left the scene.

A juvenile probation officer acting as a private citizen later arrested Hardin off reservation and turned him over to the tribal police. No evidence stemming from the arrest was used against Hardin.

. . .

Hardin alleges his sentence was harsh and unusual. The RSIC Law and Order Code proscribes cruel and unusual punishment. See Constitution and By Laws Of The Reno– Sparks Indian Colony, Article VII(7). The Indian Civil Rights Act has a similar provision. 25 U.S.C. § 1302(7). The trial court's sentence for each offense was within the limits of a tribal court's jurisdiction under the Indian Civil Rights Act, which is one year per offense. 25 U.S.C. § 1302(7). The RSIC has a similar enactment and Hardin's sentence was within the limits of this provision as well. RSIC Law and Order Code, Title 5, § 10–080(1). A sentence within allowable jurisdictional limits is not cruel and unusual punishment. *Ramos v. Pyramid Tribal Court*, 621 F.Supp. 967, 970 (D.Nev.1985).

In *Spears v. Red Lake Band of Chippewa Indians*, 363 F.Supp.2d 1176, 1180–1181 (D.Minn.2005), the Court, using the federal sentencing guidelines as a model, struck down a tribal court's consecutive sentence because the offenses constituted a single criminal transaction for sentencing purposes. *Spears* held that consecutive sentencing was inappropriate for minor tribal offenses because the tribal court is a forum with limited authority to impose jail sentences and does not afford the full range of protections found in the federal constitution, such as the right to appointed counsel. Id. at 1189–1190. Hardin was convicted of offenses that constituted a single criminal transaction. Consecutive sentencing was therefore inappropriate in this case. Hardin's sentence is set aside.

The sentencing process may have been flawed in other ways. A sentencing hearing was held on February 28, 2005 and the Court made findings and imposed a jail sentence based in part on testimony introduced at this hearing. There is no transcript of this hearing and we have only the statements of counsel at oral argument about what transpired. The prosecutor said there was testimony that in fact Hardin used a real handgun, contradicting the trial finding that the purported weapon was a toy. There apparently was also testimony by a law enforcement officer about the nature and severity of the offense and the harm perceived by the victims and the community. The testimony about these matters, especially that a real weapon was involved, may well have played a significant role in the imposition of enhanced jail sentences. Since there is no transcript of the hearing in the record on appeal, we are unable to properly evaluate whether this complied with the sentencing provisions of the tribal ordinance. Nor can we determine whether Hardin was afforded due process by being given adequate notice and the opportunity to be heard on these matters. *Boykin v. Alabama*, 395 U.S. 238, 243, 89 S.Ct. 1709, 23 L.Ed.2d 274 (1969) (compliance with the law cannot be presumed from a silent record). minimal criminal history. See RSIC Law and Order Code, Title 5, § 10–010 (proscribing arbitrary and oppressive treatment of offenders); however, this Court cannot substitute its judgment for that of a judge who heard the trial evidence and is in the best position to evaluate the seriousness of the assaults, the aggravating and mitigating factors in defendant's conduct, and other circumstances that must be taken into account in imposing sentence. See RSIC Law and Order Code, Title 3, Section 1–1303. The trial court must consider each and every factor in the RSIC Law and Order Code. See Id., at § 1–1303(a). These factors must also be weighed and findings made on each one. Leyva v. Hyeoma, AC–CV–04–004, 5–6 (Intertribal Court of Appeals of Nevada, 2004). This case must therefore be remanded for further sentencing proceedings to apply these standards.

> **Conclusion**
> Hardin's convictions are AFFIRMED. Hardin's sentences are set aside and this case is remanded to the trial court for further sentencing proceedings in conformance with this opinion.

Pardon and Expungement

After a sentence has been served, there are mechanisms in state, federal, and tribal law that allow for some offenders to appeal to the executive branch to expunge their criminal record. In many cases, tribal governments have been concerned about the inability of rehabilitated offenders to secure employment due to their criminal record. For example, the Menominee Tribal Code allows for persons convicted of misdemeanors in tribal court to appeal for a pardon:

Chapter 81: Executive Pardons

Sec. 81-1 Declaration of Intent

The Legislature finds that some Indians violate law and are convicted of misdemeanor charges, serve out their punishment, and become rehabilitated over a period of time, only to find that they are prevented from tribal employment or other tribal benefits because of a record of past misdemeanor conduct. It is the declared intent of the Legislature to examine the records of tribal miscreants (as defined herein), assess their behavior following conviction, and to give serious consideration to the granting of a pardon to qualified persons in order to brings such persons back into the fabric of tribal society where they can make a meaningful contribution.

Sec. 81-3 Eligibility

A. Only Indians over whom the Menominee Tribal Court has jurisdiction and who have been convicted of a misdemeanor in Tribal Court are eligible for a pardon under this chapter.

B. Indians may petition for a pardon as many times as they may choose; provided, however, that each petition meets the requirements listed in this chapter, including the required payment of a fee. As stated herein, the filing of a petition for a pardon does not guarantee the granting of a pardon by the Tribal Legislature.

C. The Legislature shall grant pardons only for misdemeanor convictions from Tribal Court. Felony convictions are not rendered in Tribal Court and this chapter does not extend to felony convictions. Pardons will not be granted for violent offenses as determined by the Tribal Legislature after consultation with the Tribal Prosecutor.

D. Misdemeanor convictions in jurisdictions other than the Menominee Tribe are not eligible for pardons under this chapter.

Sec. 81-4 Petitions

A petition is required to be filed in the Tribal Chairperson's office by any Indian requesting a pardon. Five full years shall have elapsed since the requirements of the sentence were completed before filing a petition. The form of the petition shall be prescribed by the Legislature. Any misrepresentations, omissions or falsifications on the petition shall result in a denial of a Tribal pardon and may result in prosecution by the Tribe in Tribal Court. The filing of a petition for a pardon does not guarantee the granting of a pardon by the Tribal Legislature. The Legislature shall review each case on its individual merits. The decision by the Tribal Legislature to grant or deny a request for a pardon is final and not subject to further review of any kind. The fee for filing a petition for a tribal pardon is $150, nonrefundable, payable at the time the petition is submitted to the Tribal Chairperson's office. No petition will be accepted unless this fee has been paid to the Tribe either by cash or cashier's check.

Sec. 81-5 Action by Legislature

A. Upon submission of a completed petition by the Indian to the Tribal Chairperson's office, the petition shall be placed on the agenda for the next regular meeting of the Legislature, provided that the petition is submitted 10 days in advance of a regularly scheduled legislative meeting. The Legislature may act at this meeting or may table the matter for any reason. The petition shall be scheduled on the regular agenda as a matter of public record.

B. The Legislature shall render its decision after due deliberation and direct that a tribal resolution be prepared if a pardon is granted.

In the next case, the Hopi Appellate Court used Hopi traditional value to grant an expungement.

Appellate Court of the Hopi Tribe
Hopi v. Timms (2001)
3 Am. Tribal Law 419
Before SEKAQUAPTEWA, Chief Judge, and LOMAYESVA and ABBEY, Judges.

Opinion

Factual and Procedural Background
The issue in this case is whether the Hopi Tribal Courts have the authority to set aside or expunge a conviction after the convicted individual has demonstrated sufficient rehabilitation.

Statement of Facts
On June 3, 1990, Mr. Timms was arrested and charged with four (4) criminal offenses: possession of alcohol, resisting lawful arrest, assault, and aiding and abetting. On December 28, 1990, he entered a plea of guilty to all four charges.

He was fined $125 and sentenced to 90 days in jail, which was later reduced to one year of probation. Eight years later, Mr. Timms was dismissed from employment at Sherman High School pursuant to 25 U.S.C.A. § 3207(b), which, at that time, stated that no individual may be appointed to a position that involves regular contact with Indian children if the individual has "been found guilty of, or entered a plea of nolo contendere or guilty to, any offense under Federal, State, or tribal law involving crimes of violence." Mr. Timms' assault conviction was considered a previous "crime of violence," and he was dismissed.

Procedural History

On February 15, 1999, Mr. Timms filed a motion to dismiss his prior convictions for lack of personal jurisdiction because he was not an enrolled member of the tribe when the offenses were committed. On June 1, 1999, the Tribal Court denied Mr. Timms' motion claiming there was no legal basis upon which to grant the motion. The court held he should have appealed the conviction immediately following imposition of the sentence.

On October 19, 1999, Mr. Timms filed a motion in Hopi Tribal Court to set aside the prior convictions. The court denied the motion because Mr. Timms did not provide any legal authority in support of his motion. Mr. Timms resubmitted the motion to set aside his convictions on October 11, 2000, but the court again denied the motion for lack of legal authority. The court also found the state law cited by Mr. Timms "not binding or controlling in this case." On December 6, 2000, appellant filed a "notice of appeal" to this court.

Mr. Timms argues on appeal that the Hopi Tribal Court erred in denying the motion to set aside his conviction. He notes that, according to Hopi Resolution H–12–76, Section 2, the laws of Arizona are the sixth highest category of precedential authority in Hopi Tribal Court. Although admitting that Hopi law does not contain any provision for setting aside convictions, he argues that Hopi Resolution H–12–76 authorizes the court to import Arizona state law in cases where the five stronger categories of precedent are silent. He urges the court to follow Arizona Revised Statutes § 13–907(A), which grants Arizona state courts the discretion to set aside convictions.

Synopsis

The Court finds that this matter invokes the deeply rooted Hopi concept of ookwalni (forgiveness and mercy). It would be inconsistent with this fundamental concept to not consider the Appellant's petition to set aside his prior conviction. Hopi Resolution H–12–76 requires us to look to such "customs, traditions and culture of the Hopi Tribe." Accordingly, this court does not need to consider whether H–12–76 authorizes the court to import Arizona statutory law regarding setting aside a conviction. The case is reversed and remanded for further proceedings in accordance with this opinion.

Decision of the Court

A. The court has statutory jurisdiction to decide this case [1] This Court has jurisdiction to hear appeals from final judgments and other final orders issued by a judge of the Hopi Tribal Court "except in criminal cases where the defendant is sentenced to less than 30 days imprisonment or labor and/ or to pay a fine of less than $50." Ordinance 21, § 1.2.5. In this case, the underlying conviction involved a fine of $125.

Therefore, the court has statutory jurisdiction to decide the case.

B. The Tribal Courts may set aside convictions based on the Hopi tradition of ookwalni (forgiveness and mercy). [2] [3] Hopi Resolution H–12–76 requires the Hopi Courts to look to the "customs, traditions, and culture of the Hopi Tribe" as authoritative in determining Hopi law. One such deeply rooted tradition of the Hopi Tribe is the concept of ookwalni (forgiveness and mercy). In this case, Mr. Timms is clearly deserving of ookwalni. He was dismissed from his position at Sherman High School pursuant to 25 U.S.C.A. §3207(b), which stated that no individual may be appointed to a position which involves regular contact with Indian children if the individual has "been found guilty of, or entered a plea of nolo contendere or guilty to, any offense under Federal, State, or tribal law involving crimes of violence...."

In 1990, Mr. Timms entered a guilty plea to assault as part of a case arising from wrongful possession of alcohol when he was 18-years-old. He is now 29-years-old, has attended college, and is a respected member of the community. He has not been convicted of any other criminal offense either before or since the 1990 conviction. In addition, he has submitted numerous letters praising him as both a teacher and an individual. Sandy Dixon, Mr. Timms supervisor at Sherman High School, wrote on June 28, 1999:

Mr. Timms . . . has demonstrated professionalism . . . and outstanding integrity. I admonish you to reconsider Mr. Timms. . . . We will lose an outstanding role model for Native American children. As his supervisor, I do not wish to see this occur, nor do I want to lose an outstanding employee. His career is in your hands.

Ms. Kathy Tewawina stated in a letter dated January 22, 1999, that Mr. Timms is a "caring and sensitive person" and has a "very outgoing personality." Victoria Richardson, Mr. Timms' supervisor at the Southern California Indian Center, wrote on January 22, 1999, that Mr. Timms has a "great attitude and professional manner," is on their volunteer call list, and has volunteered to help the Indian Center with its community events. In addition, Jim Hastings, principal of Sherman High School, wrote a letter dated June 28, 1998, in which he stated:

[During the past two years] Mr. Timms has proven himself to be an exemplary employee and a very caring individual. Cameron works very well with Native American students showing a great concern for their personal and educational well being. I have the highest regard for him as an employee and friend.

> Mr. Timms acted irresponsibly on June 3, 1990. However, he has served his punishment and shown sufficient rehabilitation in order for the Court to invoke ookwalni in this case. Even the prosecutor in the motion to dismiss noted: the Tribe does not object to Defendants request for dismissal as a matter of justice. The Tribe believes that Defendant has not been before this Court since this matter occurred and that the disposition in this matter reflects in an equally positive manner on Defendant. Response to Motion to Dismiss, April 14, 1999 (R.M.D.) (Given all of these facts, the Court finds the tradition of ookwalni to be properly involved and controlling.
>
> ### Order of the Court
> It is hereby ORDERED that the judgment of the Tribal Court denying the motion to set aside judgment in the case of The Hopi Tribe v. Cameron Timms is REVERSED AND REMANDED. The Tribal Court erred in not considering the Hopi tradition of ookwalni (forgiveness and mercy).

Conclusion

Tribal sentencing laws focus on accountability for harmful behavior. There are a variety of ways that a tribal government can assure accountability, including restitution, fines, counseling, and incarceration. Some tribal governments have determined that incarceration is an important part of protecting the community and deterring others from committing crimes. Because of the consequences and stigma associated with a criminal conviction, some tribal governments also offer a process for pardon or expungement.

Questions

Makah v. Greene
1. Why do you think the Court decided to suspend the jail time in this case?
2. What were the conditions of the defendant's probation in this case? Do you agree with these conditions?

Pakootas v. Colville
1. What was the defendant's argument as to why he should not have to serve jail time? What was the Court's response?
2. What did the Court say about the authority to sentence?

Sweowat v. Colville
1. Should a tribal judge have to express findings of fact that justify the sentence? Why or why not?

2. Why was the defendant's sentence in this case vacated? Do you agree with this decision?

St. Peter v. Colville
1. How would you have ruled on the ICRA claim that St. Peter's right to due process was violated by the court's reliance on his part criminal history from the FBI?
2. The court in St. Peter said that the trial judge did not have to explain her reasoning for the sentence. Do you agree with this outcome?
3. How would you have ruled on the ICRA claim that St. Peter's right to be free from cruel and unusual punishment was violated by the imposition of the maximum sentences?

Cherokee v. Crowe
1. Why did the court provide the credentials of the judges in this case?
2. Do you agree with the court that the *Bustamante* case is more persuasive than the *Spears* case?

Pascua Yaqui v. Miranda
1. Is the phrase "any one offense" ambiguous? Explain your answer.
2. How does the court link consecutive sentencing power with tribal self-determination?

Hardin v. Reno Sparks
1. Why was the sentencing process flawed?
2. Was the sentence imposed on Hardin "cruel and unusual punishment"?

Hopi v. Timms
1. What were Mr. Timms's crimes?
2. What Hopi principle did the Court refer to in expunging Mr. Timms's conviction?

In Your Community
1. What kinds of sentences does your tribal code allow?
2. Does your tribe currently operate a jail or other detention facility? If not, where are convicted people sent to serve their time?
3. Does your tribal government have an official pardon procedure? Should there be an option for a pardon?

Terms Used in Chapter 26

Arbitrarily and capriciously: According to a person's whims or desires; not following general principles or rules.

Consecutively: Following one after the other without interruption.

Contravene: Go against the laws or rules.

Controverted: Disputed, denied, or opposed.

Deferred sentence: A sentence that has been postponed.

Dicta: Latin term meaning "digression" or discussion of a side/unreleated issue.

Erroneous: Involving error or deviating from the law.

Execution: Carrying out a course of action to its completion.

Inapposite: Not pertinent; unsuitable.

Remanded: Sent back to a lower court.

Reversible error: A mistake made by a judge that could affect the outcome of a legal proceeding.

Revoke: Wipe out something's legal effect by taking it back; cancelling it.

Vacated: Annulled; set aside.

Notes

1. We have replaced the victim's name with initials for privacy reasons.
2. We have replaced the victim's name with initials for privacy reasons.

Further Readings

Ed Hermes, "Law & Order Tribal Edition: How the Tribal Law and Order Act Has Failed to Increase Tribal Court Sentencing Authority," 45 *Ariz. State Law J.* 675 (2013).

Eileen M. Luna-Firebaugh, "Incarcerating Ourselves: Tribal Jails and Corrections," 83 *Prison J.* 51 (2003).

Tribal Restorative Justice — Chapter 27

Introduction

As discussed in Chapters 1 and 2, the American criminal justice system has been heavily focused on punishing criminals. Many traditional indigenous forms of justice have focused on restoring peace to the community. Given high rates of repeat offenders, American criminal justice systems have begun to experiment with alternatives to the criminal justice system that focus more on a restorative form of justice.

Many tribal courts are replacing adopted forms of punitive criminal justice with their own indigenous forms of justice, which focus on healing. There are a variety of terms to refer to these systems—including restorative justice, traditional justice, peacemaking, law mending—or appropriate terms from the original language of the tribe.

While the focus of traditional systems is not punitive, offenders are still held accountable for their actions. An Inter-Tribal Workgroup composed of the Navajo Nation, Hopi Tribe, and Fort McDowell Yavapai Nation, formed to assist the Senate Committee on Indian Affairs in understanding Indian justice and accountability and returning offenders to Indian communities, shared the following understanding of restorative justice.

> "Restorative justice" as used here is distinct from [the] term as commonly understood and applied. Whereas the term in the American justice system has become greatly simplified and come to mean non-convictions, no jail and no fines, restorative justice in traditional Indian justice is used in the literal sense, to "restore" in conformity with justice principles. Wrongdoers, those who are harmed, and their affected communities are engaged in search of solutions that promote repair and

rebuilding. Convictions, detention, and penalties in support of personal responsibility and community safety are not excluded.

Indian justice responsibilities include accountability and return of offenders to the community. These are in addition to community safety responsibilities. . . . These three are core elements of all traditional justice systems notwithstanding a tribe's diverse specific customs. All agencies and community members necessary to fulfill these responsibilities are part of the Indian justice system.

In Navajo, there is a term, ná bináhaazláo which means providing parties with a sense of completeness or comprehensiveness. It also means fairness and doing whatever is necessary in coming to a comprehensive solution. The tribal courts are charged with ná bináhaazláo through restorative justice. In Hopi, the offender's accountability—QaHopit qa' antipu'at—and bring the offender back into the community—QaHopit ahoy Kiimmi pavnaya—are deep-rooted justice principles.

This means there is a circle of responsibilities, beginning with law enforcement and prosecution, the judiciary being responsible for accountability and bringing the offender back into the community through sentencing, and probation and parole services ensure that the judiciary's conditions are fulfilled. These components integrate and coordinate with mental health, social service, behavioral health professionals and traditional counselors where necessary; given the very high rate of alcohol and substance abuse disorders implicated in Indian Country crime, integration is needed in almost instances.[1]

Restorative justice within tribal courts takes many different forms, such as healing to wellness courts, peacemaking, and other forms of traditional restorative justice systems based upon the nation's own customs and traditions. As Indian nations choose to use these forms of justice they are exercising their sovereignty and helping their citizens. A system based on the nation's traditions and customs, as opposed to American law which is a tool of colonization, refuses to bend to assimilation. Use of alternatives based on custom and tradition also strengthens sovereignty because foreign systems are displaced and the nation returns to its own system of justice. But perhaps more importantly, the use of alternatives strengthens individuals as it allows the justice system to focus on healing or restoring the individual not simply so he does not return to a life of crime, but becomes a positive or contributing member to the community.

Traditional indigenous forms of justice differ from American criminal justice in many ways. Former Chief Justice Yazzie of the Navajo Nation Supreme Court describes the Western adversarial system as a vertical system that transforms one party into the bad guy and the other party into the winner or the person who is right.[2] Yazzie also describes vertical justice as the judge having the most important role, as the victim and the victim's family having little say, and says that there is a preoccupation with truth rather than focusing on solving the problem.[3] But Yazzie argues that traditional indigenous legal systems are horizontal, as opposed to the vertical, hierarchal criminal justice systems where the judge is in charge. For example in the Navajo traditional system, no one person is considered more important.[4] "A better description of the horizontal model, and one often used by Indians to portray their thought, is a circle. In a circle, there is no right or left, nor is there a beginning or an end; every point (or person) on the line of the circle looks to the same center as the focus. The circle is the symbol of Navajo justice because it is perfect, unbroken, and a simile of unity and oneness. It conveys the image of people gathering together for discussion."[5]

Indigenous justice systems also focus on distributing justice or **distributive justice**, or that a justice focused on the well-being of everyone. "Distributive justice abandons fault and adequate compensation . . . in favor of assuring well-being for everyone . . . [and] the victim's feelings and the perpetrator's ability to pay are more important than damages determined using a precise measure of actual loss. In addition, relatives of the party causing the injury are responsible for compensating the injured party, and the relatives of the injured party are entitled to the benefit of the compensation."[6]

As part of focusing on the well-being, some forms of indigenous justice, such as peacemaking, use an educational process that heals relationships. Judge David Raasch explains peacemaking as "more of an educational process than an adversarial process. In peacemaking we get to learn about the feelings of the other person; we get to learn ideas. Some of the peacemaking that I've been involved in, where people can simply be at each other's throats for years and years and years simply because they've never talked—it goes on to that same simple communication process of conversing with each other like you would build relationships between state and tribal agencies or practitioners. It's the same thing with peacemaking: it's about the relationships involved and less about the law."[7]

Justice may differ in other ways as well. Professor Russell Barsh explains that indigenous law systems focus on just-ness, not necessarily justice. Barsh believes justice is often confused with order, and that justice was an afterthought to Western legal systems. "We routinely refer to the police, criminal courts, and prisons as institutions of justice, when in fact they were clearly devised to maintain order among certain social classes. . . . Justice was an afterthought historically. It arose when the governments tried to justify their methods of imposing order on society with a developing sense of 'rights' and the inevitable resistance among the people on whom order had been imposed."[8] Barsh encourages separating the "just-ness of the responses to violence and disorder from the short-term effectiveness of those responses in reducing the quality of violence and disorder."[9] A just system should feel more just to all of the participants, not only the offender. Barsh suggests several measures of just-ness:

- Victims should feel that their pain and anger are acknowledged and more effectively addressed.
- Decision makers must feel that they are able to understand the needs of the parties and respond more appropriately than would be possible in mainstream adjudication.
- Accused persons must feel that they are treated fairly and with respect and must be more willing to comply with decisions.
- Community members who are currently observers rather than participants should nonetheless have a more positive view of the legal order.
- People in the community as a whole should feel that, whether as victims or as the accused, they would expect to be treated more fairly and respectfully. In other words, those who are presently only potential participants should *expect* just treatment.[10]

Examples of Restorative or Indigenous Justice

Navajo Nation Peacemaker Courts

Institutional History of hózhóji naat'aah, from http://www.navajocourts.org/Peacemaking/Plan/insthistory.html

In 1982, the Navajo Peacemaker Court was created by Navajo judges by vote of the Judicial Conference. The judges wanted to find an alternative to Anglo-American judicial methods that had roots in Navajo common law, and which could pull in Diné wisdom, methods and customs in resolving disputes. The court that was created aspired to protect and support the customary practice of peacemaking, hózhóji naat'aah, but also imposed Anglo-American court-style procedural rules on hózhóji naat'aah. The judicial institutionalization of hózhóji naat'aah had the inadvertent consequence of changing its fundamental nature.

Over thirty years, institutionalized hózhóji naat'aah more and more resembled mediator-assisted settlement. Its teaching component, its heroic component, and its dynamic life value engagement component as hózhóji naat'aah were not included in the peacemaker court rules and, over time, fell out of practice. "Consent" to participate in the often emotional journey came to be equated with the Anglo-American notion of "consent" to lessen gains or losses through settlement. As a result of the rules, the emotional component of peacemaking came to be viewed as a complication that the peacemaker ought to quieten and diffuse.

The Judicial Conference and Council have done their best to address the relationship problems between hózhóji naat'aah and the court-style processes. In the early 2000s, the word "court" was removed from peacemaking. The late Chief Justice Claudeen Bates-Arthur replaced the peacemaking rules with "guidelines." The Council acknowledged Diné bi beenahaz'áanii, Fundamental Laws, and created the Peacemaking Division, later Peacemaking Program, to provide education and develop hózhóji naat'aah throughout the Nation.

Recent laws expand the relationship of peacemaking with Navajo Nation institutions. The Álchíní Bi Beehaz'áannii Act (ABBA) allows agencies, professionals and family to refer matters concerning children to peacemaking for a tradition-based resolution without need for court orders as a method for diversion, self- and family-accountability and for preserving or reunifying a family. The ABBA requires program guidance for agency-referred cases that will not involve the Navajo Nation courts. New federal grants also encourage the use of peacemaking in family group conferencing for school children. Previously, agency referrals other than agreements under the Navajo Nation Child Support Enforcement Act were not expressly provided for in the Navajo Nation Code.

Court referrals have also expanded. The ABBA also reinforces courts' ability to make referrals to hózhóji naat'aah at any stage in children's cases. Additionally, the Vulnerable Adult Protection Act obliges courts to discuss the peacemaking option when abuse, neglect or exploitation of elders and other vulnerable adults is involved prior to issuing a protection order. Finally, the Supreme Court in Manning v. Abeita emphasized the obligation of our courts to provide traditional options for dispute resolution at pretrial phases of adjudication. The Court emphasized the duty to use Diné methods of informal dispute resolution whenever permissible, primarily to aid horizontal decision-making by the parties themselves in pretrial during which court rules may be suspended, and for referral of all or part of a case to hózhóji naat'aah.

These last three decades, how a peacemaking case begins has added to an intricate and often confused relationship with the courts. In order to emphasize that people could choose hózhóji naat'aah over adversarial courts, all cases—even cases for which court orders are clearly required such as divorces, guardianships, and probate—were permitted to be initiated in peacemaking with the resulting agreement "acknowledged" later via court order. However, over time, many courts began requiring the Peacemaking Program to provide legal assistance to hózhóji naat'aah participants and also began requiring peacemaking agreements to be drafted in the style of legal documents. As the legal demands of the courts grew, it became evident that the program lacked the legal ability to provide such services and should not do so.

In 1993, the Domestic Abuse Protection Act authorized the "Peacemaker Court" to provide remedies in domestic violence cases and made it mandatory for courts to provide victims with the peacemaking option. However, subsequent court rules limit peacemaking to "suggestions" for remedies. Later in 2000, courts began initiating peacemaking cases themselves after amendments to the criminal code called for referrals to peacemaking to determine nályééh in criminal sentencing. This development actually helped the courts view the peacemaking method as distinct and separate from court processes in criminal sentencing matters, because in such referrals, there has never been an expectation that peacemakers provide legal assistance. However, peacemakers have been hesitant to recommend sentencing options that are not listed on the court's sentencing options checklist. The hope that the referrals would result in recommendations for community-based alternative sentencing based on nályééh, k'é ná'ásdlįį, k'é níjísdlįį, and k'eedí'nééh that would come from deep life value engagement by offenders and victims in hózhóji naat'aah has never been realized.

Over time, it has become clear that the independence of the peacemakers needs to be reinforced, the goal of peacemaking clarified, and the traditional components of hózhóji naat'aah as a distinct and separate method need to be restored for the traditional method's effective and proper use.

Kake Peacemaking Court System

Duane Champagne and Carole Goldberg, *Promising Strategies: Public Law 280*, 1-3 (2013). Available at: http://www.walkingoncommonground.org/

In 1999, the Organized Village of Kake (OVK), a Tlingit village in Southeast Alaska with an Indian Reorganization Act government, adopted the Keex' Kwaan Judicial Peacemaking Code. The code established the Kake Peacemaking Court System, which consists of Kake Peacemaking Circle, Keex' Kwan Peacemaking Panel, the Keex' Kwaan Appellate Court, and Kake Youth Circle Peacemaking. The code says that peacemakers are community volunteers and are appointed by the OVK Council to serve three-year renewable terms. Persons with felony convictions or more than two misdemeanor cases are not eligible to serve as peacemakers. A pool of a dozen peacemakers is available to take up cases.

There are multiple ways for a case to enter into the Kake Peacemaking Court System, which usually addresses minor violations or misdemeanor cases. Petitions are filed with the court clerk of the Kake Peacemaker Court. Petitions can be initiated by family and friends of a victim or offender, by either a victim or offender, or by the police, district attorney, junior police officer, Office of Family Support, or alcohol counselor. Upon receiving the petition, a review team of peacemakers considers whether to accept the proposed case. If the case is accepted, then the review team decides whether to send the case to the peacemaking circle or to a peacemaking panel.

If a wrongdoer does not meet with the peacemaker court or does not agree to peacemaking procedures, the case is referred to Alaska State Court. In state court, the police and district attorney will file a complaint. A defendant can return to Kake Peacemaking Court if the offender decides to plead no contest or guilty. If the state court agrees, the offender can petition the Kake Peacemaking Court for sentencing. The peacemaker court will consider the offender's petition for taking the case. If the peacemaker court accepts an offender's case, then the offender must waive Alaska Criminal Rule 45, the right to a speedy trial. If a defendant enters a plea of not guilty in state court, and later in the trial the defendant agrees to a guilty plea, then the judge can consider whether to accept sentencing through the Kake Peacemaking Court. If an offender does not comply with peacemaking rules or decisions, the offender is returned to state court.

When the peacemaker review team accepts a petition to use the peacemaker court, the review team decides on the appropriate format: either panel or circle. Panels are formed by at least three peacemakers who elect a presiding peacemaker and alternate by consensus. The presiding peacemaker manages the hearing of the case, and participants can speak only at the direction of the presiding peacemaker. All parties are informed of court procedures and their rights in the hearing. Petitioners and defendants may present evidence and witnesses during the hearings. The peacemakers may question anyone in the court room, and all parties are given an opportunity to speak. Decisions by the peacemaker panels are made by consensus. If there is no consensus, then decisions on sentencing are made by majority rule among the panel members. When a case involves extreme legal complications or significant conflicts of interests among the standing Kake peacemakers, then the reviewing peacemakers can choose the panel format and utilize visiting judges. Visiting judges can be judges from other tribal courts or attorneys with bar certification. At least one member of a three-member peacemaker panel must be a member of Kake. Parties can be referred to the peacemaking circles to address specific issues.

The review team may suggest a peacemaking circle for sentencing or other solutions, if the team decides that it is the most appropriate format. Peacemakers are assigned to circles by OVK staff. The offender must waive Criminal Rule 45, if they have not already done so. Circle participants are informed of their rights, circle procedures, and the goals of the circle sentencing method. Support groups, such as family members and social service counselors, are invited to provide council and advice to the participants. The circles are led by the Keeper of the Circle, a peacemaker who is recognized by the OVK Council. The rules of circle peacemaking follow traditional patterns. Participants have to show respect for each other, and each participant is allowed to speak and give voice to his or her ideas and feelings about the case. Only one person speaks at a time. The speaker holds a talking stick while speaking and none can interrupt. Speaking continues with the goal of participants arriving at an agreement or common ground. After everyone has been heard, the keeper moves the discussion toward possible solutions and sentencing for the case. Decisions are made by consensus. The Keeper of the Circle maintains order during the speaking but does not have a deciding vote. If consensus is reached, the agreements of the circle are written out as Consensus Agreements or Orders of the Keex' Kwaan Tribal Court. If a consensus cannot be reached, the case may be referred to a peacemaking panel. The keeper may set a time to revisit the case and evaluate the progress of the proposed solution or sentence, or the keeper may instead outline a specific follow-up plan that can be monitored by justice services staff. The peacemaker sessions usually start and end with prayers led by a participating elder.

The Kake Peacemaking Court sets the orders or sentences for the panel and circle cases: "The Peacemakers shall seek a **holistic** plan for the wrongdoer and shall consider the rights and wellness of any victims." Sentencing can include fines up to $5,000, a work sentence, community service, impounding of vehicles, banishment, drug and alcohol treatment, counseling by elders, traditional activities, apologies, or restitution. Banishment is temporary and used to protect village members from harm. "Restitution is defined to include payment in money, repairing property, and apologies." A person found to have violated village ordinances may be ordered to "participate in seasonally appropriate traditional activities such as fish camps, trapping, hunting, culture camps, and other tribally sponsored or approved traditional activities." Wrongdoers may be asked to make a public apology to the entire village. Apologies can be written, spoken, or both. Peacemakers may "counsel persons brought before them in a helpful spirit."[11] The court may bring village elders to the court to counsel people.

The Keex' Kwaan Appellate Court does not rehear cases but will review whether proper procedures were upheld in peacemaking circles or panels. Kake Youth Circle Peacemaking is conducted by the youth coordinator and assisted by volunteer youth from the Kake community. The Kake Youth Circle Peacemaking follows protocols similar to those used to conduct the adult circle peacemaking cases.

Tribal Healing to Wellness Courts

Tribal Healing to Wellness Courts are adaptations of state drug courts. State drug courts began in the 1980s in a response the growing number of drug-related cases and overcrowding in jails and prisons. Courts often sentenced offenders to treatment, but this approach was not addressing the problem. "The drug court approach anchors treatment with the authority of a judge who, often with team input, holds the defendant or offender personally and publicly accountable for treatment participation and progress. . . . Teams of judges, prosecutors, public defenders, treatment providers, law enforcement officials, probation officers, case managers, and a host of other community members use the coercive power of the court to promote abstinence and alter behavior. This is accomplished through a combination of intensive judicial supervision, praise for progress, sanctions for noncompliance, random drug testing, comprehensive and phased treatment, aftercare programs, and other **ancillary** human services."[12]

Healing to Wellness Courts are based on the Tribal Drug Court Key Components, adapted from State Court Key Components. "The Ten Key Components prompt the determination of what types of cases and participants enter the court and are eligible for its treatment services. They promote a shared case management role by the Team, one that necessitates detailed record keeping and data collection, intensive supervision including random drug testing, and swift responses to participant conduct. Maintaining a primary role, the judge is relied on to facilitate respectful communication through the whole collaborative process, a practice that forces a change of attitude and mindset."[13]

Tribal Healing to Wellness Courts: The Key Components, iv-v (2014). Available at: http://www.wellnesscourts.org/

Key Component #1: Individual and Community Healing Focus

Tribal Healing to Wellness Court brings together alcohol and drug treatment, community healing resources, and the tribal justice process by using a team approach to achieve the physical and spiritual healing of the individual participant, and to promote Native nation building and the well-being of the community.

Key Component #2: Referral Points and Legal Process

Participants enter Tribal Healing to Wellness Court through various referral points and legal processes that promote tribal sovereignty and the participant's due (fair) process rights.

Key Component #3: Screening and Eligibility

Eligible court-involved substance-abusing parents, guardians, juveniles, and adults are identified early through legal and clinical screening for eligibility and are promptly placed into the Tribal Healing to Wellness Court.

Key Component #4: Treatment and Rehabilitation

Tribal Healing to Wellness Court provides access to holistic, structured, and phased alcohol and drug abuse treatment and rehabilitation services that incorporate culture and tradition.

Key Component #5: Intensive Supervision

Tribal Healing to Wellness Court participants are monitored through intensive supervision that includes frequent and random testing for alcohol and drug use, while participants and their families benefit from effective team-based case management.

Key Component #6: Incentives and Sanctions

Progressive rewards (or incentives) and consequences (or sanctions) are used to encourage participant compliance with the Tribal Healing to Wellness Court requirements.

Key Component #7: Judicial Interaction
Ongoing involvement of a Tribal Healing to Wellness Court judge with the Tribal Wellness Court team and staffing, and ongoing Tribal Wellness Court judge interaction with each participant are essential.

Key Component #8: Monitoring and Evaluation
Process measurement, performance measurement, and evaluation are tools used to monitor and evaluate the achievement of program goals, identify needed improvements to the Tribal Healing to Wellness Court and to the tribal court process, determine participant progress, and provide information to governing bodies, interested community groups, and funding sources.

Key Component #9: Continuing Interdisciplinary and Community Education
Continuing interdisciplinary and community education promote effective Tribal Healing to Wellness Court planning, implementation, and operation.

Key Component #10: Team Interaction
The development and maintenance of ongoing commitments, communication, coordination, and cooperation among Tribal Healing to Wellness Court team members, service providers and payers, the community and relevant organizations, including the use of formal written procedures and agreements, are critical for Tribal Wellness Court success.

Waabshki-Miigwan is the Little Traverse Bay Bands Healing to Wellness Court. Waabshki-Miigwan targets nonviolent participants charged with drug or alcohol related offenses. Individuals are admitted into Waabshki-Miigwan if they are Indian; committed a nonviolent crime; committed a crime related to drug or alcohol or drugs or alcohol was the underlying factor; have a history of drug or alcohol use; understand and are willing to follow program requirements; and fall within the jurisdiction of the Little Traverse Bay Band Tribal Court.[14] Participants either enter a plea agreement and agree to be sentenced to the Drug Court, or are referred after committing a violation of their probation. Sanctions and incentives are used to encourage and reinforce progress. Participants enter into a forty-four-week program based on Odawa values that encourage adopting a healthy lifestyle and eliminating harmful behaviors that cause negative consequences.[15] The curriculum has four phases: the learning level, the accepting level, the willing level, and the succeeding level.

Participants engage in assignments that balance the spiritual, emotional, physical, and mental wellness. "Spiritual health activities include self-help meetings, daily prayer and meditation, and Twelve Step Work in either AA or the White Bison Medicine Wheel Teachings. Emotional health activities include assigned WMDCP cultural and wellness activities laid out in the WMDCP Workbook. These activities include various engaging tasks designed to instill Odawa culture as well as challenge the drug court client. Physical health activities include weekly physical exercise to be chosen by the client and negative random/scheduled drug and alcohol screens. Mental health activities are laid out in periodic therapy sessions with a substance abuse counselor on staff. Clients must simultaneously complete these weekly spiritual, emotional, physical, and mental health activities in order to advance to the next week's assignments. Failure to complete all assigned tasks can halt the client's progress and extend the length of time until successful completion of the WMDCP."[16] Although these activities may seem daunting, the program is laid out in weekly planners, workbooks, and the website.[17] And the WMDCP team works with the participants on their path toward wellness. The WMDCP team consists of a tribal court judge, tribal prosecutor, tribal defense attorney, court administrator, the coordinator, probation officer, a cultural resource advisor, substance abuse counselor, law enforcement, sobriety mentor, and an elder.

About the Waabshki-Miigwan Drug Court Program

Available at: http://www.ltbbodawa-nsn.gov/

To all that take interest in our program,

The Waabshki-Miigwan Program is dedicated to my grandmother, the late Hon. Rita Gasco-Shepard. Grandma was a Beautiful Odawa woman whom I have always cherished. She taught me many lessons in life about love, faith, and most importantly for me, respect. I learned by her example that I was capable of being all that I dreamed. She taught me how to respect myself and to live in Truth. She helped me to find the purpose that God has created me for which has lead to blessings far beyond what I could have imagined for myself. I will always be grateful for her love.

She was born Rita Marie Ann Gasco in 1939, the oldest of five children born to Stella Gasco of Harbor Springs, Michigan. She lived with her mother and grandparents in Indian Town until the age of nine, when she was placed in foster care. Grandma grew up in Harbor Springs and Petoskey, and lived and worked her entire life in the area. Being part of the Boarding School Era, Grandma attended Holy Childhood day school. During this time she was separated from her two sisters. She reconnected with one sister shortly after High school, and all three sisters were briefly re-united during the last years of my grandmother's life. Grandma married my Grandpa, Harvey Brubacker, during her senior year of high school and started a family. She had four children with my mother, Vicki, being her eldest. Grandma received her GED in the early 1970s and encouraged all of her children to finish school and pursue higher education. Grandma and Grandpa would later divorce and both remarry. My Mother, Aunts, and Uncle were raised by Grandma here in Northern Michigan.

It seemed that Grandma excelled in everything that she did. When I was a young child I remember seeing all of her trophies that she had been awarded for her numerous talents. Grandma played sports, she was a singer and musician, a wonderful artist, and like I said, just plain good at everything she did. She was a master in needlecraft and she is well-known for her intricate beadwork. She enjoyed watching birds and walking Duke, her miniature Doberman. She went to all of her Grandchildren's sporting events and kept very accurate stats in the meanwhile.

Her lifestyle was rich with joy in so many areas especially in her hobbies; my Grandma loved playing golf most. She began playing in the late seventies and quickly became a local legend as she would outplay most men. She was just a tiny woman at 130 pounds, but what she lacked in strength she made up on the greens. Her last year of league play was the summer before she got sick. In that year Grandma and her partner played in the championship of the local men's Tribal golf league. The opposing team was comprised of her husband Flash and his partner Harvey. At the conclusion of the match Grandma lost by a few strokes. Flash told me that she didn't talk to him for three days after the match. I guess she was just a little upset that he had beaten her. Two years after she walked on, everyone still raves about how she would beat the pants off most of the men she played against. She had a truly competitive nature and I think she strived for excellence in all areas of her life.

In the 80s, Grandma started a new chapter of her story. It was a path that would lead to her fulfilling her purpose, one in which she would touch countless lives, and leave a lasting legacy for her family and community. In 1983, grandma took a job at a local law firm. Later, when one of the attorneys left the firm to become an Emmett County Judge, he offered her the position of Probate Court Registrar. Grandma accepted the position and served the court until her retirement at the age of 62. During her career she learned many things about the workings of the legal system, and also began to develop an interest in doing what she could to give back to the Native American community. Then, in 1998 the Little Traverse Bay Bands posted the position of Appellate Justice for which my grandmother applied. She was chosen for the position and was sworn in on May 17, 1998 to serve several terms as judge before retiring again in 2008.

During her judgeship Grandma became increasingly interested in promoting the health and well-being of the tribal youth, and participated in the Tribe's Healing to Wellness Court. One component of the court was to build a peacemaking process to solve disputes among community members. While on the team my grandmother had the opportunity to attend a training in Kake, a small village on an Alaskan island in the Pacific where the local Tribe would be presenting its experience in developing a Peacekeeping program. In Kake my Grandmother learned about Peacekeeping, but more importantly learned a lesson that would change her perspective on healing and alter the way she would live out the rest of her days here with us. Not many years after her visit to Alaska, Grandma walked on with grace after a brief but intense battle with cancer.

Before Grandma walked on she asked me to pass on the story about her experience in Kake. She made me promise to memorize and tell the story when opportunities would come about. Before Grandma found out she had cancer and during a time of her life when she was the happiest, she wrote this story:

> I was on my way to Alaska, excited to be on a journey to a land I had never seen. As a member of a Tribal peacekeeping team, I was one of several who were being given the wonderful opportunity to visit Kake, a little village on a small Alaskan island in the Pacific. The purpose of our journey was to get a firsthand experience at how this community developed their peacekeeping program, which was based on traditional native values. This experience would then aid us in our own efforts to establish a Tribal peacekeeping system back home in Michigan.
>
> We were told that our visit was occurring during a time of the year when the landscape would be exposed and the wildlife would be very active. We would be visiting the island of Kake in the spring. The salmon would be running, making their own journey up into the mouth of the river to spawn. The bear and eagle would be moving about, hoping to feast on the spawning fish at river's edge. I, too, had hopes about this journey . . . hopes that I would fulfill my lifelong quest of finding my first eagle feather.

Our small plane landed on the airstrip in the village of Kake, which was tucked away on this Alaskan island. I observed my surroundings and concluded that Kake was in a very natural, depressed and untouched state. It was shortly after arrival that I shared my dream of finding an eagle feather with our facilitator and island guide, Mike. He reassured me that my search would end here in Kake because the possibilities for where a feather might be discovered were endless. Eagle feathers could be found below trees that held the favorite roosting spots, out on the ocean flats during ebb tide, and along the river where the mighty bird comes to feed.

The first day on the island was spent getting acclimated, settling in and taking in some of the local sites. With determination, I started out early the next morning enjoying a walk through the rustic village of Kake. The weather was typical for a day on an island south of Juneau. I could feel the mist on my face while my body was chilled by the dampness that hung in the air. As promised, the island's activity was occupied by the wildlife moving about. Mother bear would snag a fish and carry it off to the woods, where the noisy cubs were climbing in the trees and letting her know they were hungry. Eagles could be seen flying overhead or perched in any of the tall pine trees along the river.

I walked along the river in various paths, not venturing too far in any particular direction for fear that I might meet a bear. As I looked up to the treetops, I could spot two and three eagles at a time. I walked up into the brush, which was so thick that I felt as if I was walking through a rainforest. I reached the mouth of the river. The tide was out and my walk ended on the misty ocean flats. It is where my walked stopped for that moment that my search began. I could see eagles fishing in the little pools of water that had been left on the ocean floor after the tide had receded. If I got too close, the feeding birds would fly off. Timidly I kept walking. I was a bit uneasy about going further out onto the flats, nervous that the tide could return at any moment, but I continued walking and looking, looking and walking. There wasn't an eagle feather to be found.

I decided to go back to the hotel, ending my day's quest. Upon my return, others sensed my disappointment. A traveling companion named Jeff presented me with a beautiful immature eagle feather that he had found. I would treasure this feather but I would not give up on my quest.

After a couple of days of long walks and fruitless searches, Mike offered some encouragement. He had planned a tour for us later that evening that would take us around the island. He also said that we could make a stop at the village dump. While this sounded somewhat unattractive, this little rendezvous was planned because eagles often visited the village dump to scavenge through the garbage, which often left a trail of feathers. This could be just the place I had been waiting for.

Our group of six to seven people had a very pleasant road trip around the island, although the drive couldn't really be described as having gone "around." You see, when traveling on this remote island you would follow the roads until they simply didn't go any further. The roads we took on our tour would go just so far and then they would stop, causing us to turn around and take another route. We enjoyed the scenery and occasional spotting of wildlife. We also stopped to pick medicinal plants to accompany us on our journey home. Our tour did end at the village dump, where we all got out and started rummaging through the debris left by the villagers in hopes of finding an elusive eagle feather. A couple of pretty raven feathers were spotted and kept, which was considered a treasure as well. In Alaska, the raven and the eagle are referred to as the "lovebirds" and are often pictured together in Alaskan native art.

While everyone was preparing to depart, I was preparing myself for bringing closure to another day without having fulfilled my lifelong quest of finding an eagle feather. But just as I was walking away, I looked down at my feet and saw a quill sticking out of the muck. I reached down and pulled at the quill. Out from the rubbish came the sorriest and dirtiest feather I had ever seen.

Mike our guide, coaxed me to throw it back on the ground. He promised that he would get me another feather, explaining again how plentiful they were on the island. He even offered to share one of his feathers. I ignored his urges. As soon as I saw the feather, I knew it was from an eagle. I also knew at that moment that I was keeping it.

Later that evening, I returned to my hotel room with the dirty and mangled feather. With soap and water, I began to gently wash the feather, fanning it to dry. What appeared was the most beautiful eagle's white tail feather. It was my treasured gift from the Creator.

The next day I was given the opportunity to share the story of my feather with a group of young people from San Diego, who were also visiting Kake. Their journey to the Alaskan Village had been a reward for their sobriety. The story I shared with them was not just about the search for the feather but about the transformation of the feather, which is symbolic of our own lives. When something that is so dirty and mangled can become beautiful, clean and white, then there is hope. Each one of us gets dirty, whether we get the dirt on ourselves or other people throw it on us. But with some gentle care, and with the help of the Creator, we can make ourselves clean and pure again.

It is my own personal story that allows me to share the white feather story. I am a simple person who has lived a long life. Much of my childhood was spent in foster homes, which is a rough life for any child. I have done things I am not proud of. Over the years, bad things have happened to me, some of which have been my own doing, some of which have not. I have also had many wonderful experiences and I am proud of the wonderful accomplishments in my life. I believe that the Creator has always walked next to me. It is with the Creator's help that I have been able to walk my path and make my own transformation. Through my life experiences I have learned that the greatest lesson is forgiveness. The ability to forgive both oneself and others is truly an opportunity for healing.

Epilogue

Our own Tribal Court has a "sobriety" court, which is called the Healing to Wellness Court, which offers support and resources to young substance abusers. As a Tribal elder, I am one of the program's team members and I participate in reviewing the progress of our participants and in making recommendations for their healing path.

One of our participants was having a difficult time maintaining his sobriety. He showed so much promise; he was someone who could conceivably one day lead our tribe. I could see that he was fighting his demons and they had a strong hold. My heart was heavy with worry for him. I put down tobacco and prayed to the Creator, asking for guidance. The Creator answered me a few days later as I lay awake in bed asking again for insight on how to help this young man.

The kind and loving Creator brings people and events into our lives for a reason, which we will recognize if we pray and listen for his answer. He revealed to me that night why He gave me the white feather.

I said goodbye to the feather a few days later after telling our young man this story and presented him with the feather. I told him that I would pray for him. I also expressed my hopes that the Creator would use the feather to bring strength and encouragement as he walked his path. I also told him that I hoped one day the Creator would make it known to him that it would be time to pass the feather on to another who needs it more than he does.

Just as I had pulled the dirty and mangled feather from the muck and then transformed it into a beautiful clean feather, it is with much prayer that I hope each of our young people who are struggling can also be pulled from their troubled paths to find strength in the Creator to make their own transformation.

On May 21st, 2008 Grandma walked on. A fire was lit in the pouring rain and continued to burn until the end of the fourth day. The Thunders came rolling through as the sun went down.

It was Grandma's wish that the feather be passed on when the moment was right but even more it was Grandma's dream that, with the help of the creator, we would pass on a hope of healing and redemption to other natives. She could see the potential in our community members who struggle with addiction and she could see the potential in that "dirty mangled feather" she picked out of the muck that day. This wasn't because she had some great gift. It was simply because she could relate to the person who struggled and she could relate to that feather. When she was coaxed to throw the feather back, I believe, even at that moment, she saw herself in that feather and she saw her community in that feather. Because of her healing she knew there was hope for that feather, as she knew that everyone in our community was worth saving.

As we learn to walk on the red road we will find brothers or sisters that are stuck in the rubbish of life, dirty and mangled from the tribulations of addiction and abuse. Let us not walk any further without extending a helping hand. Many may have already passed by and, for selfish reasons, have left them behind thinking that someone else would eventually stop to help. It is time for those of us who have been blessed to experience hope again, to fulfill Grandma's last wish. You see, Grandma hoped that when faced with the decision of keeping a feather or throwing it back, her people would rise to the responsibility of providing the gentle care needed for a transformation to take place in their fellow Odawa. We should all remember that in some way we have all had dirt heaped on us and without the help of the Creator and our fellow man we would all still be buried in rubbish.

In the months leading up to her death, my Grandmother and I talked many hours about how we could help make positive changes in our community. Since then I have followed in the footsteps of my Grandmother and joined the Tribal Court Team. I was hired to develop the Adult Drug Court Program which we have since named Waabshki-Miigwan (White Feather). During this experience, the Tribal Court Team and I have kept Grandmother's story close to our hearts and in honor of her we have incorporated her story into our curriculum.

We hope our program will help you find the healing that I, my Grandmother, and many others have found on our journey to wellness. This program was developed for our brothers and sisters that struggle to find hope. Please understand that we are only passing on what was freely given to us by those who took the time to pick us out of the muck on the road to healing and wellness. We believe in our Elder's experiences and teach-

> ings because they have worked for us in extraordinary ways. Our prayer is that our Waabshki-Miigwan Program will help you to find peace. We wish you the best and hope to see you helping on the red road. Chii Miigwetch.
> Sincerely,
> Joe Lucier and the WMDCP Drug Court Team

Banishment

Banishment is often characterized as a traditional remedy because it was used before contact with Europeans. Banishment was the ultimate punishment—because without the help of family and community, a person would likely die. Today, banishment is still used to protect tribal members and the nation as a whole from serious harm. Typically, an offender can only be banished for very serious crimes. Banishment can be imposed from crimes such as child abuse, drug trafficking, or repeat offenses. Some tribes allow for banishment for violations of public trust (such as embezzlement). Banishment can be limited to a certain time period, or can be permanent.

Banishment is a controversial topic in many tribal nations—to "throw away one's family" can raise fundamental questions about identity and accountability. Some tribes completely forbid banishment. Some tribal governments characterize banishment as a punishment of "last resort" (after other efforts have failed). But note that the Sac and Fox Tribe in Iowa imposes banishment as an "automatic" punishment after conviction for murder.

Banishment also known as exclusion or removal. In some cases, it has been imposed upon non-Indians (chapter 8). This section focuses on banishing tribal members for criminal behavior.

Banishment as Authorized by Statute

Sac and Fox in Iowa

Sac & Fox Tr. in Ia Code § 13–8202
Code of the Sac & Fox Tribe of the Mississippi in Iowa
Title 13. Law and Order
Article VIII. Banishment
Chapter 2. Substantive Law
Sec. 13–8202. Grounds for Banishment; Automatic Banishment

*Any person shall be automatically banished, and the Tribal Council shall issue a banishment **decree**, upon conviction for knowingly or intentionally killing, or attempting to kill, a member of the Tribe, employee of the Tribe, or any person on the Settlement. A person may be banished by the Tribe for:*

(a) Upon conviction for recklessly killing or attempting to kill a member of the Tribe, employee of the Tribe, or any person on the Settlement;
(b) Upon conviction of raping or attempting to rape a member of the Tribe, employee of the Tribe, or any person on the Settlement;
(c) Upon conviction of having sexual contact with, or attempting to have sexual contact with, a member of the Tribe or person on the Settlement who is less than 16 years old;
(d) Stealing or unlawfully retaining possession of tribal records or destroying tribal records without authorization;
(e) Upon conviction for manufacturing or distributing illegal drugs;
(f) Desecration of Meskwaki cultural or religious sites or artifacts;
(g) Repeatedly engaging in assault intended to inflict serious bodily harm, or which does inflict serious bodily harm to a member of the Tribe, employee of the Tribe, or any person on the Settlement, or repeatedly engaging in aggravated assault of a member of the Tribe, employee of the Tribe, or any person on the Settlement; or
(h) Conspiring with others to commit any of the acts stated above.

Sac & Fox Tr. in Ia Code § 13–8103
Code of the Sac & Fox Tribe of the Mississippi in Iowa
Title 13. Law and Order
Article VIII. Banishment
Chapter 1. General Provisions (Refs & Annos)
Sec. 13–8103. Preservation of Common Law Authority to Banish

Tribal common law permits a clan or a family to banish one of its own members. This Article does not reduce that common law authority. It does not provide the grounds upon which such banishments may be based, and does not provide procedures applicable to such banishments. The family or clan banishing one of its own members shall have responsibility for enforcing the banishment decree. The family or clan shall provide a written copy of the decree or written description of the decree to the Tribal Council Secretary.

Prairie Band Potawatomi Nation
PBPN Law and Order Code Section 16-4-4
Section 16-4-4. Sentence of Banishment

(A) Banishment Defined. Banishment is the traditional and customary sentence imposed by the Nation for offenders who have been convicted of offenses which violate the basic rights to life, liberty, and property of the community and whose violation is a gross violation of the peace and safety of the Nation requiring the person to be totally expelled for the protection of the community. During the term of banishment, a person who is banished from the territory and association of the Nation shall:
(1) Be considered legally dead and a nonentity with no civil rights to engage in contracts or come before the courts of the Nation for any reason not related to the original conviction, provided, that the banished person retains all rights of a criminal defendant during any prosecution for an offense during the term of banishment, and while attending or going directly to or from any court, or a proceeding involving a criminal action to which the person is a party, including the appeal of the defendant's case.

(2) Be expelled from the jurisdiction of the Nation and not be allowed to return for any reason during the period of banishment except when required to attend court.
(3) Forfeit all positions or offices of honor or profit with the Nation.
(4) Be absolutely ineligible for any service, monies, or benefits provided by the Nation, or due as a result of citizenship in the Nation.
(5) Be absolutely ineligible to vote in any election conducted by or hold any office in the Nation.
(6) Be subject to the claims of creditors, who may apply for an order attaching the banished person's personal property within this jurisdiction and bringing execution thereon to satisfy the debt.

(B) Violation of Banishment.
(1) If the person banished be found within the jurisdiction of the Nation not going directly to, attending, or returning from a court hearing required in the person's case, such act shall be considered criminal contempt in violation of a lawful order of the court and may be punished accordingly.
(2) A person under a **decree** or judgment of banishment found unlawfully within the jurisdiction of the Nation shall, upon conviction, and in addition to any other punishment imposed for disobedience of a lawful order of the court, forfeit to the Nation all personal property brought by the person into the jurisdiction of the Nation or in the person's immediate control therein, whether ownership of said property is in the banished person or another, as civil damages for breach of the peace and safety of the Nation.

(C) Expiration of Banishment Term. Upon expiration of the term of banishment and satisfaction of any other terms imposed by the sentence, the banished person shall be restored to all rights forfeited during the banishment and shall thereafter be treated as if banishment had never been imposed.

Kalispel Tribe of Indians
Law and Order Code of the Kalispel Tribe
Chapter 5. Exclusion of Nonmembers from the Kalispel Indian Reservation
Section 5-2. Procedure for Exclusion (Refs & Annos)
5-2.01. PROCEDURE FOR EXCLUSION

The Kalispel Tribal Business Council has the authority to exclude persons not entitled to reside within the boundaries of the Reservation. The procedure for such exclusion will be as follows:

(1) Where there appears to be reasonable grounds to believe that cause exists to exclude a person or persons from the Kalispel Indian Reservation the Tribal Business Committee shall pass a resolution stating the name(s) of the person or persons to be excluded and the reasons for the exclusion.
(2) The resolution shall direct a Business Committee member to petition the Kalispel Tribal Court for an order of exclusion.
(3) Upon the filing of said petition the Tribal judge shall issue a notice to the person or persons named in the petition to appear before the Court at a designated place and time to show cause why an order excluding him or them from the Reservation should not be issued. Said notice shall state the reason for the proposed exclusion.

(4) Notice shall be served personally upon the person or persons to be excluded in the same manner as personal service is obtained in civil cases.

(5) A hearing will be held not less than three (3) days nor more than ten (10) days after service of the notice.

(6) The hearing may be held in less than three (3) days if the Court has reasonable cause to believe that an emergency exists. In such cases a hearing may be held after 24 hours from the time of service, provided the notice to the person gives the time and date of such hearing.

Tribal Cases Analyzing Banishment Law

Review the following court decisions regarding banishment. Determine whether the outcome is beneficial for the community

Passamaquoddy Tribal Appellate Court
Passamaquoddy v. Francis (2000)
Passamaquoddy Tribe v. Dean Francis, Sr.
2000.NAPA.0000001 (VersusLaw)
The opinion of the court was delivered by: Jill E. Shibles Appellate Judge
[Excerpts]

Decision of Appellate Division

Dean Francis, Sr. appeals from an order of the Passamaquoddy Tribal Court (Irving, J.) denying his motion for correction of sentence. Pursuant to a plea agreement, Francis plead guilty to two counts of assault in violation of 17-A M.R.S.A. § 207, and one count of terrorizing in violation of 17-A M.R.S.A. § 210. The court sentenced the defendant to ninety days in jail, all but three days suspended, and one-year probation. Included among the conditions of probation, was the condition that Francis not have any contact with the Pleasant Point reservation unless given permission by his probation officer. Francis argues on appeal that the court erred in failing to remove that condition of probation because the condition violates the tribal constitutional prohibition against banishment and because the condition is not related to a legitimate **criminological** goal. Finding no error, this Court affirms.

I. Factual Summary

During the latter half of 1998, Francis and his wife, Janice Francis, both of whom are Passamaquoddy tribal members and resided on the Pleasant Point reservation ("Sipayik"), were engaged in a bitter and volatile breakup. A central issue for the couple was the care and custody of their minor children. Virginia Aymond is the Director of Social Services for the Passamaquoddy Tribe: On December 29, 1998, Francis came into Aymond's office area in an agitated state requesting some assistance. He began swearing at another Social Services employee, which drew the attention of Aymond who came to the employee's defense. Francis then verbally accosted Aymond. He stepped toward Aymond during his tirade. Aymond then told Francis that she was going to get the Lieutenant Governor. As he turned to leave, Francis shouldered Aymond. Shortly after the assault on Aymond, Francis went to a tribal office down the hall asking for a food voucher. He entered the office of Richard Doyle, Governor of the Passamaquoddy Tribe at Sipayik, where he was told that there were no funds available. Upon hearing this, Francis began slamming doors and swearing at Governor Doyle. Francis told the governor that he better go home and hide and continued to swear and yell at him. On April 4, 1999, while at their residence, Francis and his wife became involved in an altercation at which time Francis grabbed his wife and hit her in the arm.

On September 10, 1999, pursuant to a plea agreement, Francis pled guilty to two counts of assault, one count of criminal threatening. Additional charges of assault and violation of a protection order were dismissed. At the sentencing hearing, counsel for Francis, Attorney John Mitchell, stated that the recommended sentence and conditions of probation were not objected to and were appropriate. He noted on the record that Francis would be required to have the permission of his probation officer before he could come onto the Pleasant Point reservation. Chief Judge Irving inquired on the record of Francis whether he understood the plea agreement, to which he responded that he did.

Francis subsequently filed a motion for correction of sentence, which came for hearing before the Tribal Court on March 10, 2000. Francis sought to have stricken the special condition of probation that prohibited him from having any contact with the Pleasant Point Reservation on the grounds that it violated the Sipayik Tribal Constitution's prohibition against the banishment of tribal members by the Pleasant Point government. The court denied Francis' motion finding that the sentence was not an illegal one because he was not banished by the government, rather that "[Francis] made a voluntary agreement to reside off reservation, in order to avoid a lengthy jail sentence." The court further ruled that not enough justification had been offered by Francis to set aside the condition. Chief Judge Irving then reminded Francis that he still had access to the reservation for medical treatment and other necessities so long as he received his probation officer's permission. Francis then brought this appeal.

II. Discussion of Law

The Passamaquoddy Tribe has existed as a sovereign Indian nation since time immemorial. In 1979, the Tribe was federally recognized. The Maine Indian Land Claims Settlement Act of 1980 settled the Tribe's claims to territory transferred in violation of law, including the federal Trade and Intercourse Act of 1790. 25 U.S.C. § 1721. The Settlement Act also served to ratify the Maine Implementing

Act, which defines certain aspects of the relationship between the Tribe and the State of Maine. 30 M.R.S.A. §6201 et seq. The Tribe retained exclusive jurisdiction over misdemeanor crimes committed by Native Americans on its reservations.

30 M.R.S.A. § 6209. In exercising its exclusive criminal jurisdiction, the Tribe is deemed to be enforcing tribal law, "provided, however, the definitions of criminal offenses . . . the punishments applicable thereto . . . shall be governed by the laws of the State." As a consequence, the Passamaquoddy Tribal Court has utilized the sentencing statutes of the State of Maine in its criminal dispositions.

Maine law provides that a court may order a split sentence where the convicted person serves an initial period of incarceration followed by a suspended period of imprisonment and probation. 17-A M.R.S.A. § 1152. As a condition of probation, the court may require the convicted person to "refrain from frequenting specified places." Id. at § 1204 (2-A) (F). The court may impose "any other conditions reasonably related to the rehabilitation of the convicted person, or to public safety or security." Id. at § 1204 (2-A) (M). Francis was convicted of multiple offenses of assaultive and threatening behavior occurring at various locations on Sipayik against a variety of tribal members and tribal officials. Aymond expressed her continuing fear of Francis at both the sentencing hearing and at the hearing on the motion to correct the sentence. Given the totality of the circumstances underlying the sentence, the condition of not contacting the Pleasant Point reservation is clearly related to the criminological goal of protecting the safety of the tribal community.

Francis argues that the limitation on his presence on Sipayik is a violation of the Sipayik Constitution. In 1993, the Sipayik members of the Passamaquoddy Tribe adopted a Constitution to govern the Pleasant Point Reservation and its tribal government. The Constitution left in place any ordinance previously adopted by the Joint Tribal Council of the Passamaquoddy Tribe or by the Pleasant Point Governor and Council in effect at the time of its adoption, "except to the extent that it may be inconsistent with the rights and privileges secured by this Constitution." Article IX, Section 3. Article IV, Section 2 of the Constitution provides that, "Notwithstanding any provision of this Constitution, the government of the Pleasant Point Reservation shall have no power of banishment over tribal members." The term "banishment" is not defined.

In effect at the time of the adoption of the Sipayik Constitution were the sentencing and probation provisions mentioned above. Also in effect were tribal resolutions adopting, as Passamaquoddy tribal law, the Protection from Abuse and Protection from Harassment provisions of Maine law. (Joint Council Resolutions dated May 28, 1981 and January 3, 1983.) See 19-A M.R.S.A. § 4011(1) (violation of a protective order of the Passamaquoddy Tribal Court is a Class D crime under Maine law). The Tribal Court may grant relief to a victim of abuse or harassment in the form of an order "directing the defendant to refrain from going upon the premises of the plaintiff's residence . . . [and/or] from repeatedly and without reasonable cause . . . being at or in the vicinity of the plaintiff's home, school, business or place of employment." 19-A M.R.S.A. § 4007 (I) (B), (C) (2); 5 M.R.S.A. § 4655 (I) (B), (C-I) (2). Given the small area of Sipayik, where the victim is a resident tribal member employed on the reservation such an order could effectively restrict the abuser from most, if not all, areas of Sipayik. If this Court were to find that the geographical restriction placed on Francis constituted the act of banishment, then similar restrictions ordered in the context of protection from abuse and harassment cases may also be construed to be illegal banishments. The Court should be reluctant to summarily invalidate tribal ordinances. Thus, the Court looks for ways in which to interpret the Sipayik Constitution in such a way as to avoid violence to existing tribal laws.

Francis did not present any legislative history that would explain what the Sipayik membership meant by the term banishment. Given the close communal and interdependent relationships of the Wabanaki tribes, it has been said that historically the imposition of banishment by a tribal community was the equivalent of a death sentence. No longer would the tribal member receive the protection and benefits of being part of a tribal community. Rather the banished person would be forced to make their way alone, isolated and excluded from his or her people. A Passamaquoddy man once explained the continuing vital importance of the tribal community as follows, "With us the sense of community goes right down to an extended family. What you do is governed by your neighbors. Issues are common, you can't isolate your neighbor. So, when we achieve or when we succeed, we succeed as a community. When we get sick, we get sick as a community . . . we still seem to function as a unit." "A Passamaquoddy Man From Indian Township," The Wabanakis of Maine and the Maritimes, p. C-65.

The question becomes then, does simply requiring a tribal member to receive permission to step onto the reservation rise to the level of banishment?

A review of local tribal practices and laws reveals that there is a distinction made between "banishment" and "exclusion" of persons. The Mashantucket Pequot Tribal Constitution grants to its Elders Council the authority to "hear and determine any matter concerning the banishment or exclusion of any person from the Mashantucket Western (Pequot) Reservation and tribal lands as necessary to preserve and protect the safety and well-being of the Tribe and the Tribal Community, and the removal of any Tribal benefits and membership privileges. . . ." Mashantucket Pequot Constitution, Article XII, Section I(d). The Mashantucket Pequot "Elders Council Guidelines Governing Banishment, Exclusion and Suspension or Termination of Tribal Benefits and Privileges" further explains that, "[b]anishment orders shall apply to tribal members and exclusion orders shall apply to non-tribal members. A tribal member may be banished or have his or her tribal benefits or privileges suspended or terminated and any non-tribal member may be excluded for conduct that occurs either on or off the Mashantucket Pequot reservation." Sections 1.1 and 1.4. From these provisions, it may be concluded that banishment includes not only exclusion from tribal lands, but also the loss of tribal benefits.

There are many privileges that arise from being [a] Passamaquoddy tribal member, apart from the right to reside on the reservation. "Some of these rights include: the right to vote in tribal elections, to vote in tribal referendums, to attend and participate in tribal meetings, to share in any per capita distributions, to receive benefits, such as health care and educational assistance, through tribal programs." It is uncontested that Francis retains many of these privileges.

In the case Poodry v. Tonawanda Band of Seneca Indians, 85 F.3d 874 (2d Cir. 1996), members of the Tonawanda Band of Seneca Indians of New York petitioned the federal district court for writs of habeas corpus under the Indian Civil Rights Act [ICRA] of 1968, 25 U.S.C. § 1301 and sought to challenge the legality of orders issued by members of the Seneca tribal council purporting to banish them from the tribe and its reservation. The order of banishment at issue in Poodry read in part as follows:

It is with a great deal of sorrow that we inform you that you are now banished from the territories of the Tonawanda Band of Seneca Nation. You are to leave now and never return. . . . According to the customs and usage of the Tonawanda Band of the Seneca Nation and the HAUDENOSAUNEE, your name is removed from the Tribal rolls, your Indian name is taken away, and your lands will become the responsibility of the Council of Chiefs. You are now stripped of your Indian citizenship and permanently lose any and all rights afforded our members. Id. at 878.

Clearly, the permission requirement contained in the Tribal Court's conditions of probation does not come anywhere close to severity and breadth of the banishment order at issue in Poodry. The burden was on Francis to demonstrate that the condition of probation requiring him to receive permission from the probation officer before coming onto the Pleasant Point constituted a "banishment," the Court finds that he failed to meet his burden.

Even if the condition of probation did constitute banishment, Francis voluntarily and knowingly accepted the condition as a means of avoiding prolonged incarceration for his multiple convictions. In the case Ex Parte Snyder, 81 Okla. Cr. 34, 159 P.2d 752 (1945), a state constitutional challenge was brought to a condition of parole that required the petitioner to, "immediately upon his release [from prison], leave the said State of Oklahoma; and shall remain out of said state for a period of twenty years. . . ." It was argued that the condition violated the provision of Section 29, Article 2 of the Oklahoma Constitution, which provides: "No person shall be transported out of the State for any offense committed within the State. . . ." The Snyder court held that the provision applied to the involuntary transportation of a person out of the state, as punishment for crime. It further found that, "In the instant case, there was no involuntary transportation of the petitioner out of the state. The parole, with all of the conditions set forth therein, was a matter which the petitioner could accept or reject. He gave his written acceptance and, pursuant to its terms, voluntarily left the state." Id. at 39.

The Tribal Court properly found that the Constitution of the Sipayik Members of the Passamaquoddy Tribe prohibits the tribal government, including the Tribal Court, from involuntarily banishing its members. Francis was advised by competent legal counsel at the time of sentencing and voluntarily agreed to reside off the Pleasant Point reservation in exchange for freedom from jail. Just as in Snyder, the condition of probation was a matter that Francis could accept or reject. This Court holds that the voluntary agreement of a criminal defendant to a condition of probation not to have contact with the Pleasant Point reservation does not constitute a banishment. The condition was rationally related to the protection of the tribal community, its members, employees and governmental officials. The trial court did not abuse its discretion in declining to vacate the condition.

The entry is: Judgment affirmed.

Non-Removable Mille Lacs Band of Ojibwe Indians Court of Appeals
Mille Lacs Band of Ojibwe Indians vs. Darrick DeWayne Williams Jr. (2006)
No. 11-APP 06

Darrick Williams petitioned this Court for interlocutory review of the August 17, 2011 order of the Court of Central Jurisdiction, the Honorable Richard Osburn presiding, finding the Band's exclusion law constitutional under the Band and MCT Constitution and valid under the Indian Civil Rights Act.

The facts in this case have not yet been fleshed out because Williams opted to assert a "facial" challenge to the Band's Exclusion and Removal ordinance, codified at Chapter 4 of the Mille Lacs Band Code. A "facial" challenge is when a party seeks to vindicate not only his own rights, but those of others who may also be adversely impacted by the statute in question.

This Court is somewhat confused why Williams wishes to assert a facial challenge to the removal ordinance rather than an "as applied" challenge. At oral argument his attorney noted that he is a Band member living on the Mille Lacs reservation. He has a small child whom lives with him and he has expressed a desire to learn and practice the cultural and spiritual ways of the Anishinabe. He appears to have substantial rights that would be impaired by the application of the removal ordinance to him. This Court notes that the lower court held that he could not present a facial challenge to the removal ordinance because he has not asserted first amendment rights that would be impaired or impacted by his removal from the Mille Lacs reservation. This Court does not necessarily agree with this assessment.

Of course the first amendment to the United States Constitution has no applicability in this Court or the lower court because the United States Constitution in no way restrains the exercise of sovereign tribal powers, but it would be appropriate for this Court to analyze this facial challenge by examining whether the Band's Exclusion and Removal ordinance abridges the rights preserved Band members and others under the provision of the Indian Civil Rights Act most comparable to the First amendment to the United States Constitution. That provision is 25 U.S.C. §1302 which provides in relevant part:

§ 1302. Constitutional rights

(a) In general. No Indian tribe in exercising powers of self-government shall—

(1) make or enforce any law prohibiting the free exercise of religion, or abridging the freedom of speech, or of the press, or the right of the people peaceably to assemble and to petition for a redress of grievances.

This Court also notes that this same right is preserved Band members in the Band's Civil Rights Code at Title I, Section I and the language there mirrors the language in the Indian Civil Rights Act.

The question thus becomes whether the removal of a Band member or other person from the Mille Lacs Indian reservation, pursuant to the Band's Exclusion and Removal Ordinance, may potentially impair the exercise of this right. The answer to that question appears obvious to this Court—it could certainly potentially impair a Band member's rights to participate in the exercise of his "religion" if he was desirous of learning the traditional ways of the Anishinabe and his access to the **patrimony** necessary for practicing these ways was defeated by his inability to come on to the reservation. The Court also believes that the right of a person to live with his child and raise his child is that type of intimate relationship that many Courts have recognized as being within that core group of persons whom a person has a first amendment right to live with and associate with. See *Moore v. City of East Cleveland*, 431 U.S. 434 (1976).

The Court therefore concludes that the Band's removal ordinance potentially impacts fundamental rights similar to those protected by the First amendment to the United States Constitution and is therefore subject to a facial challenge. That said the Court does not conclude that the Band is denied the right to enact and enforce an Exclusion and Removal ordinance merely because it may impair a fundamental right to practice one's religion or raise one's child. Every right that the Band must extend to its members or non-members is subject to forfeiture by any person who fails to comport himself with the standards expected of them while interacting with the Band and its members.

The federal courts have recognized the inherent rights of Indian tribes to exclude non-members from their reservations.

To the extent, therefore, that Williams may have standing to assert a facial challenge to the exclusion of non-members the Band's ordinance is clearly valid. It is the fact that the Band ordinance also applies to its own members that causes some concern. There have been few federal court decisions discussing the inherent rights of Indian tribes to banish their own members. Several courts that have taken jurisdiction over such challenges in habeas corpus actions have held that banishment is a type of "detention" that authorizes a person to challenge his "banishment" in federal court under the provisions of 25 U.S.C. §1303, permitting federal court review of tribal court actions under the Indian Civil Rights Act. The first court to rule such was the United States Court of Appeals for the Second Circuit in *Poodry v. Tonawanda Band of Seneca Indians*, 85 F.3d 874 (2d Cir. 1996) in which the federal court of appeals reversed a lower court's order dismissing a habeas corpus challenge to a banishment of certain Seneca Indians.

The Court did not address whether a Tribe could banish its own members consistent with the Indian Civil Rights Act, but only that federal courts could review such banishments. In one unreported federal court decision, *Sweet v. Hinzman*, 2009 U.S. Dist. LEXIS 36716 (W.D. Wash. 2008) a federal court held that the banishment and disenrollment of certain tribal members violated the Indian Civil Rights Act. However, that case seems to turn on procedural due process violations and not on the ground that the Tribe involved therein had no right to banish its own members. The fact that the Court ruled that banishment could only be accomplished when due process is afforded, however, is relevant to the analysis this Court undertakes later in this decision relevant to the particular notice provisions of the banishment ordinance being reviewed herein. Nothing in the Minnesota Chippewa Tribe's Constitution expressly grants to the respective Bands the right to banish its members. Conversely, nothing in the MCT Constitution prohibits the Bands from banishing its own members. Judge Osburn found that banishment is an inherent right of Indian tribes and this Court can certainly agree with that concept. Banishment is a traditional form of punishment many Indian tribes have resurrected in an attempt to deal with a burgeoning crime problem in their communities. In certain circumstances, especially vis a vis non-members, Indian tribes have been preserved in treaties the right to remove certain persons from their reservations, oftentimes with the promised assistance of the United States government. These treaty provisions, oftentimes referred to as "bad man" clauses, implicitly permit Indian tribes to remove those nonmembers who violate tribal norms or values and are also require the Tribes to turn over to the United States those tribal members who violate the rights of non-members in the Community. Those members who were turned over to the United States were essentially "banished" from the tribal communities. Neither party has pointed the Court to any provision of the 1855 Treaty between the United States and the Band that addresses "banishment"—although Article 9 of that Treaty does bind Band members to certain lawful conduct on the reservation—but merely because the right is not expressly preserved by treaty does not mean that the right did not exist prior to the treaty being executed.

The Court therefore concludes that the Mille Lacs Band has the inherent right to banish members and non-members from its lands, provided it does so in accordance with the Indian Civil Rights Act and the Minnesota Chippewa Tribal Constitution. The question thus becomes whether the ordinance enacted by the Band and which it being utilized as the basis for the requested banishment of Williams passes ICRA and constitutional muster. This Court concludes that it does not.

This Court acknowledges that it is the responsibility of this Court and the lower court to make every attempt to reconcile Band law with the ICRA and the MCT Constitution and to interpret Band law so as to avoid constitutional problems. Judge Osburn attempted to do just that when he held that the Band Solicitor could proceed with banishment efforts against Mr. Williams under the current ordinance. Judge Osburn also held that the ordinance should not be assessed under the due process rules Courts utilize to assess whether a "criminal" statute is void for vagueness grounds because banishment is a civil proceeding. Although that may be correct under procedural rules it is clear under federal court rulings that banishments are being considered as quasi-criminal proceedings subject to federal court review under 25 U.S.C. 1303. Banishment penalties can be just as severe as criminal penalties, especially since the penalty apparently for violating a banishment order would be incarceration.

Also, because this Court has found that banishment may also potentially deny free expression of religious rights under the ICRA this Court finds that it is appropriate to assess the Band's ordinance using the same level of judicial scrutiny that Courts pay to criminal statutes.

Williams argues that the Band's ordinance should be struck down because it is so vague that it does not apprise Band members and others of what conduct may lead to banishment and also fails to give the fact-finder, the Tribal Court, any standards for assessing whether banishment is the appropriate penalty. This is oftentimes referred to as the void for vagueness doctrine, which permits Courts to strike down laws that relate to speech or conduct that the government attempts to punish. Consistent with that approach, the United States Supreme Court has steadfastly applied the void-for-vagueness doctrine only to statutes or regulations that purport to define the lawfulness of conduct or speech.

Ordinances that may have a chilling effect on the exercise of free speech or religious freedom rights, or those that attempt to punish conduct, must clearly define that conduct which may result in penalties being imposed, or rights denied, in order to satisfy due process of law. Otherwise persons are not put on notice of what behavior may result in the denial of their freedoms or rights. In addition, if no standards are laid out in the law persons may be subjected to arbitrary enforcement of the law based upon the personal predilections of each Judge that may hear a case. One Judge may feel, for example, that drug use is having such a deleterious impact on the tribal community that such use justifies banishment, while another may feel that such a remedy is an overreach for drug activity. It is therefore up to the Band Assembly to define for the Tribal Court when banishment would be appropriate to avoid conflicting value judgments.

This doctrine is referred to as the "overbreadth" or void for vagueness doctrine. Although they are distinct concepts, overbreadth and vagueness challenges are closely related in the principles they vindicate, and courts often discuss them together.

The void-for-vagueness doctrine is rooted in the basic guarantees of due process, a concept incorporated both into the Indian Civil Rights Act and the underlying premise of fairness set out in the Mille Lacs Band Code. This Court notes that Band law directs this Court and the lower court to:

> Section I. Purpose. The Purpose of this Act is to promote the general welfare, preserve and maintain justice and to protect the rights of all persons under the jurisdiction of the Non-Removable Mille Lacs Band of Chippewa Indians consistent with a judicial philosophy of a search for truth and justice. MLBSA Title V, Section I

The void for vagueness doctrine requires that a statute punishing conduct define the conduct with sufficient definiteness that ordinary people can understand what conduct is prohibited and in a manner that does not encourage arbitrary and discriminatory enforcement. . . . Although the doctrine focuses both on actual notice to citizens and arbitrary enforcement the United States Supreme Court [has] recognized . . . that the more important aspect of vagueness doctrine is not actual notice, but the other principal element of the doctrine—the requirement that a legislature establish minimal guidelines to govern judicial officers attempting to enforce them.

The void-for-vagueness doctrine is premised on the notion that [v]ague laws offend several important values. First, because we assume that a person is free to steer between lawful and unlawful conduct, we insist that laws give the person of ordinary intelligence a reasonable opportunity to know what is prohibited, so that he may act accordingly. Vague laws may trap the innocent by not providing fair warning. Second, if arbitrary and discriminatory enforcement is to be prevented, laws must provide explicit standards for those who apply them. A vague law impermissibly delegates basic policy matters to policemen, judges, and juries for resolution on an ad hoc and subjective basis, with the attendant dangers of arbitrary and discriminatory application.

With those concepts in mind this Court must examine the Band's Exclusion and Removal Ordinance to determine if it establishes minimal guidelines to govern judicial officers attempting to enforce them. In the findings and determinations section of the Ordinance the Band Assembly states that the reason for the law is to "provide a means to exclude or remove such persons from said lands in the event that they violate Band law or do other acts harmful to the Band, its members or other residents...." This is certainly laudable and within the authority of the Band to enact. It is somewhat vague, however, for the judiciary to enforce.

The real gist of the Ordinance is Section 3004, laying out the grounds for exclusion and removal. That section lays out 14 grounds for potential exclusion and removal with one ground specified even more with five descriptive subtitles (Section 3004(e)). Ground one allows this Court to exclude and remove any person who commits a crime as defined under Band law or federal law. Ground two allows this Court to exclude and remove any person who causes physical loss or damage to a Band member, his property, or to a non-Band member or his property. The remaining grounds are more specific as they describe particular conduct which would clearly apprise a Band member or non-member of conduct that may subject them to removal.

Williams argued at hearing that Section 3004(1) is so broad that it could permit a person to file a removal petition against a person who, for example, litters on the reservation or commits a speeding infraction. Section 3004(2) would allow a person to file a removal complaint against someone, for example, who accidentally backs into a person's vehicle at the Casino.

The Ordinance is extremely broad also with regard to who has standing to bring a removal petition. Section 3005 allows any "member, officer, agent or employee of the Band" to bring a complaint and the only requirement for its prosecution is that its execution be attested to by a Judge, Clerk or law enforcement officer. There is no requirement that the petition be screened by the Solicitor's office or law enforcement and it appears that once filed the matter is prosecuted by the individual filing it. In addition the Ordinance does not permit the Court to review it and summarily deny it if the Court were to find that it is frivolous because Section 3006 states that upon receipt of the exclusion petition the Court "shall" cause notice to be served upon the person who the petition seeks to exclude. The hearing must also be held "no less than three days after the time of the service or mailing."

Potentially this ordinance permits Band employees who feel aggrieved by the actions of other employees to take their dispute to Court and seek removal instead of working through the personnel policies and procedures of the Band and its economic enterprises. Nothing in the Removal ordinance would permit the lower court to merely dismiss the removal petition based on that ground as all petitions must be heard by the Court.

This Court does not point out these concerns out of disrespect to the Band Assembly or the Solicitor's office, which ultimately is charged with defending the laws of the Band. This Court is also appreciative of the efforts of the Court of Central Jurisdiction to craft the ordinance in a way to preserve its constitutionality. This Court also gave serious consideration to the Solicitor's request at oral argument—that this Court and the lower Court essentially "rewrite" the Ordinance in a way that it felt would survive Indian Civil Rights Act scrutiny—but ultimately this Court feels that rewriting the law so as to render the ordinance enforceable would subject this Court to criticism by Band members and the Band Assembly. This Court has been criticized in the past for interfering into the prerogative of the Band Assembly, see *Benjamin v. Weyaus*, 08-APP- 07 (Solicitor's Office—not the present Solicitor however—advises Court during oral argument on case involving Court's stay of removal proceedings against Melanie Benjamin that Band Assembly had created the Court and could dissolve it if the Court interfered in the removal efforts of Benjamin), and is mindful that the separation of powers between this Court and the Band Assembly goes both ways. The Bands' laws clearly stipulate that there is a separation of powers and the law-making branch is the Band Assembly:

> Section 1. Purpose. The purpose of this act is to promote the general welfare of the Non-Removable Mille Lacs Bands of Chippewa Indians and its members by establishing duties, purposes and procedures for the conduct of domestic and external affairs of the Band by a form of government based upon the principle of division of powers. This statute is enacted by the authority vested in the Mille Lacs Reservation Business Committee under Article VI, Section 1 of the Constitution of the Minnesota Chippewa Tribe. MLBSA Title 2

In order for the present Ordinance to clearly give direction to this Court on when a person, especially a Band member, should be excluded from the lands under the Band's jurisdiction the law should define which crimes would warrant removal and exclusion. For example, the Fort McDowell Tribal Code, which permits the exclusion of nonmembers only, allows exclusion for the following crimes:

> Commission of criminal offenses classified as a felony in the State of Arizona or a misdemeanor involving injury or damages or threats to persons or property in violation of Federal, State or Tribal law, regardless of whether such offense has been expunged or otherwise forgiven. Section 15.2(B)

The Ordinance before this Court would permit the exclusion of Band members from the reservation for far less than that required to exclude a non-member from the Fort McDowell reservation. It appears to the Court that the Mille Lacs Band Ordinance permitting removal and exclusion was based upon the removal ordinances of other Tribes that addressed the removal of non-members only, whereas the Band here has expanded those who can be excluded to Band members. There has to be a heightened standard for removal of Band members from their home because they possess unique interests in remaining on the Mille Lacs reservation that non-members may not possess. To allow Band members to be excluded from the reservation on the same grounds as non-members strikes this Court as potentially violative of the rights of Band members who have familial and spiritual interests on the reservation that non-members may not possess.

The few Tribes that do permit exclusion of their own members have a much heightened standard for removal than that contained in the Band's exclusion ordinance. For example the Fort Peck Tribal Code permits the exclusion of all persons for the following reasons:

> Chapter 7. Exclusion from the Fort Peck Reservation
> Sec. 701. Grounds for Exclusion.
> Any person may be excluded from the Reservation for:
>
> > (a) Conduct which substantially threatens the life, the physical health or the safety of an Indian or Indians residing on the Reservation.
> > (b) Conviction in Tribal Court of at least three felonies or Class A Misdemeanors which involve acts of violence against persons under the laws of the Tribes.

In addition most Tribal Exclusion Codes require the screening of a complaint by some agency of the Tribe before the matter can be filed in the Court. Again the Fort Peck Tribal Code is instructive:

> Sec. 702. Initiation of Exclusion Proceedings.
>
> > (a) Exclusion proceedings shall be initiated by written charges of specific conduct justifying exclusion made by the Tribal Civil Prosecutor or a member of the Tribal Executive Board. Such charges shall also include the text of a proposed exclusion order. The charges and order must then be adopted by a majority vote of the Tribal Executive Board at a meeting at which a quorum is present.

This Court points out these ordinances not because the Court believes that the Band should merely mimic what other Tribes have done, but to point out that most Indian Tribes that have implemented the sovereign right of exclusion have treated their members differently than non-members. The Band's Ordinance does not do that.

In conclusion this Court finds that because the present Exclusion Ordinance gives too much discretion to the lower court to decide what crimes or other conduct warrants exclusion, that because the exclusion ordinance does not distinguish between Band members and non-members, and because the Ordinance does not provide for any screening of exclusion petitions by any entity of the Executive branch of government, that the current Ordinance violates the due process provision of the Indian Civil Rights Act. This Court will remand this matter back to the lower court to stay the removal petition against Mr. Williams until such time as a revised Exclusion Ordinance is enacted by the Band Assembly that addresses the issues raised in this case.

Chief Justice Rayna J. Churchill-Mattinas

Conclusion

Indigenous justice may be defined differently based upon the various laws and customs of each Indian nation. The preceding examples are a small sample of the various forms of indigenous justice practices that are being employed to replace Western forms of criminal justice that focuses on punishment. By focusing on a distributive justice that includes everyone affected, working to heal and restore relationships, and using a horizontal system that is inclusive, these systems work better to solve problems, as opposed to punishing a person for committing a crime.

Questions

1. For each of the preceding examples of indigenous or restorative justice practices, determine whether they will meet Barsh's measures of "just-ness."
2. Explain how tribal culture, language, and practices can be incorporated in a contemporary tribal justice system.
3. What are the advantages and disadvantages of imposing banishment as a punishment?

In Your Community

1. What forms of indigenous or restorative justice are used by your nation to address crime?
2. Does your Nation have banishment laws? Do they impose permanent banishment or temporary banishment?

Terms Used in Chapter 27

Ancillary: Something that functions in a supplementary or supporting role.
Criminological: Related to crimes or the criminal justice system.
Decree: an official order issued by a legal authority.
Distributive justice: justice that is concerned with the apportionment of privileges, duties, and goods in consonance with the merits of the individual and in the best interest of society.
Holistic: Emphasizing the importance of the whole and the interdependence of its parts.
Patrimony: Items inherited from one's father.

Notes

1. Memorandum to the Senate Committee on Indian Affairs on the proposed Indian Country Crime Bill, 2–3 (April 21, 2008). http://www.navajocourts.org/intertribal workgroup/WorkgrpMemo1.pdf.

2. The Honorable Robert Yazzie, *"Life Comes From It": Navajo Justice Concepts*, 24 NEW MEXICO LAW REVIEW 178.
3. Ibid., 178–80.
4. Ibid., 180.
5. Ibid.
6. Ibid., 185.
7. Interview, David Raasch, Judge Stockbridge-Munsee Tribal Court, Bowler, Wisconsin, 2 *Journal of Court Innovation* 381, 389 (2009)
8. Russel L. Barsh, "Evaluating the Quality of Justice," in *Justice as Healing, Indigenous Ways, Writings on Community Peacemaking and Restorative Justice from the Native Law Centre*, ed. Wanda D. McCaslin, 167 (Living Justice Press 2005)
9. Ibid., 168.
10. Ibid., 168–9.
11. All quotes are from the *Keex' Kwaan Judicial Peacekeeping Code: Organized Village of Kake*. The code can be found at http://www.kakefirstnation.org/OVKTribalCourts/judical_peacemaking_code.pdf.
12. "Healing to Wellness Courts: A Preliminary Overview of Tribal Drug Courts," 1 (1999), http://www.wellnesscourts.org/files/Pub_THWC%20-%20Overview1999.pdf.
13. Joseph Thomas Flies-Away and Carrie E. Garrow, "Healing to Wellness Courts: Therapeutic Jurisprudence," 2013 *Mich. St. L. Rev.* 403, 412–13.
14. Waabshki-Miigwan Policy Book, 2.
15. http://www.ltbbodawa-nsn.gov/Departments/DrugCourt/Curriculum%20Summary.html.
16. http://www.ltbbodawa-nsn.gov/Departments/DrugCourt/Curriculum%20Summary.html.
17. http://www.ltbbodawa-nsn.gov/Departments/DrugCourt/DCIndex.html.

Suggested Further Reading

Ronald Eagleye Johnny, "The Duckwater Shoshone Drug Court, 1997–2000," 26 *American Indian Law Review* 261 (2001).

Patrice Kunesh, "Banishment as Cultural Justice in Contemporary Tribal Justice Systems," 37 *New Mexico Law Review* 85 (2007).

Wanda D. McCasin, *Justice as Healing, Indigenous Ways* (Living Justice Press, 2005).

Marianne O. Nielsen and James W. Zion, *Navajo Nation Peacemaking: Living Traditional Justice* (University of Arizona Press, 2005).

Kay Pranis, Barry Stuart, and Mark Wedge, *Peacemaking Circles from Crime to Community* (Living Justice Press, 2003).

Glossary of Terms

A

Abuse of discretion: A failure to use sound, reasonable judgment when a person is under a legal duty to do so.

Affidavit: A written statement, usually about the truth of a set of facts, sworn to before a person who is officially permitted by law to administer an oath.

Alibi: Evidence that a defendant was in a different place during the commission of a crime.

Allotments: Shares or portions; distribution of land.

Ambiguous: Having more the one reasonable interpretation.

Amicus curiae: Latin term meaning "friend of the Court"; a person who is allowed to appear in a lawsuit even though the person is not a party to the lawsuit.

Anachronistic: Chronologically misplaced.

Ancillary: Something that functions in a supplementary or supporting role.

Apprehension: Fear.

Arbitrarily and capriciously: According to a person's whims or desires; not following general principles or rules.

Articulable: Capable of being articulated; expressed easily.

Articulable Suspicion: The officer can articulate (explain) what raised suspicion about a person's behavior.

Assimilation: Made similar; caused to resemble. A tribal government is "assimilated" if it looks and operates exactly like the Anglo-American government.

Atonement: Amends or reparation made for an injury or wrong.

Attendant circumstances: Facts surrounding an event.

Attenuate: To lessen the amount, force, or value, or to reduce the severity.

B

Bail: The temporary release of a prisoner in exchange for security given for the due appearance of the prisoner.

Beyond a reasonable doubt: The level of proof required to convict a person of a crime.

Bootlegger: Someone who makes or sells illegal liquor.

Burden: The requirement that to win a point you must show that the weight of the evidence is on your side.

Burden of persuasion: The requirement of obligation of a party to convince the judge or jury.

Burden of production: The requirement of obligation of a party to present the evidence.

Buttress: Make stronger or defensible.

C

Capital Crime: A crime punishable by death.

Case of first impression: A new case; a case that presents an entirely new issue or problem to the court.

Circumstantial: Consisting in, or pertaining to, circumstances or particular incidents.

Civil law: The norms and rules that are supposed to be followed in the legal relationships that individual citizens or corporations have with each other or the government.

Coercion: Compulsion or force; making a person act against free will.

Cognizable: Capable of being known.

Complaint: A formal document charging a person with a crime.

Complicity: Fact of being an accomplice.

Compulsory process: Official action to force a person to appear in court as a witness.

Concurrent jurisdiction: Two or more governments can exercise power or jurisdiction over an issue.

Condonation: The implied forgiveness of an offense by ignoring it.

Conscious: Possessing the faculty of knowing one's own thoughts or mental operations.

Consecutively: Following one after the other without interruption.

Consummating: Bringing to completion or fruition.

Contempt: An act that obstructs a court's work or lessens the dignity of the court.

Contravene: Go against the laws or rules.

Controverted: Disputed, denied, or opposed.

Corroborate: Add to the likely truth or importance of a fact; give additional facts or evidence to strengthen a fact or assertion.
Corroborative: Strengthening or supporting with other evidence; making more certain.
Criminal law: The norms or rules that, when violated, are considered to be an offense against the community as a whole rather than against an individual party.
Criminological: Related to crimes or the criminal justice system.
Cross-deputization: An agreement that facilitates law enforcement to cross borders in criminal cases.
Culpability: Deserving blame or punishment for violating the law.
Culminate: To come to completion; end.
Custody: A suspect is "in custody" for purpose of determining necessity of Miranda warnings if police, by word or by conduct, have expressed to the suspect that he is not free to leave.

D

Decorum: Appropriate behavior or conduct.
Decree: an official order issued by a legal authority
Deferred: Postponed or delayed.
Deposition: The process of taking a witness's sworn, out-of-court testimony.
Depredation: A destructive action.
Derogation: A partial repeal or abolishment of law by a later law
Deterrence: The theory that punishment of an individual will discourage others from doing wrong.
Deviation: Departure from established procedure or philosophy.
Dichotomy: A division or the process of dividing into two mutually exclusive or contradictory groups.
Dicta: Latin term meaning "digression" or discussion of a side/unrelated issue.
Dispositive: Relating to or having an effect on disposition or settlement, especially of a legal case or will.
Distributive justice: justice that is concerned with the apportionment of privileges, duties, and goods in consonance with the merits of the individual and in the best interest of society.
Docket: A list of the legal cases that will be heard in court.
Dominion: Legal ownership plus full actual control.
Double jeopardy: Putting a person on trial more than once for the same crime.
Due Process: Refers to the legal right to have notice, a chance to present his/her side in a legal dispute, and to have a fair hearing.
Duress: Unlawful pressure on a person to do what he or she would not otherwise do.

E

Egregious: Conspicuously bad or offensive.

Elements: Basic parts. Elements of a crime are the basic parts that are required in order to convict someone of a crime.

Enumerated: Mentioned specifically; listed one by one.

Erroneous: Involving error or deviating from the law.

Exclusionary rule: Statements or evidence obtained in violation of a person's civil rights are not admissible in criminal prosecutions against the defendant as proof of the defendant's guilt.

Exclusive jurisdiction: Only one government can exercise power or jurisdiction over an issue.

Execution: Carrying out a course of action to its completion.

Exhausted (in reference to tribal remedies): Tribal courts are given full opportunity to make the initial determination of all claims raised in the case.

Exigent circumstances: Situations that demand unusual or immediate action.

Exonerated: Cleared of a crime or other wrongdoing.

Ex post facto: After the fact.

Extradition: To give up (an alleged fugitive or criminal) to another state or nation at its request.

F

Fee land: Land that is owned free and clear without any trust or restrictions.

Forfeiture: Losing the right to do something or own something because of an offense.

Frisk: A superficial running of hands over a person's body to do a quick search, usually for weapons.

Full Faith and Credit: Recognition and enforcement of the public acts, records, and judicial proceedings of other sovereigns.

G

Gauntlet: A form of punishment in which people armed with sticks or other weapons arrange themselves in two lines facing each other and beat a person forced to run between them.

Gerontocracy: Government based on rule by elders.

H

Habeas corpus: A judicial order normally given to a jail or detention facility to bring a person to court so a decision regarding whether the imprisonment is legal can be made.

Hearsay: Legal term for an out of court statement, made in court, to prove the truth of the matter asserted. Hearsay is generally inadmissible in a trial.
Holistic: Emphasizing the importance of the whole and the interdependence of its parts.
Homicide: The killing of a person.
Hybridization: A combination of two dissimilar systems to form a new system that is a mixture of the originals.

I
Imminent: Just about to happen; threatening.
Impeach: To show that a witness is being untruthful.
Implicit: Implied or understood although not directly expressed.
Implied Consent: A presumption or inference, based on signs, actions, facts, or inaction or silence, that consent has been given.
Inadvertent: Without intention; especially, resulting from heedless action.
Inapposite: Not pertinent; unsuitable.
Incapacitation: The theory that punishment will prevent a particular criminal from continuing the criminal behavior, at least during the period of the punishment.
Incommunicado: A condition in which a person accused of a crime does not have the right to communicate with anyone other than the custodian.
Indicia: Latin term meaning indications; pointers; signs.
Information: A formal accusation of a crime made by a prosecuting attorney.
Inherent: A natural part of; a permanent feature of.
In rem: Latin term meaning "thing." Describes a lawsuit brought to enforce rights in a thing.
Insanity: A legal word regarding a person's mental capacity—sometimes invokes mental illness. It has different meanings in different court systems.
Intent: The resolve or purpose to use a particular means to reach a particular result.
Interlocutory: A judicial opinion given during an intermediate stage of a case.
Interrogation: The questioning by police of a person suspected of a crime.
Inventory: A detailed list of articles of property.
Irreparable: Impossible to repair, rectify, or amend.

J
Junta: A closely knit group united for a common purpose and usually meeting secretly.

M
Majority Rule: In an appellate court case, the decision of the majority of the justices becomes law.

Maxim: A saying that is widely accepted.
Menace: To threaten, cause danger.
Merits: The substance or real issues of a lawsuit, as opposed to the form or legal technicalities it involves.
Misdemeanor: A criminal offense less serious than a felony that is usually punishable by a fine or less than a year in jail.
Motion to suppress evidence: Usually brought by the defendant in a criminal case, the motion asks the judge to disallow certain evidence that was obtained illegally.

N
Negate: To make ineffective or invalid; nullify.
Negligent: Failing to exercise a reasonable amount of care in a situation.
Nonmember Indians: Indians who are citizens of a different tribe.
Notarization: Certification of or attestation to.

O
Overt: Out in the open; not secret.

P
Patent: A grant of land by the government to an individual.
Paternalistic: Like a father; benevolent but intrusive.
Patrimony: Items inherited from one's father.
Penal: Concerning a penalty for breaking a law.
Per capita: Per unit of population.
Perjure: To lie while under oath, especially in a court proceeding.
Personal recognizance: Permission to go free before trial without putting up a bail bond.
Plea agreement: An agreement between the prosecutor and defendant whereby the defendant agrees to plead guilty to a particular charge in return for some concession from the prosecutor.
Predilections: Strong likings; predispositions in favor of something.
Presumption: A conclusion or inference drawn.
Presumption of innocence: The rule that all persons are innocent until proven guilty.
Privilege: The right and duty to withhold information because of some special status or relationship of confidentiality.
Promulgate: Formally put a law into effect.
Proscribed: Prohibited or forbidden.

Pro se: Latin term meaning "for oneself"; applied to the actions of a person handling his or her own case in court without a lawyer.
Prospecting: To look over; explore or examine something (such as the prospect a district for gold).
Provoked: Acted in a way that triggered a reaction of anger or rage in another person.

Q
Quasi: Latin term meaning "sort of."

R
Rational: Based on reason.
Reciprocal: Interchanged, given or owed to each other.
Reckless: Can mean "careless and inattentive" or "a willful disregard for the life of others"—usually involving more than negligence.
Rehabilitation: The restoration of someone to a useful place in society.
Remanded: Sent back to a lower court.
Renunciation: The process of rejecting, casting off, or giving up something openly and in public.
Repressive: Restrictive of action; exerting strict control on the freedom of others.
Restitution: Act of restoring a wronged or injured person to the person's condition before the wrong, loss, or injury.
Retribution: Punishment or revenge for a previous act.
Reversible error: A mistake made by a judge that could affect the outcome of a legal proceeding.
Revoke: Wipe out something's legal effect by taking it back; cancelling it.

S
Self-incrimination: Anything said or done by a person that implicates herself in a crime.
Sequester: To isolate, hold aside, or take away. For example, to sequester a jury is to keep it from having contact with the outside world during a trial.
Sociolinguistic: Pertaining to the study of relationships between language and the social and cultural factors that affect it.
Solicit: To ask for; entice; strongly request.
Standing: The right of a person (or party) to bring (start) or join a lawsuit because they are directly affected by the issue raised.
Stare Decisis: (Latin term meaning "Let it stand.") The rule that when a court has decided a case by applying a legal principle to a set of facts, the court

should stick by the principle and apply it to all later cases with clearly similar facts.

Status: A basic condition of a person.

Sting: An operation organized and implemented by undercover law enforcement to apprehend criminals.

Stipulation: A condition or requirement in a contract or agreement.

Strict liability: Guilt even without criminal intention.

Summons: A formal written notice to show up in court.

T

Totality of the circumstances: Test used to determine the constitutionality of various search and seizure procedures. The standard focuses on all the circumstances of a particular case rather than just one factor.

Tort: A civil violation where one person causes damage, injury, or harm to another person.

Transitory: Continuing for only a short time.

U

Unilaterally: Performed or undertaken by only one side.

V

Vacated: Annulled; set aside.

Veracity: Truthfulness; accuracy.

Voir dire: The preliminary in-court questioning of a potential juror to determine that person's suitability to decide a case.

Volitional: By a conscious choice or decision.

W

Warrant: A document issued by a court that gives the police the power to do something.

Watershed: A place where two things separate.

Writ of mandamus: Used by courts of superior jurisdiction to require a lower court to perform a certain act.

Index

ABBA. *See* Álchíní Bi Beehaz'áannii Act
Aboriginals, xvii. *See also* Indians
Abraham, Robert, 95
Absentee-Shawnee Tribe, 245–46
abuse. *See* assault; domestic violence
abuse of discretion, 333
accessory, 257
accidental homicide, 237
accomplice liability, 257–59
accountability, 555–56
Acosta, Melissa, 179
actus reus (act), 210, 213
admissibility: confession, 345, 356–62, 409; search and seizure, 368–69, 370–73
adoption fraud case, 221–31
advocates: counsel effectiveness, 181–82, 439–43; victim, 494–96
affidavit: for arrest warrant, 377; for search and seizure warrant, 370–71, 375–77
affirmative defenses, 262
after the fact, 311
aggravated assault, 251–54, 356–57
Aginsky, Burt, 18
Aginsky, Ethel, 18
aiding and abetting: defining, 223, 224, 257–58; tribal court cases on, 221–31, 258–59

Alabama. *See* Poarch Band of Creek Indians
Alaska Native Language Center, 96–97
Alaskan Natives: Cup'ik seal hunting rules, 211–13; Huslia, 301–2; identity terminology for, xvi; Kake, 560–63, 568–70; non-U.S. citizen jurisdiction in, 96–97; peacemaking by, 560–63; Venetie, 102; Yup'ik, 238–39, 337–39
Alaska v. Native Village of Venetie Tribal Government, 102
Álchíní Bi Beehaz'áannii Act (ABBA), 559
alcohol-related incidents: arrest rate for, 125; bootlegging, 384–86, 472–73, 476; consumption defined for, 291; involuntary intoxication defense for, 280–84; Miranda rights case with, 347–56; peacemaking success for, 59, 60; reasonable doubt and, 289–92; sobriety tests for, 246, 354, 411–12; strict liability of, 234–35; tribal court cases on, 116–17, 132–33, 154, 234–35, 289–92, 384–86, 472–73, 475–76; underage, 154, 289–92; undercover operations for, 284–85; voluntary intoxication defense for, 279–80. *See also* driving while impaired; healing to wellness court; rehabilitation

599

alerquutet (rules of living), 238–39
Alfred, Taiaiake, 300
Algonikan. *See* Menominee Indians
alibi, 263, 286
allotments, *109*, 111
ambiguity: banishment law, 584–86; of consecutive sentences, 533–34; defining, 364; due process protection from, 67–68, 457–60; of right to counsel notification, 427–31; of right to counsel request, 342–43; of search and seizure warrant, 373–78; of statute translation, 359–60, 457–60; of tribal Miranda rights, 354–55, 359–60
American criminal law: civil law compared to, 2, *2*, 108; civil rights defined by, 299–301; criminal offense defined by, 6; defining, 1, 14; enforcement in, 7; entrapment defense in, 144; failure of, 37–38; hybridization of, 69–70; individual harm concept of, 2, *2*; individual rights concept of, 299–301; justice concept of, 7, 7–8, 556–57; procedure in, 8–9, *10*; punishment theories of, 7, 7–8; restorative justice differences from, 556–57; social harm concept of, 2, *2*, 5–7, *6*; structure of, 8–9, *10*; tribal law parallels to, 350–51; wrongdoing response in, 7–8. *See also* federal jurisdiction; federal system; state jurisdiction
American Indian Politics and the American Political System (Kiiwetinepinesiik Stark and Wilkins), xvi–xvii
American Indians, xvii. *See also* Indians
American Tobacco Co. v. United States, 532
amicus curiae, 162
Ami v. Hopi Tribe: discussion, 432–37; on due process and guilty pleas, 465–69; facts, 431; issues, 432, 465–69; order, 438, 469; as precedent, 448–51; precedents for, 431–32, 437–38; on right to counsel, 431–38, 448–51

Amnesty International, 166
Amundson v. Colville Confederated Tribes, 255–57
anachronistic, 49, 54
ancillary, 563, 589
Anderson, Louella, 226
Anishinaabe Indians. *See* Ojibway Indians
anonymous tips, 330–31
anthropologists, non-Indian, xvi
Apache Tribe, in *New Mexico v. Mescalero Apache*, 134. *See also* White Mountain Apache Tribe
apology, public, 509
appeal. *See* right to appeal
apprehension, 241, 247
Aquinnah. *See* Wampanoag Tribe of Gay Head
Arapaho Indians, 61–63
arbitrary and capricious sentence, 519, 554
Arizona: *Bustamante v. Valenzuela* in, 533–34; counsel effectiveness rules in, 441, 445; Indianness burden of proof in, 157; *Miranda v. Arizona*, 344–45, 533; waiver of counsel rules in, 435. *See also* Hopi Tribe; Navajo Nation; Oglala Sioux Tribe
Arizona State ex rel. Merrill v. Turtle, 128
Arizona State v. Bullington, 331
Arizona State v. Hampton, 182
Arizona State v. Lucas, 441
Arizona State v. Nash, 441
Arkansas, in *Ex parte Kenyon*, 138
Army, U.S., 130
Arneson, Ron, 252–53
Aroostook Band of Micmacs, 105
arraignment. *See* trial rights
arrest: alcohol-related rate of, 125; defendant rights in, 313–31; defining, 313; ICRA on, 313, 314; of non-Indians, 131, 191, 194; peace officer authority to, 193–94; stop and frisk compared to, 324–25; summons

compared to, 320; tribal code example on, 131; warrantless search for, 321–24, 387
arrest warrant: affidavit for, 377; example of, *316*; probable cause for, 314–15; search and seizure warrant or, 377. *See also* warrantless arrest
arrows: Cleansing the Arrows ritual, 237; *Sacred Arrows matter*, 61–63
arson, 3–5
articulable facts, 400, 404
articulable suspicion, 473, 483
assault: aggravated, 251–54, 356–57; attempt of, 251–54; child abuse, 116, 213, 214–16, 496; defining, 210, 241–42; hypotheticals, 242; juvenile, 480; threatening, 242; tribal court cases on, 123–24, 179–80, 251–54, 463, 480. *See also* domestic violence; sexual assault
assimilation, 49, 54, *109*
Assimilative Crimes Act, *109*
Assiniboine Tribe. *See* Fort Peck Tribes
Athabascan Indians, 96–97
atonement, 22
attempt: defining, 250–51; tribal court case on, 251–54
attendant circumstances, 232, 240
attenuated circumstances, 210, 217
attorney. *See* right to counsel
Augustine Komalestewa v. The Hopi Tribe, 475–79
Austin, Raymond D., 56
Austin v. United States, 144–45
automobile search and seizure, 143–47, 326–27, 329–31, 388–401, 416–20
Aymond, Virginia, 576–77

"bad men" clause, 42, 128, 129–30
bail, 11
Baker, Robert, 395
banishment: ambiguity of, 584–86; exclusion compared to, 579, 587–88; expiration of, 575; ICRA on, 582–84; of non-Indians, 141–42, 587–88; of nonmember Indians, 575–76, 587–88; of parents, 581–82; probation, parole and, 580–81; religious expression and, 582, 584; traditional law of, 235–39, 487–89, 573; tribal codes of, 141–42, 573–76, 579–80, 587–88; violation of, 575
Banko, Richard, 79
Barnhart, in *United States v. Barnhart*, 520
Barsh, Russell, 557–58
battery, 242–44. *See also* assault; self-defense
"Battle with the Snakes" (Bruchac), 26–28
benchbooks, 202–3
Benjamin v. Weyaus, 587
beyond reasonable doubt, 297. *See also* reasonable doubt
BIA. *See* Bureau of Indian Affairs
Big Man, Lance, 346–56
Biolsi, Thomas, 38–39
Bitsui, Jeremiah, 124, 126
Blackfeet Indians, 20
Blake, in *Navajo Nation v. Blake*, 3–5
Blockburger v. United States, 542
Bolstrom, James L., 406–7
bootlegging, 384–86, 472–73, 476
Bottchenbaugh, Frankie, 397–98, 400
Boundaries and Passages (Fienup-Riordan), 238–39
Bowen, John C., 258–59
Bowstring Soldiers, 23–26
Boyum, William, 530
Brant, Clare, 336
Brave Wolf, 487–89
British Columbia, 95–96
Broken Landscape (Pommersheim), 535–36
Bruchac, Joseph, 15–17, 26–28
Brule Sioux, 41–45, 47–50, 52–53
Budd, James, 50–51
Building on Common Ground, 201–2

Bullington, in *Arizona State v. Bullington*, 331
burden, 163
burden of persuasion, 288, 297
burden of production, 287–88, 297
burden of proof: allocation error, 418–20; of child abuse, 215; of counsel effectiveness, 441, 445; on defendant, 419; defenses using, 262–64; exclusionary rule and, 414–20; of *habeas corpus*, 304, 310; of Indianness, 154–61; of intent, 221–31, 263; of Miranda rights waiver, 345–46; on prosecution, 287–88, 419–20; reasonable doubt and, 288–93; of search and seizure legality, 414–20; of self-defense, 272–75, 293–96; types of, 287–88; for warrantless search and seizure, 415–20
Bureau of Indian Affairs (BIA): CFR and, 4, 38; federal deputization of, 168; on fish and game rights, 79; IRA proposal beyond, 45–47; Major Crimes Act proposed by, 41, 45–52; OIA predecessor to, 38–40
burglary, 244–45, 268–69
Burke, in *Washington State v. Burke*, 275
Burland, Donelda, 214–16
Bustamante v. Valenzuela, 533–34
buttress, 422

Canada: legal parallels with, xvii; Witsuwit'en of, 95–96
capital crime: murder as, 20, 22, 31; right to appeal for, 44; treason as, 22; witchcraft as, 31–32
capricious sentence, 519–20
Carama, in *Washington State v. Carama*, 274
caretakers, failure to act by, 213, 214–16
case of first impression, 407, 422
cases. *See* Supreme Court; tribal court cases
Cass County Wellness Court, 195–98, *198–201*
Catawba Indians, 105

ceremonies and rituals: Cleansing the Arrow, 237; cultural sanctions for, 509; dances, 40, 236–37; Harvest Festival, 94; membership reinstatement, 236–37; *Sacred Arrows matter*, 61–63; smoking, 236; smudging, 197; tribal-state cultural exchange and, 197, 205; Two Row Wampum, 205
CFR. *See* Code of Federal Regulations
Champagne, Duane, 192–94, 195–98, 202–5, 207
Champagne v. the People of the Little River Band of Ottawa Indians: conclusion, 77–78; discussion, 73–77; introduction, 71–73; order, 78
Chatter, Bennett, 379–80, 431, 443, 444
Chehalis Indians, 172–77. *See also* Salish and Kootenai Tribes
Cherokee Indians: Choctaw and, 94; deviations recognized by, 28–33; *Eastern Band of Cherokee Indians v. Crowe*, 528–37; *Eastern Band of Cherokee Indians v. Cruz*, 302–4; *Eastern Band of Cherokee Indians v. Lambert*, 152–54; *Eastern Band of Cherokee Indians v. Reed*, 396–401; *Eastern Band of Cherokee Indians v. Torres*, 116–22; murder law of, 30–31; spirituality in criminal law of, 28–33, 216; treaties with, 119, 121; women and laws of, 30, 32, 33
Cheyenne Indians: Cheyenne-Arapaho District Court case, 61–63; domestic violence victim response of, 487–89; intent according to, 235–38; membership reinstatement by, 235–37; OIA Pine Ridge control of, 39; restorative justice by, 23–26; stories of, 23–26, 235–38, 487–89
The Cheyennes: Indians of the Great Plains (Hoebel), 487–89
The Cheyenne Way (Llewellyn and Hoebel), 23–26, 235–38
Chickasaw Indians, 94

chief. *See* clan leader
child abuse, 116, 213, 214–16, 496
children. *See* juveniles
Chinle District Court, 123–30
Chippewa Indians: banishment rules of, 583–84; *Mille Lacs Band of Ojibwe Indians vs. Darrick DeWayne Williams Jr.*, 581–88; *People of the Grand Traverse Band v. Raphael*, 264–66; Red Cliff Band, 131, 143; *Spears v. Red Lake Band of Chippewa Indians*, 532, 533–34; *Turtle Mountain Band of Chippewa v. McGillis*, 480–81. *See also* Sault Ste. Marie Tribal Code
Choctaw Indians: jurisdiction of, 94; theft rare among, 244; treaties with, 94, 118
circumstances: attendant, 232, 240; attenuated, 210, 217; exigent, 324, 333, 389; totality of the, 377, 404
circumstantial: defining, 297; evidence, 315
citizenship. *See* non-U.S. citizens; tribal membership
civil forfeiture: defined, 148; overview, 142; tribal code examples on, 143; tribal court case on, 143–47
civil law: on banishment, 141–42; contempt power, 140–41, 148; defined, 2, *2*, 11; for non-Indians, 130–47; state jurisdiction in, 105, *108*
civil rights: federal protection of, 305–11; tribal and American criminal law definitions of, 299–301; tribal protection of, 301–4. *See also* Indian Civil Rights Act; *specific types of rights*
civil rights violations. *See* exclusionary rule
Clairmont, Bonnie, 494–95
clan leader: characteristics of, 57; enforcement level of, 19; as peacemaker, 57; as pipe-holder, 20
Cleansing the Arrows, 237
cocaine, 179, 255–57, 374
Code of Federal Regulations (CFR), 4, 38

coercion: confession admissibility and, 356–62, 409; as defense, 261, 278–79; defining, 286; "fruits of the poisonous tree" from, 411–14; scope of, 409
cognizable, 54
Cohen, Felix S., 84, 156
Colorado-New Mexico Indian Court Judges Association, 203–4
Colville Confederated Tribes: *Amundson v. Colville Confederated Tribes*, 255–57; *Condon v. Colville Confederated Tribes*, 289–92; *Davisson, et al. v. Colville Confederated Tribes*, 267–75; *Henry Pakootas v. Colville Confederated Tribes*, 515–16; *John Manuel v. Colville Confederated Tribes*, 321–24; *Joseph Sweowat v. Colville Confederated Tribes*, 518–22; *Julie R. Swan v. Colville Confederated Tribes*, 373–78; *Laurie Watt v. Colville Confederated Tribes*, 63–65; *Louie v. Colville Confederated Tribes*, 460–62; *St. Peter v. Colville Confederated Tribes*, 470–71, 521, 523–28; *Sam v. Colville Confederated Tribes*, 469–71, 521; *Shane C. Innes v. Colville Confederated Tribes*, 234–35; *Waters v. Colville Confederated Tribes*, 276–77
Colville Confederated Tribes v. Peter P. George, 328–29
Colville Confederated Tribes v. Swan, 221–31
Comanche Indians: enforcement by, 20; individual harm concept of, 19; restorative justice by, 22; theft rare among, 244
Common Ground, 201–2
Commonwealth v. Webster, 288
communication. *See* informants; peacemaking; sociolinguistics; tribal-state collaboration
community: individual responsibility to, 17–19, 299–300, 305; private property as part of, 367–68; restorative justice and, *21*, 21–26,

556, 558; social harm concept and, 15–17, 26–28, 238–39; stop and frisk involvement of, 389–92; victim right to have a voice and, 493
community service, 500, 508
compensation. *See* fines; restitution
complaint, 287, 297, 460–65
complicity, 260
compulsory process, 479–81
concurrent jurisdiction, 87, 104–5
condonation, 22
Condon v. Colville Confederated Tribes, 289–92
Confederated Chehalis v. Lyons, 172–77
Confederated Salish and Kootenai Tribes v. Burland, 214–16
Confederated Salish and Kootenai Tribes v. Daniel Felix Finley, 294–96
Confederated Salish and Kootenai Tribes v. William Conko, 411–14
Confederated Tribes of Warm Springs, 193, 350
Conference of Chief Justices, 201–2
confession: accuracy of, 335; admissibility of, 345, 356–62, 409; cultural values impact on, 335–39; voluntariness, 340, 409. *See also* Miranda rights; right to remain silent
confidentiality, 495
Conko, William, 411–14
conscious choice, 232, 240
consecutive sentences: ambiguity of, 533–34; in *Eastern Band of Cherokee Indians v. Crowe*, 528–37; in *Hardin v. Reno Sparks Indian Colony*, 546–48; in *Pascua Yaqui v. Miranda*, 537–45; in *St. Peter v. Colville Confederated Tribes*, 523–28; Supreme Court on, 532, 533
consent: implied, 163; to jurisdiction, non-Indian, 130–40; to peacemaking, 558–59; terms of, 386–87; for warrantless arrest, 322–23; for warrantless search and seizure, 386–87

conspiracy: defining, 254–55; tribal court case on, 255–57
Constitution, U.S., 68–69, 300–301. *See also specific amendments of Constitution*
constructive intent, 231–32
consummating, 260
contempt of court, 140–41, 148
contravene, 554
controverted matter, 521, 554
Coochyouma, William, 416–20
Coquille Tribe, 498
Corn Woman, 487–89
corroborate, 260, 333
counsel. *See* right to counsel
court cases. *See* Supreme Court; tribal court cases
Courts of Indian Offenses: criminal offense defined by, 39–40; formation of, 38
Coushatta Tribe, 105
Craig, Vincent, 57
Creator. *See* spirituality
Creek Indians, 94
Cries Yia Eya, 237
crime: elements of, 209, 217; Indian translation of, 13–14; rate, violent, 125, 166, 485
criminal, as *haksi*, 14
criminal defense. *See* defendant rights; defense
criminal identification, 363, 446
criminal law: American structures of, 8–9, *10*; defining, 11. *See also* American criminal law; traditional criminal law; tribal criminal law
criminal offense. *See* offense
criminal procedure: American, 8–9, *10*; defining, 299; traditional, 20–21
criminology, 576, 589
cross-deputization: defined, 207; federal, 168; state, 191–94
cross-examination, 479–81

Crow Dog: *Ex parte Crow Dog*, 41–45, 52–53, 103, *109*; Major Crimes Act and, 47–50, 103
Crow Dog's Case (Harring), 41–45
Crowe, Jon Nathaniel, 528–37
Crow Flies High, 394–96
Crow Tribe: *Montana v. United States*, 137; *National Farmers Union Ins. Cos. v. Crow Tribe of Indians*, 137
Crow Tribe v. Lance Big Man, 346–56
Cruz, in *Eastern Band of Cherokee Indians v. Cruz*, 302–4
culmination, 260
culpability: defining, 210, 217; Pueblo of Laguna Tribal Code for, 232–33
cultural sanctions, 509
cultural values: eagle feathers and, 568–72; eye contact and, 336; of humility, 336–37; of individual responsibility to community, 17–19, 299–300, 301; interrogations and confessions impacted by, 335–39; private property search impact on, 367–68; respect and exchange of, 197, 203–4, 205, 207; right to remain silent clash with, 335–39
Cup'ik People of the Western Tundra, 211–13
custody: defining, 333; Miranda rights in, 345

dances, 40, 236–37
dating violence, 169, 171
Davisson, et al. v. Colville Confederated Tribes: conclusion, 275; due process and, 269–71; equal protection and, 271–72; procedural history for, 267–68; relevant facts in, 268–69; self-defense burden of proof in, 272–75
Dawahoya, Beauford, 329–31
Dawes Act, *109*
death penalty. *See* capital crime

decorum, 302, 311
decree, 589
Deep Valley (Aginsky and Aginsky), 18
defendant rights: to appeal, 44, 527; in arrest, 313–31; civil, 299–311; exclusionary rule and, 405–21; to jury trial, 75–76, 533; Miranda, 344–62; to remain silent, 335–63; in search and seizure, 367–402. *See also* trial rights
defense: affirmative, 262; categories of, 261; coercion, 261, 278–79; entrapment, 144–45, 284–85; excuse, 278; insanity, 261, 279; justification, 264–66; mistake of law, 263–64; necessity, 277–78; self-defense, 261, 266–77
deferred, 85
deferred sentence: defining, 508, 554; expungement after, 512; for restitution, 510
Delaware Treaty, 118
deposition, 505
depredation, 51, 54
deputization. *See* cross-deputization
derogation, 69, 85
detainment. *See* search and seizure
detainment legality. *See habeas corpus*
deterrence, 7, 7
deviations: Cherokee types of, 28–33; defining, 34, 240
Devils Lake Sioux Tribe v. Frederick, 319–20
dichotomy, 422
dicta, 554
discretion, abuse of, 333
dismissals. *See* pardons
disorderly conduct: self-defense in, 276–77; tribal court cases on, 443–46
dispositive, 436, 453
distributive justice, 557, 589
dockets, 194, 208
domestic violence: banishment and, 487–89, 576–79; consecutive sentences for,

529; peacemaking for, 60, 560; self-defense case against, 267–75; stories of, 487–89; tribal court cases on, 251–54, 321–22, 529, 576–79; tribal response to, 22–23, 96–97, 487–89; victim support systems for, 491–92, 494–95; voluntary intoxication defense for, 280; warrantless arrest for, 316, 319–20. *See also* Violence Against Women Act
dominion, 367, 404
Dorszynski v. United States, 521
double jeopardy: confusion over, 471–72; tribal court case on, 472–74; tribal sovereignty and, 105–6, 107
Doyle, Richard, 577
driving incidents: accident fraud, 71–78; automobile search and seizure, 143–47, 326–27, 329–31, 388–401, 416–20; negligent, 66; non-Indian jurisdiction via, 131; reckless, 66, 85, 131; search and seizure warrant for, 326, 329–31; stop and frisk for, 326–27, 329–31, 388–89; without valid license, 63–65, 116–17, 411–14, 427–31
driving while impaired (DWI): elements, 245; healing to wellness court for, 195–96, 198; hypotheticals, 246; peacemaking success for, 59; reasonable doubt on, 292–93; tribal code examples on, 245–46; tribal court cases on, 116–17, 292–93, 346–47, 411–14, 427–31, 470
drug courts. *See* healing to wellness court
drug possession: cocaine, 179, 255–57, 374; involuntary intoxication defense for, 280–84; marijuana, 143–44, 326, 379–82, 415–16, 417; methamphetamine, 398; punishment theory for, 8; search and seizure of, 373–78, 379–82, 397–98; stop and frisk for, 326–27, 417; tribal court cases on, 143–47, 179, 255–57, 341–43, 373–78, 379–82, 397–98, 417, 518; undercover operations for, 144–45, 255–57, 284–85; voluntary intoxication defense for, 279–81. *See also* driving while impaired
"The Duck Dinner," 71–72
Duckwater Shoshone Tribe, 243
due process: American-tribal parallel requirements in, 350; conclusion, 482; criminal identification and, 363; defining, 85, 287, 297, 455; double jeopardy and, 471–74; ex parte and, 464–65; guilty pleas and, 465–69; ICRA rights to, 67, 70, 140, 269–71; offense complaint and, 460–65; scope of, 455–57; in self-defense case, 269–71; sentence and, 469–71; statute ambiguity and, 67–68, 457–60. *See also* burden of proof
Duhamel, George (Skip), 265
DUI (driving under the influence). *See* driving while impaired
Dupris, C. J., 63–65
Dupuis, Georgia, 462–63
duress. *See* coercion
Duro v. Reina: case, 106–7, 110, 306; in establishing Indianness, 152–53; in non-Indian consent case, 135–36, 138
DWI. *See* driving while impaired

Eagle (Cheyenne chief), 237–38
Eagle Down Is Our Law (Mills), 95
eagle feathers, 568–72
Eastern Band of Cherokee Indians v. Crowe, 528–37
Eastern Band of Cherokee Indians v. Cruz, 302–4
Eastern Band of Cherokee Indians v. Lambert, 152–54
Eastern Band of Cherokee Indians v. Reed, 396–401

Eastern Band of Cherokee Indians v. Torres, 116–22
Eastman, Galen, 128
education assistance act, *110*
egregious, 440, 453
Elmo Nevayaktewa and Emily Verna Mutz v. The Hopi Tribe, 379–82
emergency search and seizure, 324, 389
enforcement: in American criminal law, 7; in traditional criminal law, 19–20
entrapment, 144–45, 284–85
enumerated powers, 54, 68–69
equal protection, 271–72, 349
erroneous, 554
error, reversible, 520, 554
Eskimos. *See* Alaskan Natives; Yup'ik Eskimos
Evans, Tom, 214
Evans, William, 289
evidence: alibi as, 263, 286; burden of persuasion of, 288, 297; burden of production of, 287–88, 297; circumstantial, *315*; failure of proof defenses, 262–64; hearsay, 173, 189; for insanity defense, 279, 281–84; motion to suppress, 369, 396–401, 408–9, 422; nonverbal, 363; oath or affirmation of, 370–71; pedigree, 156; sobriety tests as, 354, 411–14; standing to suppress, 369, 396–401, 408–9; TLOA rules of, 176. *See also* burden of proof; exclusionary rule; search and seizure
Evil Mind, 15–17
excessive fines doctrine, 145–47
exclusion, 141–42, 579, 587–88. *See also* banishment
exclusionary rule: burden of proof and, 414–20; defining, 422; "fruits of the poisonous tree," 410–14; good faith exception to, 377, 421; impeachment exception to, 421; involuntary statements and, 409; Miranda violations and, 409–10; purpose of, 405; scope of, 405–6; search and seizure violations, 408–9; tribal court cases on, 406–7, 411–14, 415–20
exclusive jurisdiction, 87, 89
excuse defense, 278
execution, as course of action, 519, 546, 554. *See also* capital crime
executive pardons, 548–49
exhausted remedies, 309, 311
exigent circumstances: defining, 333; for warrantless search, 324, 389
exoneration, 264, 286
ex parte, due process and, 464–65
Ex parte Crow Dog, 41–45, 52–53, 103, *109*
Ex parte Kenyon, 138
Ex parte Snyder, 580–81
ex post facto (after the fact), 302, 311
expungement: after rehabilitation, 551–52; tribal code example of, 512, 548–49; tribal court cases on, 549–52
extradition, 94, 98
eye contact, 336

failure of proof defenses, 262–64
failure to act: defining, 210, 213; tribal court case on, 214–16
family: incest, 172–77; responsibility to, 18; stop and frisk requested by, 389–92; tribal probate officer role of, 58–59; victim's advocate for, 494. *See also* banishment; parents
Federal Enclaves Act, 159–60
federal jurisdiction: General Crimes Act for, 102–3, *109*; Indian country defined for, 101–2; Major Crimes Act for, 41, 45–52, 103–4, *109*; over non-Indians, 102–3, 106, 107, *108*, *109–10*; over nonmember Indians, 106–7; state jurisdiction over, 105; statute overview, *109–10*; summary map, *108*

federal system: civil rights in, 305–11; cross-deputization in, 168; sentence vacating in, 520–21; tribal criminal law recognized by, 41–45, 52–53, 103, 105–6; tribal jurisdiction limitations by, 41, 45–52, 101–4, 108, 109–10; tribal jurisdiction support from, 165–88, 201–2, 204–5. *See also* Supreme Court; United States District Court

Federal Youth Corrections Act, 526

fee land, 111

Fienup-Riordan, Ann, 238–39

Fifth Amendment. *See* right to remain silent

fines: defining, 508; tribal code on payment of, 511–13. *See also* restitution

Finley, Daniel Felix, 294–96

Finley-Justus, Deborah, 221–31

Finley-Justus, Jacob Riley, 221–31

The Fire and the Spirits (Strickland), 28–33

First Amendment, 582

First Descendents, 153

first impression, case of, 407, 422

First Nations: terminology issue for, xvii. *See also* Canada

fish and game rights: accomplice liability and, 258–59; BIA, 79; justification defense and, 264–66; non-Indian jurisdiction via, 131, 132, 137; seal hunting rules, 211–13; spirituality and, 80; stop and frisk, 394–96; tribal court cases on, 78–84, 258–59, 264–66, 406–7

Fletcher, Tami, 79

Florida, 105

foreigners. *See* non-U.S. citizens

forgiveness: condonation, 22; Hopi concept of, 550, 551; Ojibway concept of, 23

Fornsby, in *Swinomish v. Fornsby*, 280–84

Fort Berthold Reservation, 394–96

Fort McDowell Yavapai Nation: banishment code of, 587; victim protection code of, 493

Fort Peck Assiniboine and Sioux Tribes v. Jesse Martell, 149–51

Fort Peck Assiniboine and Sioux Tribes v. Stiffarm, 457–60

Fort Peck Tribes: banishment code of, 588; due process scope by, 456

Fort Peck Tribes v. Joseph Harold Jones, 292–93

Fort Peck Tribes v. Morales, 462–65

Fort Peck Tribes v. Victor and Patti Grant, 415–16

Fort Peck Tribes v. William Turcotte, 251–54

Fourteenth Amendment. *See* due process

Fourth Amendment. *See* arrest warrant; search and seizure warrant

Francis, Dean, Sr., 576–81

Frank, Johnny, 96–97

Franklin, Marie, 384–86

fraud: adoption, 221–31; aiding and abetting, 221–31; defining, 222; driving accident, 71–78

Frederick, Adrian, 319–20

freedom with responsibility, 56

free speech, 582, 584

Freidman, Lawrence, 7

frisk, 333. *See also* stop and frisk

"fruits of the poisonous tree," 410–14

full faith and credit, 204, 208

Gardner, Jerry, 205

Gasco-Shepard, Rita, 566–68

gauntlet, 56, 85

General Allotment Act, *109*

General Crimes Act, 102–3, *109*

general intent, 219–20

genocide, 38

George, Peter P., 328–29

George, Richard, 440

Georgia, in *Worcester v. Georgia*, 41, 49, *109*

Georgiadis, in *United States v. Georgiadis*, 520

gerontocracy, 29, 34
Gila River Tribal Code, 317
Gilmore, Ray, 123
Gishey v. Hopi Tribe, 431–32, 437–38
Goldberg, Carol, 192–94, 195–98, 202–5, 207
good faith exception, 377, 421
Good Mind, 15–17
Goodrich, in *Romero v. Goodrich*, 535
Goss (chief of police), 326–27
Grand Traverse Band of Ottawa and Chippewa Indians, 264–66
Grant, Gloria, 126
Grant, Leon, 123–24, 126
Grant, Patti, 415–16
Grant, Victor, 415–16
Great Law, 14, 15, 93, 492
Greene, Jonathan, 513–15
Greyeyes, in *Thompson v. Greyeyes*, 304
guilty mind, 209, 219. *See also* intent
guilty pleas: due process and, 465–69; waiver of counsel and, 435. *See also* confession
Guswhenta, 205
Gwis Gyen, 95–96

habeas corpus (you may have the body), 54, 303–4, 310
haksi (criminal), 14
Hampton, in *Arizona State v. Hampton*, 182
Handbook of Federal Indian Law, 84, 155–56
Hardin v. Reno Sparks Indian Colony, 546–48
Hare, Bishop H., 48
Harring, Sidney L., 41–45
Harvest Festival, 94
Haudenosaunee. *See* Iroquois Confederacy
hazhó'ógo (respectful patience), 361–62
healing to wellness court: dedication story of, 566–73; individual agency responsibilities in, *199–201*; juvenile program in, 571; key components of, 563–65; Leech Lake Band and Minnesota, 195–98, *198–201*; Little Traverse Bay Band, 565–73; memorandum example, *198–201*; mission statement, *198–99*; process and curriculum, 565–66; success of, 197–98; tribal-state collaboration in, 194; Waabshki-Miigwan, 565–73
Heap-of-Birds, Alfrich, 61–62
Heap-of-Birds, Cheevers, 61–62
Heap-of-Birds, Edgar, 61
hearsay: defining, 189; juvenile victim exception to, 496–98
Henry Pakootas v. Colville Confederated Tribes, 515–16
Hepfer, Russell N., 406–7
Hester, in *United States v. Hester*, 159–60
Hewankorn, Shannon, 294–96
Hicks, in *Nevada v. Hicks*, 137–38
High Backed Wolf, 23–26
Hill, Brenda, 494–95
Hjert, Michael, 123–30
Hoebel, E. Adamson, 23–26, 235–38, 487–89
holistic, 562–63, 589
homicide, accidental, 237. *See also* murder
Hopewell Treaty, 119
Hopi Tribe: *Ami v. Hopi Tribe*, 431–38, 448–51, 465–69; *Augustine Komalestewa v. The Hopi Tribe*, 475–79; *Elmo Nevayaktewa and Emily Verna Mutz v. The Hopi Tribe*, 379–82; *Gishey v. Hopi Tribe*, 431–32, 437–38; *Nathan J. Navasie v. The Hopi Tribe*, 439–43; *Norris v. Hopi Tribe*, 456–57; *Pavatea v. Hopi Tribe*, 432; *Sinquah v. Hopi Tribe*, 446–52; *Taylor v. Hopi Tribe*, 443–46; *Timothy Randolph v. The Hopi Tribe*, 416–20
Hopi Tribe in Matter of Certified Question, 157–61
Hopi Tribe v. Beauford Dawahoya, 329–31
Hopi Tribe v. Kahe, 389–92
Hopi Tribe v. Marlon Huma, 472–74

Hopi v. Timms, 549–52
horizontal justice, 557
hot pursuit, 324, 389
hózhóji naat'aah (talking things out), 3, 56–58, 558–60. *See also* peacemaking
Huma, Marlon, 472–74
Hunter, Cynthia, 154–57, 158
hunting. *See* fish and game rights
Huron Indians, 22
Huslia. *See* Native Tribe of Huslia
Hutchinson, Margie, 224–25
hybridization, 69–70, 85
hypotheticals: answers to, 247; assault, 242; battery, 243–44; DWI, 245–46; theft, 245

ICRA. *See* Indian Civil Rights Act
ICWA. *See* Indian Child Welfare Act
Idaho tribal-state collaboration, 202–3
identification, criminal, 363, 446
Illinois v. Rodriguez, 323
imminent, 266, 286
impeachment: defining, 364; exclusionary rule exception of, 421
implicit, 106, 111
implied consent, 163
inadvertent discovery, 404
inapposite, 521, 554
incapacitation, 7, 7
incarceration: consecutive sentences of, 528; credit for, 513, 516–17; suspended sentence of, 508, 512–15
incest, 172–77
incommunicado, 340, 364
Indian Child Welfare Act (ICWA), 70, 157, 197, 204
Indian Civil Rights Act (ICRA): on arrest, 313, 314; on banishment, 582–84; code, 306–8; on double jeopardy, 107, 473; on due process, 67, 70, 140, 269–71; Duro amendment to, 106–7, 110, 135–36, 138, 152–53, 306; on equal protection, 271–72, 349; on excessive fines doctrine, 145–47; on guilty pleas, 466; *habeas corpus* in, 310; on Indianness, 152–53; individualistic approach of, 305; Miranda rights and, 348–50; on nonmember Indian jurisdiction, 107; overview, *109, 110*, 305–6; on private property determination, 367–68; purpose of, 309–10; on restitution, 504; on right to counsel, 425–26; on right to remain silent, 339; on right to speedy trial, 476; on search and seizure, 368–69; on seizures, 368–69; sentence limitation amendment of, 103, 167–68, 305–6, *307*, 522–23; Supreme Court interpretation of, 308–9, 349; TLOA amendment of, 167–68; VAWA amendment of, 169–71
Indian country, 101–2, 149–51
Indian Country Crimes Act, 102–3, *109*
Indian Law, 83–84
Indianness: burden of proof of, 154–61; establishing, 151–54; type and degree of, 160–61
Indian Rights Association (IRA), 45–46
Indians: crime defined by, 13–14; First Descendent, 153; genocide against, 38; nonmember Indian crime between, 106–7, 123–30; terminology issue for, xvii; violence rate among, 125, 166, 485
Indian Self-Determination and Education Assistance Act, *110*
indicia, 333
indigenous justice. *See* restorative justice
indigenous peoples, xvi. *See also* Indians
individual: American concept of harm, 2, *2*; responsibility to community, 17–19, 299–300, 301; traditional concept of harm, 17–19
inerquutet (warnings of harm), 238–39

informants: anonymous, 330–31; as probable cause source, *315*; veracity of, 330–31, 373, 376–77
information document, 287, 297
inherent authority, 111, 117, 136–39. *See also* tribal sovereignty
Innes, Shane C., 234–35
innocence. *See* presumption of innocence
in rem jurisdiction (property jurisdiction), 87, 89, 148
insanity, 261, 279, 286
insanity defense: defining, 261, 279; involuntary intoxication or, 280–84
intent, 209, 217; burden of proof of, 221–31, 263; constructive, 231–32; culpability and, 232–33; executive pardons, 548; general, 219–20; offense regardless of, 233–38; in solicitation, 249; specific, 220; strict liability without, 233–35, 240; traditional criminal law and, 235–39; transferred, 232; tribal code example on, 232–33; tribal court cases on proving, 221–31
intentionality, 230
interlocutory, 178, 189
interrogation: coerced confession in, 356–62; cultural values impact on, 335–39; defining, 335, 364; notice of rights before, 339, 344; right to counsel at, 340–43; on scene or in custody, 345. *See also* Miranda rights; right to remain silent
intertribal marriage, 124–25, 129, 309
intoxication defense: involuntary, 280–84; voluntary, 279–80
Inventing the Savage (Ross), 38
inventory, 390, 404
involuntary intoxication defense for, 280–84
involuntary statements, 340, 409. *See also* coercion
Iowa, Sac and Fox Tribe in, 573–74

IRA. *See* Indian Rights Association
Iroquois Confederacy: enforcement by, 19; Great Law of, 14, 15, 93, 492; individual harm concept of, 17, 19; jurisdiction of, 93; murder law of, 22; offenses under, 211; restorative justice by, 22–23; theft rare among, 244; treason law of, 22
Iroquois Stories: Heroes, Heroines, Monsters and Magic (Bruchac), 15–17, 26–28
irreparable, 363, 364
irresistible impulse test, 279
Irvin, Rosemary, 67
Itasca County Wellness Court, 195–98

jail time. *See* incarceration
Jarred, Jeanne, 226–27
Jimerson, Tom, 18
John C. Bowen v. Upper Skagit Indian Tribe, 258–59
John Manuel v. Colville Confederated Tribes, 321–24
Johnny, Merle K., 325–27
Joint Powers Agreements, 195–98
Jones, Joseph Harold, 292–93
Joseph Sweowat v. Colville Confederated Tribes, 518–22
judges: Conference of Chief Justices, 201–2; counsel waiver role of, 434–37, 450–51; mistrial disqualification of, 462–65; sentence vacating by poor discretion, 519–20
judgment. *See* sentence
Julie R. Swan v. Colville Confederated Tribes: conclusion, 378; opinion and order for, 373; on search warrant affidavits, 375–77; summary and discussion of, 374
junta, 483
jurisdiction, 87–90. *See also specific types of jurisdiction*
jury duty, 126; voir dire for, 337, 364

jury trial. *See* right to jury trial
justice: in American criminal law, 7, 7–8, 556–57; by Courts of Indian Offenses, 40. *See also* restorative justice
Justice as Healing Indigenous Ways (McCaslin), 55–60
justification defense, 264–66
just-ness, 557–58
juveniles: assault by, 480; child abuse, 116, 213, 214–16, 496; failure of proof by age, 263; healing to wellness court for, 571; ICWA for, 70, 157, 197, 204; molestation of, 439–43; parental enforcement for, 19; peacemaking for, 559; rehabilitation of, 526; restitution by, 499–504; separate system for, xvii; sexual assault of, 439–43, 497–98; tribal court cases on, 289–92, 439–43, 480–81, 499–504; underage drinking, 154, 289–92; victim rights for, 496–98

Kagama, in *United States v. Kagama*, 104, 109
Kahe, Thomas E., 389–92
Kake village: peacemaking court, 560–63; Waabshki-Miigwan dedication story of, 568–70
Kalispel Tribe, 575–76
Kansas, 104–5
Kaye, Judith S., 204
Keating, Darrell, 371–73
Keating, Diane, 371
Keepers of the Faith, 19
Keex' Kwaan, 560–63
Kenyon, in *Ex parte Kenyon*, 138
Kickingbird, Kirke, 20
Kiiwetinepinesiik Stark, Heidi, xvi–xvii
Kirkland, Brian, 392–94
Kirkwood, Samuel, 47–48
Klallam Tribe: *Lower Elwha Klallam Tribe v. James L. Bolstrom and Russell N. Hepfer*, 406–7; *Port Gamble S'Klallam Tribe v. Michael Hjert*, 132–40
Klamath River, 79, 80, 81–82
knowingness, 230, 232
Komalestewa, Augustine, 475–79
Kootenai Tribe. *See* Salish and Kootenai Tribes

Lakota. *See* Oglala Sioux Tribe
Lamar, L. Q. C., 48
Lambert, in *Eastern Band of Cherokee Indians v. Lambert*, 152–54
Lamone, Eugene, 317–19
Lance Big Man, in *Crow Tribe v. Lance Big Man*, 346–56
Lane, Barbara, 71
language. *See* sociolinguistics; terminology
Lara, in *United States v. Lara*, 107, 110, 120, 135–36
Laurie Watt v. Colville Confederated Tribes, 63–65
Law and Order Regulations. *See* Code of Federal Regulations
law enforcement officers, 7. *See also* tribal police
lay advocate effectiveness, 181–82, 439–43. *See also* right to counsel
LeClair, Valerie, 427–31
Leech Lake Band, 195–98, 198–201
Leon, in *United States v. Leon*, 377
let it stand, 45, 54, 418, 422
Lewis, Leroy, 379
liability: accomplice, 257–59; strict, 233–35, 240
lineups, 363, 446
Listening Conference, 204–5
Little Old Men, 93–94
Little River Band of Ottawa Indians, 71–78
Little Traverse Bay Band Healing to Wellness Court. *See* Waabshki-Miigwan Drug Court Program

INDEX 613

Llewellyn, Karl N., 23–26, 235–38
Louie v. Colville Confederated Tribes, 460–62
Lower Elwha Klallam Tribe v. James L. Bolstrom and Russell N. Hepfer, 406–7
Lucas, in *State v. Lucas*, 441
Lucier, Joe, 572–73
Lummi Nation, 185–86
Luongo, Alfred, 143–44
lying, as tribal offense, 335–36
Lyons, in *Confederated Chehalis v. Lyons*, 172–77

Maho, Rachel, 443
Maine Indian Land Claims Act, 105, 577–78
Major Crimes Act, 41, 45–52, 103–4, 109
majority rule, 420, 422, 562
Makah Tribe v. Jonathan Greene, 513–15
MaliSeet Indians, 105
malum prohibitum (prohibited wrong as strict liability), 233, 234–35
mandamus. *See* writ of mandamus
Manuel, John, 321–24
"A Man without Family" (Aginsky and Aginsky), 18
Maricopa Indians. *See* Salt River Pima-Maricopa Indian Community
marijuana, 143–44, 326, 379–82, 415–16, 417
marriage: Courts of Indian Offenses on, 39, 40; intertribal, 124–25, 129, 309; licenses, 39
Marshall, John, 41, 49
Martell, Jesse, 149–51
Martin, Harry C., 530
Martin, J. Matthew, 531
Martinez, Julia, 309–11
Martin v. Ohio, 295
Mashantucket Pequot Tribe: banishment code of, 579–80; juvenile victim rights in, 496; right to counsel in, 426

Massachusetts Settlement Act, 105
Matthews, Stanley, 42
maxim, 260
"Maze of Injustice" (Amnesty International), 166
McCaslin, Wanda D., 55–60
McDonald, in *Navajo Nation v. McDonald*, 358–59
McDonald, Selanhongva, 380
McGillis, Deborah, 480–81
McNaughten test, 281
Means, Russell, 123–30
medicine men, 40
membership. *See* nonmember Indians; tribal membership
menace, 243, 247
Menominee Indians, 20–21, 548–49
mens rea (guilty mind), 209, 219. *See also* intent
mental healing therapy. *See* healing to wellness court
mental illness. *See* insanity defense
mental state. *See* intent
mercy, 550, 551
merits, 309, 311
Merrill, in *Arizona State ex rel. Merrill v. Turtle*, 128
Mescalero Apache, 134
methamphetamine, 398
Mexican citizen, jurisdiction over, 116–22
Miccosukee Tribe, 105
Michael Stepetin, III v. Nisqually Indian Community, 66–71
Michigan. *See* Chippewa Indians; Ottawa Indians
Micmacs. *See* Aroostook Band of Micmacs
mike-suk (police society member), 20
Mille Lacs Band of Ojibwe Indians vs. Darrick DeWayne Williams Jr., 581–88
Miller, Bruce, 18
Mills, Antonia, 95
Mills, Rutherford, 502–4

Minnesota. *See* Ojibway Indians
minors. *See* juveniles
Miranda, Bernice, 537–45
Miranda rights: confession admissibility and, 345, 356–62, 409; in custody, 345; exclusionary rule and, 407, 409–10; failure to read, 346–56, 407, 409–10; ICRA and, 348–50; Supreme Court on, 344–45; translation ambiguity of, 354–55, 359–60; tribal court cases on, 346–62, 538–39; waiver of, 345–62, 353, 538–39; warning limitations, 352–54
Miranda v. Arizona, 344–45, 533
misdemeanor: defining, 54; warrantless arrest for, 315–16, 319–20
Mississippi, Sac and Fox Tribe in, 574
mistake of law defense, 263–64
mistrial, 462–65
Mohawk Indians, 300, 335
Mohegan Tribe, 105
Molina, Lourdes Salomon, 178–84
Montana. *See* Salish and Kootenai Tribes
Montana v. United States, 137
Morales, John, 462–65
Morgan, in *United States v. Morgan*, 521
Morris, Lindy Lee, 184–88
Morris, Loretta, 58
Morrison v. United States, 161
Morrow, Phyllis, 337–39
motion for mistrial, 462–65
motion to suppress evidence: defining, 422; standing for, 369, 396–401, 408–9
murder: Blackfeet law for, 20; blood revenge, 30–31, 50; as capital crime, 20, 22, 31; Cherokee law for, 30–31; Cheyenne intent and, 237–38; Crow Dog, 41–45, 47–50, 52–53; Iroquois law for, 22–23; Navajo restitution for, 501; Osage law for, 19–20; peacemaking for, 19–20, 22, 237–38; threatening, 253–54; Yurok law for, 22

Mutz, Emily Verna, 379–82

naat'aanii (peacemaker), 57
NAICJA. *See* National American Indian Court Judges Association
nályééh (restitution), 3, 58, 560
Nambe. *See* Pueblo of Nambe Tribal Court
Nanabozho, 71–72
Narragansett Indians, 105
Nash, in *State v. Nash*, 441
Nathan J. Navasie v. The Hopi Tribe, 439–43
National American Indian Court Judges Association (NAICJA), 482
National Congress of American Indians, 166
National Farmers Union Ins. Cos. v. Crow Tribe of Indians, 137
Nations, John, 397–98, 401
Native Americans, xvi–xvii. *See also* Indians
Native Tribe of Huslia, 301–2
Navajo Nation: civil rights defined by, 299–300; on confession admissibility, 356–62; *Eugene Lamone v. Navajo Nation*, 317–19; Indianness proof for, 154–57; jurisdiction of nonmember Indians, 123–30; membership acquisition to, 129; respectful patience concept of, 361–62; on restitution, 3–5, 499–504; restitution under, 501; restorative justice by, 55–60, 556–57, 558–60; size and demographics of, 124–25; talking things out concept of, 3, 56–58, 558–60; terminology, 3, 55–58, 361–632, 558–60; *Thompson v. Greyeyes*, 304; treaties, 123, 127–29, 130; *United States v. Wheeler*, 105–6; Ute and, 128
Navajo Nation in the Matter of the Interest of D.P., 499–504
Navajo Nation v. Blake, 3–5
Navajo Nation v. Cynthia Hunter, 154–57, 158
Navajo Nation v. Marie Franklin, 384–86

Navajo Nation v. McDonald, 358–59
Navajo Nation v. Rafael Rodriguez, 356–62
Navasie, Nathan J., 439–43
Nebraska. *See* Oglala Sioux Tribe
necessity defense, 277–78
negate, 264, 286
negligence, 85, 232, 233
Nelson v. Yurok: background and issues, 79; Harvest Management Plan and, 81; Indian Law and, 83–84; personal jurisdiction for, 78; tribal constitutional issues of, 79–83
Nevada, in *Hardin v. Reno Sparks Indian Colony*, 546–48
Nevada v. Hicks, 137–38
Nevayaktewa, Elmo, 379–82
Newell, William, 17
New Mexico: Pueblo of Laguna Tribe of, 232–33; *Santa Clara Pueblo v. Martinez*, 309–11, 349; Tribal–State Judicial Consortium, 203–4
New Mexico v. Mescalero Apache, 134
New York: concurrent jurisdiction of, 105; federal-state-tribal collaboration, 204–5; *Patterson v. New York*, 274; *Poodry v. Tonawanda Band of Seneca Indians*, 580
Nez Perce Tribal Code: on accomplice liability, 257–58; on battery, 243; on civil rights, 302; on coercion, 278–79; on elements of offense, 210, 211; on mistake of law defense, 264; on reasonable doubt, 288; on self-defense, 266–67; on solicitation, 250; on victim advocacy, 496
Nisqually Tribe, 66–71
non-Indians: anthropologists, xvi; arrest of, 131, 191, 194; banishment of, 141–42, 587–88; civil laws used for, 130–47; *Eastern Band of Cherokee Indians v. Torres*, 116–22; exclusion of, 141–42, 587–88; federal jurisdiction over, 102–3, 106, 107, *108*, *109–10*;

General Crimes Act for, 102–3, *109*; non-U.S. citizen, 96–97, 116–22; *Oliphant v. Suquamish*, 106, 107, *110*, 118–22, 134–38; overview, 115; *Port Gamble S'Klallam Tribe v. Michael Hjert*, 132–40; *Russell Means v. District Court of the Chinle Judicial District*, 123–30; tribal court cases on, 116–30, 132–40, 143–47; tribal jurisdiction over, 106–7, 123–47; VAWA exception for, 108, *110*, 170, 171–72
nonmember Indians: banishment of, 575–76, 587–88; defined, 111; federal jurisdiction over, 106–7; residence requirements for, 129; tribal jurisdiction over, 123–30; VAWA exception for, 170
non-U.S. citizens, 96–97, 116–22
nonverbal evidence, 363
Nordwick, Randy, 463
Norris v. Hopi Tribe, 456–57
North Carolina. *See* Eastern Band of Cherokee Indians
North Dakota, 319, 394–96
Northern Plains Intertribal Court of Appeals: *Devils Lake Sioux Tribe v. Frederick*, 319–20; *Turtle Mountain Band of Chippewa v. McGillis*, 480–81
notarization, 404

oath, 370–71
Obama administration, 165
observation expertise, *315*
Odawa. *See* Ottawa Indians
offense: accessory defined for, 257; accomplice defined for, 257–58; aiding and abetting defined as, 223, 257–58; assault defined as, 210, 241–42; battery defined as, 242–44; complaint, 287, 297, 460–65; conspiracy defined as, 254–55; elements of, 210–11; failure to act as, 210, 213–16; fraud defined as, 222; intent disregarded for,

233–38; lying defined for, 335–36; preliminary, 249–54, 260; spiritual omission as, 216; statute of limitations on, 94, 474–75; strict liability defined as, 233–34, 240; theft defined as, 244–45; types of, by American criminal law, 6; types of, by Cheyenne deviations, 28; types of, by Courts of Indian Offenses, 39–40. *See also* intent
offense, same. *See* consecutive sentences
Office of Indian Affairs (OIA), 38–40. *See also* Bureau of Indian Affairs
Oglala Sioux Tribe: assault defined by, 242; exclusion code of, 141–42; OIA control of, 39; Pine Ridge Reservation, 39, 131, 142; police removal rights of, 131; Rosebud Reservation, 39, 44, 491; in *Russell Means v. District Court of the Chinle Judicial District*, 123, 126
Ohio, in *Martin v. Ohio*, 295
OIA. *See* Office of Indian Affairs
Ojibway Indians: "The Duck Dinner" story of, 71–72; eye contact among, 336; forgiveness concept of, 23; Leech Lake Band of, 195–98, *198–201*; *Mille Lacs Band of Ojibwe Indians vs. Darrick DeWayne Williams Jr.*, 581–88; Sandy Lake Band of, 23
Oklahoma: banishment law in, 580–81; DWI code of, 245–46; Major Crimes Act exclusion of, 52. *See also* Cheyenne Indians
Oliphant v. Suquamish: case, 106, 107, *110*; in non-Indian consent case, 134–38; in non-U.S. citizen case, 118–22
omission, 216
Oneida Indians, 205
ookwalni (forgiveness, mercy), 550, 551
oral argument. *See* right to remain silent
oral customs. *See* stories
Oregon, cross-deputization agreement in, 193–94

Organizing the Lakota (Biolsi), 38–39
Osage Indians: enforcement by, 19–20; jurisdiction of, 93–94; murder law of, 19–20; restorative justice by, 22
Ottawa Indians: *Champagne v. the People of the Little River Band of Ottawa Indians*, 71–78; *People of the Grand Traverse Band v. Raphael*, 264–66; Waabshki-Miigwan Drug Court Program, 565–73
overbreadth, 585
overt, 260

Paiute Indians, 105, 128, 129
Pakootas, Henry, 515–16
Pancoast, Henry, 45–46
pardons, 548–49
parents: adoption fraud by, 221–31; banishment of, 581–82; enforcement role of, 19; failure to act as, 213, 214–16; juvenile assault contribution of, 480
Parker, Isaac C., 138
Parker, Vickie, 537
parole: banishment and, 580–81; revocation of, 512
Pascua Yaqui v. Miranda, 537–45
Pascua Yaqui writ of mandamus, 177–84
Passamaquoddy v. Francis, 576–81
patent, 101, 111
paternity: Cheyenne view of, 32; documentation of, 39; OIA offenses of, 39; policy by, 43, 46–47, 54
patience, respectful, 361–62
Patnaude, Carol, 480
patrimony, 582, 589
Patterson v. New York, 274
Pavatea v. Hopi Tribe, 432
peacemaker, 57
peacemaking: for domestic violence, 60, 560; juvenile, 559; Kake, 560–63; for murder, 19–20, 22, 237–38; Navajo Nation, 3, 55–58, 361–632, 558–60;

process, 57–58, 59–60, 561–63; sentence, 59–60, 562–63; traditional probation officer role in, 58–59; tribal court systems for, 56–58, 558–63
peace officer status, 192–94
pedigree evidence, 156
penal, 11
Penobscot Indians, 105
People of the Grand Traverse Band v. Raphael, 264–66
Pequot Tribe. *See* Mashantucket Pequot Tribe
per capita, 166, 189
perjure, 422
personal jurisdiction: defined, 87, 87; establishing, 151–54; in *Nelson v. Yurok*, 78; in Poarch Band of Creek Indians' Code, 88. *See also* non-Indians
personal recognizance, 505
persuasion. *See* burden of persuasion
Philo, Steven E., 531
physical acts, 210
Pima-Maricopa Indians. *See* Salt River Pima-Maricopa Indian Community
Pine Ridge Reservation, 39, 131, 142
Pingayak, John, 211–12
pipe-holder, 20
plain view search and seizure: scope of, 383–84; tribal court case on, 384–86, 399–401
plea agreement: defined, 11; disregarding, 5. *See also* guilty pleas
plural marriage, 39, 40
Poarch Band of Creek Indians: civil rights code of, 302–3; jurisdiction code of, 88–89; statute of limitations code of, 475
police. *See* law enforcement officers; tribal police
police society member, 20
polygamy, 40
Pommersheim (professor), 535–36

Pomo Indians, 18
Poodry v. Tonawanda Band of Seneca Indians, 580
Port Gamble S'Klallam Tribe v. Michael Hjert, 132–40
Prairie Band Potawatomi Nation, 574–75
predilections, 67, 85
preliminary offense: attempt as, 250–54; solicitation as, 249–50, 260
presumption of innocence: defining, 297; right not to testify and, 482; Supreme Court on, 287; tribal code example on, 288
presumptions, 245, 247
Price, Anastasia Snyder, 221, 227
prison system, 46
private property: automobiles as reduced level of, 393; ICRA determination of, 367–68; surveillance of, 415–16; warrantless arrest on, 321–24. *See also* property destruction; search and seizure
privilege: advocate-victim, 496; defining, 505
probable cause: for arrest warrant, 314–15; defining, 315; for search and seizure warrant, 370, 371–73, 375; sources of, 315; for summons, 320
probation: banishment and, 580–81; defining, 508–9; example terms of, 514–15, 578; right to counsel scope for, 447–52; warrantless search and seizure under, 396–401
probation officers: healing to wellness court role of, 200; traditional restitution role of, 58–59
production. *See* burden of production
prohibited wrong as strict liability, 233, 234–35
Promising Strategies (Champagne and Goldberg), 192–94, 195–98, 202–5, 207

promulgation, 54
proof. *See* burden of proof; evidence
property destruction: Courts of Indian Offenses on, 40; restitution for, 3–5, 502–4; tribal court cases on, 3–5, 317–19, 502–4
property jurisdiction, 87, 89, 148
property rights. *See* private property
property theft, 244–45, 268–69
proscription, 67, 85
pro se (representation for oneself): counsel waiver and, 177–84, 431–38, 447–52; defining, 453
prosecution: burden of proof on, 287–88, 419–20; enforcement role of, 7, 20; failure of proof by, 262–63; federal deputization of tribal, 168; statute of limitations for, 94, 474–75
prospecting, 141, 148
protection order: terms, 169–70, 171; violation case, 184–88
protective sweep, 400–401
provocation, 267, 286
public apology, 509
Public Law 101-511, 107
Public Law 280: description of, 104, *108*, *109*; TLOA expansion of, 168; tribal-state jurisdiction collaboration and, 192, 195
Pueblo of Nambe Tribal Court, 535
Pueblo Tribe: Laguna, 232–33; Santa Clara, 309–11, 349
punishment. *See* restorative justice; sentence
punishment theories, 7, 7–8
purposefulness, 230, 232
Puyallup Tribe v. Darrell Keating, 371–73

Qualla Boundary, 117, 152–54. *See also* Eastern Band of Cherokee Indians
quasi, 163
quasi-sovereigns, 69–70, 106

Quick, Brenda Jones, 72, 75, 76, 78
Quileute Indian Tribe v. Valerie LeClair, 427–31

Ramirez, Daniel, 179
Randall v. Yakima Nation Tribal Court, 350, 527
Randolph, Timothy, 416–20
rape, tribal court cases on, 149–51, 172–77
Raphael, in *People of the Grand Traverse Band v. Raphael*, 264–66
rational: basis review, 270, 271; defined, 217
reasonable cause: for stop and frisk, 324, 327, 328, 330; for warrantless arrests, 317
reasonable doubt: defining, 288; tribal court cases on, 289–93
reciprocal obligation, 94, 98
recklessness: constructive intent, 231–32; driving, 66, 85, 131; negligence compared to, 66
recognizance, personal, 505
records: expungement of, 512, 548; oral traditional law, 14; TLOA rule of keeping, 177
Red Cliff Band, 131, 143
Red Lake Band of Chippewa Indians, 532, 533
Reed, Gerri Lynn Smith, 396–401
Reed, in *Eastern Band of Cherokee Indians v. Reed*, 396–401
rehabilitation: American view of, 7, 7; deferred sentence laws for, 510; expungement after, 551–52; juvenile, 526; tribal view of, *21*, 21–26. *See also* healing to wellness court
Reid, Vincent Lee, 341–43
Reina. *See Duro v. Reina*
religious expression, 582, 584
remand, 520, 554

renunciation, 255, 260
reparation, restitution compared to, 503
reparative justice, 56. *See also* peacemaking; restitution
representation for oneself. *See* pro se
repressive action, 54
reservations. *See* territorial jurisdiction
respectful patience, 361–62
restitution: defining, 85, 508; failure to pay, 512–13; ICRA on, 504; improper amount of, 500; by juveniles, 499–504; *nályééh* concept of, 3, 58, 560; reparation compared to, 503; right to, 499–504; stories, 235–38; time limit for, 515; traditional probation officer role in, 58–59; tribal code examples of, 511–12; tribal court cases on, 3–5, 499–504, 513–15; victim rights to, 498–504
restorative justice: American criminal law differences from, 556–57; banishment controversy in, 573; Cheyenne, 23–26; Comanche, 22; cycle of, *21*, 557; distributive nature of, 557, 589; elements of, 555–58; examples of, 22–26, 558–63; healing to wellness courts for, 194–98, *198–201*, 563–73; Iroquois, 22–23; Kake, 560–63; Navajo Nation, 55–60, 556–57, 558–60; Osage, 22; talking things out for, 3, 56–58, 558–60; tribal criminal law integration of, 55, 61, 555, 558–63; Yurok, 22. *See also* peacemaking; rehabilitation
retribution, 7, 7
revenge: blood, 30–31, 50; in Navajo treaty, 130
reversible error, 520, 554
revocation, 512, 554
right not to testify, 482. *See also* Miranda rights
rights, civil. *See* civil rights

right to advocacy, 494–96
right to appeal, 44, 527
right to compulsory process, 479–81
right to counsel: ambiguous notification of, 427–31; ambiguous request for, 342–43; conclusion, 452; effectiveness and, 181–82, 438–46; ICRA on, 425–26, 447–48; at interrogation, 340–43; scope of, 446–52; sentence and denial of, 470–71; Supreme Court on, 426, 433; TLOA rules of, 181; tribal code example on, 426; tribal court cases on, 177–84, 341–43, 427–38, 439–52; waiver, 177–84, 431–38, 447–52. *See also* Miranda rights
right to free speech, 582, 584
right to have a voice, 493–94
right to jury trial, 75–76, 533
right to privacy. *See* private property
right to religious expression, 582, 584
right to remain silent: cultural values clash with, 335–39; nonverbal evidence and, 363; right to counsel and, 340–43; tribal code example on, 359. *See also* Miranda rights
right to safety: overview of, 492; protection order terms, 169–70, 171; protection order violation, 184–88; tribal code examples of, 493
right to self-governance. *See* tribal sovereignty
right to speedy trial: assertion of, 478–79; ICRA on, 476; length of delay in, 477; overview, 475; prejudice in, 479; reason for delay in, 477–78
rituals. *See* ceremonies and rituals
Rodriguez, in *Illinois v. Rodriguez*, 323
Rodriguez, Jose, 397
Rodriguez, Rafael, 356–62
Rogers, in *United States v. Rogers*, 153
Romero v. Goodrich, 535
Rosebud Reservation, 39, 44, 491

620 INDEX

Ross, Luana, 38
rules of living, 238–39
Russell Means v. District Court of the Chinle Judicial District, 123–30
Russians, "Taa'ii'ti" story of, 96–97

Sac and Fox Tribe, 573–74
Sacred Arrows matter, 61–63
safety. *See* right to safety
St. Peter v. Colville Confederated Tribes, 470–71, 521, 523–28
Sakiestewa, Howard, 329–31
Salish and Kootenai Tribes: civil rights code of, 303; *Confederated Chehalis v. Lyons*, 172–77; *Confederated Salish and Kootenai Tribes v. Burland*, 214–16; *Confederated Salish and Kootenai Tribes v. Daniel Felix Finley*, 294–96; *Confederated Salish and Kootenai Tribes v. William Conko*, 411–14; restitution code of, 511; sentence code of, 509–13
Salt River Pima-Maricopa Indian Community, 106–7, 317
same offense. *See* consecutive sentences
Sam v. Colville Confederated Tribes, 469–71, 521
sanctions, cultural, 509
Sanders (deputy sheriff), 325–27
Sandy Lake Band of Ojibway, 23
Santa Clara Pueblo v. Martinez, 309–11, 349
Sault Ste. Marie Tribal Code: on affirmative defenses, 262; on assault, 242; on civil forfeiture, 143; on presumption of innocence, 288; on reasonable doubt, 288; on right to remain silent, 345; on substantial step, 250; on theft, 244; on victim rights, 493, 494
Saunooke, Kirk G., 530–31
Saunooke, Robert, 528
schizophrenia, 279
Schurz, Carl, 47
seal hunting rules, 211–13

search and seizure: admissibility of, 368–69, 370–73; of automobiles, 143–47, 326–27, 329–31, 388–401, 416–20; conclusion, 402; consent to, 386–87; cultural values impacted by, 367–68; of drugs, 373–78, 379–82, 397–98; emergency, 324, 389; exclusionary rule and, 408–9; exclusionary rule and violations of, 408–9; plain view, 383–86, 399–401; scope of, 379–82; of weapons, 398, 400
search and seizure warrant: affidavits for, 370–71, 375–77; ambiguity of, 373–78; arrest warrant or, 377; defining, 369–70; probable cause for, 370, 371–73, 375; purpose of, 368; serving, 378; totality of the circumstances for, 377. *See also* warrantless search and seizure
seizure. *See* search and seizure
self-defense: burden of proof of, 272–75, 293–96; defining, 261, 266–67; due process in, 269–71; equal protection in, 271–72; Supreme Court on, 295; tribal court cases on, 267–75, 276–77
self-determination. *See* Indian Self-Determination and Education Assistance Act
self-governance. *See* tribal sovereignty
self-incrimination, 339, 364. *See also* Miranda rights
Seminole Indians, 94
Senate Committee on Indian Affairs, restorative justice defined by, 555–56
Seneca Indians, 580
sentence: arbitrary and capricious, 519–20, 554; defining, 507; due process and, 469–71; execution of, 511; expungement after, 512, 548–52; ICRA limitations amendment, 103, 167–68, 305–6, 307, 522–23; imposition of, 509–10; options and types, 508–9; peacemaking, 59–60, 562–63; remanded, 520; right to

counsel denial and, 470–71; tribal code example for, 509–13; vacating, 517–22; victim right to have a voice in, 494. *See also* consecutive sentences; deferred sentence; suspended sentence
sequestration, 441, 453, 494
sexual assault: of juvenile, 439–43, 497–98; rape, 149–51, 172–77; rate of, 166; victim support systems for, 491–92, 494–95
shame, 26–28, 32
Shane C. Innes v. Colville Confederated Tribes, 234–35
Sharing Our Stories of Survival (Clairmont), 494–95
Shawnee. *See* Absentee-Shawnee Tribe
Sherman, William T., 128, 130
Shoshone Tribe. *See* Duckwater Shoshone Tribe
Sinquah v. Hopi Tribe, 446–52
Sioux Tribes: *Devils Lake Sioux Tribe v. Frederick*, 319–20; *Ex parte Crow Dog*, 41–45, 52–53, 103, *109*; treaties with, 41, 42–43; Yankton Sioux Tribal Code, 497. *See also* Fort Peck Tribes; Oglala Sioux Tribe
Sipayik, 576–81
Sitting Bull, 39
Sixth Amendment. *See* right to counsel
Skagit. *See* Upper Skagit Indian Tribe
S'Klallam Tribe, 123–30
Sky-Woman, 15–16
Smith v. Confederated Tribes of Warm Springs, 350
smoking ceremonies, 236
smudging ceremonies, 197
Snyder, Kirk, 356, 358
sobriety court. *See* healing to wellness court
sobriety tests, 246, 354, 411–14
social harm: American concept of, 2, *2*, 5–7, *6*; traditional concept of, 15–17, 26–28, 238–39

sociolinguistics, 337–39, 364. *See also* terminology
soldiers, 20
solicitation, 249–50, 260
Song Pumpkin, 44–45
South Carolina, 105
South Dakota. *See* Oglala Sioux Tribe
sovereignty. *See* jurisdiction; tribal sovereignty
Spears v. Red Lake Band of Chippewa Indians, 532, 533–34
specific intent, 220
speedy trial, 475–79
spirituality: ceremonial artifact cases, 61–63; fish and game rights and, 80; in healing to wellness courts, 196, 566; omission of, 216; tribal criminal law foundation of, 14–17, 28–33, 216. *See also* stories
Spotted Tail, 49–50, 52–53
Spotted Tail, Jr., 44–45
stacked sentences. *See* consecutive sentences
standing: defining, 404; for motion to suppress evidence, 369, 396–401, 408–9. *See also* exclusionary rule
stare decisis (let it stand), 45, 54, 418, 422
state collaboration. *See* tribal-state collaboration
state jurisdiction, 104–5, 106, *108*, *109*–10, 168; tribal jurisdiction with, 201–8
statements, involuntary, 340, 409. *See also* affidavit
status, 210, 217
statute of limitations, 94, 474–75
statutes: ambiguity of, 359–60, 457–60; consecutive sentences for different, 532; federal and state jurisdiction, *109*–10; tribal, caveat on, xv–xvi
Stepetin, Michael, III, 66–71
stereotypes, 56
Sticks Everything Under His Belt, 235–37

Stiffarm, Johnny Lee, 457–60
stigma, social harm, 26–28
sting, 284, 286. *See also* undercover operations
stipulation: defined, 54, 148; non-Indian consent to jurisdiction or, 131
stop and frisk: arrest compared to, 324–25; automobile searches, 143–47, 326–27, 329–31, 388–401, 416–20; for drugs, 326–27, 417; family and community involvement in, 389–92; fish and game, 394–96; Supreme Court on, 324, 388; tribal court cases on, 325–31, 389–96
stories: Alaskan Native, 96–97; banishment, 235–39, 487–89; "Battle with the Snakes" (Bruchac), 26–28; Cheyenne, 23–26, 235–38, 487–89; domestic violence, 487–89; "The Duck Dinner," 71–72; healing to wellness court, 566–73; jurisdiction over non-Indians, 96–97; "A Man without Family" (Aginsky and Aginsky), 18; restitution, 235–38; "Taa'ii'ti" (Frank), 96–97; tribal law recording by, 14; "The Two Brothers" (Bruchac), 15–17; Waabshki-Miigwan, 566–73
Strickland, Rennard, 28–33
Strickland test, 441–43, 444–46
strict liability: defining, 233–34, 240; tribal court case on, 234–35
subject matter jurisdiction: defined, 87, *87*; establishing, 151–54; example, 89, 152–53
subpoenas. *See* summons
substantial step, 250, 251–54
sukanahowao (pipe-holder, chief), 20
summons: arrest warrant or, 320; defining, 333; witness, 479–81
Sun Dance, 236–37
Supreme Court, U.S.: *American Tobacco Co. v. United States*, 532; *Austin v. United States*, 144–45; on automobile searches, 393; *Blockburger v. United States*, 542; on confession voluntariness, 340; on consecutive sentences, 532, 533; on counsel effectiveness, 441, 444; *Dorszynski v. United States*, 521; on double jeopardy, 105–6, 107, *110*, 473; *Duro v. Reina*, 106–7, *110*, 135–36, 138, 152–53, 306; exclusionary rule scope defined by, 405–6; *Ex parte Crow Dog*, 41–45, 52–53, 103, *109*; on good faith exception, 377; ICRA interpretation by, 308–9, 349; on Indianness, 156, 161; on jurisdiction over non-Indians, 102–3, 106, 107, *108*, *109–10*; on jurisdiction over nonmember Indians, 106–7; on jurisdiction over non-U.S. citizens, 118–19; on *Miranda v. Arizona*, 344–45; *Montana v. United States*, 137; *Morrison v. United States*, 161; offensive acts defined by, 210; *Oliphant v. Suquamish*, 106, 107, *110*, 118–22, 134–38; on presumption of innocence, 287; on private property entry, 321, 324; on reasonable doubt, 288; right to appeal to, 44; on right to counsel, 426, 433; on right to remain silent, 344–45; on right to speedy trial, 477; *Santa Clara Pueblo v. Martinez*, 309–10, 349; on self-defense, 295; on sentence vacating, 521; on stop and frisk, 324, 388; tribal court cases reviewed by, 308–11; on tribal membership, 309–10; tribal sovereignty recognized by, 41–45, 52–53, 103, 105–6; *Tsosie v. United States*, 129–30; on warrantless search and seizure, 388, 398–99, 400–401, 416
Suquamish Indians. *See Oliphant v. Suquamish*
surveillance, 415–16
suspended sentence: defining, 508; revocation of, 512; tribal court cases on, 513–15

suspicion, articulable, 473, 483
Sutton, George, 61–63
Swan, Julie R. *See Julie R. Swan v. Colville Confederated Tribes*
Swan, Richard, 221–31
Sweowat, Joseph, 518–22
Swinomish Indian Community v. Fornsby, 280–84
Swinomish Indian Community v. Reid, 341–43
sworn statements. *See* affidavit
sworn testimony, 370
Synder, in *Ex parte Snyder*, 580–81

"Taa'ii'ti" (Frank), 96–97
TAH-BONE, 61–63
talking things out, 3, 56–58, 558–60. *See also* peacemaking
Tatshama, Amelia, 322
Taylor, Julius, 397
Taylor v. Hopi Tribe, 443–46
Teller, Henry M., 48
Ten Commandments, 14
terminology: Indian identity, xvi–xvii; Indian translation of crime, 13–14; Navajo Nation peacemaking, 3, 55–58, 361–632, 558–60. *See also* ambiguity
territorial jurisdiction: in *Champagne v. the People of the Little River Band of Ottawa Indians*, 73–75; defined, 87, 87; establishing, 149–51; Indian country defined for, 101–2; Poarch Band of Creek Indians' Code of, 89; of states, 104–5; of Witsuwit'en, 95–96
Terry stop, 324, 328, 330
testimony: right not to testify, 482; victim rights to, 494, 496–98
Texas, 105
theft, 244–45, 268–69
Thompson v. Greyeyes, 304
Three Affiliated Tribes v. Crow Flies High, 394–96
Thunder Hawk, 44–45

Timms, Cameron, 549–52
Timothy Randolph v. The Hopi Tribe, 416–20
TLOA. *See* Tribal Law and Order Act
Toineeta Pipestem, Brenda, 530
Tonawanda Band of Seneca Indians, 580
Torres, in *Eastern Band of Cherokee Indians v. Torres*, 116–22
tort liability, 193, 208
totality of the circumstances, 377, 404
Trade and Intercourse Act, *109*
traditional criminal law: administration in, 20; banishment in, 235–39, 487–89, 573; enforcement in, 19–20; hybridization of, 69–70; individual harm concept in, 17–19; intent in, 235–39; procedure in, 20–21; social harm concept in, 15–17, 26–28, 238–39; spiritual foundation of, 14–17, 28–33, 216; victim rights in, 486–89, 493; wrongdoing response in, 21–26. *See also* restorative justice
traditional probation officers, 58–59
training, tribal police, 193
transferred intent, 232
transitory, 54
treason, 22
treaties: Cherokee, 119, 121; Chippewa-Ottawa fishing, 264–65; Choctaw, 94, 118; construction of, 127; Delaware, 118; Holston River, 119; Major Crimes Act conflicts with, 51–52; Mille Lacs Band, 583–84; Navajo Nation, 123, 127–29, 130; Shawnee, 118; Sioux, 41, 42–43
Tree of the Great Peace, 93
trial rights: compulsory process, 479–81; double jeopardy, 105–6, 107, 471–74; due process and guilty pleas, 465–69; due process and offense complaint, 460–65; due process and sentence, 469–71; due process and statute ambiguity, 67–68, 457–60; due process scope, 455–57; not to testify,

624 INDEX

482; speedy trial, 475–79; statute of limitations, 94, 474–75
tribal court cases, by case name: *Ami v. Hopi Tribe*, 431–38, 448–51, 465–69; *Amundson v. Colville Confederated Tribes*, 255–57; *Augustine Komalestewa v. The Hopi Tribe*, 475–79; *Benjamin v. Weyaus*, 587; *Champagne v. the People of the Little River Band of Ottawa Indians*, 71–78; *Colville Confederated Tribes v. Peter P. George*, 328–29; *Colville Confederated Tribes v. Swan*, 221–31; *Condon v. Colville Confederated Tribes*, 289–92; *Confederated Chehalis v. Lyons*, 172–77; *Confederated Salish and Kootenai Tribes v. Burland*, 214–16; *Confederated Salish and Kootenai Tribes v. Daniel Felix Finley*, 294–96; *Confederated Salish and Kootenai Tribes v. William Conko*, 411–14; *Crow Tribe v. Lance Big Man*, 346–56; *Davisson, et al. v. Colville Confederated Tribes*, 267–75; *Devils Lake Sioux Tribe v. Frederick*, 319–20; *Eastern Band of Cherokee Indians v. Crowe*, 528–37; *Eastern Band of Cherokee Indians v. Cruz*, 302–4; *Eastern Band of Cherokee Indians v. Lambert*, 152–54; *Eastern Band of Cherokee Indians v. Reed*, 396–401; *Eastern Band of Cherokee Indians v. Torres*, 116–22; *Elmo Nevayaktewa and Emily Verna Mutz v. The Hopi Tribe*, 379–82; *Eugene Lamone v. Navajo Nation*, 317–19; *Fort Peck Assiniboine and Sioux Tribes v. Jesse Martell*, 149–51; *Fort Peck Assiniboine and Sioux Tribes v. Stiffarm*, 457–60; *Fort Peck Tribes v. Joseph Harold Jones*, 292–93; *Fort Peck Tribes v. Morales*, 462–65; *Fort Peck Tribes v. Victor and Patti Grant*, 415–16; *Fort Peck Tribes v. William Turcotte*, 251–54; *Gishey v. Hopi Tribe*, 431–32, 437–38; *Hardin v. Reno Sparks Indian Colony*, 546–48; *Henry Pakootas v. Colville Confederated Tribes*, 515–16; *Hopi Tribe in Matter of Certified Question*, 157–61; *Hopi Tribe v. Beauford Dawahoya*, 329–31; *Hopi Tribe v. Kahe*, 389–92; *Hopi Tribe v. Marlon Huma*, 472–74; *Hopi v. Timms*, 549–52; *John C. Bowen v. Upper Skagit Indian Tribe*, 258–59; *John Manuel v. Colville Confederated Tribes*, 321–24; *Joseph Sweowat v. Colville Confederated Tribes*, 518–22; *Julie R. Swan v. Colville Confederated Tribes*, 373–78; *Laurie Watt v. Colville Confederated Tribes*, 63–65; *Louie v. Colville Confederated Tribes*, 460–62; *Lower Elwha Klallam Tribe v. James L. Bolstrom and Russell N. Hepfer*, 406–7; *Makah Tribe v. Jonathan Greene*, 513–15; *Michael Stepetin, III v. Nisqually Indian Community*, 66–71; *Mille Lacs Band of Ojibwe Indians vs. Darrick DeWayne Williams Jr.*, 581–88; *Nathan J. Navasie v. The Hopi Tribe*, 439–43; *Navajo Nation in the Matter of the Interest of D.P.*, 499–504; *Navajo Nation v. Blake*, 3–5; *Navajo Nation v. Cynthia Hunter*, 154–57, 158; *Navajo Nation v. Marie Franklin*, 384–86; *Navajo Nation v. McDonald*, 358–59; *Navajo Nation v. Rafael Rodriguez*, 356–62; *Nelson v. Yurok*, 78–84; *Norris v. Hopi Tribe*, 456–57; *Pascua Yaqui v. Miranda*, 537–45; Pascua Yaqui writ of mandamus, 177–84; *Passamaquoddy v. Francis*, 576–81; *Pavatea v. Hopi Tribe*, 432; *People of the Grand Traverse Band v. Raphael*, 264–66; *Poodry v. Tonawanda Band of Seneca Indians*, 580; *Port Gamble S'Klallam Tribe v. Michael Hjert*, 132–40; *Puyallup Tribe v. Darrell Keating*, 371–73; *Quileute Indian Tribe v. Valerie LeClair*, 427–31; *Randall v. Yakima Nation Tribal Court*, 350, 527; *Russell Means v. District Court of the Chinle Judicial District*, 123–30; Sacred Arrows matter, 61–63; *St. Peter v. Colville Confederated Tribes*, 470–71, 521, 523–28; *Sam v. Colville Confederated Tribes*, 469–71, 521; *Shane C. Innes v. Colville Confederated*

INDEX   625

Tribes, 234–35; *Sinquah v. Hopi Tribe*, 446–52; *Smith v. Confederated Tribes of Warm Springs*, 350; *Spears v. Red Lake Band of Chippewa Indians*, 532, 533–34; *Swinomish Indian Community v. Fornsby*, 280–84; *Swinomish Indian Community v. Reid*, 341–43; *Taylor v. Hopi Tribe*, 443–46; *Thompson v. Greyeyes*, 304; *Three Affiliated Tribes v. Crow Flies High*, 394–96; *Timothy Randolph v. The Hopi Tribe*, 416–20; *Tulalip Tribes, Petitioner and Appellee, v. 2008 White Ford Econoline Van*, 143–47; *Tulalip Tribes v. Lindy Lee Morris*, 184–88; *Tulalip Tribes v. Merle K. Johnny*, 325–27; *Turtle Mountain Band of Chippewa v. McGillis*, 480–81; *Ute Mountain Ute Tribe v. Mills*, 502–4; *Waters v. Colville Confederated Tribes*, 276–77

tribal court cases, by topic: accomplice liability, 258–59; aiding and abetting, 221–31, 258–59; alcohol-related incidents, 116–17, 132–33, 154, 234–35, 289–92, 384–86, 472–73, 476; assault, 123–24, 179–80, 251–54, 463, 480; attempt, 251–54; automobile search and seizure, 143–47, 326–27, 329–31, 388–401, 416–20; banishment, 576–88; burden of proof allocation error, 418–20; case of first impression, 407, 422; ceremonial artifacts, 61–63; child abuse, 214–16; civil forfeiture, 143–47; confession admissibility, 356–62; conspiracy, 255–57; disorderly conduct, 443–46; domestic violence, 251–54, 321–22, 529, 576–79; double jeopardy, 472–74; driving accident fraud, 71–78; driving recklessly, 66–68; driving without license, 63–65, 116–17, 411–14, 427–31; drug possession, 143–47, 179, 255–57, 341–43, 373–78, 379–82, 397–98, 417, 518; due process ambiguity, 457–60; due process and guilty pleas, 465–69; due process and offense complaint, 460–65; due process and sentence, 469–71; due process scope, 455–57; DWI, 116–17, 292–93, 346–47, 411–14, 427–31, 470; exclusionary rule, 406–7, 411–14, 415–20; expungement, 549–52; failure to act, 214–16; fish and game rights, 78–84, 258–59, 264–66, 406–7; "fruits of the poisonous tree," 411–14; *habeas corpus*, 304; incarceration credit, 516–17; Indianness, establishing, 151–54; Indianness, proving, 154–61; insanity defense, 280–84; intent, proving, 221–31; interrogation right to counsel, 341–43; involuntary intoxication defense, 280–84; jurisdiction, non-Indian consent to, 132–40; jurisdiction establishment, personal, 151–54; jurisdiction establishment, subject-matter, 151–54; jurisdiction establishment, territorial, 149–51; jurisdiction over non-Indians, 116–30, 132–40, 143–47; jurisdiction over non-U.S. citizens, 116–22; justification defense, 264–66; juvenile, 289–92, 439–43, 480–81, 499–504; lay advocate ineffectiveness, 439–43; Miranda rights, 346–62, 538–39; mistrial judge disqualification, 462–65; peacemaking, 558–63; property destruction, 3–5, 317–19, 502–4; protection order violation, 184–88; reasonable doubt, 289–93; research caveats on, xv; restitution, 3–5, 499–504, 513–15; right to compulsory process, 480–81; right to counsel, effectiveness and, 181–82, 439–46; right to counsel, scope, 446–52; right to counsel ambiguity, 427–31; right to counsel at interrogation, 341–43; right to counsel waiver, 177–84,

431–38, 447–52; right to speedy trial, 475–79; search and seizure, plain view, 384–86, 399–401; search and seizure admissibility, 371–73; search and seizure emergencies, 389–401; search and seizure legality, 415–20; search and seizure scope, 379–82; search warrant ambiguity, 373–78; self-defense, 267–75, 276–77; sentence, suspended, 513–15; sentence, vacating, 518–22; sentences, consecutive, 523–44; sexual assault, 149–51, 172–77, 439–43; stop and frisk, 325–31, 389–96; strict liability, 234–35; Supreme Court review of, 308–11; TLOA used in, 172–84; VAWA used in, 172–77, 184–88; warrantless arrest, 317–20, 321–24; warrantless search and seizure, 325–31, 384–86, 389–401, 415–20; witness summons and cross-examination, 480–81

tribal court cases, by tribe: Chehalis, 172–77; Cherokee, 116–22, 152–54, 302–4, 396–401, 528–37; Cheyenne-Arapaho, 61–63; Chippewa, 264–66, 480–81, 532, 533–34; Crow, 137, 346–56; Fort Peck, 149–51, 251–54, 292–93, 415–16, 457–60, 462–65; Kake, 560–63; Klallam, 132–40, 406–7; Makah, 513–15; Navajo Nation, 3–5, 154–57, 158, 317–19, 356–62, 384–86, 499–501, 558–60; Nisqually, 66–71; Ojibway, 581–88; Ottawa, 71–78, 264–66; Pascua Yaqui, 177–84, 537–45; Passamaquoddy, 576–81; Puyallup, 371–73; Quileute, 427–31; Reno Sparks Indian Colony, 546–48; Salish and Kootenai, 214–16, 294–96, 411–14; Swinomish, 280–84, 341–43; Three Affiliated Tribes of Fort Berthold, 394–96; Tonawanda Band of Seneca Indians, 580; Tulalip, 143–47, 184–88, 325–27; Ute, 502–4; Warm Springs, 350; Yakima Nation, 350, 527; Yurok, 79–84. *See also* Colville Confederated Tribes; Hopi Tribe; Sioux Tribes

tribal criminal law: American law parallels to, 350–51; BIA rejection of, 41, 45–52; civil rights defined by, 299–301; civil rights protection by, 301–4; Constitution, U.S., and, 68–69, 300–301; federal recognition of, 41–45, 52–53, 103, 105–6; hybridization of, 69–70; OIA rejection of, 38; omissions and, 216; restorative justice integration with, 55, 61, 555, 558–63. *See also* traditional criminal law

tribal jurisdiction: of Alaskan Natives, 96–97; in British Columbia, 95–96; of Choctaw Indians, 94; civil law used for, 130–47; cross-deputization for, 168, 191–94; of Eastern Band of Cherokee Indians, 116–22, 152–54; establishing personal, 151–54; establishing subject-matter, 151–54; establishing territorial, 149–51; federal limitations on, 41, 45–52, 101–4, *108, 109–10*; federal support and collaboration for, 165–88, 201–2, 204–5; of Fort Peck, 149–51; healing to wellness court expansion of, 194–95; Indian country defined for, 101–2; of Iroquois Confederacy, 93; of Little River Band of Ottawa Indians, 73–75; Major Crimes Act and, 41, 45–52, 103–4, *109*; of Navajo Nation, 123–30; of Osage Indians, 93–94; over non-Indians, 106–7, 123–40; over nonmember Indians, 123–30; over non-U.S. citizens, 96–97, 116–22; of Poarch Band of Creek Indians, 88–89; of S'Klallam Tribe, 123–30; state jurisdiction with, 191–208; state limitations on, 104–5, 106, *108, 109–*

10, 168; TLOA expansion of, *108*, 166–68, 172–84; VAWA expansion of, 108, *110*, 169–77, 184–88; violence rate argument for, 125, 166; of White Mountain Apache, 131, 132; of Witsuwit'en, 95–96; of Yurok Indians, 78
Tribal Law and Order Act (TLOA): cases involving, 172–84; overview, *108*, 167–68; right to counsel rules of, 181; rules of evidence, 176; rules of record keeping, 177
Tribal Law and Policy Institute, 205–6
tribal membership: adoption fraud, 221–31; banishment from, 141–42, 235–37, 487–89, 573–88; establishing Indianness and, 151–54; gender bias in, 309; intertribal marriage and, 129, 309; Navajo acquisition of, 129; proving Indianness and, 154–61; reinstatement of, 235–37; Supreme Court on, 309–10
tribal police: cross-deputization of, 168, 191–94; entrapment by, 144–45; role of, 20–21; training, 193; undercover operations of, 144–45, 255–57, 284–85, 384–85
tribal sovereignty: double jeopardy and, 105–6, 107; federal recognition of, 41–45, 52–53, 103, 105–6; incarceration credit and, 513, 516–17; jurisdiction extension of, 89–90; quasi-, 69–70, 106. *See also* tribal jurisdiction
tribal-state collaboration: benchbooks for, 202–3; by cross-deputization, 191–94; cultural respect and exchange in, 197, 203–4, 205, 207; forums for, 201–5, 206; on healing to wellness courts, 194; in Idaho, 202–3; lessons learned, 205–7; in Minnesota, 195–98, *198–201*; in New Mexico, 203–4; in New York, 204–5; in Oregon, 193–94; process for, 194; Public Law 280 and, 192, 195

Tsanaloo, 95
Tsosie v. United States, 129–30
Tulalip Tribes, Petitioner and Appellee, v. 2008 White Ford Econoline Van: discussion, 143–44; entrapment, 144–45; excessive fines doctrine, 145–47
Tulalip Tribes v. Lindy Lee Morris, 184–88
Tulalip Tribes v. Merle K. Johnny, 325–27
Turcotte, Linda, 252–53
Turcotte, William, 251–54
Turtle, in *Arizona State ex rel. Merrill v. Turtle*, 128
Turtle Mountain Band of Chippewa v. McGillis, 480–81
"The Two Brothers" (Bruchac), 15–17
Two Row Wampum (Guswhenta), 205

undercover operations, 144–45, 255–57, 284–85, 384–85
unilateralism, 165, 189
United States District Court: *United States v. Barnhart*, 520; *United States v. Driver*, 161; *United States v. Georgiadis*, 520; *United States v. Hester*, 159–60; *United States v. Kagama*, 104, *109*; *United States v. Lara*, 107, *110*, 120, 135–36; *United States v. Leon*, 377; *United States v. McBratney*, *109*; *United States v. Morgan*, 521; *United States v. Rogers*, 153; *United States v. Washington*, 69; *United States v. Wheeler*, 105–6, *110*, 135; *United States v. Winsor*, 416. *See also* Supreme Court
Upper Skagit Indian Tribe, 258–59
Utah, 105
Ute Indians: on civil contempt power, 141; Navajo Nation and, 128; on search and seizure warrants, 369–70
Ute Mountain Ute Tribe v. Mills, 502–4

vacating sentence: overview, 517–18; tribal court case on, 518–22; vacated, defined, 554
vagueness. *See* ambiguity

Valenzuela, Ignacio, 179
Valenzuela, in *Bustamante v. Valenzuela*, 533–34
validity, 333
VAWA. *See* Violence Against Women Act
vehicles. *See* driving incidents
Venetie Tribe, 102
veracity, 330–31, 373, 376–77, 404
verbal acts, 210, 242
vertical justice, 556–57
victim compensation. *See* restitution
victimization demographics, 485
victim rights: to advocacy, 494–96; civil, 299–311; contemporary, 489–90; juvenile, 496–98; protection order terms, 169–70, 171; protection order violation and, 184–88; to restitution, 498–504; to safety, 169–70, 171, 184–88, 492–93; sequestration, 494; to testify, 494–96; traditional, 486–89, 493; trial presence, 494; tribal code examples of, 490, 493, 494, 496–98; to voice, 493–94; warrantless arrest consent and, 322–23
victim support systems: advocate, 494–96; for domestic violence, 491–92, 494–95; need for, 486; for sexual assault, 491–92, 494–95; White Buffalo Calf Woman Society example of, 491–92; for women, 491–92, 494–95; Yurok example of, 489
Villegas, Avis, 460–61
violence: dating, 169, 171; rate, 125, 166, 485; types of, 486. *See also* assault; domestic violence
Violence Against Women Act (VAWA) reauthorization, 108, *110*; ICRA terms of, 169–71; in protection order violation case, 184–88; in rape case, 172–77; requirements, 172
voice. *See* right to have a voice

void-for-vagueness doctrine, 585. *See also* ambiguity
voir dire, 337, 364
volitional, 235, 240
voluntary confession, 340, 409
voluntary guilty plea, 465–69
voluntary intoxication defense, 279–80

Waabshki-Miigwan Drug Court Program (WMDCP): dedication story of, 566–73; process and curriculum, 565–66
Wabanaki Confederacy, 579
Wahwassuck, Korey, 196, 198
waiver: of counsel, 177–84, 431–38, 447–52; of Miranda rights, 345–46, 353, 538–39
Walking Eagle, Carletta, 319
Walking on Common Ground initiative, 202
Wampanoag Tribe of Gay Head, 105
war captives, 94
Warm Springs. *See* Confederated Tribes of Warm Springs
warnings of harm, 238–39
warrantless arrest: consent for, 322–23; occasions for, 315–16; tribal code examples on, 317; tribal court cases on, 317–20, 321–23
warrantless search and seizure: for arrest, 32–324, 387; of automobiles, 143–47, 326–27, 329–31, 388–401, 416–20; burden of proof for, 415–20; consent for, 386–87; exigent circumstances for, 324, 389; "fruits of the poisonous tree" for, 410–14; motion to suppress evidence from, 422; overview of, 382–83; plain view, 383–86, 399–401; probation condition for, 396–401; for protective sweep, 400–401; standing to suppress evidence from, 369, 396–401, 408–9; for stop and frisk, 324–31, 388–96; Supreme Court on,

388, 398–99, 400–401, 416; tribal court cases on, 325–31, 384–86, 389–401, 415–20
warrants, 11. *See also* arrest warrant; search and seizure warrant
Washa, Jasper H., Sr., 61
Washington state: *Michael Stepetin, III v. Nisqually Indian Community* in, 66–71; *State v. Burke*, 275; *State v. Carama*, 274; *Tulalip Tribes, Petitioner and Appellee, v. 2008 White Ford Econoline Van*, 143–47; *United States v. Washington*, 69. *See also* Colville Confederated Tribes
watershed, 42, 54
Waters v. Colville Confederated Tribes, 276–77
Watt, Laurie, 63–65
WBCWS. *See* White Buffalo Calf Woman Society
weapons search and seizure, 398, 400
Webster, in *Commonwealth v. Webster*, 288
Weeks, Glen, 397–98, 399
welfare stops. *See* stop and frisk
wellness court. *See* healing to wellness court
Welsh, Herbert, 45
Weyaus, in *Benjamin v. Weyaus*, 587
Wheeler, in *United States v. Wheeler*, 105–6, 110, 135
White Bear, 237
White Buffalo Calf Woman Society (WBCWS), 491–92
White Head, William, 463
White Mountain Apache Tribe: conspiracy code of, 254–55; jurisdiction code of, 131, 132; victim rights under, 490
White Thunder, 44–45
Wilkins, David E., xvi–xvii
willfulness, 230
Williams, Darrick DeWayne, Jr., 581–88

Williams, Sherman, 258–59
Williams, Stanley, 95–96
witchcraft, 15, 19, 31–32
witness: criminal identification by, 363, 446; sequestration, 441; summons and cross-examination of, 479–81
Witsuwit'en, 95–96
WMDCP. *See* Waabshki-Miigwan Drug Court Program
women: Cherokee laws for, 30, 32, 33; clan leaders, 57; immoral cohabitation with, 40; Navajo membership through, 129; social status dependence on, 32; tribal membership bias against, 309; victim support system for, 491–92, 494–95. *See also* domestic violence; sexual assault
Worcester v. Georgia, 41, 49, 109
work release, 508
writ of mandamus, 177–78, 180, 189
wrongdoing response: American, 7–8; traditional, 21–26

Yakima Nation Tribal Court, 350, 527
Yankton Sioux Tribal Code, 497
Yava, Albert, 17
Yavapai Nation. *See* Fort McDowell Yavapai Nation
Yazzie, Robert, 55–60, 556–57
you may have the body. *See habeas corpus*
youth. *See* juveniles
Ysleta del Sur Pueblo, 105
Yup'ik Eskimos, 238–39, 337–39
Yurok Indians: individual harm concept of, 18–19; murder law of, 22; *Nelson v. Yurok*, 79–84; restorative justice by, 22; victim support system by, 489

Zion, James W., 299–300

About the Authors

Sarah Deer (Mvskoke), a 2014 MacArthur Fellow, is a professor at William Mitchell College of Law in Minnesota. She received her Juris Doctor and Tribal Law certificate from the University of Kansas School of Law. She has been an instructor at UCLA Law School, the University of Minnesota School of Law, and Lewis and Clark Law School. In 2013, she was appointed Associate Justice of the Prairie Island Indian Community Court of Appeals. Formerly she worked at the Tribal Law and Policy Institute. She is the co-author of Introduction to Tribal Law and co-editor of Sharing Our Stories of Survival: Native Women Surviving Violence.

Carrie E. Garrow received her B.A. from Dartmouth College in 1991, her J.D. from Stanford Law School in 1994, and her M.P.P. from Harvard University Kennedy School of Government in 2000. Ms. Garrow is a Visiting Assistant Professor at Syracuse University College of Law and the Chief Appellate Judge at the St. Regis Mohawk Tribal Court. She has served as a deputy district attorney in Riverside County, California, Chief Judge of the St. Regis Mohawk Tribal Court, and Executive Director of the Center for Indigenous Law, Governance & Citizenship at Syracuse University College of Law. Currently she works as a consultant for Tribal Law and Policy Institute.

Made in United States
Troutdale, OR
11/23/2024